Mysteries
of the
Unexplained

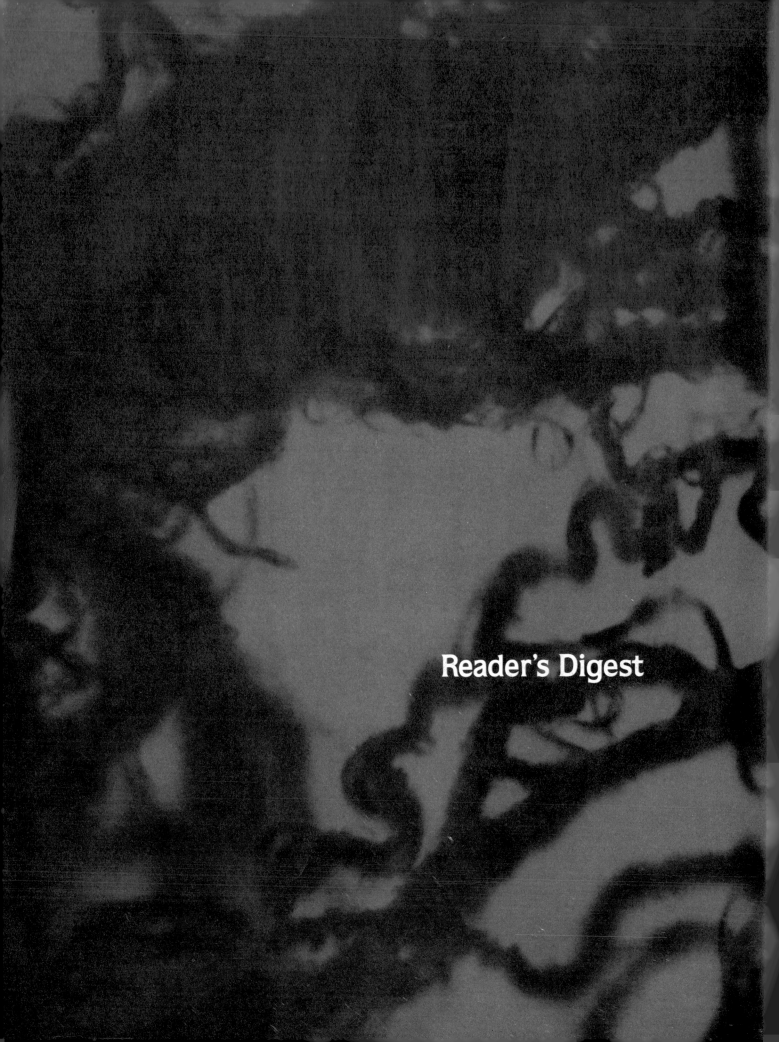

Reader's Digest

Mysteries of the Unexplained

The Reader's Digest Association, Inc.
Pleasantville, New York/Montreal

MYSTERIES OF THE UNEXPLAINED

Project Editor: Carroll C. Calkins
Art Editor: Vincent L. Perry
Associate Editors: Noreen B. Church;
    Susan Brackett, Susan Parker
Research Editors: Hildegard Anderson;
    Shirley Miller, Georgea Pace, Tanya Strage
Copy Editors: Zahava Feldman;
    Rosemarie Conefrey, Diana Marsh
Picture Editor: Robert J. Woodward
Picture Researcher: Marion Bodine
Art Associate: Larissa Lawrynenko
Editorial Assistant: Dolores H. Damm

Chief Contributing Writer: Richard Marshall
Contributing Writers: Monte Davis, Valerie Moolman,
    Georg Zappler
Contributing Researchers: Amy Daly,
    Helen M. Hinkle, Sara M. Solberg, Jozefa Stuart

*The editors of Reader's Digest General Books
wish to express their gratitude for the help
and advice of the following:*

American Museum–Hayden Planetarium
American Museum of Natural History
Eileen J. Garrett Library of the
    Parapsychology Foundation, Inc.
The Library of The American Society
    for Psychical Research
Lowell Observatory
The Metropolitan Museum of Art
Mississippi Department of Archives and History
The New York Public Library

Library of Congress Catalog Card Number 82-60791
ISBN 0-89577-146-2

Printed in Great Britain

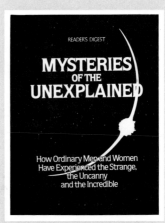

*An eclipse of the sun by the
planet Earth, viewed from
Apollo 12 in 1969, suggests
the awesome mystery and
beauty of the unknown.*

CONTENTS

The Endless Search
For Answers

**BEYOND THE
WALLS OF TIME**

**UNEARTHLY
FATES**

**MONSTERS
AND MORE**

**THE
UNQUIET SKY**

**IN THE REALM
OF MIRACLES**

*The frescoes executed by Michelangelo
for the Vatican in the 16th century sublimely
portray the mysteries of antiquity.*

"The most beautiful thing we can experience is the mysterious. It is the source of all true art and science." —Albert Einstein

Close in importance to the basic human needs for food, shelter, and companionship comes the urge to create an orderly world governed by dependable rules and to develop a reassuring structure of beliefs. This urge, since the beginning of recorded time, has provided a receptive audience for seers, scholars, scientists, and experts of every persuasion. There has never been, nor is there likely to be, a shortage of authorities ready to find reasonable explanations for all observed phenomena and to provide solutions for the mysteries of the universe.

And yet there are events that seem to say that our rules, our beliefs, even our common sense, may sometimes let us down.

In the past, men and women believed that the world around them had a miraculous dimension—that angels and demons were real, that prayers were efficacious, that man had a special place in the universe. Today fewer and fewer people believe in such a world. For many, existence has become something defined by politics, economics, and discoveries made in laboratories. And yet an instinct for the unknown persists, and a conviction also that not everything in our lives can be cut and dried by the statisticians, controlled in the halls of government, or defined in a test tube.

For, though more has been learned about the earth and the cosmos in the past 25 years than in all the preceding years of recorded history, the more we have probed the more mysterious the world has become. In view of the strangeness persistently revealed around us, we ask if common sense does not require us to accept the uncommon. Should we not abandon our conventional notions of the laws of nature? As our scientists tune in to the reverberations of cosmic creation, must we adhere to the idea that time progresses in a linear way? Cannot past, present, and future exist simultaneously? Must every effect be preceded by a cause? Cannot psychic energy make itself manifest in physically observable ways? It is questions like these that open the doorway to the vast and intriguing world of the unknown.

The editors of Reader's Digest recognize the fascination of such questions. In *Mysteries of the Unexplained* we have gathered hundreds of reports suggesting that the miraculous, the mysterious, and the enigmatic are alive and well, and always have been. But we must also recognize and warn against the danger of exaggeration, bias, and distortion in the reporting of inexplicable happenings.

This book is an almanac of events that defy explanation in commonly accepted terms. Some of the events are chilling; some document seeming miracles. Many suggest that the human mind and body have uncanny capabilities, while others suggest that creatures unknown to science and staggering to the imagination are roaming the world. Some reports propose that the cosmos may not be so sterile or uneventful as we think. And others—incredible stories of coincidence —hint that sometimes the inorganic world conspires with life to create bizarre or meaningful patterns in the vast tracts of time and space. In short, the stories gathered here imply that what we see and know of the everyday world represents only a glimpse of how things really are.

Where have we found these stories? Our researchers sought far and wide to track down recorded accounts of the strange and remarkable—in newspapers from around the world and from the journals of learned societies; in meteorological reports and the logs of ships' captains; in the diaries of travelers and missionaries; in ancient chronicles; in police records and in the records of archeological excavations; in the testimony of ordinary men and women who have related what they themselves have seen or experienced.

And how can we judge these reports? We cannot establish that all the events related herein occurred exactly as they have been recounted; human beings are fallible, excitable, and prone to exaggeration. But we can document every report. Someone, at some specific time or place, wrote down an account of each phenomenon described. All these sources are given in this book. And so our criteria should be the same as those applied to more conventional testimony by the jury in a court of law. Like the jury, it is up to us to measure the credibility of the witnesses who speak to us in these reports. We may doubt or disbelieve. But when we find numerous witnesses to a certain class of phenomena, we may also suppose, if we choose, not that all those witnesses are lying—but that there may be shortcomings in our commonsense notions of what is, and what is not, possible.

As we read on, we may agree that many things still remain hidden from us. As the philosopher Seneca observed in the first century: "Our universe is a sorry little affair unless it has in it something for every age to investigate . . . Nature does not reveal her mysteries once and for all."

The Editors

BEYOND
THE
WALLS OF TIME

The present is our only point of reference for
the past and for the future, and our awareness of
any happening must obviously occur somewhat after
the actual event. What, then, are we to make
of the time warp that allows some people to prophesy
that which will happen in the future?
Anomalies and coincidences are related phenomena in
that they are both departures from the expected time
frame. That some prophecies do come true, that anomalies
of many kinds exist, and that coincidences abound—
all this is without question. The (as yet)
fathomless mystery is what force or forces are powerful
enough to bring them into being.

DELPHICA

The sibyl, or prophetess, of Delphi looks into the future.

PROPHECIES

Prophecy is at once among the most mundane and the most exalted of human presumptions. By it, properly speaking, we signify a transcendence of time and space that delivers to our consciousness apocalyptic landscapes, the death of kings, New Ages, Final Judgments, and the Risen Dead.

We also prophesy when we make a date for lunch the day after next or a dentist's appointment for the following week. In these cases we construe the present state of affairs—our wish to see a friend, the nagging suspicion of trouble in a lower molar—and confidently predict, despite the uncertainties of life, that a luncheon will take place, that a molar will be probed.

Between these two extremes—the Grand Apocalypse and the lunch date—lie such gradations of prophecy as premonitions, precognitions, and predictions. Premonitions are unfocused sensations that usually occur in a more or less normal waking state or as the residue of an unremembered dream. The feeling that the plane a friend is due to take will crash or that a letter from a long-lost friend will be in the mailbox is a premonition.

Precognitions, which normally occur in dreams or states of reverie, are visual and more precise than premonitions. They occur in what is felt at the time to be a normal waking state and are indistinguishable from ordinary events, though they later prove to be specters of an event in the future. In a rare form of precognitive phenomena, the Vardogr, most commonly experienced in Norway, events are sometimes prefigured by sounds: Footsteps are heard some time before an arrival. A door is heard to open or close before anyone passes through.

Prediction differs from premonition and precognition by virtue of its deliberateness and the two kinds of techniques it employs. One of these includes the use of various and numerous signs: the position of planets, lines on the palm of a hand, tea leaves in a cup, tossed coins, birds in flight, and so on. The other involves the use of mind-changing drugs, procedures, and rituals, the latter often being aimed at invoking the help of some supernatural being with the gift of prophecy.

Prophecy in the grand sense, on the other hand, is usually neither sought nor cultivated by the methods of prediction. It is usually thought of as being inspired by God or gods or other spiritual beings of an elevated kind, and its subject matter is accordingly of major significance to large numbers of people. These areas of the prophetic spectrum are actually no more distinct from each other than are the colors of a rainbow. The most mundane examples, in fact, are not normally thought of as prophecy at all, though they share with it its qualifying characteristics. They have the emotional character of premonition (the wish to see a friend, the fear of toothache), the visual and sign-reading characteristics of precognition and prediction (clear images of menus or dentist's drills), and the sense of certainty about what has not yet taken place, which is the mark of all kinds of prophecy. And, like all prophecy, they only sometimes come true.

Finally, if mundane prophecy does come true—if our appointments occur as planned, if the future unfolds as expected—it does so for reasons pertaining to memory, observation, determination, and luck: a concatenation of factors as mysterious as any investigator of the prophetic could wish to find.

Because the element of time is the essential ingredient in the phenomena of prophecy, it seems logical to present the examples here in chronological order.

Biblical Prophecies Fulfilled

Numerous references in the Old Testament of the Bible are taken by Christians as prophetic of Jesus Christ as the Messiah. Among the more striking are these:

• But you, O Bethlehem Ephrathah, who are little to be among the clans of Judah, from you shall come forth for me one who is to be ruler in Israel, whose origin is from of old, from ancient days. [Micah 5:2]

• Say to those who are of a fearful heart, "Be strong, fear not! Behold, your God will come with vengeance, with the recompense of God. He will come and save you."

Then the eyes of the blind shall be opened, and the ears of the deaf unstopped;

then shall the lame man leap like a hart, and the tongue of the dumb sing for joy. For waters shall break forth in the wilderness, and streams in the desert. [Isaiah 35:4–6]

The prophet Isaiah, who lived in the eighth century B.C., *is among the biblical figures gloriously portrayed by Michelangelo on the ceiling of the Vatican's Sistine Chapel.*

• Rejoice greatly, O daughter of Zion! Shout aloud, O daughter of Jerusalem! Lo, your king comes to you; triumphant and victorious is he, humble and riding on an ass, on a colt the foal of an ass. [Zechariah 9:9]

• And I took my staff Grace, and I broke it, annulling the covenant which I had made with all the peoples. So it was annulled on that day, and the traffickers in the sheep, who were watching me, knew that it was the word of the Lord. Then I said to them, "If it seems right to you, give me my wages; but if not, keep them." And they weighed out as my wages thirty shekels of silver. Then the Lord said to me, "Cast it into the treasury"—the lordly price at which I was paid off by them. So I took the thirty shekels of silver and cast them into the treasury in the house of the Lord. [Zechariah 11:10–13]

• He was despised and rejected by men; a man of sorrows, and acquainted with grief; and as one from whom men hide their faces he was despised, and we esteemed him not.

Surely he has borne our griefs and carried our sorrows; yet we esteemed him stricken, smitten by God, and afflicted.

But he was wounded for our transgressions, he was bruised for our iniquities; upon him was the chastisement that made us whole, and with his stripes we are healed. [Isaiah 53:3–5]

• Yea, dogs are round about me; a company of evildoers encircle me; they have pierced my hands and feet—

I can count all my bones—they stare and gloat over me;

they divide my garments among them, and for my raiment they cast lots. [Psalm 22:16–18]

These biblical verses are held by Christians to accurately predict key events in Christ's life: His birth at Bethlehem; His miraculous cures; His entry into Jerusalem on an ass; His betrayal for 30 pieces of silver; His arrest and beating; His crucifixion.

These and other such verses are, of course, not universally accepted as prophecies of Christ as the Messiah. In Jewish commentary, for example, the famous Suffering Servant passages of Isaiah (beginning in Chapter 42) are sometimes interpreted as referring to Israel itself (on the basis, for instance, of Isaiah 49:3: "And he said to me, 'You are my servant, Israel, in whom I will be glorified' "); and at least one commentator, Julian Morgenstern, has demonstrated a connection between this theme and pre-Semitic harvest rituals that indicate the very ancient salvationary role of a despised and executed figure.

Jews, then, disagree with the theological significance attached to these verses by Christians, while others disparage their worth as prophecies on the grounds that they were self-fulfilled—on the grounds, that is, that Christ and His disciples fulfilled them quite deliberately and engineered the events of the New Testament—or their account of them—to conform to a plan outlined in the Old Testament. While this view (assuming the factual veracity of the Gospels) may or may not detract from Christ's status, it does not have any logical bearing on the prophetic connection between Old and New Testament events. (Julian Morgenstern, *Some Significant Antecedents of Christianity*, pp.49–51; *The New Oxford Annotated Bible*, Revised Standard Version)

A Contest of Oracles

Oracles were an accepted part of political and personal life in the ancient world, and the most famous of them remained influential for many hundreds of years. Valuable gifts were bestowed on them by hopeful or grateful inquirers, and many of the shrines housed great wealth.

Each oracle had its own method of divination. The oracle at Dodona, for example, the oldest in Greece, was an oak tree whose oracles were interpreted by a priest from the rustling of its leaves, the cooing of doves in its branches, and the clanking of the brass vessels hung from it. The reputation and success of the oracles were as variable as their methods, and a troubled inquirer, with no previous loyalties involved, might well be uncertain as to where to turn for help.

This was the position in which Croesus, the inordinately rich king of Lydia in the mid-sixth century B.C., found himself when the strength and ambition of his Persian neighbors grew to alarming proportions under the rule of Cyrus the Great. What danger did Cyrus pose to Lydia, and with whom might the king of Lydia most profitably ally himself to forestall the threat? These were important questions facing Croesus, and he felt the need of oracular help. But which oracle could he rely on? There were six famous ones in Greece and one in Egypt, and each had its enthusiastic devotees.

Croesus therefore decided to approach the problem scientifically, by testing the oracles before committing himself. Seven messengers, one to each shrine, were dispatched from Lydia on the same day and told to pose their question exactly 100 days from the departure date. The question each was to ask was "What is King Croesus, son of Alyattes, now doing?" Each was then to return to Lydia with the answer with all speed.

The record of only one reply has survived, that given by the oracle at Delphi, at the foot of the southern slope of Mount Parnassus. Here, in the temple of Apollo, the human source of the oracle, traditionally a woman named the Pythoness, sat on a golden tripod above a deep cleft in the rock, chewing leaves of the laurel, sacred to Apollo, and inhaling the fumes that rose around her from the cleft. Her mutterings when pre-

The oracle of Delphi, a priestess traditionally known as the Pythoness, exercises her magical powers, having put herself under a spell by inhaling fumes and chewing laurel leaves.

sented with a question were frenzied and incomprehensible and were translated for the questioner, usually in verse, by the attendant priest.

Croesus' messenger had scarcely set foot inside the shrine when the oracle spoke, without even waiting for his question:

> I can count the sands, and I can measure the ocean;
> I have ears for the silent and know what the dumb man meaneth;
> Lo! On my sense there striketh the smell of a shell-covered tortoise,
> Boiling now on a fire, with the flesh of a lamb in a caldron—
> Brass is the vessel below, and brass the cover above it.

This reply was taken back to Croesus, and he unhesitatingly placed his trust in the oracle of Delphi. For after much consideration he had chosen to perform on the day of the test the most improbable act he could think of. And so he had taken a lamb and a tortoise, cut them into pieces, and set them to boil together in a brass caldron with a brass lid. (*The Unexplained: Mysteries of Mind Space & Time*, Vol. 1, Issue 4)

Synchronicity

The vexing thing about techniques of prediction that rely on signs, of whatever kind, is that no connections seem to exist between the signs and what they signify. In the disposition of planets or the condition of a sheep's liver, in the way birds fly or tea leaves settle in the cup, in none of these traditional modes of prediction is there a conceivable relationship with war or death, with fortune in love or money, or with the outcome of any other future event. Such devices, however, are still considered to be useful omens.

Professor C. G. Jung (the Swiss psychotherapist and cofounder, with Sigmund Freud, of 20th-century psychiatry) was persuaded that such methods of prediction do produce meaningful results. His work had brought him into repeated contact with the stranger shores of the human psyche, and he was aware that the lives of many people are punctuated by the phenomena of coincidences and fulfilled prophecies.

Jung became convinced that some linking process, distinct from causality but complementary to it, is at work in the universe and that its manifestation is in seeming collaboration between the human psyche and the external world. He named this principle "synchronicity" and spent much of the latter part of his life trying to explain its workings.

In doing so he was keenly aware of the difficulty of describing a noncausal process for an audience that has been deeply conditioned by an exclusively causal view of the world. His systematic essay on the subject, entitled *Synchronicity: An Acausal Connecting Principle* and published in 1952, was a heroic attempt to avoid giving the impression that the agents of synchronicity are causal agents.

In Jung's view, the agents of synchronicity are to be found in what he called the archetypes of the human psyche. An archetype appears to the conscious mind as a special kind of symbol. It is not conceived by the conscious mind but rises into it, fully potent, from what Jung called the collective unconscious, a repository of archetypes held in common by all mankind. Just as all humans have certain genetic features in common, so they share, Jung found, a wealth of psychological material that becomes conscious only in dreams and reveries.

Examples of the archetypal figures that Jung found recurring in his own dreams, in the dreams of patients, and in the folk stories and myths of every age and nation, are those of the wise old man or woman, the eternal mother, the magical child, the trickster, the tree, and the mandala (a graphic pattern symbolizing the universe). Just as genes embody order (genes are orderly arrangements of DNA molecules and are themselves disposed in an orderly way in chromosomes) and create orderly patterns of growth, so archetypes embody order at a psychological level, and in their presence new order ensues.

At this point Jung's difficulty was to explain how the archetype, by virtue of its inherent order, creates order in a noncausal way. A medical example may provide an approximate model of the process. Penicillin is helpful in cases of bacterial infection because penicillin molecules are a partial match for molecules in the bacterial cell wall. When a bacterium is "deceived" by this near match into incorporating a penicillin molecule into its cell wall, the wall is weakened at that point (because of the inexact fit) and ruptures, killing the bacterium.

The penicillin molecule has been instrumental in this process but not actively so: in the presence of the penicillin molecule the bacterium has developed a new fatally flawed molecular pattern. Thus the role of the penicillin is contingent but not causal.

In a similar way an archetype serves as a psychic catalyst, in whose presence orderly psychical experiences unfold and in a way that often entails the physical world.

How can this be possible? Another biological example may be helpful. It is established that some migratory birds are guided by the stars. The birds' genetic time sense and mental image of the star patterns can be considered as the psychic level. The stars themselves represent the physical level. When the two levels mesh to put the birds on their proper route at the proper time, we see evidence of the psychic catalyst or archetype. And here, too, the archetypes (the genetic inner clock and mental image) are contingent, not causal.

So, in a similar way, many human beings, responding to the force of inherited psychological patterns, find themselves in various, altering relationships with the external world.

Jung himself was well aware that his theory was a tentative first step to the understanding of something profoundly difficult to formulate. The most important question he left unanswered: the real and precise nature of the synchronistic connection between the psychic and the physical.

For Jung this relationship was the psychological equivalent of the physicist's mathematical equations, and he realized that the lack of an appropriate contribution from mathematical physics rendered his theory incomplete as an attempt to account for "the relative or partial identity of psyche and physical continuum." While the theory of synchronicity has not been proved right, it has also not been proved wrong. And people may have genetic (archetypal) subconscious information that is related to their seeming ability to foretell the future.

A Papal Forecast

A well-known prophecy regarding the papal succession has often been erroneously attributed to Saint Malachy of Ireland, who lived from 1095 to 1148 and was famous for his prophetic gifts.

The prediction, actually a forgery first published in 1595, consists of a series of brief descriptions—two- and three-word phrases in Latin—of 111 popes, in sequence, from 1143 to the presumed end of the papacy. Some are opaque, and others are strikingly accurate:

- *Montium custos* ("Guardian of the hills"): Alexander VII (1655–67) had as his family crest three hills with a star above them.
- *Rosa Umbriae* ("The rose of Umbria"): Clement XIII (1758–69) served in Umbria before becoming pope; Umbria's emblem is a rose.
- *Ursus velox* ("Swift bear"): Clement XIV (1769–74) had the image of a running bear on his family crest.
- *Peregrinus apostolicus* ("Apostolic wanderer"): Pius VI (1775–99) spent the last years of his life as a fugitive from the political aftermath of the French Revolution.
- *De balneis Etruria* ("From the baths of Etruria"): Gregory XVI (1831–46) held office in Etruria before his election.
- *Religio depopulata* ("Religion laid waste"): the pope to whom this applied, in the sequence of the prophecy, was Benedict XV (1914–22), whose reign spanned World War I and the subsequent world influenza epidemic.
- *Pastor angelicus* ("The angelic shepherd"): Pius XII (1939–58) was a devoted student of Saint Thomas Aquinas, traditionally known as The Angelic Doctor.
- *Pastor et nauta* ("Shepherd and navigator"): John XXIII (1958–63) was the "shepherd and navigator" of the Second Vatican Council.
- *Flos florum* ("Flower of flowers"): Paul VI (1963–78) had the fleur-de-lis as his personal coat of arms.

The prophecy described only four more popes after Paul VI. *De medietate lunae* ("From the half-moon," or "Of the middle moon") referred to John Paul I, who was elected to the papacy on August 26, 1978, and died 33 days later, on September 28—approximately in the middle of the lunar month marked by the full moons of September 16 and October 16. The present pope, John Paul II (1978–   ), is signified by *De labore solis* ("From the toil of the sun"), the import of which, so far at least, is not clear. The two remaining popes are signified as *De gloria olivae* ("The glory of the olive") and *Petrus Romanus* ("Peter of Rome"). After, or perhaps during, the reign of the last pope, Rome will be destroyed and the day of Final Judgment will arrive. (Joe Fisher, *Predictions*, pp.36–39; David Wallechinsky and Irving Wallace, *The People's Almanac*, p.12)

The Plowboy Prophet

Robert Nixon, a rural visionary who, by reputation, was held to be mentally retarded, was born around 1467 on a farm in the county of Cheshire, England. He began his working life as a plowboy, being too stupid, by all appearances, to do anything else. He was mostly a silent youth, though sometimes given to strange, incomprehensible babblings that were taken to be a sign of his limited mentality.

One day, however, while he was plowing a field, he paused in his work, looked around him in a strange way, and exclaimed: "Now Dick! now Harry! Oh, ill done, Dick! Oh, well done, Harry! Harry has gained the day!" This outcry, more cogent than most, though still incomprehensible, puzzled Robert's fellow workers, but the next day everything was made clear: at the very moment of Robert's strange seizure King Richard III had been killed at Bosworth Field, and the victor of that decisive battle, Henry Tudor, was now proclaimed Henry VII of England.

Before long, news of the bucolic seer reached the new king, who was much intrigued and wanted to meet him. An envoy was sent from London to escort Nixon back to the palace. Even before the envoy left the court, Robert knew he was coming and was thrown into a fit of great distress, running about the town of Over and crying out that Henry had sent for him and he would be *clammed*—starved to death!

In the meantime Henry had decided on a method of testing the young prophet, and when Nixon was shown into his presence the king appeared to be greatly troubled. He had lost a valuable diamond, he explained. Could Nixon help him locate it? Nixon calmly replied, in the words of a proverb, that those who hide can find. Henry had, of course, hidden the diamond and was so impressed by the plowboy's answer that he ordered a record to be made of everything the lad said. What he said, duly interpreted, forecast the English civil wars, the death and abdication of kings, and war with France. He also forecast that the town of Nantwich, in Cheshire, would be swept away by a flood, though this has not yet happened.

But the prophecy that most concerned Nixon was the most improbable of all: that he would starve to death in the royal palace. To allay these fears, Henry ordered that Nixon should be given all the food he wanted, whenever he wanted it, an order that did not endear the strange young man to the royal kitchen (whose staff, in any case, envied his privileges).

One day, however, the king left London, leaving Robert in the care of one of his officers. To protect his

16

When Henry Tudor was crowned King Henry VII after the defeat and death of Richard III at Bosworth Field, the event was "seen" from afar by a clairvoyant plowboy.

charge from the malice of the palace domestics, the officer thoughtfully locked him safely in the king's own closet. The officer was then also called away from London on urgent business and forgot to leave the key or instructions for Robert's release. By the time he returned, Robert had starved to death. (Charles Mackay, *Extraordinary Popular Delusions and the Madness of Crowds*, pp.277–80)

The Prophecies of Nostradamus
The most famous of all nonbiblical prophets, Michel de Nostredame, or Nostradamus, was born at St. Rémy in the south of France in 1503. He first became famous for his medical work with victims of the plague that broke out at Aix-en-Provence and Lyons in 1546–47 and only after this began making prophecies. His first collection was published as an almanac of weather predictions in 1550, and in 1555 he published the first of 10 collections of prophecies (almost 1,000 in all) under the title of *Centuries*. He died at Salon, in southern France, in 1566.

Nostradamus wrote his prophecies in verse, for the most part in a highly symbolic style. This, and the fact that he chose not to arrange them in any particular order, makes their interpretation, in many cases, a matter of conjecture. Nonetheless, a number of the prophecies do seem to point rather clearly to events that had not yet occurred when *Centuries* appeared.

The first prophecy to bring Nostradamus fame as a seer was the following:

> The young lion will overcome the older one, in a field of combat in a single fight: He will pierce his

eyes in their golden cage; two wounds in one, then he dies a cruel death.

Four years later, in July 1559, King Henry II of France, who sometimes used the lion as his emblem, engaged in a jousting contest. The lance of his young opponent pierced the king's gilt helmet and wounded him; Henry died after prolonged agony.

Few of Nostradamus's prophecies contain anything so precise as a date, or even a partial date. But he seems to have given one for the great fire of London in 1666, saying it would occur "in three times twenty plus six."

Most of Nostradamus's prophecies concern large-scale political movements and the affairs of the high and mighty. The French Revolution seems to be the subject of several verses, including this:

> From the enslaved populace, songs, chants and demands, while Princes and Lords are held captive in prisons. These will in the future be received by headless idiots as divine prayers.

The first sentence is straightforward. The "headless idiots" of the second sentence are thought to refer to the early leaders of the revolution, who perceived the demands of the French populace as "prayers," and who, ultimately corrupted by their new power, were themselves overthrown and guillotined.

In a letter to King Henry II, Nostradamus also predicted 1792 as a key date in the affairs of state. In September of that year, at the culmination of the revolution, France was declared a republic. The deaths of Queen Marie Antoinette and Madame Du Barry, a mistress of Louis XVI, also appear to have been forecast by this remarkable seer.

Like most prophets, Nostradamus seems to have had a particular talent for predicting disasters and falls from power. He is held to have described the fate of Napoleon, whose rule over the French Empire ended with his imprisonment on the tiny island of St. Helena in 1815, and to have predicted the abdication of King Edward VIII of Great Britain in 1936.

In two quatrains Nostradamus came close to naming Adolf Hitler and described his calamitous activities with some accuracy. According to the first one:

> Liberty shall not be recovered, a black, fierce, villainous, evil man shall occupy it, when the ties of his alliance are wrought. Venice shall be vexed by Hister.

The second quatrain was even more vivid:

> Beasts wild with hunger will cross the rivers, the greater part of the battlefield will be against Hister. He will drag the leader in a cage of iron, when the child of Germany observes no law.

travelers from outer space—in this case, inhabitants of the moon (though originally from the sun) who could change their shape at will.

Cyrano also, and far more remarkably, described the following items of moon technology: houses that could be withdrawn into the ground on huge screws in cold weather (though the retractable screw is something not yet attempted by builders of berm houses); houses that moved about with the seasons, driven by sails filled by bellows; devices to record and play back speech; and radiant bulbs that made the lunar night as bright as day.

Although many science-fiction writers have forecast new technology, none was so early in the field as Cyrano, with his prevision of such electrical and electronic inventions as the phonograph and tape recorder, mobile homes and light bulbs. He may, indeed, have equals in the field, but we shall have to wait another two or three hundred years to find out. (Sam Moskowitz, *Explorers of the Infinite*, pp.23–27)

Illustrating the prophetic works of Cyrano de Bergerac on space travel were these depictions of a spacecraft sailing to the sun and a man flying with the aid of a special belt.

In content the verses are remarkably apt. Liberty was seized, or occupied, by an evil (black-hearted and black-haired) man. Venice, along with the rest of Italy, was indeed eventually "vexed" by her former ally. Hitler's troops did cross rivers, and other boundaries, like ravening beasts, even though the majority of countries were against them. The last sentence is unclear but may refer to the German naval blockade of Britain, which, before Pearl Harbor, was the lone leader of the free world's battle for survival. (Erika Cheetham, *The Prophecies of Nostradamus*, passim)

Cyrano's Amazing Predictions

The French author Savinien Cyrano de Bergerac, whom fate and Edmond Rostand's play have made immortal for the size of his nose and his superlative swordsmanship, should properly be remembered as a lively science-fiction writer, a competent playwright, an inquiring scholar, and also, perhaps, as a prophet.

His two romances on trips to the moon and the sun (which usually appear in a single volume under the English title *Voyages to the Moon and the Sun*) were published posthumously in 1656 and 1662, respectively. In them, only a few years after Galileo had recanted the fact before the Inquisition, Cyrano described the orbit of the earth and other planets around the sun, and the weak gravitational field of the moon, and he proposed, among seven fanciful methods of interplanetary travel, a form of rocket propulsion. He also proposed, 300 years before the idea was borrowed by the writer Erich von Däniken, that the gods and mythological beings with whom earth's history is intertwined were actually

The Seaforth Doom

Some called him the Warlock of The Glen, and others the Brahan Seer. His real name was Coinneach Odhar, in Gaelic, or Kenneth Mackenzie, in English. He lived in Scotland in the 17th century. The seer, who looked into the future through a hole in a white stone, is said to have foreseen the bloody battle of Culloden and the cutting of the Caledonian Canal, the narrow, loch-linking waterway that runs across Scotland from Loch Linnhe in the southwest to the Moray Firth at Inverness. But what Mackenzie is most famed for is undoubtedly the Doom of the Seaforths.

The story of the Doom begins in 1660, when the earl of Seaforth traveled from Brahan Castle, his home, to Paris, leaving behind his wife, Isabella, a woman reputedly as ugly as she was violent and uncouth. Time passed. The day of the earl's scheduled return to Brahan came and went, and still he remained in Paris. Slowly it dawned on Isabella that her husband might have found more pleasant company in Paris than she had been providing at Brahan Castle.

Day by day the certainty that the earl was deceiving her grew stronger and so did her jealousy. One night, when the big hall at Brahan was crowded with guests, she summoned the seer and asked him if he could see her husband through his viewing stone. Mackenzie put the stone to his eye—and was overcome with laughter. What was he laughing at, Isabella demanded. He refused to tell her. Her fury mounting, Isabella insisted, and at last the Brahan Seer told her that he saw the earl with one girl on his knee and another stroking his hair.

Isabella's rage at the news was uncontrollable, and she ordered her servants to seize the sage. Some accounts say that she had him hanged there in Brahan Castle, and others that she charged him before the authorities with practicing witchcraft and that as a result he was burned to death in a barrel of tar.

In either case, all sources agree that before he died in 1663 Mackenzie pronounced the famous Doom of the Seaforths, as follows:

> I see into the future and I read the doom of the race of my oppressor. The long-descended line of Seaforth will, ere many generations have passed, end in extinction and sorrow. I see a chief, the last of his house, both deaf and dumb. He will be the father of four fair sons, all of whom he will follow to the tomb. He will live careworn and die mourning, knowing that the honours of his line are to be extinguished for ever, and that no future chief of the Mackenzies shall bear rule at Brahan or in Kintail. After lamenting over the last and most promising of his sons, he himself shall sink into the grave, and the remnant of his possessions shall be inherited by a white-coifed lassie from the East, and she is to kill her sister. And as a sign by which it may be known that these things are coming to pass, there shall be four great lairds in the days of the last deaf and dumb Seaforth—Gairloch, Chisholm, Grant and Raasay—of whom one shall be buck-toothed, another hare-lipped, another half-witted, and the fourth a stammerer. Chiefs distinguished by these personal marks shall be the allies and neighbors of the last Seaforth; and when he looks around him and sees them, he may know that his sons are doomed to death, that his broad lands shall pass away to the stranger, and that his race shall come to an end.

For the next 135 years the fortunes of the Seaforth family waxed and waned. In the revolution of 1688 they supported James II, the Roman Catholic king who fled to France, and in 1715 they supported his son James, the Old Pretender. For their pains they were stripped of their lands and title. By the mid-18th century the political loyalties of the Seaforths brought them back into royal favor, and by 1783, when Francis Humberston Mackenzie inherited the estates, their lands and forfeited title had been restored.

By this time the Doom of the Seaforths was little more than a vague memory. The new lord had four sons and six daughters, and though scarlet fever had left him deaf and dumb in his childhood (he later recovered his power of speech), there seemed little chance that the Seaforth line was coming to an end. As for his neighbors, it could be no more than a sinister coincidence that Mackenzie of Gairloch should be buck-toothed, that Chisholm of Chisholm should have a harelip, that Grant of Grant should be a half-wit, and Macleod of Raasay an incurable stammerer.

Then one of Seaforth's sons died, then another, and then still another. The fourth boy was now in poor health, and his father sent him to England for medical treatment. Despite this, the fourth and last son also died. As the Warlock had prophesied, the deaf-and-dumb lord outlived all his sons, and when he died in 1815 the Seaforth title lapsed. The first part of the Doom had been fulfilled precisely.

Seaforth's estates were inherited by his daughter Mary Elizabeth Frederica. She had married Sir Samuel Hood, an admiral who, after serving with Nelson in the Battle of the Nile, had become commander in chief of the East Indies, a position that took him and Mary to India. Sir Samuel died at Madras shortly before Lord Seaforth. Mary came home wearing the traditional widow's white cap: as the Doom said they would, the Seaforth lands had passed into the hands of "a white-coifed lassie from the East."

In fact, the Seaforth estate was by now much diminished by mismanagement, extravagance, and government fines. Mary found herself obliged to sell still more of the property, including the Isle of Lewis. Piece by piece the broad lands of the Seaforths were indeed passing away to the stranger.

The last chapter in the fulfillment of the Doom of the Seaforths occurred a few years later as Mary was taking her young sister Caroline for a drive through the woods in a pony carriage. Without warning the ponies bolted and the carriage was overturned. Mary was cut and bruised, but her sister died from her injuries. The "lassie from the East" had killed her sister—or had, at least, been instrumental in her death—just as Kenneth Mackenzie had foretold. (J. G. Lockhart, *Curses, Lucks and Talismans*, pp.27–37)

The Fatal Salute

If a person dreams that he will die in a certain situation and then takes care to avoid that situation, we have, of course, no means of knowing if the warning was false or if fate has been cheated. Sometimes, though, fate gives a warning and then refuses to be cheated.

One night in July 1750 Robert Morris, Sr., the father of the Robert Morris who managed the financial affairs of the American Revolution, dreamed that he would be killed by cannon fire from a naval ship he was to visit. The dream made him so nervous that he was persuaded to board the vessel only by the captain's promise that no guns would be fired until he was safely back on land.

The visit was made, and at its conclusion the captain gave instructions that no salute be fired until he signaled that the rowboat had returned Morris safely to shore. But while the boat was still within range of the ship's gun, a fly settled on the captain's nose and he thoughtlessly raised his hand to brush it away. This gesture was taken as a sign that the salute should be fired, and so it was. A fragment of the blast struck Morris and wounded him fatally. *(Journal of the American Society for Psychical Research,* April 1970, p.193)

Swedenborg's Vision

Emanuel Swedenborg (1688–1772) was equally famous in his native Sweden as a scientist, a mystical theologian, and a clairvoyant. A well-authenticated instance of the latter ability, investigated by the German philosopher Immanuel Kant, occurred on July 19, 1759, in Goteborg, a port on Sweden's southwest coast. It was a Saturday, about four o'clock in the afternoon, and Swedenborg had just returned to Goteborg from a visit to England when he became restless and upset. He excused himself to his friends and went for a walk. Upon his return he told them that he had seen, in a vision, a fire that had broken out near his house, 300 miles away, and was now raging through his hometown. He remained distressed until 8 P.M., when he informed his friends that the fire was now extinguished.

News of the vision spread quickly, and Swedenborg was asked to describe it in person to the governor. On Monday morning a royal messenger arrived in Goteborg with news of the fire, and confirmed Swedenborg's vision in all particulars. (*The Unexplained: Mysteries of Mind Space & Time,* Vol. 1, Issue 4)

Truth Follows Fiction

In 1838 Edgar Allan Poe published a grim tale called "The Narrative of Arthur Gordon Pym of Nantucket." In it, three survivors of a shipwreck, dying of thirst and

---

The Intermediate Present

Most theories of prophecy concentrate on what are professed to be ambiguities and uncertainties in our conventional notion of what the future is and claim that the future either unfolds in or coexists with the present. A somewhat novel approach to the problem, focusing on ambiguities in what we call the present, was proposed in 1934 by H. F. Saltmarsh.

Saltmarsh begins by pointing out that what we conventionally name the present is nothing of the kind. For when we perceive something—the fall of a leaf, the prick of a pin—we regard our perception and what it reveals as occurring simultaneously in time. But sensory impressions do not occur all at once. We feel the pinprick an instant after it happens; the leaf touches the ground an instant before we register the landing. For in addition to the time it takes for sensory impressions to reach our brain is the time it takes our brain to process the signals when they arrive. Thus, based on Saltmarsh's proposal, our perception of any happening is inevitably a bit later than the event itself. Consequently, we have two kinds of present. The interval between these two presents might well be considered a third level, or intermediate present, in which events can occur or begin to occur. We can further conjecture that it is in this third level of time that certain people receive intimations of the future.

Because all transitions take time, we can hardly suppose that the contents of the intermediate present pass into our awareness intact or unchanged. We can therefore say that the intermediate present, like the real present, is unavailable to ordinary consciousness and that its contents can never be quite the same as those of our normal awareness. It is in this nether area between an event and the perception of it that precognition might occur.

In Poe's tale of horror on the high seas, the shipwrecked Pym and his companions joyously greet an approaching brig, only to find that all aboard are dead of a virulent disease.

starvation, kill and eat their companion, Richard Parker, who lost when they drew lots.

In 1884 three survivors of a shipwreck were tried for the murder of a fourth. Adrift, and facing starvation, they had killed and eaten their companion, a cabin boy named Richard Parker. (Alan Vaughan, *Incredible Coincidence*, pp.22–23)

The Murder of Hart Northey

The following vision of a brother's murder was recorded by the English journalist William T. Stead (1848–1912), editor of the *Pall Mall Gazette* and founder of the *Review of Reviews*. Stead was a champion of social reform and in later life became interested in psychical research. He had been given the story by persons intimately acquainted with George Northey, the brother of Hart, the murdered man.

From childhood their lives had been marked by the strongest brotherly affection. They had lived in St. Eglos, in Cornwall, England, which is situated about 10 miles from the Atlantic and not quite so far from the old market town of Trebodwina.

George and Hart had never been separated since their birth until the former became a sailor. Hart at the same time joined his father in business. In February 1840 George Northey's ship was lying in port at St. Helena. While he was there George had a strange dream, which he himself related:

"I dreamed that my brother Hart was at Trebodwina Market, and that I was with him, quite close by his side, during the whole of the market transactions. Although I could see and hear everything which passed around me, I felt sure that it was not my bodily presence which thus accompanied him, but my shadow, or rather my spiritual self, for he seemed quite unconscious that I was near him.

"I felt that my being thus present in this strange way betokened some hidden danger which he was destined to meet, and which I knew my presence could not avert, for I could not speak to warn him of his peril. . . .

"[Brother having collected a considerable sum of money then started on his ride homeward.] My terror gradually increased as Hart approached the hamlet of Polkerrow, until I was in a perfect frenzy, frantically desirous, yet unable, to warn my brother in some way and prevent him going further. . . .

"I suddenly became aware of two dark shadows thrown across the road. . . . Two men appeared whom I instantly recognized as notorious poachers, who lived in a lonely wood near St. Eglos. . . . The men wished him 'Good Evening, maister,' civilly enough. . . . He replied and entered into conversation with them about some work he had promised them.

"After a few minutes they asked him for some money. . . . The elder of the two brothers, who was standing near the horse's head, said:

" 'Mr. Northey, we know you have just come from Trebodwina Market with plenty of money in your pockets, we are desperate men, and you bean't going to leave this place until we've got that money; so hand over.'

"My brother made no reply, except to slash at him with the whip and spur the horse at him.

"The younger of the ruffians instantly drew a pistol and fired. Hart dropped lifeless from the saddle, and one of the villains held him by the throat with a grip of iron for some minutes, as though to make assurance doubly sure, and crush out any particle of life my poor brother might have left.

"The murderers secured the horse to a tree in the orchard, and, having rifled the corpse, they dragged it up the stream, concealing it under the overhanging banks of the water-course. They then carefully covered over all marks of blood on the road, and hid the pistol in the thatch of a disused hut close to the roadside; then, setting the horse free to gallop home alone, they decamped across the country to their own cottage."

George Northey's vessel left St. Helena the next day and reached Plymouth in due course. During the entire voyage back home George Northey was constantly under the firm conviction that his brother, Hart, had been murdered and that the vision had shown him the details and the murderers. He eventually reached port and his family. His brother, Hart, had been murdered! Exactly as he had visioned!

The crime had aroused widespread horror and indignation, and every effort of the authorities had been bent upon discovering the murderers and bringing them to justice. Two brothers named Hightwood were suspected. A search was made of their cottage, which revealed blood-stained garments, but no trace of the pistol was to be found, although the younger brother admitted having one but said he had lost it.

The brothers were arrested and brought before the magistrates. The evidence against them was certainly not strong, but their manner seemed that of guilty men. They were ordered to be tried at the forthcoming assizes at Trebodwina. Each confessed, in the hope of saving his life, and both were sentenced to be hung. There was, however, some doubt about the pistol.

Before the execution, George Northey arrived from St. Helena and declared that the pistol was in the thatch of the old cottage close by the place where his brother, Hart, had been murdered and where the Hightwood brothers had hidden it.

"How did you know?" he was asked, after the weapon had been found at the place he stated.

"I saw the foul deed committed in a dream which I had the night of the murder," he declared. (William T. Stead, *More Ghost Stories,* pp.35–36)

Mark Twain's Dream
In the late 1850's young Mark Twain and his brother Henry worked together on the riverboats then plying the Mississippi between St. Louis and New Orleans. One night, during a stay at his sister's house in St. Louis, Twain had an unusually vivid dream. In it he saw his brother's corpse lying in a metal coffin in his sister's sitting room. The coffin rested on two chairs, and a bouquet with a single crimson flower at its center had been placed on Henry's chest.

When Twain awoke, he was quite convinced that his brother had died and was lying in the sitting room. He dressed, thought of visiting the corpse, but decided to take a walk first. He left the house and had gone half a block before he realized he had been dreaming. He then returned and told his sister of the dream.

A few weeks later Twain and his brother were together in New Orleans but took different boats back to St. Louis. Henry's passage was on the *Pennsylvania,* whose boilers exploded not far from Memphis, killing many people. Henry was badly injured and taken, in great pain, to Memphis, where he died a few days later. Although most victims of the accident were buried in wooden coffins, a number of Memphis women, moved by pity for the young man, raised the money to provide a metal coffin. Thus, when Mark Twain came to say his last farewells to his brother, he found the body lying in a metal coffin, just as it had been in his dream. The bouquet, however, was missing. But as Twain stood beside the body a woman entered the room and placed on Henry's chest a bouquet of white flowers. At its center was a single red rose. (*Journal of the American Society for Psychical Research,* 64:187–88, 1970)

The Priest of Bel
Dr. Hermann V. Hilprecht was tired. It was the middle of March 1892, and for weeks he had been working on his new book. Now the proofs had arrived, and he would soon have to send his brainchild out into the world. Its full title was *The Babylonian Expedition of the University of Pennsylvania, Series A: Cuneiform Texts, Vol. 1, Part 1: Old Babylonian Inscriptions Chiefly From Nippur,* and Hermann Hilprecht, professor of Assyriology at the University of Pennsylvania, was not entirely satisfied. Two small fragments of inscribed agate—he thought they were parts of finger rings—had resisted his best efforts as translator. Numerous similar fragments had been found in the temple of Bel at Nippur, but in the present case he had not even been able to examine the originals, only a sketch of them.

Despite these difficulties, Hilprecht, after weeks of study, had assigned to the fragments a date of between 1700 and 1140 B.C., the Kassite period of Babylonian history. On one fragment he thought he could decipher the cuneiform character *KU* and ascribed the piece, very tentatively, to King Kurigalzu. The other fragment, with much regret, he had to assign to the large group of unclassified Kassite fragments. The final proofs of his discussion of these unclassified pieces were now awaiting his approval. There was no more he could do, and he reluctantly signed the proof sheets. It was around midnight, he was exhausted, and he went to bed.

He fell asleep almost immediately and dreamed a strange dream. A tall figure appeared to him, thin and clad in a simple robe: a priestly phantom from the Babylonian era, it seemed, a man about 40 years old.

"Come with me," the figure said and beckoned the professor. Together they traveled in time until they came to the treasure chamber of the temple of Bel. They entered a low-ceilinged room without windows. It was furnished with a large wooden chest, and the floor was strewn with fragments of agate and lapis lazuli.

The figure turned to him and said:

"The two fragments which you have published separately on pages 22 and 26, belong together. They are *not* finger rings. Their history is as follows: King Kurigalzu (c. 1300 B.C.) once sent to the temple of

The maxim Mark Twain scrawled beneath this 1897 photograph of himself reveals his celebrated humor. The writer was deeply interested in psychical phenomena.

Be good + you will be lonesome

Mark Twain

The chief center for the worship of the god Bel, king of Heaven and Earth, was the city of Nippur in ancient Babylonia. In 1892 a priestly phantom took Dr. Hermann V. Hilprecht back through time to the temple of Bel there and helped him to solve an archeological mystery. This depiction of Bel is believed to be from a Babylonian relief.

Bel—among other articles of agate and lapis-lazuli—an inscribed votive cylinder of agate.

"Then we priests received a command from him to make a pair of earrings of agate for the statue of the god Ninib. We were in great dismay, since there was no agate as raw material at hand. In order to carry out the King's command there was nothing for us to do but cut the votive cylinder into three parts, thus making three rings, each of which contained a portion of the original inscription.

"The first two rings served as earrings for the statue of the god. The two fragments which have given you so much trouble are portions of them. If you will put the two together you will have the proof of my words to you. But the third ring you have not yet found during your excavations—and you never will find it."

So saying, the priest disappeared. Hilprecht woke up and immediately told his wife what had happened.

The next day, a Sunday, he again examined the fragments. The dream was true! By placing them together he could read the original inscription: "To the God Ninib, son of Bel, his Lord, has Kurigalzu, Pontifex of Bel, presented this."

Still tingling with excitement, Professor Hilprecht told his friend and colleague Prof. William Romaine Newbold of the experience and showed him the account of the dream he had written down while it was still fresh in his mind. Together they pored over the translation and the notes made when the fragments were discovered. Suddenly Newbold noticed a problem: according to the original descriptions by the archeologist Dr. John P. Peters, the two fragments were of different colors. How could they originally have been part of the same piece?

Professor Hilprecht acknowledged the difficulty and determined to examine the fragments themselves that summer, when he visited the Istanbul museum where they were housed.

His journey to Istanbul was made on behalf of the Committee on the Babylonian Expedition, to catalog and study those objects preserved there from the Nippur excavations. He related his dream to Halil Bey, the director of the museum, and asked if he might examine the fragments. Halil Bey agreed enthusiastically.

I found one fragment in one case, and another in a case far away from it [Hilprecht wrote]. When I put them together the truth of my dream was demonstrated *ad oculos* ["before my eyes"]. They had in fact once belonged to one and the same votive cylinder!

As it originally had been of finely veined agate, the stone-cutter's saw had accidentally divided the object in such a way that the whitish vein of the stone appeared only upon one fragment and the larger grey surface upon the other. Thus I was able to explain Dr. Peters' discordant description of the two fragments!

Perhaps Professor Hilprecht had, in his subconscious mind, solved the riddle of the fragments during his hours of study and devised the dramatic dream to bring its findings to his conscious attention. Perhaps Professor Hilprecht's subconscious was clever enough to construe a votive cylinder from two small fragments of agate.

Or could it be that the priest of Bel traveled through 32 centuries to guide the latest guardian of his ancient treasures? (Sylvan Muldoon, *Psychic Experiences of Famous People*, pp.136–40)

The News in Advance

In 1896 Madame de Ferriëm, a noted German psychic of the period, had a vision of an impending disaster. Her description of what she saw—or was seeing—has a curiously rapid and selective quality, as though she were scanning a fast-moving newsreel:

All these people here at the mine entrance! How white they are! Like corpses!—Ah! That is what they are, all corpses! Yes, they are coming out—all being now carried out. The whole region is so black, nothing but small huts all about. The people that I see speak a different language.... Now they are bringing out one wearing a belt with a shining buckle on it. It will soon be Christmas—it is so cold! There is one who has a lamp with a little wire grating about it. Ah, this is a coal-mine.... Now I understand what one of them is saying. He says, "The doctors are all coming from Brüx!" Oh! This is a Bohemian place.... They are Bohemians. The women and children all wear kerchiefs.... Are those physicians, applying friction? Many of them have bands with crosses on their arms.... Oh, that is a rosary.... "In the coal-mines of Dux" he is saying. But what I read is Brüx. Why, I see it on his arm-band—Oh, they are from the health department.

Three years after Madame de Ferriëm's vision, in 1899, a German newspaper published an account of it. The following year, in September 1900, hundreds of people were killed by an explosion in a coal mine at Dux, near Brüx in Czechoslovakia. A month after the explosion, during an unusually cold October, bodies were still being brought out of the mine. Madame de Ferriëm's only error was in thinking that the calamity occurred at Christmas. (Both towns were, as Madame de Ferriëm had said, in Bohemia, an ancient region of western Czechoslovakia. Dux is now called Duchkov, and the name of Brüx has been changed to Most.) (Herbert R. Greenhouse, *Premonitions: A Leap Into the Future*, pp.50–51)

Futility and the Future

In 1898 Morgan Robertson published a novel about pride, greed, and stupidity. It was called *The Wreck of the Titan, or Futility,* and it described the maiden voyage of a transatlantic luxury liner named *Titan*. Although reputedly unsinkable, the *Titan* strikes an iceberg and sinks, with enormous loss of life.

In 1912 the *Titanic,* a transatlantic luxury liner widely touted as unsinkable, made her maiden voyage. She struck an iceberg and sank, with enormous loss of life. The following similarities pertained:

On Tuesday, April 16, 1912, The New York Times *announced the sinking of the* Titanic. *The disaster was strangely similar to a fictional tragedy published in 1898.*

	Titan	*Titanic*
Month of wreck	April	April
Passengers and crew	3,000	2,207
Lifeboats	24	20
Tonnage	75,000	66,000
Length	800 ft.	882.5 ft.
Propellers	3	3
Speed at impact	25 knots	23 knots

(Martin Ebon, *Prophecy in Our Time*, p.11)

The Death of the Archduke

The assassination of Archduke Francis Ferdinand of Austria at Sarajevo, Yugoslavia, on June 28, 1914, was one of the immediate causes of World War I. In the early morning of June 28 the archduke's former tutor Bishop Joseph Lanyi woke from a terrible dream:

I dreamed that I had gone to my desk early in the morning to look through the post that had come in. On top of all the other letters there lay one with a black border, a black seal and the arms of the Archduke. I immediately recognized the latter's writing, and saw at the head of the notepaper in blue colouring a picture like those on picture postcards which showed me a street and a narrow side-street. Their Highnesses sat in a car, opposite them sat a general, and an officer next to the chauffeur. On both sides of the street, there was a large crowd. Two young lads sprang forward and shot at their Highnesses. The text of the letter was as follows: "Dear Dr. Lanyi, Your Excellency, I wish to inform you that my wife and I were the victims of a political assassination. We recommend ourselves to your prayers. Cordial greetings from your Archduke Franz, Sarajevo, June 28th, 3.15 A.M." Trembling and in tears, I sprang out of bed and I looked at the clock which showed 3.15. I immediately hurried to my desk and wrote down what I had read and seen in my dream. In doing so, I even retained the form of certain letters just as the Archduke had written them. My servant entered my study at a quarter to six that morning and saw me sitting there pale and saying my rosary. He asked whether I was ill. I said: "Call my mother and the guest at once. I will say Mass immediately for their Highnesses, for I have had a terrible dream." My mother and the guest came at a quarter to seven. I told my mother the dream in the presence of the guest and of my servant. Then I went into the house chapel. The day passed in fear and apprehension. At half-past three, a telegram brought us news of the murder.

Bishop Lanyi's dream was inaccurate in two details: there was only one assassin, and the officer was not sitting next to the chauffeur—he was standing on the car's running board because of an earlier unsuccessful bomb attack on the archduke. (Keith Ellis, *Prediction and Prophecy*, pp.101–02)

Dimensions of Time

That time has many dimensions is a concept often advanced to account for prophecy. The gist of the idea is that time—which seems to unfold in a linear way, with the past coming before the present and the present before the future—might, in another dimension, not be experienced sequentially. The past, present, and future could exist simultaneously.

The concept that there are unfamiliar dimensions of time is most easily approached by way of those dimensions with which we are already familiar, those of length, height, and breadth. These, in turn, are best approached, quite literally, from a starting point, which, geometrically speaking, has a location but no dimensions. It does, however, relate to figures with dimensions in the following way:

If a point is moved through space, it marks a line, with the one dimension of length. If a line is moved through space, it traces the figure of a plane, with the two dimensions of length and breadth. And if a plane is moved in space, it traces a figure with the three dimensions of length, breadth, and height.

We can also work backward from a three-dimensional body and find that the cross section of the three-dimensional cube is a two-dimensional plane, that the cross section of the plane is a one-dimensional line, and that the cross section of the line is a dimensionless point.

From this we can can infer that a body of three dimensions is the cross section of a body of four dimensions and that a three-dimensional body, when moved in a certain way, will produce a body of four dimensions. Then comes the question, of what sort of body could a three-dimensional shape be the cross section? And in what sort of new direction could a three-dimensional shape be moved to produce one of four dimensions, since a movement other than up and down, backward and forward, or side to side would simply produce a larger figure, not one of a different dimension. The answer, of course, is the feature duration. For as soon as something ceases to endure, it ceases to exist. To the three familiar dimensions, then, we should add duration in time as a fourth dimension. Ordinary three-dimensional bodies should therefore be properly described as four-dimensional, and a body with three dimensions must be defined as having only length, breadth, and height but no duration. Is such a thing possible? It is, but only hypothetically. For, in fact, the point, line, and plane do not truly exist as such. Any line that can be seen has breadth as well as length (and duration), just as any physical plane has a certain thickness as well as length and breadth. What movement, then, must a figure of three dimensions

undergo to produce a body of four dimensions?

We moved a plane in the dimension of height to produce a cube; so the movement of a (hypothetical) cube in the dimension of time should produce a (real) figure of four dimensions. What does movement in the dimension of time mean?

As we said, it must mean movement in a new direction, not up, down, or sideways. Are there any other kinds of movement? For a start, there is the movement that the earth's rotation imparts to everything upon it and that puts even apparently motionless objects in motion. We can thus say that a three-dimensional body is the hypothetically motionless cross section of a real body whose fourth dimension, duration, is inseparable from the motion that the turning world inevitably imparts to everything. Further inevitable motions are that of the earth around the sun, of the sun around the center of the galaxy, and, perhaps, of the galaxy itself around some unknown point. Since any perceptible body is, in fact, undergoing all these motions simultaneously, we can say that everything has these dimensions, though in a way that is ordinarily imperceptible. Because motions and the dimensions they imply are only perceptible in a framework of time, they can be referred to as dimensions of time.

If duration is one aspect of time, what might the others be? Among several possibilities, we can suggest appearance and disappearance, change and recurrence. Of all possibilities, only duration is perceptible. When we say that something appears, we mean that we suddenly note its existence; when something disappears, we note its lack of existence. We perceive no intermediate condition of "appearing" or "disappearing." In the same way, we talk of change but actually only develop the concept as we perceive aggregates of characteristics that exist—or cease to exist. And so we infer, but do not observe, the recurrence of sunset and sunrise, the passage of seasons, the growth of a child.

And yet, things really do appear and disappear, change and recur, although not actually perceived to do so. They are, so to speak, hypothetical to us and must have their reality in other dimensions of time, just as the hypothetical three-dimensional body becomes real, that is, perceptible, in the dimension of time we call duration.

If access to higher dimensions of time belongs to one body, it is at least theoretically possible that it belongs, though invisibly, to all bodies. We can further assume that such access is by way of unfamiliar modes or levels of consciousness—and that the name we give to one of these is prophecy.

Man Overboard!

J. B. Priestly, the English novelist and playwright, was fascinated by the philosophical and psychological enigmas of time and collected many stories from his friends on this subject. One of these was related to him by Sir Stephen King-Hall, a fellow writer who had for many years been an officer in the Royal Navy.

The event Sir Stephen remembered so vividly took place in 1916, during World War I. He was then serving aboard the *Southampton* and, on the day in question, was officer of the watch. As the *Southampton* and the convoy she was guarding approached a small island off the Scottish coast, Sir Stephen experienced a premonition that a man was about to fall overboard. Thus prompted, he gave orders to prepare to rescue a man overboard, but since there was, as yet, no such person, his order was immediately challenged by the commodore, who inquired, "What the hell do you think you are doing?" Sir Stephen continues the story:

> We were abreast the island. I had no answer. We were steaming at 20 knots and we passed the little island in a few seconds. Nothing happened!
>
> As I was struggling to say something, the cry went up "man overboard!" from the *Nottingham* (the next ship in the line, 100 yards behind us) then level with the island. Thirty seconds later "man overboard!" from the *Birmingham* (the third ship in the line, and then abreast the island). We went full speed astern; our sea boat was in the water almost at once and we picked up both men. I was then able to explain to a startled bridge why I had behaved as I had done.
> [Angus Hall, *Signs of Things to Come,* p.17]

Twenty Years Notice

In the middle of August 1918 Eugene P. Lyle, Jr., an American journalist, wrote an article entitled "The War of 1938," which was published in *Everybody's Magazine* the following September. At that time World War I was drawing to a close; the German Marne offensive had been halted in July, and the Germans had suffered major losses at Amiens on August 8. Pershing was in command of the American troops, and by every indication peace could not be far away. In fact, the war came to an end with the signing of the armistice on November 11, less than two months after *Everybody's* published its curious story.

In the article, Lyle offered a warning that unless Germany were crushed beyond all hope of revival she would rise to plague the world again with a war of monstrous proportions. "And our soldiers, climbing out of the trenches," Lyle wrote, "warn the politicians: 'God help you if you haven't let us finish our work!'"

The article unfolds by way of flashbacks from the war of 1938 to the years immediately following World

World War I was still being waged in September 1918 when Everybody's Maga-zine *featured a chilling article forecasting "The War of 1938." This illustration appeared on the cover.*

War I. Germany concedes defeat, repents, expresses a wish to join the family of nations; the war-weary allies are delighted and take her words at face value. But they are deceived. Germany begins to rearm, surreptitiously but on a massive scale. She stockpiles the raw materials of war: nitrates from Chile, copper from Mexico, iron from Sweden. "Germany must not be merely efficient, but self-sufficient!" her leaders say and put the country in a state of permanent rationing.

The years go by and rumors spread of the vast arsenal that Germany has secretly compiled and of the new weapons her scientists have developed. Still more alarming are the stories that the Pan-Germanic gun clubs have been a successful front for the training of highly disciplined young soldiers, whose "sporting events" are paramilitary maneuvers involving 50,000 men. And in addition to all these warnings, "Flying clubs were common. To skill in flying was added sham combat, governed by rules and regulations to make for proficiency in the real thing."

At last Germany has an army of 20 million men equipped and ready for action. Europe, totally unprepared, falls in three weeks. England is taken by an airborne invasion, leaving the United States and the British overseas dominions to face the enemy as best they can: "It is the Night—the Prussian Night—the Consummation!" Lyle wrote portentiously.

Lyle was wrong about a few things in his scenario for the next 20 years. He did not, for example, foresee that the harshness of the Treaty of Versailles would plunge Germany into the social and economic conditions that fostered, according to the hindsight of many contemporary historians, the rise of Hitler and German militarism. Nor did he get the date of the beginning of World War II quite right—unless one regards the British and French capitulation to Hitler at Munich in 1938 as the event that made the war inevitable. And though Lyle did, remarkably, forecast the aerial invasion of England—the Battle of Britain—he was wrong about the outcome. And though it took Hitler more than three weeks to subdue mainland Europe, his blitzkrieg took Poland in three weeks in 1939, and in 1940 France fell after a six-week invasion.

In other details Lyle was uncannily accurate. Arms and raw materials were stockpiled; soldiers and pilots were trained in "youth camps," "gun clubs," and "flying clubs"; German scientists did develop new weapons; and Hitler's intended victims were woefully unprepared.

If Eugene Lyle's gift of prophecy had been recognized on this occasion, the world might today be a very different place. (*American History Illustrated*, November 1976, pp.35–43)

Cheiromancy

In 1925 "Count" Louis Hamon, the celebrated palmist and clairvoyant whose professional name was Cheiro, made the following prediction about Edward, prince of Wales: "It is within the range of possibility . . . that he will fall victim of a devastating love affair. If he does, I predict the Prince will give up everything, even the chance of being crowned, rather than lose the object of his affection."

In 1936 King George V died and the prince of Wales became King Edward VIII. His abdication 325 days later (and more than 10 years after Cheiro's prophecy) in favor of his future wife, the twice-divorced Mrs. Wallis Simpson, was made, he said, because he could not give up the woman he loved.

Cheiro also warned the well-known English journalist William T. Stead that he should on no account travel by water in mid-April 1912. Surprisingly, because of his deep interest in psychical phenomena (see page 21), Stead ignored the warning, booked a passage on the *Titanic*, and was drowned on April 14.

Even earlier, in 1905, Cheiro "read" the future of the powerful and hated Rasputin, the Mad Monk of Russia, telling him, "I foresee for you a violent end within the palace. You will be menaced by poison, by knife, and by bullet. Finally, I see the icy waters of the Neva closing above you." Eleven years later the prophecy was fulfilled. (For the story of his death, see page 272.) (Omar V. Garrison, *The Encyclopaedia of Prophecy*, pp.77–78; Herbert B. Greenhouse, *Premonitions: A Leap Into the Future*, pp.102–03)

Preview of an Air Raid

In 1932 two German newspapermen, reporter J. Bernard Hutton and photographer Joachim Brandt, were sent to do a story on the Hamburg-Altona shipyards. An executive showed them around the place, and by the end of the afternoon their assignment was finished. Just as they left the yards, the two men heard the drone of aircraft overhead, and in a short while the noise of antiaircraft guns drowned out all other sounds. Darkness had fallen and soon the two men saw bombs exploding all around them. Before long the place was an inferno, and what they had at first taken for a

Two newspapermen claimed they witnessed an air raid that devastated Hamburg's shipyards—11 years before it happened. This 1945 photograph shows the damage they "saw."

practice drill was all too clearly a full-scale air raid. They turned back to ask the guard at the gate if they could do anything to help. They were threateningly told to go about their business, and so the two newspapermen drove back to Hamburg.

Although the sky had been dark throughout the attack, they were surprised to find Hamburg going about its everyday business by the light of an ordinary late afternoon. They stopped their car and looked back toward the shipyards. They, too, lay intact and unharmed in the fading daylight.

When Brandt's photographs were developed—he had kept on shooting throughout the air raid—they showed nothing unusual, and when the editor heard their story he accused them of being drunk on the job.

Just before World War II broke out, Hutton left Germany to live in England. There, in 1943, he saw a newspaper account of a highly successful night raid by the Royal Air Force on the Hamburg shipyards. He sought more details of the attack and confirmed what he had guessed: the scene of destruction that he and Brandt had witnessed in the spring of 1932 had been real after all; they had seen it 11 years before it happened. (J. Bernard Hutton, *On the Other Side of Reality*, pp.171–75)

Flight Into the Future

Victor Goddard of the Royal Air Force was lost. Somewhere over Scotland a heavy storm had caught him, and now he needed to find a landmark. He eased his Hawker Hart biplane down through the clouds, hoping to find clear weather below him and perhaps to catch a glimpse of Drem, an abandoned airfield that he thought was somewhere in the vicinity.

His instincts were good. Drem was not far ahead of him, and from it he could take new bearings. Then, when he was about a quarter of a mile from the airfield,

As he flew low over Drem airfield in 1934, Sir Victor Goddard apparently glimpsed the future when he saw the abandoned site as the busy airport it would become in 1938.

something extraordinary happened. "Suddenly," he wrote later, "the area was bathed in an ethereal light as though the sun were shining on a midsummer day." Drem was not deserted, was not abandoned and falling into ruin at all. It was a hive of activity, of mechanics in blue overalls at work on yellow planes, all bright in the sunlight. He flew over them at an altitude of no more than 50 feet—a little surprised that no one looked up as his plane went over—and headed back into the clouds, now confident of his direction. The year was 1934.

In 1934 Drem airfield was an abandoned ruin.

In 1938, with the threat of war growing daily, Drem was reopened as an air force flying school, and the color of British training planes changed from silver to yellow.

Victor Goddard had flown out of the clouds and, briefly, four years into the future. (Angus Hall, *Signs of Things to Come,* p.17)

A Gift From the Grave

When the famous beauty—and the fame—of Mrs. Patrick Campbell was beginning to fade (she had been the first to play Eliza Doolittle in Shaw's *Pygmalion*), she was nursed through a period of sickness by another actress, Sarah Allgood. Mrs. Campbell was grateful for the loving care she had received from her colleague and, as a token of thanks, gave Miss Allgood a watercolor painting of a heron.

Afterward Mrs. Campbell went to France and Miss Allgood to Hollywood, where she moved into a house. The year was 1940. Sarah Allgood's first dream in the new house was of Mrs. Campbell, who said, "Have you found my gift from the grave? Look behind the picture." Miss Allgood was puzzled by the dream, since she had no reason to believe that Mrs. Campbell was not still alive. But she looked behind the painting of the heron and there found a caricature of Mrs. Campbell by

Sir Max Beerbohm, worth about $2,000 at the time.

Sarah Allgood later learned that Mrs. Patrick Campbell had died on the day of her inexplicable dream. (Stuart Holroyd, *Dream Worlds,* p.127)

Winston Churchill's Inner Voice

Air raids were such a regular feature of life in London during World War II that many Londoners became, if not quite indifferent to the danger they posed, at least rather casual about them. Prime Minister Winston Churchill, a naturally courageous man who had often come under enemy fire during his years of active service, was as pugnacious as anyone else in the capital city and perhaps even less disposed than most to let himself be disturbed by Hitler's bombs. In any case, he was supposed to be the embodiment of Britain's unyielding resistance to the enemy, and he took the role seriously, but when his inner voice told him that danger was real and imminent, he listened and—figuratively, of course—jumped for the dugout with all due agility.

One night he was entertaining three government ministers at 10 Downing Street, the prime minister's traditional residence in London. An air raid was in progress, but this had not been allowed to interrupt the dinner. Suddenly Churchill left the table and went into the kitchen, where the cook and a maid were at work. On one side of the kitchen was a large plate glass window. He told the butler to put the food on a hot plate in the dining room and ordered the kitchen staff to go immediately into the bomb shelter. He then returned to his dinner guests.

Three minutes later a bomb fell behind the house and completely destroyed the kitchen. But the prime min-

An inner voice once warned Winston Churchill to avoid his usual seat in the car, and saved his life. Here he is shown exiting from his customary place in the car.

ister and his guests were, miraculously, unharmed.

One of the ways in which Churchill fulfilled his role as an inspirer of confidence was by personally visiting antiaircraft batteries during night attacks. On one occasion, having watched the gunners in action for a while, he walked back to his car, perhaps intending to visit two or three more gun crews before daybreak.

The door on the side of the car where he normally sat was standing open for him. But for once he ignored it, walked around to the other side of the car, opened the door, and got in. A few minutes later, as the car was making its way through the blacked-out streets, a bomb exploded nearby, lifting the car and causing it to careen perilously on two wheels, within an ace of overturning. At last, though, it righted itself and continued safely on its way. "It must have been my beef on that side that pulled it down," Churchill said later.

When his wife asked him about his brush with death, he said at first that he did not know why, on this occasion, he had deliberately chosen the other side of the car. Then he added: "Of course I know. Something said 'Stop!' before I reached the car door held open for me. It then appeared to me that I was told I was meant to open the door on the other side and get in and sit there—and that's what I did." (*The Unexplained: Mysteries of Mind Space & Time*, Vol. 2, Issue 14)

Unconscious Premonitions

According to a study made in the 1950's by W. E. Cox, fewer people travel on trains that are destined to have an accident than on trains that are not. Since train accidents are an unknown quantity until they occur, Cox was forced to conclude that many people, consciously or unconsciously, avoid taking a train on the day that it has a crash.

Cox obtained from railroad companies figures for the number of passengers on a given train on the day of an accident, for each of the six days preceding the crash, and for the corresponding day in each of the four preceding weeks. The *Georgian,* for example, a Chicago and Eastern Illinois train, had an accident on June 15, 1952. On that day only nine coach passengers were aboard the train. For the six days preceding the crash the numbers of passengers were 68, 60, 53, 48, 62, and 70. A week earlier, on June 8, there had been 35 passengers, and for the other days considered, 55, 53, and 54 passengers. For the 10 days examined, the average number of passengers on the *Georgian* was 55.8. On the day of the accident, however, the number dropped by 84 percent.

Another example of what Cox calls accident-avoidance appears in the figures he gathered for train No. 15 of the Chicago, Milwaukee and St. Paul, and Pacific line, which was wrecked on December 15, 1952, with 55

people on board. On five of the previous seven days chosen by Cox's method there were more than 100 coach passengers on the train and on the other two days at least 30 more passengers than on the day of the accident. The average number of passengers on the train on the 10 accident-free days was 50 percent higher than the number of passengers on the day when the wreck had occurred. (*Journal of the American Society for Psychical Research,* 50:99–109, 1956)

A Date With Destiny

In 1954 Eva Hellström, founder of the Swedish Society for Psychical Research, dreamed that she and her husband were flying over the streets of Stockholm. As she looked down, she saw a traffic accident: a green train had just crashed into a blue trolley.

At that time all Stockholm's trains were painted brown, so when new green trains were introduced a few months later, Eva Hellström felt sure her dream would be fulfilled. She had sketched the position of the two vehicles and made a note in her diary: "The accident will happen when the train from Djursholm and the Number 4 trolley meet at Valhallavägen. This is a place where there have been accidents between autos and trains but so far as I know, never with a trolley. . . ."

On March 4, 1956, almost two years after the dream, a blue No. 4 trolley and the green Djursholm train collided at Valhallavägen. The position of the crashed vehicles was precisely as shown in Eva Hellström's sketch. (Stuart Holroyd, *Dream Worlds,* pp.123, 127)

Double Vision

Precognitive apparitions are rare, and when they occur they are rarely shared. But that's what happened to Mr. and Mrs. Paul McCahen of Inglewood, California, on the evening of September 4, 1956. They had arrived earlier that day at the Grand Canyon, and as dusk fell they saw a woman, accompanied by a man and a boy carrying luggage, walk up to a nearby cabin. To Mrs. McCahen's surprise, she recognized the woman as an acquaintance, a Mrs. Nash with whom she had served on a jury a year before. She mentioned this to her husband, and the fact that Mr. Nash had only one arm. Supposing that Mrs. Nash would be tired after her journey, Mrs. McCahen decided to wait until morning before talking to her friend.

"The next day," she wrote in her report to the American Society for Psychical Research, "I saw her sitting on the veranda, and I went to talk to her. Our husbands met each other and we had a pleasant chat until I mentioned I had seen her the evening before, but didn't speak then. Mr. and Mrs. Nash both looked astonished and said they had just gotten there with a busload of tourists. . . ."

Mr. McCahen confirmed his wife's story and added that the apparitional Mrs. Nash had not been more than 10 or 15 feet away when his wife pointed her out.

The McCahens's experience is rare not only in being shared but in having occurred in the absence of any emotional pressure. Mrs. McCahen and Mrs. Nash knew each other only slightly and had not seen each other for a year. No danger threatened either of them, and Mr. McCahen had had no previous connection whatsoever with the Nash family. (Martin Ebon, *Prophecy in Our Time*, p.142)

Seen in a Crystal Ball
On the night of January 16, 1969, Joseph DeLouise walked into a Chicago cocktail lounge and asked to see a newspaper. He wanted to read about the two trains that had crashed somewhere south of Chicago. The men at the bar suddenly paid attention. What crash? They'd heard nothing about it. There hadn't been anything in the newspapers. Where?

"Somewhere south of here," DeLouise said, "two trains hit each other in the fog. It was the worst train disaster we have had since World War II, 25 years ago. Many people were hurt and killed."

The bartender turned on the radio. It was 11 o'clock and there was no news of a train wreck.

Two hours later, at 1 A.M. on January 17, two Illinois Central trains collided head-on in the fog, 45 miles south of Chicago. Forty-seven people were hurt and three killed. It was the worst train disaster in the area in the last 25 years.

DeLouise had spoken on a radio show on December 14, 1968, in Gary, Indiana, and predicted that the crash would occur in five or six weeks.

What sort of man is Joseph DeLouise?

He works as a hairdresser, never finished the eighth grade and, like many scryers, uses a crystal ball to make his predictions (see page 302). On television and in the press he has foretold many disasters.

On November 25, 1967, he predicted the collapse of a bridge. Three weeks later, on December 16, the Silver Bridge across the Ohio River at Point Pleasant, West Virginia, collapsed. Thirty-six people were killed, and another 10 were reported missing.

On January 8, 1968, DeLouise predicted that there would be no major riots in the country in the coming year but that there would be an actual "insurrection." On April 7, 1968, the governor of Illinois declared an outbreak of violence in Chicago to be an insurrection; 5,000 federal troops were flown in.

On December 15, 1968, DeLouise predicted that the Kennedy family would be involved in a tragedy connected with water. Later, he "saw" a woman drowning in that context. On July 18, 1969, Mary Jo Kopechne

The psychic Joseph DeLouise uses a crystal ball to see into the future. He focuses on the shiny surface until it becomes misty, and in the cloudlike shapes that form over the crystal he can perceive what is filtering through his senses.

was drowned at Chappaquiddick in a car accident involving Senator Edward Kennedy.

On May 21, 1969, DeLouise predicted the crash of a jet plane near Indianapolis. He said that 79 people would be killed and that somehow the number 330 would be involved. At 3:30 P.M. on September 9, 1969, an Allegheny Airlines DC-9 collided with a private plane near Indianapolis. The 4 crew members and 78 passengers were killed, as well as the pilot who had flown the private plane. (Joseph DeLouise with Tom Valentine, *Psychic Mission*, passim)

Abducting the Future
In 1972 Regency Press published a novel called *Black Abductor* by Harrison James, the pen name of James Rusk, Jr. In the novel a group of terrorists, led by a black, kidnap the daughter of a wealthy and well-known man with right-wing sympathies. The daughter, a college student named Patricia, is kidnapped near her college campus. Her boyfriend, who is with her at the time, is beaten by the kidnappers and briefly becomes a suspect in the case. At first Patricia resists her captors but soon succumbs to their ideology and dark charm. They send Polaroid photographs of her to her father and describe their act as America's "first political kidnapping." In the end, they predict, they will be surrounded by the police, tear-gassed, and wiped out.

A month after Patricia Hearst (student daughter of wealthy, right-wing Randolph Hearst) was kidnapped from her apartment near her college campus by members of the Symbionese Liberation Army (a terrorist group whose leader was a black) in 1974, the FBI visited James Rusk, Jr. By then Miss Hearst's former boyfriend, Steven Weed, who had been with her when she was kidnapped, and badly beaten by the kidnappers, was no longer a suspect in the case, but James Rusk, Jr., was. The FBI had read his novel.

Whether the terrorists were familiar with the novel too and took it as the scenario for their crime—thus making the book in part a self-fulfilling prophecy—will never be known. The terrorists were surrounded by the police, tear-gassed, and killed. (Alan Vaughan, *Incredible Coincidence*, pp.55–56)

Cognition of the Future

Attempts to explain prophecy must make suppositions about the future. The most fundamental supposition is that events in the future do not yet exist and cannot, therefore, produce effects in the present. The path of explanation that stems from this view leads, of necessity, to various ideas of the future as a potential that somehow exists in the present.

In their simplest form these ideas follow the analogy of the seed and flower. A gardener can examine a seed and predict what flower it will produce.

Some premonitions may indeed stem from clues scarcely noticed in a conscious way. An unfamiliar noise in a car, for example, may give rise to an accurate premonition of danger. The weakness of the theory, in this form, is that it requires of the precognizer an uncanny ability to analyze signs and indications that are not only imperceptible to the ordinary eye but impossible to deduce theoretically. What clues in a dreamer's environment could prompt an accurate precognition of a disaster six months and 3,000 miles away? Some extraordinary suggestions have been made to explain how the future may be unrealized but cognizable in the present.

One such suggestion, by Gerhard Dietrich Wasserman, a mathematical physicist at the University of Durham in England, is that all events exist as timeless mental patterns, with which every living and nonliving particle in the universe is associated.

This idea owes something to the ancient belief that the universe—the macrocosm—contains innumerable microcosms, each recapitulating the features and order of the large whole. Thus man was seen as a microcosm of the earth, his veins and arteries corresponding to streams and rivers, and so on.

By the end of the 17th century the idea had undergone many transformations but was still potent. The great philosopher and mathematician Baron Gottfried Wilhelm von Leibniz, for example, wrote:

> All the different classes of beings which taken together make up the universe are, in the ideas of God who knows distinctly their essential gradations, only so many ordinates of a single curve so closely united that it would be impossible to place others between any two of them, since that would imply disorder and imperfection.

Accordingly, the various orders of beings, animate and inanimate, so gradually approximate each other in their attributes and properties that they form a single chain, "so closely linked one to another that it is impossible ... to determine precisely the point at which one ends and the next begins."

In this concept of a "chain of being," then, the animate, and therefore the spiritual or psychic, are connected with the inanimate by a gradation of shared attributes. For Leibniz the implication was that someone with enough insight "would see the future in the present as in a mirror."

Another version of the idea that the future lies hidden in the present was advanced by Adrian Dobbs, a mathematician and physicist at the University of Cambridge, in 1965. As events unfold, he proposed, they actualize a relatively small number of the possibilities for change that exist at a subatomic level. In the process disturbances are caused that create, in another dimension of time, what Dobbs calls a psitronic wavefront. This wavefront can be registered by the brain's neurons, at least in certain especially sensitive people, and interpreted. A metaphor may help to clarify the process:

Imagine a pond, at one side of which a toy ship is launched. At the other side of the pond is a very small person. He is unable to see the ship, but as the ship travels forward, the waves it makes reach the shore on which he stands. As they travel across the pond, these waves pass around certain objects—weeds, leaves, a log—that are fixed or slowly drifting on its surface. The objects thus create disturbances in the wavefront, which the small person, who has a lifetime's experience in these things, is able to note in fine detail. From what he learns of the wavefronts he not only obtains an image of the objects that produced them but calculates how long it will be before they drift to the shore.

In this metaphor the toy ship represents an event unfolding in time. Its course across the pond represents one of many paths it might have taken and the dimension of time it occurs in. The pond itself represents another dimension of time in which other factors are having an influence. The ship's bow wave represents Dobbs's "psitronic wavefront," and the small person is, of course, the neuronal apparatus that receives the wavefront and converts it to a prediction.

Granting that Dobbs's theory is purely hypothetical and that no psitronic wave has been discovered, the difficulty is in suggesting a neuronal mechanism by which the observer distinguishes the wavefront of a particular event from the presumable maelstrom of wavefronts produced by simultaneously unfolding events. Again, the farther away the event is in the future, the more numerous the wavefronts and the more complex the problem.

Such, in general, are some of the theories that regard the future as being, in some way, a potential implicitly accessible in the present, and such are the difficulties and limitations attending them.

An Unemployed Prophet

On December 4, 1978, Edward Pearson was arrested for traveling by train from Inverness to Perth, in Scotland, without a ticket. He duly appeared in court at Perth, where he was described as "an unemployed Welsh prophet," and said that he had been on his way to London to warn the minister of the environment of an earthquake that was soon to strike Glasgow.

Edward Pearson's story was duly reported in the Dundee *Courier & Advertiser* for December 6 under the headline "Prophet Didn't Have a Ticket." Three weeks later the *Courier & Advertiser*'s readers were shaken in their beds by an earthquake that damaged buildings in Glasgow and other parts of Scotland.

Earthquakes are a very rare phenomenon in any part of the British Isles. (*The Unexplained: Mysteries of Mind Space & Time,* Vol. 1, Issue 6)

No Questions Asked

His child was due to be born in three months time, but Jaime Castell, a Spanish hotel executive, heard a voice in a dream tell him that he would never see it. Castell, convinced that he was going to die soon, took out an insurance policy for more than $100,000 (7 million pesetas), payable only in the event of his death and with no other benefits.

A few weeks later he was driving home from work at a steady 50 mph when a car going in the opposite direction at over 100 mph struck a safety barrier, somersaulted in midair, and landed on top of his own car. Castell and the other driver were instantly killed.

The insurance company paid Mrs. Castell without delay, though normally the death of someone who had so recently taken out such a specific policy would have been investigated at length. "But this incredible accident rules out any suspicion," a spokesman for the company said; "a fraction of a second either way and he would have escaped." (*The Unexplained: Mysteries of Mind Space & Time,* Vol. 1, Issue 6)

The Nightmare That Came True

Night after night David Booth had the same nightmare. First he heard the sound of huge engines failing; then he saw the plane, a passenger liner belonging to American Airlines, swerve and roll in the air, plunging to the ground in a red inferno. And every day—he had the nightmare 10 nights in a row—23-year-old David, an office manager in Cincinnati, Ohio, was haunted by what he had seen. "There was never any doubt to me that something was going to happen," he said. "It wasn't like a dream. It was like I was standing there watching the whole thing—like watching television."

On Tuesday, May 22, 1979, David phoned the Federal Aviation Administration (FAA) at the Greater

The worst air accident in U.S. history was the crash of an American Airlines DC-10 only moments after it left the runway at Chicago's O'Hare International Airport (above) in May 1979. Earlier that month the disaster was unreeled in the nightmares of David Booth (left) for 10 haunting nights in a row.

Cincinnati International Airport. He also called American Airlines—and a psychiatrist at the University of Cincinnati. On May 26 an American Airlines DC-10 jetliner crashed at Chicago's O'Hare International Airport. Two hundred and seventy-five people were killed in the worst air accident in U.S. history.

The Federal Aviation Administration had taken David Booth seriously enough to try to match his nightmare with the information available, but they had too little to go on. "It was uncanny," said Jack Barker, public affairs officer for the FAA's southern region. "There were differences, but there were many similarities. The greatest similarity was his calling the airline and the airplane [the FAA had guessed from Booth's description that the plane was a DC-10] . . . and that [the plane] came in inverted." In retrospect the dream description of the site of the crash resembled O'Hare International Airport but not closely enough for anyone to guess in advance that that was where the accident would occur. (*The Unexplained: Mysteries of Mind Space & Time,* Vol. 1, Issue 6)

The Warning That Wasn't

At five o'clock one morning in 1979 Helen Tillotson was awakened by an urgent knock at the door of her Philadelphia apartment and the sound of her mother calling, "Helen, are you there? Let me in!"

When she opened the door, her mother, who lived across the street, asked why Helen had been knocking on her door a few minutes earlier. Helen explained that she had gone to bed at 11 o'clock the night before and had not awakened until her mother's arrival. "But I *saw* you! I *spoke* to you!" Mrs. Tillotson said, insisting that Helen had told her to follow her back to her house and not ask any questions.

Then they heard the explosion.

A gas leak in Mrs. Tillotson's block had caused the blast. Her apartment was badly damaged.

"If she had been asleep there at the time," a fire chief said later, "I doubt whether she would have got out alive." (*The Unexplained: Mysteries of Mind Space & Time,* Vol. 1, Issue 6)

Fatal Prediction

During an interview taped on August 23, 1980, for later broadcast, the psychic Alex Tanous made a prediction that came true before the year was out.

The interview, conducted by Lee Speigel, host of the NBC radio show *Unexplained Phenomena*, took place at the American Society for Psychical Research, located on West 73rd Street, New York City, directly across the street from the Dakota Apartments. Speigel, who planned to use the tape on an upcoming program, asked Tanous if he could predict something that would occur in the next few months and would be of interest to the many rock music fans in the audience. Tanous replied:

> The prediction that I will make is that a very famous rock star will have an untimely death, and this can happen from this moment on. I say untimely death because there is something strange about his death, but it will affect [the] consciousness of many people because of his fame.

The taped interview was played on the show September 5, 1980. On December 8 John Lennon, the world-famous rock musician, was shot to death at the door of the Dakota, where he resided. Since Tanous had not named a specific person, Speigel had drawn up a list of six possibilities; rock star John Lennon was at the head of the list. (*American Society for Psychical Research Newsletter,* 7:22, October 1981)

A psychic's prophecy of the untimely demise of a famous rock star seemed to come true when John Lennon was shot to death in 1980. This photograph of Lennon with his wife, Yoko Ono, in New York City appears on their last album.

ANOMALIES

Any departure from the expected arrangement, general rule, or usual method is considered to be an anomaly and, as such, is dismissed as largely suspect by the scientific community. This, however, does not keep the evidence of inexplicable events and relationships from cropping up in a wondrous variety of ways and in a wide range of places.

The world is a museum of anomalous history, filled with the curious and the incredible. In this chapter let us take a look around. In one corner (Sayre, Pennsylvania, for example) are found the skulls of giants with small horns protruding from their brows. In another spot (Clearwater, Minnesota) a burial mound discloses seven skeletons, all with double rows of teeth in the upper and lower jaws. Meanwhile, staring blankly from a ledge of rock (Casper, Wyoming), is a mummified human 14 inches tall.

Nearby (Antelope Spring, Utah) is the imprint of a sandaled foot that trod on a living trilobite. Not surprising, perhaps, except for the fact that trilobites became extinct about 280 million years ago. Not far away (Glen Rose, Texas) humans and dinosaurs have left adjacent tracks—another "impossible" relationship, since dinosaurs vanished some 60 million years before man is thought to have existed.

Across the ocean (Rutherford, Scotland) a piece of gold thread protrudes from a solid chunk of newly quarried rock: how could it possibly have gotten there? Far to the south (Mali, West Africa) a farming people impart to visitors their ancient knowledge of Sirius B, a star invisible to the naked eye—and only just discovered by astronomers. In the meantime, far to the east (in the Ural Mountains of the U.S.S.R.) the world's oldest living creatures are suddenly reanimated beneath the eyes of scientists, after being locked in a piece of ore for 250 million years.

The curators and scholars of the world are predisposed to look askance at this collection of improbable objects. Inscribed above the entrance to our hypothetical museum could be letters from a mysterious alphabet, perhaps Phoenician, that would translate as "Abandon certitude all ye who enter here."

As rational beings, we tend to feel uneasy with things we can't explain. But in the future, as has been true in the past, some of our most fondly held beliefs may be shattered beyond repair.

Anomalous findings are many and diverse. Those found on the following pages are mysterious tracks, strange skeletons, living animals locked in stone, out-of-place artifacts, and unaccountable knowledge. The discoveries are first grouped regionally, moving from north to south, and then chronologically.

MYSTERIOUS TRACKS FROM THE PAST

A highly detailed footprint, thought to be that of a young boy, was found fossilized in clay stone on the east bank of the Connecticut River, just south of Hadley, Massachusetts, in 1852. Also preserved in the clay were tracks of birds, four-footed animals, and snails. Even the impressions of raindrops were preserved "and were not entirely obliterated by the foot of the boy. All the striae and lines upon the sole of the foot appear distinctly...." Alongside the boy's footprint were those of a crow, and the pattern of skin on the bird's feet could be seen clearly.

The bed of clay stone bearing these imprints lay under some 20 feet of alluvial sand until it was exposed by the current of streams. (*The American Journal of Science and Arts*, 2:19:391–96, May 1855)

A large stone bearing the perfect imprint of a human foot 14½ inches long was shown to members of the Ohio State Academy of Science in 1896. The stone had been taken from a hill four miles north of Parkersburg, West Virginia, some 20 years earlier. (*The American Anthropologist*, February 1896, p.66)

At the summit of Big Hill in the Cumberland Mountains in Jackson County, Kentucky, is a layer of carboniferous sandstone. In the 1880's it was crossed by a wagon trail that in time broke up the surface of the rock. When the resulting debris was cleared away, a series of tracks was discovered in this carboniferous layer about 300 million years old. There were imprints of bear, something resembling a large horse, and two "tracks of a human being, good sized, toes well spread, and very distinctly marked." The prints were examined by Prof. J. F. Brown of Berea College, Kentucky. (*The American Antiquarian*, 7:39, January 1885)

In 1938 Dr. Wilbur Burroughs, head of the geology department of Berea College, Kentucky, announced that he had discovered 10 humanoid footprints in carboniferous sandstone on a farm belonging to Mr. O. Finnell in the hills in the northern part of Rockcastle County. The prints were 9½ inches long and 6 inches across the toes; the length of the stride was 18 inches. No marks of a tail or forefeet were found. Photomicrographs and infrared photography revealed no signs of carving or artificial marking in or around the prints, and a microscopic count of sand grains indicated that material within the prints had been impacted. This would be the natural result of a print made by the pressure of a human foot but could in no way be duplicated by carving.

The rock in which the prints were found was estimated to be some 250 million years old. In recent years the prints were destroyed by vandals. (Brad Steiger, *Mysteries of Time and Space*, pp.6–7)

A carnival of horses, bears, turkeys, and six-toed humans left its tracks in what is now solid rock near the headwaters of the Tennessee River, a few miles south of Braystown, North Carolina. According to Josiah Priest, a 19th-century writer on antiquities, the strange human tracks included one of a giant—16 inches long, 13 inches wide at the toes, and 5 inches wide at the ball of the heel. (Josiah Priest, *American Antiquities*, p.150)

A pair of human footprints once graced a slab of limestone on the west bank of the Mississippi River at St. Louis. In 1816 or 1817 the slab was quarried from its position and removed by a Mr. George Rappe to the

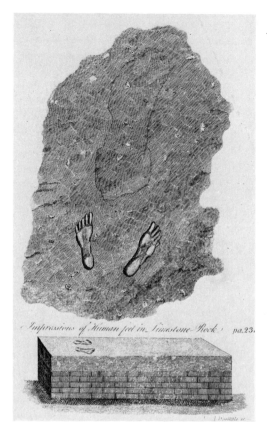

Sketches of the human footprints found in limestone at St. Louis were made by the noted ethnologist Henry R. Schoolcraft and were printed with his report in 1822.

village of Harmony (now New Harmony), Indiana.

The prints were 10½ inches long and 4 inches wide at the toes, 6¼ inches apart at the heels, and 13½ inches apart at the toes, reported Henry R. Schoolcraft,

the toes being very much spread, and the foot flattened in a manner that happens to those who have been habituated to go a great length of time without shoes. Notwithstanding this circumstance, the prints are strikingly natural, exhibiting every muscular impression, and swell of the heel and toes, with a precision and faithfulness to nature, which I have not been able to copy, with perfect exactness, in the present drawing....

Every appearance will warrant the conclusion that these impressions were made at a time when the rock was soft enough to receive them by pressure, and that the marks of feet are natural and genuine.

In the geologic scheme of things, this limestone hardened about 270 million years ago. Both the rock and the prints in it were said to show the same evidence of wear and aging. (*The American Journal of Science and Arts*, 1:5:223–31, 1822)

On the north slope of a boulder-strewn hill near the mouth of the Little Cheyenne River, South Dakota, lies a flat, dazzlingly white rock of magnesian limestone, which geologists say was laid down and hardened some 100 million years ago. On it are three prints of moccasined feet. In size they seem to be those of a woman or adolescent, and to judge from the length of the stride (4½ and 5½ feet) the person who made them was running. In one of the prints, moreover, the impression made by the heel is deeper than that made by the ball of the foot, again suggesting that whoever made them was running at some speed.

The depth of the prints varies from ½ inch to 1 inch. All three clearly show the instep and faint toe marks, and all show the same degree of weathering as the unmarked surface of the rock. According to an interview obtained in 1882 with a Mr. Le Beau, who had lived in the area for 26 years, local Indians knew nothing of the origin of the prints but viewed the stone as a "medicine rock." (William R. Corliss, *Ancient Man: A Handbook of Puzzling Artifacts,* p.649)

Dinosaur tracks and human tracks exist in the riverbed of the Paluxy River, near Glen Rose, Texas. There also exists an admission of fraud. The authenticity of dinosaur tracks at several sites along the Paluxy River has remained largely unchallenged for more than 50 years. However, the discovery of manlike prints in the same rock stratum—in one case a human print actually overlaps that of a three-toed dinosaur—is unacceptable to orthodox paleontology, since the giant reptiles were supposedly extinct some 60 million years before man first walked the earth.

But the supposition of fraud is based on something more substantial than the simple wish to be rid of objectionable evidence. The refutation of the Glen Rose man-tracks rests on the admission that during the Depression a number of local people made money by carving human footprints and selling them with the (real) dinosaur prints. The carving procedure—which involved aging the carved stone with acid—was described by the nephew of one of the footprint artists. For those wishing to see an end to the whole improbable story, such admissions are enough to close the case.

On the other hand, Mr. Jim Ryals, who has said that

he and his wife sold prints to tourists, has also stated that they had removed several of the human tracks from the Paluxy riverbed, using a chisel and a sledgehammer and then hauling the blocks of rock with a team of horses. Mr. Ryals told investigators how real prints might be distinguished from fakes:

> First, the pressure of the foot usually pushed up a ridge of mud around the outside of the track. Second, if the track is broken open or sawed, pressure lines can be found beneath the surface....

These tracks of a three-toed dinosaur and a man were photographed in 1971 at the Paluxy River. A flood in 1979 washed away the man track and eroded the dinosaur's trail.

A controversial Paluxy River footprint (left) is measured by geologist Jack Walper, who believes it was made by a bipedal dinosaur dragging his toes as he walked in mud.

Furthermore . . . when the [real] tracks were chiseled out of the riverbed, the workman was usually very careful to do his chiseling a good distance from the track for fear of damaging it. This resulted in a rather wide circle of the limestone surrounding the footprint.

The implication here, of course, is that those engaged in the sale of prints were well aware of the difference between the real thing and the imitation. In other words, the fake carvings were made to resemble genuine human tracks; this corresponds to the testimony of other, apparently reliable, Glen Rose residents.

Far more disturbing than self-interested testimony for those who wish to be rid of the prints is the fact that a number of prints have been found in areas normally submerged by the Paluxy River. In 1976 Jack Walper, a professor of geology at Texas Christian University, and John Green examined areas of the riverbed. By building dikes and using pumps, they were able to expose a number of dinosaur and human prints. Significantly, all the prints had a ridge around them where the pressure of the footfall had forced the mud upward. Anyone wishing to duplicate this effect would have had to carve away a large area of rock around the print to leave the raised ridge and would, in the sites that Green and Walper discovered, have had to work underwater.

On average, the submerged prints were 18 inches long and 5 to 7 inches wide. (Frederick P. Beierle, *Man, Dinosaur and History*, pp.22–29; *Bible-Science Newsletter*, April 15, 1971; *Pursuit*, 9:83–85, Fall 1976)

Giant tracks, seemingly of a human being, were found by a government trapper in the Alkali Flats area of Great White Sands, New Mexico, in 1931. A year later a party of four, including O. Fred Arthur, supervisor of Lincoln National Forest, set out to investigate the tracks, with the trapper Ellis Wright as their guide. They found 13 imprints crossing a relic desert basin in the eastern foothills of the San Andres Mountains. Despite the great size of the tracks, the investigators were convinced that they were left by humans, "for the print was perfect and even the instep plainly marked." Oval shaped, the prints are 16 to 22 inches long and 8 to 12 inches wide, with a distance between them of about 5 feet and a separation in width of 2 feet.

The site was revisited in 1972, 1974, and 1981, and more tracks were found. When they were first studied, it had been noted that the imprints were 2½ inches deep. But in 1974 (42 years later) they were 1 to 1½ inches above the level of the ground! The compacting of the soft earth by the heavy tread of the creature had preserved the prints while the surrounding soil had been eroded by wind and occasional rain. By 1981 the tracks stood pedestallike a few inches above the desert floor.

There is no doubt that the prints were those of living creatures. One suggestion is that they were made as recently as the 1850's by U.S. Army camels; a more considered view is that they are at least 10,000 years old and belong to a now-extinct native camel or mammoth. But the spacing of the footprints seems to suggest a two-legged creature. The mysterious tracks have been protected for further study by archeologists. (U.S. Army report, 1981)

What may be the oldest fossil footprint yet found was discovered in June 1968 by William J. Meister, an amateur fossil collector. If the print is what it appears to be—the impression of a sandaled shoe crushing a trilobite—it would have been made 300 to 600 million years ago and would be sufficient either to overturn all conventionally accepted ideas of human and geological evolution or to prove that a shoe-wearing biped from another world had once visited this planet.

Meister made his potentially disturbing find during

The giant tracks found at Great White Sands form stepping stones across the desert floor. The diagram below shows how erosion of the loose soil around the compacted imprints has left them standing 2½ to 4 inches above ground.

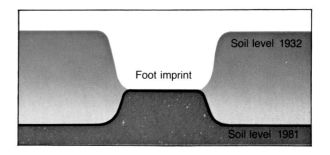

a rock- and fossil-hunting expedition to Antelope Spring, 43 miles west of Delta, Utah. He was accompanied by his wife and two daughters, and by Mr. and Mrs. Francis Shape and their two daughters. The party had already discovered several fossils of trilobites when Meister split open a two-inch-thick slab of rock with his hammer and discovered the outrageous print. The rock fell open "like a book," revealing

> on one side the footprint of a human with trilobites right in the footprint itself. The other half of the rock slab showed an almost perfect mold of the footprint and fossils. Amazingly the human was wearing a sandal!

Trilobites were small marine invertebrates, the relatives of crabs and shrimps, that flourished for some 320 million years before becoming extinct 280 million years ago. Humans are currently thought to have emerged between 1 and 2 million years ago and to have been wearing well-shaped footwear for no more than a few thousand years.

The sandal that seems to have crushed a living trilobite was 10¼ inches long and 3½ inches wide; the heel is indented slightly more than the sole, as a human shoe print would be. Meister took the rock to Melvin Cook, a professor of metallurgy at the University of Utah, who advised him to show the specimen to the university geologists. When Meister was unable to find a geologist willing to examine the print, he went to a local newspaper, *The Deseret News*. Before long, the find received national publicity.

In a subsequent news conference the curator of the Museum of Earth Science at the University of Utah, James Madsen, said:

> There were no men 600 million years ago. Neither were there monkeys or bears or ground sloths to make pseudohuman tracks. What man-thing could possibly have been walking about on this planet before vertebrates even evolved?

Madsen then went on to say that the fossil must have been formed by a natural process, though of what kind

he was unable to suggest. Dr. Jesse Jennings, of the university's anthropology department, guessed (rather boldly, considering the absence of any supporting visual evidence) that the print might have been made by one large trilobite coming to rest on three smaller ones.

On July 20, 1968, the Antelope Spring site was examined by Dr. Clifford Burdick, a consulting geologist from Tucson, Arizona, who soon found the impression of a child's foot in a bed of shale. "The impression," he said, "was about six inches in length, with the toes spreading, as if the child had never yet worn shoes, which compress the toes. There does not appear to be much of an arch, and the big toe is not prominent." The print was shown to two geologists and a paleontologist. One of the geologists agreed that it appeared to be that of a human being, but the paleontologist's opinion was that no biological agent had been involved. Dr. Burdick stuck to his guns:

> The rock chanced to fracture along the front of the toes before the fossil footprint was found. On cross section the fabric of the rock stands out in fine laminations, or bedding planes. Where the toes pressed into the soft material, the laminations were bowed downward from the horizontal, indicating a weight that had been pressed into the mud.

In August 1968 Mr. Dean Bitter, an educator in the Salt Lake City public schools system, claimed to have discovered two more prints of shoes or sandals in the Antelope Spring area. According to Professor Cook, no trilobites were injured by these footfalls, but a small trilobite was found near the prints in the same rock, indicating that the small sea creature and the sandaled wanderer might have been contemporaries. (*Bible-Science Newsletter*, August–September 1969; *Creation Research Society Quarterly*, December 1968)

In 1882 huge footprints, strongly resembling those of a human wearing shoes, were found in a layer of sandstone in the yard of the state prison near Carson City, Nevada, during quarrying operations. The prints were from 18 to 20 inches long and about 8 inches wide; the stride was from 2½ feet to more than 3 feet, and the distance between the left and right tracks—the straddle—was 18 or 19 inches. Numerous other tracks, of animals resembling horses, deer, elephants, and wolves, were found in the same layer of sandstone.

Since the size of the prints and the age of the rock in which they were found (from 2 to 3 million years) argued against a human or even a hominid origin, the

This impression of a seemingly sandaled foot with a trilobite in the heel may be the oldest footprint yet discovered. It was found in a split rock at Antelope Spring.

prints were ascribed to a more acceptable source—a giant ground sloth. It is thought that these animals could stand upright but only by using their tails as additional support. However, no track of a tail was found at this site. It was also suggested that the animal may have walked on four feet but that its hind feet fell almost exactly into the tracks left by its front feet, thereby creating a bipedal impression. But this fails to account for the fact that the prints showed no evidence of toe marks. (*The American Journal of Science*, 3:26:139–40, July–December 1883)

The imprint of a leather shoe was found in Triassic limestone in Fisher Canyon, Pershing County, Nevada, in 1927 by Alfred E. Knapp. According to microphotographs of the print, the leather was hand stitched with a finer thread than was customarily used by shoemakers in 1927. Triassic limestone is conventionally dated as between 180 and 225 million years old. (Brad Steiger, *Mysteries of Time and Space*, p.18)

The footprint of a human being, apparently fleeing toward the Gediz River from a volcanic eruption, was

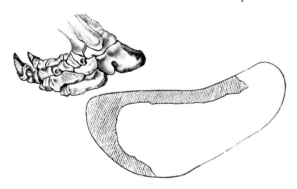

The outline of one of the Carson City footprints was sketched in 1882 with the shaded portion added to match it to others in the series. The drawing above it, in the same scale, is of the foot of a large sloth.

discovered in volcanic ash during the construction of a dam near Demirköprü, Turkey, in 1970. The age of the ash was determined to be 250,000 years by the Turkish Mineral Research and Exploration Institute in Ankara, and the print was pronounced human by the National Laboratory of Forensic Science in Sweden. If so, whoever made the print was an antecedent of Neanderthal man. (*Nature*, 254:553, April 17, 1975)

STRANGE AND IMPROBABLE SKELETONS

Human skulls with horns were found in a burial mound at Sayre, Bradford County, Pennsylvania, in the

This human footprint found near Demirköprü, Turkey, in volcanic ash deposited some 250,000 years ago may have been left by an antecedent of Neanderthal man.

1880's. Except for the horny projections some two inches above the eyebrows, the men to whom these skeletons belonged were anatomically normal, though at seven feet tall, well above average height. It was estimated that they were buried about A.D. 1200.

The find was made by a reputable group of antiquarians, including a Pennsylvania state historian and

---

Phase-Two Fossils: Burroughs's Conjecture

The most cogent explanation of anomalous fossil footprints is perhaps that offered by Dr. William Greely Burroughs, of Berea College in Kentucky. Dr. Burroughs's conjecture is that a depression in fossil-bearing rock may, long after the original fossils have been formed, be filled with a sediment that in its turn may also become the medium in which the impression of a footprint or the body of a creature is fossilized. When this second period of fossilization is complete, the newly formed rock may be indistinguishable from the older formation, and the new fossils may appear to have been formed at the same time as those that are actually much older.

There are two problems with this explanation. First, anomalous fossils are found not only at the junction of sedimentary layers but deep within rocks that show no sign at all of discontinuous formation. Second, out-of-place fossils are often inconsistent not only with the ages of associated fossils but also with the rock strata and the age conventionally ascribed to them.

---

dignitary of the Presbyterian Church (Dr. G. P. Donehoo) and two professors (A. B. Skinner, of the American Investigating Museum, and W. K. Morehead, of Phillips Academy, Andover, Massachusetts). Some of the bones were sent to the American Investigating Museum in Philadelphia, where they seem to have disappeared. (*Pursuit*, 6:69–70, July 1973)

A burial ground of pygmies was discovered in 1837 near Coshocton, Ohio. The skeletons were from 3 to 4½ feet long and seemed to have been buried in wooden coffins. No artifacts were found by which the culture of the pygmies might be dated, but the number of graves led observers to suppose that they "must have been tenants of a considerable city." (*The Gentleman's Magazine,* August 1837, p.182)

At the center of one of the large Ohio burial mounds, excavators in 1891 found the skeleton of a massive man wrapped in copper armor. On the head was a copper cap, and copper moldings encased the jaws. The arms were clad in copper, and so were the chest and stomach. On either side of the head were wooden antlers encased in copper, and the mouth cavity was filled with immense but decayed pearls. Around the neck was a necklace of bear's teeth inlaid with pearls. Beside the skeleton of the giant lay that of a woman.

The remains were found at a depth of 14 feet in a mound 500 feet long, 200 feet wide, and 28 feet high. (*Nature,* 45:157, December 17, 1891)

A skeleton nine feet eight inches tall was recovered from a stone burial mound at Brewersville, Indiana, in 1879. A mica necklace was around the neck, and a crude human image of burnt clay embedded with pieces of flint stood at the feet. The mound, between 3 and 5 feet high and 71 feet in diameter, was excavated by Indiana archeologists, scientific observers from New York and Ohio, a local physician, Dr. Charles Green, and the owner of the property on which the mound stood, a Mr. Robison.

The bones were kept by the Robison family in a basket in a nearby grain mill. They were lost when a flood swept away the mill in 1937. (*The Indianapolis News,* November 10, 1975)

Seven skeletons were found in a burial mound near Clearwater, Minnesota, in 1888. They had double rows of teeth in the upper and lower jaws and had been buried in a sitting position, facing the lake. The foreheads were unusually low and sloping, with prominent brows. (The *Saint Paul and Minneapolis Pioneer Press,* July 1, 1888)

He was found sitting cross-legged on a ledge in a small cave in a granite mountain. His hands were folded in his lap, in the timeless attitude of a Buddha. He appeared to be middle-aged. His skin was brown and wrinkled, his nose flat, the forehead low, the mouth broad and thin-lipped. And he was 14 inches tall.

The mummy was discovered in 1932 by gold prospectors blasting the walls of a gulch in the Pedro Mountains, 60 miles southwest of Casper, Wyoming. After studying it, puzzled scientists ventured the theory that it was a mummified pygmy and possibly the

progenitor of the American Indian. When it died, it was given a ceremonial burial.

Displayed in sideshows for several years, the Pedro Mountain Mummy was eventually purchased by Ivan T. Goodman, a Casper businessman, and taken to New York City. The remains, X-rayed by Dr. Harry Shapiro of the American Museum of Natural History and certified as genuine by the Anthropology Department of Harvard University, were thought by some to be those of a 65-year-old person. The speculation generated interest in the legends of the Shoshone and Crow Indians of Wyoming about a miniature people, only inches tall.

Following Goodman's death in 1950 the mummy passed into the hands of one Leonard Wadler and disappeared, but interest in it continued nationwide. In 1979 pictures of Shapiro's X-rays were given to Dr. George Gill, professor of anthropology at the Univer-

The Pedro Mountain Mummy, amazing because of its adult bodily proportions, has helped perpetuate stories of "little people."

sity of Wyoming. The withered little body, he concluded, was that of an infant or a fetus, possibly of an unknown tribe of prehistoric Indians. He believed that the infant had been afflicted with anencephaly, a congenital abnormality that would account for the adult proportions of its skeleton. Discoveries of mummified remains are not uncommon in Wyoming, which has an arid climate. As Dr. Gill pointed out, the Indians may have found other mummies of similarly diseased infants and quite naturally assumed that they were the remains of small adults. This in turn would tend to support the legend of a "little people."

But Pedro, as the mummy is known, remains a scientific curiosity. "All we have are tantalizing bits of information," Dr. Gill remarked. He and other anthropologists still hope to locate the missing mummy for further examination. (The *Casper Star-Tribune*, July 22 and July 24, 1979; The *Casper Tribune Herald*, October 22, 1932; C. J. Cazeau and Stuart D. Scott, *Exploring the Unknown*, p.222)

In 1973 two human skeletons were found on a rock plateau that had been cleared by bulldozers for mining operations near La Sal, Utah. The discovery was made by a party of rock collectors, who noticed teeth and bone fragments lying on the plateau surface. Before long they found an area of discolored sand, indicating that organic material had decayed there. They began scraping and soon exposed the surface of a large bone. At this point the leader of the party, Lin Ottinger, realized that the find might be worthy of professional excavation and called a halt. Back at the Salt Lake City University in Utah, Ottinger enlisted the help of anthropology professor J. P. Marwitt, and a week after the original find they returned to the site with a photographer, a journalist, and a number of interested observers. Professor Marwitt's excavation, recorded in movies and still photographs, revealed the lower halves of two human skeletons.

In Marwitt's opinion, the formation in which the skeletons lay buried was at least 100 million years old. The bones were neither jumbled nor broken, indicating that they had not been carried to the site by floodwater and that whoever they belonged to had died where the bones were found. To further confound things, these bones, apparently about 100 million years old, had a relatively modern appearance. They were the bones of a man, not of some distantly related, shambling anthropoid (which would, in any case, have also been wildly out of place).

The excavation complete, the skeletons were packed up and taken to the University of Utah for laboratory examination and dating.

At this point the story becomes mysterious in another way. According to Ottinger, Marwitt simply lost interest in the bones. If dating tests were made, the results were not released, and before long Marwitt left the university for a position at a college in one of the eastern states. A year later Ottinger recovered the still untested bones and let the matter rest. (Jim Brandon, *Weird America*, p.221)

In 1911 miners began to work the rich guano deposits in Lovelock Cave, 22 miles southwest of the Nevada town of Lovelock. They had removed several carloads of guano when they came upon some Indian relics. Soon afterward a mummy was also found; reportedly it was that of a 6½-foot-tall person with "distinctly red" hair.

According to the legends of the local Paiute Indians, a tribe of red-haired giants—the Si-te-cahs—were once the mortal enemies of the Indians in the area, who had joined forces to drive the redheads out. John T. Reid of Lovelock, a mining engineer avidly interested in Indian lore, became convinced that the mummy substantiated the Paiute legend, and in the years that followed devoted himself to proving it. Included in his growing file on redheaded giants were descriptions of hair robes once worn by a few Paiutes: the hair was human, and it was of a reddish-brown color.

In the meantime the discoveries at Lovelock had generated interest among archeologists, and in 1912 the University of California at Berkeley and the Nevada State Historical Society sent Mr. L. L. Loud to investigate the cave. Loud found the archeological deposits so disturbed in the rough-and-tumble of the mining operation that he only salvaged artifacts, which he took back to the University of California.

Twelve years later, in 1924, the Museum of the American Indian in New York sent out a Mr. M. R. Harrington to excavate the cave. He too collected artifacts and no bones. He apparently requested that one

The gigantic size of this skull from the Lovelock Cave area, on display along with artifacts and photographs of the gravesite at the Humboldt Museum in Winnemucca, Nevada, mystifies all who see it.

whole skeleton be reburied. Probably this was to appease the Indian employees, who were upset that such disrespectful treatment was accorded the remains of the deceased.

But the legend of the red-haired giants persisted. In the next few years more skeletal remains were found in the Lovelock area. Measuring the length of the unearthed femurs, Reid and others deduced that they belonged to a people ranging from 6 to 9½ or 10 feet in height.

Anthropologists, however, have stated that the tallest skeleton studied so far in the region was only 5 feet 11 inches, a not inconsiderable size in that time and place, but hardly a giant. Furthermore, they have pointed out, when mummies with black hair are removed from a dark cave into daylight, the hair often turns red. No one has been able to establish whether this happened to the Lovelock mummies.

Today a few of the remains—a skull, some bones, and artifacts—can be seen at the Humboldt Museum in Winnemucca, Nevada. Artifacts from the Lovelock area are also displayed at the Nevada State Historical Society's museum in Reno, but no bones. And no mention is made of a giant people. Anthropologists concede, however, that redheaded Indians did exist in the West. (*Nevada State Historical Society Quarterly*, Fall 1975, pp.153–67; telephone interview with Amy Dansie, Nevada State Historical Society, Reno, Nevada)

The origins of the Zapotec civilization, which flourished in southwest Mexico from 200 B.C. until the Spanish invasion in 1519, are shrouded in uncertainty, for even its earliest known remains are those of a culture already at a high level of urban and agricultural development. In art and architecture, mathematics and calendrical science, the Zapotecs have clear affinities with the earlier Olmec and Mayan civilizations to the south, but their history contains no record of migration from those or any other parts. Instead, and to the contrary, the Zapotecs believed themselves to be descended from trees, rocks, and jaguars.

The Zapotec capital was at Monte Albán, seven miles from the present-day city of Oaxaca. It lies at the top of an artificially leveled mountain promontory and is centered on a huge plaza, roughly 1,000 feet long and 650 feet wide, flanked on all sides by terraced steps, sunken courtyards, and low, handsome buildings. The first systematic excavation of the site began in 1931, and treasures of gold, jade, rock crystal, and turquoise were soon found in several of the tombs. But the most remarkable discovery was of something more mysterious than fine artwork and rich materials: a complex network of stone-lined tunnels, far too small to be used by adults or children of average stature.

The first of these tunnels, discovered in 1932 but not explored until 1933, was 20 inches high and 25 inches wide—so small that the excavators could make their way along it only on their backs. After they had inched through it in this way for 195 feet, they came to a skeleton, an incense burner, and funeral urns; there were also ornaments of jade, turquoise, and stone, and a few pearls. Some yards beyond this the tunnel was blocked, and to enter it again the explorers had to dig a 25-foot shaft from the surface beyond the blockage.

As they wormed along this next stretch, they found even smaller passages, no more than a foot high, branching off the main tunnel. Leading down into one of these was a tiny flight of steps. At a distance of 320 feet from the main entrance, the archeologists found another skeleton, and a few yards beyond this, at the edge of the northern terrace of the great plaza, the tunnel came to an end.

Further excavations revealed two similar tunnels, both packed with clay. Finally, to the east of tomb number seven, where the richest treasures had been found, a complex network of miniature tunnels was discovered, all lined with stone and some of them less than a foot high. Smoke was blown into these in an effort to trace their course and "revealed a number of unexpected exits."

The excavators' initial guess that they had discovered a drainage system was abandoned. Also ruled out was the idea that the tunnels had been a network of emergency escape routes (or had been of any other service to humans of ordinary size), and official speculation about their purpose ceased. Since then, the pygmy tunnels of Monte Albán have remained one of the major mysteries of the unexplained. (William R. Corliss, *Ancient Man: A Handbook of Puzzling Artifacts*, pp.360–61)

When the great breakwater at Plymouth, England, was being built in the early part of the 19th century, stone for the job was brought from the duke of Bedford's marble quarries at Oreston, on the eastern shore of the Plym estuary. These quarries then covered some 25 acres and were known for the close-grained, finely variegated Devonian marble that they produced. The only defect was that here and there wide seams of clay wandered through the 400-million-year-old stone and in places gave way to partially clay-filled caverns.

In one of these caverns, completely surrounded by solid rock, the fossil bones of three rhinoceroses were found. Rhinoceroses were common in this area 2 million to 65 million years ago.

The cave was 15 feet wide, 45 feet long, and 12 feet deep. It lay 70 feet below the surface, 60 feet, horizontally, from the edge of the quarry, and 160 feet from the edge of the estuary. It contained no stalactites or stalagmites nor any other indication of a former opening. In short, the cave contained no indication—except for the perfectly preserved rhinoceros bones—that it had ever been anything but hermetically sealed. (*The American Journal of Science and Arts,* 1:2:144-45, 1820)

The Tools of Tiny People

In the last years of the 19th century hundreds of flint tools were found beneath the moorland peat of east Lancashire's Pennine hills. By their minute size, they seemed to belong not to the province of ancient man but rather to the world of dwarfs or gnomes.

None of the tools found—scrapers, borers, and tiny, crescent-shaped knives—was longer than half an inch, and many were smaller than a quarter of an inch. The flaking by which they were shaped and brought to a sharp edge was so fine that, in many cases, it could only be appreciated through a magnifying glass.

That the flints were not "bird points"—used for bird hunting—seems evident from the fact that nothing resembling an arrowhead was found among them. And while the scrapers and borers may conceivably have been fitted with wooden handles (they are far too small to be used by ordinary human hands), two observations suggest that this was not done: no bored or engraved materials were found in conjunction with the flints; and even with handles, the scrapers would have been hopelessly impractical for the task of scraping flesh from animal hides. The same observations apply to the crescent-shaped knives, which were, in any case, clearly not designed to have handles or to be placed in wooden holders.

For such reasons, some have guessed that the knives were ritual replicas of the crescent moon. But why, in that case, they should have been found alongside small versions of conventional tools is a mystery, unless those too are supposed to have had a ritual purpose. (To label ancient objects of unknown purpose as "ritual instruments" is, of course, a remedy commonly applied by puzzled archeologists.)

If the Lancashire finds had been unique, they would probably have been forgotten, but other examples of tools apparently fashioned by a miniature people were found in England, beneath the floor of a drowned forest in Devon and in the sandy heathland of Suffolk. And more finds of pygmy flints have been made in other parts of the world: in Egypt, Africa, Australia, France, and Sicily, for example, and in India, where small crescent-shaped knives of flint and agate were found in caves in the Vindhya hills.

Whoever the makers of the pygmy flints were, and whatever their purpose, they seem to have been an established class of artisans and to have plied their delicate craft from one end of the world to the other.

A race of men whose average height was just under five feet is believed to have inhabited the area between Breslau and Sobotka in Poland as recently as 1,000 years ago. Professor Thilenius of the University of Breslau came to this conclusion in 1902 after examining numerous skeletal remains. He estimated that the little people may have begun to inhabit the area around the first century B.C.

The Polish pygmies, if such they were, were not unique in Europe. A Swiss race, described by Professor Kollmann of Basel, averaged from 4 feet 5½ inches to 4 feet 11 inches. Remains found at Eguisheim in Lower Alsace were of people whose height ranged from 3 feet 11 inches to just under 5 feet. In all these cases no deformity or abnormality (except for unusual shortness) was found in the bones, which are therefore taken to represent distinct races of men rather than pathological dwarfism. (*Nature,* 66:151, June 12, 1902)

The 1935 discovery of a 15-inch fossilized man in a prehistoric well at Vadnagar, Baroda State, India, was later declared to be a hoax—the improbability of the find being increased by the simultaneous discovery of a cow 18 inches tall. The story is included here because the height of the man closely matches that of the Casper, Wyoming, mummy and because ancient legends of "little people" have a worldwide currency. Experts, however, have a way of dismissing unpalatable finds as frauds, hoaxes, or evidence of mental instability. (*The Times* [London], February 21, 1935)

LIVING ANIMALS, LOCKED IN STONE

A horned lizard that had been found alive in a block of stone "so solid as to preclude the entrance of the smallest insect" was sent to the Smithsonian Institution in Washington by Judge Houghton of New Mexico in 1853. The lizard lived for two days after its release. (*Scientific American,* 8:366, July 30, 1853)

During excavations being made for the Hartlepool waterworks in Durham, England, in 1865, workmen inadvertently freed a living toad from a block of magnesian limestone 25 feet below ground level.

> The cavity [in which the toad had been contained] was no larger than its body, and presented the appearance of being a cast of it. The toad's eyes shone with unusual brilliancy, and it was full of vivacity on its liberation. It appeared, when first discovered, desirous to perform the process of respiration, but evidently experienced some difficulty, and the only sign of success consisted of a "barking" noise, which it continues invariably to make at present on being touched. The toad is in the possession of Mr. S. Horner, the president of the Natural History Society,

and continues in as lively a state as when found. On a minute examination its mouth is found to be completely closed, and the barking noise it makes proceeds from its nostrils. The claws of its fore feet are turned inwards, and its hind ones are of extraordinary length and unlike the present English toad. . . . The toad, when first released, was of a pale colour and not readily distinguished from the stone, but shortly after its colour grew darker until it became a fine olive brown.

A local clergyman and geologist, the Reverend Robert Taylor, expressed the opinion that the toad was 6,000 years old. At the last report (1865) the creature was to be given a place of honor in the Hartlepool Museum, its "primary habitation"–the rock–being provided for accommodation should it so desire. (The *Leeds Mercury*, April 8, 1865; as quoted in *The Zoologist*, 23:9630, 1865)

A living toad was liberated from a cavity near the center of a large rock by workmen digging for ore at Paswick, Derby, England, in 1852. They came upon the rock—actually a large lump of ore—at a depth of 12 feet below ground level and since it was too large for two men to lift, they began to break it up with their picks.

The cavity in which they found the toad was nearly six inches in diameter, considerably larger than the animal itself, and was lined with crystals, perhaps of carbonate of lime. The toad died very soon after being exposed to air. (*The Zoologist*, 10:3632, 1852)

When the ground was being prepared for the London–Birmingham railway line in 1835, workers on the Coventry stretch had to deal with masses of red sandstone at a depth of about 4½ feet, which they cleared with crowbars and gunpowder. As one block of this sandstone was being lifted and thrown toward a wagon, it fell and fractured. One of the broken pieces was thrown into the wagon, and in a cavity in one of the remaining pieces a living toad was found.

When the toad was first exposed to the air, its color was a bright brown, but within 10 minutes it had become almost black. It was quite plump, though smaller than most toads, but seemed "oppressed" and frequently gasped, having, or so it seemed, sustained a head injury. It was carefully replaced in its cavity and the cracked stone was sealed with clay, but the animal died four days later. (*Report of the Fifth Meeting of the British Association for the Advancement of Science*, 1835, p.72)

In a lecture given at the University of Cambridge in 1818, Dr. Edward D. Clarke, a geologist, described some unusual newts he had found in a chalk quarry. He had

been looking for fossils, he said, and was digging in the quarry at a depth of 270 feet when he came upon a number of fossilized sea urchins and newts. Three of the newts were very well preserved, and Dr. Clarke carefully dug them out of the rock and placed them on a sheet of paper in the sun. To his considerable surprise, the newts began to move.

Within a short time two of the animals were dead, but the third seemed so lively that Dr. Clarke placed it in a pond. Its response was to promptly escape from him and disappear.

According to Dr. Clarke, the rejuvenated newts were unlike any of those living locally at the time and belonged to an extinct species previously unknown to science. (*The Unexplained: Mysteries of Mind Space & Time*, Vol. 1, Issue 8)

An hour and a half after stoking his fire, Mr. W. J. Clarke, of Rugby, England, reached over to poke the coals. As he broke open one coal, he saw something move and snatched it out of the fireplace. It proved to be a living toad and it survived for five weeks. It had no mouth and was almost transparent. Photographs of this marvel were offered for sale to the public by the London Stereoscopic Company. (*The English Mechanic and World of Science*, 73:260, May 10, 1901)

Above is a photograph of the live toad Mr. Clarke of Rugby found embedded in a coal. Frogs can hibernate in a casing of mud for months, but could they survive long enough for the mud to metamorphose into rock?

In the late 16th century Ambroise Paré, Henry III's surgeon, saw "a huge toad, full of life" emerge from a large stone just split by workmen near his house at Meudon, France. (*The Unexplained: Mysteries of Mind Space & Time*, Vol. 1, Issue 8)

An astonished toad was liberated from its snug cavity in a 14-pound nodule of flint by a workman's pickax at Blois, France, in 1851. Upon finding the wind in its nostrils for the first time in no one knows how long, the toad jumped out of its hole and began to crawl rapidly away. His escape was thwarted by the workmen, however, who put him back in the flint and sent their find to the local Society of Sciences for their study.

At the society's headquarters, the toad, within his flint, was placed in a basement in a bed of moss. If the top of the flint was removed in darkness, the toad would lie quietly where he was, but if the room was light he climbed out and tried to run away. If he was placed on the edge of the flint, he would crawl into the hole of his own accord, gathering his legs under his body and taking particular care of a foot that had been slightly hurt when he was first removed from the flint. The cavity fitted his body like a glove, except for a small area above the back, and his mouth rested on a small ledge which had produced a permanent indentation in his jawbone. (*The Zoologist*, 9:3265-66, 1851)

The last of the pterodactyls—flying reptiles with leathery wings and long, toothy beaks—died about 100 million years ago, according to established scientific opinion. But in the experience of a number of startled French workmen, the last one died in the winter of 1856 in a partially completed railway tunnel between the St.-Dizier and Nancy lines.

In the half-light of the tunnel, something monstrous stumbled toward them out of a great boulder of Jurassic limestone they had just split open. It fluttered its wings, croaked, and died at their feet.

The creature, whose wingspan was 10 feet 7 inches, had four legs joined by a membrane, like a bat. What should have been feet were long talons, and the mouth was arrayed with sharp teeth. The skin was like black leather, thick and oily.

At the nearby town of Gray, the creature was immediately identified by a local student of paleontology as a pterodactyl. The rock stratum in which it had been found was consistent with the period when pterodactyls lived, and the limestone boulder that had

---

Toads in the Coal: An Occasional Hell?

There are three ways, broadly speaking, to account for the numerous reports of living creatures recovered from cavities in solid rock thousands of years old. The most decisive way is to declare (as one Captain Buckland did when a toad supposedly released from a lump of coal in a Welsh mine was exhibited at the Great Exhibition of 1862) that such things are "a gross imposition"—the work of fools and bunglers whose words and eyes are not to be trusted.

A less impetuous explanation maintains that although the stone in which these creatures are found may appear to be solid, it actually contains fissures through which water, air, and perhaps even nutrients may enter. In the case of limestone, these fissures may become sealed by seeping carbonate of lime, the chemical from which stalactites and stalagmites are formed. To the untrained eye, the new deposits would not be distinguishable from the old rock, and the limestone would seem to be a solid, uniform mass.

The third account of such things is the most interesting but is not verifiable by any ordinary means. It can be illustrated by a story from Tibet.

In the later part of the 19th century a venerable lama named Situ Pema Wangyal Rinpoche was making a journey to Lhasa in the company of several friends. One day, much to the alarm of his companions, he fell into an unusually wrathful mood and that evening insisted on making camp on a barren plain where neither firewood nor water could be found. The next morning, still in a bad humor, he obliged the party to leave the route for Lhasa and to set out in a northerly direction that led, so far as his companions knew, to nowhere in particular. Since they held him in considerable esteem, however, they followed him without question.

After several hours they came to an enormous outcrop of rock, which, Situ Rinpoche announced, it was their task to break open. Since they had no tools but their wooden staffs, they fared poorly in this task, and—already alarmed by their leader's behavior—they withdrew some 50 to 60 feet to confer, leaving Situ Rinpoche standing by the rock.

Whereupon the lama took his staff and struck the rock a single blow. It shattered and revealed within a large, repulsive-looking creature somewhat like a salamander, its scaly black skin stuck to the rock, panting for breath. Situ Rinpoche gently lifted the animal out of the rock and set it down on the ground in front of him. He then sat down and began to perform a certain yoga on the animal's behalf.

In Tibetan this yoga is called *pho-wa* and is usually described as involving a transfer of consciousness. It is performed by lamas for the benefit of the dying.

After a while a narrow column of rainbow-colored light rose from the creature's head, and it died. Funeral rites were performed, and soon afterward the body was burned.

Afterward Situ Rinpoche explained that he had liberated the animal, which in a previous life had had a connection with him, from one of the occasional Hells. In the Buddhist description of other realms of existence, these occasional Hells lie outside the main circles of Hell and are sometimes encountered in this world. Very often, they are instanced by the enclosure of a living creature in solid rock.

imprisoned the winged reptile for millions of years was found to contain a cavity in the form of an exact mold of the creature's body. (*The Illustrated London News,* February 9, 1856, p.166)

The world's oldest living creatures were discovered by chance in 1972 in the laboratory of N. Chudinov at the Berezniki Potassium Combine in the Ural Mountains. Chudinov had dissolved a piece of potassium ore in distilled water as part of an effort to explain its red coloration. After a while he noticed that small flakes of material were beginning to float away from the rock, and when he examined one of them under a microscope he saw that it contained numerous microorganisms. This was surprising but not unduly so.

Several days later Chudinov again examined the water in his flask: it was now swarming with living organisms, apparently reanimated by their immersion. He placed some in test tubes and was staggered to see them grow and reproduce, apparently unharmed by being locked inside potassium crystals for 250 million years. (*Soviet Union,* February 1972, p.18)

OUT-OF-PLACE ARTIFACTS

During blasting work at Dorchester, Massachusetts, in 1851, the broken halves of a bell-shaped vessel were thrown by the force of an explosion from the vessel's resting place within a bed of formerly solid rock. The vase, about 4½ inches high, was made of an unknown metal and embellished with floral inlays of silver—the "art of some cunning workman," according to the local newspaper report.

The editor of *Scientific American* gave as his opinion that the vase had been made by Tubal-cain, the biblical father of metallurgy. In response, Charles Fort—a life-long connoisseur of anomalies and a dedicated opponent of scientific dogmatism—said: "Though I fear that this is a little arbitrary, I am not disposed to fly rabidly at every scientific opinion." (*Scientific American,* 7:298, June 5, 1852)

In 1851 Hiram de Witt, of Springfield, Massachusetts, accidentally dropped a fist-sized piece of gold-bearing quartz that he had previously brought back from California. The rock was broken apart by the fall, and inside it De Witt found a two-inch cut-iron nail, slightly corroded. "It was entirely straight and had a perfect head," reported *The Times* of London. (*The Times* [London], December 24, 1851)

Mrs. S. W. Culp, of Morrisonville, Illinois, was breaking coal into smaller lumps for her scuttle, one day in 1891, when she noticed a chain in the midst of the coal. When she reached down to pick it up, she saw that the two ends of the chain were firmly embedded in two separate pieces of coal that had clearly been a single lump only moments before. (The Morrisonville *Times,* June 11, 1891)

A strange tooth was found in the Bearcreek Mutual Coal Mine, Bearcreek, Montana, in 1926. According to local dentists, it looked exactly like a small human tooth, a lower second molar—but the passage of time had turned the enamel into carbon and the roots into iron. It was discovered by J.C.F. Siegfriedt, the company doctor, who collected fossils and who estimated the age of the coal deposits in which it was found as 10 million years. (The *Carbon County News,* November 11, 1926)

The tooth yielded by a lump of coal (above) at the Bearcreek mine was that of a primitive man, according to Dr. J.C.F. Siegfriedt, an expert on fossils.

This exquisitely wrought vessel (left) was broken and hurled from a bed of rock by the blasting set off at Dorchester in 1851. The whereabouts of the artifact is now unknown.

Geodes are something like oysters—not much to look at on the outside but apt to contain something valuable within. To an untrained eye, geodes look like ordinary stones, but their cavities are often filled with a small wonderland of colorful crystals and minerals. A good geode carefully sawn in half is much prized by rock collectors and by those whose business is selling rocks.

Cut in half, the Coso geode resembled a spark plug, with a shaft of metal about .08 inch thick encased in white ceramic. It was thought, however, to be half a million years old.

In 1961 Wally Lane, Mike Mikesell, and Virginia Maxey, co-owners of the LM&V Rockhounds Gem and Gift Shop in Olancha, California, went into the Coso Mountains, six miles northeast of Olancha, to look for unusual rocks. Near the top of a 4,300-foot peak overlooking the dry bed of Owens Lake they found a fossil-encrusted geode that proved to contain something very strange.

What the geode proved to contain, after Mike Mikesell had ruined a diamond saw blade in cutting it open, was something that would later be shown to resemble a spark plug.

In the middle of the geode was a metal core, about .08 inch (two millimeters) in diameter. Enclosing this was what appeared to be a ceramic collar that was itself encased in a hexagonal sleeve carved out of wood that had, presumably at a later date, become petrified. Around this was the outer layer of the geode, consisting of hardened clay, pebbles, bits of fossil shell, and "two nonmagnetic metallic objects resembling a nail and a washer." A fragment of copper still remaining between the ceramic and petrified wood suggests that the two may once have been separated by a now decomposed copper sleeve.

X-ray photographs of the objects were taken, and it was after examining these that the editor of *INFO Journal*, Paul Willis, noticed a startling similarity between the Coso artifact and a modern spark plug.

In 1963 the Coso geode was displayed for three months at the Eastern California Museum in Indepen-

dence. Wally Lane then seems to have taken possession of the object and in 1969 was reportedly offering it for sale for $25,000.

According to the estimate of a geologist unnamed in the original report of the find, the age of the geode, based on the fossils it contains, is some 500,000 years. No examination by a named professional scientist or scientific organization is on record. (*INFO Journal*, No. 4, Spring 1969, pp.4–13)

Workmen quarrying stone near the River Tweed below Rutherford, Scotland, in 1844, found a piece of gold thread embedded in the rock eight feet below ground level. A small piece of the thread was sent to the offices of the local newspaper, the *Kelso Chronicle*, "for the inspection of the curious." (*The Times* [London], June 22, 1844)

A nail partially embedded in a block of stone taken from the Kingoodie quarry in Scotland was described at a meeting of the British Association for the Advancement of Science in 1845. Sir David Brewster, who gave the report, said that about an inch of the nail was embedded, the rest lying along the stone and projecting into a layer of gravel, where it had rusted. The depth from which the nine-inch-thick block of stone bearing the nail had been removed was not on record, but the quarry was said to have been worked for some 20 years prior to the discovery. (Charles Fort, *The Complete Books of Charles Fort*, p.133)

An "iron instrument," apparently resembling the bit of a coal drill, was found inside a lump of coal taken from an excavation in Scotland in 1852. It was supposed that a miner had broken his drill while working the seam and had left the piece of metal embedded there. But the surface of the lump of coal was unbroken: it showed no sign of drilling nor any present or former opening by which a drill might have passed into its interior. If such a thing were not quite impossible, according to every date in the geology textbooks, observers would have been obliged to conclude that the coal had somehow been formed around the mysterious metal. (*Proceedings of the Society of Antiquaries of Scotland*, 1:1:121, December 13, 1852)

Extensive quarrying was done near the city of Aix-en-Provence, France, between 1786 and 1788, to provide the large quantities of limestone needed for the rebuilding of the Palace of Justice. In the quarry from which this limestone was taken, the rock strata were separated from each other by layers of sand and clay, and by the time the workmen had removed 11 layers of rock they found they had reached a depth of some 40 or

50 feet below the original ground level of the area.

Beneath the 11th layer of limestone they came to a bed of sand and began to remove it to get at the rock beneath. But in the sand they found the stumps of stone pillars and fragments of half-worked rock—the same stone and rock as they had themselves been excavating. They dug further and to their intense surprise found coins, the petrified wooden handles of hammers, and pieces of other petrified wooden tools. Finally, they came to a large wooden board, seven or eight feet long and an inch thick. Like the wooden tools, it had also been petrified into a form of agate and had been broken into pieces. When the pieces were reassembled, the workmen saw before them a quarryman's board of exactly the kind they themselves used, worn in just the same way as their own boards were, with rounded, wavy edges.

How a stonemason's yard, equipped with the kind of tools used in France in the late 18th century, had come to be buried 50 feet deep under layers of sand and limestone 300 million years old is a question even more vexing today than at the time of the original discovery. For we now know, thanks to advances in geological and anthropological dating, that such a thing is absolutely and incontrovertibly impossible. And yet it does seem to have happened. (*The American Journal of Science and Arts*, 1:145–46, 1820)

The remains of what seems to have been a pleasant village were discovered on the sunny west bank of the Danube River in 1965, at the archeological site now named Lepenski Vir, in Yugoslavia. The ancient community, perched on a sheltered horseshoe-shaped ledge at a bend in the river, has no close parallel in European prehistory.

For this tiny settlement was a model of community planning, with a fanlike arrangement of houses and streets. It also had a central marketplace and a sanctuary with carefully positioned stone sculptures of remarkable diversity and artistry. The town evinced an architectural awareness, too, with structures of trapezoidal shape and a geometric orderliness throughout.

Also impressive is the technology displayed in the construction of the floors, which were finished with a mortar. Made by baking local limestone and adding water, gravel, and sand, the substance was poured over the stone foundations, smoothed, and often polished.

Lepenski Vir has been a revelation to archeologists, who have dated the community back to about 5800 B.C. Cutting down through layers of foundations to the first settlement, they discovered that the design of the village and the methods of construction had been well worked out early in its long history and had remained almost unchanged, evidence that this culture had risen suddenly and spontaneously. In the view of archeologists, Lepenski Vir stands out in European prehistory for its monumental sculptures and for its organization of social, economic, and religious life.

Prior to these finds, it was assumed that the cultural development of Neolithic Europe had depended upon infusions of ideas from the Near East. But Lepenski Vir shows an independent flowering of creative activity that challenges traditional views. (Dragoslav Drejović, *Europe's First Monumental Sculpture: New Discoveries at Lepenski Vir*, pp.8–135 passim)

The Pacific island of New Caledonia is approximately 1,000 miles southwest of New Guinea and about 750 miles from the east coast of Australia. About 40 miles from its southern tip is the Isle of Pines. On this small island are some 400 curious tumuli—anthill-shaped mounds of sand and gravel, 8 to 9 feet high and some 300 feet in diameter. Similar mounds are found in smaller numbers in the Païta district of southern New Caledonia. On the Isle of Pines the sand has a high iron oxide content; near Païta it is rich in silica. In both cases the mounds are virtually bare of vegetation.

In the early 1960's four of the tumuli were excavated by L. Chevalier of the Museum of New Caledonia at

---

Astonishing Frauds

The easiest way to account for discoveries that are at odds with orthodox dating is to dismiss them as frauds. Some nonconformist finds are quite probably fraudulent. However, there are several problems in supposing that this solution accounts for all anomalous fossils and enclosures.

In the first place, these things have very often been discovered by perfectly respectable people who have gained nothing but ridicule and a reputation for stupidity or dishonesty for making their finds public. In the second place, the discoveries have often been made during mining or quarrying operations, sometimes at great depths, and have been revealed by the random breaking of a piece of coal or stone in the presence of witnesses. To suppose that anonymous tricksters have somehow penetrated to such depths, inserting their handiwork in solid seams of rock and coal without leaving a trace, and, having done this, arranged to have precisely the right piece of material broken open in the presence of appropriate witnesses by mining equipment or someone's hammer—to suppose all this strains belief. To suppose that such a complex scenario has been performed numerous times, by tricksters who remain anonymous and who therefore fail to enjoy to the full the embarrassment of those they have gone to such pains to embarrass—stretches credulity quite as much as the anomalies themselves.

Lepenski Vir has no close parallel in European prehistory for its orderly, planned architecture or its stone sculptures, such as this figure from a sanctuary.

A place of enchanting lagoons, the Isle of Pines is also the site of curious cement pillars reputedly formed long before humans are known to have stepped ashore.

Noumea, the island's capital. The mounds are strange in their own right, but what Chevalier found in them was even stranger. At the centers of three mounds he discovered an upright cement pillar, and in a fourth, two such pillars side by side. No bones, charcoal, or any other remains were found. The pillars, or cylinders, which range from 40 to 75 inches in diameter and 40 to 100 inches in height, are composed of a lime-mortar compound containing bits of shell. These have been dated by the radiocarbon process at between 5120 B.C. and 10,950 B.C.. The use of lime-mortar compounds is almost unheard of prior to the classical period, a few hundred years B.C. As far as is currently known, the first human arrived in New Caledonia from Indonesia around 2000 B.C.

The outer surface of the cylinders is speckled with fragments of silica and iron gravel that seem to have set in the mortar as it hardened. Chevalier's guess is that they were formed by pouring mortar into narrow pits dug into the top of the mounds and allowing it to harden in place. Why anyone should do such a thing (there appears to be no natural explanation for the pillars) is entirely mysterious. And given the apparent age of the cylinders and the fact that there are no signs of life, human or otherwise, associated with them, so is the nature of those who made them. (*INFO Journal,* No. 2, Autumn 1967, pp.15–16)

UNACCOUNTABLE KNOWLEDGE

The Efe pygmies, who live in the Ituri forest in Central Africa, refer to the planet Saturn as "the star of the nine moons," *Bibi Tiba Abuutsiua'ani*. This term was made known to a French anthropologist named Jean Pierre Hallet, who lived with the Efe for 18 months in 1957–58. (Saturn's ninth moon had been discovered by the American astronomer William H. Pickering in 1899.) In 1966 a very small 10th moon was observed in orbit around the planet, and in 1980–81 Voyager space probes discovered still others. But since all the moons are equally invisible to the naked eye, only a purist would fault the Efe on that account. The source of their knowledge is unknown. (Francis Hitching, *The Mysterious World: An Atlas of the Unexplained,* p.108)

The greatest mysteries are sometimes hidden in circumstances so unexpected that their discovery is always by chance or incidental to some other search. In southern Mali, where the Niger River makes a great bend, live the Dogon people, poor farmers who still live, many of them in caves, in the Hombori Mountains. The nearest cities are Timbuktu, to the north, and Ouagadougou, to the south, in Upper Volta.

In outward appearance there is little to distinguish

the Dogon from other West African peoples; and yet they, along with three related tribes, may have preserved, in religious secrecy for many hundreds of years, information about a phenomenon of the greatest rarity. For preserved at the core of their deepest religious teachings is detailed knowledge about a star that is quite invisible to the naked eye and so difficult to observe—even through a telescope—that no photographs of it were obtained until 1970. The Dogon say that this knowledge (which they disclosed to French anthropologists in the 1930's and 1940's) was given to them by visitors to the earth from another star system.

The star they describe is known to astronomers as Sirius B and to the Dogon as *Pŏ Tolo*. Its existence was first suspected by Western astronomers in 1844, when certain irregularities were noticed in the movements of the star Sirius—the brilliant "Dog Star" in the constellation Canis Major. To account for these perturbations, it was supposed that Sirius must be affected by the gravitational pull of an as-yet-unseen second star, and in 1862, after much observation, a faint companion star was finally detected. It seemed, however, far too small to exercise any noticeable influence on Sirius, which is twice as large as our own sun and 20 times as radiant. Today we know that Sirius B is a white dwarf that, although small and faint (white dwarfs are the smallest class of visible star), is extremely dense and quite heavy enough to exercise a gravitational influence on Sirius A.

The Dogon name for Sirius B consists of the word for star, *tolo,* and *pŏ,* the name of the smallest seed known to them (the seed of *Digitaria exilis,* a variety of crabgrass). By this name they describe the star's smallness—it is, they say, "the smallest thing there is." They also claim that it is "the heaviest star" (since in it the element earth is replaced by an immensely heavy metal called *sagala*), so heavy "that all earthly beings combined cannot lift it." And the color of the star is white. The Dogon thus attribute to Sirius B (which is, remember, quite invisible to the naked eye) its three principal qualities as a white dwarf: its smallness, heaviness, and whiteness. They go on to say that the star's orbit is elliptical, with Sirius A at one focus of the ellipse (as it is), that the orbital period is 50 years (the actual figure is $50.04 \pm .09$ years), and that the star rotates on its own axis (it does). The Dogon also describe a third star in the Sirius system, called *Emme Ya* ("sorghum female"). In orbit around this star, they say, is a single satellite. To date *Emme Ya* has not been detected by Western astronomers.

The significance of Sirius B to the Dogon is that it was the first star made by God and is the axis of the universe. From it, all matter and all souls are produced by a complex spiral movement that the Dogon symbolize in woven baskets. All souls, whatever their final

Dogon dancers (above) sometimes portray their people's belief that they were visited and taught by creatures from the Sirius system in ancient times.

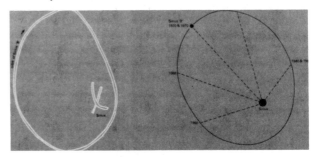

A Dogon sand drawing of the elliptical course of Sirius B around Sirius A (above left) resembles the astronomical diagram of the orbit (above right). In the photograph of Sirius A (left), Sirius B appears as a small dot. The spurs of light on Sirius A are caused by a telescopic device.

destination, first gravitate from *Pŏ Tolo* to *Emme Ya*.

In addition to their knowledge of Sirius B, Dogon astronomical lore includes the fact that Saturn has rings and that Jupiter has four major moons. They have four calendars, for the Sun, Moon, Sirius, and Venus, and have long known that planets orbit the Sun.

The Dogon say that their astronomical knowledge was given to them by the Nommos, amphibious beings sent to earth from the Sirius star system for the benefit of humankind. The name comes from a Dogon word meaning "to make one drink," and the Nommos are also called Masters of the Water, The Monitors, and

The Dogon and the Erudite Europeans

Carl Sagan, Cornell University astronomer, author of *The Cosmic Connection,* and coauthor of *Intelligent Life in the Universe,* has calculated that, given the billions of stars in the universe, the vast number of planets in orbit around those stars (assuming, conservatively, that even a small percentage have planets), and the incredible age of the universe, it is virtually a statistical certainty that intelligent life has evolved over and over again and that many civilizations must be far older and more advanced than ours.

This would seem to lend weight to the possibility that the Dogon source of information was, as they report, ancient astronauts. But Sagan, while believing in the existence and capabilities of extraterrestrials, also believes that the evidence in this case points in a different direction. He agrees that "the Dogon have knowledge impossible to acquire without the telescope. The straightforward conclusion is that they had contact with an advanced technical civilization. The only question is," he says, "Which civilization—extraterrestrial or European?"

Western astronomers first deduced the existence of Sirius B in 1844; it was not actually observed until 1862; and it was recognized as a white dwarf, incredibly dense and composed of "electron-degenerate matter," in 1928. All of this information is accurately expounded by the Dogon, but because their complex cosmology, including the Sirius B information, was not recorded by European anthropologists until the 1930's and 1940's, Sagan contends that the Dogon picked up that information from a passing European (popular information about Sirius B was published in 1928 in Sir Arthur Eddington's book *The Nature of the Physical World*) as they spent an evening around the campfire swapping Sirius myths:

> In my mind's eye I picture a Gallic visitor to the Dogon people, in what was then French West Africa, in the early part of this century.... The conversation turns to astronomical lore. Sirius is the brightest star in the sky. The Dogon regale their visitor with their Sirius mythology. Then, smiling politely, expectantly, they enquire of their visitor what his Sirius myths might be.

At first glance this might seem a plausible scenario, but several crucial problems arise.

The primary difficulty is that only the highest Dogon initiates are taught the secret calculations. The two French anthropologists, Marcel Griaule and Germaine Dieterlen, whose monograph "A Sudanese Sirius System" first described this phenomenon, were given this information only after a decade of work among the Dogon, when extraordinary mutual trust and affection had developed. Even so, the anthropologists had to piece the information together from several sources, since the highest-ranking priests were each responsible for only a part of this complex system of knowledge. Such carefully guarded secrets are not the stuff of campfire tales told to amuse strangers.

Next, consider the high degree of accuracy in modern scientific terms. It is well known that preliterate societies do, in fact, have extremely accurate oral traditions, with stories handed down virtually unchanged for hundreds of years. But the Dogon add a third star to the Sirius system, a star with a satellite in orbit around it. Since Western astronomy has no knowledge of such a star, what would account for the accurate retelling of one segment of the explorer's myth, in combination with the total fabrication of another segment?

And in what language were the Dogon and our hypothetical explorer conversing? After all, communicating such sophisticated and precise scientific information to pretechnological people would be difficult even if there were a common language. Yet Griaule and Dieterlen list the languages of their informants as Sanga and Wazouba; no mention is made of French or of Arabic.

Another European has his own explanation of the Sirius mystery as reported in 1973 in the *Journal of the British Astronomical Association.* Its author, W. H. McCrea, suggested that all the information the Dogon have about Sirius B could have been derived from a mirage of Sirius A observed over the desert during its annual heliacal setting (that is, when Sirius and the sun set together at almost the same time and at the same point on the horizon). At such a time, McCrea suggests, a mirage of Sirius A would be seen below the actual star. Setting first, this "second star" would seem to be heavier than the main star; it would also seem fainter and, therefore, smaller.

The defects in this attempted explanation are as follows: (1) McCrea is wrong in supposing that the Dogon say that Sirius B is visible once a year; they claim no observations of the star. (2) McCrea says that Sirius A and its mirage would both seem red at the heliacal setting; the Dogon have never said that Sirius B is anything but white in color. (3) The mirage thesis does not explain why or how the Dogon accurately describe an elliptical orbit for Sirius B. (4) Nor is their knowledge of the 50-year orbital period explained. McCrea admits this and can only suppose that the figure given by the Dogon is accurate by coincidence.

The Instructors. They came to earth somewhere to the northeast of the Dogon's present homeland. When their vessel landed (after a "spinning or whirling" descent and with a great noise and wind), it skidded to a stop, scoring the ground and "spurting blood" (perhaps a reference to a rocket's fiery exhaust). At that time a new star (perhaps a mother ship) was seen in the sky. After the landing, something with four legs appeared and dragged the vessel to a hollow, which filled with water until the vessel floated in it.

According to Dogon art, the Nommos were more fishlike than human, and they had to live in water. They were saviors and spiritual guardians:

> The Nommo divided his body among men to feed them; that is why it is also said that as the universe "had drunk of his body," the Nommo also made men drink. He gave all his life principles to human beings.

The Nommo was crucified and resurrected and in the future will again visit the earth, this time in human form. Later he will assume his amphibious form and will rule the world from the waters.

If the Dogon accounts record something as momentous as a landing on this earth by beings from another star system, one would expect to find comparable descriptions elsewhere. Do such descriptions exist? They do, in Babylonian accounts of the Oannes, amphibious beings who came to this planet for the welfare of the human race. Their vehicle was egg shaped, and they landed in the Red Sea. The following descriptions are taken from a history of Mesopotamia written in the third century B.C. by Berossus, a Babylonian priest whose work survives only in fragments recorded by later Greek historians.

The Oannes "had the shape of a fish blended with that of a man," a "complicated form between a fish and a man"; they were "semi-demons—halfway between men and gods." Their appearance was repulsive:

> The whole body of the animal was like that of a fish; and had under a fish's head, another head and also feet below, similar to those of a man, subjoined to the fish's tail. His voice too, and language, was articulate and human. . . .
>
> This Being in the daytime used to converse with men, but took no food at that season; and he gave them an insight into letters and sciences, and every kind of art. He taught them to construct houses, to found temples, to compile laws, and explained to them the principles of geometrical knowledge . . . in short, he instructed them in everything which could tend to soften manners and humanize mankind. . . . When the sun set, it was the custom of this Being to plunge again into the sea, and abide all night in the deep, for he was amphibious.

One further account of the Oannes is preserved, in summary form, by Saint Photius (c. A.D. 820–892), patriarch of Constantinople. In his *Myriobiblon* he says that the historian Helladius

> recounts the story of a man named Oe who came out of the Red Sea having a fish-like body but the head, feet and arms of a man, and who taught astronomy and letters. Some accounts say that he came out of a great egg, whence his name, and that he was actually a man, but only seemed a fish because he was clothed in "the skin of a sea-creature."

Is it possible that the Dogon Nommo and the Babylonian Oannes are different representations of the same event? The Dogon themselves insist that their people did not always live in their present homeland, and evidence suggests that they are descendants of Berbers who began a southward migration from Libya in the 1st and 2nd centuries A.D. and who, having intermarried with local blacks, were fully established in the Mali area by the 11th century.

If the Dogon did indeed come to Mali from the northeast, they may originally have been close enough to the Red Sea for a connection between the Nommo and Oannes to be geographically feasible. If so, however, it is curious that the Dogon alone should preserve the Sirius B information, while the Egyptians, who were certainly in contact with Babylonian culture, should preserve only a high regard for Sirius A, and that largely because it helped them to predict the Nile floods.

On these grounds, then, it seems likely that Dogon and Babylonian history record separate but similar events. (Robert Temple, *The Sirius Mystery*, passim)

India's national epic, *The Mahābhārata,* a poem of vast length and complexity, achieved its present form in the second century A.D. Depending on one's point of view, either it contains some of the earliest known examples of science fiction, or it records conflicts between beings whose armaments were just as advanced as those employed today.

In one episode, for example, the Vrishnis, a tribe whose warriors include the hero Krishna, are beset by the forces of a leader named Salva:

> The cruel Salva had come mounted on the Saubha chariot that can go anywhere, and from it he killed many valiant Vrishni youths and evilly devastated all the city parks.

The Saubha is at once Salva's city, flagship, and battle headquarters. In it he can fly wherever he chooses. In contemporary terms the Saubha might best be described as the mother ship from which Salva makes sorties against the enemy. Fortunately, the Vrishni heroes are comparably well equipped and at one point have Salva at their mercy. The hero Pradyumna is about to finish him off with a special weapon, but the highest gods intervene: "Not a man in battle is safe from this arrow," they say, and in any case tell Pradyumna it has been ordained that Salva shall fall to Krishna.

Krishna takes to the skies in pursuit of Salva, but

his Saubha clung to the sky at a league's length. . . .
He threw at me rockets, missiles, spears, spikes,
battleaxes, three-bladed javelins, flame-throwers,
without pausing. . . . The sky . . . seemed to hold a
hundred suns, a hundred moons . . . and a hundred
myriad stars. Neither day nor night could be made
out, or the points of compass.

Krishna, however, wards off Salva's counterattack with the equivalent of antiballistic missiles:

I warded them off as they loomed towards me
With my swift-striking shafts, as they flashed
through the sky,
And I cut them into two or three pieces with mine—
There was a great din in the sky above.

Nonetheless, Krishna is sorely pressed. He rallies, but the Saubha, by technological or other magic, becomes invisible. Krishna then loads a special weapon, an ancient version of a "smart bomb":

I quickly laid on an arrow, which killed by seeking out sound, to kill them. . . . All the Danavas [troops in Salva's army] who had been screeching lay dead, killed by the blazing sunlike arrows that were triggered by sound.

But the Saubha itself has escaped the attack, and at last Krishna hurls against it his "favorite fire weapon," a discus having the shape of the "haloed sun." Severed in two by the impact, the aerial city falls down.

Salva himself is killed, and with his death this episode of *The Mahābhārata* comes to an end. One of the most intriguing things in it is the suggestion that the use of one especially terrible weapon—Pradyumna's special arrow, from which "not a man in battle is safe"—is outlawed by the gods. What sort of weapon could this have been? Another episode may provide the answer in its description of the effects of the fearful Agneya weapon used by the hero Adwattan. When the weapon, a "blazing missile of smokeless fire," is unleashed:

Dense arrows of flame, like a great shower, issued
forth upon creation, encompassing the enemy. . . . A
thick gloom swiftly settled upon the Pandava hosts.
All points of the compass were lost in darkness.

The Mahābhārata *contains many references to air travel. In this illustration of its account of the hero Rajah Karna, deities arrive on flying carpets to observe him in battle.*

Fierce winds began to blow. Clouds roared upward, showering dust and gravel.

Birds croaked madly . . . the very elements seemed disturbed. The sun seemed to waver in the heavens. The earth shook, scorched by the terrible violent heat of this weapon. Elephants burst into flame and ran to and fro in a frenzy . . . over a vast area, other animals crumpled to the ground and died. From all points of the compass the arrows of flame rained continuously and fiercely.

Worse is still to come. If the effects of Adwattan's weapon resemble those of a fire storm, the results of one fired by Gurkha seem to describe nothing less than a nuclear explosion and poisoning by radioactive fallout:

Gurkha, flying in his swift and powerful Vimana, hurled against the three cities of the Vrishnis and Andhakas a single projectile charged with all the power of the universe. An incandescent column of smoke and fire, as brilliant as ten thousand suns, rose in all its splendor. It was the unknown weapon, the iron thunderbolt, a gigantic messenger of death which reduced to ashes the entire race of the Vrishnis and Andhakas.

The corpses were so burnt they were no longer recognizable. Hair and nails fell out. Pottery broke without cause. . . . Foodstuffs were poisoned. To escape, the warriors threw themselves in streams to wash themselves and their equipment.

If this description is science fiction, its author was surely a prophet. (*The Mahābhārata,* J.A.B. van Buitenen, ed. and trans., Vol. 2, pp.182–267; Rene Noorbergen, *Secrets of Lost Races,* pp.137–38)

Babylonian astronomers have long been recognized as preeminent in the ancient world. A few thousand years before Copernicus they realized that the earth and the other planets were spherical and that they revolved around the sun. With this knowledge they could accurately predict eclipses of the sun and moon. Many modern scholars assumed that the Babylonians developed their astronomy themselves, to meet the need for accurate calculations for their complex astrology. Surprisingly, newly translated Babylonian texts indicate that the positions and motions of the stars and planets were calculated instead according to complex equations inherited from the Sumerian civilization. The Babylonians seem not to have understood the theoretical basis of these formulas, only how to use them.

The Sumerians had even more exact knowledge of the solar system and its place in the universe than their Babylonian heirs, whom they predate. Their calendar, devised as early as 3000 B.C., is the model for our calendar today, and they evidently understood a number of more arcane astronomical matters.

For example, as the earth spins, it wobbles on its axis; this causes a very gradual change—1 degree every 72 years—affecting which star the north pole points to. The phenomenon is called precession. A Great Year—the time it takes before the north pole points to the same north star again—is 25,920 years, calculated by multiplying the 72 years it takes to move each degree by the 360 degrees in a full circle. The Sumerians understood precession and knew the length of the Great Year—an extraordinary feat, given the lengthy observations involved and the instruments available to them.

The Sumerians were also able to measure the distances between stars very precisely. But how would earthbound, pretechnological people learn to do this, and, even more mysterious, why? Such star maps are clearly a necessity for space travelers, but what use could the Sumerians have made of them?

Given the extraordinary accuracy of Sumerian astronomical calculations, we should, perhaps, have another look at those areas where their information differs from ours. The Sumerians assign 12 "celestial bodies" to the solar system—the sun, the moon, and 10 planets, including Earth. Today we recognize 11 of these, but it was not always so. Until the late 18th century Western astronomers knew only of the existence of six planets—Mercury, Venus, Earth, Mars, Jupiter, and Saturn. Uranus was discovered in 1781, Neptune in 1846, and Pluto only in 1930. In this light, is it possible that the Sumerians' 12th planet is yet to be discovered? Interestingly, in 1972 Joseph L. Brady, an astronomer at the Lawrence Livermore Laboratory, Livermore, California, discovered a perturbation in the orbit of Halley's comet that could be accounted for by the gravitational pull of a planet about the size of Jupiter that orbits the sun every 1,800 years. (Zecharia Sitchin, *The Twelfth Planet,* passim)

A star in the southern constellation Hydra and a lion, the zodiacal symbol for the constellation Leo, are represented on this clay tablet from ancient Babylonia.

Radiohalos: The Glow of Youth?

The oddities assembled in this chapter are so regarded because they bring one scientific method of dating into conflict with another. And not just methods of dating; each method carries an enormous baggage of dependent ideas and descriptions, which are sometimes rather roughly jostled and shoved together but which constitute, for better or worse, a generally accepted picture of how things have come to be as they are.

For example, the science of geology has established a more or less comprehensive account of the earth's evolution, distinguishing kinds and periods of rock formation and the time scales appropriate to them. Industrial and technological archeology has performed a similar service for the history of man's technical ingenuity, and paleontology and zoology have done the same thing for classes of animals. All these systems work reasonably well and, in fact, sometimes depend on each other for their development.

But when a housewife finds a piece of chain inside a lump of coal, or when a well digger finds a living toad inside a flint nodule, the systems come into conflict. And so they do when a relatively obscure African people is found to be in possession of sophisticated astronomical knowledge, or when ancient Indian poets write—with what seems to be something close to personal knowledge—of an event that resembles the explosion of a nuclear weapon.

When any of these things happen, a conflict arises, and since chains, toads, obscure Africans, and long-dead poets are feeble things when set beside folded mountain ranges and eons of geologic time (to say nothing of the vast weight of invested academic opinion), they usually lose the contest. No one whose opinion counts is going to set it aside for a hatful of toads or a few feet of chain. No one is going to agree that the technology of metal chain making seems to be millions of years old, after all, or that some "ancient" coal beds seem to have been formed only a few hundred or thousand years ago.

Until the last decade or so the physicists have remained largely aloof from these grubby squabbles. But it now seems that they may have thrown a radioactive monkey wrench into the geological works.

Specifically, the geological bulwarks are threatened by something far less substantial than toads or chains. The new siege weapons are tiny bubbles of color, called radiohalos, found in mica, coal, and other minerals.

Radiohalos occur when radioactive matter infiltrates a mineral deposit during the early stages of its formation. Uranium and polonium particles, for example, may infiltrate deposits of organic material that are in the process of becoming coal. When the process of coalification is complete, the radioactive particle continues to emit radiation and produces rings of discoloration whose sequence and radii relate directly to the energy level of the radiation and to the length of time that the process has been going on.

The problem from a geologist's point of view is that the radiohalos are too small. Given the energy of the radiating particle and the length of time it has been enclosed in its mineral matrix, the radiohalos should be larger than they are. From the physicist's point of view, the implication is that the mineral matrices are nowhere near as old as the geologist tells him they are. As far as the geologists are concerned, there must be something wrong with some of the very basic premises in modern physics, and this the physicists are unwilling to admit.

In either case, it seems that radical revisions of scientific chronology may soon be in order and that the case for toads, chains, and other outcasts from the halls of science may yet be advanced by the dim light of radioactive decay.

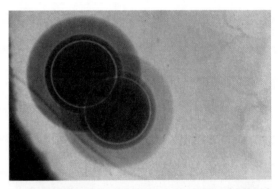

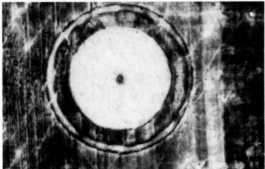

These photographs show polonium halos in mica (above) and a uranium halo in fluorite (below). The formation of polonium halos defies explanation by current physical laws.

COINCIDENCES

As a race, the English are said to value the welfare of their animals rather more than that of their children. The French, supposedly, regard indifference to culinary pleasure as the sign of the clod, while the Italians revere bicycle racing and the opera to the same degree. Such national stereotypes—Japanese ingenuity, German efficiency, Danish gloom—are numerous, come readily to mind, and many even contain a grain of truth. In view of this, the lack of such stereotypes for humankind in general is surprising. We can safely suggest that humans seek pleasure and avoid pain, but what else can we claim without hedging?

We could say that humans, in general, enjoy humor—but only in its place; that they admire courage—but not the unthinking kind; that they dislike meanness— providing it be distinguished from fiscal prudence. We could also say that motherhood meets with general approval—providing the world population does not threaten to explode. But what can we say that humans approve in an unqualified way?

They approve coincidence. Human beings enjoy, universally and without qualification, a good coincidence.

For several reasons. First, because coincidence is democratic; it has no regard for wealth or station in society. Second, coincidence suggests that the world—meaning that vastness of time and space in which a human being can easily feel less important than a grain of sand in the Sahara—is not indifferent to us. Indeed, coincidence suggests that the world, whatever it may be, is not only uncannily attentive to us and ours but sometimes goes to extraordinary lengths to prove it. Third, as a consequence, coincidence creates an impression of mysterious potentials, mostly unrealized, to be sure, but still a possible source of relief from the dreariness of mundane comings and goings of everyday life.

Finally, and it is a consideration of great importance, none of the foregoing virtues offends any social, political, religious, or scientific preoccupation that we may have. Even stern-faced statisticians, anxious to persuade us that the arm of coincidence is not so long as we like to believe, are titillated by the challenge it offers to their professional skill.

Granted all this, that coincidence does enjoy a rare kind of unequivocal, universal popularity, it is not surprising that all kinds of opinions and theories about it should abound. Are all events, in the supposed absence of provable causal connections, in fact coincidences? Are coincidences spurred into being by our latent psychic abilities? Do they exploit, or reveal, unities ultimately traceable to the mind of God, or to the Collective Unconscious, or to the infinite kinship systems of innumerable rebirths? Does their value lie solely in what we learn from them of the mind's tendency to create the patterns it observes and to then invest them with meaning? Will coincidence eventually yield to the picklock of correct statistical procedure? And so on.

With nets such as these being cast, perhaps the elusive coincidence creature will someday be captured and identified. But if it is, shall we ever be quite sure that the evidence that becomes available has not merely fallen into place by virtue of the mystery we call coincidence?

To bring a modicum of order to a subject that, by its very nature, violates our sense of the expected, the examples here are arranged by category. They fall into three groups: coincidences involving people, objects, and animals.

CONCERNING PEOPLE

The odds seem even more dramatic when two or more people are involved in coincidences. For this to happen, the paths of all the parties concerned must cross in some unpredictable and unexpected ways.

Twenty-one

When Louis XVI of France was a child, an astrologer warned him to be always on his guard on the 21st of every month. The advice terrified the young child, and thereafter he refused to undertake any important business on that day.

In spite of his precautions in regard to business, he was caught up in larger events on that date. It was on June 21, 1791, that Louis and his queen were arrested at Varennes as they tried to escape the revolution. On September 21 the following year, France abolished the institution of royalty and proclaimed itself a republic. And on January 21, 1793, Louis XVI was executed. (*Holiday*, November 1962, p.52)

Led to the guillotine on a charge of treason, Louis XVI of France faced his death with courage. The tricolored flag of the new French Republic flies above his head.

A Sense of Occasion

Thomas Jefferson was the author of the Declaration of Independence, and John Adams was one of its chief promulgators. Adams became the second president of the United States and Jefferson the third. The two men

Louis XVI and Marie Antoinette were captured by antiroyalists at Varennes as the couple attempted to flee France. Louis then tied his hopes to foreign intervention.

Thomas Jefferson sat for this portrait in 1791 when he was the secretary of state. The painting, by Charles Willson Peale, hangs in Independence Hall, Philadelphia.

died in the same year, 1826, and on the same day, the 50th anniversary of the most important day in their lives: July 4. Jefferson apparently willed himself to live until then. Before breathing his last, he asked whether it was the Fourth. Adams, whose famous last words were "Thomas Jefferson still survives," outlived his compatriot by only five hours. (Dumas Malone, *The Sage of Monticello,* Vol. 6, pp.497-98)

Although President John Adams (above) retired from public life in 1801, he maintained a lively correspondence with Thomas Jefferson until their last days.

The Anniversary

Augustus J. C. Hare, a well-known writer and artist in the Victorian period, had been given up for adoption in the 1830's when he was only 14 months old. Following his graduation from Oxford he lived chiefly in Europe, making occasional visits to England. In his autobiography Hare tells the following story:

> On the anniversary of my adoption, we all went over to Mannheim, and dined at the hotel where, seventeen years before, I, being fourteen months old, was given away to my aunt, who was also my godmother, to live with her forever as if I were her own child.... When we returned to the station in the evening . . . on the platform was a poor woman, crying very bitterly, with a little child in her arms. Emmie Penrhyn . . . went up to her and said she was afraid she was in some great trouble. "Yes," she said. "It is about my little child, who is only fourteen months old, is going away from me forever in the train which is coming. It is going away to be adopted by its aunt, who is also its godmother, and I shall never, never have anything to do with it any more." [Augustus J. C. Hare, *The Story of My Life,* Vol. 1, pp.383-84]

The Monk and the Painter

When Joseph Aigner, who became a well-known portrait painter, was 18 years old, he tried to hang himself but was prevented by the mysterious arrival of a Capuchin monk. This took place in Vienna in 1836. Four years later, in Budapest, Aigner again tried to hang himself and was again prevented by the sudden appearance of the same monk. Eight years went by and Aigner, who had espoused a revolutionary cause, was sentenced to the gallows for his political activities. He was reprieved, however, at the instigation of a monk— the same Capuchin. Finally, in 1886 when he was 68 years old, Aigner fulfilled his death wish and killed himself with a pistol. His funeral ceremony was conducted by the Capuchin monk, whose name, to the very last, Aigner had never learned. (*Ripley's Giant Book of Believe It or Not!*)

Augustus J. C. Hare, who was reared from infancy by an aunt, moved in fashionable circles and became popular for his anecdotes about society and his well-told ghost stories.

Fate Plays a Hand

In 1858 Robert Fallon, of Northumberland, England, was accused of cheating in a poker game at the Bella Union saloon in San Francisco and shot dead. Since money won by cheating—$600 in this case—was thought to be unlucky, the other players called in the first available passerby to take the dead man's place, confident that they would soon win the money back. By the time the police arrived, though, the new player had turned the original $600 into $2,200. When the police asked for the $600, so that they could pass it on to the dead man's next of kin, the young stranger proved that he was Fallon's son, who had not seen his father for seven years. (*Ripley's Giant Book of Believe It or Not!*)

No Secret

During the Civil War a group of Yankee prisoners was being transferred by train to a prison camp in Salisbury, North Carolina. One of the guards on the train was a 17-year-old named Beverley Tucker, and his duty was to guard a number of prisoners who spent the journey whispering together in a foreign language. As it turned out, they were speaking the dialect of their native Swiss canton and were plotting their escape. At a way station they made their bid for freedom—and found themselves encircled by the bayonets of the entire guard. They had the misfortune to be put in the charge of Bev Tucker—probably the only man in the entire Confederate Army who understood their language. He had gone to school in their native canton. (Joseph Bryan III, *The Sword Over the Mantel*, p.69)

The Duelist

Henri Tragne, of Marseille, France, fought five duels between 1861 and 1878. In the first four his opponents fell dead before a single shot had been fired; in the fifth, Tragne himself died—again before shots had been exchanged. (Max Jouvenot, *Champs d'Honneur*, p.113)

The Unfortunate Bride

The wedding day of Princess Maria del Pozzo della Cisterna, who married Amadeo, the Duke D'Aosta, the son of the king of Italy, in Turin on May 30, 1867, was marred by these events:

- Her wardrobe mistress hanged herself.
- The palace gatekeeper cut his throat.
- The colonel leading the wedding procession collapsed from sunstroke.
- The stationmaster was crushed to death under the wheels of the honeymoon train.
- The king's aide was killed by a fall from his horse.
- The best man shot himself.

The couple did not live happily ever after. (Roger L. Williams, *Gaslight and Shadow*, pp.156–57)

A life of marital bliss was hardly augured by the events that occurred on the wedding day of Princess Maria del Pozzo della Cisterna and the Duke D'Aosta (above).

Similar Assassins

An assassin named Claude Volbonne murdered Baron Rodemire de Tarazone, of France, in 1872. Twenty-one years earlier the baron's father had also been murdered—by a Claude Volbonne. The two assassins were not related. (*Ripley's Giant Book of Believe It or Not!*)

The Man Who Broke the Bank at Monte Carlo

Charles Wells was so famous that they wrote a music-hall song about him: "The Man Who Broke the Bank at Monte Carlo." In fact, Wells broke the bank three times. He was not a well-known gambler, he used no "system," he was not in the least bit dashing (he was, in fact, a fat Englishman), and after his staggering successes he was never again seen in the casino.

The first two times he broke the bank in 1891—that is, won the 100,000 francs "bank" allocated to each table—he did so by putting even-money bets on black and red and winning nearly every time. On the third occasion he placed his opening bet on the number five, at odds of 35 to 1, and won. He left his original bet on the number, added his winnings to it, and won again. He did this five times, all told, and each time the number five came up for him. The bank was broken again, and Charles Wells left quietly with his winnings.

He was said by some who had met him to be a slightly sinister man. (*The Unexplained: Mysteries of Mind Space & Time*, Vol. 3, Issue 32)

The Causal Figment

A striking coincidence is much like a small drama: the participants arrive exactly on cue, wear the right makeup, know their lines, and produce results that are significant or trivial, amusing or, sometimes, awe-inspiring. The problem is that no scriptwriter, no director, no stage manager, and no collusion on the part of the actors are involved in the performance; it unfolds, without reason but with perfect order, as though by magic.

Coincidences are baffling because they seem to represent order arising by chance: they resemble the results of an orderly causal process, but they do not have a causal connection that fits our experience. For example, the beetle (see "The Golden Scarab," p.77) that flies into the psychiatrist's consulting room just as a patient is recounting a dream in which such an insect enters her room has no discernible connection with the patient. It could not have known how to enter the room on cue. Furthermore, the patient who dreams of this liberating encounter has no way of knowing that it will occur or any means of ensuring that her response will be the one predicted by the dream.

The problem with coincidences is that they violate our notions of cause and effect. But supposing our notions of causality are wrong?

In 1739 the Scottish philosopher David Hume published *A Treatise of Human Nature,* an analytical rejection of the commonly established ideas of causation. In philosophical terms, his arguments have never been fully rebutted; in scientific terms, much of what he maintained has been justified.

Since Greek philosophers first turned their attention to causality in the fifth century B.C., it had been almost universally accepted that everything that has a beginning must be caused by something else. Hume rejected this. On the contrary, he maintained, it is not certain that every object which begins to exist must owe its existence to a cause. To believe, said Hume, that every being must be preceded by a cause is no more valid than believing that because every husband must have a wife, every man must therefore be married.

Hume aimed to show that the traditional starting point for theories of causation is incapable of proof; he was not, of course, trying to prove its reverse or any other position. All we can justly say of causality is that what we take to be a cause always precedes what we take to be its effect and that there is always contiguity between the two. Beyond this, he said, nothing could be claimed, and the view that a necessary connection exists between a cause and its effect is nothing more than a habit of mind.

For example, while watching a game of billiards, we

The Scottish philosopher David Hume held that the idea of a causal relationship between two events occurring in sequence is nothing more than a habit of mind.

confidently expect that when one ball strikes another, the ball that has been struck will move, and we therefore persuade ourselves that there is a connection between the motion of the first ball and the motion of the second—between cause and effect. Such an idea, however, is not based on logic or observation, Hume said. All we observe is that contact—contiguity—occurs; the rest is assumption. Our expectation that a stationary ball will move in a predictable way when struck by another ball may well be correct in most cases, but this is not a certainty. The momentum and inertia of the two balls must be considered—too little momentum or too much inertia, and the effect will not be what we expect. The materials from which the balls are made must also be taken into account, and so must their soundness—is one of the balls apt to shatter rather than move? We must also consider the shape of the balls, the nature of the surface on which they lie, and the stability of the situation in which the event takes place. Among all these variables and many more, we look in vain for an identifiable principle connecting cause and effect; and since we look in vain for it, we are under no compulsion to assert its existence or to accede to such assertions.

Although Hume's arguments may appear to fly in the face of common sense, they have to some extent been vindicated by 20th-century physics. At the sub-atomic level, ideas of predictability (which should pertain, at least theoretically, if causal connections could be found or even theoretically established) have been replaced by those of statistical probability.

Established ideas of causality have also come under fire at a macroscopic level, particularly among evolutionary biologists. For example, how can we describe the evolution of the reptilian egg in terms of cause and effect? Evolutionary theory holds that changes in organisms occur as the result of random genetic mutations; if one of these changes confers an advantage that allows the organism to produce more offspring, the change is likely to be inherited by the offspring and may eventually become normal for the species. But when we look at the reptilian egg (or the mammalian eye or any number of other features and organs), we see that numerous events must have occurred *simultaneously* for the development to succeed. The shell, for instance, had to be impermeable and strong enough to protect the embryo. But unless the embryo had at the same time developed some means of liberating itself from the shell, this durable egg would have become a tomb. In addition, the embryo had to develop a means of absorbing nutrition while in the egg. But unless it had also developed some means of storing its own waste products safely, it would soon have created a poisonous environment.

Each of these developments—the durable shell, egg tooth, and so on—had to arise, according to evolutionary theory, as the result of random mutations. But between the mutations that produced the shell and those that produced the egg tooth there could have been no connection (they arose at random), nor between those concerning nutrition and waste disposal. And if there were no such connections, how was the whole process orchestrated? From this point of view, the reptilian egg must be seen as appearing without causal benefit and as representing the culmination of a series of wildly improbable coincidences.

David Hume was well aware that his view of causality would be hard for people to accept when he ascribed the difficulty to the force of mental habits that condition our outlook. If he was right—if we expect causal connections—we have only ourselves to blame (or congratulate) when we find coincidences a tantalizing and titillating affront to the commonsense view we hold of the world.

The King's Double

On July 28, 1900, King Umberto I of Italy and his aide-de-camp Gen. Emilio Ponzio-Vaglia arrived in the town of Monza, a few miles outside Milan. The next day the king was to present the prizes at an athletic meet. The night of their arrival he and his aide went to a small restaurant for dinner. As the owner was taking their order, the king noticed that he and the padrone were virtually doubles, in both face and build. He remarked on this, and as the two men talked an extraordinary series of parallels emerged which caused both of them to marvel.

The two men were born on the same day of the same year (on March 14, 1844) and in the same town, and each was named Umberto. They had both been married on April 22, 1868, each to a woman called Margherita. Each had named his son Vittorio. And on the day of Umberto's coronation, the other Umberto had opened his restaurant.

The king was staggered by these coincidences and asked the restaurant owner how it could be that their paths had never before crossed? In fact, Umberto told

While in Monza in 1900, King Umberto I of Italy learned that his double had just been shot dead. Moments later the king himself was the victim of an assassin's bullet.

him, they had been decorated for bravery together on two occasions, the first time in 1866, when Umberto had been a private and the king a colonel, and the second time in 1870, when each had been promoted, to sergeant and corps commander. With this final revelation the padrone returned to his duties, and the king, turning to his aide, said, "I intend to make that man a Cavaliere of the Crown of Italy tomorrow. Be sure he comes to the meet."

The following day, true to his word, the king asked for his double—only to be told that the man had died that day in a shooting accident. Shocked, the king asked his aide to find out when the funeral was to take place so that he might attend. At that very moment three shots rang out, fired by an assassin. The first of them missed the king, but the second two pierced his heart and killed him instantly. (*Ripley's Ghost Stories and Plays*, pp.30–33)

The Perfect Day

Everyone, from time to time, experiences one of those perfect days when everything seems to fall into place, a day that exceeds the most optimistic expectations—the kind of day that persuades one that one's guardian angel is working overtime. One of the most extraordinary of these "perfect days" is recorded by Prof. C. E. Sherman, longtime chairman of the Civil Engineering Department of Ohio State University at Columbus, in his book *Land of Kingdom Come:*

In 1909 while preparing the originals for the Ohio State Highway Atlas, we were hard put to it to get maps of the southwestern counties. . . . The United States Geological Survey had not yet mapped this area, and the only suitable data . . . to be had were in the form of old county atlases about 15 inches square and half an inch thick. . . .

Much correspondence had secured the data for every county in the state except Pike and Highland. These two could not be had, nor could I discover by all my written enquiry whether any maps of these regions existed. In the absence of any data at all, it would be quite a task to make a complete survey of all the roads in a county. In fact it was out of the question with the appropriation we had. So I left Columbus, resolved to search the county seats and the homesteads nearby, for a week or two, if necessary, to get the lost data. We also wanted a good map of the Ohio River for adjusting the data we had already gathered.

The following events then happened during the next 12 hours, that Saturday in August: Taking an early morning train for Cincinnati, I found an excellent map of the Ohio at the first place visited, the United States Engineers Office. . . . Proceeding at once to Highland County, I had to wait at Norwood for the Hillsboro car. When I happened to mention the nature of my quest to the ticket agent at Norwood, he said, "There's an old book like that in the rear room, I think." We searched the dusty pile together, and fished out the long-sought Highland County Atlas!

Two ways then offered of reaching Pike's capital that afternoon. I ate lunch and took the B.&O. [railroad] to Chillicothe. In the short wait there, for the N.&W. south, I strolled up the street to call on an old friend, if perchance he were in town. He came toward me as I started, just as if the whole thing had been prearranged. After our chat, as I was mounting the southbound train, a gentleman who had written the day before, hailed me. As his letter was of a nature much more easily answered orally, it was gratifying to give him the immediate information.

I was personally acquainted with but two citizens of Waverly [the county seat of Pike County], one a mechanical, the other a civil engineering student, but hardly expected either of them to be in town. When I stepped off at Waverly, the mechanical engineer stepped off the car in front, and as we walked toward the hotel together he said he would send around the other man if he were home. I had just leisurely finished dinner at seven o'clock when Gehres appeared. Did he know of any Pike County map? "No, but perhaps father does," he said, "and here comes father now." Mr. Gehres, senior, said he thought the county auditor had one. The auditor came walking up the street as he spoke. After introductions, and in accord with the happenings of the whole day, he took us across the street to his office in the court house, where hung a fine old map of the county. I had written the county surveyor of that same county, but he knew nothing of this map.

I am actually afraid to record here all the incidents of that trip that I have on the memorandum here before me. It would be straining credulity too much. . . . You see, every step taken during the day was as much to the purpose as if planned with foreknowledge. I had gone directly to the Ohio River maps . . . had gone directly to a Highland County Atlas without knowing one existed, by the shortest traveled route; and when from that point two ways might be taken, I had chosen the one that led most directly to the remaining data sought.

Even the smallest incident, during the day, seemed to fit perfectly into a harmonious whole. I suppose much of this was psychological. I had for months been on the quest for all the data for the state, and when this last, hardest problem began to unravel so easily, it put me in a humor to notice only favoring circumstances, such for instance as the following:

The Norwood agent didn't want to sell, but would gladly lend his book—this saved us the purchase price; my Chillicothe friend was just leaving town on the car after instead of the car before my arrival; again, the tracing paper I picked up at random that morning, before leaving home, just fitted the large Pike County wall map; then again, the one person that I hoped might be at home to help at Waverly if needed, was on the spot to make the Pike County tracing. Who would expect to get into the court house in a strange town on Saturday night? Yet along came just the right persons, at just the right time, to take me to that map, which I didn't know existed. The train from Chillicothe to Waverly was full of men excursionists; they filled the aisles, yet as I stepped on, a seat was vacant for me, and I had uninterrupted privacy and comfort all the way down to reflect on the events of the day. I retired that night with the sensation of having experienced a perfect day. [C. E. Sherman, quoted in Alan Vaughan, *Incredible Coincidence*, pp.92-94]

Franz Richter Times Two
Franz Richter, a 19-year-old volunteer in the Austrian Transport Corps following World War I, was admitted to the hospital suffering from pneumonia. In the same hospital was another patient named Franz Richter, also 19 years old, also suffering from pneumonia, and also a volunteer in the Transport Corps. Both men were born in Silesia. (*Scientific American*, October 19, 1972, p.110)

Three Men on a Train
Three Englishmen traveling by rail in Peru, one day in the 1920's, found themselves to be the only occupants of their passenger car. Introducing themselves, they discovered that the first man's surname was Bingham, and the second man's, Powell; the third man was Bingham-Powell. (A firsthand report to the Editors)

A Bouncing Baby
Joseph Figlock was walking down a street in Detroit in the 1930's when a baby fell on him from a high window. A year later the same baby fell on him again from the same window. Figlock and baby both survived. (Telephone interview with Mrs. Arthur Figlock, Harper Wood, Michigan)

One Good Tourniquet...
One June night in the 1930's Allan Falby, captain of the El Paso County Highway Patrol, was in hot pursuit of a speeding truck in El Paso County, Texas. The truck slowed to take a corner, and Falby rammed into it at full speed. The collision ruptured an artery in his leg, and if Alfred Smith had not stopped to give him first aid he would almost certainly have died. As it was, the tourniquet that Smith applied stopped the blood flow and an ambulance reached Falby in time to save his life and his leg. After several months in a hospital, Falby

was well enough to return to his job.

Five years later Falby was again working the night patrol when he received a radio message to assist at a bad accident on U.S. 80. A car had smashed into a tree, and the man was in critical condition. Falby arrived at the scene before the ambulance and found an unconscious man in the car; he had severed an artery in his right leg and was bleeding to death. Falby applied a tourniquet and managed to stop the bleeding. Then he stared at the victim: it was, of course, Alfred Smith.

"It all goes to prove," Falby said later, "that one good tourniquet deserves another." (Telephone interview with Allan Falby's widow, Doris Falby, Truth or Consequences, New Mexico)

Twice fate brought motorcycle patrolman Allan Falby and motorist Alfred Smith together on a highway in El Paso County, Texas, each time in a brush with death.

Kup-Links
When TV talk-show host and columnist Irv Kupcinet—"Kup" to his friends—was in London to cover the coronation of Elizabeth II in 1953, he stayed at the Savoy Hotel. In one of the drawers in his room he was surprised to find some articles belonging to an old

On the television show Forum in June 1964, columnist Irv Kupcinet (left) and TV newsman Frank Reynolds (center) interview Richard Nixon about his presidential plans.

friend of his, the basketball impresario Harry Hannin, then with the Harlem Globetrotters. He was even more surprised when, two days later, he received a letter from Hannin, who was staying at the Hotel Meurice in Paris just then. "You'll never believe this," Hannin wrote, "but I've just opened a drawer here and found a tie with your name on it." (Telephone interview with Irv Kupcinet, Chicago, Illinois)

On a Woodland Path
Eric W. Smith, a metallurgist with the English Steel Company, lived in a quiet suburb of Sheffield called Ecclesall. Behind his house were woods where people used to ride, and in the spring and summer it was Smith's habit to stroll there, enjoying the peace and quiet and collecting horse manure for his tomato plants. For this purpose he carried with him a small dustpan and an old oilcloth shopping bag.

One day in the late 1950's, as he was quietly making his way along a woodland path, pausing now and then to scoop up some manure for his tomatoes, he saw a figure slowly approaching him along the path, a man whose progress was also interrupted by stooping and shoveling. Clearly, Smith thought, here was another man who appreciated the virtues of horse manure.

Midway between the two men was a bench, and, reaching it simultaneously, they sat down. By a remarkable coincidence the stranger was carrying an oilcloth bag identical to Smith's, as well as a little dustpan. Both men, it turned out, had gone to the woods to collect manure for their tomatoes.

With a bond now established, Smith reached for his pipe and tobacco tin. The stranger also took out a pipe, and Smith offered him a fill of tobacco. "No thanks," the stranger said, "I have my own brand." He did. It was the same as Smith's.

At this point both men had the sense that something eerie was happening to them.

"My name's Smith," Smith said.

"So's mine," said the stranger.

"Eric Smith," said the first Smith.

"Me too," said the second Smith.

"Eric W. Smith."

"Yes."

"The *W* stands for Wales," said number 1 Smith.

"Ah, " said number 2, "there we differ. I'm Walter." (A firsthand report to the Editors)

D for Double
Dr. Warren Weaver tells the following story in his book *Lady Luck: The Theory of Probability*. The probable date was the late 1950's:

My next-door neighbor, Mr. George D. Bryson, was making a business trip some years ago from St. Louis to New York. Since this involved weekend travel and he was in no hurry, since he had never been to Louisville, Kentucky, since he was interested in seeing the town, and since his train went through Louisville, he asked the conductor, after he had boarded the train, whether he might have a stopover at Louisville.

This was possible, and on arrival at Louisville he enquired at the station for the leading hotel. He accordingly went to the Brown Hotel and registered. And then, just as a lark, he stepped up to the mail desk and asked if there was any mail for him.

The girl calmly handed him a letter addressed to "Mr. George D. Bryson, Room 307," that being the number of the room to which he had just been assigned.

It turned out that the preceding resident of room 307 was another George D. Bryson, who was associated with an insurance company in Montreal but came originally from North Carolina. The two Mr. Brysons eventually met, so each could pinch the other to be sure he was real. [Warren Weaver, quoted in Alan Vaughan, *Incredible Coincidence*, pp.58–59]

Generation Gap
The author J. Bryan III describes a curious bridging of time and space that occurred around 1960 when he was in Majorca writing about the American Civil War:

I finished my book. The very last passage I typed was the inscription on a tablet that stands on my grandfather's old place:

"At this point, where the intermediate line of the Richmond defences crossed Brook Road, Confederate forces on March 1, 1864, repulsed Kilpatricks raid, undertaken to release federal prisoners in Richmond. . . ."

That done, I bundled up the manuscript, left it at the post office and drove to a luncheon given by some Austrian friends. I arrived late; the party—16 or 18—was already moving toward the dining room. I knew scarcely a soul, but there was no time for introductions. I slid into my chair and was about to take a tranquilizing swallow of wine when the hostess announced to those at her end of the table, "Mr. Bryan here is from Richmond."

The gentleman across from me said pleasantly, "Richmond? I've often wanted to go there, but at the last minute something has always prevented it." He smiled, then went on. "Come to think of it, my grandfather had the same experience."

I have no explanation for what I said next, except that the inscription I had just transcribed was fresh in my subconscious. I asked, "Is your name Kilpatrick, sir?"

"No," he said, "but my grandfather's was." He was *that* Kilpatrick, too!

Savor it for a moment—the two of us meeting on a small island in the Mediterranean and discovering that 4000 miles away and almost a hundred years before, his grandfather had been "repulsed" from my grandfather's place in a minor skirmish of the Civil War! [Joseph Bryan III, *The Sword Over the Mantel,* quoted in *Holiday,* November 1962, p.50]

Lincoln and Kennedy

Two of the most tragic and dramatic deaths in American history, the assassinations of Presidents Abraham Lincoln and John Fitzgerald Kennedy, involve the following astonishing parallels:

A handsewn teardrop expresses the grief felt after Lincoln was murdered in 1865. Like most presidents, he was fatalistic about the possibility of assassination.

The above dollar bill, issued in Dallas only two weeks before JFK was killed there, is now known as the Kennedy assassination bill. Since Dallas is the location of the 11th of the 12 Federal Reserve Bank districts, the bill bears the letter K, the 11th letter of the alphabet, and the number 11 appears in each corner. The serial number begins with K and ends with A, standing for Kennedy Assassination. Eleven also stands for November, the 11th month of the year; two 11's equal 22, the date of the tragedy. And the series number is 1963, the year the assassination occurred.

1) Lincoln was elected president in 1860. Exactly one hundred years later, in 1960, Kennedy was elected president.

2) Both men were deeply involved in civil rights for Negroes.

3) Both men were assassinated on a Friday, in the presence of their wives.

4) Each wife had lost a son while living at the White House.

5) Both men were killed by a bullet that entered the head from behind.

6) Lincoln was killed in Ford's Theater. Kennedy met his death while riding in a Lincoln convertible made by the Ford Motor Company.

7) Both men were succeeded by vice-presidents named Johnson who were southern Democrats and former senators.

8) Andrew Johnson was born in 1808. Lyndon Johnson was born in 1908, exactly one hundred years later.

9) The first name of Lincoln's private secretary was John, the last name of Kennedy's private secretary was Lincoln.

10) John Wilkes Booth was born in 1839 [according to some sources]. Lee Harvey Oswald was born in 1939, one hundred years later.

11) Both assassins were Southerners who held extremist views.

12) Both assassins were murdered before they could be brought to trial.

13) Booth shot Lincoln in a theater and fled to a barn. Oswald shot Kennedy from a warehouse and fled to a theater.

14) LINCOLN and KENNEDY each has seven letters.

15) ANDREW JOHNSON and LYNDON JOHNSON each
has 13 letters.
16) JOHN WILKES BOOTH and LEE HARVEY OSWALD
each has 15 letters.

In addition, the first public proposal that Lincoln be the Republican candidate for president (in a letter to the Cincinnati *Gazette*, November 6, 1858) also endorsed a John Kennedy for vice president (John P. Kennedy, formerly secretary of the navy). (Martin Gardner, *The Incredible Dr. Matrix*, pp.42–45)

Lucky Seven
The following memoir, sent to Arthur Koestler after the publication of his book *The Roots of Coincidence* in 1973, may be too good to be true. The author of the letter, Anthony S. Clancy of Dublin, Ireland, writes:

> I was born on the seventh day of the week, seventh day of the month, seventh month of the year, seventh year of the century. I was the seventh child of a seventh child, and I have seven brothers; that makes seven sevens. On my 27th birthday, at a race meeting, when I looked at the race-card to pick a winner in the seventh race, the horse numbered seven was called Seventh Heaven, with a handicap of seven stone. The odds were seven to one. I put seven shillings on this horse. It finished seventh. [Alan Vaughan, *Incredible Coincidence*, quoted in *Reader's Digest*, August 1979, p.120]

Paging Mr. Pape
On May 5, 1974, *The Sunday Times* of London published the results of a competition for the best story of a coincidence. Among the more than 2,000 letters submitted was the following from Mr. D. J. Page, of Surrey, England:

> About the month of July, 1940, I was a young soldier in the service of His Majesty at the time somewhere in England. I was to discover that my long awaited wedding photographs had been opened in mistake by a soldier in another Troop (A), my Troop being "B." He was most apologetic, having opened the letter, and, realizing his error, which was not surprising, seeing that our names and numbers were so similar. His name being Pape No. 1509322 and my name being Page No. 1509321. This mix up in the mail being frequent until I was posted to another Battery. Some time after the war had ended I was employed as a driver with London Transport at the Merton depot, Colliers Wood, S.W. London. One particular pay day I'd noticed that the tax deduction was very heavy, and duly presented myself to the superintendent's office. . . . Imagine my amazement when I discovered that my wages had been mixed up with a driver who had been transferred to the garage, not so surprising when I

> found out that his name was Pape, yes, the very same chap. . . . The weirdest thing of all, our P.S.V. License Nos. were—mine 29222, Mr. Pape 29223. [*The Sunday Times* (London), May 5, 1974]

Mr. D. J. Page of England, shown here in his uniform during World War II, found his life inexplicably mixed up with that of a stranger with a similar name.

The Prophetic Picture
Mrs. Eileen M. Bithell, of Portsmouth, England, tells the following story of a long-hidden but prophetic photograph:

> For over twenty years there hung in the window of my parents' grocery shop a framed sign which stated the one day of the week on which the shop was closed. Two weeks before my brother's wedding, the sign was taken down to be altered and was removed from its frame.
> Behind the sign was found a large photograph showing a small girl held in her father's arms. The small girl was my brother's bride-to-be and the man his future father-in-law. No one knows how this particular photograph came to be used as a backing for the shop sign as none of the people in the photograph were then known to my family, yet now, twenty years later, the two families were to be joined by marriage. [*The Sunday Times* (London), May 5, 1974]

Heart to Heart

John and Arthur Mowforth were twins. "What happened to one," their sister said, "usually happened to the other. On the evening of May 22, 1975, each experienced severe chest pains and was rushed (unbeknown to the other or their families) to the hospital—one in Bristol and the other in Windsor, 70 or 80 miles away as the crow flies. Each man died of a heart attack shortly after arrival. (Luigi Gedda and Gianni Brenci, *Chronogenetics: The Inheritance of Biological Time*, Louis Keith, trans., p.90)

The Unfortunate Anagram

Sir Peter Scott, one of Britian's best-known naturalists, is an enthusiastic believer in the Loch Ness monster and has lent the weight of his reputation to the debate about it for a good many years. So great, in fact, is his confidence in the creature's existence that he has promoted the use of a Greek name for it: *Nessiteras rhombopteryx*. This name, which he and underwater photographer Robert Rines coined in December 1975, may be roughly translated as "The Ness monster with diamond-shaped fin." As London newspapers quickly pointed out with some glee, the name is also an anagram for the words "Monster Hoax by Sir Peter S." (*Nature*, 258:466–68, December 11, 1975)

The T-shirts worn by British naturalist Sir Peter Scott and his wife, Christmas presents from their daughter, say it all. Scott is an expert on the elusive "Nessie."

A Shared Fate

A man riding a moped was killed by a taxi in Bermuda in 1975, exactly a year after his brother had been killed—on the same street, by the same taxi driver carrying the same passenger, and on the same moped. (John Michell and Robert J. M. Rickard, *Phenomena: A Book of Wonders*, p.90)

Wanda Marie Johnson Times Two

The following story appeared in *The Washington Post* for April 20, 1978:

> Wanda Marie Johnson, of Adelphi, Maryland, Prince Georges County, is a baggage clerk at Union Station in Washington.
>
> Wanda Marie Johnson, of Suitland, Maryland, Prince Georges County, is a nurse at D.C. General Hospital in Washington.

The nearly duplicate lives of Wanda Marie Johnson of Suitland (left) and Wanda Marie Johnson of Adelphi (right) finally brought the two women together in 1978.

Both Wanda Maries were born on the same day, June 15, 1953; both moved from Washington, D.C., to Prince Georges County; both have two children, delivered in the same hospital, and both own two-door Ford Granadas; the 11-digit serial numbers on their cars are the same except for the last three digits.

...And Dogs Named Toy

Identical twin boys, born in Ohio some 40 years ago, were adopted by different families shortly after birth. In 1979, after 39 years apart, they were reunited. It was discovered that each had been named James; that each had had law-enforcement training; that each liked

When identical twins Jim Lewis (left) and Jim Springer (right) met after 39 years, they found the similarities in their lives, habits, and ideas "downright spooky."

mechanical drawing and carpentry. Each married a woman named Linda, had a son—one named James Alan and the other James Allan—had divorced, and then married a second wife, named Betty. Both had had dogs named Toy. Also, both favored the same St. Petersburg, Florida, vacation beach. (*Reader's Digest*, January 1980, p.78)

COINCIDENCES WITH OBJECTS INVOLVED
The objects that figure in coincidental happenings are as remarkably diverse as kimonos, clocks, guns, plum puddings, scarabs, and watchboxes.

Deadly Kimono

A kimono, successively owned by three teenage girls, each of whom died before she had a chance to wear it, was believed to be so unlucky that it was cremated by a Japanese priest in February 1657. As the garment was being burned, a violent wind sprang up, fanning the flames and spreading them beyond control. The ensuing fire destroyed three-quarters of Tokyo, leveling 300 temples, 500 palaces, 9,000 shops, 61 bridges, and killing 100,000 people. (Noêl Nouet, *Histoire de Tokyo*, p.98)

Whether started by a burning kimono or by an earthquake, Tokyo's great fire of 1657 quickly leaped out of the control of its anguished residents and consumed most of the city, a tinderbox of wooden houses, temples, and bridges.

Clocking Out

An ornate clock belonging to King Louis XIV of France stopped at the precise moment of his death, 7:45 A.M., on September 1, 1715, and has never run since. (*Ripley's Giant Book of Believe It or Not!*)

A magnificently ornate clock is presented to Louis XIV by Christiaan Huygens, a Dutch scientist who was the first to use a pendulum to regulate a clock movement.

Double Jeopardy

Jabez Spicer, of Leyden, Massachusetts, was killed by two bullets in the attack on the federal arsenal at Springfield on January 25, 1787, during Shays's Rebellion. At the time, he was wearing the same coat his brother Daniel had been wearing when he, too, was killed by two bullets on March 5, 1784.

The bullets that killed Jabez Spicer passed through the holes made by the bullets that had killed his brother Daniel three years earlier. (*Official History of Guilford, Vermont, 1678–1961*, p.94)

Monsieur de Fortgibu and the Plum Puddings

Plum puddings are an English rather than a French specialty, and the French poet Émile Deschamps—who as a child at a boarding school in Orléans, around 1800, had been urged to try a slice by a M. de Fortgibu (who had just returned from England)—remembered the dessert very well.

Ten years later Deschamps was passing by a restaurant in Paris when he noticed inside it a plum pudding of fine appearance. He went in to order a slice but was told that the pudding had already been ordered by another customer. "Monsieur de Fortgibu," the lady at the counter called out to an approaching customer, "would you have the goodness to share your plum pudding with this gentleman?" Deschamps's old plum-pudding benefactor was now an elderly man with powdered hair and wearing the uniform of a colonel. He was more than willing to share his pudding, again, with Deschamps. Greeting each other, the two men reminisced about the earlier plum pudding.

Many years went by, and Deschamps found himself invited to a dinner party at which, he was told, plum pudding would be served. "Then I know M. de Fortgibu will be there," Deschamps told his hostess and amused her with the story.

The evening of the dinner party arrived, and at the conclusion of the meal a magnificent plum pudding was served to the 10 guests. At that very moment the door opened and in wandered M. de Fortgibu. By now very old, and somewhat disoriented, he had mistaken the address he was aiming for and had arrived at the party by error. (Camille Flammarion, *The Unknown*, p.194)

The importance of plum puddings in English households at Yuletide is depicted in this 1838 Christmas scene of a family welcoming the appearance of that traditional dessert.

The Pertinent Papyrus

The Angel of Libraries, whose task is to look after deserving authors and scholars, is perhaps an Egyptologist at heart, for one of her choicest gifts of coincidence was bestowed on Dr. Thomas Young, the English physicist who, with Jean François Champollion, was largely responsible for deciphering the Rosetta stone, the first and major key to our understanding of hieroglyphics.

Decipherment of the Rosetta stone, inscribed in hieroglyphic, demotic, and Greek characters, was the key to understanding ancient Egyptian manuscripts.

One evening in 1822 (the year in which Champollion, taking his cue from Young's research, published his own study of the Rosetta stone), Dr. Young was poring over a manuscript written in hieroglyphics. Except for three names written in Greek characters—Apollonius, Antigonus, and Antiochus (which he read as Antimachus)—he could make neither head nor tail of it. He put the papyrus away and in another shipment found another papyrus. This one proved to be written entirely in Greek. As Young scanned it quickly before putting it aside, his eye caught the same names that he had just read in the Egyptian manuscript, though in a slightly different form: Portis Apollonii and Antimachus Antigenis. With a shock, he realized that he had before him a translation of the hieroglyphs. Somehow the document had survived for 2,000 years and, from an entirely different part of the world, had come to him at the moment when it was most desirable. Such a conspiracy of events, he wrote later, would have been quite sufficient, in an earlier age, to convince people that he had learned not only hieroglyphics but the secrets of Egyptian sorcery as well. (Thomas Young, *An Account of Some Recent Discoveries in Hieroglyphical Literature and Egyptian Antiquities*, pp.55–58)

The Golden Boxes

When King Edward VII of England was a young man, and still the prince of Wales, he was a keen fox hunter. One of his frequent companions in the hunt was an actor named Edward A. Sothern. One day, as a mark of esteem and affection, the prince gave his friend a golden matchbox designed to be attached to a watch chain. Sothern carried the matchbox with him wherever he went, but one day when he was out hunting he was thrown from his horse, and the box, despite all efforts to find it, was lost. Sothern had a duplicate made and later gave it to his son Lytton as a present.

Lytton Sothern was also an actor, and during a tour of Australia he gave the duplicate matchbox to a friend there named Labertouche.

Back in England, Lytton's brother George, a fox hunter like his father, was riding to hounds one day when he came upon the old farmer whose land the hunt was using. Learning that George was the son of Edward A. Sothern, the farmer presented him with the golden box lost 20 years earlier and found only that morning by a farmhand who had been out plowing.

Lytton and George's brother, Edward H. Sothern—the third actor in the family—was on tour in America when this incident occurred, and George found the

Edward, prince of Wales, who became king of England when he was 59, was an enthusiastic sportsman. This painting shows him taking part in a fox hunt.

incident striking enough to write to him about it. When Edward read the letter he was traveling by train with another actor, Arthur Lawrence, whom he had met for the first time that day. He told Lawrence the curious story and wondered, out loud, what had become of the duplicate box. Whereupon, to his astonishment, Lawrence dangled a chain in front of him. On it was the golden matchbox given to Lawrence by Mr. Labertouche. (Edward H. Sothern, *My Remembrances: The Melancholy Tale of "Me,"* p.341)

Written on the Wind
Camille Flammarion, the celebrated 19th-century French astronomer, was also a student of the occult, in particular of how the appearance of ghosts might relate to the question of life after death. In his book *The Unknown*, published in 1900, he records how, when he was writing the chapter on the wind in his major work on the atmosphere (*L'Atmosphère*), a gale blew open his window, lifted the loose pages he had just written, and carried them off. A few days later he was mystified to receive proofs of the vanished chapter from his publisher. The wind had carried the papers into a street traversed by the publisher's porter, who often acted as a messenger for Flammarion. The porter had simply picked up the scattered pages of the chapter and taken them to the publisher in the usual way. (Camille Flammarion, *The Unknown*, p.192)

Camille Flammarion, the French astronomer, wrote prodigiously in his field, as the papers before him suggest. In later years he became preoccupied with psychical research.

The Persistent Pistol
The following story is told by Sir Harold Nicolson in his essay "Coincidences":

In May of 1866 Prince Bismark, while riding on the Unter den Linden, was approached by a student of the name of Cohen Blind, who pulled out a revolver and fired four shots at point-blank range. Two of the bullets missed their mark, one entered Bismark's shoulder, and one penetrated the lung. The Iron Chancellor was not a man to be disturbed by a little thing like that, and in six days he could again be observed, erect and dominant, riding down the Unter den Linden. Herr Blind, meanwhile, had been arrested and the revolver had been taken from him. It was presented to Bismark as a souvenir of the occasion.

In 1886 the father of my friend Leopold was staying with Bismark, to whom he was related by marriage. There were several ladies staying in the house, and after luncheon the Princess Bismark took the ladies around the rooms, showing them the historical objects which they contained. Bismark himself and the men guests remained in the

The artist who made this engraving of the attempt on Bismarck's life has taken liberties, showing the German prince and chancellor on foot rather than on horseback.

smoking-room puffing Hamburg cigars. The voices of the ladies could be heard in the Chancellor's study. "And this," a voice said, "is the pistol which Blind used in 1866." There was a murmur of interest followed by a loud report. Bismark leapt from his chair and dashed into the adjoining room: the ladies were standing looking at each other in astonishment; a smell of powder hung in the air. The pistol, still smoking, lay upon the ground. The Chancellor gave way to one of his rare outbursts of fury. How could, he thundered, anyone have been so foolish as to touch the revolver? It was a mere miracle that no one had been killed. Never must anyone be allowed to touch that weapon again.

In 1906 my friend Leopold was also staying with his cousins at Friedrichsruh. It was a wet afternoon, and some young people had come over to luncheon. He showed them the Chancellor's study. He took up the pistol from the writing table. "This," he said, "is the pistol with which Blind shot at Bismark in 1866. Twenty years later, when my father was staying here, some ladies were visiting the house and one of them took up the pistol and foolishly pulled the trigger—like this . . ." There was a flash and a report. They leapt aside and stared at each other with white faces. One of the girls had been slightly hurt in the hand: Leopold himself was bleeding at the finger, and his hand was burnt and black with gunpowder. The bullet, the sixth and last bullet in the revolver of Herr Blind, was imbedded in his biceps. [Harold Nicolson, *Small Talk*, pp.99–101]

The Bullet That Found Its Mark
In 1883 Henry Ziegland, of Honey Grove, Texas, jilted his sweetheart, who then killed herself. Her brother tried to avenge her by shooting Ziegland, but the bullet only grazed his face and buried itself in a tree. The brother, believing that he had killed Ziegland, then took his own life.

In 1913 Ziegland was cutting down the tree with the bullet in it. It was a difficult job, so he used dynamite. The explosion sent the old bullet through Ziegland's head and killed him. (*Ripley's Believe It or Not!*, p.133)

No Escape
At the beginning of World War I, French intelligence agents arrested a German spy, Peter Karpin, as soon as he entered the country. They kept the arrest secret, however, and for the next three years, until Karpin's escape in 1917, sent fake reports to his superiors and intercepted all funds sent to France on his behalf. These funds were used to buy an automobile, which, in 1919, ran down and killed a man in the Ruhr, at that time still occupied by the French. The victim of the accident was none other than the escaped spy Peter Karpin. (*Ripley's Giant Book of Believe It or Not!*)

Reunion in Paris
When the novelist Anne Parrish first visited Paris in the 1920's, she and her husband spent some time browsing among the secondhand bookstalls that line the banks of the River Seine near the Île de la Cité. In one stall she found an old copy of *Jack Frost and Other Stories,* a book she had loved as a small child in Colorado Springs and had not seen since her nursery days. Excited to meet such an old friend again after so many years, she showed the book to her husband. He opened it and on the flyleaf found an inscription: "Anne Parrish, 209 N. Weber Street, Colorado Springs." (Alexander Woollcott, *While Rome Burns,* pp.20–23)

Anne Parrish, who was born in 1888 and died in 1957, became well known in the 1920's for her deftly written novels, among them The Perennial Bachelor, *which won a prize in 1925. She always treasured the storybooks of her childhood and collaborated on two books for children, including* Knee High to a Grasshopper.

A Book With a View
During World War II, Yorkshireman Arthur Butterworth was stationed at an army camp on the grounds of Taversham Hall, near Norwich. He had ordered a secondhand book on music from a London bookseller, and when the parcel eventually arrived he opened it in his hut, standing at his window. As he did so, a picture postcard fell out of the book, evidently placed there as a bookmark by the previous owner. Butterworth saw that the card had been written on August 4, 1913, and he turned it over to look at the picture. To his astonishment the photograph showed exactly what he could see from his window—Taversham Hall.

Since army camps during the war were signified solely by a post code, and not by name, the bookseller could not have known where he was sending the parcel and therefore could not deliberately have included the card as a friendly gesture. In a book about music, Arthur Butterworth found not an ordinary gift but a baffling resonance of time and space. (*The Sunday Times* [London], May 5, 1974)

The Deadly Double

On November 22, 1941—16 days before the Japanese attack on Pearl Harbor—*The New Yorker* ran two advertisements for a new dice game called The Deadly Double. One of the advertisements carried the headline ACHTUNG. WARNING. ALERTE! At the foot of the column were the words THE DEADLY DOUBLE, and beneath the words a double-headed heraldic eagle (in the manner of the armorial device of Germany) with a shield on its breast bearing a double cross. The other advertisement showed two dice, one black and the other white, each with three faces visible. On the faces of the white dice were the numbers 12 and 24 and the double-cross sign; on the black dice were the numbers 0, 5, and 7. Above the dice the headline words ACHTUNG. WARNING. ALERTE! were repeated.

After the Pearl Harbor attack there was much speculation that these advertisements had been placed by the Axis powers to alert their agents: the numbers 12 and 7 could have referred to the date of the attack (December 7), the numbers 5 and 0 could have indicated the planned time of the attack, and the XX (20 in Roman numerals) might have stood for the approximate latitude of the target; the significance of the 24 was unknown. So strong were these suspicions that FBI agents visited the people who had placed the advertisements, Mr. and Mrs. Roger Craig.

The game of Deadly Double was legitimate and was being sold by several New York department stores in 1941. The government's suspicions were kept quiet until 1967 when Ladislas Farago, formerly with U.S. naval intelligence, revealed the story in the press release for his book *The Broken Seal*. Interviewed by a reporter shortly after, Roger Craig's widow said that any connection between the advertisements and Pearl Harbor "was just one big coincidence." (*Scientific American*, 227:111-12, October 1972)

In 1941 it was suspected that these advertisements for the dice game The Deadly Double gave clues to the bombing of Pearl Harbor. More recently it has been suggested that the numbers shown on the dice (right) predicted Kennedy's assassination by Oswald. Because of the many variants that can be tried in numerology games, the probability of finding apparent coincidences is high.

Achtung
WARNING!
alerte
See Advertisement Page 86

MONARCH PUBLISHING CO.
New York

Achtung
WARNING
alerte!

We hope you'll never have to spend a long winter's night in an air-raid shelter, but we were just thinking . . . it's only common sense to be prepared. If you're not too busy between now and Christmas, why not sit down and plan a list of the things you'll want to have on hand. . . . Canned goods, of course, and candles, Sterno, bottled water, sugar, coffee or tea, brandy, and plenty of cigarettes, sweaters and blankets, books or magazines, vitamin capsules . . . and though it's no time, really, to be thinking of what's fashionable, we bet that most of your friends will remember to include those intriguing dice and chips which make Chicago's favorite game

THE DEADLY DOUBLE

The Crossword Codebreaker

The Allied preparations for the invasion of Europe in 1944 were cloaked in unprecedented secrecy. Each phase of the operation, which was coded as Operation Overlord, was assigned its own code name. Among the most important of these were Neptune, code for the naval initiative, Omaha and Utah, the designations of two French beaches where landings were to take place, and Mulberry, the code name for the artificial harbors to be used for beachhead supply.

Thirty-three days before the scheduled date of the invasion, these code names began to crop up in the London *Daily Telegraph* crossword puzzle. On June 2, only four days before the invasion was launched, the code Overlord appeared, given as the solution for the clue reading "some big-wig like this has stolen some of it at times."

Security men descended on the *Telegraph*'s Fleet Street offices, certain that a Nazi spy had given the game away. Instead they found a bewildered schoolteacher named Leonard Dawe, who had been compiling the paper's crossword puzzle for 20 years. Eventually he managed to convince the interrogators of his innocence: he had been guilty of nothing but an outrageous coincidence. (*The Unexplained: Mysteries of Mind Space & Time*, Vol. 3, Issue 31)

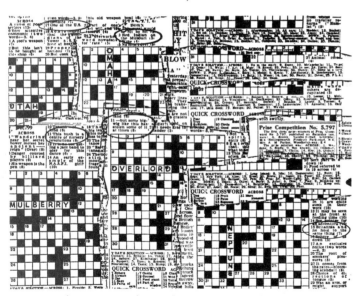

These crossword puzzles appeared in the London Daily Telegraph *just before D day in World War II. By coincidence, the solutions to the encircled clues were Allied code words for the planned invasion of Europe.*

Wet Winner

When the Jersey Central train plunged from a bridge into Newark Bay in 1958, cameramen rushed to the scene. One front-page newspaper photograph showed the rear coach being winched out of the water, with the number 932 clearly visible on its side. That day, 932 was the number chosen by thousands in the New York numbers game, and that day 932 was the winning number. (*Scientific American*, 227:112, October 1972)

September 17, 1958, brought tragedy to many commuters on a Jersey Central train when it plunged into Newark Bay, but for bettors it brought good fortune: thousands playing the New York numbers game chose the coach's number, 932, which is shown in this grim scene—and won.

Against All Odds

Best-selling author and pilot Richard Bach was barnstorming in the Midwest in 1966 with a rare biplane, a 1929 Detroit-Parks P-2A Speedster, only eight of which were ever built. In Palmyra, Wisconsin, Bach loaned

Old planes are a special fondness of Richard Bach, author of the novel Jonathan Livingston Seagull. *A 1973 photograph shows him with his 1947 Widgeon seaplane.*

the plane to a friend, who upended the craft as he came in for a landing. "They were able to fix everything except for one strut. That repair looked hopeless because of the rarity of the wanted part."

Just then the man who owned the hangar near them came up and asked if he might help, offering to let them have any of the bits and pieces stored in his three hangars. When Bach explained what rare parts he needed, the man walked over to a pile of junk and pointed to the parts. Bach concludes:

The odds against our breaking the biplane in a little town that happened to be home to a man with the forty-year-old part to repair it; the odds that he would be on the scene when the event happened; the odds that we'd push the plane right next to his hangar, within ten feet of the part we needed—the odds were so high that coincidence was a foolish answer. [Richard Bach, *Nothing by Chance*, quoted in *Reader's Digest*, August 1979, p.118]

Memory Lapse?

Dr. Lawrence LeShan, a psychologist who has written extensively on meditation and paranormal phenomena, published the following letter in the *International Journal of Parapsychology* in 1968:

In the very first days of December, 1967, I sent the draft of a manuscript dealing largely with mysticism to the well-known psychologist Dr. Nina Ridenour. Although she is best known for her professional work in mental health, Dr. Ridenour is also an expert on mysticism.

At noon of December 11, Dr. Ridenour and I met for lunch to discuss my paper. I was taking notes of her comments and criticisms throughout the discussion. Her central argument was that my manuscript reflected my less than perfect knowledge of mysticism. When she suggested a number of books on the subject I should read, I took down the entire list. She mentioned eight works, books by Nicoll, Stace and Ouspensky among them. The fifth book Dr. Ridenour mentioned was Byng's *The Vision of Asia*. To my clear recollection, she said, after I had written down both the author's name and the title: "Until you read this, you won't understand the difference between Eastern and Western mysticism." Although I did not record this particular comment of hers, I can still hear her voice saying precisely these words, and my notes contain the reference with a check mark after it.

Dr. Ridenour's comment had impressed me, for the differences between Eastern and Western mysticism are crucial to the idea I have been trying to explore. Consequently, I went straight from our luncheon meeting to the library of the Parapsychology Foundation to see whether they had this book, but they did not. From the Foundation, I went directly to the library of Union Theological Seminary to find the book, again without success.

That evening, on my way home, I was in a hurry as I was late. Yet on sheer impulse I took a route I had never taken before, because it is about 50 paces longer. Pausing for a moment at a traffic light next to a trash basket, my eye was caught by a book lying on the ground. Prompted by idle curiosity, I bent down and picked it up. The volume I held in my hand was entitled *The Vision of Asia*, and the author's name was L. A. Cranmer-Byng.

The next morning I called Dr. Ridenour and said:

"I have a funny story to tell you about the book you recommended." She replied, "Which book?" I said, "*The Vision of Asia* by Byng." "I never heard of it," she answered.

And there, as Kipling would put it, the matter rests. Dr. Ridenour, who is a serious and highly responsible person, is quite clear about the fact that she does not remember ever having heard of the book until I mentioned it to her. I have the book (a library copy removed from the Columbia University Oriental Library in 1960) and my notes taken as she was talking, including the reference to the book.

I must say that I am unable to classify this experience into any general category. [*International Journal of Parapsychology*, 10:223–24, 1968]

Return of *The Girl From Petrovka*

When early in the 1970's the British actor Anthony Hopkins signed a contract to play one of the leading roles in a film version of George Feifer's *The Girl From Petrovka*, he scoured the bookshops in London's Charing Cross Road for a copy of the original novel. His search was in vain, and in some frustration he went into the Leicester Square subway station to catch a train home. And there, lying on a bench in the station, he found a copy of the book, apparently forgotten by some fellow traveler.

Two years later Hopkins was in Vienna, working on the film production, and was visited by George Feifer. Feifer told him that he had no copy of his own book—he had given his last one to a friend who had lost it in London. "Is this the one," Hopkins asked, handing him the book, "with the notes scribbled in the margins?" It was, indeed, Feifer's own copy. The girl from Petrovka had come home at last. (*The Sunday Times* [London], May 5, 1974)

After Anthony Hopkins (above, with Goldie Hawn), agreed to play in George Feifer's The Girl From Petrovka, *he happened upon the author's lost copy of the book.*

Odds Can Be Figured

Dr. Tom Leonard, a professor of statistics at the University of Warwick, England, provided the following observations and story to Arthur Koestler in 1974:

> A particular coincidental event has, by definition, an infinitesimally small probability of occurring. However, there are infinitely many events which might possibly occur coincidentally to a particular person but, as it happens, do not occur. If we summed over all possible coincidental events, then we would find the probability of at least one of them occurring during the person's lifetime to be quite sizeable. I would indeed be surprised if many people could say that they had never experienced an extreme coincidence.
>
> The best coincidence yarn I know of runs as follows. In his first lecture at this university, a new professor of statistics was describing the laws of probability to his students. To illustrate them, he removed a coin from his pocket and tossed it in the air. It landed on a polished floor, spun around a few times, and to a thunderous applause came to rest—vertically on its edge! The point is that this was one of many coincidences that might have happened.

The chances of a (perfectly rounded) coin coming to rest on its edge after being tossed have been calculated by mathematician Warren Weaver at approximately one billion to one. (Alan Vaughan, *Incredible Coincidence*, pp.198–99)

An Iceberg in the Sky

In July 1975 a large block of ice fell through the roof of the Melkis home in Dunstable, Bedford, England. At the time of the incident the family was engrossed in a TV movie about the *Titanic*. As the ice crashed through their ceiling, they were tensely waiting for the ship to strike the fateful iceberg. (John Michell and Robert J. M. Rickard, *Phenomena: A Book of Wonders*, p.91)

The Two Walter Kellners

In 1979 *Das Beste*, the German edition of *Reader's Digest*, ran a competition for the best story of a personal experience by one of its readers. The winner, chosen from 7,000 entries, was a pilot named Walter Kellner, of Munich. Kellner had described how his plane, a Cessna 421, had crashed into the Tyrrhenian Sea between Sardinia and Sicily and how he had survived the ordeal in a rubber dinghy. *Digest* researchers checked the story carefully against German and Italian reports of the accident and satisfied themselves that Kellner's account was true. His Cessna, registration number D-INUR, had indeed plunged 10,000 feet to the bottom of the Tyrrhenian Sea as he described. The date of the prize-giving was set for December 6, and Kellner was to bring the rubber dinghy to the *Das Beste* offices.

On the morning of the presentation a letter arrived at *Das Beste* for Editor-in-Chief Wulf Schwarzwäller, who was to hand Kellner his prize. The letter was from Walter Kellner—another Walter Kellner, who lived in Kritzendorf, Austria. This Kellner was also a pilot. The story was a fake, he said. He had flown that same Cessna for four years over Europe and the Mediterranean, and though he had once had to make a forced landing with engine trouble at the Cagliari airstrip in Sardinia, he had never once gone down at sea. Some imposter had taken his story, invented a new ending, and was about to make off with the prize money.

Schwarzwäller was dumbfounded. How could this be when the story had been so carefully checked? And what to do now? The author of the story was due to arrive for lunch soon. . . .

Just as scheduled, a smiling Walter Kellner arrived at the *Das Beste* offices, was welcomed—and then promptly shown the letter from his namesake.

At first he laughed. Yes, he knew from the plane's records that another Kellner had flown it, but he had had no idea that they shared the same first name. Then he came to the part of the letter describing the other Kellner's forced landing in Sardinia—and' turned pale. The same plane, the same area, the same engine problem, and a pilot with the same name. What jinx had been at work? Why should the Cessna seem to have a grudge against Walter Kellners, and why should it—apparently—have been determined to destroy itself and its pilot, in the vicinity of the Tyrrhenian Sea?

The questions were unanswerable. The two Walter Kellners had been touched by a mystery they were lucky to survive. The *Das Beste* editors had unwittingly nudged open a door onto the unknown, and through it they could feel blowing, throughout the presentation, a chill and eerie wind. (*Courier*, April 1980, pp.12–13)

ANIMALS ARE NOT EXEMPT
Fish, beetles, grasshoppers, and geese are the unwitting (one supposes) parties to some mysterious coincidences.

The Voice of the Fish

On Midsummer Eve, 1626, a Mr. Mead of Christ's College, Cambridge, England, was walking through the city marketplace when he heard a commotion coming from a fishmonger's stall. A small crowd had gathered and was examining a book that the fishwife had just discovered inside a large codfish:

> I saw all with mine own eyes [Mr. Mead wrote]—the fish, the maw [stomach], the piece of sailcloth, the book—and observed all I have written. Only I did not see the opening of the fish, which not many did, being on the fish-woman's stall in the

market, who first cut off its head, to which the maw was hanging, and seeming much stuffed with somewhat, it was searched, and all found as aforesaid. He that had had his nose as near as I yester morning would have been persuaded there was no imposture here without witness. The fish came from Lynn [King's Lynn, in Norfolk].

The book, which Mr. Mead took charge of, had been bound in sailcloth and, though slimy and dog-eared, was perfectly legible. It proved to be a theological treatise written by John Frith during his imprisonment at Oxford a hundred years before. So highly did the Cambridge authorities think of this remarkable mode of book distribution that they had the volume reprinted under the title *Vox Piscis* ("the voice of the fish") or, *The Bookfish,* and embellished it with an engraving of the fish, the book, and the fishmonger's knife.

Young Frith had been imprisoned in a cellar where fish were stored and where the stench was so great that several of his fellow prisoners had actually died of it. Frith himself was burned at the stake as a heretic in 1533. (John Michell and Robert J. M. Rickard, *Phenomena: A Book of Wonders,* p.92)

The Golden Scarab
Carl Gustav Jung, one of the founding fathers of 20th-century psychology, told the following story in his treatise "Synchronicity: An Acausal Connecting Principle," written in 1960:

A young woman I was treating had, at a critical moment, a dream in which she was given a golden scarab. While she was telling me this dream I sat with my back to the closed window. Suddenly I heard a noise behind me, like a gentle tapping. I turned around and saw a flying insect knocking against the window pane from the outside. I opened the window and caught the creature in the air as it flew in. It was the nearest analogy to a golden scarab that one finds in our latitudes, a scarabaeid beetle, the common rose-chafer *(Cetonia aurata),* which contrary to its usual habits had evidently felt an urge to get into a dark room at this particular moment....

There ... seems to be an archetypal foundation to the ... case. It was an extraordinarily difficult case to treat, and up to the time of the dream little or no

Dr. Carl G. Jung's theories of synchronicity and of the collective unconscious were among his major concepts. The great psychiatrist, who lived from 1875 to 1961, was 60 years of age when this portrait of him was drawn.

progress had been made. I should explain that the main reason for this was my patient's animus, which ... clung so rigidly to its own idea of reality that three doctors—I was the third—had not been able to weaken it. Evidently something quite irrational was needed which was beyond my powers to produce. The dream alone was enough to disturb ever so slightly the rationalistic attitude of my patient. But when the "scarab" came flying in through the window in actual fact, her natural being could burst through the armour of her animus possession and the process of transformation could at last begin to move. Any essential change of attitude signifies a psychic renewal which is usually accompanied by symbols of rebirth in the patients' dreams and fantasies. The scarab is a classic example of a rebirth symbol. [C. G. Jung, quoted in C. G. Jung and W. Pauli, *The Interpretation of Nature and the Psyche,* pp.31–33]

Alter Ego
The English novelist J. B. Priestley, who is married to the well-known archeologist Jacquetta Hawkes, related this experience to Arthur Koestler in a letter dated February 7, 1972:

My wife bought three large lithographs by Graham Sutherland. When they arrived here from London she took them up to her bedroom, to hang them up in the morning. They were leaning against a chair and the one on the outside, facing the room, was a lithograph of a grasshopper. When Jacquetta got into bed that night, she felt some sort of twittering movement going on, so she got out and pulled back the clothes. There was a grasshopper in the bed. No grasshopper had been seen in that room before, nor has been seen since. No grasshopper has been seen at any other time in this house. [*Research in Parapsychology,* W. G. Roll, R. L. Morris, and J. D. Morris, eds., p.209]

The author J. B. Priestley and his wife, Jacquetta Hawkes, pose before the mantelpiece of their drawing room. Priestley, who has a wide range of interests, has experimented with psychological themes in some of his writings.

A Wild-Goose Case
As Noel McCabe, of Derby, England, was listening to a record of Frankie Laine singing "Cry of the Wild Goose," in 1974, a Canada goose crashed through his bedroom window and two more fell to the ground outside. (John Michell and Robert J. M. Rickard, *Phenomena: A Book of Wonders,* p.91)

UNEARTHLY FATES

Unearthly, indeed, is the fate of bursting into flame
without benefit of ignition from any known
source—an occurrence shared by an impressive number
of unfortunates. Another manifestation of attack
by agencies unknown is the rash of cattle mutilations
on western ranches, the explanations for which
are as strange as the events themselves.
Examples of demonic possession and curses that can
kill are almost too fanciful to believe, but in the minds
of the victims their power is all too real.
Unearthly, also, are the cases of people who appear
seemingly from nowhere and those who suddenly
and inexplicably disappear into the unknown.

The artist masterfully portrays a soul facing the fate of damnation.

SPONTANEOUS HUMAN COMBUSTION

Spontaneous human combustion is a well-documented phenomenon in which a human body ignites and burns without any known contact with an external source of fire. In some cases the damage is slight. In others the victim is reduced to ashes. And in some of the strangest cases nearby objects escape relatively unscathed. The chair or bed on which the victim was sitting or lying, and even the clothes on the charred body, may be undamaged or only slightly singed. Often, too, a single foot, a leg, or the tips of some fingers remain intact, although the rest of the body is consumed.

Cases of spontaneous human combustion (SHC) began to appear in medical reports as far back as the 17th century, and by the 20th century the literature abounded in detailed accounts of inexplicable human incineration. Over a span of four centuries more than 200 such incidents have been reported.

In earlier times the classical targets of this fiery fate were believed to be alcoholic and usually corpulent elderly women who lived alone. They almost always incinerated indoors on winter nights and were usually found near an open fire. Needless to say, there were no witnesses. Their deaths were attributed to God's punishment of their sins.

But even in those days there were exceptions, as some of the cases related in this chapter show. In fact, recent research into this strange phenomenon shows a fairly equal representation of the sexes among the victims, with ages ranging from infancy to 114 years; many were abstemious and thin. Some have combusted in the proximity of a source of fire, but others have ignited while they were driving, or simply walking in surroundings devoid of any external source of fire.

Contemporary scientific and medical opinion rejects the idea of spontaneous combustion, dismissing the many instances of inexplicable deaths by burning as simply "puzzling" or "unsolved." Although a number of theories have been proposed, there is no sound physiological model that can explain how a human body could possibly self-ignite or how it could burn fiercely enough to be reduced to ashes. Such consumption of human tissue and bone is only possible at the extreme temperatures (over 3000°F) provided by a pressurized crematorium. And, of course, when it comes to explaining unscorched clothing, or a fully fleshed limb associated with the ashy or charred remains, the inexplicable becomes the bizarre.

BEFORE 1800

One of the earliest well-attested cases of spontaneous human combustion was recorded by Thomas Bartholin in 1673. A poor "woman of the people" was mysteriously consumed by fire in Paris. She had been a heavy drinker of "strong spirits" to the point of not taking any nourishment for three years. One evening she went to sleep on a straw pallet and was burned up during the night. In the morning only her head and the ends of her fingers were found; all the rest of her body was reduced to ashes. The incident was recounted by Pierre-Aimé Lair, who in 1800 published the first comprehensive essay on the subject of human combustion. (*American Medicine*, 9:657, April 22, 1905; Pierre-Aimé Lair, *Essai sur les combustions humaines*, pp.10–11)

An unusually vivid and detailed report of inexplicable human incineration was given by Claude-Nicolas Le Cat, a physician serving as an apprentice surgeon in Rheims, France, where he stayed at a local inn. The innkeeper, Jean Millet, had a nagging wife who got drunk every day. On the night of February 19, 1725, the inn was full of people in anticipation of a big fair the next day. Millet and his wife, Nicole, retired early. Mme. Millet could not sleep and got up to go downstairs into the kitchen, probably to follow her usual habit of drinking herself insensible in front of a warm fire. Her husband fell asleep, but around 2 o'clock in the morning he woke up with a start. He smelled fire and rushed downstairs, banging on doors along the way to wake up any sleeping guests. When the panicked group arrived in the big kitchen, what they found burning was not the inn but the innkeeper's wife, Mme. Millet, who was lying close to the fireplace and was almost totally consumed by fire. Only part of her head, her lower limbs, and a few vertebrae remained. A small section of the flooring under the body had been burned through and the chair she usually sat on next to the fireplace was slightly scorched, but nothing else in the room was even touched by fire.

A police lieutenant accompanied by two gendarmes was making his rounds when he heard the commotion from the inn. He quickly went inside, saw the smoldering remains, and promptly arrested Jean Millet on suspicion of murder. It was well known that Mme. Millet was not only a drunkard but a shrew who made life miserable for her hardworking husband. The suspicion around town was that Jean desperately wanted to be rid of his wife so that he could marry a servant girl who worked at the inn. The charges leveled against him were that the innkeeper had poured the remaining contents of the liquor bottle over the body of Nicole Millet, who was presumably unconscious by then, deliberately set her on fire, and then tried to make it look like an accident.

Le Cat, the young physician, was among those who had rushed downstairs and seen the charred body of Mme. Millet. During the court proceedings that followed, he testified on behalf of the innkeeper. He stated that he did not believe that any human agency could account for the total combustion of the unfortunate victim's body so that only the skull and extremities

This portrait is of Claude-Nicolas Le Cat, the physician whose testimony helped free a convicted murderer. The wife of the accused had burned to death, and Le Cat persuaded the court that the fire had been visited upon her as punishment for her alcoholism and shrewish ways.

remained and in such a way as to leave nearby objects unburned. The court proceedings were very heated, the prosecution insisting that Jean Millet was a murderer. He was declared guilty and condemned to death. However, Le Cat's repeated testimony that this could not have been a "normal" fire but was instead "the visitation of God" finally persuaded the court. Jean Millet's sentence was reversed and he was released. But by then the poor man's life was ruined. Deeply depressed, he lived out the rest of his years in a hospital. (Theodoric R. and John B. Beck, *Elements of Medical Jurisprudence*, 10th ed., Vol. 2, pp.94–105; Michael Harrison, *Fire From Heaven: A Study of Spontaneous Combustion in Human Beings,* passim; Pierre-Aimé Lair, *Essai sur les combustions humaines,* pp.22–25)

The celebrated case of the Countess di Bandi of Cesena, Italy, was first described by the Reverend Joseph Bianchini of Verona in an account dated April 4, 1731, and brought to the notice of the Royal Society of London in 1745:

> The Countess Cornelia [di] Bandi, in the sixty-second year of her age, was all day as well as she used to be; but at night was observed, when at supper, dull and heavy. She retired, was put to bed, where she passed three hours and more in familiar discourses with her maid, and in some prayers; at last, falling asleep, the door was shut. In the morning, the maid, taking notice that her mistress did not wake at the usual hour, went into the bed-chamber, and called her, but not being answer'd, doubting some ill accident, open'd the window, and saw the corpse of her mistress in this deplorable condition.
>
> Four feet distance from the bed there was a heap of ashes, two legs untouch'd, from the foot to the knee, with their stockings on; between them was the lady's head; whose brains, half of the back-part of the scull [*sic*] and the whole chin, were burnt to ashes; amongst which were found three fingers blacken'd. All the rest was ashes, which had this particular quality, that they left in the hand, when taken up, a greasy and stinking moisture.
>
> The air in the room was also observed cumber'd with soot floating in it: A small oil-lamp on the floor was cover'd with ashes, but no oil in it. Two candles in candlesticks upon a table stood upright; the cotton [wick] was left in both, but the tallow was gone and vanished. Somewhat of moisture was about the feet of the candlesticks. The bed receiv'd no damage; the blankets and sheets were only raised on one side, as when a person rises up from it, or goes in: The whole furniture, as well as the bed, were spread over with moist and ash-coloured soot, which had penetrated into the chest-of-drawers, even to foul the linnens [*sic*]: Nay the soot was

also gone into a neighbouring kitchen, and hung on the walls, moveables [furniture], and utensils of it. From the pantry a piece of bread cover'd with that soot, and grown black, was given to several dogs, all of which refused to eat it. In the room above it was moreover taken notice, that from the lower part of the windows trickled down a greasy, loathsome, yellowish liquor; and thereabout they smelt a stink, without knowing of what; and saw the soot fly around.

It was remarkable, that the floor of the chamber was so thick smear'd with a gluish moisture, that it could not be taken off; and the stink spread more and more through the other chambers.

It should be noted that this was an upper-class woman of good character, not a poor old creature addicted to alcohol. However, some connection with alcohol did exist. A few days after the countess's demise, an Italian nobleman who passed through Cesena said that he had heard on good authority that the countess was in the habit of washing her body in camphorated spirits of wine when she felt indisposed and that it was very likely she had done so on the evening before her accident. After a great deal of speculation by the medical authorities of the time, the final opinion was that, although lightning could conceivably be blamed, it was more likely that a naturally caused internal combustion had taken place in her body; that she had risen from her bed to cool herself; and that on her way to open the window, she had been overcome. Her body was consumed from within, and no external flames were produced that could set fire to the furniture in the room. The internal combustion was ascribed to

> inflamed effluvia of her blood, by juices and fermentations in the stomach, by the many combustible matters which are abundant in living bodies for the uses of life; and, finally, by the fiery evaporations which exhale from the settlings of spirit of wine, brandies, and other hot liquors in the tunica villosa of the stomach, and other adipose or fat membranes; within which (as chemists observe) those spirits ingender a kind of camphire; which, in the night time, in sleep, by a full breathing and respiration, are put in a stronger motion, and, consequently, more apt to be set afire.

(*American Medicine*, 9:657–58, April 22, 1905; *Gentleman's Magazine*, 16:369, 1746)

Don Gio Maria Bertholi, an Italian priest who caught fire during his devotions, was one of the few victims to survive his ordeal for several days. The case was reported by Dr. Battaglia, the surgeon who attended him, in a journal from Florence dated October 1776.

The priest, who had been traveling about the country, arrived in the evening at the house of his brother-in-law and asked to be shown to his apartment. Once inside he requested a handkerchief to be placed between his shirt and shoulders. (Devout priests often wore shirts made of scratchy horsehair for penance, and the handkerchief served to relieve any discomfort and distraction during devotions.) He was left alone to pray. A few minutes later an extraordinary noise was heard from the room, with the cries of the priest ringing out in agony. The people of the house, rushing into the room, found Bertholi extended on the floor surrounded by a light flame that receded as they approached and finally vanished. On the following morning the patient was examined by Dr. Battaglia, who found the skin of the right arm almost entirely detached and hanging from the bone. From the shoulders to the thighs, the skin was equally injured. On the right hand, the part most seriously burned, putrefaction had already begun. Despite immediate treatment, the condition worsened. The patient complained of burning thirst and was horribly convulsed. His stool was described as full of "putrid and bilious matter," and he was exhausted by continual vomiting accompanied by fever and delirium. He died on the fourth day in a state of unconsciousness. Dr. Battaglia could not find a trace of any known disease. A horrifying aspect of the priest's condition was that, even before he died, the odor of the putrescent flesh had become insufferable. Dr. Battaglia said he saw worms crawling from the body onto the bed and that the nails had fallen off the fingers.

When the priest was first brought to Dr. Battaglia, he said that all he remembered was a stroke like the blow of a cudgel on the right hand. At the same time he saw a "lambent flame" attach itself to his shirt, which was immediately reduced to ashes, although his cuffs remained untouched. The handkerchief that had been placed on his shoulders was, astonishingly, also intact. His trousers, too, were unharmed, but although not a hair on his head was singed, his cap was totally consumed. There had been no fire in the room. An oil lamp, however, which had been full of oil, was completely dry, and the lamp's wick was reduced to a cinder. (Theodoric R. and John B. Beck, *Elements of Medical Jurisprudence,* 10th ed., Vol. 2, p.98; *Journal of Criminal Law, Criminology and Political Science,* 42:794–95, March-April 1952)

An English source from 1788 told of a man who entered a room where, to his amazement, he beheld a young chambermaid scrubbing the floor with fire blazing from her back. He cried out in alarm, and it was only then that the girl became aware of the fire and started to scream. She was dead before he could put out the flames. (Vincent H. Gaddis, *Mysterious Fires and Lights*, p.265; *True*, May 1964, p.112)

The phenomenon *of spontaneous human combustion was recognized in the 19th century and may have inspired this dramatic engraving, "Lady Ablaze."*

FROM 1800 TO 1900

Mrs. Wright, the mother of John Wright, a London linen draper, was hospitalized for severe burns from which she was not expected to recover. Her injuries were the culmination of a series of strange spontaneous fires that had been plaguing the Wright household since January 5, 1820. On that date there was an unexplained small fire; then, on January 7, Mrs. Wright, who had been sitting with a servant girl by the kitchen hearth, noticed her own clothes were on fire as she stood up to walk away. On January 12 her clothes flamed up again, in the presence of the same girl, but this time Mrs. Wright had been nowhere near the hearth. Then sometime on the following day

> Wright heard screams from the kitchen, where his mother was, and where the girl had been. He ran into the room, and found his mother in flames. Only a moment before had the girl left the kitchen, and this time Wright accused her. But it was Mrs. Wright's belief that the girl had nothing to do with her misfortunes, and that "something supernatural" was assailing her. She sent for her daughter, who arrived, to guard her. She continued to believe that the girl could have had nothing to do with the fires and went to the kitchen, where the girl was, and again "by some unknown means, she caught fire. She was so dreadfully burned that she was put to bed." When she had gone to sleep, her son and daughter left the room—and were immediately brought back by her screams, finding her surrounded by flames. Then the girl was told to leave the house. She left and there were no more fires. This seemed conclusive, and the Wrights caused her arrest. At the hearing, the magistrate said that he had no doubt that the girl was guilty, but that he could not

pronounce sentence, until Mrs. Wright should so recover as to testify. [Charles Fort, *The Complete Books of Charles Fort*, pp.927-28]

A mysterious, though not spontaneous, case of human combustion was reported by a Dr. De Brus in the *Edinburgh Medical and Surgical Journal* dated March 1829. The subject's hands burst into blue flames when he attempted to help his brother, whose clothes were on fire. The flames continued for several hours to leap up and flicker over the hands, and only constant immersion in water finally extinguished them. (Theodoric R. and John B. Beck, *Elements of Medical Jurisprudence*, 10th ed., Vol. 2, pp.98–99)

A professor of mathematics at the University of Nashville, in Tennessee, was described as a victim of "partial human combustion" by John Overton, M.D., in the *Transactions of the Medical Society of Tennessee*. On January 5, 1835, James Hamilton had just returned home from the university, a walk of three-quarters of a mile, and had decided to check a hygrometer hanging outside his house. It was a very cold day; the thermometer registered 8° above zero.

Suddenly he felt a sharp pain like a hornet's sting, together with a sensation of heat, in the thigh of his left leg. When he looked down, he saw a bright flame several inches high, about the diameter of a dime, and somewhat flattened at the top. He immediately slapped it with his hand but to no avail. Hamilton kept his head and, reasoning that cutting off the oxygen supply should extinguish the flame, he cupped his hands over the spot of burning flesh. His presence of mind saved his life, because, indeed, the flame went out.

The pain, however, continued and felt as though it was coming from deep within his thigh. The professor, remaining calm throughout this ordeal, went back into the house, removed his pants and underpants, and examined the wound. The injury resembled an abrasion about three-fourths of an inch in width and three inches long. The burn was livid but dry and extended obliquely across the lower portion of his left thigh. He examined his underpants and noted that they were burned through at the point corresponding to the injury but were not scorched in the slightest around the hole. What was most amazing, however, was that the trousers were not burned at all. Opposite the hole in the underwear the fibers on the inside of the pants leg were slightly tinged with a dark yellow fuzz, which the professor was able to scrape off with a penknife.

The examining physician treated the wound as he would any ordinary burn, although it was unusual in some respects. The injury was very deep and took 32 days to heal. The muscles around the area also remained sore for a long time, and the scar was unusually livid. Dr. Overton stated that the patient had always been in excellent health and continued to be so throughout his period of recovery. (Vincent H. Gaddis, *Mysterious Fires and Lights*, pp.265–66; Michael Harrison, *Fire From Heaven: A Study of Spontaneous Combustion in Human Beings*, p.84)

In 1847 a French couple was indicted for murdering the man's father and burning his body to conceal the crime. They claimed that the 71-year-old man was found in a "state of combustion" in his bed on January 6 of that year. According to the account given in court:

> The chamber was filled with a dense smoke, and one of the witnesses asserted, that he saw playing around the body of the deceased, a small whitish flame, which receded from him as he approached. The clothes of the deceased, and the coverings of the bed were almost entirely consumed, but the wood was only partially burnt. There were no ashes, and only a small quantity of vegetable charcoal; there was, however, a kind of mixed residue, altered by fire, and some pieces of animal charcoal, which had evidently been derived from the articulations.

The victim's son and daughter-in-law declared that the deceased, according to his usual practice, had a hot brick placed at his feet when he went to bed the previous evening. When they passed his door two hours later, they noticed nothing out of the ordinary. However, early the next morning the victim's grandson entered his grandfather's room and found the old man burning up as described.

The inquest established that the victim was not addicted to drunkenness and that he had been in the habit of carrying "lucifer" matches (an early type of friction match) in his waistcoat pocket. A Dr. Masson, who was commissioned to investigate the case, had the body exhumed and examined. A partially burned cravat was found around the neck, and part of the sleeve of his nightshirt was intact. His burned hands were attached to the forearms only by some carbonized tendons, which gave way when touched. The legs were detached from the torso and looked as though they had been deliberately cut off, except for the presence of some charring around their edges.

The doctor gave evidence to the effect that he thought it impossible for the victim to have died of accidental burning or as a result of having been deliberately set on fire after he had been killed. He concluded that the burning resulted from "some inherent cause in the individual" and that perhaps the hot brick had touched something off. All in all, Dr. Masson could not put the facts together as they stood. The case was, as far as he could tell, to be classed as one of spontaneous combustion. The son and daughter-in-law were acquitted. (Theodoric R. and John B. Beck, *Elements of Medical Jurisprudence*, 10th ed., Vol. 2, pp.104–05)

On Christmas Eve, 1885, near Ottawa, Illinois, Mr. and Mrs. Patrick Rooney, their son John, and their hired hand, John Larson, sat around the kitchen table celebrating the holiday with a jug of whiskey farmer Rooney had just brought back from town. Larson had a few drinks and went off to bed. John Rooney stayed for a while but eventually left for his farm, a mile away.

Larson, rising early, came down Christmas morning to do his chores. He tried to strike a match on the iron kitchen stove but found to his surprise that the stove was covered with a layer of greasy soot. Alarmed, he quickly struck the match against his thumbnail and lit the lamp. To his horror he saw Patrick Rooney sitting dead in a chair; there was no sign of Mrs. Rooney. Larson rushed out, saddled a horse, and galloped madly to John Rooney's farm. When Larson and young Rooney got back, they found what remained of Mrs. Rooney under a three- by four-foot hole in the floor. On the bare ground, a couple of feet below, were a burned piece of skull, two charred vertebrae, a foot, and a small pile of ashes—all that remained of the 200-pound woman. No other part of the floor was burned and neither was any of the furniture. The only damaged item was the corner of the tablecloth hanging over the hole, which was slightly scorched.

The police were summoned. They found that the soot, drifting upstairs, had outlined Larson's head on the pillow while he slept. Although suspicion fell on Larson, no case could be made against him. The coroner, Dr. Floyd Clemens, pointed out to the bewildered jury that this was a classic instance of spontaneous combustion: a body consumed by intense heat in the absence of any kind of fire. The jury, however, could not reach a verdict on the cause of Mrs. Rooney's death other than calling it accidental. But the cause of her husband's death was quite clear: he had been asphyxiated by the fumes of his wife's burning body. (Vincent H. Gaddis, *Mysterious Fires and Lights*, pp.217–18; Michael Harrison, *Fire From Heaven: A Study of Spontaneous Combustion in Human Beings*, pp.79–80; *Pursuit*, 10:80, Fall 1976; *True*, May 1964, p.33)

An old soldier climbed up into a hayloft in Colchester, England, on Sunday, February 19, 1888, to sleep off his drunkenness. He was found completely consumed by fire, while the highly flammable hay around him, both loose and in bundles, was not even scorched. (*The British Medical Journal*, April 21, 1888, pp.841–42)

Dr. B. H. Hartwell, a New England doctor of medicine, reported that a child beckoned him for help on the road near Ayer, Massachussets, on May 12, 1890. Standing in a clearing in a wood was the crouched form of a woman, the child's mother, with flames blazing from her shoulders, abdomen, and legs. Hartwell saw no evidence that she had set herself on fire and noticed that the ground was wet from a recent rainfall. So far as he could tell, she seemed to have just burst into flames without any apparent cause. The doctor was able to put the flames out by throwing earth onto the woman's badly burned body. (*The Boston Medical and Surgical Journal,* 126:135–36, January–June 1892)

FROM 1900 TO 1950

Some odd things happened in Binbrook, Lincolnshire, England around the end of 1904. In December the Reverend A. C. Custance said that objects were being hurled about and sometimes catching fire at the rectory. A month later a Binbrook farmer walked into his kitchen and saw the servant girl busy sweeping, oblivious of the flames leaping from the back of her dress. He shouted to her and rushed to smother the flames, but she was badly burned. (Charles Fort, *The Complete Books of Charles Fort,* pp.663–65)

A most peculiar fire took the lives of Mr. and Mrs. John Kiley, a retired couple, at Butlock's Heath, a village near Southampton, England. On the morning of February 26, 1905, neighbors heard a "scratching sound" issuing from the Kiley house, and on entering the house, they found the interior in flames.

Mr. Kiley was lying on the floor, totally consumed by fire. His wife was in an easy chair in the same room, also "badly charred, but recognizable." The police investigators noted an overturned table and an oil lamp with its glass chimney smashed on the floor, but it was not clear how this lamp could have been the cause of such an intense fire. The easy chair on which Mrs. Kiley was found was not burned or even singed. The jury brought in a verdict of "accidental death, but by what means we are unable to say." (Michael Harrison, *Fire From Heaven: A Study of Spontaneous Combustion in Human Beings,* pp.34–36, 109)

Two constables found the burned corpse of a woman in the village of Manner, near Dinapore, India, in 1907. The two men carried the corpse, still smoldering *inside unscorched clothes,* to the district magistrate's office. The Indian press said that the officers had seen no signs of fire in the room where the body was. (Charles Fort, *The Complete Books of Charles Fort,* p.930)

The Reverend A. C. Custance reported that on three occasions small objects in the Binbrook Rectory (above) had burst into flames with no apparent cause.

Two retired schoolteachers, Margaret and Wilhelmina Dewar of Whitley Bay, near Blyth, England, were involved in a sensational "accident case" reported in the British press in 1908. On the evening of March 22 Margaret Dewar ran to her neighbors' house in great distress and told them that she had found her sister burned to death. When the neighbors entered the Dewar house, they found the charred body of Wilhelmina lying on a bed. The sheets and bed showed no sign of fire—nor, for that matter, did any part of the house.

At the inquest Margaret repeatedly testified that she had discovered her sister's body on the bed exactly as observed by the neighbors. The coroner refused to believe such a preposterous story—how could a body burn up on an unscorched bed? He accused Margaret of lying, threatened her with prosecution for perjury, and postponed the inquest to a later date.

Poor Margaret was placed under a tremendous amount of local pressure from both her neighbors and the newspapers; no one would believe her tale. When the inquest resumed, she admitted to lying. She said that what had actually happened was that she had found Wilhelmina on fire, but still alive, on the ground floor of their house; that she had put out the flames and had helped her sister upstairs; and that there she had put Wilhelmina on the bed, where she died. Somehow, this story satisfied the coroner more than Margaret's original testimony, although there had been no signs of fire downstairs either.

After pronouncing a verdict of "accidental death by fire," the coroner noted that the case was one of the most extraordinary he had ever investigated. (Charles Fort, *The Complete Books of Charles Fort*, pp.909, 929–30; Vincent H. Gaddis, *Mysterious Fires and Lights*, p.222; Michael Harrison, *Fire From Heaven: A Study of Spontaneous Combustion in Human Beings*, pp.87–89)

A curious case of spontaneous combustion was reported from Antigua in the British West Indies in August 1929. The woman involved was luckier than most victims of such fires—her clothing would ignite without any apparent cause, but she was always unharmed. Her bedding, too, was affected—the sheets above and below her were frequently scorched when she woke up. Her story was corroborated by the neighbors who had helped replace her burned-up wardrobe. (Michael Harrison, *Fire From Heaven: A Study of Spontaneous Combustion in Human Beings*, p.228)

On a cold January morning in 1932 in Bladenboro, North Carolina, the cotton dress of Mrs. Charles Williamson suddenly flared into flames. She was not standing near any kind of fire, and her dress had not been in contact with cleaning fluid or any other flammable substance. Her husband and daughter tore off the flaming dress with their bare hands. Remarkably, not one of the three was even slightly burned. Soon after this, a pair of Mr. Williamson's pants, hanging in a closet, burst into flames. Then a bed caught fire, as did the curtains in an unoccupied room. Various articles in the house were found burning with bluish, jetlike flames, but oddly enough, adjacent objects were never affected. There was no smoke or smell associated with the flames, which could not be extinguished—they just vanished after the "attacked" object was totally consumed.

The authorities were called in, but the arson experts, police, and special investigators from the gas and electric companies were at a total loss to explain the erratic fires. On the fifth day the fires suddenly stopped. A newspaper report stated: "The fires started, burned out and vanished as mysteriously as if guided by invisible hands. There has been no logical explanation." (Michael Harrison, *Fire From Heaven: A Study of Spontaneous Combustion in Human Beings*, pp.166–67)

The sudden combustion of Mrs. Mary Carpenter, who perished while vacationing on a cabin cruiser off Norfolk, England, on July 29, 1938, took place in full view of her husband and children. She "was engulfed in flames and reduced to a charred corpse" in minutes. No one else was burned and the boat was undamaged. "I suppose her clothes caught fire," the investigating officer said, "but I can't understand how it happened." (Vincent H. Gaddis, *Mysterious Fires and Lights*, p.224;

Michael Harrison, *Fire From Heaven: A Study of Spontaneous Combustion in Human Beings*, p.94)

Phyllis Newcombe burst into flames in the middle of a dance floor on the evening of August 27, 1938, at the Chelmsford Shire Hall in Chelmsford, England. The 22-year-old girl was wearing a dress "modeled on an old-fashioned crinoline." At midnight, just as she was leaving the dance floor, her dress flared up, and within seconds she was a blazing mass of blue flames. The young woman's fiancé, Henry McAusland, tried valiantly to beat out the flames with his bare hands, but it was already too late. Phyllis was fatally burned before the ambulance arrived.

At the inquest the coroner initially surmised that a light from a cigarette must have set the gown on fire, but the young woman's father was able to demonstrate to the court that the dress was not that flammable. Using a piece of the same material, he showed that only an open flame would set the cloth on fire and that a cigarette by itself would not ignite it. Since all the witnesses swore that no one had used a lighter or struck a match at midnight in the Shire Hall, the case remained unsolved. (Vincent H. Gaddis, *Mysterious Fires and Lights*, p.224; Michael Harrison, *Fire From Heaven: A Study of Spontaneous Combustion in Human Beings*, pp.92–93; *True*, May 1964, pp.32–33, 104–07, 112)

One of the youngest victims of unexplained death-by-fire, 11-month-old Peter Seaton of London, had been put to bed as usual one evening in January 1939. Soon after, a visitor, Harold Huxstep, heard screams of terror. Rushing upstairs to Peter's room, Mr. Huxstep opened the door to face an inferno of leaping flames that flung him back across the hall. There was no way he could rescue the baby.

After the firemen had put out the blaze, a thorough investigation of the nursery revealed nothing that could have caused such a conflagration. What was especially remarkable was that despite the intensity of the fire, hardly any of the furniture was damaged. (Michael Harrison, *Fire From Heaven: A Study of Spontaneous Combustion in Human Beings*, pp.6–7)

The burned body of Allen M. Small, age 52, was found in his home at Deer Isle, Maine, on January 13, 1943. The carpet beneath the body was scorched, but there was no other sign of fire anywhere in the house. In the kitchen the stove lids were all in place, and Small's unlit pipe was resting on a shelf. (Vincent H. Gaddis, *Mysterious Fires and Lights*, p.227)

On December 15, 1949, the police reported a 53-year-old woman, Mrs. Ellen K. Coutres, dead from burns in her home in Manchester, New Hampshire. Her horribly disfigured body was discovered lying on the floor in an unscorched room. The fireplace had not been used, and no other source of fire could be found. The Associated Press release stated: "There was no other sign of fire, and although ... the woman must have been a human torch, flames had not ignited the wooden structure [of the frame house]." (Vincent H. Gaddis, *Mysterious Fires and Lights*, p.227; Michael Harrison, *Fire From Heaven: A Study of Spontaneous Combustion in Human Beings*, pp.94–95)

SINCE 1950

The 1951 death of Mrs. Mary Reeser of St. Petersburg, Florida, who was found reduced to ashes in a practically undamaged apartment, was a landmark case of spontaneous combustion because it was the first instance where every possible tool of modern scientific investigation was used to determine the cause of this mysterious phenomenon. Yet despite the efforts of the FBI, fire officials, arson experts, and pathologists, a year after the incident Detective Cass Burgess of the St. Petersburg police commented as follows:

> Our investigation has turned up nothing that could be singled out as proving, beyond a doubt, what actually happened. The case is still open. We are still as far from establishing any logical cause for the death as we were when we first entered Mrs. Reeser's apartment.

To which Police Chief J. R. Reichert added:

> As far as logical explanations go, this is one of those things that just couldn't have happened, but it did. The case is not closed and may never be to the satisfaction of all concerned.

And Dr. Wilton M. Krogman, a physical anthropologist at the University of Pennsylvania's School of Medicine and a world-renowned expert on the effects of fire on the human body, finally gave up trying to understand what had happened. Dr. Krogman said: "I regard it as the most amazing thing I've ever seen. As I review it, the short hairs on my neck bristle with vague fear. Were I living in the Middle Ages, I'd mutter something about black magic."

Here are the details of the case: Mrs. Mary Hardy Reeser, an agreeable, motherly widow of 67, was living in St. Petersburg, Florida, to be near to her son, Dr. Richard Reeser. On the evening of July 1, 1951, she had remained in her son's home with one of her grandchildren while the rest of the family went to the beach. When they returned, they found that Mrs. Reeser had already left for her own apartment. The younger Mrs. Reeser drove to her mother-in-law's to see if every-

thing was all right. According to her testimony, there was nothing in Mrs. Mary Reeser's appearance or demeanor to cause any alarm. Dr. Reeser visited his mother later that evening. She was mildly depressed over the fact that she had not heard from two friends who were supposed to rent an apartment for her in anticipation of a return trip to Columbia, Pennsylvania, formerly her hometown. His mother told him that she wished to retire early and would take two sleeping pills to ensure a good night's rest. Dr. Reeser left at about 8:30 P.M. and returned to his home.

The last person to see Mrs. Reeser alive was her landlady, Mrs. Pansy M. Carpenter, who lived in another apartment in the four-unit building (the two units between them were unoccupied). Mrs. Carpenter saw Mrs. Reeser briefly at about 9 P.M. She was wearing her nightgown, a housecoat, and black satin slippers and was lounging in a comfortable chair smoking a cigarette. The bed covers had been turned back. Mrs. Reeser's last night was a typical summer night in Florida: the sky was overcast with occasional flashes of heat lightning in the distance.

When Mrs. Carpenter woke up Monday morning at 5 A.M., she noticed a slight odor of smoke but was not alarmed, since she attributed the smell to a water pump in the garage that had been overheating lately. She got up, turned off the pump, and settled back into bed. When she got up an hour later to collect her newspaper outside, she no longer smelled any smoke.

At 8 A.M. a telegram arrived for Mrs. Reeser. Mrs. Carpenter signed the receipt and went to her tenant's apartment to bring her the telegram. The doorknob, when she placed her hand on it, was hot. Alarmed, she stepped back and shouted for help. Two painters working across the street ran over. One of them opened the door; as he entered, he felt a blast of hot air. Thinking of rescuing Mrs. Reeser, he frantically looked around but saw no signs of her. The bed was empty. There was some smoke, but the only fire was a small flame on a wooden beam over a partition separating the living room and kitchenette.

The firemen arrived, put out the small flame with a hand pump, and tore away part of the partition. When Assistant Fire Chief S. O. Griffith began his inspection of the premises, he could not believe his eyes. In the middle of the floor there was a charred area roughly four feet in diameter, inside which he found a number of blackened chair springs and the ghastly remains of a human body, consisting of a charred liver attached to a piece of the spine, a shrunken skull, one foot still wearing a black satin slipper, and a small pile of ashes.

Coroner Edward T. Silk arrived to examine the body and survey the apartment. Although deeply puzzled, he decided that the death was accidental and authorized

When Truth Is as Strange as Fiction

Spontaneous human combustion was such a well-known phenomenon during the late 18th and 19th centuries that a number of authors used it to dispose of some of their fictional characters.

In Charles Dickens's *Bleak House,* published in the mid-1800's, Krook, an old, cadaverous, gin-soaked rag-and-bottle merchant, dies gruesomely of spontaneous combustion. Krook was a symbol for all the social evils and inequities then rampant in England, and through his horrible death Dickens prophesied the self-destruction of "all authorities in all places under all names soever, where false pretenses are made, and where injustice is done." The chapter depicting Krook's demise concluded:

> Call the death by any name [you] will,
> attribute it to whom you will, or say it might
> have been prevented how you will, it is the
> same death eternally—inborn, inbred,
> engendered in the corrupted humours of
> the vicious body itself, and that only—
> Spontaneous Combustion, and none other of
> all the deaths that can be died.

When this installment of the serialized *Bleak House* appeared, the literary critic George Henry Lewes severely chided his old friend Dickens for perpetuating what he felt to be a vulgar and unscientific superstition. But Dickens vigorously defended the reality of

An illustration from Dickens's Bleak House *shows William Guppy and a friend as they arrive at Krook's house only to find he had combusted. Nothing of him remained.*

spontaneous combustion, citing many documented cases, including those of Mme. Millet of Rheims (see pages 80–81) and of the Countess di Bandi (see pages 81–82) as well as his own memories of inquests he attended when he was still a young reporter. Later, when *Bleak House* was reissued in a single volume, Dickens continued to defend the authenticity of spontaneous human combustion in his foreword:

> I shall not abandon the facts until there
> shall have been a considerable Spontaneous
> Combustion of the testimony on which
> human occurrences are usually received.

The earliest literary account of spontaneous combustion is from the 1798 novel *Wieland,* written by America's first novelist and master of the gothic, Charles Brockden Brown. The main character is a German pietist who observes the mysterious solitary rites of his religion in a tumbledown wooden shack he calls his chapel. One night his wife is startled by a bright light that bursts above the chapel and by a "loud report, like the explosion of a mine." She hears horrible shrieks, but by the time she gets to the shack, the light and cries have died away. She finds Wieland "insensible," his clothing in cinders, his body frightfully burned, but the chapel unharmed. The wretched man dies after terrible suffering:

> . . . the disease . . . betrayed more terrible
> symptoms. Fever and delirium terminated
> in lethargic slumber. . . . Yet not until
> insupportable exhalations and crawling
> putrefaction had driven from his chamber
> and the house everyone whom their duty
> did not detain.

(The reader will recognize this as a gothic version of the priest Bertholi's case, reported on page 82.)

In Frederick Marryat's 1834 novel *Jacob Faithful,* the hero's mother is a victim of spontaneous combustion. In his account Marryat closely followed the details of an 1832 case reported in London. Jacob enters his parents' cabin aboard a barge on the Thames:

> The lamp fixed against the after bulkhead,
> with a glass before it, was still alight, and I
> could see plainly to every corner of the cabin.
> Nothing was burning—not even the curtains to
> my mother's bed appeared to be singed . . .
> there appeared to be a black mass in the
> middle of the bed. I put my hand fearfully
> upon it—it was a sort of unctuous pitchy

cinder. I screamed with horror. . . . I staggered from the cabin, and fell down on the deck in a state amounting to almost insanity. . . . She perished from what is called *spontaneous combustion*, and inflammation of the gases generated from the spirits absorbed into the system.

In Gogol's *Dead Souls* (1842) there is a regretful mention of the death of a blacksmith combined with relief that the smithy itself had not burned:

He caught fire himself. Something inside him caught fire. Must have had too much to drink. Only a blue flame came out of him and he smoldered, smoldered, and turned as black as coal. And he was such a clever blacksmith. . . .

Nikolai Gogol is famous for his social commentary, in which he ridiculed Russian society and officials. Dead Souls, one of his greatest works, contains an episode in which a man catches on fire. Gogol hypothesized that the flames, presumably induced by alcohol, were the just reward of drunkenness.

Herman Melville, too, used the device. In *Redburn* (1849), Miguel, a shanghaied sailor, is found on deck in a stupor, drunk and stinking. As the rest of the horrified crew look on,

. . . two threads of greenish fire, like a forked tongue, darted out between the lips and in a moment, the cadaverous face was covered by a swarm of wormlike flames . . . the uncovered body burned before us, precisely like a phosphorescent shark in a midnight sea.

Herman Melville's Redburn is based upon his first experience at sea as a cabin boy on a merchant vessel bound for Liverpool. Could it be that he had witnessed an incidence of spontaneous combustion?

And Thomas de Quincey, in the 1856 revised edition of *Confessions of an English Opium-Eater*, included as one of the "Pains of Opium" the fear that the narcotic, like alcohol, might result in spontaneous combustion and that he might himself take leave of the literary world in that fashion.

The mysterious fiery death was also used by Mark Twain in his *Life on the Mississippi* (1883):

Jimmy Finn was not burned in the calaboose, but died a natural death in a tan vat, of a combination of delirium tremens and spontaneous combustion. When I say natural death, it was a natural death for Jimmy Finn to die.

Finally, in Emile Zola's 1893 novel, *Le Docteur Pascal*, one of the members of the degenerate Macquart family catches fire from the smoldering tobacco of his pipe while he sits in a drunken stupor, as his sister watches with horror:

At first Félicité thought that it was his linen, his underpants or his vest, which was burning. But, there was no doubt about it, it was his flesh, burning with a flickering blue flame, light, dancing, like a flame spreading over the surface of a bowl of alcohol . . . it was growing, spreading rapidly and the skin was splitting and the fat beginning to melt. . . . Now the liquid fat was dribbling through the cracks in his skin, feeding the flame which was spreading to his belly. And Félicité realized that he was burning up, like a sponge soaked in alcohol.

Emile Zola, leader of French literature's naturalist school, emphasised in many of his works the influence of heredity on the individual. In Le Docteur Pascal, one of 20 novels in his famous series, Les Rougon-Macquart, he graphically portrayed the death of Antoine Macquart, who burst into flames while in a drunken sleep.

the removal of the remains. The scooped-up ashes, the tiny shrunken head, and the slipper-encased foot were taken by ambulance to a local hospital.

The ensuing investigation included police and fire officials as well as arson experts. The facts that confronted them seemed inexplicable considering the great heat necessary to account for Mrs. Reeser's incinerated body. Little of the furniture, other than the chair and the end table next to it, was badly damaged, but the apartment had suffered some peculiar effects:

> The ceiling, draperies and walls, from a point exactly four feet above the floor, were coated with smelly, oily soot. Below this four-foot mark there was none. The wall paint adjacent to the chair was faintly browned, but the carpet where the chair had rested was not even burned through. A wall mirror 10 feet away had cracked, probably from heat. On a dressing table 12 feet away, two pink wax candles had puddled, but their wicks lay undamaged in their holders. Plastic wall outlets above the four-foot mark were melted, but the fuses were not blown and the current was on. The baseboard electrical outlets were undamaged. An electric clock plugged into one of the fused fixtures had stopped at precisely 4:20 . . . but the same clock ran perfectly when plugged into one of the baseboard outlets.
>
> Newspapers nearby on a table and draperies and linens on the daybed close at hand—all flammable —were not damaged. And though the painters and Mrs. Carpenter had felt a wave of heat when they opened the door, no one had noted smoke or burning odor and there were no embers or flames in the ashes.

Faced with such a mystery, the St. Petersburg authorities called in the FBI. Laboratory findings showed that Mrs. Reeser's estimated weight of 175 pounds had been reduced to a total of *less than 10 pounds,* including the foot and shrunken head. The final report concluded that no known chemical agents or other accelerants had been involved in starting the fire and ended by stating that the case was "unusual and improbable."

A top arson specialist of the National Board of Underwriters was also stumped. "I can only say," he admitted, "the victim died from fire. . . . " Finally, the aforementioned Dr. Krogman, an authority on different kinds of burns, was asked to help clarify the mystery. After checking the findings of the other authorities, he began eliminating possibilities. He considered lightning as a cause, but an engineer who specialized in the effects of lightning bolts on the human body flatly dismissed such a conjecture. Besides, lightning was not reported in the immediate neighborhood during the night of the accident. Another possibility was that the sedatives taken by Mrs. Reeser had made her so drowsy that she did not notice a fire set to her nightgown or chair by the cigarette she was smoking. However, neither the gown nor the chair was particularly flammable, and besides, there was not enough material available in these items to produce the intense heat necessary to reduce a human body to ashes. Dr. Krogman has burned cadavers with gasoline, oil, wood, and all kinds of other agents. He has experimented with bones encased in flesh or stripped, both moist and dry. His tests have utilized combustion apparatus ranging from outdoor pyres to the most modern pressurized crematorium equipment. He has demonstrated conclusively that it takes enormous heat to consume a body, and that only at over 3000°F would bone become volatile enough to lose its shape and leave only ashes. "These are very great heats," he said, "that would sear, char, scorch or otherwise mar or affect anything and everything within a considerable radius. . . . They say truth often is stranger than fiction and this case proves it." The remaining slippered left foot was a mystery in itself. It was established that Mrs. Reeser was in the habit of stretching out her left leg because of some physical discomfort in that limb. The foot was left unburned, apparently because it was outside the mysterious four-foot radius of incineration.

Another speculation, that the fire might have been caused by some failure in the electrical system, was also ruled out by the experts: the fuse would have blown. Finally, murder and suicide were considered. Murder was eliminated because there were no known suspects, the apartment had not been disturbed, and there was no hypothesis to account for how such a murder could have been accomplished. Suicide, too, was ruled out— Mrs. Reeser was well provided for and not depressed, and, again, how could she have set such a fire?

Eventually Dr. Krogman admitted defeat. He reported to Chief Reichert:

> I have posed the problem to myself again and again of why Mrs. Reeser could have been so thoroughly destroyed, even to the bones, and yet leave nearby objects materially unaffected. I always end up rejecting it in theory but facing it in apparent fact.

Nor could he understand the shrunken condition of Mrs. Reeser's skull:

> . . . the head is not left complete in ordinary burning cases. Certainly it does *not* shrivel or symmetrically reduce to a much smaller size. In presence of heat sufficient to destroy soft tissues, the skull would literally explode in many pieces. I . . . have never known any exception to this rule. Never have I seen a skull so shrunken or a body so completely consumed by heat.

(Vincent H. Gaddis, *Mysterious Fires and Lights,* pp.246–59; Michael Harrison, *Fire From Heaven: A*

The Case for Spontaneous Combustion

Spontaneous human combustion is not a phenomenon recognized by 20th-century science: it is not listed in the *International Classification of Diseases* compiled by the World Health Organization, nor is it a subject heading in the *Index Medicus,* the National Library of Medicine's index of biomedical literature. Despite the evidence of police and fire authorities, arson specialists, coroners, and pathologists, most doctors and scientists regard seemingly indisputable cases as simply not thoroughly investigated.

However, such skepticism was not always prevalent. In the 17th and 18th centuries spontaneous combustion, especially of drunkards, was regarded as divine retribution, but by the 19th century, advances in biology and chemistry encouraged researchers to look for more mundane causes for these seemingly inexplicable fires. A number of additional possibilities were suggested that might, alone or in various combinations, account for such bizarre occurrences:

- Intestinal gases are flammable.
- Cadavers produce gases that are flammable.
- Haystacks and compost heaps can build up enough heat for spontaneous combustion.
- Certain elements and compounds spontaneously burst into flames when exposed to air. This is true of phosphorus, for example, which is a constituent of the human body.
- Some chemicals that are inert alone combine to form explosive compounds.
- The luminescence emitted by certain insects and fishes proves the possibility of internal "fire" of some kind.
- Fats and oils, which the human body contains in abundance, are excellent fuels.
- Static electricity produces sparks that could, under certain conditions, set a body on fire.

Mounting evidence indicated, however, that none of these hypotheses could really account for spontaneous human combustion. In 1851 a German chemist pointed out that overweight imbibers of brandy generally do not burn when they are close to a fire.

Toward the end of the 1800's several doctors said it was difficult to comprehend how the body, which has a high water content and relatively little fat, could combust. Finally, the April 22, 1905, issue of *American Medicine* dealt a harsh blow to SHC believers, noting: "Of the total number of cases published, nearly half have been reported from the neurotic land of France."

To test the theory that alcohol renders the body highly combustible, a rat was soaked in alcohol for a year, then set on fire. The skin blazed up fiercely, charring some outer layers of flesh, but the rat's internal tissues and organs were hardly affected. The experiment was repeated on museum specimens that had been immersed in alcohol for even longer periods; the results, however, were the same.

It may be possible for flammable gases produced by digestion to accumulate in the body and present a hazard. An English pastor with such a condition was once warned not to blow out the altar candles following church services for fear his breath might be ignited.

Static electricity seems a good candidate for starting these fires, no matter what might fuel them thereafter. The human body can, according to the *Fire Protection Manual* of the National Fire Protection Association, accumulate a static charge of several thousand volts. Some people have been known to build up far greater charges, occasionally generating up to 30,000 volts. Ordinarily this electricity is harmlessly discharged through the hair, but in certain volatile situations, such as factories for combustible materials or hospital operating rooms using gaseous anesthetics, these people can spark off explosions. But these explosions have never been known to burn one person to ashes, leaving the room and furnishings undamaged.

A number of other physical causes for spontaneous combustion have been suggested, including fireballs, lightning, internal atomic explosions, laser beams, microwave radiation, high-frequency sound, and geomagnetic flux, but the mechanisms through which any of these might work are unexplained. And, for now, so is spontaneous human combustion.

Study of Spontaneous Combustion in Human Beings, pp.120–36; Francis Hitching, *The Mysterious World: An Atlas of the Unexplained,* p.21; *True,* May 1964, pp.32, 106–07, 112)

A particularly bizarre case of death-by-burning was that of 46-year-old Glen B. Denney, owner of a foundry and a resident of Algiers, Louisiana. On September 18, 1952, a neighbor called the fire department when she noticed smoke coming from the apartment above her. When the firemen forced open the door, they found the burning body of a man in the living room. The flames were quickly put out with a blanket. Lt. Louis Wattingney recounted:

> The man was lying on the floor behind the door and he was a mass of flames. Not another blessed thing in the room was burning. He was dead. I don't know

what caused the fire to burn so hot. He could have been saturated with some oil. I did not smell anything, however. In all my experience, I never saw anything to beat this.

There was no evidence that Mr. Denney was a smoker, and no matches were found. The windows were all closed. There were no traces of flammable liquids anywhere. But the most startling discovery was that Denney had cut his wrists before he collapsed in flames: both wrist arteries were severed, and there was a pool of blood and a bloody knife in the kitchen. It was determined that Denney had been depressed and drinking heavily: he had had the "shakes" when last seen alive. The final verdict stated that Denney had cut his wrists and then set fire to himself to "make sure." Both the evidence and logic, however, strongly contradicted such a finding. How could a man rapidly losing blood from five deep cuts walk from the kitchen to the living room, drench himself with kerosene that was never detected, from a can that was never found, and then set himself on fire with a nonexistent match? (Vincent H. Gaddis, *Mysterious Fires and Lights,* p.271)

The body of Waymon Wood of Greenville, South Carolina, was found "crisped black" in the front seat of his closed car on March 1, 1953. The car was parked on the side of Bypass Route 291. Although little remained of Wood, the car, which contained a half tank of gas, was unaffected except for the windshield, which had bubbled and sagged inward from the intense heat. (Vincent H. Gaddis, *Mysterious Fires and Lights,* pp.227–28; *True,* May 1964, p.112)

In December 1956 a 78-year-old cripple, Young Sik Kim of 1130 Maunakea Street, Honolulu, was found enveloped in blue flames by his next-door neighbor. The heat was too intense for her even to approach him. By the time the firemen got there, 15 minutes later, the victim and his overstuffed chair were reduced to ashes. His feet, however, remained undamaged and were still propped up on his wheelchair facing the chair in which he had been sitting. Nothing else in the room, even the curtains and clothing nearby, had suffered any damage. (*True,* May 1964, p.32)

Children are rarely mentioned as victims of spontaneous combustion, but Ricky P. Pruitt of Rockford, Illinois, may have been one of the few unfortunate exceptions. The four-month-old infant died of severe burns in the spring of 1959, but there were no clues as to what had caused them. His garments showed no scorch marks, nor did the bedding of the crib in which he was found. (Vincent H. Gaddis, *Mysterious Fires and Lights,* p.229; *True,* May 1964, p.112)

On an October evening in the late 1950's, 19-year-old Maybelle Andrews was dancing with her boyfriend, Billy Clifford, in a London discotheque. Suddenly she burst into flames. The fire blazed from her back and chest, enveloping her head and igniting her hair. Her boyfriend and some of the bystanders tried to beat out the flames, but they could not save her. She died on the way to the hospital.

According to Clifford's testimony:

I saw no one smoking on the dance floor. There were no candles on the tables and I did not see her dress catch fire from anything. I know it sounds incredible, but it appeared to me that the flames burst outwards, as if they originated within her body.

Other witnesses agreed. The final verdict was "death by misadventure, caused by a fire of unknown origin." (Michael Harrison, *Fire From Heaven: A Study of Spontaneous Combustion in Human Beings,* pp.93–94)

Billy Peterson, about 30 years old, an automobile factory worker from Pontiac, Michigan, had been very depressed over the state of his health for several months. On December 13, 1959, at 7:45 P.M., he was found dead in his car, an apparent suicide. When he was discovered, the right front seat of the car was smoldering where the exhaust pipe had been bent to lead into the closed car. Peterson's body was seated several feet away from the smoldering upholstery.

His body was taken to the Pontiac General Hospital, where he was pronounced dead of carbon monoxide poisoning, a finding consistent with the idea of suicide. But what could not be explained were the third-degree burns on Billy's back, legs, and arms and the seared condition of his nose, throat, and lungs. What was even more startling was that Peterson's clothing—even his underwear—was in no way damaged and that unsinged hairs stuck up through the charred flesh. The investigators first suggested heated exhaust fumes, and one detective proposed the idea of a "torture killing," but neither explanation could account for Billy's condition. (Vincent H. Gaddis, *Mysterious Fires and Lights,* pp.273–76; *True,* May 1964, p.104)

A former actress, Mrs. Olga Worth Stephens, age 75, of Dallas, Texas, was sitting in a parked car in October 1964 when witnesses saw her burst into flames. She was fatally burned before anyone could come to her rescue. Firemen said that the automobile was not damaged and contained nothing that could have started the fire. (Vincent H. Gaddis, *Mysterious Fires and Lights,* p.230; Michael Harrison, *Fire From Heaven: A Study of Spontaneous Combustion in Human Beings,* p.153)

Horrified witnesses saw Mrs. Olga Worth Stephens suddenly ignite into a "human torch" while sitting in her parked automobile. The car was not damaged by the flames.

In the small town of Coudersport, Pennsylvania, Don E. Gosnell, a meter reader for the North Penn Gas Company, set out on his accustomed rounds on the morning of December 5, 1966. His first call was on Dr. John Irving Bentley, a 92-year-old retired physician, who was a semi-invalid but still able to get around his house with the aid of a walker. Gosnell opened the doctor's front door, yelled, but received no answer. He proceeded downstairs to the basement to read the meter. There he became aware of a "light-blue smoke of unusual odor . . . like that of starting up a new central heating system . . . somewhat sweet."

In the corner of the dirt-floored basement was a pile of fine ash about 14 inches in diameter and about 5 inches high, perhaps enough to fill a bucket. Idly he kicked and scattered the stuff. He did not notice the hole in the ceiling—an irregular area about 2½ feet wide and 4 feet long, charred around the edges—burned clear through the floorboards above. He read the meter and then went upstairs to look in on the doctor. There the smoke was denser, but Dr. Bentley was nowhere in sight. Don Gosnell stuck his head into the bathroom. He was appalled at the sight that greeted him. The doctor's walker was tilted over the burned hole in the floor, and alongside it was all that remained of Dr. Bentley—his right leg from the knee down, browned but not charred. The shoe was still intact. Gosnell ran out of the house, white as a sheet, yelling at the top of his lungs: "Doctor Bentley burnt up!"

The coroner, John Dec, had too many unanswered questions to determine how the accident could have happened. One theory was that the doctor had set his robe on fire in the living room while striking a match to light his pipe, then used his walker to get to the bathroom for water to put out the flames. (His robe

was found in the bathtub next to the drain, singed but not badly burned.) But even if the robe had burst into flames, how could it have generated enough heat to set a body on fire? If the fire had started in the living room, why was there no trace of it? And how was it possible for a body to be consumed so completely with so little else being affected?

The coroner's certificate finally gave "asphyxiation and 90 percent burning" as the cause of Dr. Bentley's basically inexplicable death. (Francis Hitching, *The Mysterious World: An Atlas of the Unexplained,* pp.20–21; *Pursuit,* 9:75–79, Fall 1976)

Two cases of infant spontaneous combustion were reported in England in 1973 and 1974.

In 1973 seven-month-old Parvinder Kaur and the baby carriage in which he was sitting suddenly burst into flames in his parents' living room. He was treated in the Burns Unit at the Birmingham Hospital, Birmingham, England. Officials were unable to determine any cause for the fire.

The following year the Birmingham [England] *Evening Mail* of August 26, 1974, reported the death of six-month-old Lisa Tipton. She was found burned to death in an unexplained fire confined to one room of her parents' home in Highfields, Staffordshire. (Michael Harrison, *Fire From Heaven: A Study of Spontaneous Combustion in Human Beings,* p.261)

Not just one but six people were involved in what appears to be an instance of multiple victims of spontaneous combustion. The following account is from the *Nigerian Herald* of December 27, 1976:

> The death of six members of a family of seven by fire in Lagos . . . has now become the greatest mystery.
>
> An on-the-spot investigation yesterday revealed that everything in the small wooden room at Iponri on the Lagos Mainland remained intact.
>
> Among the articles left untouched by fire were two cotton mattresses carefully placed on two iron beds. . . .
>
> Altogether, the room looked unaffected by the fire which killed the six persons. . . . It was also expected [from the condition of the fire victims] that nothing, including the wooden walls and iron sheets on the roof, would have remained. . . .
>
> And although earlier reports claimed that the fire came from petrol which was sprinkled on the family through an opening in the wooden wall while they were asleep [this was claimed by the mother who survived] it became known yesterday that this might not be true at all. . . . [Michael Harrison, *Fire From Heaven: A Study of Spontaneous Combustion in Human Beings,* pp.262–63]

INEXPLICABLE CRIMES AND ASSAULTS

At various times, and from various parts of the world, have come convincing reports of crimes and of assaults on people—and sometimes on animals—for which there is no generally acceptable solution. The cases described on the following pages do not have definable perpetrators, to use the time-honored jargon of the police. These are all crimes and assaults that have been carried out in mysterious ways and by agencies that often remain unidentified.

Included herein are some seemingly ordinary crimes: a stabbing, shootings, and a theft, committed by extraordinary and unknown means. There are also some extraordinary crimes, such as instances of cattle mutilation and mystical enslavement, for which there seem to be no clear explanations.

On another level are assaults by demons and similar malevolent spirits. Some of these attacks may be induced by outside agencies and simply strike the victim without warning. There are others that, strangely enough, may be self-induced by the victim's own fearful belief in a curse or hex that has been proclaimed by another. Only if one believes in curses of this category will their evil intention be fulfilled.

As we read about these strange and inexplicable happenings, we should be reminded of the limits of our knowledge and not be too impressed with what we think we know. As we discover that some of our most cherished beliefs are questionable, we may well become more receptive to the heretical idea that we are not infallible in other areas of our life and thought.

INEXPLICABLE CRIMES

Notwithstanding the experience, sophisticated equipment, and networks of communication shared by police departments all across the country, there are still some crimes in which the evidence is so puzzling as to defy logical solution. Sherlock Holmes himself would have had trouble with such examples as the following:

An Impossible Suicide?

In 1872 Capt. George M. Colvocoresses was found shot to death on a well-frequented street in Bridgeport, Connecticut. A pistol and a satchel lay beside the body, and the police at first assumed they had a clear case of murder. When they examined the body more closely, however, they discovered that no bullet hole was to be found in the dead man's jacket or vest, while the hole and powder burn in his shirt indicated that the pistol had been inserted beneath the outer garments before being fired. Police and journalists were at a loss to explain why a murderer should go to this trouble.

The next conclusion was that Captain Colvocoresses had taken his own life, a thought reinforced by the discovery that not many months earlier he had insured his life for $193,000. But when his will revealed bequests of only a few thousand dollars, this thesis seemed

doubtful. Even more doubt was cast by the captain's character; he was, according to *The New York Times,* "a man of high character and stainless life," unlikely, in the highest degree, to take his own life.

And then there were the technical difficulties of the suicide theory. Why did Colvocoresses carefully place the gun inside his vest before pulling the trigger? Not, presumably, because he was afraid of spoiling his jacket and vest. But if he did do that, perhaps precisely to shroud his death in mystery, how could he be sure that, having shot himself in the heart, he would have time to extricate his hand from his vest before he died? And if he could not be sure of this, and yet wished his suicide to appear as murder, why choose this method? And finally, if he wished to kill himself without the appearance of suicide, why would he decide to do it in the early evening hours on a well-frequented street? (*The New York Times,* July 1, 1872)

How Did It Happen?

In July 1891 Carl Gros was shot dead near Maspeth, Long Island. The bullet had penetrated his body but had left no holes in his clothing. (Charles Fort, *The Complete Books of Charles Fort,* p.913)

No Verdict

The death of 72-year-old Lavinia Farrar, a woman "of independent means," was reported in the *Cambridge Daily News* in England on March 16, 1901. She had been found on the floor of her kitchen, fully dressed, her face bruised, and her nose broken. Beside her were a blood-stained knife and a few drops of blood. An examination revealed that she had been stabbed in the heart.

At the inquest an open verdict was returned for these reasons: Although the dead woman had been stabbed, her clothing had not been penetrated by the knife and was unmarked by blood except for the innermost garment, which was slightly bloodstained. Since death had been almost instantaneous, she could not possibly have first stabbed herself and then dressed before dying. Moreover, the blood on the knife and on the floor beside her seemed not to be hers, since the wound was "almost bloodless." (Charles Fort, *The Complete Books of Charles Fort*, p.916)

Missing: Ireland's Crown Jewels

One of the most daring thefts of the 20th century occurred in 1907 when Ireland's crown jewels (valued at $250,000) were stolen from a safe kept in the strong room of Bedford Tower at Dublin Castle—practically under the eyes of the four men who had been assigned to guard them.

Sometime between June 28 and July 6, the thief had first obtained keys to the tower's main door and then to the strong room and finally to the safe, where he must have spent at least 10 or 15 minutes freeing the jewels from their cases. And yet no suspicions had been aroused. A long investigation by Scotland Yard came to naught. The whereabouts of the treasure and the identity of the thief are still unknown. (*The New York Times*, September 6, 1931; Reader's Digest, eds., *Strange Stories, Amazing Facts*, p.354)

Mystery of the Locked Room

Isidore Fink was shot dead at 10:30 P.M. on March 9, 1929, in the back room of the Fifth Avenue Laundry (which he owned) at 4 East 132nd Street in New York City. The police were alerted by a neighbor, Mrs. Locklan Smith, who had heard screaming and the sounds of a struggle. When the officers arrived, they found that the doors to the room in which Fink lay were locked, and so they gained entry by lifting a small boy into the room through a transom window.

Fink had been shot twice in the chest and once through the left hand, which showed powder burns. No gun was found in the room. There was money in Fink's pocket and in the cash register.

At first police theorized that whoever shot Fink, who always bolted the laundry doors when he worked at night, had climbed through the transom window. But the window was small, as was the boy who was hoisted through it; and the question of why an escaping murderer should climb through a small window instead of leaving by the door seemed unanswerable. A second theory was that Fink had been shot from the hallway through the transom, but the powder burns on Fink's body showed that he had been shot from close range. More than two years after the crime, New York Police Commissioner Edward P. Mulrooney called the murder an "insoluble mystery." (Charles Fort, *The Complete Books of Charles Fort*, p.916; *The New York Times*, March 10, 1929)

A Heavy Question

At the end of a day's work in 1974, workers for the Dowling Construction Company of Indianapolis left a five-ton steel wrecking ball hanging from a crane 200 feet above the ground. When they came back the next morning, the ball was gone. Police and all concerned were baffled, and the ball was never found. (Telephone interview with Loran Dowling, Indianapolis, Indiana)

Could anyone have stolen a five-ton steel ball, or did it simply float away? René Magritte's 1953 painting, "The Infinite Search," suggests the mystery of such an event.

Inexplicable Revelations

A limited, but fascinating, antidote to inexplicable crimes are examples of inexplicable solutions and revelations. There is a considerable body of information on the subject and, in some cases, disagreement as to the true value of the psychics and seers who claim to have the ability to solve crimes and locate missing persons by extrasensory perception.

But about the psychic power of one clairvoyant, a New Jersey housewife, the local police have no question. To these conscientious well-trained investigators, whose powers of perception are limited to the ordinary, the psychic ability of Dorothy Allison must seem to be from another realm.

Her gift, which might also be considered a burden, is to visualize events, environments, and situations in her mind's eye as if they were projected on a TV screen. The visualizations are sometimes the result of specific queries about a missing person. At other times the "news" of a tragedy comes to her mind unbidden.

One such case occasioned her first involvement with the police. At 6 A.M. on December 3, 1967, she awoke from a vivid dream in which she had visioned the body of a young boy caught in a pipe. After a few days of worrying about it, she decided to report her dream to the Nutley, New Jersey, police. They established that five-year-old Michael Kurcsics had drowned in the Third River about two hours *after* her dream, but his body had not yet been found. Mrs. Allison also confided that she was psychic. But because the tragedy had been reported in the newspapers, the police were unimpressed. Upon further questioning, however, Mrs. Allison revealed details about the child's clothing that had not been reported in the papers and offered the surprising information that the child's shoes were on the wrong feet.

In order to draw more specific information from Mrs. Allison, the investigator, patrolman Donald Vicaro, elicited the help of Dr. Richard Ribner, a New York City psychiatrist. The doctor put her in a semihypnotized state, and she revealed that she saw the figure 8, a school with a fence around it, a gray house, a set of offices with gold lettering on a door, and a

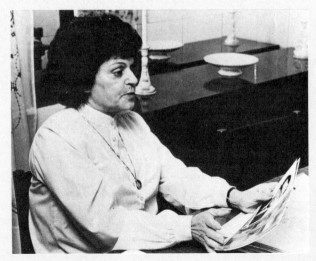

Psychic Dorothy Allison cannot explain how she sees unknown people and events so clearly in her mind. But several times her gift has helped locate missing persons.

factory. On February 7 the body was found in a pond fed by the Third River, about three miles from the spot where the boy had fallen in. Standing at the scene, Vicaro was astounded to see Public School No. 8, fence-encircled, a gray house, and a plant with a parking lot. Every detail given by Dorothy Allison, including the shoes on the wrong feet, was accurate. It was later learned that large pipes had been laid into the stream feeding the pond, over which a bridge had been improvised. Possibly the boy's body had become wedged in a pipe for a while.

On another occasion, in Dr. Ribner's office, Dorothy confided that a young man in the outer waiting room, through which she had just passed, had a gun and was contemplating suicide. She also noted that he had great potential and would become very successful once his illness was overcome. Later, during his session with the doctor, the young man admitted to having the gun and planning to use it. He was dissuaded and continued with his therapy. He later

CATTLE MUTILATION

There is no question that numbers of cattle, and in a few instances other livestock, were found mutilated in the 1970's on the vast reaches of the western plains. There is, however, a hotly debated controversy as to whether this was the work of natural predators or of agencies unknown. A few case histories are offered here.

Zapped, but by Whom?

The prelude to a long, gruesome sequence of cattle mutilations was the mysterious death in 1967 of a horse named Snippy. The three-year-old gelding was a pet saddle horse of Mr. and Mrs. Berle Lewis of Alamosa, Colorado, who pastured him on the ranch of Mrs. Lewis's brother a few miles away.

went on to become a successful industrial designer.

Another success story had to do with Charles Little Eagle's 18-year-old daughter who vanished November 6, 1975. Her disappearance was reported to the police, but after two days the father, who knew of Dorothy Allison, called on her for help. She immediately told him that his daughter was safe and that she was living in a filthy house with a red door and the number 106, 186, or 168. She said that the house would be found before January 21 and added, "One more thing. You're going to become a grandfather."

In due course a private investigator who had been hired to find the girl asked for Dorothy's help. She got in a car with the detective and his colleague and directed them around a maze of New York streets and then into Brooklyn, where she suddenly said: "We have to look for something connected with taxis. And something connected with a President's name." They found Monroe Street, where she directed them to turn at the corner. On the next street they found a house, number 186, with a storefront office that took calls for a taxi service. The woman who ran the service denied that the missing girl was inside. Dorothy knew better.

On January 21 Charles Little Eagle asked Dorothy to go to the house with him and get his daughter. "Not today," she replied. "I don't want to be involved in an accident. I'll go with you tomorrow."

The father and two investigators decided not to wait. As they drove into Brooklyn, another car skidded on the ice and crashed into them. They were only bruised, but their car was demolished.

The next day Dorothy did accompany them. The girl was found and was, indeed, pregnant—which she had not been on the date that Dorothy had told the father he was to have a grandchild.

Dorothy, whose mother was also clairvoyant, has been aware of her psychic gifts since childhood. Direct and candid, she has no explanation for this power and sees no point in speculating about it. She refuses to take money for her time and efforts. "If I have been blessed with this gift," she says, "it would be wrong to use it for anything but humanitarian purposes."

Snippy was last seen the evening of September 7, frisky and capering about as usual. The next morning, when he failed to appear at the ranch house for his breakfast ration of grain and water, there was some concern. The second morning, a search for the missing animal began. Snippy was found dead in a pasture about a quarter of a mile from the house. The horse,

lying on his left side, presented a gruesome sight. His neck appeared to have been cut all the way around down to the bone, as if with a sharp knife, and the flesh above the shoulders was gone. Nothing remained of the head but the skull.

Several dark spots were found on the ground just southeast and northwest of the body. Two bushes near the animal had been flattened, and close by one bush were small holes that seemed "punched" into the ground. On one of the two bushes Mrs. Lewis discovered a bit of the horse's mane.

The most remarkable thing of all, people noted, was the total absence of tracks—even those of Snippy—within a 100-foot radius of the dead horse. Imprints in the ground seemed to show that two other horses had been running with Snippy up to a certain point, where they apparently veered off to race to the ranch house. Snippy's tracks appeared to continue a short distance beyond and then stop—approximately 100 feet short of the spot where his body lay.

In the flurry of news reports about the shocking case, it was said that the carcass was devoid of blood, spinal fluid, and brain tissue and that the internal organs were gone. It was also pointed out that although brain tissue is known to liquefy quickly in a warm climate, the September weather in the high valley was quite chilly. And except for two coyotes that came around the carcass a week after the horse was found, there was no evidence of scavengers. Furthermore, the idea that birds, ants, and other predators would feed only on the neck and head seemed preposterous.

References were made to UFO sightings in the area. Was it possible that Snippy was a UFO casualty? The Aerial Phenomena Research Organization (APRO) sent Don Richmond of Pueblo, Colorado, to look into the matter. Neither his investigation nor the laboratory tests that were made provided answers—or even a clue—as to the cause of Snippy's death.

A month went by before a thorough postmortem examination was made of the carcass. The veterinarian, Dr. Robert O. Adams of the College of Veterinary Medicine and Biomedical Science at Colorado State University, said that he found nothing unusual about the internal organs being missing: small scavengers commonly burrow into a carcass through one of the body's apertures to devour those parts. The blood, he pointed out, had simply coagulated, and the brain tissues had liquefied and evaporated in the normal course of decomposition.

But Dr. Adams did find evidence of a bad infection in the horse's right flank and indications that the skin by the shoulder "had been incised." He speculated that perhaps someone had come upon the horse in agonizing pain and had cut its throat to end its misery. Natural predators, Dr. Adams said, could have done the rest.

Soon afterward the carcass was given to Dr. Wallace Leary, a private veterinarian in Alamosa. Working on the skeleton, Dr. Leary was startled to discover wounds in the pelvic bone that were undoubtedly bullet holes. Convinced that the animal had been shot, he theorized that the horse had proceeded to run himself to death and had torn through a barbed wire fence, which inflicted the wounds found on the body.

Snippy's skeleton was put on display in the Luther Bean Museum at Adams State College in Alamosa. The true story of how the horse died remains unknown. (*Esquire,* 84:64, December 1975; *Penthouse,* 12:121–22, September 1980; Kenneth M. Rommel, Jr., *Operation Animal Mutilation,* pp.172–75; Ronald D. Story, ed., *Encyclopedia of UFO's,* pp.338–39)

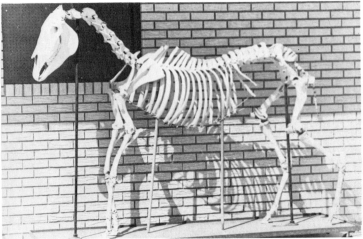

The mutilated carcass of the horse Snippy, whose skeleton is shown above, was discovered on ground devoid of tracks. No explanation was found for the manner of his death.

Geometric Surgery
In the fall of 1974 a Minnesota farmer came upon a dead cow in his fields and found that the udder, the sexual organs, and one ear were missing. According to the farmer, the udder had been removed by a diamond-shaped incision. (*Esquire,* 84:62, December 1975)

Unwanted Visitations
Many western farmers had the notion that extraterrestrials in spaceships were responsible for the cattle crimes, and numerous sightings of UFO's in areas where mutilations were reported seemed to confirm their suspicion. Early in 1975 near Copperas Cove, Texas, for instance, an orange light was seen hovering over farmland on the night that a calf was mutilated. Some witnesses said they had observed shafts of bluish-white light passing from a UFO to the ground.

An examination of the mutilation site was made by officials of the Texas Department of Public Safety. They found that the vegetation around the dead calf had been curiously flattened into leaf-shaped patterns arranged in concentric circles, as though under the impact of a strong blast of air from above. About 40 yards away from the dead calf the same leaf-shaped marks appeared in a circular area some 30 feet in diameter. (Michael D. Albers, *The Terror,* pp.54–55)

Double Strike
At Whiteface, Texas, in an area where UFO's had been reported for weeks in early 1975, police examined a mutilated heifer that rancher Darwood Marshall had found lying within a 30-foot circle of flattened vegetation on March 10. The animal's neck was twisted so that its head pointed grotesquely to the sky, its tongue and external organs were missing, and its navel appeared to have been cored out. No traces of blood were found on the ground near the calf.

A few days earlier Marshall had discovered a mutilated steer lying in a circle of scorched young wheat. Sheriff Richards tested the site for radiation, got a positive reading, and enlisted the help of experts at Reese Air Force Base. Their tests revealed that radiation at the site was one-half of 1 percent higher than normal—not a dramatic or dangerous difference. But why was there a difference at all, Sheriff Richards wanted to know, and just what had scorched that circle of wheat? (Michael D. Albers, *The Terror,* pp.55–56)

The Blue Valise
While crossing his land one day in late summer 1975, a Colorado rancher spied a blue plastic valise on the ground. Opening it, he found a cow's ear, a tongue, and a scalpel. This seemed to be the first clue to tie in with what many ranchers had begun to suspect: that satanic cultists were responsible for the cattle mutilations.

According to Carl Whiteside, the Colorado Bureau of Investigation officer, many mutilated bodies of livestock were sent to the veterinary school at Colorado State University, but only six "were fresh enough to be amenable to autopsy." Although all six had died of natural causes, it was believed that five of them had been mutilated afterward by human beings.

Whiteside, who had recently returned from a meeting attended by 300 ranchers in Kiowa, Elbert County, said that the Colorado men

> were literally up in arms. . . . The thing that's puzzling and frightening to them is that somebody can get onto their ranch and actually cut up an animal and leave no trace. What we're afraid of is that we're going to have a homicide on our hands. A person runs out of gas, wanders onto a ranch and

the next thing you know these people who are spooked become involved in a murder. (*Esquire*, 84:65, December 1975)

Aerial Delivery?

Although no direct evidence was found to link helicopter sightings with cattle mutilation, many ranchers were convinced that aircraft of some kind must be involved because the dead cattle often seemed to have fallen from a height.

In August 1975 Sheriff W. L. McDonald of Washington County, Colorado, told reporters that he had examined a mutilated heifer that appeared to have been dropped from a height of several feet into a pond. In Park County, Colorado, two mutilated cows were discovered in a pasture the gate to which was padlocked. According to Sheriff Norman Howey, the cows "couldn't possibly have been where they were found unless they had been dropped from aircraft." There were no strange tracks near the bodies. (Michael D. Albers, *The Terror*, p.59; Fredrick W. Smith, *Cattle Mutilation: The Unthinkable Truth*, p.16)

The Hooded People in Black

A forestry service employee reported seeing several people in hooded black robes near Cove Creek in Blaine County, Idaho, one day in September 1975. The following day a number of mutilated cattle were found in the area, and police launched an unsuccessful search for the supposed cultists. On October 9 a motorist told police that he had been driving along U.S. Highway 95 in northern Idaho at about 3:30 A.M. when he encountered some 15 masked people forming a roadblock with linked arms. He managed to turn his car around and escape. (Michael D. Albers, *The Terror*, pp.86–87)

A Square Cut

On October 21, 1975, a 1,500-pound bison was found dead in its enclosure at the Cheyenne Mountain Zoo, in Colorado. One ear and the udder had been cut off, the genitals were mutilated, and a 24-inch-square section of hide had been removed. The only tracks found around the carcass were those of the other animals in the pen, which maintained altogether some 50 bison and 10 American elk. "There's no doubt," said zoo director Dan Davis, "the animal was mutilated with some sort of sharp instrument handled by man."

An autopsy was performed on the bison by Dr. Rodney C. Walker, the zoo's veterinarian. His examination ruled out an attack by predators and failed to reveal any signs of a fatal disease. It did, however, uncover one curious fact: the blood of the dead animal was abnormally thin, as though an anticoagulant had been administered. "It was very, very strange," Dr.

Walker said, "There was an excessive amount of serosanguinous (blood-tinged) fluid in the abdominal and thoracic cavities and the fluid had seeped into the body tissue and even into the eyeballs."

The corpse was also examined by the El Paso county coroner, Dr. Raoul W. Urich. He found that the two-foot-square section of hide had been removed without damage to the underlying tissue. "The cutting was done neatly, cleanly, obviously with a very sharp instrument. The dissection was of the type that would eliminate any type of predator. . . . It was better than I could do if I were trying. It was really an expert job." Dr. Urich further noted that the body was found not more than 24 hours after the animal's death; the night had been cold, retarding decomposition, and the carcass was therefore in good condition when the autopsy was performed. (Fredrick W. Smith, *Cattle Mutilation: The Unthinkable Truth*, pp.11–12)

Tracks of the Unknown

A "mysterious trail of suction cup-like impressions" caught the attention of the cattle inspector and law enforcement officer investigating a typical case of cattle mutilation in Rio Arriba County, New Mexico. The incident, involving a three-year-old cow missing its sexual organs, tongue, and one ear, was reported June 13, 1976, by a rancher in the Dulce area.

The June 15 issue of *The Albuquerque Tribune* stated that the indentations were tripodlike, about 4 inches in diameter and 28 inches apart from each other. The tracks terminated about 500 feet from the dead animal, according to the law officer, "as if they had landed at that point, gone to the cow and then returned to that point." The day after the investigators had visited the site, the article continued, the rancher had returned and "found more depressions on top of the tire tracks made by his truck the day before." Several similar incidents were to occur in the Dulce area in 1978. (*The Albuquerque Tribune*, June 15, 1976; Kenneth M. Rommel, Jr., *Operation Animal Mutilation*, pp.12–13)

A Tidy UFOnaut?

A dead bull "with parts of its body lying neatly severed nearby" was found early one morning in 1976 by Manuel Gomez as he drove across his ranch near the town of Dulce, New Mexico.

Perplexed, Gomez went into town to get state police officer Gabe Valdez. Returning to the bull a while later, the two of them discovered that the severed pieces were gone and that other pieces had been removed from the carcass as well. Gomez also saw "pod-like tracks over his truck tire tracks."

Arriving at the ranch field within 48 hours of the "killing," Howard Burgess, a professional photographer and a writer for *Popular Mechanics* and *Prevention* magazines, shot a roll of black-and-white film on the site. To his astonishment, 2 of the 20 photos, "taken nine frames apart, show two little round spots about midway up in the sky. The relationship of one spot to the other changes from one picture to the other." The other snapshots on the roll show only "a blank sky above the field where the mutilated animal was found." The spots in the sky, Burgess said, were not visible to the naked eye. "It could very well be a flaw in the film, but I've never had that happen before." (The *Albuquerque News*, February 21, 1979)

New Mexico's state police were puzzled by the lack of footprints around the mutilated cattle carcasses they investigated. Here they view a cow found dead in 1978.

The round spots in the sky were not visible to the naked eye when he took this picture, says Howard Burgess. Some suspected a connection with the strange deaths of cattle.

A Preference for Ears

Something had been eating the ears off living hogs, reported *The Jasper County News* in Mississippi, in January 1977. One victim, belonging to Joseph Dickson of the Nazarene Community, had had its ears sheared off so cleanly that the job might have been done with scissors. The next night another hog was attacked in a pen, and a third hog the night following. On the third night, Dickson saw an animal in the pen; it was bigger than the biggest German shepherd, he said, and could jump farther than any dog in the world. A week later Calvin Martin, a neighbor, found that the ears of one of his sows had been pulled out by the roots. (*The Jasper County News*, January 12 and 19, 1977)

Something Else!

"Whether it's human or something else, they cut that animal and it was not a cow or horse or predator that left those tracks," swore the investigating officer who declared he was "confused as hell." The victim was an 11-month-old bull found dead and minus its sexual organs and rectum on April 24, 1978. Its owner happened to be the same rancher from Dulce, New Mexico,

who had reported a mutilated cow two years earlier.

According to the story carried in the *Albuquerque Journal*, the tracks were similar to those found on the ranch in 1976. Various people in the area claimed they saw strange lights in the sky at the supposed time of the incident, and the officer of the Department of Game and Fish reported "a large orange light in the darkness along a ridge directly south of the meadow." (Kenneth M. Rommel, Jr., *Operation Animal Mutilation*, p.14)

Menacing Helicopters

On the night of April 8, 1979, two Apache tribal officers were on patrol duty not far from Dulce, New Mexico, when they saw a mysterious aircraft "hovering about 50 feet off the ground with a powerful spotlight aimed at the cattle." A third police officer in the area also observed the craft, which, he said, "had to be connected with a series of 16 recent cattle mutilations in the Dulce area." The craft was never identified, but one person said he understood that the U.S. military had developed a comparatively quiet jet-powered helicopter to use in Vietnam, and suggested it was one of those.

Five years prior to this sighting, on July 15, 1974, a white helicopter and a black twin-engine aircraft were seen by Robert Smith, Jr. The helicopter opened fire on Smith while he was driving a tractor on his farm in Honey Creek, Iowa, not far from the Nebraska border. Neither craft had registration marks (which are required by law), and police were unable to trace them.

The presence and aggressive behavior of unmarked helicopters near numerous sites of mutilation increased the apprehension of many ranchers that cultists were collecting the organs and blood of dead cattle to use in their rituals. (Michael D. Albers, *The Terror*, pp.13–15; Kenneth M. Rommel, Jr., *Operation Animal Mutilation*, pp.22–23; Fredrick W. Smith, *Cattle Mutilation*, p.21)

Cattle Mutilation—An Explanation?

Troubled ranchers in more than a dozen states were hard put to explain the rash of cattle mutilations that were reported during the 1970's. Those who were convinced that it was not done by predators suggested that it was the work of unknown agencies, such as religious or satanic cultists, extraterrestrial beings, or even the U.S. military, suspected of carrying out secret tests on the animals in the middle of the night.

In 1979 U.S. senator Harrison Schmitt of New Mexico obtained a public hearing to investigate the hundreds of unexplained, yet remarkably similar, livestock deaths that plagued his state and others in the 1970's.

In the spring of 1979 U.S. senator Harrison Schmitt of New Mexico convened a public hearing in Albuquerque to look into the problem. As a result, a grant of $44,000 was obtained from the U.S. Law Enforcement Assistance Administration to investigate.

In charge of the investigation was Kenneth M. Rommel, Jr., a former FBI agent with a reputation for shrewdness and hard-nosed competence. In the course of his investigation he and his associates examined 27 supposed mutilations that occurred in New Mexico during that period, reviewed the reports of 90 earlier mutilations, and sought the help of governors, law agencies, and veterinarians in other states.

The classic mutilation case, Rommel found, involved, among other features, the removal by "precision surgery" of parts of the dead animal (the sexual organs, one eye, one ear, the tongue, and—with female animals—the udder), a seemingly cored rectum ("as though a large cookie cutter" had been used), and the lack of blood in the carcass.

At the end of a year's work he stated that all the mutilations he had investigated were "consistent with what one would expect to find with normal predation, scavenger activity, and normal decomposition of a dead animal." He believed this would be true for "a good many of the other reported mutilations."

The predator-scavenger explanation may be summarized as follows: In the first place, scavengers habitually take the external organs and other soft parts of a carcass before any other simply because they are accessible. Some predators—coyotes, for instance—have teeth that can shear flesh very cleanly, helping to create an impression of "surgical precision," and blowflies, picking over the wounds made by other scavengers, can clean up ragged edges in a way that further enhances the surgical effect.

Similarly, the cored-rectum effect was attributed to a combination of scavenger activity and the processes of bodily decomposition. As for the reported absence of blood, which many ranchers believed had been deliberately drained from the animals, this also was shown to be natural—the blood in a dead animal drains by gravity to the lowest parts of the body and coagulates there. And in cases where one eye or one ear was missing, Rommel pointed out that these had been removed from the side of the animal lying uppermost and hence accessible.

Finally, Rommel claimed, witnesses had often been highly inaccurate in their accounts. But how could this be, when so many of the witnesses were veteran ranchers, well used to finding dead cattle and seeing the results of scavenging and predation? According to sociology professor James R. Stewart of the University of South Dakota, the cattle mutilation story was one of collective delusion, fostered by strain, anxiety, and confusing statements by veterinarians and police officers and provoked in part by the public interest in stories of gore, mystery, and conspiracy.

Rommel's predator theory, however, gains a good deal of its force by ignoring certain pieces of evidence that have been described as calling cards.

Ignored, for instance, is the case of the bison mutilated at Cheyenne Mountain Zoo in 1975: a 24-inch-square piece of hide had been removed without damaging the underlying tissue. This was only one of several instances in which carcasses showed square, clean-cut incisions. The point, of course, is that predators do not take their meals geometrically and do not usually ignore the flesh beneath the hide.

Also difficult to explain away is the finding in 1975 by Sheriff George Yarnell of Elbert County, Colorado, of an udder whose natural contents had been removed and replaced with sand. And in February 1976, also in Colorado, the discovery of a mutilated calf with radar chaff stuffed in its mouth. The chaff, which resembled the tinsel that planes drop to confuse enemy radar, was said to be similar to the material used by the air force.

And yet, according to the predator explanation, the ranchers and cattlemen's associations have all been mistaken, and their testimony has been discounted. The divergent views are well expressed by an exchange between a rancher and Rommel. Adhering to his own theories, the rancher argued, "[If] coyotes did that, they did it with knives." To which Rommel replied, "I say that if surgeons did it, they did it with their teeth."

101

The Mounties Aren't Talking

The Royal Canadian Mounted Police of Calgary, Alberta, became fairly certain that a cult was mutilating cattle in their area. During their investigation of three cases in June 1980, they stated that two of the carcasses showed "characteristics of those observed last fall," from which the external organs had been removed. The Canadian Mounties would not give the location of the three cases or cite any further details.* (*The New York Times*, June 5, 1980)

DEMONS AND EXORCISM

For reasons unknown, perfectly normal people sometimes suddenly exhibit a dramatic change of being. Their actions become violent and seemingly inhuman. They may expel foul substances, utter shocking profanities, make strange animal sounds, and distort their bodies in extraordinary ways. In some circles such actions are considered to be evidence of possession by the Devil, for which the only antidote is the ritual of exorcism.

The Devil's Contortions

In 1865 something ghastly entered the lives of two young boys in the small town of Illfurth, in Alsace, France. They were Joseph and Theobald Bruner, nearly 8 and 10 years old respectively, the sons of a farmer. According to records kept by Father Karl Brey, the parish priest, the first signs that something was seriously wrong with the children were their fascination with diabolic things and their aversion to anything of a religious nature:

> While lying in their bed, the children used to turn to the wall, paint horrible Devil faces on it, and then speak to the faces and play with them. If, while one of the possessed was asleep, a rosary was placed on his bed, he would immediately hide under the covers and refuse to come out of hiding until the rosary was removed.

More extraordinary were the physical contortions the boys underwent.

> [They] entangled their legs every two or three hours in an unnatural way. They knotted them so intricately that it was impossible to pull them apart. And yet, suddenly, they could untangle them with lightning speed. At times the boys stood simultaneously on their heads and legs, bent backwards, their bodies arched high. No amount of outside pressure could bring their bodies into a normal position—until the Devil saw fit to give these objects of his torture some temporary peace.

By these and other bizarre manifestations Father Brey was persuaded that the brothers were the victims of demonic possession.

> At times, their bodies became bloated as if about to burst; when this happened, the boy would vomit, whereby yellow foam, feathers, and seaweed would come out of his mouth. Often, their clothes were covered with evil smelling feathers. . . .
>
> No matter how often their shirts and outer clothing were changed, new feathers and seaweed would appear. These feathers, which covered their bodies in some inexplicable way, filled the air with such a stench that they had to be burned. . . .

If further evidence that the boys were in the grip of a supernatural power had been needed, it was given in their frequent displays of clairvoyance.

> Theobald several times predicted the death of a person correctly. Two hours before the death of a Frau Müller, the boy knelt by his bed and acted as if he were ringing a mourning bell. Another time he did the same thing for a whole hour. When he was asked for whom he was ringing, the boy answered, "For Gregor Kunegel." As it happened, Kunegel's daughter was visiting in the house. Shocked and angry, she told Theobald, "You liar, my father is not even ill. He is working on the new boys' seminary building as a mason." Theobald answered, "That may be, but he just had a fall. Go ahead and check on it!" The facts bore him out. The man had fallen from a scaffold, breaking his neck. This happened at the very moment that Theobald made the bell-ringing motions. No one in Illfurth had been aware of the accident.

When their parents and Father Karl Brey decided that exorcism was the only effective way of helping the boys, Theobald was sent to the St. Charles Orphanage at Schiltigheim near Strasbourg. The orphanage was run by nuns, and its superior was one Father Stumpf. For the first three days after his arrival, Theobald—or the diabolic entity—was silent, but on the fourth day he said, "I have come and I am in a rage." One of the nuns asked, "And who are you?" A nonhuman voice answered: "I am the Lord of Darkness!" Later on Joseph was also sent to the orphanage.

Throughout the prolonged period of exorcism, performed by Father Stumpf, the demonic possession of the two brothers was manifested in many ways. Both boys, for instance, became infested with red head lice, which multiplied so quickly that three or four people with brushes and combs were not able to keep pace with them. Eventually, the priest poured holy water on the vermin, and they disappeared.

In all, the possession of Theobald and Joseph Bruner lasted four years before they were freed by the rites of exorcism. Theobald died two years later, on April 3, 1871, when he was 16. Joseph, in whom the symptoms had been less severe, died in 1882. (*Demon Children*, Martin Ebon, ed., pp.131–39)

102

Exorcising the Devil

Saint Wolfgang of Regensburg, a 10th-century German bishop, is portrayed confronting the Devil, believed to have the power to interfere in daily life.

A Pact With Satan

When Clara Germana Cele was 16 years old, she made a pact with Satan—or so she told her confessor, Father Erasmus Hörner, at the mission school she had attended since she was four years old. In the weeks following her confession, Germana began to behave wildly, and on August 20, 1906, she alarmed the sisters in charge by tearing her clothes, breaking one of the posts on her bed, growling and grunting like an animal, and seeming to converse with invisible beings. In a more lucid moment she called out: "Sister, please call Father Erasmus. I must confess and tell everything. But quick, quick, or Satan will kill me. He has me in his power! Nothing blessed is with me; I have thrown away all the medals you gave me." Later that day she again called out: "You have betrayed me. You have promised me days of glory, but now you treat me cruelly."

Until these outbursts began, the priests and nuns of the Marianhill Order mission school in Umzinto, about 50 miles south of Durban, South Africa, had considered Germana a normal, healthy, although somewhat erratic young person. As her condition worsened, Germana began to manifest the signs by which the Roman Catholic Church identifies cases of demonic possession. Holy water, for example, burned her when she was sprinkled with it or given it to drink, but when she was sprinkled with ordinary water with which the font had secretly been filled, she simply laughed. She complained vigorously whenever a cross was brought near her and could detect the presence of a religious object, such as a small fragment of a cross, even when it had been heavily wrapped or otherwise concealed.

Germana also developed a more wide-ranging clairvoyance. She was able to describe the daily details of a priest's journey from Africa to Rome, including the addresses of the places where he stayed along the way. And, to shame one young man who made fun of her, she revealed scandalous details of his private life, complete with dates, times, and names.

Among Germana's physical manifestations, her confessor reported numerous instances of levitation:

> Germana floated often three, four, and up to five feet in the air, sometimes vertically, with her feet downward, and at other times horizontally, with her whole body floating above her bed. She was in a rigid position. Even her clothing did not fall downward, as would have been normal; instead, her dresses remained tightly attached to her body and legs. If she was sprinkled with holy water, she moved down immediately, and her clothing fell loosely onto her bed. This type of the phenomenon took place in the presence of witnesses, including outsiders. Even in church, where she could be seen by everyone, she floated above her seat. Some people tried to pull her down forcibly, holding on to her feet, but it proved to be impossible.

Another curious physical capacity that astonished the attending priests and nuns was her ability to transform herself into a snakelike creature. Her whole body would become as flexible as rubber, and she would writhe along the floor. At times her neck seemed to elongate, thereby enhancing the serpentlike impression she gave. Once, while she was being restrained, she darted, like lightning, at a nun kneeling in front of her and bit the poor woman on the arm. The wound showed the marks of Germana's teeth and a small red puncture resembling a snakebite.

On September 10, 1906, permission for Germana's exorcism was given, to be performed by Father Erasmus, her confessor, and by Father Mansuet, the mission rector. The rites began in the morning, lasted till noon, began again at 3 P.M., and continued well into the night. The next morning they began at 8 and lasted until 10. Under fierce pressure from the two exorcists, the possessing demon said that he would signal his departure by an act of levitation; this occurred before 170 witnesses in the mission chapel. Prayers of thanks were later given.

In January 1907, while Father Erasmus was away, Germana suffered a relapse and made a new pact with the Devil. On April 24 a new exorcism began. It lasted for two days and was successful, the Devil's final departure being signaled by an incomparably foul smell. (*Demon Children*, Martin Ebon, ed., pp.154–64; Adolf Rodewyk, *Possessed by Satan*, pp.120–27)

The Demon's Daughter

The victim of one of the most detailed instances of demonic possession in 20th-century America was a midwestern woman whose real name was never made public. As a child she had been notably pious, but when she was 14, blasphemous inner voices interfered with her religious practice, frightened her, and caused her much shame. In the years that followed she was examined by several doctors. Finding no physical illness or abnormality, they unanimously concluded that her personality was neither nervous nor hysterical—she was "normal in the fullest sense."

Despite this diagnosis, Mary (a pseudonym) began to manifest the recognized signs of demonic possession. She would become furiously enraged and would foam at the mouth when a priest blessed her, and could infallibly tell when an object had been secretly blessed or sprinkled with holy water. She also understood languages she had never been taught.

In 1928, when she was 40 years old, Mary agreed to undergo exorcism. Her exorcist was to be Father Theophilus Riesinger, a 60-year-old Capuchin monk in the community of St. Anthony, at Marathon, Wisconsin, a man with considerable experience in the application of the ancient rite. For the place of exorcism, Father Theophilus chose a Franciscan convent in Earling, Iowa, where the pastor, Father Joseph Steiger, was an old friend of his.

On her first night in the convent, Mary became furious when she realized that holy water had been sprinkled on her food. She purred like a cat and refused to eat until unblessed food was put before her.

The next morning Father Theophilus and Father Steiger began the exorcism, for which a large room had been made ready. A number of nuns who were physically strong stood by to help, and Mary was laid on a mattress on an iron bed. The exorcism had scarcely begun when she became unconscious, with her eyes closed so tightly that they could not be forced open. They remained in this state throughout the service.

A shrill cry filled the room, loud but seemingly far-off at the same time. And then a din of howling, like wild animals, came from Mary's lips. "Silence, Satan!" Father Theophilus shouted, but the unearthly tortured clamor continued unabated.

Neither Father Steiger nor the nuns could long endure the howling or the sight of the woman's body and face, hideously twisted and distorted by the onslaught. From time to time they had to leave the room, but Father Theophilus, accustomed to the screaming of devils at the pain of exorcism, remained constant and attentive throughout.

Day after day the exorcism continued, and with it the howling, the twisted limbs, and excrement and vomit in vast quantities. Although the victim had taken only a spoonful of milk or water during the entire day to sustain her, she sometimes disgorged bowlfuls of what seemed to be shredded tobacco leaves or other unsavory materials.

At last Father Theophilus learned the names of the devils infesting his patient. One, calling himself Beelzebub, told him that Mary had been possessed since she was 14 and that she had been cursed by her own father, who had joined the company of possessing demons after his own death and damnation. This demon—Mary's father, Jacob—spoke with Father Theophilus, revealing that he had frequently tried to force his daughter into an incestuous relationship but that she had always resisted him and that he had uttered a curse that she be entered by devils to destroy her chastity. A female demon, who gave her name as Mina, in life Jacob's mistress, joined the colloquy. She was damned, she said, because she had murdered four of her own children. A fourth demon, Judas, confessed that he had intended to drive Mary to suicide.

Whatever was expressing itself in these voices at times demonstrated an uncanny knowledge of things that could not have been known to Mary. On one occasion, as a test, a piece of paper with a Latin inscription was placed on Mary's head. The nuns, thinking the words were a prayer, were surprised to see that the demons tolerated its presence. In fact, the words had no religious content at all; but when a second piece of paper, which had been secretly blessed, was placed on the woman's head, it was immediately torn to pieces.

As the painful weeks of exorcism continued, relations between the two priests deteriorated and Father Steiger began to wish he had never allowed the exorcism to take place in his parish. But Father Theophilus viewed this development as the work of the Devil, who seemed to regard Father Steiger with special malice.

"Just wait," a demonic voice said to Father Steiger one day, "until the end of the week! When Friday comes, then . . ."

On his way back from visiting a sick parishioner on Friday, Father Steiger, remembering the demon's threat, drove with special care. Suddenly, just as he was about to cross a bridge over a deep ravine, a black cloud seemed to descend on his car. He could see nothing, but he felt the car smash violently into the railing of the bridge and then teeter on the edge. A farmer plowing a nearby field heard the crash and came running. Slowly, the pastor crawled out of the debris. He had no serious injuries despite the fact that even the car's steering wheel had been crushed.

When he reached the convent, a chorus of malicious laughter greeted him in the exorcism room.

"Today," the demon screeched, "he pulled in his proud neck and was outpointed! I certainly showed him up today. What about your new auto, that dandy car that was smashed to smithereens? It served you right!"

Was it true, the nuns and Father Theophilus asked?

"Yes, what he says is true. My auto is a complete wreck. But he was not able to harm me personally."

"Our aim was to get you," the demon said, "but somehow our plans were thwarted. It was your powerful patron saint [Saint Joseph] who prevented us from harming you."

(During these and all other conversations, the lips of the possessed woman did not move at all—she was unconscious, and her lips almost never parted. The voices seemed to come from within her.)

For two weeks the solemn exorcism was repeated without any sign of success. Father Theophilus decided to continue the exorcisms throughout the night, giving Satan (and himself) no respite. For three days and nights he prayed, but the demons held their ground; by the 23rd day Father Theophilus was near collapse. But now a change began to occur in the demons' behavior. They were less aggressive and more apt to moan about the tortures the exorcism inflicted on them. Then, after Father Theophilus had demanded in the name of the Trinity that the demons depart, they agreed.

On December 23 at about 9 P.M., the possessed woman broke free from the grip of her attendants and stood before them. "Pull her down! Pull her down!" Father Steiger cried, while Father Theophilus blessed her and declaimed, "Depart ye fiends of hell! Begone, Satan! The Lion of Juda reigns!"

Then the stiffness left Mary's body and she fell onto the bed. A sound arose, so piercing that the room vibrated, and then a babble of voices, repeating the names "Beelzebub, Judas, Jacob, Mina," again and again, more and more faintly until, with the final words "Hell—hell—hell!" they disappeared.

Then, Mary sat up, opened her eyes and quietly smiled. "My Jesus, Mercy!" she said. "Praised be Jesus Christ!" (*Exorcism: Fact Not Fiction*, Martin Ebon, ed., pp.212–45; Rev. John J. Nicola, *Diabolical Possession and Exorcism*, pp.126–31)

A Tragic Case

In November 1973 Anneliese Michel, a young student at the University of Würzburg, West Germany, was taken by her parents to see the parish priest in her hometown of Klingenberg. She had developed some worrisome signs of abnormal behavior at the university—refusing to eat, flying into violent rages, screaming, and trying to attack those around her—and her parents were deeply concerned.

In the priest's view, Anneliese was possessed by demons, and he recommended a ritual exorcism. As Roman Catholic procedure requires, the case was investigated by a leading authority on exorcism and demonic possession, Father Adolf Rodewyk, an 81-year-old Jesuit. Father Rodewyk agreed with the priest's diagnosis, and on his recommendation the regional bishop, Father Josef Stangl, gave permission for the exorcism to take place. The exorcists chosen for the task were the Reverend Arnold Renz and the Reverend Ernst Alt. By then Anneliese had been receiving medical treatment for epilepsy for four years.

On July 1, 1976, after several months of exorcism, Anneliese died of malnutrition and dehydration at the age of 23. She weighed 70 pounds. On March 2, 1978, the two exorcists and Anneliese's parents were charged with negligent homicide, on the grounds that they had allowed the young girl's condition to deteriorate to the point of death without seeking medical help for her. Bishop Stangl and Father Rodewyk, who seem not to have known that medical help was being withheld, were not charged. In April 1978 the two priests were found guilty and were given suspended prison sentences of six months.

For the Roman Catholic Church, the death of Anneliese Michel was a nightmare come true, demonstrating the dangers inherent in the ritual of exorcism and the murky distinctions between priestly and medical responsibility. In Father Rodewyk's own handbook on possession and exorcism, originally published in 1963 and translated into English under the title *Possessed by Satan*, priests are urged to consider medical explanations for apparent possession. One section of the book,

Attempts to drive out demons possessing Anneliese Michel of Germany ended in tragedy when medical attention was withheld during the exorcism. The Roman Catholic Church in Germany now requires that a physician be present whenever an exorcism is performed.

in fact, is titled "Let's Not Always Think of Possession!" Father Rodewyk, outlining the bishop's responsibilities, says that he "may appoint a commission of theologians and physicians to undertake a further investigation" and warns that the exorcists "must guard against playing the role of physician when encountering physiological symptoms." He quotes the authoritative Roman Ritual (of exorcism): "The exorcist should avoid giving or recommending any sort of medication to the possessed; that is the physician's task." Although such statements clearly suggest that a physician may sometimes be needed before and during an exorcism, there is no

Possession, Epilepsy, or Hysteria?

As far as many doctors and psychiatrists are concerned, the diagnosis of demonic possession is one that reeks of medieval superstition and ignorance, and the symptoms that lead to it are subject either to a wide range of medical and psychiatric interpretations or to being dismissed as misperceptions or hallucinations.

Other medical and psychological conditions likely to produce symptoms confused with those of possession are epilepsy, hysteria, and multiple personality. During a convulsive seizure, a person with epilepsy can experience extreme muscular rigidity and foam at the mouth and is sometimes subject to rapid back-and-forth head movements. The face may be distorted, and strange, guttural noises may be produced by a spasm of the throat muscles. During the period immediately before a seizure, the patient may experience auditory and visual hallucinations and various sensory distortions. Most seizures last no more than five minutes.

All these symptoms may also be present in a person diagnosed by the church as suffering from possession. But there are distinguishing characteristics. The first of these is that a demonic attack can continue for many hours. Extreme liveliness, rather than rigidity, is characteristic and muscular reflexes tend to be strong. According to the Roman Ritual, other signs of possession include "the ability to speak with some familiarity in a strange tongue or to understand it when spoken by another; the faculty of divulging future and hidden events; and the display of powers which are beyond the subject's age and natural condition."

Hysteria also produces many of the symptoms of possession. The following description of a female hysteric was recorded at the turn of the century by Prof. Paul Richter, a doctor at La Salpêtrière, a famous hospital in Paris for mental disturbances:

Suddenly, we heard loud cries and shouting. Her body, which went through a series of elaborate motions, was either in the throes of wild gyrations or catatonically motionless. Her legs became entangled, then disentangled, her arms twisted and disjointed, her wrists bent. Some of her fingers were stretched out straight, while others were twisted. The body was either bent in a semicircle or loose-limbed. Her head was at times thrown to the right or left or, when thrown backward with vehemence, seemed to emerge from a bloated neck. The face alternately mirrored horror, anger, and some times fury; it was bloated and showed shades of violet in its coloration. . . .

One of the most striking details in this description is that of the body "bent in a semicircle." This is also known as the hysterical arch and is frequently seen in cases of possession. All the other symptoms described above have been observed by exorcists. In addition, the appearance of livid marks on the skin—sometimes resembling bites, letters, or graphic symbols—are also known to be produced by hysterics. Given this partial duplication of symptoms, how does the church distinguish between hysteria and possession? The determining factor is the context in which the symptoms occur. If they arise in relationship with a hatred of religious objects, and if they are accompanied by paranormal phenomena (the ability to detect religious objects that have been hidden, to understand languages never learned, to levitate, and so on), the church is likely to consider them manifestations of the Devil.

As mysterious as hysteria, and as likely to be confused with possession, is the multiple personality, in which the patient may at different times manifest one, two, three, or even more different personalities—each with its own goals, likes, dislikes, speech patterns, and memories. Each personality may be indifferent or opposed to the others, or ignorant of them. If one or more should have a diabolic cast, the church has no means of determining whether to treat the case as possession other than the criteria it applies to distinguish hysteria from possession.

Those criteria are the hatred of religious objects and the paranormal phenomena referred to earlier, and they are precisely the phenomena that many doctors and psychiatrists are likely to reject as misperceptions or hallucinations on the part of witnesses. Those less skeptical, on the other hand, are likely to view such things as parapsychological but not as the work of demons. Again, the church's test is likely to be whether or not the paranormal manifestations occur in the context of a general hatred of religion.

stipulation that a doctor *must* be in attendance.

This deficiency in church procedure was corrected, at least in Germany, after the conviction of the two priests in the Michel case. In May 1978 the German Bishops' Conference ruled that in the future no exorcisms would be permitted unless a doctor was present. (*The New York Times*, August 8, 1976; Adolf Rodewyk, *Possessed by Satan*, pp.11–20; *Time*, 111:80–81, August 8, 1978)

THE SPEAR OF THOUGHT

In many primitive societies there is the belief that, by some means of accepted ritual, a hex or curse can be leveled against an individual. And unless the curse is ritually canceled, the dire predictions of pain, injury, or death will be fulfilled.

Retroactive Magic

While he was in the Congo in 1682, the Italian missionary Father Jerome Merolla da Sorrento heard a curious story demonstrating the sometimes fatal effects of superstitious fear. During a journey a young black man had spent the night at a friend's house, and in the morning the friend had prepared a wild hen for breakfast. This was a food that young people were forbidden to eat, by inviolable tribal custom, and the visitor asked his friend if the dish he had prepared was really wild hen. The host replied that it was not, and the young guest ate a hearty breakfast.

A few years later the two men met again, and the friend asked his former guest if he would eat a wild hen. No, he said, that was impossible—he had been solemnly warned by a magician never to eat that food. The friend laughed and asked why he should refuse to eat the dish now, when he had been perfectly happy to eat it before. As soon as the guest learned the truth about the breakfast his host had once served him, he began to tremble violently and within 24 hours was dead, the victim of his own fear. (*American Anthropologist*, New Series 44:169–70, April–June 1942)

A Dramatic Reversal

The active ill effects of a curse can immediately cease if the victim believes that he has been released from it. This indicates that the effects of curses, as recorded since ancient times, are psychosomatic (see page 109) and thus in accord with relatively recent physiological discoveries. The following incident, which occurred in Australia around 1919, was later reported by Dr. S. M. Lambert during his association with the International Health Division of the Rockefeller Foundation. An example of a dramatic reversal, it makes the point:

> At a Mission at Mona Mona in North Queensland were many native converts, but on the outskirts of the Mission was a group of non-converts including

one Nebo, a famous witch doctor. The chief helper of the missionary was Rob, a native who had been converted. When Dr. Lambert arrived at the Mission he learned that Rob was in distress and that the missionary wanted him examined. Dr. Lambert made the examination, and found no fever, no complaint of pain, no symptoms or signs of disease. He was impressed, however, by the obvious indications that Rob was seriously ill and extremely weak. From the missionary he learned that Rob had had a bone pointed at him by Nebo and was convinced that in consequence he must die. Thereupon Dr. Lambert and the missionary went for Nebo, threatened him sharply that his supply of food would be shut off if anything happened to Rob and that he and his people would be driven away from the Mission. At once Nebo agreed to go with them to see Rob. He leaned over Rob's bed and told the sick man that it was all a mistake, a mere joke—indeed, that he had not pointed a bone at him at all. The relief, Dr. Lambert testifies, was almost instaneous [*sic*]; that evening Rob was back at work, quite happy again, and in full possession of his physical strength. [*American Anthropologist*, New Series 44:170–71, April–June 1942]

A Prophecy Self-fulfilled

On a Friday the 13th in 1946, a Georgia midwife was called upon to deliver three babies in the same area of the Okefenokee Swamp. For some malevolent reason, the woman put a curse on all three of the infant girls.

She said that one would die before she was 16 years of age, another would be dead before she reached 21, and the third would not live to see her 23rd birthday. The first two predictions were violently accurate. One girl, at 15, was in a fatal automobile accident. The second was killed by gunfire in a nightclub brawl the night before her 21st birthday.

Two years later, in 1969, the third young woman asked to enter a Baltimore hospital, declaring hysterically that she was doomed to die before her 23rd birthday, which was only three days away. Although there was apparently nothing wrong with her physically, she was obviously under great emotional stress and was admitted to the hospital for observation.

The next morning, just two days before the fateful date, the girl was was found dead in her bed—the victim, evidently, of her belief in the power of the midwife's curse. (*Science Digest*, 80:45, August 1976)

The Relentless *Kurdaitcha*

In 1953 an aborigine named Kinjika was flown from his native Arnhem Land in Australia's Northern Territory to a hospital in Darwin, the territorial capital. He had not been injured or poisoned, was not suffering from any known disease, but he was dying. Kinjika survived

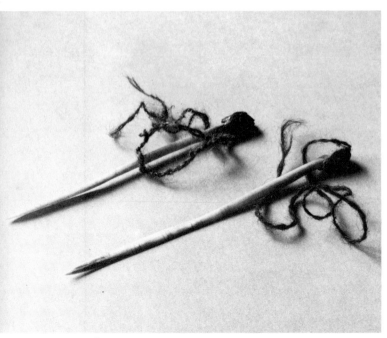

These carefully modeled implements, made of human bones and hair, are charged with psychic energy for bone pointing, a ritual execution practiced by Australian aborigines.

for four days in great pain after entering the hospital, and on the fifth day he died, the victim of bone pointing, a method of execution—or murder—that leaves no trace and almost never fails.

The dead man had been a member of the Mailli tribe and had broken one of its laws governing incestuous relationships. Following this he had been summoned before a tribal council, had refused to attend, and in his absence had been sentenced to death.

Kinjika then fled his homeland, and the tribal executioner, the *mulunguwa*, made and ritually "loaded" the killing-bone, or *kundela*.

The bone used may be human, kangaroo, or emu, or it may be fashioned from wood. The design varies from tribe to tribe. Most are from six to nine inches long, pointed at one end, and shaved to a smooth roundness. At the other end a braid of hair is attached through a hole or with a resinous gum derived from the spinifex bush. To be effective, the *kundela* must be charged with powerful psychic energy, in a complex ritual that must be performed faultlessly. The process is kept secret from women and all who are not members of the tribe. If the condemned man has fled from his village, the loaded bone is given to the *kurdaitcha*, the tribe's ritual killers.

The *kurdaitcha* take their name from the special slippers they wear when hunting a condemned man. These are woven from cockatoo feathers and human hair and leave virtually no footprints. The hunters clothe themselves with kangaroo hair, which they stick to their skin after first coating themselves with human blood, and they don masks of emu feathers. Usually operating in two's or three's, they are relentless and will pursue their quarry for years if necessary.

When the hunters finally corner their man, they approach to within 15 feet or so, and one *kurdaitcha*, or "hit man," dropping to his knee, holds the bone in his fist and points it like a pistol. At this instant, the condemned man is said to be frozen with fear. The *kurdaitcha* thrusts the bone toward him and utters a brief, piercing chant. He and his fellow hunters then withdraw, leaving the pointed man to his own devices. When they return to their village, the *kundela* is ceremonially burned.

The condemned man may live for several more days or weeks. But convinced of the *kundela's* fatal power, his relatives and members of any other tribe he may meet (who will certainly have heard that he has been pointed) treat him as though he were already dead.

The ritual loading of the *kundela* creates a psychic counterpart of the bone—a "spear of thought," as it has been described—which pierces the condemned man when the bone is pointed at him. Once he has been wounded, the victim's death is certain, as though an actual spear had been thrust through him. (John Godwin, *Unsolved: The World of the Unknown*, pp.163–76; Ronald Rose, *Living Magic*, pp.30–36)

The Song of Death (Almost)

In mid-April 1956, in Arnhem Land, Australia, a young aborigine named Lya Wulumu fell sick and was taken by airplane to a hospital in Darwin. He was unable to eat or drink because, although he tried, he could not swallow. There was, however, no apparent cause for his malady. Examinations, including X-rays, blood tests, and spinal taps, revealed nothing unusual.

What was going on in the victim's mind was another matter. He asked an attending Methodist minister to pray for him because, as he said, "me bin sung and me finish." The singing to which Wulumu referred is a form of ritual execution practiced by his people. In his case a group of women were requested by his mother-in-law to sing him to death, perhaps in reprisal for some taboo that he had broken.

To inaugurate the ritual the women stole Wulumu's spear and throwing stick (*woomera*) and put them in a ceremonial log. Then they sang the songs that are believed to put the curse of death on the owner of the captured objects. After the singing, his club (*nulla nulla*) was displayed in a treetop to signify the successful conclusion of the curse. When Wulumu saw the weapon, he knew what had transpired, and when he tried to swallow, he could not.

The Deadly Magic of Believing

From the days of ancient Egypt and Mesopotamia to modern times in Haiti, Australia, Africa, and elsewhere, healthy people have turned sick and died because a hex, curse, or spell was put upon them. There is a considerable body of literature on the subject.

The methods of declaring the curse are many and varied. It can be done by making an effigy of the victim and piercing it with pins or burning it. Wax, wood, clay, cloth, and straw have all been used for the purpose. Hair or fingernail parings from the victim can be ritually hexed. Chants and singing can declare a curse. Stones or weapons can be magically charged, or a container of magically endowed powders or herbs can be used to cast a spell.

Although methods differ, the magic works when there is sufficient belief in its power. The sorcerer must have absolute confidence in his powers, the victim must believe that his magic is unassailable, and the community at large must subscribe to the belief. The latter is especially important. One can imagine the effect in the cultures where the community looks upon the victim as dead from the moment the curse becomes known. The victim may cease to eat and drink (as befits the dead), which serves to hasten the end.

One well-documented method of killing by suggestion is "bone pointing," a form of ritual execution occasionally practiced by the aborigines of Australia. There is no physical contact with the victim, but his fate is usually as firmly sealed as if he were run through the heart with a spear.

The pointing weapon can be made of bone, wood, or stone. Belief in its magic is what counts. A graphic description of the effects of bone pointing is given in Dr. Herbert Basedow's book *The Australian Aboriginal,* published in 1925:

> A man who discovers that he is being boned by an enemy is, indeed, a pitiable sight. He stands aghast, with his eyes staring at the treacherous pointer, and with his hands lifted as though to ward off the lethal medium, which he imagines is pouring into his body. His cheeks blanch and his eyes become glassy, and the expression of his face becomes horribly distorted. . . . He attempts to shriek, but usually the sound chokes in his throat, and all one might see is froth at his mouth. His body begins to tremble and the muscles twist involuntarily. He sways backwards and falls to the ground, and for a short time appears to be in a swoon; but soon after he begins to writhe as if in mortal agony, and, covering his face with his hands, begin [sic] to moan. After a

while he becomes more composed and crawls to his wurley (hut). From this time onwards he sickens and frets, refusing to eat, and keeping aloof from the daily affairs of the tribe. Unless help is forthcoming in the shape of a counter-charm, administered by the hands of the "*Nangarri,*" or medicine-man, his death is only a matter of a comparatively short time. If the coming of the medicine-man is opportune, he might be saved.

A possible physiological explanation for the victim's response to bone pointing has been suggested. The consequences of extreme fear are similar to those of great rage: the adrenal glands increase their production of adrenalin, reducing the blood supply to the less essential parts of the body in order to ensure an adequate supply to the muscles, upon whose efficiency, for flight or fight, the life of the subject may depend. Adrenalin produces this result by constricting the small blood vessels in those parts of the body that can temporarily survive a reduced blood supply.

The advantage acquired in this way, however, is gained at some cost. When blood supply is reduced, so is the supply of oxygen, which is carried in the blood by the red corpuscles. When the fine capillary blood vessels are deprived of oxygen, they become more permeable to the blood plasma, which seeps into the tissue surrounding the blood vessel. The consequence of this, in a prolonged condition of fear or anger, is an overall reduction in the volume of circulating blood.

This, in turn, reduces the blood pressure, and a potentially disastrous cycle can then be established. The reduced blood pressure adversely affects those parts of the body responsible for maintaining the circulation of the blood, and the reduced circulation further reduces the blood pressure. This sequence of events, if unchecked, will be fatal.

That a hex, spell, or curse can rate such physiological disorders is mystery enough. Even more puzzling are cases of death in which medical examination reveals no evidence of either reduced blood pressure or an abnormal accumulation of red blood cells. One example is that of Kinjika, the Mailli tribesman whose death is described on pages 107–08. Another is a report by a Dr. P. S. Clarke concerning a Kanaka tribesman in North Queensland, Australia, who said that he was going to die soon because a spell had been put on him. The doctor's examinations revealed no medical problems, but a few days later the man was dead.

It would seem that in societies where the effects of a curse are accepted as common knowledge, there is no question that the spear of thought can kill.

Wulumu would surely have died had it not been for the iron lung. Because of its respiratory support capability he became convinced that the white man's magic was greater than that of his tribe. He was right. (John Godwin, *Unsolved: The World of the Unknown*, p.169; *The Times* [London], August 14, 1956)

A Mother's Curses
Not all curse-deaths take place in primitive places. The following events for example, occurred in Oklahoma in 1960. The case involved a man who had been raised by a very domineering mother. When he decided to open a nightclub, she helped him finance it and then stayed on to assist with the management.

Some 14 years later, at age 38, he married and soon after decided to sell the club. His mother warned that if he sold out, "something dire will happen to you."

Two days after her threat the man, with no prior history of respiratory trouble of any kind, began to experience a mild attack of asthma. Nevertheless, he went ahead and sold the club. The day after the transaction he called his mother to tell her about it. She once again told him that "Something will strike you." His asthmatic condition worsened at once, and he was rushed to the hospital.

A psychiatrist was able to help him see the link between his illness and his mother's warnings, and the asthmatic condition began to subside. Feeling better, the man began plans for another business, this time without his mother. Then one day, he called to tell her about it. She did not try to dissuade him but told him to expect more "dire results" if he persisted. Within an hour of that fateful phone call he had another attack of asthma and died. (*Psychosomatic Medicine*, 26:104-07, 1964)

Living on the Run
The *kundela* is used by the aborigines for initiation ceremonies, against enemies, and against those who have broken tribal laws. Within those spheres its power is awesome. There seems to be only one instance of a man surviving after being condemned to die by the bone without the antidote of white man's medicine.

The man, Alan Webb, a full-blooded aborigine of the Arunta tribe, had shot a fellow tribesman during a struggle over a rifle. In April 1969 the court found that Webb had been attacked and that the rifle had gone off accidentally. He was declared not guilty of the manslaughter charge. Outside the courtroom, after the verdict had been returned, Webb was met by a tribal delegation. The white men's court was irrelevant, he was told, and he would have to stand trial before his peers among the Arunta.

Webb knew very well what the tribe's verdict would be. He had killed a member of his own tribe; therefore,

he must die. He promptly left Alice Springs and was sentenced to death *in absentia* by the Aruntas.

This time the *kurdaitcha* had a more difficult task than usual. Their quarry was driving a van and living in it with his wife, two children, and three dogs. He slept with a rifle at his side, ready to be awakened at any moment by the barking of the dogs.

By 1976, the date of the last available information, Alan Webb had managed to evade the *kurdaitcha* for seven years, earning his living doing odd jobs and moving on whenever he heard that the death squad was coming his way. It is improbable that anyone has survived an aborigine death sentence for a longer period. But Webb knew—and perhaps still knows—that the *kurdaitcha* would never abandon their pursuit. And although he spent his life on the fringe of white society, he realized that if his hunters ever came close enough to point the *kundela*, he would be as good as dead—killed, without trace of injury, by nothing more substantial than a spear of thought. (John Godwin, *Unsolved: The World of the Unknown*, 175-76)

ZOMBIES—THE WALKING DEAD

There are those in Haiti who believe that voodoo priests (houngans) have the power to resurrect the dead. The houngan steals the soul from the corpse, which he then reanimates as a mindless automaton—a zombie. This poor creature will, if certain precautions are taken, do his master's bidding ever after.

The Marks of the Dead
Love and revenge play large roles in voodoo, and one must always be careful not to offend the wrong people.

A houngan made advances to a certain girl, but she, being engaged to marry a man whom she loved, rejected him completely. The enraged houngan was heard muttering threats as he departed, and within a few days the girl fell ill and died. Her family brought the body back to their village for burial and then discovered that the coffin ordered from town was too short; the neck had to be bent to fit the body inside. At the wake someone accidentally dropped a cigarette on one foot of the corpse, which left a small burn.

A few months later it was whispered that this girl had been seen in the company of the houngan she had previously rejected, but there was no evidence and the story was soon forgotten. Then, some years later, the girl reappeared at her home—the houngan had repented and released all his zombies. She was positively identified by many people who had attended her funeral and who remembered her bent neck and the burn mark on her foot. (Alfred Métraux, *Voodoo in Haiti*, Hugo Charteris, trans., pp.284-85)

Voodoo Ceremonies

Blending elements of the Roman Catholic faith with tribal religious beliefs, African slaves in Haiti developed the rituals of voodoo. Ceremonies with singing, drumming, and dancing are often held to summon and win the favor of a particular loa, or god. During these sessions the loa may take possession of some of the worshipers. In a trance they begin to dance with increasing frenzy until they finally collapse on the ground. This is taken as a sign that the loa has been propitiated and his special aid may be invoked.

Haitian voodoo is practiced in some places in the United States. This doll stuck with pins was found with a beheaded chicken, both associated with voodoo magic, in a New Orleans cemetery in 1981.

Voodoo ceremonies, led by houngans, or priests, are held on the earthen floor of a temple or in the courtyard. The houngan's aides hold rattles that will be used later for the dancing. A houngan draws veves—*symbols of the loa, or deity—on the ground with cornmeal flour. The heart shown here symbolizes Erzulie, the god of love. At the bottom is a design indicating that everything in life has a limit. As the ceremony continues, symbols of other loa are added by the houngans.*

Return to the Grave

If ever a zombie learns of what has happened to him, he is said to become totally uncontrollable, and salt is reputed to be a substance that can trigger such awareness. In his book *The Magic Island,* published in 1929, William B. Seabrook reported one such horrifying incident which took place a few years earlier:

A houngan named Joseph had a number of zombies whom he used as cane cutters at Hasco, the huge factory and plantation of the Haitian-American Sugar Company on the outskirts of Port-au-Prince. Joseph's wife, who was looking after the zombies, made the irrevocable error of feeding them some candy that contained salted peanuts.

Upon ingesting the salt, the zombies instantly realized their terrible situation and determinedly set out for their home village. When they arrived, they were recognized by their families, who tried to waylay and talk to them, but the zombies were unstoppable and pressed on until they reached the cemetery. There they tried desperately to dig their way back into their graves with their bare hands, but as they touched the earth they reverted to rotting corpses. (William B. Seabrook, *The Magic Island,* pp.95–99)

The Cotton Pickers

On a field trip in Haiti in 1930, French anthropologist Georges de Rouquet had an opportunity, most unusual for a Caucasian, to observe four zombies, although he was not allowed to touch them. De Rouquet, who had the advantage of being fluent in Creole and was accompanied by a knowledgeable Haitian guide, recorded the experience in his journal:

> Toward evening we encountered a group of four male figures coming from the nearby cotton field where they had been toiling. I was struck by their peculiar shambling gait, most unlike the lithe walk of other natives. The overseer with them stopped their progress, enabling me to observe them closely for some minutes. They were clothed in rags made from sacking. Their arms hung down by their sides, dangling in a curiously lifeless fashion. Their faces and hands appeared devoid of flesh, the skin adhering to the bones like wrinkled brown parchment. I also noticed that they did not sweat, although they had been working and the sun was still very hot. I was unable to judge even their approximate ages. They may have been young men or quite elderly. The most arresting feature about them was their gaze. They all stared straight ahead, their eyes dull and unfocused as if blind. They did not show a spark of awareness of my presence, even when I approached them closely. To test the reflexes of one I made a stabbing gesture toward his eyes with my pointed fingers. He did not blink or shrink back. But when I attempted to touch his hand the overseer prevented me, saying that this was not permitted.
>
> My immediate impression was that these creatures were imbeciles made to work for their keep. Baptiste, however assured me that they were indeed the *zombies;* that is dead persons resurrected by sorcery and employed as unpaid laborers.

De Rouquet watched as the zombies were locked up in a tiny, windowless shed (much smaller and more strongly built than the usual thatched peasant huts) and suggested to Baptiste, his guide, that they should investigate this prison. But Baptiste, who until now had shown a cool detachment, became very frightened, and insisted that they depart immediately, telling de Rouquet, who was armed, that a gun was often a useless defense in Haiti. (John Godwin, *Unsolved: The World of the Unknown,* pp.205–06, 216)

A Twelve-Dollar Slave

Although in general the educated upper classes in Haiti profess to be skeptical of voodoo, wealth and knowledge do not necessarily offer them adequate protection against sorcery.

A well-to-do society man, a "Monsieur," had a flat tire outside a small village. When he got out of the car to change the tire, he was approached by a small, white-bearded old man (actually a houngan) who offered to obtain help from a friend and suggested that meanwhile the Monsieur should return to his home for coffee. En route, the houngan confessed that he had used a spell to cause the flat tire and, over coffee, warned the Monsieur that there was a *wanga* (an evil charm) hidden in his car.

Noting the Monsieur's amused disbelief, the houngan became annoyed and asked his guest if he had known Monsieur Célestin, who had died six months earlier. Célestin had been a very good friend, the Monsieur replied. Whereupon the houngan asked the Monsieur if he would like to see his friend and, without waiting for an answer, cracked his whip six times. In response, a man entered the room backward, a figure vaguely familiar to the Monsieur. When, on the houngan's order, the man turned around, the Monsieur recognized his former friend Célestin.

But this was not quite the Célestin of old: he now stood unmoving, head hanging, face utterly expressionless, speechless, and giving no sign of recognition—a zombie. The Monsieur was stunned.

The houngan explained that Célestin's death had been caused by a spell cast by a sorcerer, who had then transformed him into a zombie and sold him to the houngan for $12. (Alfred Métraux, *Voodoo in Haiti,* Hugo Charteris, trans., pp.283–84)

Wandering Zombie

That the belief in zombies is not restricted to superstitious peasants is demonstrated by this report attested to by a Catholic priest.

It was said that one day in 1959 a zombie shambled into a village in Haiti and wandered into the courtyard of a private house, where he was apprehended by the resident. This man tied the zombie's hands and took him to the local police station. The police eventually gave the zombie a glass of salt water (to revive his memory), and the zombie, his mind cleared, told the police his name. It was discovered that he had an aunt in the village, who was then called in to help clarify the situation. As soon as she arrived, the aunt positively identified her nephew and swore that he had died four years previously and that she had attended the burial.

When questioned by the village's Catholic priest, the zombie reported that he was just one of many zombies held in thrall by a local houngan. Hearing of this, the police, who were terrified of this man's power, offered to return his zombie, but two days later the unfortunate being was found dead. Acting on the assumption that the houngan had killed the zombie for reporting his activities to the authorities, the police arrested him for murder. The other zombies were not rescued, however; the houngan's wife had herded them together and escaped with them into the hills. (*Man, Myth & Magic,* Richard Cavendish, ed., Vol. 22, pp.3095–96)

Zombies Explained

The repeated reports of zombies, people in a trancelike state working as slaves in the fields of Haiti, gain credence by virtue of a firsthand report by a former victim named Clairvius Narcisse from the village of L'Estère. (His story was related by the *National Enquirer* in 1982.) Narcisse, who had always been in excellent health, suddenly and inexplicably took sick in 1962. His sister brought him to the Albert Schweitzer Memorial Hospital in Deschabelle:

I couldn't get enough air in my lungs [Narcisse said]. My heart was running out of strength. My stomach was burning.

Then I felt myself freeze up. I heard the doctor tell my sister, "I'm sorry he's dead."

Clairvius Narcisse points to his name on the grave from which he believes he emerged as a zombie slave. One investigator suggested that Narcisse may have been drugged, buried, and later disinterred.

I wanted to cry out, to tell her that I was alive, but I was unable to move.

The doctor examined him, pulled a sheet over his head, and signed a death certificate. Later in the day friends came to pay their respects and Narcisse said that although he could see them and hear them, he felt no emotion. At the cemetery he heard the mourners lament and heard the dirt falling on his coffin. The next thing he remembered was standing next to the grave in a trancelike state. There were two men who refilled the grave, tied a rope around his wrists, and took him to a farm where he became a slave working in the fields with about 100 other unfortunate souls.

According to Dr. Lamarque Douyon, director of the Psychiatric Center in Port-au-Prince, the so-called zombies are people who have been drugged by a voodoo sorcerer, pronounced dead, buried, dug up from their graves, and kept drugged during their enslavement as agricultural workers.

Narcisse thinks he had been enslaved for about two years when one day the overseer evidently failed to administer the dose of drugs that kept the victims in their subservient condition. Some of the zombies regained their faculties, realized the state they were in, and killed the overseer. Released from the effects of the drug, Narcisse soon became his normal self. He did not go back to his native village because he believed that the brother who lived there had made the arrangement to have him drugged by a voodoo sorcerer. But when in January 1980 he heard that his brother had died, he decided to return to L'Estère.

So 18 years after he was thought to be dead and buried, Clairvius Narcisse walked back into the lives of friends and relatives who had mourned his passing nearly two decades before.

APPEARANCES AND DISAPPEARANCES

It has been estimated that in the United States today about 10 million persons are reported missing during the course of a single year. About 95 percent of them return home within hours or days, but the remaining 5 percent vanish forever. Teenagers constitute the largest group of "vanishees"; gravitating to large cities, they are usually swallowed up by a sordid underworld. Among missing adults an increasing percentage are women—an interesting aspect of women's liberation. A Tracers study has shown that in 1960 about 300 times more husbands vanished than wives, while in 1980 as many wives as husbands whisked themselves off.

It is not easy to disappear without a trace, but it is a common occurrence. On the pages that follow are the accounts of many people who have done so. They have all the ingredients of a good mystery story—except for the ending, which in these cases is left to speculation. The circumstances surrounding their disappearances are bizarre and sometimes ridiculous, and the ways in which they vanish without a trace—from a train, a ship, or an airplane, or while crossing a street or a field—are inexplicable.

We are intrigued by the possible motives—the dictates of the heart, the overriding wish to escape from a monotonous existence or unwanted responsibilities, the lures of adventure and wealth, a compromised career, political intrigue, murky connections with criminals and the attendant perils of knowing too much.

Reading, we ponder the difficulty of disappearing and leaving no trail, of abandoning old pursuits, cutting ties, and assuming new identities. And we contemplate the dark fates of those unaccountably lost on their quest for adventure and discovery. We also imagine the families whose lives are tragically affected by the loss of a relative—the gnawing uncertainties, the apprehension, the gray area of guilt, the longing for an explanation that will never be made.

Still rarer, and perhaps stranger than the stories of those who have vanished into the chasm of the unknown, are the documented cases of people who have appeared from nowhere and whose identities remain forever a mystery. Some may be long-lost amnesiacs; others may be the "wild children" who have prompted so much speculation about the nature of "human nature."

The idea of someone who disappears into oblivion, or one who has no past, is difficult to contemplate, especially today when each person is documented by a string of records, certificates, and ID cards from the hour of birth to the moment of death.

BEFORE 1800

America's colonial history is haunted by the disappearance of Roanoke colony, founded in 1587 by more than 100 English men and women. Settling on the Virginia coastal island (now in North Carolina), they intended to farm and to pay for supplies from home by selling wild sassafras, a costly import prized medicinally in England. The governor of the colony, John White, sailed back to England for supplies to sustain the colonists through the coming winter. Detained there by the war with Spain, White finally returned to Roanoke in 1591 and found all had vanished, including his daughter and her infant, Virginia Dare, the first white child born in America. Carved on a post at the abandoned stockade was "Croatan," the name of a nearby island and of a local Indian tribe. Bad weather prevented further search, and so White returned to England. The only inkling of the fate of the lost colony came a century later when colonists reported seeing Indians with gray eyes and fair hair. (Reader's Digest, eds., *American Folklore and Legend*, p.31)

114

A double mystery combining a strange disappearance with an even stranger appearance took place October 24, 1593, when a soldier stationed in Manila reported for palace-guard duty in Mexico City. Instantly noticed because his uniform set him apart from the others, he was interrogated. The soldier, baffled at finding himself in a strange land, said that he had been

When a palace guard from Manila turned up for duty in front of the palace in Mexico City, he was questioned by the authorities. His incredible story landed him in jail.

instructed that very morning to report for duty at the palace in Manila, adding that the governor of the Philippines had been killed the night before. The incredulous authorities slapped him in jail. Two months later, news reached Mexico that confirmed his story: the governor had indeed been murdered in Manila—on the night before the soldier turned up in Mexico. The soldier was allowed to return to the Philippines. (Colin Wilson, *Enigmas and Mysteries,* p.29)

In July 1669, agents of King Louis XIV of France captured a man near the port of Dunkirk and sent him secretly to prison with stern instructions to the warden:

> It is of the first importance that he is not allowed to tell what he knows to any living person. . . . You must yourself take to him, once a day, the day's necessities and you must never listen, under any pretext whatever, to what he may want to reveal to you. You must threaten him with death if he ever opens his mouth to you on any subject but his day-to-day needs.

For 34 years the prisoner was transferred from one comfortable prison suite to another until he died in the Bastille at Paris in 1703. He always wore a black velvet mask. Once, it is said, he scratched a message on a silver plate and threw it from his window. The fisherman who found it and brought it to the gate was allowed to live only because he could not read!

All that is really known of the prisoner is contained in these facts: that his face was dangerously recognizable, that he was too valuable to dispose of but too threatening to set free, and that what he knew was so explosive that even a simple fisherman could have shaken France with the information. The best-known face in France, of course, was that of the king himself.

The great writer and philosopher Voltaire had been imprisoned in the Bastille in 1717 when he was a young man. There he had had a chance to talk with jailers who had known the masked man and all the gossip about him, but not his identity. Interested in discrediting the monarchy, Voltaire later concocted the theory that the masked man was Louis XIV's elder brother, imprisoned by the king to prevent disturbances over potential rival claimants to the throne.

In 1801, after the French Revolution, it was rumored that the prisoner was Louis XIV himself, displaced on the throne by his illegitimate half-brother. In prison he had married (not uncommon in those days), the story went on, and fathered a son who was taken to Corsica, where he grew up and became the grandfather of Napoleon Bonaparte. This version, which served to link France's revolutionary dictator to the old regime, has never been taken seriously by scholars.

The most famous treatment of the story was that of Alexandre Dumas *père,* who altered Voltaire's version, making the prisoner the king's twin brother, and also

An illustration for Alexander Dumas's tale about the man in the iron mask shows the elegantly dressed prisoner in his comfortably appointed cell in the Bastille.

changed the material of the mask. His romance, entitled *The Man in the Iron Mask,* was published in 1848. Folklore and movies have propagated this story, although it has been totally dismissed by historians.

Another version is that the prisoner was the true father of Louis XIV. The birth of Louis XIV in 1638 was thought at the time to be something of a miracle. His mother, Anne of Austria, and his presumed father, Louis XIII, had been estranged for many years and had had no children. Since the royal couple was faced with the need to produce an heir to the throne, and Louis XIII was ailing and quite likely impotent, it is possible that a surrogate father was arranged. This interpretation would explain why Louis XIV kept the mystery man a prisoner rather than having him killed, a deed which would have fixed on Louis the sin of patricide.

So many scholars and mystery lovers in the last 300 years have attempted to unravel the mystery that any conclusive evidence would surely have surfaced by now. None has. Thus it seems likely that people will continue to spin theories around the masked prisoner, who dropped out of history and into legend in 1669. (Tighe Hopkins, *The Man in the Iron Mask,* passim; Hugh Ross Williamson, *Enigmas of History,* pp.207–28)

On July 27, 1724, the boy who came to be called Wild Peter was captured near the German town of Hameln. He appeared to be about 12 years old. He could not speak and ate only vegetables and grass and sucked the juice of green stalks; at first he rejected bread. The story of the wild boy spread, and in February 1726 King George I of England (who was also the king of Hannover) sent for him. He was briefly a court favorite and learned to identify his benefactor as *ki scho* and Queen Caroline as *qui ca,* although he never learned to speak articulately.

A German naturalist and scholar later examined all the earliest documents on Wild Peter and concluded that he must have lived with people until shortly before he was captured, because he wore a rag around his neck and parts of his body were pale rather than tanned, suggesting that he had worn breeches. But not all agreed. Peter's case (like that of other "wild children," see page 119) strongly influenced contemporary views of how humans came to be civilized. French philosopher Jean Jacques Rousseau considered Wild Peter a model of an unspoiled "natural man," and Scotland's Lord Monboddo wrote: "I consider his history as a brief chronicle or abstract of the progress of human nature, from the mere animal to the first stage of civilized life." (Roger Shattuck, *The Forbidden Experiment,* pp.194–95; *The Wild Man Within,* Edward Dudley and Maximillian E. Novak, eds., p.198; Joseph Singh and Robert M. Zingg, *Wolf Children and Feral Man,* pp.182–97)

Count Saint-Germain

He was a confidant of two kings of France, a dazzlingly rich and gifted social figure, the subject of a thousand rumors—but no one knows to this day where or when he was born, who he was, or when he died. A few believe that he still lives.

It has been supposed that Saint-Germain was the natural son of the widow of Charles II of Spain, although theosophists have made a good case for his being the son of Francis Racoczi II, the prince of Transylvania. Either genealogy would place the year of his birth at about 1690. The musician Jean-Philippe Rameau was certain, however, that he had met the count in 1710, under the name of the Marquis de Montferrat, and stated that he appeared to be in his forties at the time.

The life of the self-styled count is as shadowy as his origin. He seems to have become a celebrity in the 1750's as a friend of Louis XV and his mistress Madame de Pompadour, who together spent evenings with him simply for the pleasure of his conversation. Not only was he remarkably knowledgeable, but he had other attributes—artistry as a violinist, talent as a painter, skill in alchemy and chemistry, and a largesse with precious stones.

He was known to carry jewels sewn into his clothing and was said to have presented a cross ornamented with gems to a woman he scarcely knew, because she had idly admired it. The count claimed that he had learned how to turn several small diamonds into one large one and to make pearls grow to spectacular size. It was widely suspected that he also knew the secret for making gold out of base metal.

Whether he was a genius or a charlatan, Saint-Germain had the talent to make himself noticed and the subject of gossip. But in Versailles and Paris he was embraced as the confidential adviser of Louis XV. The position earned him the envy and enmity of the king's ministers, who denounced him as an adventurer with a smooth line of talk. Matters came to a head in 1760, when the count—at the behest of the king—involved himself in foreign affairs, going behind the back of the ministry. Threatened with arrest, he was obliged to flee to England, where he stayed for a while, possibly for a period of two years.

From England Count Saint-Germain apparently went to Russia, where—it is claimed—he took part in a conspiracy that put Catherine the Great upon the throne in 1762. After that nothing much is known of the count until 1774, when Louis XVI and Marie Antoinette came to the throne.

Saint-Germain now returned to France. It is said that he warned the royal couple of the revolution then 15 years in the future, saying, "There will be a blood-

Count Saint-Germain, whose longevity and young appearance made him seem immortal, was described as "A man who knows everything and who never dies" by his contemporary Voltaire. Some thought the count had found the "Elixir of Youth."

thirsty republic, whose sceptre will be the executioner's knife." On the other hand, he consorted with many whose dabbling in the occult was actually a cover for revolutionary activities, and his real political leanings—if he had any—are still debated.

Secret societies were the fashion in prerevolutionary France, and some of them recognized Saint-Germain as an "adept," one who knew the ancient wisdoms hinted at in the rites of the Freemasons, Rosicrucians, and Knights Templars. And it was no wonder. In relating events of centuries past, the count would deliberately lead credulous listeners to believe that he had been present. "These fools of Parisians believe that I am five hundred years old," he once remarked to a friend. "I confirm them in this idea because I see that it gives them much pleasure—not that I am not infinitely older than I appear." He attributed his youthful appearance in part to his abstemiousness and a diet that consisted principally of oatmeal.

Later he lived in Germany as a protégé of Prince Charles of Hesse-Kassel. Close friends, they worked together at alchemy. Most reference works say that the count died at the prince's court in February 27, 1784. According to Maurice Magre, author of *Magicians, Seers, and Mystics* (1932), Prince Charles was uncommunicative about his friend's death "and turned the conversation if anyone spoke of him. His whole behaviour gives colour to the supposition that he was the accomplice of a pretended death."

Many continued to insist that the count was very much alive. Documents of the Freemasons indicate that he represented French Masons at a meeting in 1785. Madame de Genlis claimed to have seen him in Vienna in 1821. Several travelers in the 1800's were sure they saw him in the Far East and other parts of the world. Theosophist Annie Besant said that she met the count in 1896, incarnated as a "Master," or spiritual leader. Finally, in 1972, a Frenchman named Richard Chanfray claimed to be Saint-Germain, and to prove it, he appeared on television to demonstrate that he could turn lead into gold as the legendary count was believed to have done.

FROM 1800 TO 1830

In 1809 England sought to persuade Austria to join the confederation opposing Napoleon. Benjamin Bathurst, a 25-year-old diplomat who had already distinguished himself in foreign service, went to Vienna to promise an attack on the French who were occupying Spain in return for Austria's alignment with England. It proved a bad bargain: Napoleon was victorious at Wagram on the Danube River, and Austria was forced to cede territory to him.

That fall, Bathurst began to make his way back home through Germany. On November 25, traveling under the name of Koch and posing as a wealthy merchant, he and his secretary and valet stopped at an inn in Perleberg. A witness at the inn reported that he seemed very nervous. He asked the commander of the local garrison to provide armed guards against mysterious pursuers—perhaps agents of Napoleon.

In the middle of the evening, as his coach was preparing to leave, Bathurst went out into the otherwise deserted street, walked around his horses....

And was gone.

His valet, who had been at the rear of the coach with the baggage, cast a look down each side of the coach and saw only the hostler who had harnessed the horses. His secretary, standing in the doorway of the inn to pay the bill, had not seen him return. The soldiers stationed at each end of the street had seen no one pass.

The authorities searched first the inn and then all of Perleberg. Inquiries from the British Foreign Office brought a denial from Napoleon that his agents had been involved. Stories circulated that Bathurst had been robbed and murdered, that he had secretly gone on to a port and been lost at sea, and so on—but all that is known about Benjamin Bathurst's disappearance from a quiet street in a small German town is summed up in the words of Charles Fort, that tireless collector of events that have no rhyme or reason: "Under observation, he walked around to the other side of the horses." (*Dictionary of National Biography,* Vol. 1, p.1327; Charles Fort, *The Complete Books of Charles Fort,* p.681; Colin Wilson, *Enigmas and Mysteries,* p.37)

Benjamin Bathurst, a British envoy sent on a secret mission to Austria in 1809, was on his way back to England when he vanished forever in a small German town. The distinguished young diplomat, who was traveling incognito, may have been trailed and assassinated by French soldiers.

The monotonous routine of the inmates of the Prussian prison at Weichselmunde was surprisingly disrupted in 1815. A valet named Diderici, locked up for impersonating his master after the latter had died of a stroke, was walking in chains in the walled exercise yard with other prisoners marching ahead of and behind him. Suddenly Diderici began to fade. According to both prisoners and guards, within seconds he was invisible—then his manacles and ankle irons clinked to the ground. Nothing more was ever seen of Diderici, who somehow had made a reality of every prisoner's dream. (Jay Robert Nash, *Among the Missing*, p.331)

Not one, but two fabulous treasures disappeared somewhere on rocky, inhospitable Cocos Island, 200 miles off the Pacific coast of Costa Rica, in 1819 and 1820. The first was that of the pirate Benito Bonito, who captured a Spanish ship laden with some 150 tons of gold. After the booty was buried, Bonito killed most of his crew and sailed off with the rest. The British Royal Navy said he was killed soon afterward in a sea battle, but some believe that he alone made it to shore—although he never returned to the island.

Soon afterward, officials in the Spanish colony of Peru gathered the state and church treasures of Lima together to prevent them from falling into the hands of a liberation army. Loaded on board the British ship *Mary Dier*, the treasure was dispatched to Panama—but the *Mary Dier*'s captain, Charles Thompson, changed course and sailed to Cocos. There he and his crew buried the treasure. Unlike Bonito, Captain Thompson did not slaughter his men to safeguard the secret, yet the *Mary Dier* and all aboard her vanished.

In 1840 Thompson—or someone claiming to be Thompson—appeared in Newfoundland with a map of Cocos and a feverish desire to raise an expedition to recover the treasure. No one would believe him, and a little later he disappeared. The reputed hoard of Cocos has never been found despite many searches. (Jay Robert Nash, *Among the Missing*, pp.190–92)

The 47-year-old Czar Alexander I of Russia died on November 19, 1825. When news of his death reached the capital, a handful of St. Petersburg troops rebelled against the succession of his brother Nicholas. The uprising was quickly put down, but the "Decembrists," as the troops were called, became heroes to Russian liberals during the harsh reign of Czar Nicholas.

Perhaps because Nicholas's power was questioned at the very beginning of his reign, rumors soon spread that Alexander had not died at all but had secretly abdicated in order to take up the life of a holy hermit. A man named Fedor Kuzmich appeared in Tomsk far to the east, and local residents whispered that Alexander

Alexander I, czar of Russia for 24 years, was succeeded upon his death in 1825 by his unpopular brother. But persistent rumors that Alexander had in fact escaped to Siberia led to the opening of his tomb a century later. It was empty.

Romanov was living among them. On his deathbed in 1864 the hermit Kuzmich told them: "God knows my real name." The following year, when Alexander II attempted to quell the rumors by having his uncle's casket opened, many said that it proved to be empty. The tomb was opened again in 1926 and was found empty. (Ian Grey, *The Romanovs*, pp.262–68, 367–68)

A teenage boy wandered into Nuremberg, Germany, on May 26, 1828, wearing tattered clothes and ill-fitting boots that had cut and blistered his soft feet. He could hardly speak but on a sheet of paper scrawled the name Kaspar Hauser.

Kaspar would sit still for hours on end and seemed to prefer darkness. He would eat only bread and water. He played contentedly with a toy horse (he called all animals "horse," as he called all human beings "boy"). Yet within weeks he acquired many adult skills, and soon he recounted a strange tale: he had been confined for years in a dark cell too small for him to stand in, drugged while his clothing was changed, and isolated from human contact—indeed, he said, the only human being he had seen before entering Nuremberg had been a mysterious man who taught him to write his name and to say, "I want to be a soldier like my father."

Popular belief held that Kaspar was a legitimate son of the royal house of Baden, put aside and imprisoned in favor of another heir. In October 1829 he was found unconscious with a wound in his forehead. When he recovered, he spoke of a masked attacker.

A famous lawyer, Anselm von Feuerbach, took up his cause and pursued the displaced-heir theory. But in 1833 Feuerbach died, and soon afterward Kaspar stumbled into his teacher's home, bleeding from multiple wounds, and claimed that a stranger had attacked him in the park. Skeptics attempted to get him to admit that he had stabbed himself to renew public interest in his case, but three days later Kaspar died, saying to the end: "I didn't do it myself." (Francis Hitching, *The Mysterious World: An Atlas of the Unexplained*, pp.210–13; Colin Wilson, *Enigmas and Mysteries*, pp.134–36)

All the Wild Children

From time to time through history, apparently wild children have appeared in society, children who seem to have grown up by themselves or to have been reared by animals. Could an infant survive alone in the wild? Could he be "adopted" by wolves or bears, monkeys or gazelles? And if nature's child were brought into human society, would he be hopelessly retarded and a reminder of the bestial part of human nature—or a noble savage, free of the corruptions of civilization?

Scores of times since the first documented case, that of a "wolf boy" captured in the German principality of Hesse in 1344, children have been found whom many people believed were reared by animals; others have countered that these were simply orphans, perhaps abandoned because of retardation or retarded because of their isolation from human contact.

The studied case in modern times is that of Kamala and Amala, the wolf children of Midnapore, India. The Rev. J.A.L. Singh, who administered an orphanage and church school, was touring his district in 1920 when he heard stories of *manush-baghas,* or man-beasts: ghostlike figures seen among the wolves who had made their den in an abandoned termite mound. He saw them himself one night and returned with helpers to dig into the mound in daylight. Two wolves darted out and ran off; a third, a female, attacked the intruders who instantly shot it. Inside the mound Singh found two girls, approximately eight and two years old, curled up with two wolf cubs. He took the girls to the orphanage and began what he saw as his Christian duty to humanize them. It was no easy task, for they ran on all fours, shunned daylight, howled as much like wolves as human vocal cords allowed, and preferred meat, even carrion, to grains and vegetables. Amala, the younger, died less than a year later. Kamala lived for nine years, and learned to walk upright and to speak a few simple phrases, although she never learned at the pace of the other children.

The veracity of Singh's account has been substantiated by most investigators. Arnold Gesell, an expert on childhood development, based a book on it. The writer Charles Maclean, who had been skeptical about the story of wolf children when he went to India in 1975, concluded that "the Reverend Singh's diary account of what happened in the forest is true, though perhaps not the whole truth."

Psychologist Bruno Bettelheim presented a differing view in a paper published in 1959. He argued that Singh's wolf girls were in fact autistic children abandoned by their parents. He based his conclusion on the similarities of behavior in autistic children in his care and the behavior of Amala and Kamala as described by Singh. Bettelheim and others pointed out, plausibly

enough, that to observers who already believe they are watching children reared by animals, any animallike behavior is seized upon as confirmation.

That caution would not seem to apply to the gazelle boy of the Spanish Sahara, whom French anthropologist Jean-Claude Armen first saw about 1970 as "a naked human form . . . slender and with long black hair, galloping in gigantic bounds among a long cavalcade of white gazelles." According to Armen, the boy (who was never captured) left tracks with "the weight resting on the front part of the foot and hardly making any impression on the sand, revealing a rare suppleness." His observations left him in no doubt that the boy, about 10 years old, had adapted completely to the life of the herd, even to the point of sniffing and licking the gazelles as they did each other. The boy's adaptation to his world was so remarkable that Armen asked himself, "How could a retarded child, even though 'aided' by animals, continue to exist in the harsh environment of the desert?" He then suggested that possibly the trauma and disorientation of capture made wild children appear to be retarded.

The popularity of the idea of wild children is clear in the myth of Romulus and Remus, suckled by a wolf, and in the enduring appeal of Edgar Rice Burroughs's Tarzan and Rudyard Kipling's Mowgli, the jungle boy. We take it for granted that children are fascinated by animals, treating them as equals. And we are entertained when we hear of a puppy adopted by a cat or of the gosling that adopted behavioral scientist Konrad Lorenz and followed him about. But so much is brought into question—our view of ourselves and our place in nature—that reports of human children adopted by wild animals will always intrigue us.

In Rudyard Kipling's The Jungle Books, *an Indian boy named Mowgli is adopted by wolves. This illustration is from a French edition of the classic.*

The disappearance of New York State Supreme Court Associate Justice Joseph F. Crater (see pages 127–28) has been highly publicized, but few realize that a predecessor in that office had vanished just as mysteriously as Crater, 100 years before.

John Lansing had fought in the American Revolution and served as a legislator, mayor of Albany, and state chancellor. From 1790 to 1801 he sat on the New York Supreme Court and was chief justice in 1798. For years he was part of the political group around the wealthy Clinton family, but he alienated them by refusing to run for governor as they desired. Instead, he remained as chancellor until his retirement in 1814, then became a regent of the state university and a business consultant to Columbia College. It was in the second capacity that he was staying at a hotel in New York City on December 12, 1829. He went out that evening to mail some letters so that they would catch the night boat up the Hudson to Albany, and he was never seen again. The search was extensive, for Lansing had been one of the best-known figures in the public life of the state. Yet the 75-year-old man had disappeared into the winter night as completely as if he had never lived. (*Dictionary of American Biography*, Vol. 5, p.608; Jay Robert Nash, *Among the Missing*, p.166)

FROM 1830 TO 1860

The *Times* of London on November 6, 1840, printed this account from a correspondent in the Bahamas:

> A large French vessel, bound from Hamburgh to Havanah, was met by one of our coasters, and was discovered to be completely abandoned.... The cargo, composed of wines, fruits, silks, etc., was in the most perfect condition. The captain's papers were all secure in their proper places.... The only living things on board were a cat, some fowles, and several canaries half-dead with hunger.... The vessel, which must have been left within a very few hours, contained several bales of goods addressed to different merchants in Havanah. She is very large, recently built, and called *Rosalie*. Of her crew and passengers no intelligence has been received.

A search of insurance records at Lloyd's of London revealed what at first looked like a simple confusion: Lloyd's files described the *Rossini*, a ship on the Hamburg-Havana run, as going aground in the Bahama Channel on August 3. Those aboard the vessel were taken ashore, and on August 17 the *Rossini* was towed into Nassau by salvage ships.

And yet, what had given the *Times* correspondent the impression that the *Rosalie/Rossini* (if indeed only one ship was involved) had been abandoned "within a very few hours," especially if the canaries aboard were

starving? Would not the captain have taken his ship's papers when he was rescued? Would not the arrival of the rescued passengers have been fresh news in Nassau? And what were the "curious circumstances" alluded to in the salvage court's records concerning the *Rossini*? (Paul Begg, *Into Thin Air*, p.52)

An expedition led by Ludwig Leichhardt set out to cross the central desert of Australia in March 1848. No trace of the men or their more than 70 pack animals was ever found. In 1975 a ranger named Zac Mathias came into Darwin, Northern Territory, with photos of aboriginal cave paintings showing white men and an animal, but before a trip could be arranged to the caves where he said he had found the drawings, Mathias himself disappeared. (Paul Begg, *Into Thin Air*, p.17; *Dictionary of National Biography*, Vol. 11, p.807)

The Dutch schooner *Hermania* was discovered off England's Cornish coast in 1849, her masts blown away, her crew gone without a trace, and the lifeboat still aboard. Had all the crew been swept overboard by a single wave while fighting a storm? Had they hastily abandoned ship, thinking that the *Hermania* was about to sink? Or had they been ... taken? (Colin Wilson, *Enigmas and Mysteries*, p.44)

The *James B. Chester*, unlike the *Hermania*, was in fine condition when she was found in mid-Atlantic on February 28, 1855. The compass and ship's papers were gone, and there were signs that possessions had been hastily gathered from drawers, but all the lifeboats were in place. (Paul Begg, *Into Thin Air*, p.56)

FROM 1860 TO 1880

The Mississippi riverboat *Iron Mountain*, more than 180 feet long and towing barges loaded with a cargo of cotton and molasses, set out in June 1872 from Vicksburg. Later the barges came floating downstream; the tow rope had been cut rather than snapped or cast off. No one ever saw the *Iron Mountain* or her 52 passengers again. No trace of wreckage or floating cargo from the riverboat's deck load was ever found. (Paul Begg, *Into Thin Air*, pp.56–57)

On December 4, 1872, the brigantine *Mary Celeste* was discovered east of the Azores, bobbing along at half-sail, and deserted. Capt. Benjamin Briggs, his wife, Sarah, their two-year-old daughter, Sophia, and seven crewmen were gone. An entry written on a slate but not yet entered in the ship's log, dated November 25, put her almost 370 miles west of where she was found. Her cargo was in good order. Two hatch covers were off, the

A deceptively peaceful painting of the Mary Celeste *gives no hint of the misfortune that plagued the ship and those associated with her. From the time of her launching in 1861 the ship was jinxed, as death, fire, collision, a grounding, and bankruptcy followed in the brigantine's wake.*

ship's boat was gone, the fore-upper-topsail was lost, and the binnacle was overturned. Most important, the wheel was not lashed, an indication that the ship was abandoned in a hurry.

By coincidence, the captain of the *Dei Gratia*, who had made the discovery, was a friend of Briggs's and had dined with him less than a month earlier, toasting Briggs's new command. Capt. David Morehouse and the crewmen who helped salvage the *Mary Celeste* testified at length during the three-month inquiry at Gibraltar concerning the abandoned brigantine.

From the beginning legends and rumors wrapped themselves around the case. The attorney general of Gibraltar theorized that the crew had broken into the commercial alcohol, which was the cargo, then killed Briggs and his family in a drunken fury, and escaped by lifeboat. In fact, the alcohol would have blinded or killed anyone foolish enough to drink it. Others whispered that Morehouse and Briggs had plotted the *Mary Celeste*'s abandonment to get salvage money, then quarreled on board the *Dei Gratia* with fatal results. But the two men's friendship was well established, and there was no evidence whatsoever for this story. Yet the naval court saw fit to award the *Dei Gratia* a salvage fee that was only a fraction—one-fifth—of what it should ordinarily have been. According to one account, Briggs had feared that the flammable cargo was leaking and hastily abandoned ship, then had become separated from it as a vagrant wind filled its sails. Possibly the best explanation is that a waterspout hit the *Mary Celeste*. The atmospheric pressure inside a waterspout is very low; the difference between that pressure and the normal pressure inside the ship could have caused the hatch covers to blow open and forced bilge water up into the pump well; it would appear the ship had taken on six to eight feet of water and was sinking fast.

Over the years a number of "true explanations" were published, several purporting to be by survivors of the *Mary Celeste*'s crew. One clearly fictional account was by Arthur Conan Doyle, the creator of Sherlock Holmes. Published in 1884, it was reprinted as fact by many newspapers, and every investigator since has had to cut through the fables Doyle put forth: that tea on

The Movable Mysteries

Can some people suddenly vanish from sight by ceasing to exist? Orion Williamson was a farmer near Selma, Alabama. One day in July 1854 he got up from his chair on the farmhouse porch and set out across a field to bring his horses in from the pasture. His wife and child watched from the porch, and on the far side of the field two neighbors riding by waved to him. Before their very eyes, Williamson vanished.

The witnesses searched the field but found no hole in the ground and no trace of Williamson. Searchers came from town, and bloodhounds nosed about, but to no avail. Journalists came, too, including the young Ambrose Bierce, who wrote of the incident in the story "The Difficulty of Crossing a Field."

On September 23, 1880, the Williamson disappearance was repeated: David Lang, a farmer living near Gallatin, Tennessee, set out across the field in front of his house and vanished while in the full view of his wife. His disappearance was also witnessed by two arriving visitors (Judge August Peck from Gallatin and the judge's brother-in-law), who had just waved to Lang from their buggy. A search of the field revealed no sinkholes or hidden caves.

The Lang story, supposedly related by his daughter years later, appeared in *Fate* magazine in 1953. It was not until then that the case was researched. A check into the 1880 census records of Sumner County where the Langs lived turned up neither Lang's name nor Peck's. Nor was the farm nor any other evidence found to substantiate the story. Had Bierce's narrative been appropriated and embroidered with new detail?

A third farmer, Isaac Martin of Salem, Virginia, strode into a field and disappeared, according to the *New York Sun* of April 25, 1885. Whether anyone saw him vanish is unknown.

A nighttime trip to the well for water seemed to be as hazardous as crossing a field, according to three accounts of such errands.

In November 1878, 16-year-old Charles Ashmore of Quincy, Illinois, went out into the night with a water bucket. When he did not return after a few minutes, his father and sister went to look for him. They found his footprints clear in fresh snow, leading halfway to the well, where they abruptly stopped.

On Christmas Eve, 1889, 11-year-old Oliver Larch of South Bend, Indiana, went to get water, cried out for help, and vanished.

On Christmas Eve, 1909, 11-year-old Oliver Thomas of Rhayader, Wales, also went into the yard for water and cried out, "Help! Help! They've got me." His footprints ended halfway to the well.

In his anthology of strange disappearances, *Into Thin Air*, Paul Begg wrote that these incidents "must be duplicate accounts of the same story, although which if any is the original is anyone's guess."

the galley table was still warm when the *Dei Gratia*'s crew boarded, that a crucial page had been torn from the log, and that breakfast was still cooking.

The case of the *Mary Celeste* remains the classic nautical mystery. Adding a note of poignancy is Briggs's last letter to his mother in Maine: "Our vessel is in beautiful trim. I hope we shall have a fine passage; but as I have never been in her before, I can't say how she'll sail." (Paul Begg, *Into Thin Air*, pp.88–117; Greshom Bradford, *The Secret of Mary Celeste*, passim; Jay Robert Nash, *Among the Missing*, pp.334–37)

In 1873 English shoemaker James Worson accepted his friends' bet that he could not run from their hometown of Leamington Spa to Coventry and back, a distance of 16 miles. He set out at a jog, with his three friends following in a cart. After several miles, still moving easily, the shoemaker seemed to stumble, then pitch forward—and disappear.

The three men searched in panic, knowing there was no rational explanation for what they had seen. When they failed to find any sign of their friend, they returned to Leamington Spa and told the police what had happened. Despite prolonged questioning they could add nothing to their simple story, but neither would they retract any part of it. Worson had been there, running a few yards ahead of them, and then he was gone. (Paul Begg, *Into Thin Air*, p.31)

One reason the parental advice "never accept candy from strangers" became a very familiar phrase was the sensational July 1874 kidnapping of Charlie Ross, the four-year-old son of a wealthy businessman in Germantown, Pennsylvania.

Charlie and his six-year-old brother, Walter, were accustomed to playing near the road in front of their home. During the last week of June, two strangers in a carriage stopped each day to talk to them and offer candy. Then, on July 1, they offered to take the boys into Philadelphia to buy fireworks for Independence Day. In the city they sent Walter into a store with 25 cents, a princely sum for a six-year-old in those days. When Walter came out of the store, the carriage, the two men, and Charlie were gone.

Two days later the boys' father, Christian K. Ross, received an illiterate, barely legible note warning him: "...dont deceiv yuself an think the detectives can git him from us for that is one imposebel—you here from us in few day." Soon there came a demand for a $20,000 ransom, but an attempt at a rendezvous for the delivery of the money fell through.

The New York City police identified the handwriting of the notes as that of William Mosher, a dock thief, but before they could track him down Mosher and his accomplice, Joseph Douglass, were shot during a burglary in Bay Ridge, New York. Mosher died at once; Douglass survived long enough to confess but claimed that only Mosher had known Charlie's whereabouts. Little Walter Ross identified the two dead men as the kidnappers of his brother.

Mosher's brother-in-law, a former policeman named William Westervelt, was tried for his alleged part in the crime. Sentenced to seven years of solitary confinement, he never admitted guilt, and on his release in 1882 he dropped out of sight. (*Frank Leslie's Illustrated Newspaper*, August 15, 1874; June 18, 1875; *Harper's Weekly*, August 8, 1874, p.652)

After three years of marriage, Anna M. Fellows of Cambridge, Massachusetts, left her husband, William, in 1879. There was no trace of her for 20 years. Then Fellows came home one day to find her in the kitchen preparing a meal as if she had never been gone. She would offer no explanations, and somehow they settled down together once more, but after three years Anna departed again, this time for good. (Jay Robert Nash, *Among the Missing*, pp.250–51)

FROM 1880 TO 1900

In August 1880 a young man who had given his name as Henry Edward disappeared overnight from the Florida coastal steamer *City of Dallas*. Although the night was quiet and the water calm, none of the watch or the ship's officers heard a splash or saw Edward go overboard. (Jay Robert Nash, *Among the Missing*, p.245)

The story of the green children found in Spain is remarkably similar to that of two green children—a boy and a girl—who emerged from a cave in Woolpit, England, in the 11th century; the girl said they came from a sunless land.

Two children appeared from a cave near Banjos, Spain, in August 1887. Their skin was green, and their clothes were of an unfamiliar material. They could not speak Spanish, and their eyes appeared Oriental.

At first they would not eat, and the boy died, but the girl survived and learned enough Spanish to explain that they came from a sunless land, where one day a whirlwind had swept her and her companion away and deposited them in the cave. Understandably, this did little to dispel the wonder surrounding her. She died in 1892, her origins still unknown. (Colin Wilson, *Enigmas and Mysteries*, p.131).

A distraught young Englishwoman came to the British Embassy in Paris one day in May 1889. She and her mother, on their way home from India, had checked into a hotel not long before, taking two single rooms, and the mother had fallen ill. The hotel doctor had examined her and sent the daughter out for medicine. When she returned, the hotel staff denied ever having seen her mother! Only the younger woman's name was in the hotel register. When she insisted on seeing the room her mother had occupied, she found it was not the one she remembered. Even the hotel doctor denied having met her before.

Unable to make her story believed, the young woman ended up in an asylum in England. Some have speculated that the mother had contracted plague in the Far East and that the hotel staff had conspired to suppress the news—even going so far as to redecorate the mother's hotel room and to dispose of her corpse—rather than lose business. But the only evidence to support the case of the vanished matron was the young woman's own testimony: a sign of madness, possibly, but if true, surely enough to drive her mad. (Reader's Digest, eds., *Strange Stories, Amazing Facts*, p.361)

The man who should have been known as the father of motion pictures, Louis Le Prince, disappeared from a French train in September 1890. He had demonstrated his process for making movies—which used a technique later credited to Thomas Edison—at the Paris Opera House earlier in the year. His patent was in order and he had a brilliant future when he stepped onto the train. But he never stepped off as far as anyone could determine. Seven years later he was officially declared dead. (Jay Robert Nash, *Among the Missing*, p.158)

Grace Marian Perkins vanished from her New England home in 1898. After a fruitless search, her parents identified a murder victim in Bridgeport, Connecticut, as their daughter. On September 17, 1898, the eve of the funeral, however, Grace Perkins showed up to explain that she had merely eloped—and that now the publicity

would spoil her honeymoon! (*The New York Times*, September 18 and 19, 1898)

FROM 1900 TO 1920

As the supply ship *Hesperus* approached the island of Eilean Mor off Scotland's West Coast, there was no sign of life ashore. One passenger, lighthouse keeper Joseph Moore from a nearby island, who was also relief lighthouse keeper on Eilean Mor, was especially concerned: the lighthouse had been dark for 11 days, since December 15, 1900.

Moore and others searched the lighthouse, finding everything in order, although oilskin foul-weather gear belonging to two of the three keepers was missing. Storm damage to a jetty suggested the possibility that the three men had been swept away by a giant wave—but would they have been so incautious as to go onto the jetty at the height of a storm? There were no answers, for none of the three was ever found. (Colin Wilson, *Enigmas and Mysteries*, p.44)

The lighthouse on the Scottish isle of Eilean Mor, found unattended but in perfect order in 1900, yielded no clues as to the fate of its three missing keepers.

"Be back shortly. Keep supper for me," said Charles E. Austin of Yonkers, New York, to his wife the evening of March 28, 1905, as he left his house. That was the last that she—or anyone—saw of him. (Jay Robert Nash, *Among the Missing*, p.253)

July 4, 1906, was the wedding day of New Jersey engineer William McKeekin. An hour after the ceremony he told his bride that he was going to get a carriage. Instead, it seems, he had second thoughts about the wedding, for he never returned. The instantly "widowed" Mrs. McKeekin searched for more than 17 years before seeking an annulment. (Jay Robert Nash, *Among the Missing*, p.374)

Dorothy Arnold set out from her family's Manhattan home on the morning of December 12, 1910, to shop for a dress to wear to her younger sister's coming-out party. She was a Bryn Mawr graduate, daughter of a prosperous importer and a socially prominent mother. Acquaintances who saw her walking west to Fifth Avenue, then south toward a bookstore at 27th Street, said later that she seemed cheerful. The salesgirl who sold her a box of chocolates noticed nothing amiss, nor did the friend who encountered her outside the bookstore. Yet Dorothy Arnold was never seen again, despite an international search for the "vanishing heiress."

In 1910 Dorothy Arnold, an attractive society girl and Bryn Mawr graduate, set out from her Manhattan home for a day of shopping and never returned. Although a world-wide search was conducted, not a trace of the "vanishing heiress" was ever found.

At first the Arnold family kept her disappearance a secret, conducting private inquiries through a friend of the family and the Pinkerton detective service. But after six weeks they turned to the police, and Mr. Arnold summoned reporters to his office to announce his conviction that she had been attacked in Central Park on her way home and her body cast into the reservoir. Horrible as that thought was, the rigid and respectable Mr. Arnold apparently preferred it to another possibility—that his daughter had run away with George Griscom, Jr., with whom she had spent a clandestine week several months before.

Griscom denied any knowledge of Dorothy's whereabouts. He returned to her family a letter she had written him, in which she had lamented a magazine's rejection of a story she had submitted, concluding, "All I can see ahead is a long road with no turning." Had she concealed a deep depression at the blow to her hopes for a career as a writer—one that was deep enough to make her take her own life?

Still another suggestion was that she had slipped and fallen on the icy pavement and suffered amnesia from a concussion and had been hospitalized. But no Manhattan hospital had admitted anyone resembling her.

The more investigators looked into Dorothy Arnold's life, the more they found behind the facade of the refined, well-brought-up young lady. But they found no reason to suspect suicide or foul play.

And they never found Dorothy Arnold. (*American Heritage*, 11:5:21–95, August 1960; Allen Churchill, *They Never Came Back*, pp.33–50; *The New York Times*, December 11 and 12, 1911)

"I am going to Mexico with a pretty definite purpose which is not at present discloseable," Ambrose Bierce wrote to his literary secretary on December 16, 1913. At 71, the mordant ironist of *In the Midst of Life* and *The Devil's Dictionary* was still energetic and curious enough to want to see for himself the rebellion of Pancho Villa, although he knew the risk he was taking: "If you hear of my being stood up against a Mexican stone wall and shot to rags, please know that I think that's a pretty good way to depart this life. It beats old age, disease, or falling down cellar stairs. To be a Gringo in Mexico—ah, that is euthanasia!"

His secretary and acquaintances never heard from Bierce again, and his case became a classic in the annals of mysterious disappearances.

Later developments may have provided an answer. In 1923 his friend Adolphe de Castro went to Mexico to question Villa, who said he had ordered Bierce to leave the rebel camp after the writer had uttered some indiscreet words in favor of Villa's enemy Carranza. And what happened to him then? "Who knows?" shrugged the old bandit.

Later, though, Villa's brother Hippolito and his comrade General Reyes took De Castro aside and confided that two gunmen had been sent after the aged American iconoclast. That may have been simply a tale concocted to give De Castro what he obviously expected to hear, but it is the nearest thing to an explanation for Bierce's disappearance. Few deaths would have better merited the trite old funeral-goer's phrase "He would have wanted it that way." (Allen Churchill, *They Never Came Back*, pp.51–69; *The New York Times*, November 29, 1914; *The New York Times Magazine*, January 1, 1928)

This caricature of the iconoclastic writer Ambrose Bierce, affectionately known as San Francisco's favorite curmudgeon, was executed by Swennerton in 1911. Two years later Bierce disappeared in Mexico during a revolutionary upheaval there.

James Regan, a passenger aboard the liner *Prinz Heinrich* bound from Marseilles to Naples on January 28, 1914, unaccountably disappeared with his luggage in midvoyage. A suicide with suitcases? (Jay Robert Nash, *Among the Missing,* p.378)

According to many writers on UFO's and on the occult, hundreds of British troops were mysteriously "abducted" by a cloud that settled over them as they advanced toward the Turkish positions during one of the battles of the Gallipoli campaign in 1915. The source for this story is a statement written 50 years after the incident by three New Zealand soldiers, who deposed that they had watched a dense, solid-looking cloud shaped like a loaf of bread settle on the ground in the path of an advancing column of troops. After the men walked into it, the account went on, the cloud lifted, leaving no one behind.

Most of the 34,000 Allied troops who died at Gallipoli in the First World War have no known grave. Some said that the soldiers walked into a cloud and disappeared.

In *Into Thin Air* Paul Begg concluded that this disappearance could not have happened as described. The battalion named by the New Zealanders was not unaccounted for. Another battalion had been decimated in battle, but that was nine days before the date given in the statement, and the report of the postwar commission that investigated the disastrous Gallipoli campaign included mention of an unseasonable mist that blinded Allied artillery gunners but aided their Turkish counterparts in wiping out a British unit. Significantly, that report was only fully declassified in 1965 and its publication may have brought forth a confused recollection by the New Zealanders.

Although the details are questionable, a mystery concerning the fallen still remains. As Begg notes: "Of the 34,000 British and Empire troops who died at Gallipoli, 27,000 have no known grave. In the light of such widespread carnage, how many more 'strange disappearances' do those bald statistics hide?" (Paul Begg, *Into Thin Air,* pp.40–51; *The Unexplained: Mysteries of Mind Space & Time,* Vol. 3, Issue 31)

The crew of the ship *Zebrina* disappeared in October 1917, during a short voyage across the English Channel in good weather. There were no clues aboard. (Paul Begg, *Into Thin Air,* p.60)

British missionaries in Nepal were summoned to the deathbed of a Hindu priest in 1917. In the room they found a 14-year-old Caucasian boy. The dying priest gestured toward him and said, "I took this child from a street in Wimbledon, England, in 1910." He gave no more details before dying.

The missionaries informed the authorities, who were unable to identify the boy's parents. All that the boy himself could say was that his name was Albert. He spent the rest of his life in India without ever learning anything more about his origins. (Charles Fort, *The Complete Books of Charles Fort,* pp.691–92; Jay Robert Nash, *Among the Missing,* p.107)

The Romanov dynasty that had ruled Russia since 1613 came to an end with the Bolshevik Revolution. Czar Nicholas II, his wife, Alexandra, and their son and four daughters were imprisoned at Ekaterinburg in the Ural Mountains, guarded by secret police of the new

The last czar of Russia, Nicholas II, and his family were supposedly executed in 1918. Were his son, Alexei, and his youngest daughter, Anastasia, secretly spared?

government. By most accounts they were shot and their bodies burned on July 16, 1918, as a counterrevolutionary army fought its way toward Ekaterinburg to rescue them. But from that day on, rumors of their survival never ceased. Some said they escaped to Poland in a sealed train with Lenin's tacit permission.

Over the years there have been several claimants to the Romanov name, notably Col. Michael Goleniewski, a Polish officer who defected to the United States in 1960. His claim that he was Nicholas's son, the Grand Duke Alexei, was supported by a former research director of the CIA. Several women have said they were Anastasia, the youngest daughter of the czar. The spice of royal mystery and the lure of the missing Romanov fortune (which is supposedly still held in Western banks) have flavored many fanciful versions of the unlikely escape from the Bolsheviks at Ekaterinburg. (LeRoy Hayman, *Thirteen Who Vanished*, p.37; Jay Robert Nash, *Among the Missing*, p.381)

Ambrose J. Small, a Toronto theater owner and man-about-town, had just concluded the sale of his theater chain and his wife had deposited a check for $1 million. That evening, December 2, 1919, he walked through a heavy snowstorm to pick up *The New York Times* and swore loudly when he found that the train that usually brought the newspaper had been delayed. Those curses were the last words anyone ever heard from the irate Ambrose Small.

The case was a nine-day wonder, for Small was known to have kept several mistresses and to have gambled heavily. His secretary, John Doughty, gave the story another twist by absconding with $100,000 in bonds on the same day. Captured and tried a year later for this offense, Doughty seemed to have had nothing to do with his employer's disappearance.

As in the case of the Romanovs, the lure of money brought forth many imposters, but Small was pronounced dead in 1923. Many connoisseurs of the mysterious remember him best for Charles Fort's whimsical linkage of his disappearance with that of Ambrose Bierce (see page 124): "[W]hat could the disappearance of one Ambrose, in Texas [*sic*], have to do with the disappearance of another Ambrose, in Canada? Was somebody collecting Ambroses?" (Charles Fort, *The Complete Books of Charles Fort*, pp.844–45, 847; *The New York Times Magazine*, January 1, 1928)

FROM 1920 TO 1940

In February 1920 the naked body of a man in his late thirties was found in a field in Hampshire, England. Tracks showed that he had wandered for some distance before collapsing and dying of exposure. No investiga-

tion could link the body to any disappearance, nor was there any evidence that it was a case of murder. Wrote the London *Daily News*:

> Although his photograph has been circulated north, east, south, and west, throughout the United Kingdom, the police are still without a clew, and there is no record of any missing person, bearing the slightest resemblance to this man, presumably [from his grooming] of education and good standing.

(Charles Fort, *The Complete Books of Charles Fort*, pp.692–93)

Mountain climbers George Leigh-Mallory and Andrew C. Irvine were less than a thousand feet below the peak of Mount Everest on June 8, 1924. Then swirling, wind-driven snow and mist hid them from the telescope in the base camp below—and they were never seen again. Everest was conquered "for the record" in 1953, but the tantalizing possibility remains that two men had reached its summit almost 30 years before.

Leigh-Mallory, 36, had participated in two earlier attempts on Everest. The leader of this third expedition described him as "the living soul of the offensive; the thing had become a personal matter with him." Irvine, 22, had little mountaineering experience but was skilled with the balky, cumbersome oxygen gear. They had made camp the night before at 26,800 feet, sending their Sherpa bearers down to tell the others that they hoped to reach the peak early the next morning.

For some reason they got a late start or were held up in the early part of the climb, for it was 12:50 P.M. on the eighth when they were observed at 28,227 feet. Then the clouds closed in—and the only evidence ever found was Leigh-Mallory's or Irvine's ice axe, discovered along their route in 1933. Perhaps they fell into an icy crevasse or were swept away by an avalanche that entombed them far below the challenging peak of Everest. The answer, like the climbers themselves, was lost in clouds at the top of the world. (*Climbing Everest*, Geoffrey Broughton, ed., pp.54–67, 70)

When we hear of expeditions seeking lost cities, we think of the Spanish and Portuguese conquistadores's 16th-century dream of El Dorado. But another such expedition set forth into Brazil's little-known Mato Grosso on April 20, 1925. It was led by Lt. Col. Percy Fawcett, an archeologist, geographer, and adventurer whose dreams of discovery were no less vivid and alluring than those of the conquistadores. They led him, his son Jack, and their companion Raleigh Rimell to an unknown fate in a forbidding land.

Fawcett had served in Great Britain's Indian Army in Ceylon at the turn of the century, spending his free time searching for ancient tombs and treasures. Going to

South America, he spent the years 1906 to 1909 surveying "a long and excessively unhealthy sector of the Brazilian-Bolivian frontier." At the end of that period he carefully studied an 18th-century Portuguese account of a great city that lay in ruins but was purportedly rich in gold and gems.

Convinced that the city existed—indeed, that Brazil's lost cities predated even those of Egypt—Fawcett and his party started out from Cuyabá, traveling light and planning to live off the country. His last dispatch, dated May 30, stated in part:

> We have cut our way through miles of *cerraba,* a forest of low dry scrub; we have crossed innumerable small streams by swimming and fording; we have climbed rocky hills of forbidding aspect; we have been eaten by bugs. . . . We shall not get into interesting country for another two weeks.

The world heard no more from Fawcett and his companions. Because he had warned they would be gone for at least two years, and because his wife was convinced he was well, there was no search party until May 1928, and by then the trail was cold. Indians from several of the mutually hostile tribes in the area accused each other of killing the explorers. Others told of seeing the Englishmen near death from disease and exhaustion. For more than a decade travelers returned with stories that Fawcett had "gone native," a half-mad old man in rotting rags among the Indians, but no convincing evidence ever emerged to resolve the mystery. (Peter Fleming, *Brazilian Adventure,* pp.6–13, 40–43, 187–90; Francis Hitching, *The Mysterious World: An Atlas of the Unexplained,* pp.235–36)

An extraordinary case of amnesia, covering a span of 40 years, was reported in 1927. Albert Mayfield, a British subject traveling aboard the steamer *Siam,* collapsed after bleeding from the nose and ears. When he regained consciousness, he knew himself as Albert Gurney of Rose, Minnesota—but his most recent memory was of a day when he was 14 years old and a schoolmate threw a rock that hit him on the head. According to *The New York Times* for July 16, 1927:

> Gurney had to be calmed when he saw his first airplane and has never heard jazz. He is assured by people who met him before his collapse on the steamer that he talked several languages, but he does not know them now nor does he know anything about his wife and two grown-up boys of whom he talked on the steamer.

His neighbors in the Bronx saw Dr. Charles Brancati as an immigrant who had made good as a doctor and an investor in the spiraling stock market of the late 1920's. But after his disappearance on November 19, 1928, they learned that his career had an element of something sinister—perhaps sinister enough that someone had wanted him dead.

On that Sunday morning Brancati had his handyman drive him to a nearby subway station. He said he was in a hurry to get to his Manhattan office. For the next four months, his brothers received letters from him postmarked, first, New Jersey, then Canada, then England. When the police were called in, they found Brancati's house in disarray, littered with scraps of paper and overturned furniture. There were bullet holes in a wall, and an unsigned threatening letter referring to a woman who had spurned the writer.

The police were developing a kidnap theory when federal law-enforcement officers informed them that Brancati had a long record of association with counterfeiters and the high-rolling gangster Arnold Rothstein, who had been murdered two weeks before Brancati's disappearance. Had Brancati feared the same would happen to him? Had he betrayed Rothstein? Was the threatening letter a real clue or a clumsy attempt at misdirection? The possibilities were so varied that they could hardly be narrowed down without first learning of Brancati's fate—and that remains unknown. (Jay Robert Nash, *Among the Missing,* p.147)

No disappearance in American history stirred so much speculation as that of New York Supreme Court associate justice Joseph F. Crater on August 6, 1930. Tall, imposing, and dapper, the 41-year-old Crater was a rising figure in the city's corrupt Tammany Hall Democratic organization. He had withdrawn more than $20,000 from the bank at about the time of his appointment as interim justice. The sum was close to a year's salary, the standard Tammany payoff for a lucrative post. It was not a fruitless investment, according to investigators who later looked into his role as receiver of a bankrupt hotel. Crater sold it to a

Sally Lou Ritz (left) was among the last people to see Judge Crater (right). Her own disappearance a few weeks later led to the speculation that she knew too much.

bond-and-mortgage firm for $75,000, and two months later the city agreed to buy it back for a planned street widening at a condemnation price of nearly $3 million.

In June 1930 Judge Crater and his wife went to their summer cottage in Maine. At the end of July he got a telephone call and told his wife he had to get back to the city "to straighten those fellows out." He made a trip to Atlantic City with one of the showgirls he favored and was back in Maine by August 1. On August 3 he returned to New York, and on August 6 he had checks for more than $5,000 cashed, then spent the afternoon collecting papers from his office. That evening, with a ticket for a Broadway show in his pocket, he dined at a midtown chophouse, sitting with lawyer friend William Klein and his companion, a stunning showgirl named Sally Lou Ritz. Then Crater hailed a taxi, stepped inside, and disappeared forever.

The purported explanations for Crater's exit would fill a book: his shady political friends got rid of him before he could be summoned to testify in a graft investigation; he died in the company of his mistress or a prostitute; he was lured to Westchester and killed in a dispute over a payoff; or he decided to start a new life in Quebec, the Caribbean, or Europe. For decades after his disappearance his name was a slang term for dodging one's responsibilities: to "pull a Crater" was to slip away for good. All that can be said today was said in the 1930's: Joseph F. Crater is either securely dead or else alive (he would be in his nineties) and perhaps pleased at having carried off one of the most thoroughly investigated—and mysterious—vanishing acts on record. (*Harper's*, 219:41–47, November 1959; *Life*, 47:42–44, November 16, 1959)

Bank robber John Dillinger, according to authorities, was shot down by federal agents in Chicago on July 22, 1934. But according to Jay Robert Nash, a crime historian, the autopsy report showed that the corpse was shorter and stockier than Dillinger, had brown rather than blue eyes, and showed signs of a rheumatic heart condition, which Dillinger did not have. Was there a cover-up for publicity purposes? Catching him greatly enhanced the prestige of J. Edgar Hoover's Bureau of Investigation (later known as the FBI). Did Dillinger in fact live on, secure in the knowledge that no "dead man" would appear in the "wanted alive" placards plastered on the post office wall? (Jay Robert Nash, *Among the Missing*, p.394; Julian Symons, *A Pictorial History of Crime*, pp.140–42)

In 1936, just a few blocks from where Judge Crater was last seen stepping into a taxi, financier Fred Lloyd dropped a friend off after a shared cab ride and then rode uptown. He was never seen again. His wife

The Last Flight of Amelia Earhart

They called her Lady Lindy after Charles A. Lindbergh, but to establish herself as a great flier she had to overcome opposition that Lindbergh and other men never faced. Amelia Earhart, who was born in 1898, was in college planning to be a doctor when she became entranced with flying. She learned quickly and in 1922 set a women's altitude record.

Becoming in 1928 the first woman to go on a transatlantic flight, she found herself at the center of a publicity blitz orchestrated by George Putnam, whom she married in 1931. The following year she flew the Atlantic solo and in the next few years undertook other long-distance solo ventures, all the while advocating women's rights.

The pinnacle of her career was to be an eastward round-the-world flight in a specially equipped twin-engine plane. Departing from California on May 20, 1937, she and her copilot-navigator, Fred Noonan, skimmed over Florida, Brazil, West Africa, Pakistan, India, Burma, Singapore, Australia. All went well until July 2. That morning, fuel tanks topped off, Earhart and Noonan left Lae, New Guinea, for the 2,556-mile flight to tiny Howland Island in the central Pacific. There the Coast Guard cutter *Itasca* waited to send homing signals, while other ships patrolled the area.

As the scheduled time of arrival drew near, the *Itasca* received fragmentary messages: "Cloudy and overcast . . . want bearings." Nothing more was heard.

The moment Putnam learned that his wife was missing, he went to one of her closest friends, Jacqueline Cochran, also an outstanding pilot. Cochran, in the past, had successfully located lost planes, and Earhart was convinced that she had extrasensory perception. Before taking off, she asked her friend to employ these powers on her behalf if needed. In her autobiography, *The Stars at Noon*, Cochran recalled that she at once told Putnam that Amelia was alive. She specified the area in the Pacific where her plane was floating, and named two boats nearby, one of them the *Itasca* (which she had not heard of at the time) and the other a Japanese fishing vessel. She begged Putnam, Cochran wrote,

continued to believe, until her death in 1945, that he would return. Three uncashed insurance policies on Lloyd were found in her hotel suite. (Jay Robert Nash, *Among the Missing*, p.395)

The puzzling disappearance of an aircraft in a densely populated region occurred on April 17, 1938. Andrew Carnegie Whitfield, nephew of the steel tycoon, took off from Roosevelt Field, Long Island, for another

Admirers of Amelia Earhart, the first woman to fly the Atlantic alone, were reluctant to attribute her disappearance over the Pacific in 1937 to pilot error.

to keep my name out of it . . . but to get planes and ships out to the designated area. Navy planes and ships in abundance combed that area but found no trace. I followed the course of her drifting for two days. It was always in the area being well combed.

A massive search revealed nothing, but the nation, unwilling to accept the loss of its heroine, held on to its hopes. Stories circulated for weeks that radio messages had been picked up, stating, "On coral southwest of unknown island." As time went by it was suggested she had been forced down on a volcanic isle that later sank or on a Japanese-held island, off limits to the U.S.

Following the outbreak of World War II it was theorized that Earhart had been on a mission of military surveillance, perhaps ordered by President Roosevelt, and that she was held as a prisoner of war. According to Fred Goerner, author of *The Search for Amelia Earhart,* Adm. Chester Nimitz told him that the fliers had in fact been picked up (and presumably executed) by the Japanese. After the war a California resident who had lived on Saipan Island in 1937 claimed she had seen two fliers there, one of whom resembled Amelia. The story surpassed belief, but the speculation about the fate of Lady Lindy and Fred Noonan still continues.

A massive air-and-ground search was conducted when the wealthy young flier A. C. Whitfield disappeared on a short hop over densely populated Long Island in 1938. No trace of the man or his airplane was ever found.

airfield 22 miles away. He had logged 200 hours of experience in the air and his small craft had enough fuel for a 150-mile flight, but neither he nor the airplane ever showed up again. The public imagination, whetted by the 1930's rash of disappearances and kidnappings, spotted the missing 28-year-old flier everywhere—including Council Bluffs, Iowa, where more than a year later railroad detectives thought they saw him riding a freight car, wearing a soiled flying suit, waving a handful of large bills at them, and smiling. (Jay Robert Nash, *Among the Missing,* p.333)

Richard Halliburton, the world-famous adventurer and writer, disappeared with a crew of 13 aboard his specially built Chinese junk *Sea Dragon* during a Pacific typhoon in late March 1939. The voyage had begun in Hong Kong on March 4 and was to have ended in San Francisco, site of the World's Fair that summer, but his last message was received on March 23.

Halliburton's seven books and widely syndicated newspaper column had acquainted millions of readers with his derring-dos, in romantic and exotic settings, from the Hellespont (where he swam from Europe to Asia as Lord Byron had done) to the Yucatan (where he swam in a *cenote,* a sacred pool once used for sacrifices by Mayan priests). His *Sea Dragon* voyage was to have provided authentic color for a new book on the possibility of Pacific crossings to America in ancient

After receiving priestly invocations for a safe voyage, Richard Halliburton set sail from Hong Kong in 1939 to cross the Pacific in a junk and was apparently lost at sea.

129

times—but the ocean ruled otherwise. Efforts to locate his bravely painted ship were eventually abandoned. (Jay Robert Nash, *Among the Missing*, pp.93-96)

FROM 1940 TO 1960

The casualties of World War II included, of course, the millions of soldiers and civilians who died, and the tens of thousands of orphaned children and shell-shocked amnesiacs. Countless others inexplicably disappeared, among them Glenn Miller, Leslie Howard, and other well-known personalities. For adults and children alike, one of the most poignant disappearances was that of Antoine de Saint-Exupéry, the French aviator and writer whose book *The Little Prince*, now a classic of gentle fantasy, was published in 1943.

Saint-Exupéry charmed and overwhelmed all who knew him with his energy and enthusiasm. The oldest son of a noble family, he threw himself into military flight training in the 1920's and then into civilian mail flights in North Africa and across the Atlantic. His books *Night Flight* and *Wind, Sand and Stars* were highly acclaimed. After the fall of France in 1940, he spent three years in the United States, and then—at 43 and with a left arm disabled by an early plane crash—argued his way into the Free French Air Force and began flying reconnaissance missions over Italy and the Mediterranean. On July 31, 1944, while in radio contact

Antoine de Saint-Exupéry, whose exuberant love of flying led him to become an airmail pilot in North Africa, conveyed in his writings the romance of winging over strange and distant places. The French aviator vanished while on a mission for the Free French Air Force in 1944.

with his base in Corsica, Saint-Exupéry disappeared—perhaps no more mysteriously than the others who had been lost on military missions, but leaving behind a legacy of the romance of flying. (LeRoy Hayman, *Thirteen Who Vanished*, pp.49-60)

As a trusted aide of Adolf Hitler's, Martin Bormann was with him in the Berlin bunker when the dictator and a woman believed to be Eva Braun killed them-

selves on April 30, 1945. Loyally, Bormann helped take the bodies outside and burn them in the shell-blasted garden. The next night he and others of the staff made their way through tunnels to a railway station, then walked beside German tanks through the firelit streets. One of the group later testified that he had seen Bormann lying on the ground, unwounded but not breathing. The Nuremberg war-crimes tribunal, unconvinced, sentenced him to death *in absentia*.

Rumors circulated that Bormann had been shot in Denmark while attempting to reach Adm. Karl Doenitz, Hitler's legal successor; that he escaped through the Alps to Italy; and that a submarine had carried him to South America. Simon Wiesenthal, the well-known pursuer of Nazi war criminals, believes that Bormann had exchanged Nazi loot for false passports and a new identity in Argentina, and then in Chile. Writer Ladislas Farago claimed he visited Bormann in a hospital in Bolivia in 1973. Bormann would be in his eighties today if he is still alive; he has the best of reasons for staying out of sight. (Hugh Trevor-Roper, *The Last Days of Hitler*, pp.212-17)

Six people vanished on or near Vermont's Long Trail between November 1945 and December 1950. The body of only one of them was found.

The first disappearance was that of Middie Rivers, a 75-year-old deer hunter who knew the region of the trail near Mount Glastenbury very well. State police, soldiers, boy scouts, and local residents combed the woods after he failed to return from a day's hunting on November 12, 1945, but to no avail.

On a December day in 1946 Bennington College student Paula Welden told her roommate that she was going for a walk. The last person to see the 18-year-old alive was a watchman at the local newspaper, who gave her directions to the Long Trail. Despite a thorough search and nationwide publicity, no trace of Paula Welden could be found, and rumors of a "mad murderer" began to spread.

James Telford, the third victim (if that is the word), was last seen on the trail on December 1, 1949.

Early in 1950 Frieda Langer, who was described as an

Vermont's Long Trail, shown on this map, runs along the spine of the Green Mountains. No explanation has been found for the disappearance of six persons on or near this wilderness trail over a period of five years.

experienced woodswoman, disappeared while hiking the trail. Her body was finally found on May 12, 1951, in an open spot in the woods that was apparently overlooked in earlier searches.

When Martha Jones disappeared on November 6, 1950, it was thought at first that she had run off to join her boyfriend in Virginia. When this proved not to be the case, a search was launched, with no results.

The last of the six was Frances Christman, who set out on December 3, 1950, to visit a friend three miles away and was never seen again.

If the six cases had no connection other than their location, coincidence was at work on a grand scale. If, on the other hand, there was a "mad murderer of the Long Trail," we will never know why the crimes began or ended: the Vermont forest has yielded no secrets. (Paul Begg, *Into Thin Air*, pp.19–30)

The lore of the Bermuda Triangle, the area east of Florida where ships and planes are said to disappear in numbers too large to be happenstance, grew with the loss of Flight 19 on December 5, 1945. Five TBM Avenger torpedo bombers took off from Fort Lauderdale on a 320-mile navigation training exercise that should have taken them east, then north, over Grand Bahama Island, then southwest back to base.

Leading Flight 19 was Lt. Charles Carroll Taylor, one of two experienced crewmen aboard the planes. The 12 other pilots, radiomen, and gunners were all students in training. Less than two hours after the 2:10 P.M. takeoff, radio messages indicated that Taylor had become disoriented: "Both my compasses are out. . . .

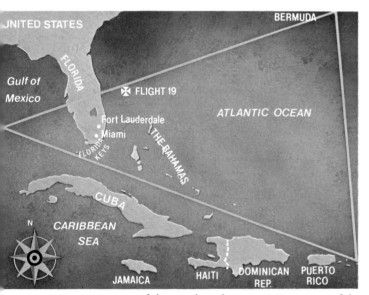

Disappearances of ships and airplanes in various parts of the ocean expanse outlined above have fostered a superstitious dread of the so-called Bermuda Triangle.

I'm over land, but it's broken. I'm sure I'm in the Keys, but I don't know how far down and I don't know how to get to Fort Lauderdale." In fact, anything like the planned course should have put Flight 19 near Great Sale Cay, 200 miles northeast of the Florida Keys.

For the next two hours, fragmentary radio contacts revealed, Flight 19 flew chiefly north and east in the apparent belief that it was over the Gulf of Mexico and would soon encounter the west coast of Florida. One of the last transmissions from Taylor announced: "All planes close up tight . . . we will have to ditch unless landfall . . . when the first man gets down to 10 gallons we will all land in the water together." One flying boat set out from Miami to search for the presumably ditched airmen but had to turn back when its antenna iced over. Another took off from the Banana River Naval Air Station. Half an hour later a tanker observed a burst of flames and investigated a patch of oil and debris where the flying boat must have crashed.

As for Flight 19, a five-day search of 250,000 square miles of ocean failed to discover any trace of it.

Over the years, exaggeration and legend have made the story of Flight 19 even more puzzling than it was, embellishing it with hints of UFO's and alleged radio messages such as "Even the ocean doesn't look as it should" and "Don't come after me. . . . It looks like. . . ." Still, there are questions at the core that even the 400-page naval inquiry record could not answer. Why did both of Taylor's compasses fail shortly after they were checked out in the preflight inspection? Even though the northernmost Bahamas look much like the Florida Keys from the air, how did the airmen become convinced that the first leg of their flight had taken them so far south rather than east? All the evidence points to the conclusion that Flight 19 ran out of fuel and that its crews were unable to get into rafts before the ditched planes sank in rough water. But the evidence does *not* explain how their planned two-hour training flight became a wandering, five-hour journey to nowhere. (Lawrence David Kusche, *The Bermuda Triangle Mystery—Solved*, pp.97–122)

Cadet Richard Cox, a 22-year-old sophomore at West Point, vanished on January 14, 1950. Cox had enlisted in the army in 1946 and served in occupied Germany. Upon entering the academy he had become a strong long-distance runner and a better-than-average student. None of his comrades knew of any shadowy side to Cadet Cox's life.

On January 7, 1950, he had a visitor who called himself "George" and said he had served in Germany with Cox. The two had dinner and drinks together. The next morning Cox told friends that his visitor had spun morbid tales about bloody fighting and the murder of a German woman "George" had lived with.

Nonetheless, a week later, when the visitor showed up again, Cox met with him and said they would meet for dinner. "He didn't act apprehensive," recalled Cox's roommate, "just sort of disgusted. I guess he just figured it was an excuse to get out to eat at the hotel, the Hotel Thayer, adjacent to the academy." That night Cadet Richard Cox disappeared: no one remembered seeing him leave West Point or dining at the hotel.

Army investigators and the FBI were unable to make any headway in the long search that followed, although they pursued more than a thousand potential leads. The academy grounds and the surrounding region were searched. Military records turned up no serviceman in Germany who could be identified with "George." Unlike most missing persons whose police case files remain open, Richard Cox is officially (and inexplicably) AWOL—absent without leave. (Allen Churchill, *They Never Came Back*, pp.149-69; Jay Robert Nash, *Among the Missing*, p.262)

Father Henry Borynski vanished on July 13, 1953, from his parish in a suburb of Bradford, England. Borynski had made himself well known among Polish emigrants and refugees in England for his denunciation of the Communist regime in postwar Poland.

The apparent occasion of Borynski's disappearance was a telephone call. "Now this has come. . . . I must go," he told his housekeeper enigmatically. Without gathering any of his papers or taking any of his possessions, he left the rectory and was observed a few minutes later waiting on a street corner.

One unproved theory is that some family or other connection in Poland had left Father Borynski subject to pressure from the Polish Communists and that he had been taken to a Russian ship sailing for Leningrad. It was rumored that there were two unidentified men on the passenger list, one of them the priest and the other a professional assassin. The British government later refused to respond to a parliamentary question about the Borynski case, saying that disclosure of any facts "would not be in the public interest." (Jay Robert Nash, *Among the Missing*, pp.228-29)

Although the captain and officers of the Joyita *had often claimed she was unsinkable, they and the passengers abandoned the vessel. Their story remains unknown.*

The small ship *Joyita* sailed from Apia in Western Samoa in early October 1955, bound for another island 270 miles away. More than a month later she was found abandoned, with an awning stretched as if to collect rainwater. A broken pipe had caused flooding, but the cork-lined hull would have kept her afloat indefinitely. The radio and one of the twin engines had failed. Bloody bandages suggested an injury, or perhaps a fight on board. But neither the captain, Dusty Miller, nor his crew and passengers were ever found to answer questions about the last voyage of the *Joyita*. (Colin Wilson, *Enigmas and Mysteries*, p.48)

The disappearance of the activist scholar Jesús María de Galíndez in New York City on March 12, 1956, led to investigations that revealed a tangled international web.

A page from the notebook of pilot Gerald Murphy indisputably linked him with Professor Galíndez, who vanished in 1956, possibly the victim of a murderous plot.

Galíndez, a refugee first from Franco's Spain and then Rafael Trujillo's Dominican Republic, was a teacher of Hispanic-American history and politics at Columbia University. He was well known for speeches attacking Trujillo and had written a 750-page doctoral thesis documenting the dictator's crimes.

Galíndez disappeared on the way to the subway after an evening class at Columbia. Nine months later a young American pilot by the name of Gerald Murphy vanished in the Dominican Republic. Local authorities said that Murphy had been killed in a quarrel with a Dominican citizen who subsequently hanged himself in jail, but inquiries pressed first by Murphy's family and then by the U.S. State Department, and finally by *Life* magazine led to a reconstruction in which Murphy had been hired to fly the kidnapped Galíndez first from Long Island to Miami, then on to Trujillo's island. Murphy later told acquaintances that on the night of

March 12 an ambulance had delivered a "wealthy invalid" to the Long Island airport, and there is no doubt that after the flight Murphy lived in unwontedly high style in the Dominican Republic.

The Trujillo government denied any link between Galíndez and Murphy, and their fate was still a mystery when Trujillo himself was assassinated in May 1961, bringing his 30-year tyranny to an end. (*Life*, 42:24–31, February 25, 1957; 45:70, July 7, 1958; *Newsweek*, 47:46, June 4, 1956; 47:65, June 11, 1956; 50:49, July 29, 1957; *Time*, 67:41, April 2, 1956; 67:45, June 4, 1956; 68:30, July 16, 1956; 69:21, February 11, 1957)

A family visit was the last journey investment counselor Bruce Campbell ever took. On April 14, 1959, he and his wife drove from their home in Massachusetts to see their son. They stopped at a motel in Jacksonville, Illinois, where Mrs. Campbell awoke to find her husband gone—in his pajamas, leaving behind their car, money, and all his clothes. Campbell was never found. (Jay Robert Nash, *Among the Missing*, p.406)

SINCE 1960

The offshore waters of a Pacific island or one of the most hostile jungles in the world claimed the life of Michael Rockefeller, the 23-year-old son of New York State's governor (and later vice president) Nelson Rockefeller, in November 1961.

Michael Rockefeller, a Harvard graduate, had been seeking "something romantic and adventurous" before going to business school and becoming a banker. So he joined an expedition from Harvard's Peabody Museum to the jungles of Dutch New Guinea, where he spent six months helping to tape native chants. After a brief return to the United States, he went back to the jungle to seek native artifacts for the Museum of Primitive Art in New York, an institution sponsored and largely supported by the Rockefeller Foundation.

On November 16 Rockefeller, a Dutch anthropologist named René Wassink, and two guides were traveling along the southern coast of Dutch New Guinea aboard a catamaran (two dugout canoes lashed together) mounted with an outboard motor. A large tidal wave swept over the boat, tipping it over and leaving it to drift. The guides swam ashore and reported the accident, while the catamaran drifted three or four miles out to sea. Finally Rockefeller decided to follow the guides, despite Wassink's warning of sharks and saltwater crocodiles. Taking a jerry can and an empty gasoline can as floats, he struck out to swim to shore.

Many hours later a search plane spotted and rescued the anthropologist, still clinging to the catamaran. Soon after, Nelson Rockefeller and Michael's twin sister, Mary, were on their way to the Pacific island. Dutch, Australian, and native search parties were sent out to cover every square mile of offshore waters and go to all the coastal villages, offering large rewards for any word of the young American, but the only clue found was a floating gasoline can. Remembering that Rockefeller was a strong swimmer, some resident officials and missionaries were inclined to think that he reached shore and that he lost his life in the jungle. His fate will probably never be known. (John Godwin, *Unsolved: The World of the Unknown*, pp.1–16; LeRoy Hayman, *Thirteen Who Vanished*, pp.136–43)

Three Germans connected with Egypt's rocket program vanished from the Munich area in September 1962. Dr. Wolfgang Pilz and Prof. Paul Görke, both of whom worked at the Egyptian rocket plant in a Cairo suburb, dropped out of sight at about the same time as Dr. Heinz Krug, whose Stuttgart trading company had supplied parts for the rockets. Krug was last seen in Munich in the company of an Arab who called himself Mr. Saleh. A few days after the two had been spotted together, Krug's car was found abandoned.

Many Egyptians believed that the Germans had been abducted by Israeli agents seeking to block the military progress of an enemy state. The fate of all three might as well have been another riddle of the Sphinx. (*Newsweek*, 60:36–37, October 1, 1962)

Three airplanes and eight passengers vanished over the Bermuda Triangle, a patch of ocean associated with a succession of perplexing and sinister disappearances, in a single week in January 1967. Searches turned up no floating debris for two of the planes. Debris from the third plane was found, but the cause of the crash could not be determined. (Lawrence David Kusche, *The Bermuda Triangle Mystery—Solved*, pp.211–15)

Sometime in early July 1969 Donald Crowhurst went overboard from his sailboat, the *Teignmouth Electron*, in mid-Atlantic. He had entered a round-the-world race sponsored by *The Times* of London with high hopes, although his newly built trimaran (named for its home

Michael Rockefeller, shown here on a river in Dutch New Guinea months before he disappeared, is believed to have drowned in an attempt to swim ashore from a drifting, overturned boat, but his death has never been proved.

port and Crowhurst's failing marine-electronics firm) was hardly ready for such a strenuous challenge when he started the race on October 31, 1968.

Month after month cabled messages and position reports indicated that Crowhurst was making good time on a voyage around Africa, across the Indian and Pacific oceans, and around Cape Horn at the tip of South America. In fact, he had fallen behind schedule in the first weeks of the voyage and decided to loiter in the South Atlantic while faking his messages and logbook. (In a second, genuine logbook he recorded his arguments with himself over what he was doing.)

By April 1969 Crowhurst seems to have decided to let the only other boat still in the race claim victory, so that nobody would look too closely at his own account. But on May 21 his competitor's ship sank near the Azores. Crowhurst found himself in an impossible position, for the publicity surrounding his widely anticipated victory would surely be too much for his story to withstand. His logbook became more incoherent, filled with rambling philosophical discourses and meditations on "the sin of concealment." His last radio message was on June 30. On July 11 a British freighter found the *Teignmouth Electron* abandoned. (LeRoy Hayman, *Thirteen Who Vanished,* pp.24–36)

On May 15, 1970, Edward and Stephania Andrews attended a trade association's cocktail party at the Chicago Sheraton Hotel. Both 63 years old, they were archetypal solid citizens, respectively a bookkeeper and a credit investigator, with a comfortable home in suburban Arlington Heights.

At the party Edward Andrews complained of mild illness, ascribing it to hunger pangs: there were only hors d'oeuvres to eat. They went downstairs to the hotel garage, where the attendant noticed that Stephania seemed to be crying and that Andrews acted somewhat under the weather—as they drove out, he scraped an exit door with the car fender. No one ever saw Mr. and Mrs. Andrews again.

Police theorized that Andrews might have driven off a bridge into the Chicago River, but dragging and metal detectors could not lead them to the car. (Telephone interview with the Arlington Heights, Illinois, Police Department)

Skyjacker Dan Cooper parachuted from a Northwest Airlines Boeing 727 into a rainy Thanksgiving night in 1971. Cooper had taken over the jetliner after it took off from Portland, Oregon, and ordered that it land at Seattle to pick up a parachute and $200,000 in cash. His demands were met and the plane took off again.

After takeoff Cooper sent the stewardess forward to the cockpit and used her intercom to repeat his instruc-

Above is an artist's composite drawing of Dan Cooper, who hijacked a Boeing 727 (top) over Washington state in 1971. The map shows approximately where Cooper bailed out and where some of the ransom was found. Cooper has not been seen since.

tions that the pilot hold the 727 at 200 mph. When they were approximately over the Lewis River, Cooper opened the rear exit door and jumped, without protective gear against the wind and freezing rain outside but apparently confident.

Over the years a plastic notice sign from a 727's rear door and a parachute were found in the woods. Then, in 1980, some of the marked bills from Cooper's haul were found in mud dredged from the Columbia River. That confirmed the belief in some quarters that Cooper had not survived his escape and that his skeleton lies somewhere underwater or in the deepest woods. But to others, captivated by Cooper's coolness and planning, he is a heroic scoundrel who deserves to be living well, wherever he is today. (*The New York Times,* November 26, 27, 28, and 30, 1971; February 13, 14, and 22, 1980)

Two aging Japanese soldiers emerged from Pacific jungles in 1972 and 1974 to find the world almost unrecognizable since the end of their war a generation earlier. In late January 1972 Shoichi Yokoi was apprehended by fishermen on the island of Guam, where he and nine comrades had hidden when American troops landed in 1944. The others had eventually died or given themselves up, but Yokoi had ignored a leaflet announcing his nation's surrender because, he said, "we Japanese soldiers were told to prefer death to the disgrace of getting captured alive."

Lt. Hiroo Onoda held out two years longer, emerging from the Philippine jungles on March 10, 1974. Unlike Yokoi, he had never been informed that World War II was over; when asked why he had not come out before, Onoda said, "I had not received the order." Both old soldiers were hailed as heroes when they returned to Japan. The Pacific conflict took in so many tiny islets, many of them still only rarely visited, that more of the emperor's faithful troops may still appear. (*The New York Times*, March 11 and 12, 1974; *Time*, 99:41–42, February 7, 1972)

Jimmy Hoffa, photographed at a Teamsters Union convention in Miami, vanished in 1975. He is thought to have been murdered in a power struggle within the union.

Sgt. Shoichi Yokoi of the Japanese Imperial Army as he looked in 1941 and as he appeared when he was captured on Guam in 1972. He had hidden in the jungle for 28 years rather than suffer the disgrace of surrender.

Jimmy Hoffa, president of the Teamsters Union from 1957 until he went to prison in 1967, disappeared on July 30, 1975. He had been paroled, some say, after a deal in which union vice president Frank Fitzsimmons assured the White House that Hoffa would not resume his office until 1980, the end of his prison term. According to this version, Hoffa was furious when he found out about the deal Fitzsimmons had made and was beginning to "spill the beans" about connections between the union and organized crime.

Hoffa was at his summer home north of Detroit in 1975, and on the 30th he drove to a luncheon meeting with alleged mob leader Tony "Jack" Giacalone and Tony "Pro" Provenzano, a Teamster who had been in prison with Hoffa. Apparently they stood him up, for several hours later he called home to see if they had left any message for him. His last call was to an old friend and business partner, Louis Linteau. The last witness to see him said that Hoffa was in the back seat of a car with

several others, leaning forward to talk to the driver.

When Hoffa did not return, a manhunt began. Authorities questioned their mob contacts, dug up cornfields, and broke through cement basement floors searching for his body. Half a dozen books have connected the murder (for nobody believes Hoffa is still alive) to various aspects of the continuing, corrupt relationship in which union pension funds have been mixed with the proceeds of gambling, prostitution, and illegal drugs. But a corpse, after all, is not as hard to dispose of as many people are inclined to believe—certainly not for professionals—and many of those Hoffa associated with were professionals at murder. (Lester Velie, *Desperate Bargain*, passim)

The long drive between Miami, Florida, and Scarsdale, New York, was routine for Charles R. Romer and his wife, Catharine. The retired couple, both in their seventies, had spent the winter of 1980 in their Florida apartment, and on April 8 they started home. That afternoon they checked into a motel in Brunswick City, Georgia. A little later a highway patrolman saw their black Lincoln Continental on the road. Perhaps they were going to a restaurant for dinner.

If so, they never arrived. They and their car disappeared. Three days later, finding the room had not been slept in, the motel management notified authorities. Baffled police could only guess that the Romers had gone off the road into a swamp or that they had been robbed and killed. Other than luggage in a motel room and a fleeting glimpse of their car, there were no clues. Said their son: "It's incredible that two people can . . . totally disappear." Incredible—but true. (*The New York Times*, April 19, 20, and 27, 1980)

MONSTERS
AND
MORE

Unknown creatures of monstrous size have been seen
and occasionally photographed in various seas,
lakes, and mountainous regions of the world. Nessie
and the Abominable Snowman have been described
so often that they have almost become
household words. As for ghosts, the countless numbers
of sober citizens who have seen or heard what
they could only define as a spectral presence suggest
that there must be some kind of etheric manifestation
beyond our understanding. Those who have encountered
apparitions are convinced this is so,
and never to have seen one is hardly proof
that they do not exist.

From the mouth of hell a terrifying monster glowers at lost souls.

MONSTERS

Anthropologists, psychiatrists, and other students of human behavior tend to interpret man's belief in monsters in terms of man's need for them. These experts hypothesize that we create monsters to give acceptable form to our unnamed anxieties; that we invent our monsters by projection, constructing brutish repositories for whatever is savage, libidinous, or otherwise undesirable in ourselves; or that we attempt to justify our fear of the unknown by exaggerating characteristics of any odd-looking and seldom-seen creatures to make them more terrifying than they actually are.

But modern man seems to have another need: to resist belief in the bizarre or paranormal, to deny the existence of what cannot be explained. Giants in fairy tales and Godzillas and King Kongs may very well serve as repositories for the nastiness in us, but we know these monsters are fiction. They are inventions of individuals. It does not follow that the Yeti is a creation of the imagination.

The combined fear and attraction of man for monster is as old as the existence of either. Throughout the ages human beings have told of such prodigies as fire-breathing dragons, reptilian oddities with many appendages, man-shaped beings with hairy coats and bestial faces, and underwater colossuses with a penchant for overturning boats. These incredible creatures were not inventions; they were seen. Doubtless many were colored by faulty observation, by exaggeration, even by a touch of poetic elaboration that wove them into myth to serve as foils for heroes—symbols clashing with symbols. But the raw materials, the observed phenomena, were there. And something still is there, in spite of our postmedieval need to ridicule monster sightings as hallucination or hoax.

The truth is that few of us in this scientific age really want to see or experience the inexplicable, and when we do, we distort the perception into something we can cope with. Many observers have gone through extraordinary mental gymnastics to persuade themselves that they did not see what they thought they saw. Bigfoot was a bear or a joker in a monkey suit. The sea serpent must have been a trick of light, a breaking wave, a floating log, a tangle of seaweed, or 50 porpoises swimming in single file. As for skeptical nonwitnesses, they would rather devise and swallow the most tortuous "explanation" than believe the most straightforward report.

Current thinking about what we call monsters is that the ones still with us are probably explainable in terms of relicts or fossil species that have taken refuge in remote and almost impenetrable regions. This attitude, too, may be an expression of our need to demystify the mysterious in order to accept the unacceptable.

Monsters come in two basic types: aquatic and terrestrial (although some monster buffs suggest an extraterrestrial link). Once in a while an odd creature may turn out to be amphibious, or ambiguous; and on occasion something flies past our startled vision and appears to be an incredible winged Unknown. Both categories are treated here according to the habitat of their choice—first water, then land—and presented in chronological order within each category.

The skeptic who feels inclined to say, "Yes, but—" after reading these reports should note that hundreds of sightings have been omitted for each one included and that many viewers are converted scoffers.

BEFORE 1900

In July 1734 a Norwegian missionary named Hans Egede, voyaging to Greenland, spotted something incredible as his vessel neared the Danish colony of Good Hope on the Davis Strait. "On the 6th," as he subsequently reported in straightforward terms,

> appeared a very terrible sea-animal, which raised itself so high above the water, that its head reached above our maintop. It had a long, sharp snout, and blew like a whale, had broad, large flappers, and the body was, as it were, covered with a hard skin, and it was very wrinkled and uneven on its skin; moreover on the lower part it was formed like a snake, and when it went under water again, it cast itself backwards, and in doing so it raised its tail above the water, a whole ship-length from its body. That evening we had very bad weather. [Richard Carrington, *Mermaids and Mastodons*, pp.23–24]

Missionary Hans Egede, a person of unquestioned integrity, supplied one of the earliest reliable firsthand accounts of a sea serpent, sighted near the coast of Greenland.

"Incontestibly the largest Sea-monster in the world" was described by Erik L. Pontoppidan, bishop of Bergen, in *The Natural History of Norway* (1752–53). The kraken, as fishermen and the bishop called it, was so enormous that even when it surfaced its whole body did not appear. Wrote Pontoppidan:

> . . . its back or upper part, which seems to be in appearance about an English mile and a half in circumference, (some say more, but I chuse [*sic*] the least for greater certainty) looks at first like a number of small islands, surrounded with something that floats and fluctuates like sea weeds. . . . at last several bright points or horns appear, which grow thicker and thicker the higher they rise above the surface of the water, and sometimes they stand up as

high and large as the masts of middle-siz'd vessels.
It seems these are the creature's arms, and, it is said, if they were to lay hold of the largest man-of-war, they would pull it down to the bottom. [Bernard Heuvelmans, *In the Wake of the Sea-Serpents*, pp.49–50]

A sea serpent of impressive size was reportedly seen in and around Gloucester Harbor, Massachusetts, by many persons during the .month of August 1817. Prompted by heated debate between believers and skeptics, a special committee of the Linnaean Society of New England collected a sheaf of sworn statements from purported eyewitnesses. The affidavit of Matthew Gaffney, ship's carpenter, typically deposed:

> That on the 14th day of August, A.D. 1817, between the hours of four and five o'clock in the afternoon, I saw a strange marine animal, resembling a serpent in the harbor in said Gloucester. I was in a boat, and was within 30 feet of him. His head appeared full as large as a four-gallon keg, his body as large as a barrel, and his length that I saw I should judge 40 feet at least. The top of his head was of a dark color, and the underpart of his head appeared nearly white, as did also several feet of his belly that I saw. . . . I fired at him when he was the nearest to me.

The creature, Gaffney went on, turned as if to charge the boat, then sank like a stone and reappeared some 100 yards away. It moved at a rate of about one mile per two or three minutes. (Reader's Digest, eds., *American Folklore and Legend*, pp.245–46)

Capt. Peter M'Quhae and most of the officers and crew of H.M.S. *Daedalus* were treated to the sight of "a sea-serpent of extraordinary dimensions" while on passage from the East Indies to Plymouth, England, in 1848. In a detailed, matter-of-fact statement dated October 11, Captain M'Quhae advised the lords of the admiralty that at 5 P.M. on August 6—the *Daedalus* then being in the South Atlantic 300 miles off the western coast of Africa—"something very unusual was seen by Mr. Sartoris, midshipman, rapidly approaching the ship from before the beam."

Mr. Sartoris immediately reported the circumstance to Captain M'Quhae and two officers walking the quarterdeck. What they and several other incredulous viewers saw was an enormous, undulating, snakelike thing "with head and shoulders kept about four feet constantly above the surface of the sea." As nearly as the men could judge by making a comparison with the length of their main topsail yard, the serpent's visible length was a good 60 feet; its diameter behind the head was 15 or 16 inches, and there seemed to be some kind of mane down the creature's back.

A 60-foot-long sea monster passed just yards from the H.M.S. Daedalus, according to Capt. Peter M'Quhae in his official report to the British admiralty.

Maintaining its course to the southwest at a pace of 12 to 15 miles per hour, the creature passed the *Daedalus* rapidly but, stated M'Quhae, "so close under our lee quarter, that had it been a man of my acquaintance, I should easily have recognized his features with the naked eye." (Bernard Heuvelmans, *In the Wake of the Sea-Serpents*, pp.198–217)

During passage from Cádiz, Spain, to Tenerife, the French sloop *Alecton* encountered a monstrous sea creature on November 30, 1861. Though there was something of a swell, the weather was extremely favorable, and Lieutenant Bouyer, commander of the ship, resolved to attempt the capture of what he later reported to have recognized "as the *Poulpe géant* [giant squid] whose existence has been so much disputed and

The Alecton *crew members slung a noose around the tail of this giant squid and were about to haul it aboard when the rope slipped; they were left with only a 40-pound fragment.*

now seems to be relegated to the realms of myth." But the swell caused the *Alecton* to roll wildly, and the few bullets that hit the creature had no effect.

Eventually Bouyer and his men managed to harpoon the thing and sling a noose around its tail. Tentacles waving violently, the quarry snapped the harpoon and tore most of its body free. The crew hauled aboard a mere portion of the tail, weighing about 40 pounds.

Yet both officers and men had come close enough to the creature to give a detailed description of it. Reporting to the minister of the navy, Bouyer wrote:

> It was in fact the giant calamary, but the shape of the tail suggested it belonged to a species not yet described. The body seemed to measure about 15 to 18 feet in length. The head had a parrot-like beak surrounded by eight arms between 5 and 6 feet long. In aspect it was quite appalling; brick red in colour, shapeless and slimy, its form repulsive and terrible.

(Richard Carrington, *Mermaids and Mastodons*, p.54)

An inland water monster that has never been hooked, though reportedly several times seen, is an elusive creature dwelling in 100-mile-long Lake Champlain, which links Vermont and New York State with Canada. One of the first descriptions of it was made on August 30, 1878, by six people on a small yacht. What they saw was an extraordinary living thing with, as one observer said, "two large folds just back of the head projecting above the water, and at some distance, say 50 feet or more behind, two or more folds at what was apparently the tail." Later this monster—or perhaps a descendant—would become known as Champ. It has consistently been reported over the years, and as recently as 1981. (Roy P. Mackal, *Searching for Hidden Animals*, pp.217–18)

Thimble Tickle, Newfoundland, was the scene of a monstrous fish sighting on November 2, 1878. Three local fishermen were out in a boat not far off shore when they saw a bulky object which they took to be part of a wreck. Rowing up to it, they found to their disbelief that it was a huge marine creature, glassy-eyed and frenziedly thrashing its tentacles and tail, for it had been grounded by the ebbing tide. They snagged the monster with a barbed grapnel and attached the hook to a rope, which they lashed to a tree. The creature struggled for a while; then, as the water continued to recede, it died. The length of the body, as estimated by the three men, was 20 feet from its beak to the tip of the tail. A tentacle measured 35 feet. Unmindful of scientists or skeptics, the fishermen chopped their catch into dogmeat. (Bernard Heuvelmans, *In the Wake of the Sea-Serpents*, pp.63–65)

It must have been a vastly surprised Mr. Hoad of Adelaide, Australia, who, while walking along Brungle Creek one day in the early fall of 1883, came upon the remains of an unworldly creature. The thing was piglike in form, with a headless trunk and an appendage that curved inward like the tail of a lobster. Needless to say, it has never been identified. (Charles Fort, *The Complete Books of Charles Fort*, p.609)

FROM 1900 TO 1970

Surveying the Amazon basin for the Royal Geographical Society of London in 1907, Maj. Percy Fawcett could not at first credit local tales of outsize snakes inhabiting the swamps and rivers. But, as he was to write in his memoirs, personal experience convinced him they were true. Fawcett and his Indian crew were slowly drifting down the sluggish Rio Abuná when, almost under the bow of their flimsy boat,

> . . . there appeared a triangular head and several feet of undulating body. It was a giant anaconda. I sprang for my rifle as the creature began to make its way up the bank, and hardly waiting to aim smashed a .44 soft-nosed bullet into its spine, ten feet below the wicked head. At once there was a flurry of foam, and several heavy thumps against the boat's keel, shaking us as though we had run on a snag. . . . We stepped ashore and approached the reptile with caution. It was out of action, but shivers ran up and down the body like puffs of wind on a mountain tarn. As far as it was possible to measure, a length of forty-five feet lay out of the water, and seventeen feet in it, making a total length of sixty-two feet.

On a return trip to London, Fawcett was branded a liar for his claim that he had bagged a 62-foot anaconda. That animal, scientists declared, could not possibly measure more than about 45 feet; therefore the observer's story was fantastic. (Bernard Heuvelmans, *On the Track of Unknown Animals*, pp.284–86)

Father Victor Heinz, while going about the Lord's work in South America, saw what he thought was a water snake very much larger than Fawcett's anaconda. The priest, who happened to be a close friend of Lorenz Hagenbeck, a famous German animal dealer and zoo director, reported:

> During the great floods of 1922, on May 22 at about 3 o'clock . . . I was being taken home by canoe on the Amazon from Obidos [Brazil]; suddenly I noticed something surprising in midstream. I distinctly recognised a giant water-snake at a distance of some 30 yards. . . .
> Coiled up in two rings the monster drifted quietly

and gently downstream. My quaking crew had stopped paddling. Thunderstruck, we all stared at the frightful beast. I reckoned that its body was as thick as an oil-drum and that its visible length was some 80 feet. When we were far enough away and my boatmen dared to speak again they said that the monster would have crushed us like a box of matches if it had not previously consumed several large capybaras [giant rodents].
[Bernard Heuvelmans, *On the Track of Unknown Animals*, pp.292–94]

Driving south from Inverness along the shore of Loch Ness on their way to the little town of Foyers were Mr. and Mrs. George Spicer, a London businessman and his wife. It was the afternoon of July 22, 1933, and the Spicers were enjoying a relaxing Scottish vacation. Suddenly the bracken on the hillside about 200 yards ahead became agitated, and from it emerged an enormous, long-necked animal. Moving jerkily, the hulk crossed the narrow road. Astounded, Spicer stepped on the gas for a closer view, but by the time he and his wife reached the spot, the creature had lumbered through the bushes on the loch side and disappeared.

Describing their encounter to the press shortly afterward, the Spicers said that the creature was about 6 feet long and stood—or lumbered—4 feet high (in later tellings the animal grew to a length of 25 or 30 feet). They also recalled that its neck undulated "in the manner of a scenic railway." In addition to these oddities, the extraordinary creature was a "terrible, dark elephant grey, of a loathsome texture, reminiscent of a snail." Thus, possibly maligned as to its looks, did the Loch Ness Monster become a public figure.

The creature had been seen many times before by people frequenting the loch and its environs, including the Irish Saint Columba in A.D. 565, but Mr. Spicer's description of it in a letter to the press publicized what has become the world's most famous monster—Nessie. Many more such sightings were to follow. (Peter Costello, *In Search of Lake Monsters*, pp.8–19)

Road-running was an uncharacteristic performance by Nessie, but one that it repeated on the brightly moonlit night of January 5, 1934. At about 1 A.M. a young medical student named Arthur Grant was whizzing along the loch road near Lochend when he saw a large, dark blob shadowed by the bushes along the road ahead. As he approached, the object bounded across the road, almost colliding with Grant's motorcycle. In the moonlight the young man saw a creature with a small eellike head with oval eyes, a long neck, a bulky body thickening toward a long, rounded-off tail, and four flipperlike legs. It was, he thought, about 18 to 20 feet long and had a dark skin rather like a whale's.

Leaping off his machine, Grant pursued the creature as it loped rapidly away and splashed into the loch. Grant marked the spot by the road and, upon reaching home, drew a sketch of the monster.

"Knowing something of natural history," Grant declared some time later, "I can say that I have never seen anything in my life like the animal I saw. It looked like a hybrid—a cross between a plesiosaur and a member of the seal family." (Peter Costello, *In Search of Lake Monsters*, pp.30–32)

Two Canadian duck hunters, who were working on the rocky shore of South Pender Island off Vancouver, British Columbia, flushed unlikely game on the morning of February 4, 1934. Bringing down a duck that flopped, badly wounded, into the water, Cyril H. Andrews and Norman Georgeson hopped into their small boat to retrieve it. As they approached their bird, they saw "a head and two loops or segments" of something quite unfamiliar rising clear of the water.

Mesmerized, the hunters watched the monster—which was only 10 feet away—as it opened its large mouth, gulped down the duck, snapped at several seagulls, and then sank from view. They noted its sawlike teeth, its pointed tongue, its gray-brown coloration, and the horselike shape of the head.

Andrews leaped ashore and ran for a phone. Rushing to the loch, Justice of the Peace G. F. Parkyn of Bedwell Harbor and several others arrived in time to see the creature swimming about 20 yards from the shore, its body undulating rhythmically and its head apparently resting on the water. Andrews estimated it to be about 40 feet in length and 2 to 3 feet in diameter at the thickest part, with a head some 3 feet long. (Roy P. Mackal, *Searching for Hidden Animals*, pp.19–21)

For 15 minutes on October 8, 1936, the alleged resident monster of Loch Ness showed itself near Urquhart Castle, a ruin on a promontory jutting into the lake. First seen about 500 yards from shore by a cottager who lived above the shore road, the beast soon attracted two tour buses and several carloads of viewers. About 50 people, several of them armed with telescopes or binoculars, watched the creature's sedate passage through the calm loch waters. Their concurring description was of something with two humps behind a head and neck. Then, suddenly, the creature was no longer there. (Dennis L. Meredith, *Search at Loch Ness*, p.105)

Okanagan Lake in British Columbia, connected to the Pacific via the Columbia River, is said to be the habitat of a huge aquatic animal popularly known as Ogopogo. Reported about 200 times since the year 1700, the creature was observed at close range by several people

This model of Ogopogo, Canada's Okanagan Lake Monster, was based upon descriptions given by several people who claim to have seen the creature.

on July 2, 1949. Mr. Leslie L. Kerry of Kelowna, having left his wife at their house overlooking the lake, was treating the W. F. Watson family of Montreal to a boat ride when they spotted a large, snakelike form in the water. Undulating vertically, the object traveled sometimes above and sometimes below the surface of the lake. The people in the boat—adults and children—saw a body about 30 feet long and perhaps a foot in diameter, with a forked tail that lashed up and down.

Mrs. Kerry saw the event from the shore and called her neighbors, Dr. and Mrs. Stanley Underhill. All rushed down to the beach and trained binoculars upon the creature, which remained in view for at least 15 minutes. Dr. Underhill described it as smooth and black and having "undulations or coils" about seven feet long. He thought there were at least two creatures because of the distance between some of the coils. Ogopogo, it would seem, is not alone. (Roy P. Mackal, *Searching for Hidden Animals*, pp.222–27)

Representatives of the media seldom have the good fortune to be present at a monster sighting, but one journalist boating on Okanagan Lake near the town of Vernon got lucky on July 17, 1959—although not lucky enough to have a camera handy. Mr. R. H. Miller, editor of the *Vernon Advertiser*, was accompanied by his wife, their friends Mr. and Mrs. Pat Marten, and the Martens's son Murray. They were on their way home early that evening when Miller noticed a large creature following in the wake of their motor cruiser at a distance of about 250 feet. Pat Marten, who was steering, turned the boat around for a better view.

As they slowly drew closer, the Millers and Martens studied the creature through binoculars and were unable to reconcile its blunt-nosed, snakelike head with that of any animal they knew. Itself apparently none too pleased at what it saw, the creature gradually submerged and disappeared from view. (Janet and Colin Bord, *Alien Animals*, pp.6–8)

One man who became a devoted pursuer of the Loch Ness Monster began his search in the spring of 1960.

Tim Dinsdale of Reading, England, arrived at the loch equipped with camping gear and a 16mm movie camera, prepared to spend all of six days watching for the creature. On April 23, his last day of surveillance, he was staring out across the loch from an elevation of 300 feet when he saw a motionless object on the surface of the water. Estimating the range at about 1,300 yards, Dinsdale trained his binoculars on the object and saw a mahogany-colored shape with a dark blotch on its left side. It began to move. Dinsdale turned to his camera and started filming, following the shape as it zigzagged across the loch and submerged, resurfacing and submerging again over a distance of 500 yards.

The result was a grainy but exciting piece of film showing a living creature whose appearance matched many eyewitness descriptions of the creature in the lake. At least one previously skeptical scientist was persuaded that there was indeed something unaccountable and worth searching for in the waters of Loch Ness. Dinsdale was understandably gratified by his success and conveyed something of what he had felt while filming when he later wrote: ". . . through the magic lens of my camera I had reached out across a thousand yards, and more, *to grasp the Monster by the tail.*" (Tim Dinsdale, *Loch Ness Monster,* pp.78–104)

This exposure from monster-investigator Tim Dinsdale's film made in April 1960 shows the strange shape that he watched for some four minutes as it floated across Loch Ness.

An expedition from Moscow University, surveying the mineral deposits of eastern Siberia from June to October 1964, paused at Lake Khaiyr to check out rumors of a resident monster. According to a *Komsomolskaya Pravda* article written by G. Rokosuev, deputy leader of the team, biologist N. Gladkikh "literally ran into it quite unexpectedly." Rokosuev explained:

> Here is how it happened. Gladkikh went out to the lake to draw water and saw a creature that had crawled out onto the shore, apparently to eat the grass—a small head on a long gleaming neck, a huge

Загадка озера

Biologist N. Gladkikh drew this sketch, published in a Russian newspaper in 1964, of the monster he and other Moscow University researchers saw in Lake Khaiyr.

body covered with a jet-black skin, a vertical fin along the spine.

Greatly alarmed, Gladkikh hurried back to the team's base with his news. Members of the unit, arming themselves with cameras and rifles, rushed down to the lakeshore. But the monster was gone; nothing remained of its passage but trampled grass and a slight ripple on the surface of the water. Quickly, Gladkikh made a sketch of what he had seen, little knowing that his monster would have looked remarkably familiar to witnesses of the creature in Loch Ness.

Any doubts about Gladkikh's credibility vanished when the creature reappeared and was seen by the leader of the expedition and several team members as well. Wrote Rokosuev:

> Suddenly a head appeared in the centre of the lake, then a dorsal fin. The creature beat the water with its long tail, producing waves on the lake. You can imagine our astonishment when we saw with our own eyes that the stories were true.

(Peter Costello, *In Search of Lake Monsters,* pp.224–25; Tim Dinsdale, *Monster Hunt,* pp.36–38)

Two paratroopers on leave from the British Army, Capt. John Ridgway and Sgt. Chay Blyth, spent 92 days rowing across the Atlantic in 1966 on a self-imposed survival test that, as it turned out, included a strange encounter. In the predawn of July 25 the sergeant was sound asleep and Ridgway, drowsy himself, was mechanically pulling at the oars of their 20-foot open boat when something disturbed the still darkness. As Ridgway wrote afterward:

> I was shocked to full wakefulness by a swishing noise to starboard. I looked out into the water and suddenly saw the writhing, twisting shape of a great creature. It was outlined by the

John Ridgway and Chay Blyth, who rowed across the Atlantic in the summer of 1966, were threatened by a sea serpent almost twice the length of their open boat, as depicted in this artist's rendition of the encounter.

phosphorescence in the sea as if a string of neon lights were hanging from it.

It was an enormous size, some thirty-five or more feet long, and it came towards me quite fast. I must have watched it for some ten seconds. It headed straight at me and disappeared right beneath me.

Almost paralyzed by this apparition, Ridgway stopped rowing. After a moment he forced himself to turn and look for it. He saw nothing, but a few seconds later he heard "a most tremendous splash," as if the monster had surfaced and then crashed back into the sea. Ridgway was shaken. His account continues:

I am not an imaginative man, and I searched for a rational explanation. . . . Chay and I had seen whales and sharks, dolphins and porpoises, flying fish—all sorts of sea creatures but this monster in the night was none of these. I reluctantly had to believe that there was only one thing it could have been—a sea serpent.

Rightly expecting incredulity, Ridgway concluded: "I can only tell what I saw with my own eyes, and I am no longer a disbeliever." (John Ridgway and Chay Blyth, *A Fighting Chance,* pp.12, 131–32)

Seven members of an Irish family, who lived among the lakes and peat bogs of Connemara in west Ireland, watched a large beast disport itself in Lough Nahooin from sunset until dark on the evening of February 22, 1968. Farmer Stephen Coyne, accompanied by one of his sons and the family dog, had gone down to a bog near the lough early that evening to get some dry peat when he noticed something black in the water. As he and the boy stared at it, they saw that it was an animal, but an altogether strange kind of creature. It had a polelike neck and head close to a foot in diameter, a flat tail, and a slick skin. It was swimming about aimlessly, turning from one direction to another, when the dog started barking excitedly. Attracted by the yapping, the creature glided toward the shore and opened its mouth in an intimidating manner; but when Coyne reached for his dog, the thing swerved off and continued swimming about in a desultory way. Coyne went on watching while the boy ran home to get his mother.

Mrs. Coyne and the rest of the small Coynes hastened to the lough to see the extraordinary sight. As the creature ducked and reared, the family saw that it was about 12 feet long, had two humps on its back and hornlike protuberances on its head, but had no eyes. Once the creature's tail flipped up close to the head, so that the body formed an almost complete loop or circle. Clearly, it was not only long but very flexible.

All seven Coynes watched until the daylight faded, then went home with a great deal to talk about. (Janet and Colin Bord, *Alien Animals,* pp.3–6)

Five young water skiers, ranging in age from 14 to 21, were cutting a swath across Okanagan Lake when, they said, they had a close-up view of Canada's Ogopogo on July 23, 1968. Sheri Campbell, on skis behind the motorboat, was the first to see the long shape floating lazily on the surface of the water. Startled at the sight of 20 feet of unexpected creature, she let go of the towrope and nervously trod water until her friends in the boat came back to pick her up.

By that time Ogopogo was moving. The youngsters decided to follow the beast for a closer look, and, as they claimed afterward, got within five feet of it—close enough, according to Sheri, to see "blue-green-grey scales" that glittered in the sun. At that point Ogopogo abruptly submerged and swam off with surprising speed, leaving a wake of V-shaped waves. Although they chased it in their motorboat at 40 mph, the young people fell behind and soon lost sight of the monster. (Janet and Colin Bord, *Alien Animals*, pp.8–9)

Loch Morar in Inverness County is one of a group of lakes in northern Scotland that is frequently reported to be inhabited by creatures similar to those said to be living in Loch Ness. Although sightings at Loch Morar can be traced back to 1887, it was not until 1969 that Nessie's competition came to be named Morag.

The occasion was a nerve-shattering one for Duncan MacDonnell and William Simpson, who were heading home across the loch in their motor cruiser on a hot summer's afternoon on August 19, at the end of a pleasant day of fishing. The two men reckoned it was time for a cup of tea, and Simpson went into the cabin to put the kettle on while MacDonnell steered. As MacDonnell later told author Elizabeth Campbell during her inquiry into Morag:

> I heard a splashing or disturbance in the water astern of us. I looked up and about twenty yards behind us this creature was coming directly after us in our wake. It only took it a matter of seconds to catch up on us. It grazed the side of the boat, I am quite certain this was unintentional. When it struck the boat it seemed to come to a halt or at least slow down. I grabbed the oar and was attempting to fend it off, my one fear being that if it got under the boat it might capsize it.

Bill Simpson felt the impact and saw the teakettle slide and fall, spilling water over the burner and drowning the flames. He turned off the gas and leaped to the deck, where he saw MacDonnell shoving at the creature with his oar. For several moments the two men struggled to keep the monster from overturning the boat. It was an enormous, unprepossessing thing and utterly strange, being 25 to 30 feet long and having a large, snakelike head about a foot wide, a back with three humps raised about 18 inches above the surface of the water, and rough-textured dirty-brown skin.

The oar snapped. One of the men grabbed a rifle, loaded it, and fired. The creature slowly sank.

The two fishermen went home with all possible speed, as much appalled by their encounter with the impossible as by the beast's appearance. "I don't want to see it again—" Bill Simpson would say. "I was terrified." (Janet and Colin Bord, *Alien Animals*, pp.1–2)

SINCE 1970

In 1970, after almost 40 years of sightings reported by reputable witnesses, Loch Ness was visited by a well-equipped expedition, consisting of members of the Boston-based Academy of Applied Science in coopera-

tion with the British Loch Ness Investigation Bureau.

The team's primary mission was to find evidence of large, moving objects in the loch. Using a new high-frequency, side-scan sonar designed by underwater engineer Martin Klein, himself on the scene as one of the academy's monster hunters, the investigators made a number of intriguing contacts with moving but unidentifiable targets of various sizes.

At the end of October a series of particularly successful sonar hits was made while the apparatus was rigged near a pier in Urquhart Bay. Something massive moved through the sonar beam not far from the pier. Then, at successive intervals of 10 or 15 minutes, similar but larger objects were detected from greater distances. Whatever they were, these objects apparently moved of their own accord and were from 10 to 50 times larger than the fish registered by the apparatus.

The contacts were compelling if not conclusive evidence of large, mysterious creatures in Loch Ness. (*Technology Review*, 8:27, March–April 1976; telephone interview with Martin Klein, Salem, New Hampshire)

California is richly endowed with almost everything, but it is unaccountably short of water monsters. One, however, has reportedly been seen from time to time in Lake Elsinore, near Riverside, since 1884. A lakesider named Bonnie Pray said she saw it twice in 1970. According to her, it is a snakelike 12-footer about 3 feet thick that travels through the water with an up-and-down undulating motion, unlike a snake, which wiggles horizontally. Subsequently, three Elsinore State Park officials crossing the lake claimed that they saw a similar creature surface about 50 feet from their boat. Too bemused for accurate observation, they gave conflicting descriptions but agreed that the thing was very odd. (Janet and Colin Bord, *Alien Animals*, p.10)

The White River at Newport, Arkansas, was the scene of several sightings in the 1970's. On July 28, 1971, Cloyce Warren of the White River Lumber Company went fishing with two friends. Mooring their boat just south of the White River bridge, they cast their lines. Suddenly the three men were astounded to see a huge column of water belching skyward from a point about 200 feet away. "I didn't know what was happening," Warren later told reporters:

> This giant form rose to the surface and began moving in the middle of the river, away from the boat. It was very long and gray colored. . . . We had taken a little Polaroid Swinger camera with us to take pictures of the fish we caught.
> I grabbed the camera and managed to get a picture right before it submerged. It appeared to have a spiny backbone that stretched for 30 or more

Cloyce Warren, one of several people who have seen the White River Monster as it surfaced, was able to take this photograph just before it submerged.

feet. It was hard to make out exactly what the front portion looked like, but it was awful large.

The *Newport Daily Independent* published the picture two days later. The White River Monster, seen in the distance, was slightly blurred around the edges but appeared to be a large creature as yet unidentified. (*Newport Daily Independent,* July 30, 1971)

Unshakable in his faith, Father Gregory Brusey entertained no doubts about his sighting of a creature in Loch Ness on October 14, 1971. He and a visitor were enjoying the view of the serene loch from the grounds of the Benedictine abbey at Fort Augustus when both were startled by the sudden, violent agitation of its waters. About 300 yards away a great beast loomed before them, rearing its head as much as seven feet above the water, and then swam idly away. The two men, hardly believing their eyes, stood watching it for

Father Gregory Brusey stands on the bank of Loch Ness, near the place where he and a friend were startled to see a huge creature rise out of the water in 1971.

about 20 seconds before the creature submerged.

The monster had been seen by many monks at the abbey but never before by Father Gregory. "We felt a sort of awe and amazement," he related. "In fact, my friend said if I hadn't been with him he'd probably have run." But not from a sense of personal danger; rather from a sense of the inexplicable. "It gave us a feeling of something from another world." (Dennis L. Meredith, *Search at Loch Ness,* p.110)

Mrs. Robert A. Green did not have all the corroboration she really wanted when she reported seeing Champ of Lake Champlain, but that was not her fault. At an unspecified date in 1971 Mrs. Green, her mother, and a friend were stopping at a hotel overlooking the lake. As they gazed at the tranquil waters, they saw a snakelike head and three dark humps gliding serenely by. Seeking a witness outside her own little group, Mrs. Green called the hotel bartender to come and see it. He took one swift, incredulous look. Returning to his bar, he shook his head and firmly said: "I'll never say I saw it." (Janet and Colin Bord, *Alien Animals,* p.9)

The problem of proving the existence of an unidentified monster in Loch Ness—difficult because of the creature's own elusiveness and the need of disbelievers to explain it away by any farfetched means—is compounded by the characteristics of the lake itself. Because of the labyrinthine loch bottom, in places 700 to 975 feet deep, underwater creatures can easily escape electronic detection. Added to that is the murkiness of the water, which is clotted and discolored with vast amounts of suspended peat particles. Even a short distance below the surface, maximum underwater visibility may extend only a few feet.

It was with these difficulties in mind that the 1972 expedition of the Academy of Applied Science, led by Dr. Robert H. Rines, arrived at the loch with advanced sonar equipment supplemented by a camera strobe light system developed by Dr. Harold E. Edgerton of MIT for photographing underwater life. This system consisted of a 16mm-time-lapse motion-picture camera with a synchronized flash unit of some 50-watt-seconds power. The objective—the almost impossible dream—was to obtain a combination of sonar and photographic evidence of the Scottish "beastie" known as Nessie.

Luck would be as important as equipment, for, obviously, the investigators had no idea where their legendary target might be. They could only set up their equipment in areas where the creature had most often been seen, and hope it might come by again.

The loch's surface on the night of August 8 was unusually flat and calm. Members of the investigating team waited in boats anchored in Urquhart Bay a short distance from shore. A sonar transducer was lowered from one boat and gently settled on an underwater slope with its beam aimed out into the loch. The stroboscopic camera was placed slightly farther down the slope and aimed, the strobe flashing periodically, at the area encompassed by the sonar beam.

At about one in the morning the team began to see the heavy, dark traces of a large moving object on the sonar beam. The traces were similar to those obtained by the 1970 expedition. Excitement rose, and with it a sense of something ominous. At 1:40 A.M. the sonar recorded the flight of some salmon (shown by lighter, discontinuous traces)—*and* the appearance of two large objects. At the same time the stroboscopic camera photographed the blobs picked up by the sonar beam.

Because of the cloudiness of the water the photographs were vague, but with computer enhancement several astounding images became apparent. Two frames of film showed a flipper. Taken 45 seconds apart, the flipper pictures showed what seemed to be the same appendage in two different positions, indicating movement. A third picture revealed two objects that seemed to be large creatures. Correlation and analysis of the findings indicated that the flipper was about 4 to 6 feet long and that the two bodies were about 12 feet apart.

Here it was at last: simultaneous sonar and photographic evidence of a large, long, flippered creature—two of them—inhabiting Loch Ness. And yet, of course, there are still people who are not impressed. (Dennis L. Meredith, *Search at Loch Ness,* pp.25–28; *Technology Review,* 8:25–30, March–April 1976)

Russian lake monsters were in the news again in the 1970's. Hearing tales of a huge water snake in the Dzhambul region of the Soviet republic of Kazakhstan in Central Asia, geographer Anatoly Pechersky and his son Volodya spent their 1975 vacation beside Lake Kok-kol in that area.

One day while Pechersky and his son were on the shore, the surface of the lake about 25 feet out broke into deep ripples, and a snakelike monster reared up through the churning water. Its massive head was about 6 feet long, and its thick, serpentine body was, by Pechersky's estimate, 50 feet long.

Terrified, Pechersky called a warning to his son and scrambled up a steep embankment to get his gun. The monster was still in view by the time father and son returned to the lakeshore, but within moments it began to submerge. As it sank and the water swirled over it, Pechersky realized that he could easily have picked up either the still camera or the movie camera instead of his gun. (Janet and Colin Bord, *Alien Animals,* p.12)

Triumph at Loch Ness climaxed the June 1975 expedition mounted by the Academy of Applied Science. Added to the team's arsenal of detection equipment was an improved camera-strobe system incorporating new techniques designed to correct some of the technical problems that had hampered the 1972 investigation. The 1972 apparatus was taken along to serve as an auxiliary system. Both cameras were provided with higher-speed, more sensitive film. The main camera system, which was to be triggered by the sonar, was

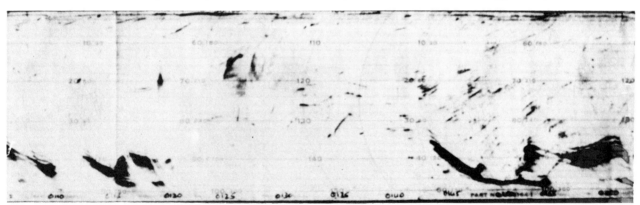

A sonar probe of Loch Ness in 1972 recorded movement of large objects as bold black traces. Numbers at the bottom show that the movement began at 1 and 1:40 A.M.

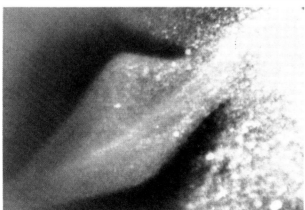

The image at left, said to resemble a large flipper, was picked up by an underwater camera at about 1:40 A.M.; the time coincided with the movement recorded on the sonar trace.

147

placed on a bottom ledge at a depth of 80 feet. The backup camera-strobe was suspended from a boat at a level of 40 feet above the primary system.

Repeatedly, the sonar record showed large objects near the sophisticated camera, but the film revealed nothing. Something on the bottom had stirred up clouds of silt that blocked the underwater view, and the only pictures were—of silt.

But the simpler backup system at 40 feet functioned faithfully throughout a 24-hour period beginning late on June 19 and ending late on June 20, shooting frame after frame at preset intervals.

Several pictures show large objects within the strobe light beam. One includes a portion of a pinkish body; another shows what looks like the upper torso, neck, and head of a living creature with two stubby append-

ages. Sandwiched between shots of eels and fish is a sequence of frames revealing that the camera had been disturbed and set in a violent rocking motion so that at one stage it pointed directly upward and photographed the bottom of the boat.

Then, in the next frame, facing the camera, is the head of the monster—or something resembling an underwater dragon. The head is in half profile, showing nostrils, an open mouth, and several hornlike projections. A study of the several frames showing body segments suggests a living creature with an overall length of 20 feet, a neck about 1½ feet thick, a mouth 9 inches long and 5 inches wide, and horns about 6 inches long, set about 10 inches apart. Other specimens may, of course, be considerably bigger.

Whether or not this manifestation is the famous

The World's Most Famous Monster

Perhaps no picture of Nessie is more provocative than Robert Rine's 1975 underwater photograph (bottom, left) of what may be a head and upper torso. Other pictures are, clockwise, surgeon R. K. Wilson's 1934 picture of a head and neck, a *1934 shot of a vague form in the lake, an unexplained shape in the water near Urquhart Castle, and a headlike form photographed in 1977. In the center is a 1951 picture of what may be three of Nessie's humps.*

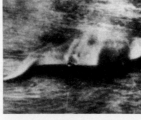

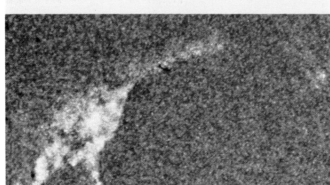

Loch Ness Monster, it is undeniably an unexplained phenomenon that begs to be explained. (*Technology Review*, 8:28, 31–40, March–April 1976)

Nessie sightings were frequent in the months following the June 1975 expedition. Two occurrences, reported by science editor Dennis L. Meredith after a season at Loch Ness, stand out from the rest for their almost carnivallike extravagance.

On July 8, 1975, teacher Allen Wilkins and his son Ian, at lochside about a mile and a half south of Invermoriston, established what was probably a record for repeated sightings. At 7:20 A.M., and for some moments thereafter, Wilkins saw a 20-foot-long black shape appear and disappear some distance down the loch. At 10:12 Wilkins, accompanied by his wife and several other watchers, saw and photographed three large triangular humps moving about in the water in a playful manner. The humps vanished when a motorboat appeared. At 9:25 P.M. Mr. Wilkins and others watched a black patch as it emerged from the water, revealing two humps. The thing rolled forward seconds later and disappeared. At 10:25 Wilkins and his fascinated companions saw three closely spaced humps about four feet high, one following the other in a graceful curve in and out of the water. Finally, they all submerged together.

On July 12, 1976, two Inverness mechanics were in a boat about a quarter mile off Abriachan Pier when they saw a hump trailing in their wake. Curious without being especially surprised, Ian Dunn and Billy Kennedy turned around and headed back for a closer view. Then they *were* surprised. Weaving and bobbing around them were five black humps, about 10 to 12 feet long and 2 to 3 feet high. Scared but spellbound, Kennedy and Dunn put on their life jackets, held on to their rocking boat, and watched the display for 15 minutes. "It was like getting caught in the center of a school of whales," Dunn said afterward. Then a rainstorm swept down the loch, and the men started shoreward—followed for a while by one of the beasts. (Dennis L. Meredith, *Search at Loch Ness*, pp.108–09, 116)

Nearly a year later, on April 25, 1977, and many thousands of miles away, the Japanese fishing vessel *Zuiyo Maru* hauled aboard a huge carcass that no one has been able to identify. It was while trawling for mackerel off the coast of New Zealand that the fishermen netted it, at a depth of 900 feet, only to discover that they had caught a rotting corpse. The blob was definitely neither fish nor whale nor any other recognizable mammal. Nor was it a figment of imagination—it weighed about 4,000 pounds, measured 32 feet, and was observed by 18 crewmen.

Despite its decomposition, it was seen to have a long neck, longish tail, four fins, and a well-developed spine. Aboard the vessel was Michihiko Yano, assistant production manager of Taiyo Fisheries, Ltd., who measured the body, clipped tissue samples, and took colored snapshots of it. Then the carcass was heaved overboard and Yano went back to Japan to baffle the scientists with his remarkable relics. (*Oceans*, 10:56–59, November–December 1977)

A Japanese fishing trawler hauled the decomposing body of an unidentified sea creature, its long neck dangling, from the waters off New Zealand in 1977.

One day in early July 1977 Sandra Mansi and a friend were enjoying the tranquil beauty of Lake Champlain when they noticed the water begin to seethe. Then, to their disbelief, a head and a long, willowy neck emerged, curving above a dark, floating mass. This, they realized, was no fish.

Almost paralyzed with fear, Sandra nonetheless managed to aim her camera at the creature and take a quick snapshot. The result was a clear photograph of an apparently animate object, gray-brown in color and with serpentine features.

Sandra Mansi saw a terrifying form, with a massive body and a long neck, surface in Lake Champlain. She managed to take one picture before it disappeared.

Some time later a public hearing was held at Montpelier, the capital of Vermont, to support the passage of legislation to protect the creature. Attending the session, Sandra fervently declared: "I just want you to know that 'Champ' is there. Believe me, 'Champ' is there." (*The New York Times*, August 31, 1981; *Pursuit*, 14:51-58, Second Quarter 1981)

Two official Chinese newspapers reported in 1980 that unknown life forms had been sighted in lakes in Manchuria and Tibet. The first report, appearing in the *Peking Evening News*, stated that a strange creature resembling a dinosaur had been seen on a number of occasions in Wenbu Lake in a remote part of Tibet. Once it allegedly seized and swallowed a yak that had paused at the lakeshore to graze. Lending credence to the tale is the fact that it was told by a local Communist Party official, who said that he had been taking the yak to market when the incident occurred.

Other sightings, according to reports in the *Peking Evening News*, were made at a crater lake near the peak of a mountain in northeastern Jilin province. Visitors to the crater and the staff of a nearby weather station claimed to have seen a creature with a head shaped like a cow's head but much bigger, and a flat beak shaped like a duck's. They said the creature traveled at a speed that churned up a wake like that of a motorboat.

In late 1980 the *Guangming Daily* reported that a respected Chinese author named Lei Jia had twice seen a lake creature in the Changbai mountain region of Manchuria. The author said that the unknown animal looked like a black reptile about two yards in length, with a long neck and oval head. Three local weather bureau officials announced that they had also seen it. They shot at it and missed, and the creature disappeared. (*Fate*, 34:60, September 1981)

On the basis of two investigatory expeditions, made in 1980 and 1981, Dr. Roy P. Mackal, a research biologist at the University of Chicago, is convinced of the existence of a legendary monster in the swampy Ubangi-Congo basin of central Africa. Known as mokele-mbembe and described by the Congo pygmies as half-elephant, half-dragon, and much more fearsome than a crocodile, the creature has been dodging hunter-explorers since the start of the 20th century—although reports of something weird in central African rivers and swamps go back to the 1800's.

In 1980 Roy Mackal and James H. Powell, Jr., a crocodile specialist, went deep into the heart of the wild Likouala region to track the tales to their source and try to identify the beast. They arrived at the remote outpost of Impfondo early in February, and although they were appalled by the trackless swamps and jungles that lay ahead, they were heartened to hear locally that the mokele-mbembe was often spoken of as a well-known phenomenon if unfamiliar beast.

One of the older eyewitness reports was given by one Firman Mosomele, who said that about 45 years earlier, when he was a 14-year-old, he had seen the creature while paddling his canoe around a bend on the Likouala aux Herbes River near the town of Epéna. He waited only long enough to see a reddish-brown snakelike head and neck about six to eight feet long before he paddled briskly away, but the image was burned on his brain. When shown a book of animal pictures, Mosomele picked a sauropod (or dinosaur) as the creature he had seen.

The next report, by a woman from Epéna, confirmed that such a creature was indeed a habitué of that area. Two of the beasts, she said, had recently entered Lake Tele from the Bai River. One had been killed by lakesiders, then cut up and eaten in spite of a local belief that people eating its flesh would soon die.

The explorers and their porters spent most of the rest of the month "slogging" through mokele-mbembe territory, hunting the creature and collecting many more eyewitness accounts. One of the most circumstantial was given by Nicolas Mondongo, a Congolese from the village of Bandéko. During a journey on the Likouala aux Herbes between Mokengui and Bandéko he saw a mokele-mbembe "making the water run backwards as it rose out of the river."

The water at that point was only three to six feet deep, and virtually the whole animal was visible. Mondongo said he saw its back, neck, head, part of a long tail, and short legs. The head was topped with something like a cockscomb. As nearly as he could judge, the length of the creature was 32 feet, about 6 to 10 feet of which were head and neck.

Convinced by such reports that "although rare, the *mokele mbembes* do exist and that they correspond to no other living forms known to science," Dr. Mackal returned to Africa in 1981 on a six-week expedition with a group of French, American, and Congolese scientists. Their foray was highlighted by the discovery of "huge footprints and a wide swath of bent and flattened vegetation. The track led into a river." In size the footprints compared with those of an elephant, according to Dr. Mackal, but the flattened vegetation suggested that the trail had been made by a reptilian creature "taller and larger than any known crocodile."

Dr. Mackal, who is "more convinced now than ever" of the creature's existence, thinks that it inhabits swamps but uses the rivers to facilitate moving about. Further ventures in search of the beast are expected. (*Animal Kingdom*, 83:4-10, December 1980; *The New York Times*, October 18 and December 10, 1981)

Neither Fish nor Fantasy

The very names "sea serpent" and "lake monster" have an aura of myth about them, suggesting that the strange animals referred to are beyond reality. Yet there are thousands of reputable reports of the creatures' existence, from Siberia to Scotland and wherever else the waters are deep. One or another of the ubiquitous monsters has been seen repeatedly by groups of unrelated viewers and on occasion by crowds of up to 200. A few creatures have even returned daily as if to give everyone in the neighborhood a chance to gawk. In the view of some authorities, including Dr. Frederic A. Lucas, for years the director of the American Museum of Natural History, "there is more sworn evidence for the beast than a court of law would need to prove any ordinary case."

But what is this mysterious life form?

For one thing, it is not *a* creature.

It seems clear from eyewitness reports that there are several distinct species of enormous underwater beasts, a few of which have been tentatively identified. The gigantic tentacled creatures so often encountered in Greek and Roman times, and called kraken by Norwegian sailors, are reckoned by most authorities to be giant squid. Zoologist Bernard Heuvelmans, who distinguishes nine different types of sea serpents, has documented the existence of squid that reach an overall length of 240 feet from tentacle to tentacle. Dr. Roy Mackal, mokele-mbembe hunter, suggests another kraken candidate may be a type of giant octopus, which he believes measures up to 200 feet.

Some mystifying manifestations turn out to have simple if surprising explanations. Dr. Mackal has no hesitation in identifying the White River Monster of Arkansas on the basis of the many eyewitness descriptions: "The White River case," writes Mackal, "is a clear-cut instance of a known aquatic animal observed outside of its normal habitat or range and therefore unidentified by the observers unfamiliar with the type. The animal in question clearly was a large male elephant seal"—a loner that had strayed up the Mississippi and into the White River. (See pages 145–46.)

Mackal has some other interesting suggestions, based on physical appearance and the possible persistence of some archaic forms. The large, vertically undulating type of sea serpent, he contends, may well be the zeuglodon, a primitive toothed whale long thought to be extinct. Dr. Mackal believes that a small population of zeuglodons may yet survive—living fossils no older than the ancient coelacanth, the crocodile, or the venerable giant tortoise of the Galapagos Islands. The monster of Okanagan Lake fits the description of the zeuglodon, as do the monster of Lake Champlain and the sea serpents off British Columbia.

Pictures suggest that the elusive creature sought in Loch Ness is linked to the elasmosaur, a type of plesiosaur that lived more than 70 million years ago.

When the Japanese scientists were through with the decomposing mass hauled in by the *Zuiyo Maru* (see page 149), they reached a tentative agreement. It "looks very like a plesiosaur," said one, and none of the others came up with a better idea.

Interestingly, the pictures of the Loch Ness Monster show a remarkable resemblance to a plesiosaur, a large water reptile of the Mesozoic era, presumed to be extinct for more than 70 million years. According to Dennis Meredith, member of the 1976 Loch Ness expedition, "One particular type of plesiosaur, the elasmosaur, is the best candidate of the lot."

There is a stupefying quality about water monsters, be they plesiosaurs or zeuglodons or whatever. On seeing one, some viewers are stunned into total inaction. Petrified and revolted, they forget to use the cameras in their hands or bungle the operation of focusing the lens. Even F. W. Holiday, a seasoned monster buff, feels that there is something very peculiar about Nessie and admits to feeling "a mixture of wonder, fear and repulsion." And yet this monster, which some people find "obscene," is affectionately known as Nessie, as if it were lovable and cute.

Many aquatic monsters have such comforting nicknames: Champ of Lake Champlain; Ogopogo of Okanagan Lake; Igopogo of Lake Simcoe near Toronto; Manipogo of Lake Manitoba; Chessie, the Chesapeake Bay sea serpent; Slimy Slim or Sharlie of Payette Lake in Idaho; and Whitey, the White River Monster of Arkansas. One wonders if these pet names suggest a companionable feeling toward local attractions or an attempt to reduce the unbelievable to something that does not boggle the mind— to level these terrors down to overgrown water Muppets with nursery school names.

By official resolution on October 6, 1980, the town fathers of Port Henry, New York, a village at the southern end of Lake Champlain, forbade the harassment of sea monsters. Champ's champions resolved "... that all the waters of Lake Champlain which adjoin the Village of Port Henry are hereby declared to be off limits to anyone who would in any way harm, harass or destroy the Lake Champlain Sea Monster."

As if heartened by this proclamation, the monster made generous appearances in 1981.

Mayor Robert Brown of Port Henry was not displeased with the boost to the tourist trade. At least three dozen people saw the creature during the year, according to *The New York Times*, including "17 people in a Bible class." One young woman, said the mayor, had taken four pictures of Champ, which were being analyzed. Mayor Brown proudly added that a summer seminar of Ph.D. candidates concluded: "there's definitely something there." (*The New York Times*, October 4, 1981; *Pursuit*, 14:51, Second Quarter 1981)

LAND MONSTERS, MAINLY TWO-LEGGED

BEFORE 1900

An English adventurer named Andrew Battel spent many years in Africa during the 16th century and upon returning home gave a detailed account of his experiences to his friend Samuel Purchas. That account appears in a famous compilation of travel writings entitled *Purchas his Pilgrimes*, published in 1625. According to Battel, who was amazed by all the baboons, monkeys, and apes in the jungles, two kinds of monsters were also common, both of them very dangerous:

> The greatest of these two Monsters is called, *Pongo,* in their Language: and the lesser is called, *Engeco.* This *Pongo* is in all proportion like a man, but that he is more like a Giant in a stature, then a man: for he is very tall, a hath a mans face, hollow eyed, with long haire vpon his browes. His face and eares are without haire, and his hands also. His bodie is full of haire, but not very thicke, and it is of a dunnish colour. He differeth not from a man, but in his legs, for they haue no calfe. Hee goeth alwaies vpon his legs, and carrieth his hands clasped on the nape of his necke, when he goeth vpon the ground. ... They goe many together, and kill many *Negroes* that trauaile in the Woods. Many times they fall vpon the Elephants, which come to feed where they be, and so beate them with their clubbed fists, and pieces of wood, that they will runne roaring away from them. Those *Pongoes* are neuer taken aliue, because they are so strong, that ten men cannot hold one of them. ... [Bernard Heuvelmans, *On the Track of Unknown Animals,* p.43]

"The Devil's hoof-marks" were so called by the astounded villagers who saw them appear overnight in rural England in 1855. On the morning of February 8 countless numbers of unidentifiable prints were discovered in the snow around 18 communities in the county of Devon. They were shaped like small horseshoes and ran in absolutely straight lines—one directly behind another, as if whatever had made them had only one leg, or a peculiarly mincing gait.

In a single night the unknown beast had traveled about 100 miles, crossing a wide river, and had skulked around houses. In some places it had apparently walked right up walls and along rooftops, and here and there the tracks gave the impression that the thing had actually passed through walls and roofs.

For some time thereafter people feared to go out after dark, and the superstitious believed that the tracks were made by Satan himself. (Bernard Heuvelmans, *On the Track of Unknown Animals*, pp.324–25)

Two eyewitnesses drew these sketches of "the Devil's hoof-marks," strange tracks seen in Devon, England, in 1855.

A possibly amphibious wormlike animal of gigantic size was seen in various parts of Brazil during the 1860's. Late in the decade one Francisco de Amaral Varella saw something like a huge earthworm on the banks of the Rio das Caveiras. It was three feet thick and had a piglike snout on what was presumably its head. When the witness called out to his neighbors, the creature disappeared into the ground, leaving in its wake deep furrows about three feet wide. (Bernard Heuvelmans, *On the Track of Unknown Animals*, pp.298–99)

In 1889, in northeastern Sikkim, Maj. Laurence Austine Waddell of the Indian Army Medical Corps found large footprints in the Himalayan snows at 17,000 feet. In his book *Among the Himalayas* (1899), he wrote:

> These were alleged [by his Sherpa porters] to be the trail of the hairy wild men who are believed to live amongst the eternal snows, along with the mythical white lions, whose roar is reputed to be heard during storms. The belief in these creatures is universal among Tibetans. [Bernard Heuvelmans, *On the Track of Unknown Animals*, pp.127–28; John Napier, *Bigfoot*, pp.34–35]

Theodore Roosevelt was no pushover for a tall tale, but he was impressed by a story he recounted in his book

An encounter with an ape-man in the wilderness of the Pacific Northwest left a young trapper so shaken that years later he still shuddered when he talked about it.

The Wilderness Hunter, published in 1893. The incident, which had occurred many years before, was related to Roosevelt, as the latter wrote,

> by a grisled, weather-beaten old mountain hunter, named Bauman, who was born and had passed all his life on the frontier. He must have believed what he said, for he could hardly repress a shudder at certain points of the tale. . . .
>
> When the event occurred Bauman was still a young man, and was trapping with a partner among the mountains dividing the forks of the Salmon from the head of Wisdom River. Not having had much luck, he and his partner determined to go up into a particularly wild and lonely pass through which ran a small stream said to contain many beaver. The pass had an evil reputation because the year before a solitary hunter who had wandered into it was there slain, seemingly by a wild beast, the half-eaten remains being afterwards found by some mining prospectors . . . only the night before.

But Bauman and his partner were adventurous and untroubled by the tale. They made camp in a small glade and went upstream to set their traps. At dusk the young men returned.

> They were surprised to find that during their short absence something, apparently a bear, had visited camp, and had rummaged about among their things, scattering the contents of their packs, and in sheer wantonness destroying their lean-to. The footprints of the beast were quite plain, but at first they paid no particular heed to them. . . .

Later they examined the tracks more closely and saw that the intruder had walked upright—but the footprints were not those of a human being.

> At midnight Bauman was awakened by some noise, and sat up in his blankets. As he did so his nostrils were struck by a strong, wild-beast odor, and he caught the loom of a great body in the darkness at the mouth of the lean-to. Grasping his rifle, he fired at the vague, threatening shadow, but must have missed, for immediately afterwards he heard the smashing of the underwood as the thing, whatever it was, rushed off into the impenetrable blackness of the forest and the night.

The two men slept but little after that and the next day stayed together as they worked. When they got back to camp they saw that it had again been destroyed and all their camp kit and bedding tossed about. Two-legged footprints showed plainly in the soft earth along the nearby stream. The trappers spent the night sitting by a blazing fire, one or the other on guard, listening uneasily to the sound of branches crackling and something uttering a "harsh, grating, long-drawn moan, a peculiarly sinister sound."

In the morning they decided to pick up their traps and leave that afternoon. They worked together as before, until there were only three traps yet to be collected. The sun was high, the traps were only a couple of miles from camp, and the men agreed that Bauman would gather them while the other went back to the lean-to to pack their gear.

There were three beavers in the traps, and it took Bauman some time to prepare them. With considerable uneasiness he noted how low the sun was as he started for the campsite.

> At last he came to the edge of the little glade where the camp lay, and shouted as he approached it, but got no answer. The camp fire had gone out, though the thin blue smoke was still curling upwards. Near it lay the packs, wrapped and arranged. At first Bauman could see nobody; nor did he receive an answer to his call. Stepping forward he again shouted, and as he did so his eye fell on the body of his friend, stretched beside the trunk of a great fallen spruce. Rushing towards it the horrified trapper found that the body was still warm, but that the neck was broken, while there were four great fang marks in the throat.
>
> The footprints of the unknown beast-creature, printed deep in the soft soil, told the whole story.
>
> The unfortunate man, having finished his packing, had sat down on the spruce log with his face to the fire, and his back to the dense woods, to wait for his companion. . . . It had not eaten the body, but apparently had romped and gambolled around it in uncouth, ferocious glee, occasionally rolling over and over it; and had then fled back into the soundless depths of the woods.
>
> Bauman, utterly unnerved, and believing that the creature with which he had to deal was something either half human or half devil, . . . abandoned everything but his rifle and struck off at speed down the pass, not halting until he reached the beaver meadows where the hobbled ponies were still grazing. Mounting, he rode onwards through the night, until far beyond the reach of pursuit.

Although Roosevelt himself had no similar experience during his years in the West, he did not seem to dismiss the story as farfetched. (Theodore Roosevelt, *The Wilderness Hunter,* pp.441–47)

FROM 1900 TO 1970

An eight-foot hairy upright monster, wielding a club, terrified a party of skaters near Chesterfield, Idaho, in 1902. Its tracks, four-toed, were later measured as 22 inches long and 7 inches wide. (Janet and Colin Bord, *Alien Animals,* p.175)

A Sydney surveyor named Charles Harper, encamped with several companions on Currockbilly Mountain in New South Wales, Australia, had an unnerving experience one night in 1912.

Disturbed by sounds from the nearby woods, the men threw extra branches on their fire, and the circle of flickering light enlarged to include a monstrous stranger. As Harper subsequently told the press:

> A huge man-like animal stood erect not twenty yards from the fire, growling . . . and thumping his breast with his huge hand-like paws. I looked round and saw one of my companions had fainted. He remained unconscious for some hours. The creature stood in one position for some time. . . .
>
> I should say its height when standing erect would be 5 ft 8 in to 5 ft 10 in. Its body, legs, and arms were covered with long, brownish-red hair, which shook with every quivering movement of its body. The hair on its shoulder and back parts appeared in the subdued light of the fire to be jet black, and long; but what struck me . . . was the apparently human shape, but still so very different.
>
> . . . The body frame was enormous, indicating immense strength and power of endurance. The arms and forepaws were extremely long and large, and very muscular, being covered with shorter hair. The head and face were very small, but very human. The eyes were large, dark and piercing, deeply set. A most horrible mouth was ornamented with two large and long canine teeth. When the jaws were closed they protruded over the lower lip. . . . All this observation occupied a few minutes while the creature stood erect, as if the firelight had paralysed him.
>
> After a few more growls, and thumping his breast, he made off, the first few yards erect, then at a faster gait on all fours through the low scrub. Nothing would induce my companions to continue the trip, at which I was rather pleased than otherwise. . . .

Mr. Harper hastened from the territory of what he thought to be a gorilla, but there is no Australian gorilla. There does seem to be a two-legged hairy beast, or wild man, locally known as the Yowie. (Janet and Colin Bord, *Alien Animals,* pp.151–52)

Lt. Col. C. K. Howard-Bury and his companions, making their way from Kharta to Lhakpa La in Tibet on the first Everest reconnaissance expedition in 1921, saw several dark shapes moving about in a snowfield far above them. On September 22, when they reached the place where the creatures had been, they saw—at more than 20,000 feet up—numbers of enormous footprints. Lt. Col. Howard-Bury stated that at first they looked human yet they were about three times the size of normal human footprints; then he declared that they must have been made by a very large stray, gray wolf.

But several creatures had been seen. The Sherpa porters were sure the tracks had been made by an upright semihuman they called *metoh* or *mehteh kangmi* ("snow or wild creature"). A journalist later gave it the appellation Abominable Snowman.

According to the Sherpas, the Snowman is a huge, hairy, half-man half-beast that lives in caves high in the mountains. It is bowlegged, its apelike arms reach down to its knees, and it is so muscular that it can rip up trees by the roots. The body hair is thick and dark, but the face appears to be white and humanoid. Ordinarily the creatures feed off yaks and snowworms, but when desperately hungry they go down into the valleys and carry off human beings.

And thus began an avalanche of intriguing Snowman stories. (Bernard Heuvelmans, *On the Track of Unknown Animals*, pp.128–29; Ivan Sanderson, *Abominable Snowmen*, pp.51–52)

American miners underwent a harrowing ordeal in Ape Canyon on the east side of Mount St. Helens in the state of Washington. In 1924 Fred Beck and several fellow prospectors noticed huge footprints around their cabin from time to time and were puzzled by them. Then, one day, they saw a large apelike creature watching them from behind a tree. One miner fired at it and the thing ran off, apparently wounded in the head. Next, Fred Beck spotted another such creature standing by the edge of the canyon wall and shot it in the back. It fell off the cliff and was lost to view.

That night at least two creatures attacked the cabin, battering at the roof and walls in an attempt to break in. A strip of wood was gouged out from between two logs of the cabin, and the men inside heard thumps on the roof that sounded like the blows of large rocks. But the cabin was sturdily built to withstand heavy snow-falls and windowless, and with the door braced from the inside the creatures were unable to force their way in. Neither were they frightened off by gunshots.

About five hours later, when dawn was approaching, the frustrated callers went away, leaving a muddle of big footprints around the cabin. The miners also left, abandoning both their cabin and their mine.

A creature of this type was to become known in the United States and Canada as Bigfoot, or Sasquatch. (John Green, *On the Track of the Sasquatch*, p.59)

In 1924 one Albert Ostman, a logger and construction worker, decided to spend his vacation looking for a lost gold mine rumored to be at the head of Toba Inlet in British Columbia, opposite Vancouver Island. On his way, an old Indian boatman told him tales of huge hairy beings—"big people"—living in the mountains near the supposed mine, but Ostman refused to believe Indian fables about mountain giants. Yet he would remember the name: Sasquatch.

Starting off on foot from the inlet with his rifle, packsack of food, cooking utensils, sleeping bag, and ground sheet, Ostman hiked for a week before settling down in an exceptionally fine campsite between two tall cypress trees and near a freshwater spring.

The camp turned out to be perfect except that, in the mornings, Ostman would wake up to find that his supplies had been disturbed and some food taken. One night, attempting to stay awake to find out who his visitor was, he climbed into his sleeping bag fully dressed but for his boots, which he put loosely into the bag along with his rifle. "I was awakened," he wrote,

> by something picking me up. I was half asleep and at first I did not remember where I was. As I began to get my wits together, I remembered I was on this prospecting trip, and in my sleeping bag.
> My first thought was—it must be a snow slide, but there was no snow around my camp. Then it felt like I was tossed on horseback, but I could feel whoever it was, was walking.

Hours of uncomfortable travel passed. Stifled and cramped inside the bag, Ostman tried in vain to reach his knife to cut his way loose. Eventually his bearer let him down, dropping his packsack beside him, and he heard a strange kind of chatter he could not understand.

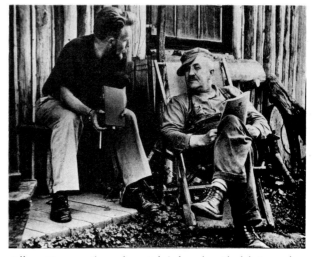

Albert Ostman (seated at right) has described being taken prisoner for six days by a family of giant half-human creatures he encountered in the British Columbia wilderness.

At dawn he struggled out of his bag and made out the forms of four people—covered with hair and wearing no clothes at all. Ostman knew he must be among the Sasquatch giants the Indian had told him about. As it got lighter he could see that he was in a valley with mountains all around and that the hairy people seemed to be a family: "old man, old lady and two young ones, a boy and a girl." They made no effort to hurt him, but they seemed intent on keeping him. All except for the girl, who was flat-chested and immature, were quite enormous—yet Ostman thought them human.

> The young fellow might have been between 11–18 years old about seven feet tall and might weigh about 300 lbs. His chest would be 50–55 inches, his waist about 36–38 inches. He had wide jaws, narrow forehead, that slanted upward round at the back about four or five inches higher than the forehead. The hair on their heads was about six inches long. The hair on the rest of their body was short and thick in places. The women's hair was a bit longer on their heads and the hair on the forehead had an upward turn like some women have—they call it bangs, among women's hair-do's. Nowadays the old lady could have been anything between 40–70 years old. She was over seven feet tall. She would be about 500–600 pounds.
>
> She had very wide hips, and a goose-like walk. She was not built for beauty or speed. . . . The man's eyeteeth were longer than the rest of the teeth, but not long enough to be called tusks. The old man must have been near eight feet tall. Big barrel chest and big hump on his back—powerful shoulders, his biceps on upper arm were enormous and tapered down to his elbows. His forearms were longer than common people have, but well proportioned. His hands were wide, the palm was long and broad, and hollow like a scoop. His fingers were short in proportion to the rest of his hand. His fingernails were like chisels. The only place they had no hair was inside their hands and the soles of their feet and upper part of the nose and eyelids. I never did see their ears, they were covered with hair hanging over them.

After six days in such company Albert Ostman decided that he had had enough. Choosing his moment, he fired his rifle, which so startled the Sasquatch family that he was able to cut and run.

Ostman did not tell his story for many years, fearing—with some reason—that he might be disbelieved. But his account of the family of giants rings true, as do the myriad details of his amazing story. (John Green, *On the Track of the Sasquatch*, pp.13–21)

As Russian troops penetrated the soaring Vanch mountains of the Pamirs in pursuit of White Army soldiers in 1925, they heard stories from the local people of "Beast-men" who lived in the higher reaches. The soldiers also found footprints and other evidence of some manlike beings. Then, one day, they shot one.

The Red soldiers had fired into a cave where they thought the Whites were hiding. To their surprise a wild, hairy creature ran out, crying inarticulately, and was killed instantly by the blazing machine guns.

Looking at the corpse, the leader, Gen. Mikhail Stepanovich Topil'skiy, thought at first it was that of an ape. "It was covered with fur," he said. "But I knew there were no apes in the Pamirs, and, moreover, the body looked far more human than ape-like, indeed, fully human." On closer examination, however, their medical officer declared otherwise: the creature was *not* a man. But what was it? Could the wild thing they had shot have been the Snowman?

The corpse, that of a male, was about 5½ feet long and covered with dense grayish-brown hair except for the face (there were a few straggly hairs on the upper lip), ears, palms, knees, feet, and buttocks. The skin on the hands, knees, and feet was coarse and thickly calloused. The face was dark, with dark eyes, a heavy, sloping brow, prominent cheekbones, a flattened nose, and a massive lower jaw. Although the teeth were quite large, they seemed to be those of a human. The creature had a broad, unusually muscular chest, but otherwise its torso was much like that of a man.

Unable to carry the body with them down the steep slopes, the soldiers covered it with a pile of stones. (Odette Tchernine, *The Yeti*, pp.104–05)

An Indian of the Nootka tribe, on the west coast of Vancouver Island, British Columbia, claimed in 1928 to have been kidnapped by a band of Bigfeet.

Muchalat Harry, a trapper of powerful physique, was an intrepid fellow who enjoyed spending long weeks alone in the woods with his canoe, his traps, and his camping gear. Heading for the Conuma River to spend the autumn in his favorite hunting ground, he was afraid of nothing, although others in his tribe spoke warily of the giants in the nearby hills. But Harry was a changed man after being scooped up from his camp one night, in his underwear and blankets, and carried two or three miles by a Bigfoot.

At daybreak, after being put down, he saw that he was encircled by perhaps 20 of the big hairy creatures, males and females, at a campsite littered with large bones. Frightened to begin with, he became terrified with the thought that his captors planned to eat him.

As they studied him, one or another came forward and touched him, pulling lightly at what they apparently assumed to be his skin. To their amazement, they found it loose—for it was his undershirt. All the while

The Abominable Snowman and His Far-flung Family

Since the sensational term "Abominable Snowman" burst upon a startled and delighted world, it has become clear that there is not just one big hairy upright hominid haunting the wild places but a varied and widespread clan.

As reports of sightings accumulate, it seems that there may be three distinct types of Yeti in the Tibetan-Himalayan area: small, large, and extra-large, all or none of which may be related. Only the large one seems to have any relationship to Bigfoot, Sasquatch, the Skunk Ape of the Everglades, Momo the Missouri Monster, and other American varieties. The Chinese ape-man bears a strong resemblance to this group, but the Russian Kaptar seems to be in a class by itself.

Are these different geographic races of the same species or several different types with nothing in common but an upright stance and a lot of hair? Indeed, how *do* they compare? John Green, famous Sasquatch hunter, takes a stab at answering:

> In very approximate terms, the North American variety is a good deal larger than the others, while the Russian one is taller than the Himalayan but perhaps not heavier. The Himalayan creature, on the evidence both of its description and its footprint, is entirely unlike a human. The Russian variety, on the other hand may be very human indeed.

For the benefit of those who fear that the killing of a Bigfoot for study would constitute not only murder but the elimination of a rare creature, Green adds firmly that "there is not the slightest possibility that Sasquatches can be considered human or near-human, neither are they an endangered species. . . ." He believes that they are numerous. With a few, suspect exceptions, Bigfoot is a gentle giant, unduly monsterized by people who cannot conceive of it as a member of the animal kingdom.

The Yeti has also been sensationalized out of all proportion to reality. To the Sherpas there is nothing mysterious about it: the creature has been part of their lives and recollections for at least 200 years. Himalayan villagers and hunters include it as just another animal when discussing local fauna. If it seems elusive, it is because its habitat lies far from human paths.

Himalayan hunters say that the Yeti is not a man, nor does it live in the snow zone. Its home is in the highest Himalayan forests, deep in almost impenetrable thickets. There it reputedly moves about on all fours or swings from tree to tree. When it ventures into the snow area, where mountaineers may glimpse it or its tracks, it walks upright with a rolling gait. The Sherpas suggest that its reason for crossing the snow-fields is to seek a saline moss that grows on the rocks of moraines. Ivan Sanderson says that it is not moss they seek but lichens, which are rich in food value.

The American creature appears to be slightly more gregarious and considerably more inquisitive than its Asian counterpart, but it, too, seems to enjoy a reclusive life-style. Skeptics may wonder how it is that so large and supposedly common an animal is able to elude searchers with such ease. In reply Peter Byrne, founder of The International Wildlife Conservation Society, Inc., points out that much of the 125,000 square miles of Sasquatch territory in the Pacific Northwest is heavily forested mountain with few roads, a sparse human population, and almost no visitors. There is plenty of room in this kind of biological sanctuary for Sasquatches and other retiring creatures to live in peaceful, unthreatened isolation.

The question of identity remains. Living in impenetrable woods appears to be characteristic of the larger, hairy, upright creatures everywhere and suggests that they may be evolutionary dropouts seeking refuge from an inimical world. If a few zeuglodons and plesiosaurs have slipped through the net of time, perhaps the two-legged enigmas are relicts too.

Bernard Heuvelmans suggests that the "wild men" of Asia may be leftovers of the race of *Pithecanthropus,* which occupied southeast Asia at the end of the Pliocene period—particularly the larger specimens of the ancient ape-man group, called *Pithecanthropus robustus* and *Meganthropus palaeojavanicus.* Even pygmy varieties of the species may have survived, accounting for the smaller unidentified apelike creatures that are occasionally seen.

Zhou Guoxing of the Peking Museum of Natural History speculates that the apelike animals seen in and near Hubei province in the 1970's might have been descendants of *Meganthropus,* "a giant apeman that died out because it lacked sufficient intelligence to adapt to its environment." Other ancients are equally likely contenders. In 1935 Dutch paleontologist Ralph von Koenigswald unearthed a collection of fossil teeth of Asian origin that were "virtually identical to human teeth, but six times larger." He decided that the specimens must have come from a species of giant ape, probably extinct for half a million years, which he called *Gigantopithecus.*

But *Gigantopithecus* may not be extinct. Zoologist Edward Cronin suggests that, during the Pleistocene Age, Asian *Gigantopithecus* sought safety from *Homo erectus* in the almost inaccessible valleys of the Himalayas. And the relatives of the giant ape, distant or near, may well have found sanctuary in the still-unexplored fastnesses of the New World.

Harry sat motionless. By late afternoon the Bigfeet seemed to grow tired of Harry as a curiosity, and most of them departed on what he assumed to be a food-gathering expedition. Left almost unattended, Harry jumped to his feet and bolted.

In panic, he plunged right past his camp, ran another dozen miles to the mouth of the Conuma River, where he had hidden his canoe, and paddled 45 miles nonstop back to Nootka. He arrived there nearly frozen in his torn and soggy underwear and, uttering wild cries, collapsed with exhaustion. Harry was eventually nursed back to health by the brothers of a Benedictine mission in Nootka, but he never again went trapping in the woods—never again so much as stepped out of the village. (Peter Byrne, *The Search for Bigfoot*, pp.31-34)

Stationed in Dagestan Autonomous Soviet Socialist Republic during the last three months of 1941, a Soviet Army lieutenant colonel named V. S. Karapetyan was asked by local authorities to examine a man captured in the mountains near Buinaksk. A strange-looking individual, the captive was suspected of being a disguised spy. It was hoped that Karapetyan, a medical officer, would be able to determine whether or not the suspect was wearing a disguise. As the colonel reported:

> I can still see the creature as it stood before me, a male, naked and bare-footed. And it was doubtlessly a man, because its entire shape was human. The chest, back, and shoulders, however, were covered with shaggy hair of a dark brown colour. . . .
>
> The man stood absolutely straight with his arms hanging, and his height was above the average—about 180 cm [about six feet]. He stood before me like a giant, his mighty chest thrust forward. His fingers were thick, strong, and exceptionally large. On the whole, he was considerably bigger than any of the local inhabitants.
>
> His eyes told me nothing. They were dull and empty—the eyes of an animal. . . .
>
> When kept in a warm room he sweated profusely. While I was there, some water and then some food was brought up to his mouth; and someone offered him a hand, but there was no reaction. I gave the verbal conclusion that this was no disguised person, but a wild man of some kind.

No doubt he would have been surprised to learn that such creatures were quite well known in the Caucasus, by the name Kaptar. (Ivan Sanderson, *Abominable Snowmen*, pp.292-99)

A compelling piece of evidence in the case for the Yeti was discovered on November 8, 1951, by British mountaineers Eric Shipton and Michael Ward. The two climbers, returning from a reconnaissance expedition on Everest, were exploring the southwestern slopes of

While crossing a high pass near Mount Everest in 1951, Eric Shipton (above) discovered and photographed a trail of huge footprints, possibly the tracks of an Abominable Snowman. A pickax shows one footprint's size.

the Menlung Glacier when they came upon a fresh trail of enormous but human-looking footprints leading along the edge of an ice mass.

Shipton photographed the trail. Close-ups of one particularly crisp imprint indicate a not-quite-human foot about 13 inches long and considerably broader than a mountain boot. This would suggest a biped about eight feet tall. It must have been limber, too: "Where the tracks crossed a crevasse," Shipton wrote afterward, "one could see quite clearly where the creature had jumped and used its toes to secure purchase on the snow on the other side." (Bernard Heuvelmans, *On the Track of Unknown Animals*, p.127)

According to the Communist Chinese News Agency, a Chinese film director named Pai Hsin, of the Chinese People's Army film studies, saw a pair of strange two-legged creatures in the Pamirs in 1954. The exact location is unknown.

Returning from a filming trip to the Himalayas, Pai Hsin and three colleagues were traveling at an elevation of some 19,600 feet very early one morning when they saw two unfamiliar upright figures walking "one behind the other up a slope" not far away. They were short, walked with their backs hunched, and moved among the rocks with ease. The men shouted and fired shots into the air, but the two figures paid no attention and were soon lost from view. The film director later said that he had heard many reports about wild men in the Pamirs. (Odette Tchernine, *The Yeti*, pp.86-87)

A Sasquatch encounter was reported by a hunter in October 1955 near the little town of Tête Jaune Cache in British Columbia, Canada. William Roe, armed with his rifle, was climbing Mica Mountain one afternoon—"just for something to do"—when he saw what he took to be a grizzly bear on the far side of a small clearing. Moments later, as he watched, the animal stepped out into the open, and Roe realized it was not a bear. In a sworn affidavit he later declared:

> This, to the best of my recollection, is what the creature looked like and how it acted as it came across the clearing directly towards me. My first impression was of a huge man, about six feet tall, almost three feet wide, and probably weighing somewhere near three hundred pounds. It was covered from head to foot with dark brown silvertipped hair. But as it came closer I saw by its breasts that it was female.
>
> And yet, its torso was not curved like a female's. Its broad frame was straight from shoulder to hip. Its arms were much thicker than a man's arms, and longer, reaching almost to its knees. Its feet were broader proportionately than a man's, about five inches wide at the front and tapering to much thinner heels.

The creature came within 20 feet of Roe, who was crouched behind a bush, and squatted on its haunches. As it stripped and munched leaves from some bushes, Roe noted the way its head peaked at the back, the flat nose, protruding chin, and beady eyes, and he was struck by the short, thick "unhuman" neck.

All at once the wild thing caught Roe's scent and looked directly at him through an opening in the brush. A look of comical amazement crossed its face as it rose to its full height and started to walk away.

> The thought came to me that if I shot it, I would possibly have a specimen of great interest to scientists the world over. I had heard stories about the Sasquatch. . . . Maybe this was a Sasquatch. . . .
>
> I levelled my rifle. The creature was still walking rapidly away, again turning its head to look in my direction. I lowered the rifle. Although I have called the creature "it," I felt now that it was a human being and I knew I would never forgive myself if I killed it.

As it crossed into the brush at the far side of the clearing it made a whinnying sound, "half laugh and half language." Beyond a stand of lodgepole pines it tipped its head back briefly and uttered the same cry. Then it disappeared into the woods. (John Green, *On the Track of the Sasquatch*, pp.10–12)

The women of a village in the sparsely settled east China province of Zhejiang had a close encounter with an ape-man one May afternoon in 1957, when all the local men were laboring in the hills. Xu Fudi, hearing a scream from her young daughter, rushed out to where the girl had been tending cattle and saw her struggling in the grip of an apelike creature about four feet nine inches tall. The mother grabbed a stick of wood and flailed frantically at the creature.

It sprang into a paddy field and tried to run but was hampered by the mud. Xu Fudi hit it again before it could turn to attack her. By that time a crowd of excited women had arrived on the scene, and about a dozen joined Xu Fudi in beating the animal into a stupor. But it was not quite dead; it recovered consciousness, tears in its eyes, and began to grunt. This time the women killed it. Later they cut it to pieces—and the next day heard woeful gruntings from the hills.

The *Sonyang Daily* made inquiries and subsequently described the creature as a young male weighing about 88 pounds and covered with long, dark-brown hair. Its chest was big, its nose sunken, its teeth white; the tongue, ears, and eyebrows, humanlike; the navel, genitals, and calves were similar to a man's; and the skin under the hair was soft and white.

A young biology teacher from a nearby village took away the creature's hands and feet and carefully preserved them. (See page 164.) (*Pursuit*, 14:64–66, Second Quarter 1981)

During the fall of 1958 the wire services in northwestern California hummed with the story of Jerry Crew and the enormous human tracks he and his buddies had been seeing around their bulldozers for several weeks. The stir of excitement followed an attempt by Crew, of Humboldt County, to prove the existence and authenticity of the outsize tracks. An Associated Press story dispatched from Eureka on October 6 read:

> Jerry Crew, a hard-eyed catskinner who bulldozes logging roads for a living, came to town this weekend with a plaster cast of a footprint.
>
> The footprint looks human, but it is 16 inches long, seven inches wide, and the great weight of the creature that made it sank the print two inches into the dirt.
>
> Crew says an ordinary foot will penetrate that dirt only half an inch.
>
> "I've seen hundreds of these footprints in the past few weeks," said Crew.
>
> He added he made the cast of a print in dirt he had bulldozed Friday in a logging operation in the forests above Weitchpeg, 50 miles north and a bit east of here in the Klamath River country of northwestern California.
>
> Crew said he and his fellow workmen never have seen the creature, but often have had a sense of being watched as they worked in the tall timber. . . .
>
> "Every morning we find his footprints in the fresh earth we've moved the day before," Crew said.
>
> Crew said Robert Titmus, a taxidermist from Redding, studied the tracks and said they were not made by any known animals. [John Green, *On the Track of the Sasquatch*, p.24]

Conducting fieldwork in the isolated valleys of the Caucasus in the 1960's, Prof. Jeanne Josefovna Kofman came close to running to earth the hairy upright creature known sometimes as the Almas.

Professor Kofman and her team collected hundreds of eyewitness reports from peasants, villagers, tea-pickers, and haymakers of an almost-human being with a receding brow and chin, flat nose, flat feet, and a coat of reddish or black body hair. One day they made an unprecedented discovery: two nests, or animal lairs, shaped out in the midst of "tall, ordinarily impenetrable weeds"—and a larder nearby.

In the pile of food were two pumpkins, some blackberries, eight potatoes, part of a sunflower, three apple cores, and a half-chewed corncob. Mixed in with these items were a few pellets of horse dung, a delicacy said to be enjoyed by the Almas because of its salt content. Other corncobs found later showed the imprints of near-human teeth from a jaw of nonhuman width. (Odette Tchernine, *The Yeti*, pp.18–21)

During a salmon run in the Nooksack River near Marietta, Washington, in mid-September 1967, several local anglers reported Sasquatch sightings.

Early one morning Harold James was going upriver

While searching for signs of Sasquatch along Bluff Creek in northern California, Roger Patterson came upon a hairy creature squatting at the edge of the stream. Stills from a film that Patterson was able to make show the creature ambling away and then turning to look back. Patterson also made casts of the creature's footprints, which he compares with his own foot (left).

about 15 feet from shore when he became aware of a strong wet-animal odor that was vaguely familiar. Looking across a bog, he saw something sitting on a stump; and when it rose and walked away, he saw that it was a dark creature twice the size of a man.

That afternoon a married couple who were also fishing saw a creature standing in the river about 200 yards away. Up to its knees in water, it stood about eight feet tall and was slightly stooped. Its body was black, its face flat, and it had no neck. As the couple watched, the creature bent down and submerged. Tracks found on a sandbar showed a five-toed foot 13½ inches long and a stride measuring 45 inches.

Drifting his gill net down a channel one night, Johnny Green discovered that it was disappearing over the edge of his boat. The powerful spotlight Green wore on his head played on a big hairy beast standing in the water, pulling at the net. Green shouted to his friends, Reynold James and Randy Kinley, who came down and shone more lights upon the creature. It let go of the net and lumbered away on the shore. (John Green, *The Sasquatch File*, p.36)

Roger Patterson, a Bigfoot buff for many years, set up camp at the bottom of Bluff Creek valley, in northern California, in October 1967 with the intention of filming fresh tracks with his 16mm movie camera.

Accompanied by his colleague Bob Gimlin, Patterson made daily horseback patrols of sandbars on which tracks had previously been seen. One day the men rounded a bend and saw a large, dark animal squatting on the bank at the far side of the creek. The horses reared at the sight and Patterson fell. As he scrambled to his feet he frantically clawed open his saddle bag to get out the movie camera, but by then the creature was walking away. Patterson ran after it, then stopped and filmed from a distance of about 80 feet.

He managed to shoot a few clear frames that show a heavily built creature, about seven feet tall and three feet across the shoulders, covered with black hair. It strides smoothly, with its knees bent. As it turns to look

at Patterson, it reveals large, drooping breasts. The face is flat and hairy, with heavy brow ridges. The head is peaked at the back and sits right on the shoulders.

The creature—she—went off into the brush, leaving footprints 14½ inches long. Patterson and Gimlin made two crisp casts and several still photographs of the tracks. According to one investigator, John Green, analysis of the material revealed no evidence of fraud. (John Green, *On the Track of the Sasquatch*, pp.51–57, and *The Sasquatch File*, p.39)

The deputy sheriff for Grays Harbor County in the state of Washington described a late-night encounter with an unknown animal to Sasquatch investigator John Green. It happened at 2:35 A.M. on July 26, 1969, as 30-year-old Deputy Verlin Herrington was driving home to Copalis Beach along the Deekay Road after handling an incident at the town of Humptulips.

As his car rounded a corner, Herrington saw a huge figure standing in the middle of the road. His first impression was that it was a bear. To avoid slamming into the animal, Herrington hit his brakes and "came to a screeching halt." He then saw that the animal was not a bear: "It had a face on it." Its eyes, like the eyes of a night creature, reflected the headlights; it had feet instead of paws, and it had breasts.

It walked to the edge of the road, "upright, as a person would." But it was not a person.

Herrington turned his spotlight on it and got out of his car with revolver in hand. He saw that the creature's body was covered with brownish-black hair, except for the face—which had "a dark leathery look"—and the soles of the feet. The feet and toes were quite distinct, as were the fingers on the creature's hands. The deputy cocked the hammer of his gun, and the creature went off into the brush. Its stride seemed short for its size but was long for a human.

In daylight, Herrington went back to the scene and photographed a footprint 18½ inches long. "The animal itself," he judged, "was around seven to seven and a half feet tall and weighed approximately 300 to 325 pounds." (John Green, *Year of the Sasquatch*, pp.27–29)

SINCE 1970

A similar encounter unnerved Mrs. Louise Baxter of Skamania, Washington, on August 19, 1970. Driving in the vicinity of the Beacon Rock trailer park, Mrs. Baxter began to suspect that she had a flat tire, and so she got out of her car to check:

> I kicked the tire, which was okay, and then bent over to see if possibly something was stuck under the fender to make the noise.
>
> I suddenly felt as if I was being watched and

without straightening up I looked toward the wooded area beside the road and looked straight into the face of the biggest creature I have ever seen except the one the time nearly a year before.

> The creature was coconut brown and shaggy and dirty looking. . . . The mouth was partly open and I saw a row of large square white teeth. The head was big and seemed to set right onto the shoulders. The ears were not visible due to the long hair about the head. It seemed the hair was about two inches long on its head.
>
> It had a jutted chin and receding forehead. The nose and upper lip were less hairy and the nose was wide with big nostrils.
>
> The eyes were the most outstanding as they were amber color and seemed to glow like an animal's eyes at night when car lights catch them.
>
> It seemed contented there and seemed to be eating as the left fist was up toward the mouth as though it had something in it.
>
> I screamed or hollered but whether I made any noise I can't tell I was so terrified. I know it didn't move while I looked. I don't remember how I got back in the car or how I started it. As I pulled out I could see it still standing there, all 10 or 12 feet of him. [John Green, *The Sasquatch File*, p.53]

A new element had begun to filter into the worldwide composite portrait of large upright monsters by the 1970's: a possible connection between *some* unidentified bipeds and the UFO phenomenon. A curious episode of the UFO kind occurred one night in August 1972 at Roachdale, Indiana, where a family named Rogers lived in a trailer home.

The sequence of events began when one of the Rogers saw a luminous object hovering in the sky over a nearby cornfield. On several occasions thereafter all the Rogers heard noises in the yard at night, and when one of the men went outside to investigate, he caught a glimpse of a large, heavily built creature parting the cornstalks. Once, Mrs. Rogers saw it looking in through her trailer window and observed that it stood like a man but ran on all fours.

The sightings were never very clear, for they always took place at night, but the Rogers could tell that the creature was covered with black hair—and it had an odor "like dead animals or garbage." A unique feature of the beast was that it appeared to lack substance:

> What was weird was that we could never find tracks, even when it ran over mud. It would run and jump but it was like somehow it wasn't touching anything. When it ran through weeds, you couldn't hear anything. And sometimes when you looked at it, it looked like you could see *through* it.

Yet the monster was not altogether insubstantial. Among the others who saw it were several farmers, who found dozens of mutilated—though uneaten—chickens after visits from the beast. The Burdines found dead chickens, trampled grass, and a broken fence on their property. The pigs' food bucket, the Burdines further noted, had been emptied of tomatoes and cucumbers. One night they saw the apparent culprit standing in the doorway of their chicken house. According to Junior Burdine:

> This thing completely blocked out the lights inside the chickenhouse. The door is 6' x 8'. Its shoulders came up to the top of the door, up to where the neck should have been. But this thing didn't have a neck. To me it looked like an orang-utan or a gorilla. It had long hair, with kind of a brownish cast to it. Sort of rust-lookin' color. I never saw its eyes or its face. It was making a groaning racket.

The Burdine men chased and shot at the creature when it ran, but though the range was short and they were certain they had hit it, it appeared to be unhurt. (Janet and Colin Bord, *Alien Animals*, pp.170–71)

Among the cases found credible by Oregon's Bigfoot Information Center in The Dalles was that related by Jack Cochran, a logger from Parksdale who at the time of the sighting in 1974 was working with a crew in the Hood River National Forest.

On May 12 of that year Mr. Cochran was taking a 10 A.M. break in the cab of his crane when he looked across a clearing and saw "a big hairy thing" standing silently some 50 yards away. A hunter as well as an amateur artist specializing in wildlife studies, Cochran—after recovering from his initial chill—studied the creature with a practiced eye. It "was covered with thick black hair . . . stood about six and a half feet tall, and had massive shoulders." As he watched, it walked away gracefully, "like an athlete," as Cochran recalled, and disappeared into the trees.

The next day at about the same time, according to a *New York Times* report, the loggers were again taking a break. Cochran stayed with his crane, keeping his eyes on the forest but seeing nothing unusual:

> His two companions, however, said that they walked into the woods for a little shade and were startled to see a big creature rise up out of the bushes and stride quickly away on two legs. One of the two men, Fermin Osborne, gave chase and even picked up some rocks to throw.
>
> Later investigators from the Bigfoot Information Center conducted a thorough search of the area. They found the creature's track—indistinct impressions of a soft but heavy foot leading from the edge of the clearing off across some wooded hills.

Commenting on the mildness of the creature and the tameness of the tale, the *Times* writer observed: "Many people have said that hallucinations or hoaxes would be unlikely to yield so tame and dull a story." (*The New York Times*, June 30, 1976)

On a dark night in May 1976 six Communist Party officials were being transported through southern Hubei province in central China when the driver of their jeep suddenly saw a large, hairy animal on the road ahead. The driver blew the horn, and the creature started to clamber up a steep slope but skidded back down to the road. It crouched there on all fours, staring into the headlights with the look of a wild man.

The driver stopped but kept honking, and his passengers got out to surround the creature—at a safe distance. One tossed a stone at it. The creature rose to its hind legs, lumbered off into a gully, and then scrambled up a slope into the woods.

The men agreed afterward that the creature had fine, soft hair like a camel's, with a dark-red streak down its back, and a face the color of flax. The legs were long and thick, the thighs heavy, and the soles of the feet were so soft that the animal made no sound while walking. The face was long, broad across the brow and narrow at the chin, and had a wide mouth.

Although the creature had vanished long before the investigators arrived to study it, an anthropologist with the Peking Museum of Natural History—a Mr. Zhou Guoxing—suggested that it might well have been a distant relative of the abominable snowman or Bigfoot. (*International Wildlife*, 11:18–19, January-February 1981; *The New York Times*, January 5, 1980)

Gong Yulan is a peasant woman who lives in the Qiaoshang Commune in Hubei province, central China. June 19, 1976, was a day like any other, except that Gong Yulan had run out of grass for her pigs, so she took her four-year-old son and climbed up a mountain to gather a supply. As mother and son crossed a pass, they saw a large, moving red object about 20 feet away.

The woman stopped and stared at what turned out to be a strange, hairy animal rubbing its back against a tree. (Later, in an interview with scientists, she described how it had scratched itself. "It stood, just like a man, like this," she said, demonstrating by rubbing her shoulder against a wall.) Watching it, she became frightened by its strangeness. She scooped up her child and ran. To her horror, the creature came after her, uttering cries that sounded like "ya, ya."

Child in arms, Gong Yulan ran a quarter of a mile to the house of her commune brigade leader. His wife, who met her at the door, recalled: "When Gong arrived at my house, the beads of sweat on her forehead were as big as soybeans. She kept saying, 'wild man.'"

Hairs were subsequently recovered from the tree

against which the creature had scratched itself and were examined at the Beijing Medical Institute. It was decided the hairs were not from a bear but resembled those "of the higher primates, including man." (*International Wildlife,* 11:18–19, January–February 1981)

The mountainous region of Shennongjia, near the intersections of the Hubei, Shaanxi, and Sichuan provincial borders, was so often the scene of hairy-creature sightings during 1976 that the Chinese Academy of Sciences in Peking decided to organize a search. In March of 1977 it sent out a 110-member expedition consisting of biologists, zoologists, photographers, and soldiers equipped with rifles, tranquilizer guns, tape recorders, cameras, and dogs. Mr. Zhou Guoxing, of the Peking Museum of Natural History, was put in charge of scientific research for the expedition.

As reported by *The New York Times,* the search party persisted for eight months, and although it failed to capture one of the apelike creatures, the expedition did see one at close range and gathered enough other evidence to substantiate its existence:

> Many footprints, 12 to 16 inches long, were found. Feces, sometimes found beside the footprints and presumed to be from the creature, was analyzed and found to be from neither a human nor a bear, according to Mr. Zhou. Hair samples, believed to have come from the animal and found stuck to tree bark, suggest that it is some sort of higher primate, he said.
>
> From accumulated evidence, including purported witnesses, Mr. Zhou described the creature as about six feet six inches tall, covered with wavy red hair, with the hair on its head falling nearly to its waist. It walks upright, he said, and its footprints show it to have no arch, hence a clumsy gait. The three smallest of its five toes are not completely separated, he said, and because of this it may have the ability to grasp things with its feet. No tail has been detected, but some witnesses said breasts were distinguishable.
>
> The creature is believed to be omnivorous but is said to prefer walnuts and chestnuts, tender young leaves and roots, and insects. While no recording exists of its calls, those who have heard it say it emits one long and one short cry. [*The New York Times,* January 5, 1980]

An unusual Bigfoot episode occurred near Wantage in rural New Jersey in 1977. On May 12 the Sites family discovered that several of their pet rabbits had been killed overnight, apparently squeezed to death by something that had clawed at boards and ripped away a wooden barn door to get at them.

The probable culprit showed up again that night and stood, as if showing off, in the brightly lit yard. "It was big and hairy," Mrs. Sites said later. "It was brown; it looked like a human with a beard and moustache; it had no neck; it looked like its head was just sitting on its shoulders; it had big red glowing eyes." A snarling dog leaped at it; the creature swatted the dog aside with a careless gesture and sent it flying for 20 feet.

On the following night the creature reappeared under the yard lights. Mr. Sites and three companions, waiting with loaded shotguns, fired several times directly at it. The creature growled and made off through an orchard. Sites was sure he had hit it, but no trace of blood was found in daylight.

Members of the Society for the Investigation of the Unexplained made a thorough search of the area, examining the rabbit corpses and the damaged barn. They also heard a scream coming from a nearby swamp, which they were told was made by the creature, but they did not see the thing itself. Nonetheless, they were convinced of the sincerity of the Sites family.

After the SITU team left, the creature was seen again several times, once by the Sites children, who spotted it crawling in the grass with an arm outstretched as if it were hurt and appealing for help. (Janet and Colin Bord, *Alien Animals,* pp.177–78)

More tantalizing evidence of the elusive Nepalese Yeti was found during the British Hinku Expedition of 1979, after mountaineers John Edwards and John Allen spotted a possible campsite at almost 17,000 feet on their way down to base camp. On November 10 Edwards noticed an "overhanging boulder that formed a natural cave" and motioned Allen to wait while he took a closer look. He was astounded to see a set of almost-human footprints in the snow. As Dr. Allen came to join him, both men were startled by "a piercing, chilling, inhuman scream that lasted five or ten seconds." Edwards and Allen decided they must be in the vicinity of an abominable snowman.

The next day the whole team, led by John Whyte, returned to the site and photographed the still-distinct footprints with their BBC camera. The "tracks were of varying sizes," suggesting a pair or perhaps even a small

A cigarette pack shows the relative size of unidentified footprints found in the Himalayan snow by British mountaineers and photographed with a BBC camera.

family of creatures. Droppings found near the prints were gathered to be taken back to England for analysis.

"We have photographed a print," says Whyte, "that no one can satisfactorily identify. I am convinced that there is an animal . . . up there that is not yet recorded by naturalists." (*People*, 13:20–23, January 21, 1980)

In a sequel to the Chinese incidents of the previous decades, a team of scientists scoured Zhejiang province late in 1980 for solid evidence of living ape-men. At the Bihu middle school in Lishui County, Chinese investigators obtained from biology teacher Zhou Shousong the well-preserved hands and feet of the apelike creature routed by Xu Fudi in 1957. (See page 159.)

Apart from some shrinkage of the muscles the remains were in good condition. The feet, which were covered with soft, yellowish-brown hair, measured about 7½ inches in length; and the palms of the hands, about 5½ inches. It was agreed that the animal was probably a primate and possibly akin to a chimpanzee.

Exploring the woods and hills of Zhejiang with a local 60-year-old herb picker for a guide, the team actually found something like a small stockade at an elevation of about 5,000 feet. "Wedged between trees and a rock," the structure was made of branches and lined with grass and leaves. The size of the branches, broken from nearby trees, suggested tremendous strength; the construction of the nest indicated an intelligence somewhat above that of an ape.

Climbing yet higher, the team found 11 additional nests scattered over an area called Fengshuyang, some of them built in trees and others on the ground. Judging by their condition, as well as by nearby footprints and droppings, none of the nests was more than two years old. One appeared to have been built only a month before. Samples of soft brown hair were also found.

Other recently constructed nests were discovered near the rarely visited peak of Nine Dragon Mountains, along with prints of a left foot that measured about 13 inches long. The toes were separated like those of a human being. To valley villagers, the findings came as no surprise. Zhang Qilin of Xikangli Village said:

> For the past 30 years or more I have gone up to Nine Dragon Mountains every year, in September or October, to guard the maize crop against ape-men.
>
> I saw an ape-man about 10 years ago. It approached from Fengshuyang. It was about as high as a house door and it was covered in reddish-brown hair with long hair falling around its shoulders and over its face. It walked upright. . . .
>
> On another occasion I saw an ape-man lying in a nest in a tree. It was quite relaxed and it clapped its hands when it saw me. Most of the time it just lay there, eating maize. There was a big pile of cobs on the ground.

Equally unsurprised was Huang Jialiang of Chenkang Village, who had seen an ape-man on August 14, 1978. It was carrying a piece of wood and walking through the forest, about 65 feet away from Huang, in the direction of Fengshuyang. Commenting on the creature's fondness for corn, Huang added casually: "We know they also like to eat persimmons and wild pears." (*Pursuit*, 14:64–66, Second Quarter 1981)

According to Jon Erik Beckjord, founder and director of Project Bigfoot in Seattle, Washington, Bigfoot-Sasquatch sightings occur every month. On July 3, 1981, loggers in southwest Washington saw a 9- or 10-foot-tall Sasquatch at a distance of 400 feet. On October 18 a logger picking mushrooms in the same area heard growling and noticed the characteristic strong odor of the large, hairy monster.

Project Bigfoot collects not only eyewitness reports but hair and blood samples as well. Specimens obtained at the scenes of the four following incidents have been carefully tested by scholarly skeptics.

In Rock State Park, Maryland, near Bel Air, Peter Hronek was driving a sports car late one night in 1975 when he hit what he thought to be a Bigfoot. Recovering its balance, the creature loomed up over the car, made grumbling sounds, and then loped off. Hair stuck in the dented headlight was removed for analysis.

On the Lummi Indian reservation in Bellingham, Washington, a Sasquatch tried to force its way into a food storage room in the home of the Jeffersons on the night of January 14, 1976. The family woke to the sounds of breaking glass. Leaping up and grabbing a rifle, Mr. Jefferson found glass from the five-foot-high window in the storage room shattered all over the floor and blood smeared on the shards. Black hairs with white tips were found on the window and among the glass fragments on the floor. Jon Beckjord himself came to collect the blood and hair samples and gather reports of the many Sasquatch sightings and attempted entries into houses on the reservation.

Near Sacramento, California, in May 1976, a group of teenagers saw a Sasquatch breaking branches off an apricot tree and eating the fruit. The creature left 25-inch-long tracks. The youngsters collected hair from a fence and turned it over to Beckjord.

In Lebanon, Oregon, in 1977 a huge creature tore doors off a barn and ruined fences while uttering piercing screams. Hair samples were taken by Beckjord.

The one blood sample secured in the course of the incidents (from the broken glass in the Jefferson house) was tested by Dr. Vincent Sarich, physical anthropologist and biochemist at the University of California at Berkeley. He found it to be the blood of a higher primate. The hairs associated with the blood sample as well as the other hair samples were analyzed by three experts. They concluded that it had not come from a human, wolf, bear, or comparable mammal; nor did the hair match that of any primate submitted for the study, although it was close to that of a gorilla.

Beckjord says of the creatures: "They are too large to be men; too much obviously *there* to be myth. They may be man-related hominid primates." (*Frontiers of Science,* 3:22–27, March–April 1981; telephone interview with Jon Beckjord, Seattle, Washington)

Do Monsters Really Fly?

The monsters that come by land and by sea are fairly well documented, and if it is true that mankind has an innate need to believe in otherworldly creatures it is not surprising that they reportedly come by air as well. The evidence, however, is less than compelling.

Mythology has supplied some fascinating species. The ancient tales include flying fire-breathing dragons, the fearsome roc of the Arabian Nights, the rapacious winged Harpies of Greek mythology, and the awesome thunderbird of American Indian lore.

The best case for airborne beasts is made by the fossil remains of the pterodactyl, a sharp-toothed reptile with a wingspan of more than 25 feet. If mankind has, indeed, a racial memory, here, then, is a flying monster fit for the most lurid nightmares. But is that a sufficient explanation for the persistent reports of flying monsters? Or could such atavistic creatures—whether large or not so large—be a current reality?

In New Jersey there have been periodic reports of the Jersey Devil as noted in Janet and Colin Bord's *Alien Animals.* This improbable critter, said by some to be the size of a large crane, is variously described as having a long, thick neck; long back legs with cloven hooves; short front legs with paws; batlike wings with about a two-foot spread; the head of a horse, dog, or ram; and a long, scrawny tail.

In his book *In Witchbound Africa,* Frank H. Melland reports hearing repeatedly of a fearful creature called the Kongamato that resembles a flying lizard with smooth skin, a beak full of teeth, and wings with batlike skin and a span of four to seven feet. This sounds suspiciously like a cousin of the pterodactyl.

Those who tell of seeing Kongamato or the Jersey Devil are doubtless sincere about it. The sightings are currently too few to build a convincing case. But should they become as frequent as those of Nessie and the Sasquatch, we will have airborne candidates for the Society of Probable Monsters (SOPM).

From places as far removed as Washington, Texas, and West Virginia have come reports of Mothman, as noted in John A. Keel's book *The Mothman Prophecies.* This strange, winged creature is reputed to be man-shaped and gray in color, which accounts for the name. Most people who say they have seen it agree that it emanates an aura of bone-chilling fear. One witness, confessing to unreasonable terror during his encounter with Mothman, describes his reaction as follows:

> I've never had that feeling before, a weird kind of fear. That fear gripped you and held you. Somehow, the best way to explain it would be to say that the whole thing just wasn't right. I know that may not make sense, but that's the only way I can put into words what I felt.

This strange gray flying man could, however, be related to well-documented phenomena of sightings of unidentified flying objects. If mankind has need of airborne monsters, the UFO's may have to suffice.

This illustration of a "Jersey Devil," reported in 1909 by a couple living in Gloucester, New Jersey, appeared in a Philadelphia newspaper story about the sighting.

SPECTRAL INCURSIONS

Those who scorn the idea that spooks and specters prowl and shimmer through the world do so because no one has so far caught a ghost in a bottle, because they are skeptical by habit, or because they resist the notion that death may not be final.

For many the word "ghost" conjures up an anonymous white-robed figure, a spirit who has come back from the grave to haunt the living. But in the annals of ghostdom, spectral beings come in a variety of forms and shapes, and some never put in an appearance at all, although they make their presence felt. Ghosts also differ in behavior—they may be aimless, purposeful, playful, angelic, and even demonic.

There are three lines of explanation for ghostly phenomena: the spiritual, mechanical, and psychological.

The most firmly established is the spiritual thesis, which holds that ghosts are intelligent beings. The first version of this idea is that ghosts are the spirits of dead humans. They continue to resemble their earthly forms in appearance and dress and are found reenacting things they did in the past, bound to their haunting grounds by guilt, remorse, desire, or habit. They may be malevolent, kindly, or indifferent toward human beings. People who take this view of ghosts regard them as marking time in a spiritual halfway house between this world and heaven, purgatory, or hell.

According to another version of the spiritual view, a ghost's resemblance to a formerly living person or animal is actually a masquerade adopted for its own purpose, the real appearance of ghosts being quite different. Some ghosts, for instance, appear as vaporous columns or clouds of light.

In the third view of ghosts as a spiritual phenomenon, these apparitions are not beings in either of the senses described above. Instead, they are illusions created by powerful classes of angelic or demonic beings for the purpose of helping or harming those who see them. Miracles are an example of intervention by angelic or enlightened powers, while most poltergeist episodes are held to be demonic.

The mechanical interpretation is that ghosts are images without substance, somehow recorded in an etheric medium and visible under certain conditions to those of a certain cast of mind. This idea accords well with some frequently observed phenomena—the way some ghosts have of disappearing into thin air. It does not explain those cases where the ghost interacts intelligently with those who see it.

In the psychological view of the phenomenon, ghosts reveal a spectrum of powerful but not yet understood capacities of the human mind. In these terms, some ghosts are the product of telepathic powers, as when a relative or friend appears to another at the time of death; others—poltergeist phenomena—suggest unwitting and uncontrolled psychokinetic abilities. And some—the appearance of phantom doubles—suggest that out-of-body experiences may sometimes be manifest to others.

In fact, most believers in ghosts are probably willing to accept all of these theses as helping to explain a complex and varied phenomenon. Skeptics, on the other hand, resorting to the dry but sturdy arguments of what they consider to be common sense, are apt to maintain that stories of ghosts are lies, hallucinations, or earnest reports of misperceptions. But the most convincing evidence of the existence of specters still seems to be their appearance on the scene.

The Frozen Fowl of Pond Square

A ghost, sad, bizarre, and deserving a place in the annals of commercial food-preparation, is associated with Pond Square in London's Highgate. It is the ghost of a half-naked, half-frozen chicken.

The ghost maker in this tale is no less a philosopher than the great Francis Bacon, once lord chancellor of England. In 1626, though, when he was 65 years old, he had been convicted of bribery, sentenced to the Tower of London, and fined £40,000. Although later pardoned, Bacon was forbidden to hold public office again. Thus freed from the struggle for worldly powers, he turned his mind to the mysteries of the universe and to the methods by which a man might solve them.

He was riding through the streets of Highgate one snowy March day in 1626 when a universal mystery occurred to him. Why was grass that had lain under snow all winter still green and fresh when his carriage wheels exposed it to the air? Did the snow somehow act as a preservative?

Bacon instantly stopped his carriage at Pond Square and ordered his coachman to buy a chicken from a farm nearby. Next he had the coachman kill the bird, pluck off most of its feathers, and clean out the abdominal cavity. Then, to the amazement of the small crowd pressing around him, Bacon stooped down and began stuffing the bird with snow. This done, he put it in a sack and filled the sack with more snow.

While he was treating the chicken in this unnatural way, a fit of shivering seized him, and he collapsed on the snow. He was taken to the home of his friend Lord Arundel and died there within a few days.

What happened to Lord Bacon after he died, nobody knows. But the chicken, bound, it seems, to the environs of Pond Square by the sudden outrage that befell it, has been frequently seen there since its death. Stripped of its feathers and shivering, it invariably half runs, and half flaps, always in circles. "It was a big, whitish bird," according to Mrs. John Greenhill who resided at Pond Square during World War II and often saw the chicken on moonlit nights. Aircraftman Terence Long was another witness, also during the war. He was crossing the square one night when he heard the sound of hooves and carriage wheels. He looked around but saw nothing—except a shivering, half-naked chicken flapping pathetically in circles. An Air Raid Precautions fire-watcher came along and told Aircraftman Long that the bird was a habitué of the square. A man had tried to snare it a month or two earlier, he said, but it had disappeared into a brick wall.

One January night in 1969 a motorist who was delayed in Pond Square with car trouble noticed a large white bird near a wall. Seeing that most of its feathers had been plucked, and thinking that a gang of youths might have abused the bird, he looked about him before going to rescue the poor creature. When he turned back, the bird was gone. A year later, in February, a young man and woman were saying good night to each other when a big white bird alighted noiselessly on the ground beside them. It ran twice in a circle and then vanished into the darkness. (Peter Underwood, *Haunted London,* pp.125–27)

Revenge From an Unquiet Grave

Late one night in 1681 a miller, James Graeme, of County Durham, England, was accosted by the hideous ghost of a young woman. She was drenched with blood and had five open wounds on her head. She told Graeme that her name was Anne Walker and that she had been murdered, with a pickax, by one Mark Sharp acting on instruction from a relative of hers, also named Walker, by whom she was pregnant. She made clear to Graeme that unless he gave this information to the local magistrate she would continue to haunt him.

Refusing to believe what he had experienced, Graeme did nothing. But after the apparition appeared, pleaded, and threatened twice more, he went to the authorities with the grisly story. A pit identified by the ghost was searched, and Anne Walker's body was found. Sharp and Walker were arrested, tried, found guilty, and hanged. Anne's spirit, thus avenged, did not appear again. (Reader's Digest, eds., *Folklore, Myths and Legends of Britain,* pp.106–07)

Anne Walker's ghost was unable to find peace until the two men who murdered her were arrested and hanged.

The Barons' Banshee

Among Gaelic people, banshees—female guardian spirits—have been well known for centuries. A banshee will attach herself to a person or family, watch over them during their life, and foretell an imminent death by shrieking, crying, and wailing. Such is the case with the Rossmore banshee of County Monaghan, Ireland.

Her terrible wailing was first heard in 1801, when

Gen. Robert Cunningham, the first Baron Rossmore, lay dying. William Rossmore, the sixth baron, described the original appearance of the banshee, a story passed down through the family over the years:

> Robert Rossmore was on terms of great friendship with Sir Jonah and Lady Barrington, and once when they met at a Dublin drawing-room, Rossmore persuaded the Barringtons to come over the next day to Mount Kennedy, where he was then living. As the invited guests proposed to rise early they retired to bed in good time, and slept soundly until two o'clock in the morning, when Sir Jonah was awakened by a wild and plaintive cry. He lost no time in rousing his wife, and the scared couple got up and opened the window, which looked over the grass plot beneath. It was a moonlight night and the objects around the house were easily discernible, but there was nothing to be seen in the direction whence the eerie sound proceeded.
>
> Now thoroughly frightened, Lady Barrington called her maid, who straightway would not listen or look, and fled in terror to the servants' quarters. The uncanny noise continued for about half an hour, when it suddenly ceased. All at once a weird cry of "Rossmore, Rossmore, Rossmore" was heard, and then all was still.
>
> The Barringtons looked at each other in dismay, and were utterly bewildered as to what the cry could mean. They decided, however, not to mention the incident at Mount Kennedy, and returned to bed in the hope of resuming their broken slumbers. They were not left long undisturbed, for at seven o'clock they were awakened by a loud knocking at the bedroom door, and Sir Jonah's servant, Lawyer, entered the room, his face white with terror.
>
> "What's the matter, what's the matter?" asked Sir Jonah. "Is anyone dead?"

A British print shows a banshee, a female spirit said to haunt old and noble Irish families, sometimes to avenge the cruelties that had been meted out to her by an ancient ancestor.

> "Oh sir," answered the man, "Lord Rossmore's footman has just gone by in great haste, and he told me that my lord, after coming from the Castle, had gone to bed in perfect health but that about half past two this morning, his own man hearing a noise in his master's room went to him, and found him in the agonies of death, and before he could alarm the servants his lordship was dead."

Shrieking and wailing and crying, "Rossmore, Rossmore," the banshee has announced the death of every Rossmore heir since then, including that of the sixth baron, who died in 1958. (Raymond Lamont Brown, *Phantom Soldiers,* pp.80–81)

Steer to the Nor'west

In 1828 a British ship out of Liverpool, England, was heading due west toward Nova Scotia in the icy waters of the North Atlantic. The ship had been at sea for many weeks when one day the first mate, Robert Bruce, found a strange man writing on a blackboard in the captain's cabin. Bruce was astonished to discover someone he did not recognize on board and, mystified, went to report the event to the captain. The captain was incredulous. How could there be anyone on the ship whom neither he nor the mate had seen before? Nonetheless, he followed Bruce to the cabin and looked at the blackboard. Plain to see were the words "STEER TO THE NOR'WEST." The stranger, however, had disappeared. The captain asked everyone on the ship to write the same words on a slate, but nobody's handwriting matched that on the blackboard.

The captain was now altogether at a loss to explain the apparition and its message, but he ordered the ship's course changed to northwest. Some hours later the ship's lookout sighted another vessel stuck fast in ice. All her passengers were taken on board, and among them Bruce recognized the man he had seen in the cabin. The captain then asked him to write down the words "Steer to the Nor'west"; his handwriting matched that of the original message exactly.

According to the captain of the icebound vessel, the passenger concerned had fallen asleep at about the same time that his double was seen; when he awoke, he had announced with complete certainty that they would all be saved. (Robert Dale Owen, *Footfalls on the Boundary of Another World,* pp.333–40)

The Curse of the *Charles Haskell*

Between 1830 and 1892 nearly 600 ships and more than 3,000 lives were lost in the treacherous and gale-swept waters of the Grand Banks, off Newfoundland. The victims were fishermen, seeking cod in the icy shoaling grounds, and most of them drowned when their ships rammed one another as they jostled in the fierce competition for fish or were wrecked on the shoals. It was hard, nerve-wracking work, and the men who risked their lives each time they put to sea were alert to every kind of omen, good or bad, real or imagined.

In 1869 the *Charles Haskell*, a graceful schooner built and outfitted for cod fishing, was undergoing final inspection when a workman slipped on a companionway and broke his neck. There could not have been a worse omen than a death, and the captain who was to take the *Charles Haskell* to sea for her maiden voyage refused to sail in her. For a year no one would assume command of the ship; then, a Captain Curtis of Gloucester, Massachusetts, accepted the position.

During her first winter at sea—a notably harsh one—the *Haskell* and a fleet of some hundred other vessels were fishing off Georges Bank when a hurricane struck. In the confusion the *Haskell* rammed the *Andrew Johnson*. Both ships were badly damaged, but the *Haskell* managed to limp back to port; the *Andrew Johnson* was lost with all hands.

If the *Haskell*'s escape seemed to belie her early, unlucky reputation, the fishermen did not believe it: the ship had been *too* lucky; she should have gone down with the *Andrew Johnson*, and it was the Devil's work that she hadn't.

Eventually the spring came, and with it better weather and excellent catches. Once more the *Haskell* was at sea, fishing off the Banks. On her sixth day out, the two men on midnight watch were suddenly terrified: men in oilskins streaming with water from the sea were silently climbing over the rails, their eyes staring hollows. The watch called the captain, and he and the crew saw the phantoms take up positions on the fishermen's benches and go through the motions of baiting and sinking invisible lines. Then, their task done, and in single file, the 26 dead seamen climbed back over the rail and returned to the depths of the sea.

Captain Curtis immediately turned the *Haskell* toward home, but another night passed before she reached the shore. Again, at midnight, dead men climbed from the sea onto her deck and played out their ghastly charade. But this time, as dawn came and the *Haskell* approached Gloucester harbor, they climbed overboard and formed a grim, mute procession, walking across the sea toward Salem.

That was the last voyage of the *Charles Haskell*, for thereafter not a man would crew her, and she eventually fell into decay and ruin at her mooring. (Mary Bolté, *Haunted New England: A Devilish View of the Yankee Past*, pp.43-46)

The Major's Revenge

In 1876 Major Stewart died at Ballechin House in Perthshire, Scotland. He had lived there for more than 40 years and during that period had acquired something of a reputation for eccentricity. This seems to have been based on nothing more extreme than a belief in spirits, a firm conviction in the transmigration of souls, and an unusual fondness for dogs, of which he had 14 at the time of his demise. He even declared that, if possible, he wished to return to earth after his death as the tenant of the body of a favorite black spaniel. After he died, however, his family had all 14 dogs destroyed. In doing so, they made a serious mistake.

The first signs of something amiss in the house occurred not long after the major's nephew, who had inherited the place, moved in with his wife. This lady was in the habit of balancing her housekeeping books in the room the major had used for a study. One day, busy with her books, she suddenly and quite unmistakably smelled the doggy odor of the old room. Then worse: something invisible pushed her. Somehow, she felt that whatever had pushed her was an animal. Other disquieting things happened. There were noises that could not be accounted for, knockings, explosions, sometimes arguing voices, when no people were there.

By 1896 Ballechin House was said to be haunted. But its estates were wide, the grouse were plentiful, and the new owner, a Captain Stewart, had no difficulty that August in renting the house and shooting rights for the season to wealthy people devoted to the sport. Whether he warned them of the house's reputation is not recorded. He had acquired the house only the year before, when the old major's nephew had been knocked down and killed by a London cab.

In any event, the tenants moved in. They had paid in advance for a rental of several months. But soon they were pushed and snuffled at and half scared to death by animals they could not see. They stayed a few weeks and moved out, forfeiting their money.

When the marquis of Bute heard of the goings-on at Ballechin, the urge to investigate overcame him. He had a deep interest in spiritualism and was a member of the Psychical Research Society. With Captain Stewart's approval, he rented the house with a Major Le Mesurier Taylor and other members of the society and prepared for an on-the-spot investigation.

In due course the marquis, the major, and a Miss Goodrich-Freer gathered 35 guests at Ballechin, ostensibly for a house party. Most of the guests knew nothing of Ballechin's reputation. They were soon to discover how it had been earned.

At first, the consensus among the guests was that owls and water pipes, and perhaps the servants, were making the noises. When it became obvious that the raps and muffled explosions, the sounds of shuffling feet, of quarreling voices, and someone interminably reading aloud were too much of a production for even a

Stately Ballechin House gained a reputation for being haunted by a deceased owner and his dogs.

The marquis of Bute and Miss Goodrich-Freer inquired into the bizzare occurrences at Ballechin House.

forestful of owls, an army of servants, and the world's most versatile water pipes, the guests began to accuse each other. Finally the men sat up at night in grim-jawed groups, armed with pistols and pokers.

But the ghosts of Ballechin were not deterred. Something was heard to beat powerfully against the bedroom doors, and a black spaniel, which seemed to congeal out of the very air and then melt into nothing, was seen by nearly everybody in the house.

To be nudged and sniffed at by invisible dogs and to hear invisible tails thumping the wainscot was the common lot of all the guests. One night a lady sharing a bedroom with another lady was awakened by the whimpering of her pet dog. She followed the animal's gaze to a bedside table. Resting on it were two black paws, each ending in thin air. Another night a gentleman saw a disembodied hand clutching a crucifix afloat in the air at the foot of his bed. A lone nun was seen weeping in a glen beyond the house, and then two nuns together; a nun, possibly a sister of the old major, had died 16 years before.

By the time the house party came to an end, all but one of the 35 guests were convinced that Ballechin House was haunted. Whether or not the marquis and his cohosts received thank-you notes is not recorded. (Charles G. Harper, *Haunted Houses,* pp.116-20)

The Light in the Orphanage

A benign light, a motherless child, a witness of faultless rectitude: the following story is told by the Reverend Charles Jupp, warden of the Orphanage and Convalescent Home at Aberlour, near Craigellachie, Scotland. In 1878, he said, three young children, recently orphaned by the death of their mother, had been admitted to his institution. A few months later several unexpected visitors arrived, and in order to accommodate them overnight the Reverend Jupp decided to occupy an empty bed in the children's dormitory. At breakfast the following morning, the warden told his co-workers and friends what had transpired during the night:

As near as I can tell I fell asleep about 11 o'clock, and slept very soundly for some time. I suddenly woke without any apparent reason, and felt an impulse to turn round, my face being towards the wall, from the children. Before turning, I looked up and saw a soft light in the room. The gas was burning low in the hall, and the dormitory door being open, I thought it probable that the light came from that source. It was soon evident, however, that such was not the case. I turned round, and then a wonderful vision met my gaze. Over the second bed from mine, and on the same side of the room, there was floating a small cloud of light, forming a halo of the brightness of the moon on an ordinary moonlight night.

I sat upright in bed, looking at this strange appearance, took up my watch and found the hands pointing to 5 minutes to 1. Everything was quiet, and all the children sleeping soundly. In the bed, over which the light seemed to float, slept the youngest of the . . . children mentioned above.

I asked myself, "Am I dreaming?" No! I was wide awake. I was seized with a strong impulse to rise and touch the substance, or whatever it might be (for it was about 5 feet high), and was getting up when something seemed to hold me back. I am certain I heard nothing, yet I *felt* and perfectly understood the words—"No, lie down, it won't hurt you." I *at once* did what I *felt* I was told to do. I fell asleep shortly afterwards and rose at half-past 5, that being my usual time.

At 6 . . . I began dressing the children, beginning at the bed furthest from the one in which I slept. Presently I came to the bed over which I had seen the light hovering. I took the little boy out, placed him on my knee, and put on some of his clothes. The child had been talking with the others; suddenly he was silent. And then, looking me hard in the face with an extraordinary expression, he said, "Oh, Mr. Jupp, my mother came to me last night. Did you see her?" For a moment I could not answer the child. I then thought it better to pass it off, and said, "Come, we must make haste, or we shall be late for breakfast."

The Reverend Jupp never spoke of the matter to the small boy, nor did the child refer to it. Some time later, however, an account of the incident was included in the small magazine put out by the orphanage. When the boy read it, wrote the Reverend Jupp in 1883,

> his countenance changed, and, looking up, he said, "Mr. Jupp, that is me." I said, "Yes, that is what we saw." He said, "Yes," and then seemed to fall into deep thought, evidently with pleasant remembrances, for he smiled so sweetly to himself, and seemed to forget I was present.

(Edmund Gurney, Frederick W. H. Myers, and Frank Podmore, *Phantasms of the Living*, pp.493–94)

The Scent of Violets

Emperor Napoleon III, Empress Eugénie, and their son, Louis, were given refuge in England by Queen Victoria after the disastrous Franco-Prussian War of 1870. Louis was loyal to his adopted country and joined a British regiment that went to fight in South Africa. In 1879 the

Louis, son of Napoleon III, was killed in battle in South Africa (below). His mother later described how his favorite scent led her through thick jungle to his lost grave.

prince was killed in a battle with Zulus, and he was buried hurriedly in the jungle.

Eugénie was adamant that Louis's body be returned to England and buried in the family vault with Napoleon III. In 1880 she went to Africa with two companions to find the prince's grave, hiring Zulu guides to help in the search.

But the jungle regenerates quickly, and the grave could not be found. Her friends, fearing for her health, urged her to give up the seemingly hopeless mission, but she insisted on continuing.

One morning she tore into the jungle, shouting, *"Par ici! C'est la route!"* ("Through here! This is the way!") Her incredulous party followed as she ran through the jungle, over rocks and fallen logs, through grass as high as her head, as though on a clear path, until she reached a marker so overgrown as to be completely hidden. It was the grave of Prince Louis.

To her amazed companions she said that she was guided by the scent of violets. Louis had loved the scent and had always worn it. She followed the scent of violets until it faded, and arrived at the grave. (Raymond Lamont Brown, *Phantom Soldiers*, pp.101–02)

The Disappearing Admiral

Thirteen ironclad warships of Britain's Mediterranean fleet, under the command of Adm. Sir George Tryon, steamed out of Beirut for routine maneuvers on the morning of June 22, 1893. Soon after 2 P.M., just off Tripoli, Sir George from his flagship, H.M.S. *Victoria*, ordered the formation of two columns, six cables (1,200 yards) apart. The admiral, a highly respected naval tactician, then gave a strange and fateful order. He signaled the lead ships and those following to reverse direction by turning toward one another. Leading the other column in his ship, the H.M.S. *Camperdown*, Rear Adm. Albert Hastings Markham saw that the columns were too close together to turn safely. He questioned the signal, and Sir George confirmed the order. The ships turned, and the *Camperdown* crashed into the bow of the *Victoria*, which sank in less than 15 minutes.

Of the 649 men on board, 358, including the admiral, went down. As his ship was sinking, Sir George said to his flag lieutenant, "It is entirely my fault."

At the same time, some 2,000 miles away, in Tryon's fashionable London home on Eaton Square, his wife, Clementina, was giving a reception. Suddenly, to the astonishment of the guests who knew he was at sea, the tall figure of Sir George appeared and walked among them; as they stepped aside to make way, he simply vanished. The tragic news of the *Victoria* and of the admiral's death did not reach London until some days later. (Marc Alexander, *Phantom Britain*, pp.178–79; *Dictionary of National Biography*, Vol. 19, pp.1200–01).

Strange Meeting

World War I ended officially at 11 A.M. on November 11, 1918. On that day Harold Owen was an officer on the H.M.S. *Astraea*, a British cruiser then anchored in Table Bay, Union of South Africa. To celebrate the armistice, the ship's captain invited all the officers for drinks in his cabin, but Owen, then 21 years old, was unable to enter into the happy mood. A feeling of apprehension gripped him; had his brother, Wilfred, survived the war? A fit of the deepest depression settled on him. Before long the *Astraea* left Table Bay for the coast of Cameroons. There, at anchor off Victoria, Owen fell ill with malaria and, in a weakened and still depressed state, had "an extraordinary and inexplicable experience," which he later described:

> I had gone down to my cabin thinking to write some letters. I drew aside the door curtain and stepped inside and to my amazement I saw Wilfred sitting in my chair. I felt shock run through me with appalling force and with it I could feel the blood draining away from my face. I did not rush towards him but walked jerkily into the cabin—all my limbs stiff and slow to respond. I did not sit down but looking at him I spoke quietly: "Wilfred, how did you get here?" He did not rise and I saw that he was involuntarily immobile, but his eyes which had never left mine were alive with the familiar look of trying to make me understand; when I spoke his whole face broke into his sweetest and most endearing dark smile. I felt no fear—I had not when I first drew my door curtain and saw him there; only exquisite mental pleasure at thus beholding him. All I was conscious of was a sensation of enormous shock and profound astonishment that he should be here in my cabin. I spoke again: "Wilfred dear, how can you be here, it's just not possible. . . ." But still he did not speak but only smiled his most gentle smile. This not speaking did not now as it had done at first seem strange or even unnatural; it was not only in some inexplicable way perfectly natural but radiated a quality which made his presence with me undeniably right and in no way out of the ordinary. I loved having him there: I could not, and did not want to try to understand how he had got there. I was content to accept him, that he was here with me was sufficient. I could not question anything, the meeting in itself was complete and strangely perfect. He was in uniform and I remember thinking how out of place the khaki looked amongst the cabin furnishings. With this thought I must have turned my eyes away from him; when I looked back my cabin chair was empty. . . .
>
> I felt the blood run slowly back to my face and looseness into my limbs and with these an overpowering sense of emptiness and absolute loss. . . . I wondered if I had been dreaming but looking down I saw that I was still standing.

Suddenly I felt terribly tired and moving to my bunk I lay down; instantly I went into a deep oblivious sleep. When I woke up I knew with absolute certainty that Wilfred was dead.

Wilfred Owen, the famous war poet, was killed on November 4, 1918. His parents received notification of his death at 12 noon on November 11, one hour after the hostilities had ceased. He is perhaps best remembered for his poem "Strange Meeting," in which he imagined an encounter with the spirits of those who had died in the war. (Andrew MacKenzie, *A Gallery of Ghosts*, pp.139–41; Harold Owen, *Journey From Obscurity, Wilfred Owen, 1893–1918*, Vol. 3, pp.192–201)

Harold Owen has described how, on the day World War I ended, he saw his brother, Wilfred (right), sitting in his cabin on a British cruiser. Harold learned only later that his brother had been killed a week before the astonishing visit.

Happenings at the Rectory

In early August 1919, oil began to "spurt" from the walls and ceilings of Swanton Novers Rectory in Norfolk, England. At first it was supposed that the house stood over a natural oil well and that the liquid was being soaked up by the walls and then somehow ejected. But when the oil was found to be refined gasoline, this theory was abandoned. Showers of water, methylated spirits, and sandalwood oil followed. At one point the oil flow was at the rate of a quart every 10 minutes. The rector, Rev. Hugh Guy, was soon obliged to move his furnishings into another house.

A magician and his wife, a Mr. and Mrs. Oswald Williams, went to the rectory to investigate. Putting pails of salted water about, they hid and watched. On September 9 they announced that the culprit was the 15-year-old scullery maid, whom they caught throwing salt water on the ceiling. But the girl denied it and said she had been beaten to make her confess.

The foreman of an oil company went to check the house and caught two gallons of oil in four hours. And a second magician-turned-investigator stated that he observed the flow of "barrels" of oil during his visit to the premises. The source of the oil was never determined, but it seemed unlikely that the girl could have handled such copious quantities of it. (Charles Fort, *The Complete Books of Charles Fort*, pp.577–81)

Fellow Travelers

In December 1924 two crew members of the S.S. *Watertown*, a large oil tanker, were overcome by fumes while cleaning one of the cargo tanks and died. The *Watertown* was en route from the west coast of the United States to Panama when the accident happened, and the two men, James Courtney and Michael Meehan, were buried at sea on December 4.

On December 5 the first mate told Captain Keith Tracy that the faces of Courtney and Meehan were seen floating in the sea; appearing and disappearing, they were keeping pace with the *Watertown*. During the rest of the journey to Panama the faces, following alongside, were observed by every man on board.

When the *Watertown* docked at New Orleans, Captain Tracy related the story at a meeting with the officials of the Cities Services Company. It was suggested that it might be possible to photograph the faces.

When the *Watertown* set sail again, the faces reappeared, and six photographs were taken. Five showed nothing unusual, but in one the two faces were clearly visible. The negative was checked for evidence of fakery by the Burns Detective Agency, and the circumstances in which it had been taken were attested to by the *Watertown's* captain and the assistant engineer. (D. Scott Rogo, *An Experience of Phantoms*, pp.58–60)

This photograph, taken from the deck of the S.S. Watertown, seems to reveal two haunting faces in the water below. They are likenesses, crewmen claimed, of two seamen who died in an accident on the ship.

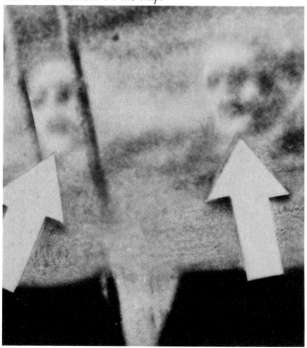

The Returning Stones

Ivan Sanderson, the well-known naturalist and author, was visiting a rubber plantation in Sumatra in 1928, where he participated in what was perhaps the most bizarre entertainment of his life. Dinner was over, and everyone gathered on the veranda. Suddenly, small stones began to shower down on the veranda deck from the darkness beyond. Then, Sanderson said,

> The host told us . . . that these small stones came all the time, particularly on certain nights and usually still ones, but not necessarily dark ones. . . . As everybody was amazed and skeptical, our host then told us to mark the stones in any way we liked and throw them back anywhere into the hopelessly thick tangle of vegetation beyond or around the garden or house. To mark them he found us chalk from his desk, a file, and pencils. The ladies used their lipsticks, and we employed all kinds of designs and devices. We all threw them back hard or lightly in every conceivable direction. Almost but not quite all of the marked stones came back onto the veranda within a matter of seconds, a few some minutes later. I would say that some fifty stones at least were so marked and thrown that night. . . . I can vouch for the fact that it would be absolutely impossible for any human . . . to trace, find, and throw back marked stones in that vegetational tangle short of clearing said tangle and sifting its entire surface. [William G. Roll, *The Poltergeist*, p.38]

Marker 239

In the late summer of 1929 a new highway was opened to traffic between Bremen and Bremerhaven, Germany. Within a year more than 100 automobiles had crashed mysteriously on the highway—all at kilometer stone 239, on a perfectly straight stretch of road. When questioned by the police, survivors described feeling "a tremendous thrill" as their cars reached the marker and said that some great force then seized their vehicles and pulled them off the road. In a single day, September 7, 1930, nine cars were wrecked at the fateful marker.

The police and other investigators were puzzled, but a local dowser, Carl Wehrs, suggested that the mysterious force was a powerful magnetic current generated by an underground stream. To test his theory he took a steel divining rod in his hands and slowly walked toward marker 239. When he was directly opposite it, and about 12 feet away, the rod suddenly flew out of his hands as if flung by some invisible force to the other side of the road, while Wehrs himself was spun halfway round in his tracks.

Satisfied that his theory was correct, Wehrs applied his own solution to the problem and buried a copper box full of small star-shaped pieces of copper at the base of the stone marker. The box remained buried there for a week, and during that time no accidents occurred. The box was then dug up—and the first three cars that passed the marker were wrecked. The box was quickly reburied, and since then there have been no accidents at kilometer marker 239.

Although Carl Wehrs made his living as a water diviner, and presumably knew something about underground streams, local farmers believed that a devil was responsible for the accidents. They said that after it had been exorcised from the road, it entered their radios, which henceforth produced nothing but static. (*The Breathless Moment,* Philip van Doren Stern, ed.)

The Ghost Bus of Ladbroke Grove
"I was turning the corner and saw a bus tearing towards me," the motorist testified before the police:

> The lights of the top and bottom deck, and the headlights were full on but I could see no sign of crew or passengers. I yanked my steering wheel hard over, and mounted the pavement (sidewalk), scraping the roadside wall. The bus just vanished.

The motorist who made this report to the local authorities in North Kensington, London, in the mid-1930's may have been drunk, hallucinating, or dreaming at the wheel when he had the accident. But if he was, so were hundreds of other motorists who complained of being forced off the road by a phantom bus careening round the corner from St. Mark's Road into Cambridge Gardens, near the Ladbroke Grove underground station. After one fatal accident, the local coroner took evidence of the apparition and discovered that dozens of local residents claimed to have seen the spectral double-decker.

In fact, there had been many ordinary accidents, several of them fatal, at the notorious junction. Eventually the local council straightened the road there, and the accident rate was greatly reduced. Thereafter there were no more reports of the ghostly red bus. (Frank Smyth, *Ghosts and Poltergeists,* p.60)

A Feeling of Terror and Panic...
Hereward Carrington was one of the pioneers of psychical research in the United States, a tireless investigator of telepathy, mediums, poltergeists, and hauntings. He claimed to have "witnessed highly curious and inexplicable phenomena in haunted houses" on several occasions. He chose the following account as one of the most striking:

> On the night of August 13, 1937, a party of seven of us spent the night in a reputed "haunted house," situated some 50 miles from New York City.... The group consisted of the former occupant [who had rented the house and left before his rental expired,

Motorists whose cars crashed at this London corner explained that they swerved to avoid a mysterious red bus. It had hurtled toward them, they said, and then suddenly vanished.

because of the disturbances], two of his friends, two friends of our own, my wife and myself. We also brought with us a dog which had lived in the house while it was occupied, and which, according to reports, had behaved in an extraordinary manner on several occasions.

Carrington suggested that the house, which was lit from top to bottom upon their arrival, be explored to make sure that it was not practical jokers, cats, bats, rats, or mice that were causing the disturbances:

> Examination of the cellar and the ground floor revealed nothing unusual. On the second floor, however, two or three of us sensed something strange in one of the middle bedrooms. This feeling was quite intangible, but was definitely present, and seemed to be associated with an old bureau standing against one wall. . . .
>
> Walking along the hall, we came to a door which had escaped our attention the first time we had passed it.
>
> "Where does this lead?" I asked.
>
> "To the servants' quarters," Mr. X. replied. "Would you like to go up there?"
>
> "By all means," I said, opening the door.
>
> Glancing up, I could see that the top floor was brilliantly lighted, and that a steep flight of stairs lay just ahead of me. Leading the way, with the others close behind me, I ascended the stairs, and made a sharp turn to the right, finding myself confronted by a series of small rooms.
>
> The instant I did so, I felt as though a vital blow had been delivered to my solar plexus. My forehead broke out into profuse perspiration, my head swam, and I had difficulty in swallowing. It was a most

extraordinary sensation, definitely physiological, and unlike anything I had ever experienced before. A feeling of terror and panic seized me, and for the moment I had the utmost difficulty in preventing myself from turning and fleeing down the stairs! Vaguely I remember saying aloud:

"Very powerful! Very powerful!"

My wife, who was just behind me, had taken a step or two forward. She was just exclaiming, "Oh, what cute little rooms!" when the next moment she was crying, "No! No!" and raced down the steep flight of stairs like a scared rabbit.

Carrington pointed out that both he and his wife were seasoned investigators, "accustomed to psychic manifestations of all kinds," and that neither had previously experienced a comparable moment of terror. He went downstairs to make sure that his wife was all right and found her sitting on the porch "slowly collecting her scattered faculties." She reassured him. The group, whose other members had all been strongly affected, then gathered in a circle in one of the bedrooms. The lights were turned out, and they waited, cameras and flashbulbs ready.

After passing an uneventful hour they ascended the stairs again, and "this time not a sensation of any kind was to be felt! The room seemed absolutely clear of all influences, clean, pure and normal. . . ." Even the dog, which had growled and bristled like a cat and refused to be coaxed upstairs on the first occasion, now ran up quite willingly, with its tail wagging.

It was only after Carrington and the others had made their original inspection of the place and experienced their "first violent reactions" that the former tenant told them "a suicide had actually been committed on the upper floor, and that these rooms were thought to be the 'seat' of the haunting." (Hereward Carrington, *Essays in the Occult*, pp.19–25)

After having spent years investigating psychical phenomena in England, Dr. Hereward Carrington came to the United States in the 1920's to continue his research. It led him to one of the most terrifying "hauntings" he ever experienced.

Stage Fright

It was a Saturday night, about midnight, and the last show was over. Bernard Mattimore and Jerry Adams, the assistant manager and the projectionist of the old Tower Cinema in Peckham, south London, were making their way to the rear exit when they stopped. They were not alone in the cinema.

A man was walking through the air about 10 feet above the floor. The figure seemed to be that of a middle-aged man wearing the clothes of another era, and he seemed to glow in the darkness. The two men watched the elevated figure as it walked slowly across the stage and disappeared into a bricked-up recess that had once held an organ.

Two years earlier, in 1953, two upholsterers told of seeing a ghost when they were working late one night in the theater. One of them had been so terrified that he had never gone back. A construction worker claimed to have seen the ghost in 1954. And when people cast their minds back, they recalled a number of strange incidents in the cinema: bags of cement inexplicably torn open during renovation work and a seepage of water from a ceiling although the weather was dry and there were no water pipes above the drip.

According to a map dating from 1819, the cinema occupied the site of an old chapel, the ground floor of which had been situated about 10 feet above the floor of the present auditorium. (Peter Underwood, *Haunted London*, pp.170–71)

The Vardogr

Erkson Gorique had never visited Norway, but he was in the importing business and in 1955 decided he must go to Oslo to investigate the possibilities of importing Norwegian china and glass. In July, therefore, he caught a plane to Oslo and promptly went to the best hotel.

"I'm glad to see you made it, Mr. Gorique," the clerk said after he had checked in. "It's good to have you back." Gorique was startled. "But I've never been here before," he said. "You must have mistaken me for somebody else."

It was the clerk's turn to be surprised. "But, sir, don't you remember? Just a few months ago you dropped in to make a reservation and said you'd be along about this time in the summer. Your name . . . well . . . is unusual. That's why, I think, I remembered it."

"That just can't be," replied Gorique. "This is the first time I have ever been here!"

"Then I must be mistaken, sir," the clerk said, realizing that he must be on delicate ground. "Please excuse me."

The next day, Gorique went to see a wholesale dealer, a Mr. Olsen.

"Ah, Mr. Gorique!" Olsen greeted him with a cordial smile. "I'm delighted to see you did get back, after all. I hoped for your return, for your visit of a few months back was, of necessity, so short. Much too short, sir."

Mind Creatures

Creatures of the mind exist in a variety of forms. There is that remarkable population of lifelike entities that inhabits the world of dreams. And there are convincing make-believe playmates, sometimes of long duration, that many children create for themselves. This is not to mention the reported menagerie of visions induced by drugs and alcohol. These manifestations are all subjective and not perceived by others.

There are, however, apparitions that make public appearances. Some of these are said to be the perceptible double—the etheric counterpart—of a living person who is undergoing an out-of-the-body experience. Even more mysterious are the externalized perceptible manifestations of something whose existence originated in the mind of its creator by virtue of that person's incredible powers of concentration, visualization, and other, more occult, efforts of mind. In Tibet, where such things are practiced, a ghost of this kind is called a *tulpa*.

A *tulpa* is usually produced by a skilled magician or yogi, although in some cases it is said to arise from the collective imagination of superstitious villagers, say, or of travelers passing through some sinister tract of country. A *tulpa*, the Tibetans claim, may sometimes be so vigorous as to produce its own secondary emanation, known as a *yang-tul*, and this may, in turn, produce an emanation of the third degree, a *nying-tul*. Adepts able to originate such multiple manifestations are rare and are usually found among the Buddhist saints, or bodhisattvas. Some are able to produce 10 different kinds of *tulpa*. These include apparently animate beings—whether human, animal, or supernatural—and those emanations that appear in the dreams of whomever the bodhisattva intends to help.

Few westerners have had an opportunity to investigate the apparently fanciful Tibetan claims outlined above. One who did was the French scholar and traveler Alexandra David-Neel, who spent 14 years in Tibet and studied the doctrines of Tantric Buddhism with a number of eminent lamas. The only woman lama at that time, she was widely honored for her contribution to the understanding of Tibetan thought. Later she published two accounts of her experiences in that remote and little-known country. The following description of her own experience with a *tulpa* is taken from her book *Magic and Mystery in Tibet*:

Besides having had few opportunities of seeing thought-forms, my habitual incredulity led me to make experiments for myself, and my efforts were attended with some success. . . . I chose for my experiment a most insignificant character: a monk, short and fat, of an innocent and jolly type.

I shut myself in *tsams* [meditative seclusion] and proceeded to perform the prescribed concentration of thought and other rites. After a few months the phantom monk was formed. His form grew gradually *fixed* and life-like looking. He became a kind of guest, living in my apartment. I then broke my seclusion and started for a tour, with my servants and tents.

The monk included himself in the party. Though I lived in the open, riding on horseback for miles each day, the illusion persisted. I saw the fat *trapa* [novice monk], now and then it was not necessary for me to think of him to make him appear. The phantom performed various actions of the kind that are natural to travellers and that I had not commanded. For instance, he walked, stopped, looked around him. The illusion was mostly visual, but sometimes I felt as if a robe was lightly rubbing against me and once a hand seemed to touch my shoulder.

The features which I had imagined, when building my phantom, gradually underwent a change. The fat, chubby-cheeked fellow grew leaner, his face assumed a vaguely mocking, sly, malignant look. He became more troublesome and bold. In brief, he escaped my control.

Once, a herdsman who brought me a present of butter saw the *tulpa* in my tent and took it for a live lama.

I ought to have let the phenomenon follow its course, but the presence of that unwanted companion began to prove trying to my nerves; it turned into a "day-nightmare." Moreover, I was . . . [going] to Lhasa . . . , so I decided to dissolve the phantom. I succeeded, but only after six months of hard struggle. My mind-creature was tenacious of life.

Gorique was now thoroughly bewildered and told Olsen why. Fortunately, Olsen was reassuring: a psychic double, he said, an apparition that goes ahead of its flesh-and-blood counterpart, was not so very uncommon, and Mr. Gorique should not be unduly alarmed.

In Norway, he said, such a thing was called a *Vardogr*, a forerunner, and was not taken *too* seriously.

Mr. Erkson Gorique's reaction to this comforting news is not recorded. (F. S. Edsall, *The World of Psychic Phenomena*, pp.12–13)

Visitor in the Night

Stationed in Asia on a U.S. government assignment during 1960–61, Mr. and Mrs. John Church spent their vacation in India. It was while they were in New Delhi, staying at the splendid old Imperial Hotel, related Mrs. Church, that she experienced the following:

One night I awoke from a sound sleep on hearing my brother, David, call my name. At the time he was living in Goshen, New York, where he operated a charter air service. Opening my eyes, I found him standing a few feet away, near the coffee table. There was enough light so that I could see him quite distinctly, and I noted that he was wearing his pilot's uniform. Curiously, though, his face was blank, lacking any features. Checking to make sure I was awake and not dreaming, I pinched myself, identified my surroundings, and touched my husband at my side. All the time I stared at my brother; there was no doubt about it—he was there in the room. I was shaken but not frightened, and I wondered whether to speak. After a moment or two his figure wavered, and then it slowly dissolved into vapor, from the head downward, until it finally vanished.

For the next several weeks we waited uneasily for mail from my family; happily, there was no bad news. Upon my return to the States a year later, I related my experience to my brother. He recalled a terrifying flight the previous year when he thought he was going to die; both engines of his twin-engine aircraft had failed, but as the plane plunged, one engine miraculously started up again. Although we were unable to synchronize the two experiences exactly, we found they had occurred very close in time. [A firsthand report to the Editors]

A Psychic Rainy Season

It began one October day in 1963, when the Francis Martin family of Methuen, Massachusetts, noticed a damp patch appearing on the wall of their TV room. They were puzzled, because it was too mild for pipes to freeze and burst. In a few moments they were more astonished than puzzled: there was a popping sound, and suddenly a spout of water burst from the wall.

After several days of popping sounds and mysterious fountains of water (the flows usually lasted about 20 seconds and were occurring every 15 minutes or so in various places), the Martins's house was so much awash that they moved into the home of Mr. Martin's mother-in-law in Lawrence, not far from Methuen.

Unfortunately, the water gremlin pursued them to Lawrence, and in a short time five rooms in the mother-in-law's place were drenched too. The deputy fire chief was asked to investigate, and the house was checked for leaky pipes; there were none. One official,

Deputy Mains, was present when a jet of water burst through a plaster wall and shot two feet into the room. He also heard the curious popping sound.

Rather than inflict their problem on his mother-in-law, Francis Martin decided to return with his wife and daughter to their home in Methuen. This time the water supply was turned off at the main, and the pipes were drained. There was no diminution of the eerie spouts, gushes, and floods of water. Once again the house became unlivable, and once again the Martins returned to Lawrence. Again the water gremlin followed them.

In time the watery assaults on the Martin family gradually came to an end. The Martins never did discover how gallons of water could jet from the dry plaster walls of their house or what kind of aqueous spirit had pursued them to Lawrence; nor could they account for the gradual cessation of the phenomena. For a while, it seemed, a kind of psychic rainy season had come upon them and then, as seasons do, had simply passed away. (D. Scott Rogo, *The Poltergeist Experience*, pp.185–86)

The Haw Branch Hauntings

At one time Haw Branch plantation, not far from the small town of Amelia, Virginia, spread over more than 15,000 acres, and the manor house, with its tall chimneys, dry moat, and numerous outbuildings, was one of the gems of antebellum architecture. As the years went by, though, the estate was reduced, the house fell into disrepair, and the gardens and rolling lawns became overgrown. Then, in 1964, Cary McConnaughey and his wife, Gibson, bought the property. Mrs. McConnaughey's grandmother had lived in the house many years before, and Gibson had visited the place when she was a child; but for 50 years no member of her family had occupied it.

By August 13, 1965, the house had been restored to the point where the McConnaugheys could move in. After four years of hard work the place had regained its old style, and in 1969 an elderly cousin gave Gibson a present: a large portrait of a distant and long-dead relative named Florence Wright. All Gibson's cousin could tell her was that the portrait had been done at a summer home belonging to the Wrights in Duxbury, Massachusetts, and that Florence had died suddenly just before it was finished, when she was still a young woman. He added that the portrait was in pastels and was beautifully colored.

When the McConnaugheys had uncrated the portrait and cleaned the glass, they were astonished to see that the work was in charcoal: instead of the glowing pastels they expected, they saw a composition of blacks, grays, and dirty whites.

Despite their disappointment, however, they hung the portrait over the library fireplace. A few days later, when Mrs. McConnaughey was in the basement, she heard women's voices coming from the library, and supposing that some friends had arrived unannounced, she called out, "I'm coming right up," and went upstairs. She continued to hear the voices until she was just outside the library door, at which point they stopped. The room was empty. She looked through the rest of the house but could find no one.

A few months later, in February 1970, Cary McConnaughey was sitting in the library reading a newspaper when he happened to look up at the picture of Florence Wright. If his eyes were not deceiving him, part of the painting—of a rose standing in a vase on a table near the young woman—was no longer a muddy gray: it was slowly turning pink. He got up to study it more closely. Not only was the rose gaining color but Florence's formerly charcoal-black hair was lightening, her gray skin was taking on the hue of living flesh, and color was creeping into almost every gray and black tone in the picture.

In the days following, the colors grew more vivid. From time to time women's voices were heard in the library, but no one was ever seen there. In a few months the portrait was fully transformed, revealing Florence Wright as a blue-eyed, red-haired girl sitting in an upholstered green chair. The vase in the painting turned a pale jade green, and the rose in it a soft pink.

Once the portrait's transformation was complete, the McConnaugheys no longer heard the sound of women's voices in the library. According to a local clairvoyant, who had heard of the portrait and examined it, Florence's spirit was locked in the picture because she died before it was finished, but she had the power to drain it of all color if she did not like the place where it hung. To restore the color, she had enlisted the help of two other spirits, and theirs were the voices heard.

If the spirit of Florence Wright was content at Haw Branch, some other entity seems to have been far from happy there. Three months after they moved in, on November 23, 1965, the McConnaugheys were awakened by a woman's scream. It seemed to come from one of the floors above them, and they rushed upstairs to investigate. Their children were standing at the foot of the stairs to the attic and said that was where the scream had come from. The family's two dogs seemed terrified. Nobody investigated the attic until daylight; when they did, they found nothing wrong.

Six months later, to the day, the McConnaugheys again heard the bloodcurdling scream and again found no source for it. This happened twice more, again at six-month intervals, on November 23 and May 23. Then the screams were replaced by the apparition of a

When Gibson McConnaughey first saw this portrait of her ancestor, it was, she said, in gray and black; only after months in the family home did it take on its original hues.

young woman. She was first seen by Gibson McConnaughey in the summer of 1967:

> I could plainly see the silhouette of a slim girl in a floor-length dress with a full skirt. It was not the wide fullness of a hoop-skirt, but one from an earlier period. I could see no features but she was not transparent, just a white silhouette. I saw her for perhaps ten seconds. In the next instant she was gone. There was no gradual fading away; she simply disappeared from one instant to the next.

Several nights later, one of the McConnaugheys's daughters was kept awake by the barking of the family dog on the porch and so she let it in. The animal instantly ran past her toward the drawing room. "When I looked into the drawing room," the girl said, "Blackie was sitting there wagging her tail and looking up at a lady in white who was standing in front of the fireplace. Before I could say anything the lady disappeared right in front of my eyes."

When the McConnaugheys discussed the Lady in White with other members of the family, they discovered that she was no newcomer to Haw Branch: Harriet Mason, their great-grandmother, had spoken of seeing her—and told how the apparition had once touched her, awakening her from a deep sleep. When November 23 came again, the McConnaugheys prepared for the anticipated screams, sitting up from midnight to dawn with flashlights and a tape recorder. They heard nothing. On May 23, 1968, they again sat up all night. This time they heard heavy footsteps crossing the yard, and Mr. and Mrs. McConnaughey went quietly out onto the porch to look around. There was nothing to see, but they heard heavy, running footsteps and then, a few seconds later, a call from behind the barn.

"Next morning," Mrs. McConnaughey said, "our son and daughter reported that they saw a giant bird standing in the yard in the moonlight under their windows. It was standing there with its wings spread out, appearing to have a wingspan of over six feet."

The bird itself was never seen again, but the unearthly screech was heard on the 23rd of May and November several times more. The woman's scream was never heard again, nor was she seen. But other curious things occurred in and around the old house. Sometimes, for example, the scent of roses or oranges would pervade the rooms, though there were no roses or oranges anywhere in the house. There were also inexplicable noises—sometimes, the heavy thud of something falling into the moat and the sound of cowbells circling the house at night. No source was ever discovered for these sounds. Another time, what seemed to be a man with a kerosene lantern came out of the barn and approached the house. As he went by the porch, the McConnaugheys saw the light bobbing and swaying in the air—but no one carrying it.

No ancient, sinister, or tragic source has so far been discovered for the Haw Branch hauntings. (Richard Winer and Nancy Osborn, *Haunted Houses*, pp.1–12)

Matthew Manning and the Mysterious Force

When the disturbances first began, in February 1967, Matthew Manning was 11 years old. He and his parents were then living in a house in Cambridge, England. The home was neither strange nor spooky and, being fairly new, had no record of hauntings. But one morning Derek Manning, Matthew's father, noticed something strange: a silver tankard that was always kept on a certain wooden shelf was found lying on the floor. He replaced it, and the next morning it was on the floor again. This strange displacement continued day after day. The children denied having anything to do with the tankard, so one night Mr. Manning carefully dusted the shelf around it with talcum powder, thinking that traces of it would identify the culprit.

The next morning the tankard was again found on the floor, but the powder was undisturbed.

A number of other odd things then began happening, though none of them were spectacular. Objects would be found in places where they should not have been and where they had not been when last seen. At length Mr. Manning became puzzled and disturbed enough to call the police. They advised him, with constabulary sang-

froid, to contact the Cambridge Psychical Research Society. The secretary of the society, Dr. A.R.G. Owen, told Mr. Manning that it seemed like the work of a poltergeist and that there was no known cure.

Meanwhile the disturbances were becoming more severe. Matthew Manning described them several years later in his book, *The Link:*

> Invariably the objects moved were lightweight ornaments, chairs, cutlery, ashtrays, baskets, plates, a small coffee table and a score of other articles, but none was ever broken or spilled. . . .
>
> As the physical manifestations increased, the house began to produce erratic and unsuspected taps and creaks. The noises would vary from a dull knocking to a sound like a small stone being thrown at the window, and they continued throughout the day and night in all parts of the house.

Dr. Owen came to investigate the phenomena, and he and Mr. Manning posted themselves in the house in the hope of seeing some object being moved by an invisible force. They never did, though things continued to be displaced. Then Dr. Owen told Mr. Manning that there often seemed to be a connection between poltergeist activity and the presence of adolescent children. The three Manning children were sent to stay with relatives, and the mysterious displacements promptly came to an end.

But only for as long as Matthew was away from home. When he returned, the strange phenomena began again, and this time with more vigor. Now furniture and other large objects were moved about and tipped over. Gradually, the mysterious force seemed to weaken. Matthew went away to boarding school, and for a time the poltergeist seemed to have run its course.

The lull was deceptive. At Christmas, 1970, Matthew heard scratching behind the wood paneling in his room and footsteps outside his window. He went back to school, and there things remained quiet. But when he returned home, the manifestations began again, and this time they acquired a sinister quality:

> I had gone to bed [Matthew wrote] . . . and I lay there restlessly. . . . I suddenly heard a scraping noise coming from the direction of the cupboard, which continued for almost thirty seconds. Having listened to it for a moment, I switched on my lamp and saw to my horror that the cupboard was inching out from the wall toward me. When it halted it had advanced about eighteen inches. I switched off the light and almost simultaneously my bed started to vibrate violently back and forth. I was now too timid to move and I lay in anticipation of whatever might happen next. The vibrating ceased, and I felt the bottom end of my bed rising from the floor to what I estimated to be about one foot. The head

end of the bed then rose two or three inches, and [at] the same time the bed pitched out toward the center of the room and finally settled at an angle to the wall.

Thoroughly scared, Matthew went to his parents' room and curled up in a sleeping bag. The rest of the night was peaceful, but when the family got up the next morning, they found the house in a shambles:

> The first room we saw was the dining room. It looked as though a bomb had hit it. Chairs were upturned or simply not in the room, the table was no longer on its feet, and ornaments were strewn around the room and on the floor. The sitting room was in a similar state as was nearly every other ground floor room in the house. Tables and chairs were piled on top of each other, pictures were dismounted, and several objects and pieces of cutlery had vanished.

During the next few days the pattern was repeated but with new twists: pools of water appeared on the floors throughout the house, and childish scrawls defaced the walls. At the peak of the onslaught the words "Matthew Beware" were discovered; and now, the family saw objects moving without visible assistance—even flying through the air and making 90-degree turns. And if they asked that a specific object be moved to a specific place, the poltergeist would often comply.

This time when Matthew went back to school, the poltergeist accompanied him, first manifesting itself only in his room and then overturning furniture and materializing pools of water throughout the dormitory. Objects would hurtle through the air toward someone, "as if to strike the person, and then either swing away at an angle, just before he was hit, or strike him so lightly that it was hardly felt." The school matron recorded her own experiences of the strange phenomena:

> In my sitting room I might be sitting quietly perhaps sewing, sometimes listening to the wireless, when I am suddenly soaked with coldness, and a shower of pebbles falls from the ceiling. Some nights it may be little chippings of wood which drop into my lap.

At about this period Matthew discovered what seemed to be a way of rechanneling the poltergeist's energy. He began, first, to undertake experiments in automatic writing and then, in an extension of that activity, to make a series of delicate drawings. He had no idea, he later said, whether these were purely the product of his own mind or whether he might sometimes serve as the medium through which other entities expressed themselves. His guess was that perhaps 5 percent of his automatic writing might be construed as

messages from the dead. Whatever the truth of it was, when Matthew began these activities the poltergeist phenomena gradually diminished, then finally ceased. Matthew continued his experiments and is said to have developed a number of convincing psychic abilities in the areas of ESP and psychokinesis. (Matthew Manning, *The Link*, passim; D. Scott Rogo, *The Poltergeist Experience*, pp.261–68)

The Ghosts of Flight 401

In December 1972 an Eastern Airlines TriStar jetliner, flight 401, crashed into a Florida swamp. One hundred and one people died in the crash, including the pilot, Bob Loft, and the flight engineer, Don Repo. On more than 20 occasions thereafter, crew members of other Eastern TriStars—especially those that had been fitted with parts salvaged from the wreck of flight 401—saw entirely lifelike apparitions of Loft and Repo. In some cases the apparitions were identified by people who had known the two men and in some cases by reference to photographs. (*The Unexplained: Mysteries of Mind Space & Time*, Vol. 3, Issue 32)

Resurrection Mary

For a number of years motorists driving along Archer Avenue in Chicago's South Side have reported giving rides to a beautiful young hitchhiker, a blonde wearing a white gown that seems to date from the 1920's or 1930's. The drivers are said to be mostly single males, and the girl often jumps into their cars uninvited, saying that she needs a ride home. Home turns out to be the Resurrection Cemetery, at 7200 South Archer Avenue, and when the car draws level with it, the hitchhiker gets out (sometimes opening the car door, sometimes passing right through it), walks up to the closed wrought-iron gates, and passes through them, disappearing into thin air once inside the cemetery.

Resurrection Mary, as the specter has been named, is said to be the ghost of a young Polish girl who was killed in an auto accident while being driven home from a dance at the O. Henry Ballroom (now named the Willowbrook Ballroom) on Archer Avenue in 1931 and buried in her party dress and dancing shoes in Resurrection Cemetery.

One night in December 1977 a motorist noticed a young woman dressed in white standing inside the cemetery gates. She was looking out and holding onto the iron bars of the gates. Thinking that the girl had been inadvertently locked inside the cemetery, the motorist called the police, but by the time the patrol car appeared the girl had vanished. The officer beamed his searchlight into the cemetery but saw nothing. He and the motorist did notice, though, that two of the iron bars in the gate were bent apart and that at the point

Poltergeists and PK

One of the best known of all psychic phenomena is that of the poltergeist, whose activities have been chronicled since ancient times. Literally translated from the German, the words *polter* and *geist* mean "racketing ghost," and this well-documented category of ghostly intervention is never a quiet one.

The activities of the rambunctious poltergeist typically include knockings, rappings, heavy trampling, the setting of fires, the hurling of stones and other objects, the breaking of crockery, the banging of doors, the jiggling of latches, the opening of windows and dresser drawers, the overturning and displacement of furniture, and the shaking and levitation of beds and their occupants. Some poltergeists have also been known to sob, moan, and scream.

As these mischievous, attention-getting, and sometimes malicious tricks would suggest, the poltergeist is almost invariably linked to the presence in the house of one specific young person, usually an adolescent boy or girl. In the Manning case, the poltergeist was associated with 11-year-old Matthew, one of the three children in the household in 1967 when the manifestations began. The disturbances—which consisted chiefly of knockings and the movement of furniture and objects—ceased when Matthew was away and resumed when he returned. Eventually the poltergeist followed him to his boarding school. It was not until 1971, when Matthew apparently siphoned the energy or force behind these manifestations into his developing artistic and psychic skills, that the poltergeist finally retreated. It should be noted that the Manning poltergeist was unusually tenacious—few visitations continue longer than two months.

Although research has shown some poltergeist cases to be fraudulent, investigators have found enough instances above suspicion to convince them that the poltergeist is a true psychic phenomenon, ungoverned by normal physical laws. Evidence suggests that the manifestations of the poltergeist are produced by bursts of psychic activity emanating from its agent, the one person whose presence is always required.

Attempting to understand the forces at work, researchers in parapsychology have hypothesized that the poltergeist's feats in moving objects (which are often seen to fly in violation of the laws of gravity, gliding, rising, and turning corners) are examples of psychokinesis, or PK—the ability to influence inanimate objects by mind power. The most widely known examples of alleged psychokinesis are those of Uri Geller, but these have now been largely dismissed as fraudulent. (Geller, for example, used a palmed magnet to control the hands on a watch.) A less-well-known but possibly more convincing exponent of PK is a Russian woman named Nina Kulagina, discovered in the 1960's. Her ability to move and otherwise affect small objects without physical contact has been witnessed by Western parapsychologists but has never been extensively tested under rigorous laboratory conditions in the West, and her feats have not been scrutinized by professional magicians.

The deficiency of the PK theory as an explanation of poltergeist phenomena, however, is that the energy involved in many poltergeist disturbances far exceeds anything claimed by the supporters of Kulagina and other PK adepts. The best they can do is to move a small object, such as a fountain pen, whereas poltergeists can cause crockery to fly across a room.

In view of this, some researchers have cast about for a source of energy that might be utilized by poltergeists. But so far their attempts to explain poltergeist phenomena have simply replaced one mystery with another. Even more mysterious is why any spirit or being that could marshal such remarkable psychic energy should expend it on such purposeless activities.

---

where they were bent were the marks, seemingly etched into the iron, of two small hands. (*U.S. Catholic,* August 1979, p.12; Richard Winer and Nancy Osborn, *Haunted Houses,* pp.75–76)

The Silent Hitchhiker

One evening in October 1979 Roy Fulton, a carpet fitter, was driving back home from a darts match in Leighton Buzzard, Bedfordshire, England. As he neared the village of Stanbridge, he stopped to pick up a young hitchhiker, a man of pale complexion, with short, curly hair, dark trousers, and a white shirt with an old-fashioned round collar. When Fulton asked him where he was going, the young man just pointed down the road. Fulton thought his passenger might be a deaf-mute and drove on in silence. After driving a mile or two, though, at a steady 45 mph, he thought a cigarette might help to break the ice, and turned to offer one to his companion.

The passenger's seat was empty. The young man had silently vanished from a moving van, whose door had never opened. Fulton drove straight to his local pub, ordered a large scotch to steady his nerves, and told his story. The landlord of the pub and the Dunstable police inspector both said later that they believed Fulton had experienced something strange—perhaps his story was true. (*Fortean Times,* No. 34, Winter 1981, p.16)

THE UNQUIET SKY

We expect rain, snow, sleet, and hail to fall
from the sky. But when fish, frogs, stones, and other
unlikely objects fall, we are dealing with other
celestial phenomena. Foremost in the
realm of aerial mysteries are the thousands of sightings
of unidentified flying objects. These have been
so widely publicized that, to the mind's eye, their saucerlike
profile is as familiar as the shape of conventional
aircraft. There are also many astronomical
and atmospheric oddities, including strange sounds, that
seem to defy explanation in spite of the proliferation
of techniques and instruments designed
to interpret such phenomena.

Mortal men gaze in awe at the sky, source of wonders and terrors.

STRANGE THINGS FROM ABOVE

Each year at the beginning of the rainy season, the people of Yoro, Honduras, gather buckets, barrels, pails, and nets in anticipation of fish that will fall from the sky. And each year, for as long as anyone can remember, sardines have fallen by the barrelful. The "shower of fish," as the natives call it, generally starts around 4 or 5 P.M. and is followed by electric storms and strong winds. The fish are left alive and jumping on a grassy plain southwest of the town.

In 1833 lumps of a woollike substance descended on miles of countryside near the French village of Montussan; elsewhere, swathes of silklike material and billowing threads have fallen, as though from a vast aerial haberdasher's warehouse.

In many parts of the world, frogs and toads have also fallen numerous times and in monstrous numbers; and so have winkles, worms, and snakes. Blood has been seen dribbling or pouring from the sky, beans and grains fall, and so do meat, muscle, and fat, as though granaries and abattoirs sailed invisibly overhead.

Reports of these and many other kinds of skyfall are included in this chapter. They range in believability from the more or less acceptable to the downright incredible. And at the farther end of this spectrum are events that may well belong to another category of the unexplained.

For example, nonmeteoritic stones may be conceived to fall from the sky, perhaps ejected by a volcano or gathered up by a whirlwind. That such falls of stones should repeatedly descend on the same two adjacent roofs (as they did at Chico, California, in 1921 and 1922) begins to stretch the imagination; and that some stone showers should single out and pursue certain people (two fishermen were such victims in 1973) is already beyond belief. But that stones should fall from undamaged ceilings in closed rooms or inside a closed tent (the victim here was an Australian farmhand in 1957) removes such incidents from the material realm to the realm of poltergeists.

BEFORE 1600

Perhaps the earliest record of a mysterious—or miraculous—fall from the sky occurs in Chapter 10, Verse 11, of the Book of Joshua in the Old Testament. The Israelites, led by Joshua, have routed the Amorite army in a surprise night attack and are in hot pursuit:

> And as they fled before Israel, while they were going down the ascent of Beth-horon, the Lord threw down great stones from heaven upon them as far as Azekah, and they died; there were more who died because of the hailstones than the men of Israel killed with the sword.

Two verses after this, incidentally, one of the most astonishing events in the Old Testament is described: the sun stands still until the Israelites have avenged themselves.

Whatever the explanation of this may be, we shall find many accounts in later centuries of motionless, bright, aerial disks.

A less explicit reference to aerial intervention on behalf of the Israelites occurs in the Book of Judges, Chapter 5, Verse 4:

> Lord, when thou didst go forth from Seir, when thou didst march from the region of Edom, the earth trembled, and the heavens dropped, yea, the clouds dropped water.

Whatever "the heavens dropped" may mean, it seems to refer to something other than rainfall, since the next clause describes that, explicitly, as an additional event. The next mention of heaven appears in Verse 20:

> From heaven fought the stars, from their courses they fought against Sisera.

In the First Book of Samuel, Chapter 7, Verses 10-12, the Lord again intervenes on behalf of the Israelites:

> As Samuel was offering up the burnt offering, the Philistines drew near to attack Israel; but the Lord thundered with a mighty voice that day against the Philistines and threw them into confusion; and they were routed before Israel. And the men of Israel . . . pursued the Philistines, and smote them, as far as below Beth-car. Then Samuel took a stone and set it up between Mizpah and Jeshanah, and called its name Ebenezer; for he said, "Hitherto the Lord has helped us."

In Hebrew, the words *eben ezer* mean "stone of help."

A fall of stones in a military context occurs in the middle of the sixth century, when the Abyssinian Army, laying siege to Mecca, was put to flight by a fall of stones, supposedly dropped by birds. However, at least one famous stonefall in ancient times occurred in the aftermath of a military action. The story is told in Chapter 31 of the first book of Livy's history of Rome, *From the Founding of the City:*

> After the defeat of the Sabines, when King Tullus [672-640 B.C.] and the entire Roman state were at a high pitch of glory and prosperity, it was reported to the king and senators that there had been a rain of stones on the Alban Mount [Mount Albanus]. As this could scarce be credited, envoys were dispatched to examine the prodigy, and in their sight there fell from the sky, like hailstones which the wind piles in drifts upon the ground, a shower of pebbles.

The envoys also thought they heard "a mighty voice issuing from the grove on the mountaintop," commanding the Albans to resume the ritual sacrifices they had neglected since the Roman victory. The Romans themselves took this order to heart, according to Livy, because thereafter "it remained a regular custom that whenever the same prodigy was reported there should be a nine days' observance." (Whether "the same prodigy" refers to all subsequent falls of stones or only to repeated falls on Mount Albanus is unclear.)

The records of ancient skyfalls are less numerous than modern accounts but are comparably diverse. The Greek historian Athenaeus, for example, refers to a three-day fall of fish and a spectacular deluge of frogs in his historical anthology, the *Deipnosophistae* ("Banquet of the Sophists"), written about A.D. 200:

> I also know that it has very often rained fishes. At all events Phenias, in the second book of his Eresian Magistrates, says that in the Chersonesus [the word means simply "peninsula" in Greek, and the exact locality referred to is uncertain] it once rained fish uninterruptedly for three days; and Phylarchus in his fourth book, says that people had often seen it raining fish, and often also raining wheat, and that the same thing had happened with respect to frogs. At all events, Heraclides Lembus, in the 21st book of his History, says: "In Paeonia and Dardania it has, they say, before now rained frogs; and so great has been the number of these frogs that the houses and the roads have been full of them; and at first, for some days, the inhabitants, endeavoring to kill them, and shutting up their houses, endured the pest; but when they did no good, but found that all their vessels were filled with them, and the frogs were found to be boiled up and roasted with everything they ate, and when besides all this, they could not make use of any water, nor put their feet on the ground for the heaps of frogs that were everywhere, and were annoyed also by the smell of those that died, they fled the country."

Accounts of fish, grain, and frogs will be found in more recent history, but the closest approximation of the plague of frogs in Paeonia and Dardania occurs in the biblical account of the second plague in Egypt, the plague of frogs (Exodus 8:1-14):

The skyfall recorded in the Book of Joshua is illustrated here. Great stones cast down from heaven upon the Amorites forced them to flee before the Israelite army. Many of the soldiers were killed by the stones.

[The Lord said] I will plague all your country with frogs; the Nile shall swarm with frogs which shall come up into your house, and into your bed-chamber and on your bed, and into the houses of your servants and of your people, and into your ovens and your kneading bowls . . . and the frogs came up and covered the land of Egypt. . . . And they gathered them together in heaps, and the land stank.

The Book of Exodus, Chapter 9, Verses 18–34, records deadly hail, and fire mingled with the hail, as the seventh plague of Egypt.

Ancient historians, including Procopius, Marcellinus, and Theophanes, record a fall of black dust in the year 472 B.C., during which the sky seemed to be on fire. The location of the fall is uncertain but may have been Constantinople.

During the reign of Charlemagne (ninth century A.D.) an enormous block of ice, 990 cubic feet of it, fell from the sky. (Camille Flammarion, *The Atmosphere,* p.398)

A burning object fell into Lake Van, Armenia, in A.D. 1110, turning the waters red. In the first plague of Egypt the Nile turned to blood (Exodus 7:15–24).

The second plague inflicted upon Egypt, related in the Book of Exodus, is depicted in this engraving of the numbers of frogs that descended upon the streets and houses.

Most falls from the sky recorded in ancient times have modern parallels, but a few are unique. There is, for example, no recent counterpart of the fall of large yellow mice that occurred in Bergen, Norway, in 1578 or the lemmings that fell there in 1579. (*The Journal of Cycle Research,* 6:3, January 1957)

FROM 1640 TO 1700

In June 1642, lumps of burning sulfur the size of a man's fist fell from the sky onto the roof of Loburg Castle, 18 miles from Magdeburg, Germany. (*Report of the Forty-fourth meeting of the British Association for the Advancement of Science,* 1874, p.272)

A luminous meteor was seen to fall in Italy in 1652 and near its landing place "star-jelly" was found. (*Annals of Philosophy,* New Series 12:93, August 1826) (See subsequent reports in this section for more falls of gelatinous material in association with presumed meteorites.)

A fibrous substance resembling blue silk fell in great quantities at Naumburg, Germany (southwest of Leipzig), on March 23, 1665. (*Annals of Philosophy,* New Series 12:93, August 1826)

On the Wednesday before Easter in 1666 a two-acre field at Cranstead, near Wrotham in Kent, England, was found covered with numerous fish the size of a man's little finger. They were believed to have fallen during a violent thunderstorm and were agreed by all who saw them to be young whiting. Mr. Ware, the field's owner, estimated that about a bushel of the fish

The Book of Exodus describes how a nightly rain of manna sustained the Israelites during their desert wanderings. This Rennaissance painting shows them gathering it to make bread. (Exodus 16:4–36)

had fallen, all in the one field, and sent samples of them to London, as a curiosity, for examination by magistrates. Whiting, members of the croaker family, are saltwater fish. Cranstead is about 10 and 7 miles respectively from the nearest bodies of brackish water, the estuaries of the rivers Thames and Medway. (John Michell and Robert J. M. Rickard, *Phenomena: A Book of Wonders*, p.12)

At Acle, a village in Norfolk, England, small toads fell from the sky in such vast numbers that the local people were greatly inconvenienced. In October 1683 it was reported that the villagers had to sweep them up by the bucketful for burning. (John Michell and Robert J. M. Rickard, *Phenomena: A Book of Wonders,* p.12)

Seeds of ivy berries were found inside hailstones that fell on Wiltshire, England, in 1687. (*Philosophical Transactions of the Royal Society of London* 16:281, January–March 1687)

Flakes of coal-black fibrous material, some as large as tabletops, fell on newly fallen snow near the town of Memel (now Klaipeda, Lithuania) on the east coast of the Baltic Sea about 1687. The flakes were damp, smelled of rotten seaweed, and tore like paper; once dry, they were odor free. Some of this material was preserved for 150 years; when it was finally examined, it was found to consist partly of "vegetable matter, chiefly *Conferva crispata* [a threadlike green algae], and partly of about 29 species of infusoria [protozoans, minute aquatic animals]." (*Proceedings of the Royal Irish Academy,* 1:381, December 9, 1839)

A foul-smelling substance, the consistency of butter, fell over large areas of southern Ireland in the winter and spring of 1696. According to the Bishop of Cloyne, this "stinking dew" fell in "lumps, often as big as the end of one's Finger"; it was "soft, clammy, and of a dark Yellow color"; the cattle in fields where it fell continued to feed as usual. According to Mr. Robert Vans of Kilkenny, the local people believed the "butter" was a useful medicine and collected it in pots and pans. (*Philosophical Transactions of the Royal Society of London,* 19:224–25, March–May 1696)

The German naturalist Alexander von Humboldt, who traveled widely in South America, provides the following account of fishfalls in the Andes, where the fish are believed to be ejected during volcanic eruptions:

> When the earthquakes which precede every eruption in the chain of the Andes, shake with mighty force the entire mass of the volcano, the subterranean vaults are opened, and emit, at the same time,

water, fishes, and tufa-mud. This is the singular phenomenon that furnishes the fish which the inhabitants of the highlands of Quito call "Preñadilla." . . . When the summit of the mountain Carguairazo, to the north of Chimborazo, and 18,000 feet high, fell, in the night between the 19th and 20th of June, 1698, the surrounding fields, to the extent of about 43 English square miles, were covered with mud and fishes. The fever which raged in the town of Ibarra, seven years before, had been ascribed to a similar eruption of fishes from the volcano Imbabura. [*Annals of Philosophy,* New Series 6:130, August 1823]

Alexander von Humboldt, who explored in South America with A.J.A. Bonpland from 1799 to 1804, learned of a fall of fish in the Andes. He believed the fish had been spewed into the air by a volcanic eruption.

FROM 1700 TO 1800

A fiery globe fell on the island of Lethy, India; gelatinous matter was found where it landed. (*The Edinburgh Philosophical Journal,* 1:234, October 1819)

An early account of the substance now known as angel hair is found in *The Natural History of Selborne* (England) by Gilbert White. He describes how on September 21, 1741, he went out into the fields before dawn and found the grass so thickly covered with "cobweb" that his dogs had to scrape it from their eyes. Then, about nine o'clock, an unusual appearance began to demand our attention—a shower of cobwebs falling from very elevated regions, and continuing, without any interruption till the close of the day. These webs were not single filmy threads, floating in the air in all directions, but perfect flakes or rags; some near an inch broad, and five or six long, which fell with a degree of velocity, that they were considerably heavier than the atmosphere.

Angel Hair and Spiders' Webs

Whatever "angel hair" may be (and the term is probably applied to several different substances), it is usually described as being like gossamer, silk, or cotton wool—white, shiny, and strong. What all accounts have in common is that when attempts are made to gather the substance for analysis it melts away and disappears into nothing. Despite this, angel hair is usually explained as being nothing more exotic than spiders' webs.

A concise statement of this view was given in *The Marine Observer* of October 1963, in reply to a letter from Captain Pape describing a fall of angel hair in the port of Montreal (see pages 205–06). The author of the explanation is D. J. Clark of the Natural History Museum in London. He told Captain Pape:

> Spiders are, I think, responsible for the phenomena you describe. The majority of these particular spiders belong to the family *Linyphiidae*, and mature in the autumn. In the autumn, on fine, warm and sunny days, especially with a fairly heavy early morning dew, the spiders begin to disperse and migrate in order to colonize new areas where the food supply is greater. The method they use is known as "ballooning." As the sun dries off the dew, upward air currents are created. The spider runs to the top of a plant, fence, etc., and lifting the tip of its abdomen emits a globule of liquid silk. This silk is drawn out in a thread by the air currents and hardens as a result of this drawing out, not simply by contact with the air. When the thread is long enough to support the spider, it lets go of its support and flies away. The spiders sometimes are carried many miles. Eventually, they come down to earth and on landing they free the "parachute." This again floats away and becomes entangled with other threads, sometimes quite thick bands are thus formed, and when this again settles down it is very conspicuous. The single thread is very fine and difficult to see unless the light is reflected from it, and when entangled together with other threads it is easy to see and quite tough and resilient.

> I cannot explain the disappearance of these strands when held in the hand. It may be that the threads of the strand you describe were not so entangled and when handled broke up into individual threads thus becoming very inconspicuous. Spider silk cannot melt because heat does not affect it, it is on the whole less soluble than true silk.

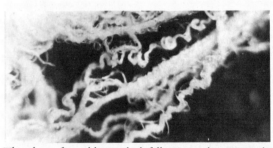

This photo of angel hair, which fell at Iwate-ken, 250 miles northeast of Tokyo, on October 4, 1957, was released by the Japan Flying Saucer Research Council.

Like many explanations, the spider thesis succeeds only at the cost of devaluing part of the evidence to be explained. In this case, for example, Captain Pape was supposedly mistaken about the substance disappearing in his hand: it was there, but he failed to see it. By the same token, spider theorists ignore a piece of negative evidence that does their theory no good: the fact that in all those yards of ballooning gossamer not a single spider is reported.

Given this general tendency to arrive at explanations by ignoring awkward observations or declaring them invalid, or by labeling them as simple coincidence, it is not surprising that advocates of the spider theory should overlook those occasions when angel hair has been seen to fall in the presence of unidentified flying objects. Nor, by the same token, is it surprising that advocates of the UFO theory of angel hair should likewise ignore the occasions when the stuff has fallen—at least according to the reports—without the benefit of cigar- or saucer-shaped dispensers.

On every side as the observer turned his eyes might he behold a continual succession of fresh flakes falling into his sight, and twinkling like stars as they turned their sides towards the sun.

How far this wonderful shower extended would be difficult to say; but we know that it reached Bradley, Selborne and Alresford, three places which lie in a sort of a triangle, the shortest of whose sides is about eight miles in extent.

On May 5, 1786, the last day of a drought that had lasted since the previous November, "a great quantity" of black eggs fell on Port-au-Prince, Haiti. They hatched the next day, and some of these strange animals from the sky were preserved in a flask of water. The creatures shed their skin several times and resembled tadpoles. (Moreau de Saint-Méry, *A Naturalist's Sojourn in Jamaica*)

The following is an account of a deluge of toads on the village of Lalain, France, in 1794:

It was very hot. Suddenly, at about 3 o'clock in the afternoon, there fell such an abundance of rain that 150 men of the grand guard, in order not to be submerged, were obliged to leave a large depression in which they were hidden. But what was their surprise when there began to fall on the ground all about a considerable number of toads, the size of hazelnuts, which began to jump about in every direction. M. Gayet [the soldier who provided this information], who could not believe that these myriads of reptiles fell with the rain, stretched out his handkerchief at the height of a man, his comrades holding the corners; they caught a considerable number of toads, most of which had the posterior part elongated into a tail, that is to say, in the tadpole state. During this rain storm, which lasted about half an hour, the men of the grand guard felt very distinctly on their hats and on their clothing the blows struck by the falling toads. As a final proof of the reality of this phenomenon, M. Gayet reports that after the storm the three-cornered hats of the men of the guard held in their folds some of the reptiles. [*Monthly Weather Review*, 45:217-24, May 1917]

FROM 1800 TO 1830

On January 21, 1803, a shooting star fell to earth in Silesia, between Barsdorf and Freiburg (now Swiebodzice); its trajectory was low, and witnesses heard a whizzing sound as it went by. For some time the meteorite seemed to lie burning on the ground, and its point of impact was therefore easily observed. In the morning a mass of jellylike material was found on the snow at the landing place.

The report of this incident makes no mention of a snowfall subsequent to the meteor's descent nor does it say whether there was any sign of melted snow at the point of impact. (*Report of the Thirtieth Meeting of the British Association for the Advancement of Science*, 30:62-63, 1860)

On June 23, 1809, M. Mauduy, curator of natural history at Poitiers, France, was caught in a heavy rainstorm. In the falling water he saw "little bodies the size of hazlenuts, which in a moment, covered the ground, and which I recognized as little toads." (*Monthly Weather Review*, 45:217-24, May 1917)

The French Academy received the following report from a M. Duparque:

In August, 1814, after several weeks of drouth [*sic*] and heat, a storm broke one Sunday about 3:30 P.M., upon the village of Fremon [Fremontiers], a quarter league from Amiens. This storm was preceded by bursts of wind so violent that they shook the church and frightened the congregation. While traversing the space separating the church from the presbytery, we were soaked, but what surprised me was to be struck on my person and my clothing by small frogs. . . . A large number of these small animals hopped about on the ground. On arriving at the presbytery, we found the floor of one of the rooms in which a window facing the storm had been left open covered with water and frogs. [*Monthly Weather Review*, 45:217-24, May 1917]

After a period of gale-force winds and an evening of heavy rain in 1817, children found three or more barrels of herring fry, 1½ to 3 inches long, scattered on mossy ground near the ferry of Shien, Argyllshire, Scotland. Although Loch Creran lies only some 300 yards from where the fish were found, it lies to the south, and in view of the northerly winds that had been blowing it was supposed that the herring had been blown from Loch Linnhe, 3 miles to the north across moorland 300 feet above sea level. However, the fish showed no sign of bruises, and there was no sign that any water had fallen with them. (Letter from Rev. Colin Smith of Appin to *The Edinburgh New Philosophical Journal*, 1:186-87, April-October 1826)

A foul-smelling object covered with a clothlike nap fell at Amherst, Massachusetts, on August 13, 1819. It was examined by Prof. Rufus Graves, who removed the nap and discovered a "buff-colored, pulpy substance" beneath it. On exposure to the air this substance became a "livid color, resembling venous blood." The object was said to have fallen with a brilliant light. (*Annual Register*, 63:687, 1821)

On **November 2, 1819,** red rain fell on Blankenberge, Belgium. The usual explanation of red rain is that it contains fine red sand caught up in a whirlwind; but when 144 ounces of the Blankenberge rain were reduced by evaporation to 4 ounces, no sand appeared. Further analysis of the rain revealed the presence of a chloride of cobalt, but no explanation of how this might have occurred was offered in the report about it. (*Annals of Philosophy,* 16:226, September 1820)

Showers of a silky substance fell in October 1820 around Pernambuco, Brazil, covering an area that extended 90 miles inland and nearly as far out to sea, where a French ship was festooned in it. (Letter from M. Laine, the French consul at Pernambuco, to the *Annual Register,* 63:681, 1821)

On a July day *in 1827, fieldworkers in Denbighshire, Wales, observed half a ton of hay sailing into the wind. Wisps fluttered down as the hay flew by.* (The Illustrated London News, *July 24, 1827*)

A shower of herring fell on a hill above Melfort House in the Lorn district of Argyllshire, Scotland, in 1821. The fish were large and of good quality, and the local people sent some of them to their landlord in Edinburgh. The weather was "exceedingly boisterous."

The prevailing wind in this area blows from Loch Melfort, toward which the hillside in question faces.

Loch Melfort is an arm of the sea and one of the few places in this part of Scotland where herring can be caught by fly-fishers, an indication that they frequently swim near the surface there. (*The Edinburgh New Philosophical Journal,* 1:186, April–October 1826)

In 1828 several districts of Persia were reported to be covered to a depth of between seven and eight inches by a fall of material that was enthusiastically eaten by livestock. (*Nature,* 43:225, January 15, 1891)

After 10 or 12 days of rain in 1828, a partially dug ditch on land belonging to Joseph Muse, of Cambridge, Maryland, was found to contain hundreds of fish, from four to seven inches long, of the species known as jack perch and sun perch. There had been no water in the ditch prior to the rainfall and there was no connection between the ditch and the nearest river (one mile away), whose level was, in any case, 10 feet below that of the ditch. (*The American Journal of Science and Arts,* 1:16:41–42, July 1829)

FROM 1830 TO 1850

Large fish fell from the sky at Faridpur, India, on February 19, 1830. The following eyewitness accounts are from nine depositions made originally in Bengali and translated into English in the December 1833 issue of *The Journal of the Asiatic Society of Bengal:*

> I had been doing my work at a meadow, when I perceived at the hour of 12 o'clock the sky gather clouds, and began to rain slightly, then a large fish touching my back by its head fell on the ground. Being surprised I looked about, and behold a number of fish likewise fell from heaven. They were saul, sale, guzal, mirgal, and bodul [all local species]. I took 10 or 11 fish in number, and I saw many other persons take many. [Testimony of Shekh Chaudhari Ahmed]
>
> On Friday, at 12 o'clock P.M., in the month of Phalgun . . . when I was at work in a field, I perceived the sky darkened by clouds, began to rain a little and a large fish fell from the sky. I was confounded at the sight, and soon entered my small cottage, which I had there, but I came out again as soon as the rain had ceased and found every part of my hut scattered with fish; they were boduli, mirgal, and nouchi, and amounted to 25 in number. [Testimony of Shekh Suduruddin]

In March 1832 a yellow substance fell on fields near Volokolamsk, Russia. At first the villagers thought that discolored snow had fallen but soon discovered that the material closely resembled cotton. Some of it was put on a fire and found to burn with a blue flame. Some was

Inexplicable Explanations

In addition to more or less scientific explanations of skyfalls are others that invoke mechanisms even more mysterious than the phenomena they explain. These explanations fall into the categories of extraterrestrial, supernatural, and time warp.

In the extraterrestrial hypothesis, alien spaceships are supposed, for unspecified but perhaps scientific or culinary reasons, to gather up supplies of earthly materials and then release them, or most of them. Or—again for undisclosed but perhaps horticultural or zoocultural reasons or perhaps simply in spasms of interplanetary generosity—materials are directed to the earth from another similar planet and jettisoned upon us in the upper atmosphere.

In the supernatural theory, gods, demons, spirits, poltergeists, or other, unnamed, entities are responsible for the skyfalls, or at least some of them. Advocates of this theory point to those cases where dry ponds or newly dug ditches have been found to contain full-grown fish after a rainstorm—as though some aching need for fish had been mysteriously satisfied—as examples of a kind of supernatural benevolence, and to prolonged showers of stones from clear skies as instances of otherworldly mischief.

In the time-warp theory, it is conceived that worlds of another dimension, but of parallel constitution, intersect occasionally with our own and that when they do, currents of fish, fields of ice, screes of stone, and mounds of jelly come tumbling into our ken.

The virtue of these theories is that they account for all contingencies, however bizarre. Their flaw is that they do so by invoking untestable powers and circumstances that are even more fantastic. This is not to say that there may not be some truth in the theories, but simply that if there is, it is a truth of the most remote kind.

On the other hand, if objects do indeed materialize in our world from other realms, perhaps those realms are subject to corresponding disappearances. Perhaps reverse skyfalls occur, in which objects are inexplicably sucked into the air. There is no evidence for this, of course, but if such events were to occur in our own world, we might feel more comfortable theorizing them in another. Therefore, the following reports of reverse skyfalls are included here.

The Times (London) of July 5, 1842, reported the following from the Scottish *Fife Herald*:

> Wednesday forenoon [June 29] a phenomenon of most rare and extraordinary character was observed in the immediate neighborhood of Cupar [Scotland]. About half past 12 o'clock, whilst the sky was clear, and the air, as it had been throughout the morning, perfectly calm, a girl employed in tramping clothes in a tub in the piece of ground above the town called the common, heard a loud and sharp report overhead, succeeded by a gust of wind of most extraordinary vehemence, and only of a few moments duration. On looking round, she observed the whole of the clothes, sheets, etc. lying within a line of certain breadth, stretching across the green, several hundred yards distant; another portion of the articles, however, consisting of a quantity of curtains, and a number of smaller articles, were carried upwards to an immense height, so as to be almost lost to the eye, and gradually disappeared altogether from sight in a south-eastern direction and have not yet been heard of. At the moment of the report which preceded the wind, the cattle in the neighboring meadow were observed running about in an affrighted state, and for some time afterwards they continued cowering together in evident terror. The violence of the wind was such that a woman, who at the time was holding a blanket, found herself unable to retain it in fear of being carried along with it! It is remarkable that, while even the heaviest articles were being stripped off a belt, as it were, running across the green, and while the loops of several sheets which were pinned down an [*sic*] snapped, light articles lying loose on both sides of the holt [a wooded hill] were never moved from their position.

From the July 10, 1880, issue of *Scientific American* comes this report from the *Plain Dealer* of East Kent, Ontario:

> Mr. David Muckle and Mr. W. R. McKay . . . were in a field on a farm of the former when they heard a sudden loud report, like that of a cannon. They turned just in time to see a cloud of stones flying upward from a spot in the field. Surprised beyond measure they examined the spot, which was circular and about 16 feet across, but there was no sign of an eruption nor anything to indicate the fall of a heavy body there. The ground was simply swept clean. They are quite certain that it was not caused by a meteorite, an eruption of the earth, or a whirlwind.

put to soak in water and became resinous; when this was put on a fire, it boiled and bubbled but did not burn. The resin was said to be amber-colored, with a rubbery texture and with a smell "like prepared oil, mixed with wax." The fall covered an area of 600 or 700 square feet to a depth of about two inches. (*Annual Register*, 74:447–48, 1832)

A 10-minute shower of toads at Jouy-en-Josas, near Versailles, France, in June 1833 was witnessed by M. Heard. They bounced off his umbrella, hopped about on the pavement, and were as numerous as the raindrops. He saw them scattered for some 1,200 feet. (*Monthly Weather Review*, 45:217–24, May 1917)

Where the citizens of Rahway, New Jersey, saw "fiery rain" fall to the ground on November 13, 1833, they found "lumps of jelly." And a woman milking a cow at West Point, New York, on the same day saw something land "with a splosh" beside her. It was a round, flattened mass the size of a teacup and perfectly transparent. This occurred at sunrise. At 10 A.M. she went out to show some people the jelly but found it had disappeared. In its place a boy found some white particles the size of a pinhead, but they disintegrated into powder and disappeared when he tried to pick them up. (Letter from Alexander C. Twining to Prof. Denison Olmsted of Yale College)

These incidents were reported in connection with a meteor shower that appeared over the eastern United States on November 13. (*The American Journal of Science and Arts*, 1:363–411, January 1834)

Peculiar hailstones fell at Padua, Italy, on August 26, 1834. Some were one inch thick and platelike. Across one surface on some of these, further plates could be seen, rectilinear or curved, transparent or opaque, while from the opposite surface, at angles of about 45°, grew four-sided crystals, 1½ inches long, interlaced at their bases, and each topped by a four-sided pyramid.

Other plates of ice were convex on both sides, irregular in outline, and bearing rudimentary four-sided crystals. Still others were circular or elliptical and formed of concentric layers of alternately transparent and opaque ice. At their center was an opaque white nucleus. The diameter of the plates in this less regular group varied from 1½ to 4 inches.

Finally, transparent pieces of ice were found that were thicker around the edge than in the middle. The edges were striped with three to five layers of opaque and transparent ice. At the center of these plates were whitish circles around a clear nucleus, which, melting before the rest, created a ring of ice. The diameter of these unusual pieces of ice was from 1½ to 3 inches. (*The Edinburgh New Philosophical Journal*, 19:83–88, April–October 1835)

At Marsala, on the western coast of Sicily, a small, dark cloud appeared in a calm sky. It gradually increased in size and eventually shed a shower of stones on the town, some of which damaged slates and roofs. (*Niles Weekly Register*, 48:397, August 8, 1835)

The appearance of a small, dark cloud, often red, yellow, or black, in an otherwise clear sky, has often been reported as heralding a deluge of bizarre material.

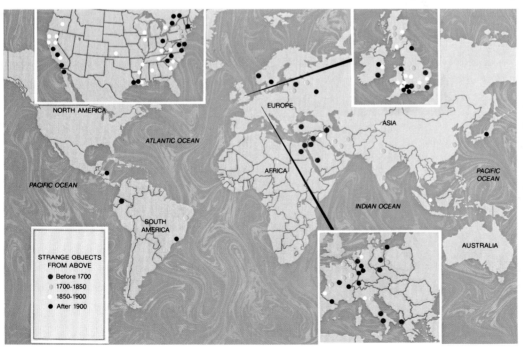

Target: Earth
For thousands of years many strange objects have fallen from the sky. Angel hair fell in Brazil, black eggs fell in Haiti, stones fell in Sicily, candy fell in California. Reports of skyfalls are almost too numerous to count. Shown here are the approximate locations in different parts of the world of many such instances observed over the centuries and described in these pages.

During a torrential thunderstorm in July 1841, hundreds of small fish and frogs fell with partially melted ice and rain on the city of Derby, England. The fish, some of them sticklebacks, were from one-half to two inches long. The frogs were the size of large beans, and many of them survived their fall onto the hard pavement; some were kept alive and "appear to enjoy themselves, in a glass with water and leaves in it." (*The Athenaeum*, July 17, 1841, p.542)

An olive-gray powder fell on Shanghai, China, on March 16, 1846. Under microscopic examination the powder seemed at first to consist of two kinds of hair. When observed through a more powerful instrument, the substance was declared to consist of confervae, a kind of algae. When the fibers were burned, however, they gave off "the common ammoniacal smell and smoke of burnt hair or feathers." According to the report, this skyfall covered an area of 3,800 square miles. (*The Journal of the Asiatic Society of Bengal*, February 1847, pp.193–99)

Nut-sized lumps of odorless, gray resinous matter fell on Vilna, Lithuania, during a rainstorm on April 4, 1846. When the material was burned, it released a pervasive sweet smell. After being soaked in water for 24 hours it swelled and seemed completely gelatinous. (*Comptes Rendus hebdomadaires des séances de l'académie des sciences*, 23:542)

On November 11 of the same year a luminous object estimated at four feet in diameter fell at Loweville, New York, leaving behind—or becoming—a heap of foul-smelling jelly. (*Scientific American*, 2:79, November 28, 1846)

Immediately after a tremendous peal of thunder in 1849, a block of ice 20 feet in circumference and "of a proportionate thickness" fell on Balvullich farm, near Ord, on the Isle of Skye, Scotland. The ice was almost entirely transparent and composed of square- and diamond-shaped crystals from one to three inches long. No other hail or snow was seen at the time. (*The Edinburgh New Philosophical Journal*, 47:371, 1849)

FROM 1850 TO 1870

At the Benicia army station near San Francisco, troops on the drill ground were showered with blood and pieces of meat, apparently beef, on July 20, 1851. Specimens "from the size of a pigeon's egg up to that of an orange" were given to the army surgeon, who described some slices as being slightly tainted. (The *San Francisco Herald*, July 24, 1851)

On June 17, 1857, a farmer in Ottawa, Illinois, heard a hissing sound and looked up to see a shower of cinders streaking toward the earth. They landed in a V-shaped pattern about 50 feet from him, causing the ground to steam. The larger cinders were almost completely buried and the smaller ones half buried. Mr. Bradley noticed a small, dense, dark cloud "hanging over the garden"; the weather had been showery, but there had been no thunder or lightning. (*The American Journal of Science and Arts*, 2:449, November 1857)

A shower of candy is recorded as having occurred in some sections of Lake County, California, on the nights of September 2 and 11, 1857. "It is said that on both of these nights there fell a shower of candy or sugar. The crystals were from one-eighth to one-fourth of an inch in length and the size of a goose quill. Syrup was made of it by some of the lady residents of the section." (Lyman L. Palmer, *History of Napa and Lake Counties, California*, p.71)

John Lewis, a sawyer of Mountain Ash, Glamorganshire, Wales, gave the following account after a rain of fish fell on his village in 1859:

> On Wednesday, February 9, I was getting out a piece of timber, for the purpose of setting it for the saw, when I was startled by something falling all over me—down my neck, on my head, and on my back. On putting my hand down my neck I was surprised to find they were little fish. By this time I saw the whole ground covered with them. I took off my hat, the brim of which was full of them. They were jumping all about. They covered the ground in a long strip of about 80 yards by 12, as we measured afterwards. That shed (pointing to a very large workshop) was covered with them, and the shoots were quite full of them. My mate and I might have gathered bucketsful of them, scraping with our hands. We did gather a great many, about a bucketful, and threw them into the rain pool, where some of them now are. There were two showers, with an interval of about ten minutes, and each shower lasted about two minutes or thereabouts. The time was 11 A.M. The morning up-train to Aberdare was just then passing. It was not blowing very hard, but uncommon wet; just about the same wind as there is today (blowing rather stiff), and it came from this quarter (which at the time was pointing to the south of west). They came down with the rain "in a body, like."

The largest fish, five inches long, died soon after being found. Some 18 or 20 living specimens, the largest of them four inches long, were sent to a Professor Owen for examination, but his observations are not recorded. (*Annual Register*, 101:14–15, 1859)

Fish tumbled down upon the residents of Singapore during the torrential rains that followed an earthquake in 1861, and *people scurried to fill their market baskets with them. Numerous dead fish were found after the puddles dried.*

Writing in *The Zoologist* magazine, W. Winter gives the following account of a toad shower in Norfolk, England, in July 1860:

> I was out insect-catching by the side of the river Waveney, about a quarter-past 9 on Friday night, when a thunder storm came on. I ran for shelter to the buildings at Aldeby Hall. The rain came down in torrents. Just before I was clear of the fens [marshland] I observed some small toads on my arms, and several fell in my net, and on the ground and paths there were thousands. I am quite sure there were none in my net before I started. I believe they fell with the rain out of the clouds. Can you enlighten me on the subject? Two other persons have told me that they met with the same occurrence some distance from the spot in which I was situated. [*The Zoologist*, 18:7146, 1860]

During a violent storm angular black pebbles fell on Wolverhampton, England, in such quantities that they had to be shoveled away. (*La Science Pour Tous,* 5:264, July 19, 1860)

On February 16, 1861, an earthquake struck Singapore. It was followed by heavy rainfalls, which became torrential on the 20th, 21st, and 22nd of the month. Francis de Castelnau, an eminent traveler and naturalist then living in Singapore, gave the following eyewitness account:

> At 10 o'clock the sun lifted and from my window I saw a large number of Malays and Chinese filling baskets with fishes which they picked up in the pools of rain water which covered the ground. On being asked where the fishes came from, the natives replied that they had fallen from the sky. Three days afterwards, when the pools had dried up, we found many dead fishes.
>
> Having examined the animals, I recognized them as *Clarias batrachi* . . . a species of catfish which is very abundant in fresh water in Singapore, and in the Malayan Peninsula, in Siam, Sumatra, Borneo, etc. They were from 25 to 30 centimeters long, and therefore adult.
>
> These siluroids, the same as Ophicephalus, etc., are able to live a long time out of water, and to progress some distance on land, and I thought at once that they had come from some small overflowing stream nearby; but the yard of the house I inhabited is enclosed by a wall that would prevent them entering in this manner.
>
> An old Malay has since told me that in his youth

Whirlwinds and Waterspouts

The standard explanation for the great majority of skyfalls is that whatever comes down was carried up by a whirlwind or waterspout. In addition to being the most logical explanation, the whirlwind theory rests on some strong observational evidence. A great variety of small plant and animal organisms, and debris, does indeed constantly circulate in the atmosphere: the spores of fungi, mosses, lichens and algae, insect eggs, bacteria, wing scales, hairs, and scraps of feathers have all been found in air samples collected in specially designed aspirators. It requires relatively little force to lift these wind-borne organisms, which may be swept up from dried-up ponds and elsewhere.

Although no great amount of energy is required to lift such small particles from the ground, enormously strong lifting forces are generated by large whirlwinds, tornadoes, and waterspouts. In the funnel of a tornado, for instance, winds may whirl at 170 to 300 miles an hour and produce a pressure of more than 300 pounds per square foot on everything that stands in their way. Such force is more than adequate for some of the more impressive tornado statistics.

On April 22, 1883, for example, a tornado at Beauregard, Mississippi, carried the 675-pound screw from a cotton press for 900 feet through the air. At Walterborough, South Carolina, a 600-pound wooden beam was carried for a quarter of a mile by the tornado of April 16, 1875, and a 75-pound chicken coop was carried for four miles. And in the Mount Carmel, Illinois, tornado of June 4, 1877, a church spire was borne through the air for 17 miles.

The action of waterspouts has been observed far less frequently than that of whirlwinds, but they too have accomplished extraordinary things. At Christiansten, Norway, for instance, the harbor was once almost entirely emptied in this way, and on a smaller scale, there are records of ponds being sucked dry. During a storm at Bassenthwaite Lake, England, fish were seen to be blown from the lake onto dry land.

Insofar as the energy generated by whirlwinds suffices to lift into the sky what has been seen to fall from it, the explanation seems sound and undoubtedly accounts for some of the skyfalls reported. Yet the theory raises some interesting questions.

How, for example, do whirlwinds and waterspouts manage to be so selective? Things that fall from the sky are usually neatly segregated: in a given shower only fish or only frogs, only stones or only mats of compacted algae fall—and, moreover, only fish of a certain kind or frogs of a certain age. But whirlwinds and waterspouts sweep up everything and anything in their path. Why, therefore, are there not falls of assorted

With a velocity of nearly 300 miles an hour, the updraft of a tornado's funnel creates a powerful suction that can lift and carry almost anything in its path.

creatures and debris—mud and waterweed along with the fish? If some kind of aerial sorting mechanism is supposed—a sorting of objects according to their weight and aerodynamics, for instance—one would then expect assorted showers, fish here, mud there, weed elsewhere, to occur in the same area at more or less the same time; but this does not happen.

How, then, do fish and other creatures survive the rigors of transport by whirlwind?

The whirlwind/waterspout theory requires one to believe, first, that fish, which often fall alive at considerable distance from their apparent point of origin, can survive for an indefinitely long period in the saturated atmosphere of a rain cloud. Second, one must believe that forces powerful enough to lift fish, frogs, toads, eels, and snakes out of their normal habitat and into the sky are insufficient to do them any physical damage and that the sudden changes of temperature and pressure are equally harmless. While such theories may appeal to common sense, they have no firm evidence to commend them.

There is the further question of how whirlwinds could hover over one spot or return to it. Since the unfailing characteristic of wind is to move, and to move whatever travels with it, the whirlwind theory fails to account for those numerous cases where the same things fall repeatedly on the same spot, as though from some stationary location in the sky.

he had seen a similar phenomenon. [*Comptes Rendus hebdomadaires des séances de l'académie des sciences*, 52:880–81, 1861]

Policemen in Dublin, on the night of May 9, 1867, took shelter from an onslaught of nuts or berries that fell from the sky "in great quantities and with great force" during a "tremendous rainfall." The "berries" were described as being "in the form of a very small orange, about half an inch in diameter, black in colour, and, when cut across, seem as if made of some hard dark brown wood. They also possess a slight aromatic odour."

According to one observer, the objects were "simply hazlenuts, preserved in a bog for centuries." How they had come to fall from the sky, however, was not explained. (*Symons's Monthly Meteorological Magazine*, 2:59, June 1867)

Fire seemed to fall from the sky like rain for about 10 minutes on the night of October 18, 1867, at Thames Ditton, Surrey, England. In the morning "waterbutts and puddles in the upper part of the village were thickly covered with a deposit of sulphur." (*Symons's Monthly Meteorological Magazine*, 2:130, December 1867)

Flesh and blood fell for three minutes and covered some two acres of Mr. J. Hudson's farm near Los Nietos, California, on August 1, 1869. The day was clear and windless, and flesh fell as fine particles as well as in strips from one to six inches long. Short fine hairs also fell with it. In the article on this phenomenon in the *San Francisco Evening Bulletin* dated August 9, 1869, it was also reported that flesh and blood had fallen in Santa Clara County some two months earlier.

FROM 1870 TO 1880

A yellowish substance fell on Genoa, Italy, on the morning of February 14, 1870. It was analyzed by M. G. Boccardo and Professor Castellani of the Genoa Technical Institute and found to consist of about 66 percent sand (mostly of the silica type, and with some of clay), 15 percent iron oxide (rust), 9 percent carbonate of lime, 7 percent organic matter, and the rest water. The organic matter contained particles resembling spores, grains of starch, fragments of diatoms (forms of algae whose cell walls contain silica), and unidentified, cobalt-blue globules. (*The Journal of the Franklin Institute*, 3:11–12, July 1870)

A deluge of "water lizards" struck Sacramento, California, in August 1870. Between two and eight inches long, they covered the roof of the opera house and swarmed over the pavements. Hundreds of them survived for several days in the rainwater that flooded a partially dug cellar belonging to a Judge Spicer. (*The Sacramento Reporter*, August 6, 1870)

Unidentified creatures apparently in a larval condition (they were encased in a gelatinous substance) fell upon the town of Bath, England, during a violent rain- and hail-storm in 1871. They were 1½ inches long and were described, after being examined "under a powerful lens," as "animals with barrel-formed bodies, the motion of the viscera in which is perfectly visible, with locust-shaped heads bearing long antennae, and with pectoral and caudal fins like feet."

Specimens of these creatures were preserved at the Derby and Midland Tavern, "where scientific men, on inspecting them, pronounce them to be marine insects, probably caught up into the clouds by a waterspout in the Bristol Channel." (*Symons's Monthly Meteorological Magazine*, 6:59, May 1871)

On Friday, March 3, 1876, flakes of meat fell over an area 100 yards long and 50 yards wide near the Kentucky home of Mr. and Mrs. Allen Crouch, not far from the Olympian Springs in southern Bath County. The sky at the time was cloudless. The flakes were from one to three or four inches square and looked like fresh beef. However, according to the opinion of "two gentlemen" who tasted it, the substance was either mutton or venison. (*Scientific American*, 34:197, March 25, 1876)

But in July, according to a Mr. Leopold Brandeis writing in the *Sanitarian*, the Kentucky meat-shower was explained: the substance that fell was nothing more than Nostoc, "a low form of vegetable existence" (though how this had dropped from a clear sky remained a mystery). Unfortunately (for the squeamish) this less alarming description did not prevail for long. Dr. A. Mead Edwards, president of the Newark Scientific Association, called on Mr. Brandeis to see if he could obtain a specimen of the original material. Mr. Brandeis kindly gave him the whole sample, with the information that he had himself obtained it from a doctor in Brooklyn, who had in turn been given it by a Professor Chandler.

Shortly after this a letter from Dr. Allan McLane Hamilton appeared in *Medical Record*, stating that he and Dr. J.W.S. Arnold had made a microscopic examination of material from the Kentucky meat-shower supplied to them by Professor Chandler. He added that they had identified the substance as lung tissue from a human infant or a horse ("the structure of the organ in these two cases being very similar").

After reading this letter, Dr. Edwards called on Dr.

Hamilton and was again rewarded with the sample in question, this time with the information that two samples had been sent from Kentucky to the editor of the *Agriculturist,* who gave them to Professor Chandler. The professor had given one to Dr. Hamilton and one to the Brooklyn doctor who had passed it on to Mr. Brandeis.

Dr. Edwards now had possession of both samples. He confirmed Dr. Hamilton's identification and identified the sample given to Mr. Brandeis as also being lung tissue, although it was less well preserved. Soon after, Dr. Edwards was shown a microscopic slide of a third sample of the Kentucky meat, which had been given to Professor J. Phin of the *American Journal of Microscopy* by a Mr. Walmsley of Philadelphia, who had in turn received it from Kentucky. This slide revealed to the observer that the material was "undoubtedly striated muscular fibre."

Subsequently Professor Phin showed Dr. Edwards a fourth specimen, this one sent to him by a Mr. A. T. Parker of Lexington, Kentucky. This sample also proved to be muscle tissue. Still not satisfied, Dr. Edwards now wrote to Mr. Parker, who sent him three more samples, two in their natural state and one prepared for the microscope. Of these, two proved to be cartilage, and one was muscle tissue with "what appears to be dense connective tissue."

Thus, of the seven samples examined, two were of lung tissue, three were of muscle tissue, and two were of cartilage.

As a postscript to the story, Dr. Edwards relayed a theory of the event passed on to him by Mr. Parker: according to the local people of Kentucky, the meat was probably disgorged by buzzards, "who, as is their custom, seeing one of their companions disgorge himself, immediately followed suit."

As to how many buzzards would be required to cover 5,000 square yards with disgorged meat, or at what height they must have been flying to be invisible, was not suggested. (*Scientific American Supplement,* 2:437, July 22, 1876)

A rain of living snakes fell over the southern part of Memphis, Tennessee, in 1877. They measured from a foot to 18 inches in length and were presumed to have been swept into the air by a hurricane; but where snakes might exist "in such abundance"–they fell by the thousands–"is yet a mystery." (*Scientific American,* 36:86, February 10, 1877)

Several acres of ground were covered by a deluge of small fish that fell from a clear sky at Chico, California, in 1878, as reported in *The New York Times* on September 2 of that year.

A heavy hailstorm, with thunder and lightning, passed over the Lomond Hills, near Falkland, Scotland, on the evening of Saturday, August 30, 1879. On Sunday "the hills were found in several places to be covered with seaweed, or some substance as nearly resembling it as possible, and it was also seen hanging from the trees and shrubberies in the district. In some places the weed lay in a pretty thick coating, so that quantities of it could be collected from the grass." The Lomond Hills are some 10 miles from the Firth of Forth. (*Symons's Monthly Meteorological Magazine,* 14:136, September 1879)

FROM 1880 TO 1890

A thunderstorm of "unusual severity" struck the city of Worcester, England, on May 28, 1881. During the early part of the storm hailstones knocked leaves from the trees, stripped peas from the vines, and generally damaged fruit and vegetable gardens. Extraordinarily heavy rain subsequently flooded an underpass at Henwick railway station to a depth of four feet.

Taking shelter from this storm in a garden shed in the suburb of St. John's, a man named John Greenall was astonished to see vast quantities of periwinkles descending with the rain, so forcefully that some buried themselves in the ground and others bounced up from it. Numerous local people came to gather up the living shellfish, and one man gathered up half a bushel of them. When dusk fell, the winkle gathering continued by lantern light.

In one large shell a living hermit crab was found; in another part of town "one or two pebbles, such as are found on the seashore, fell through a skylight at Mr. Latty's, in High Street."

Worcester is about 70 miles from the sea. (John Michell and Robert J. M. Rickard, *Phenomena: A Book of Wonders,* p. 15)

In Milwaukee, Green Bay, and other towns in Wisconsin, strong, very white spiderwebs fell in late October 1881. They ranged in size from mere specks to threads 60 feet long. The webs all seemed to float inland from Lake Michigan, sometimes being so thick as to annoy the eye, and extending upward for as far as one could see. "Curiously there is no mention, in any of the reports ... of the presence of spiders in this general shower of webs." (*Scientific American,* 45:337, November 26, 1881)

A group of railroad workers were caught in a hailstorm outside Salina, Kansas, in early August 1882. They headed back to Salina, the hailstones becoming larger and more numerous as they approached town, until they reached a place where the hailstones were as deep as winter snow. There they found one piece of ice weighing approximately 80 pounds, which they carried back to town. By evening, after it had melted somewhat, the chunk of ice measured 29 by 16 by 2 inches. (*Scientific American*, 47:119, August 19, 1882)

On October 16, 1883, a dense cloud appeared over Montussan, in the Gironde district of France. From it, a white, woolly substance fell in fist-sized lumps, leading some observers to suppose that the entire cloud was composed of this material. Samples were sent to the editor of a scientific magazine, *La Nature*, but he was unable to identify them except as something that carbonized as it burned. At the time of the fall there was a rainstorm. (*La Nature*, 1:342, October 27, 1883)

A shower of warm stones fell outside the offices of the Charleston *News and Courier* in Charleston, South Carolina, at 2:30 A.M. on September 4, 1886. Another shower occurred at 7:30 A.M., and yet another at 1:30 that afternoon. As far as could be seen the stones seemed to fall from somewhere directly above the newspaper offices, in a small area. They fell with great force, and several broke on the pavement. They were described as polished pebbles of flint, the smallest being the size of a grape and the largest the size of a hen's egg. About a quart of them were picked up. (The Charleston *News and Courier*, September 6, 1886)

The same newspaper reported earlier that Charleston had been struck by a major earthquake on August 31.

For 10 to 12 sunny, cloudless days an almost incessant deluge of rain poured down on a small area of Chesterfield County, South Carolina. (The New York *Sun*, October 24, 1886)

FROM 1890 TO 1900

An edible substance consisting of small yellowish spherules, white on the inside, fell over an area of some three square miles in the neighborhood of Mardin and Diyarbakir, Turkey, in August 1890. The local people made it into a bread that was said to be of good flavor and easily digestible. Botanists declared the substance to be a lichen, perhaps *Lecanora esculenta*. (*Nature*, 43:255, January 15, 1891)

On a day of showers and sunshine in late October 1890, a curious event took place at Dalgonar Farm in the parish of Penpoint, Dumfriesshire, Scotland. Mr. Wright was out walking on a ridge of hills, when

> I was struck by a strange appearance in the atmosphere, which I at first mistook for a flock of birds, but as I saw them falling to the earth my

curiosity was quickened. Fixing my eyes on one of the larger of them, and running about 100 yards up the hill until directly underneath, I awaited its arrival, when I found it to be *an oak leaf*. Looking upwards the air was thick with them, and as they descended in an almost vertical direction, oscillating, and glittering in the sunshine, the spectacle was as beautiful as rare. . . .

> On examination of the hills after the leaves had fallen, it was found that they covered a tract of about a mile wide and two miles long. The leaves were wholly those of the oak. No oak trees grow in clumps together nearer than eight miles. The aged shepherd, who has been on the farm since 1826, never witnessed a similar occurrence. [*Nature*, 42:637, October 30, 1890]

On several occasions during the winter of 1891 the people of the Valley Bend district of Randolph County, West Virginia, found the snow thickly covered with worms. Since the snow was two feet deep and had a hard crust, it was logically proposed that the worms could only have fallen from the sky along with the snow. They were reported to resemble "ordinary cutworms" (a nocturnal caterpillar in the family Noctuidae) and to be so abundant that "a square foot of snow can scarcely be found some days without a dozen of these worms on it." (*Scientific American*, 64:116, February 21, 1891)

White frogs fell on Mosely, a suburb of Birmingham, England, during a severe storm on the morning of June 30, 1892. (*Symons's Monthly Meteorological Magazine*, 32:107, August 1897)

A small yellow cloud passed rapidly over Paderborn, Germany, during a thunderstorm. When the cloud broke, a clattering rain of living pond mussels (*Anodonta anatina*) fell on the town. (*Nature*, 47:278, January 19, 1893)

During a severe hailstorm on May 11, 1894, a gopher turtle encased in ice fell on Bovina, eight miles east of Vicksburg, Mississippi. During the same storm a small block of alabaster, also encased in ice, fell on Vicksburg itself. (*Monthly Weather Review*, 22:215, May 1894)

On June 3, 1894, a tornado in Harney, Grant, and Union counties in eastern Oregon left sheets of icefall in its wake. They were from 3 to 4 inches square and from ¾ to 1½ inches thick. "They had a smooth surface, and in falling gave the impression of a vast field or sheet of ice suspended in the atmosphere, and suddenly broken into fragments about the size of the palm of the hand." (*Monthly Weather Review*, 22:293, July 1894)

An early-morning deluge of dead birds fell from a

clear sky on Baton Rouge, Louisiana, in November 1896, "literally cluttering the streets of the city. There were wild ducks, catbirds, woodpeckers, and many birds of strange plumage, some of them resembling canaries, but all dead, falling in heaps along the thoroughfares...." The only plausible explanation advanced for this sad event was that the birds had been driven inland by a recent storm on the Florida coast and had been killed by a sudden change of temperature that had occurred in the area of Baton Rouge. Storms and temperature changes are common, however, but bird falls are not. (*Monthly Weather Review,* 45:223, May 1917)

Something described as a "sulphur rain" fell on Mount Vernon, Kentucky, on March 21, 1898, and at several other places in Rockcastle County. The substance was flammable and smelled of sulfur. (*Monthly Weather Review,* 26:115, March 1898)

On November 21, 1898, quantities of a substance resembling spiderweb, but actually more like asbestos in texture, fell on Montgomery, Alabama. Some of the material was in strands and some in flakes several inches long and several inches broad. Most curiously, the substance was phosphorescent. (*Monthly Weather Review,* 26:566, December 1898)

FROM 1900 TO 1910

Hundreds of small catfish, trout, and perch fell during heavy rain at Tiller's Ferry, South Carolina, in June 1901. Afterward they were found swimming around in pools of water that had accumulated between the rows of cotton on a plantation belonging to a Mr. Charles Raley. (*Monthly Weather Review,* 29:263, June 1901)

A succession of curious hailstones fell during a storm over the St. Lawrence River near the village of Alexandria Bay, New York, in 1901. At first the hailstones were cylindrical, the thickness of a lead pencil and three-eighths of an inch long. These gave way to stones the size of a walnut, which in turn were followed by disk-shaped hailstones two inches thick and three inches in diameter. They were hard enough to bounce off rocks without breaking, and when they were half melted "many had the appearance of the human eye—a pupil in the center and a ring surrounding it, with fine lines radiating in all directions."

"During the storm," the observer goes on, "the river presented a beautiful appearance, there being thousands of miniature fountains from a foot to 6 feet in height spurting up where the hail plunged in." (*Monthly Weather Review,* 29:506–07, November 1901)

Above are representations of the odd variety of hailstones observed at Alexandria Bay in 1901.

On the evening of Trinity Sunday, 1908, the pastor of Saint-Étienne-les-Remiremont, a parish some miles to the west of the Vosges Mountains in eastern France, was settled comfortably in his presbytery with "a large and heavy treatise on geology." He had read no more than a few pages on the formation of ice when he heard the presbytery door open and Mlle. Marie André call out: "Monsieur le Curé, come quickly—they are melting!"

With some reluctance—he was suffering from rheumatism—L'Abbé Gueniot got up to see what was the matter. The rest of the story continues in his own words:

"Look," she said to me, "here is the image of Our Lady of the Treasure printed on the hailstones." "Come, come," I said, "do not tell me these silly tales."

In order to satisfy her, I glanced carelessly at two hailstones which she held in her hand. But, since I did not want to see anything, and, moreover, could not do so without spectacles, I turned away to go back to my book. She urged, "I beg of you to put on your glasses." I did so, and saw very distinctly on the front of the hailstones, which were slightly convex in the center, although the edges were somewhat worn, the bust of a woman, with a robe turned up at the bottom like a priest's cope. I should, perhaps, describe it more exactly by saying that it was like the Virgin of the Hermits. The outlines of the image were slightly hollow, as though they had been formed with a punch, but were very boldly drawn.

Mlle. André asked me to notice certain details of the costume, but I refused to look at it any longer. I was ashamed of my credulity, feeling sure that the Blessed Virgin would hardly concern herself with instantaneous photographs on hailstones. I said: "But do you not see that these hailstones must have fallen on vegetables, and thus received these impressions? Take them away, they are no good to me." I returned to my book, without giving any further attention to what had happened.

But my mind was disturbed by the singular formation of these hailstones. I picked up three, in order to weigh them, without looking at them closely. They weighed between six and seven ounces. One of them was perfectly round, like balls with which children play, and had a seam around it as though it had been cast in a mould. [Note: accounts of hailstones with seams or ridges are not unusual.]

During my supper (I was alone) I said to myself: "All the same, these hailstones are of unusual shape, and the imprint on the two I examined was so regular that it can hardly have been due to chance."

But I quickly stiffened myself against all thought of the supernatural, and was ashamed of having entertained it for a moment.

By the time the pastor finished supper the storm had ended, and he went into the garden to assess the damage. To his surprise he found the vegetables in good order, but he later learned that the hail had broken some 1,400 panes of glass in the area. (The storm seemed to have unleashed two kinds of hailstones, those bearing the miraculous image and a larger, destructive kind.) "What appeared most worthy of notice," the priest continued, "was that the hailstones, which ought to have been violently precipitated to the ground in accordance with the laws of acceleration of the speed of falling bodies, appeared to have fallen from the height of but a few yards, and to have only acquired the initial velocity of a falling body." The pastor continued:

Towards half-past seven the news was spread about in the vicinity of the presbytery that many persons had observed the image of Our Lady of the Treasure on the hailstones, and that a number of them were in the form of medallions. Children had collected them in their aprons, and shown them to their parents, who had verified the presence of the same image. Some even saw small details, such as the Virgin's crown, the Child Jesus, the fringes of the robe. Was this the result of imagination?

But, apart from these details, there is no doubt that the greater part of the hailstones which were examined bore distinctly the image of Our Lady of the Treasure.

The following morning the milkmen, on returning from Remiremont, reported that many persons in the town had observed the same thing.

After vespers the following Sunday the curé collected 50 signatures of persons who were "thoroughly convinced of the truth of their observations." He did not,

he said, "attach importance to these signatures which I might be suspected of having influenced, but they were spontaneously given."

The curé concluded by remarking that although the town council of Remiremont had forbidden a "magnificent procession which was in preparation" on Trinity Sunday, "the artillery of heaven caused a vertical procession which no one could forbid." (*English Mechanic and World of Science*, 87:436, June 12, 1908)

A similar rain of hailstones occurred in 1552 at Dordrecht, Holland. Here is a translation of the original report of that event, shown on the facing page:

A Prodigiously Huge Hailstone
In the year 1552—Friday the 17th of May between 4 and 5 o'clock in the afternoon—there was a particularly violent thunderstorm in a certain Dutch town called Dordrecht, driving the inhabitants in terror into their houses as if the world were coming to an end, because for more than half an hour there was a steady bombardment of horrible hailstones, so that every garden and orchard was destroyed. Some of the hailstones were of gigantic size and peculiar shape. Hundreds of people saw them, including a painter who sketched the hailstones as shown above. Several hailstones had a natural shape of a sun. On others appeared a crown of thorns. Some weighed as much as half a pound. The water from these hailstones smelled as if there were boiling water. This hailstorm was followed by a foul-smelling cloud. It is a wonder what such signs may signify. But that is known to Almighty God alone. May he protect us in Christ. Amen.

FROM 1910 TO 1950

Several hundred sand eels (*Ammodytes tobianus*) fell on an area of about one-third of an acre at Hendon, a suburb of Sunderland, England, on August 24, 1918. There was heavy rain, and the fish were not only dead but stiff and hard when picked up just after the occurrence. (*Nature*, 102:46, September 19, 1918)

Rocks began to fall from the sky upon the town of Chico, California, in July 1921, and were still falling, intermittently, in November. The falling rocks attracted no great attention until the following January, when an investigation was undertaken by Marshal J. A. Peck, a local man. His conclusions were published in the San Francisco *Examiner* on March 14. He had seen and heard the stones fall but was unable to explain them; he suspected that "someone with a machine is to blame." The origin of the stones remained a puzzle. According to Prof. C. K. Studley, writing in the same edition of the *Examiner*: "Some of the rocks are so large that they

Von einem wünder sicheu grossen hagel

welcher gefallen ist zu Dordrecht im Hollandt.

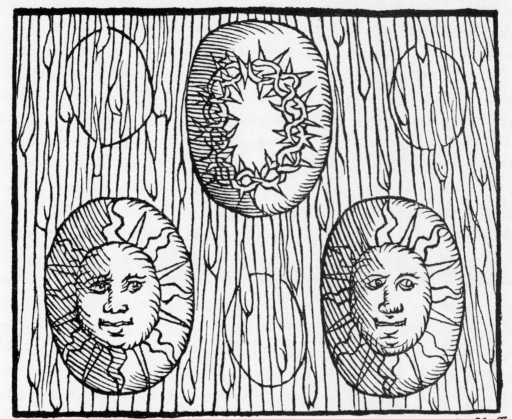

Im iare M D Lü den rvii May an einem Erichtag zwischen viere vnd fünff
nach mittag/ ist inn einer Stadt in Holland mit namen Dordrecht/ ein solchs er=
schrecklichs vngewitter gewesen/ das die burger zu dort vor grossem schrecken ir
heuser zugespert haben als wolt die welt zergehen/ vrsach ist das eine grosse halb
stunde nach einander ein gar grausamer hagel gefallen ist das es dauon alle gar
ten/ kreuter/ vnd früchte der beume verdorben.   Sölcher hagel ist mancherley
gewesen an grösse schwere vnd gestalt/ das haben vil hundert leut gesehen/ auch
vnter andern warhafftigen burgern von Antorff ein mahler. welcher die hagel
stein abcontefet ist wie hie oben verzeychent ist/ Etliche hagelsteine hetten eine na=
türliche gestalt einer Sonnen. Auff etlichen stundt ein dörnen Kron Etlich hiel
ten am gewichte ein halb pfundt etlich meh etlich weniger. Das wasser vor di
sen hagelsteinen reuchte als wehre es siedent heyss wasser.   Nach diesem hagel
fiel ein dicker stinckender fauler nebel/ das wunder ist was sölchs zeychen bedeuten
mag/ Doch weil das dem almechtigen Gott allein bekant wöl er vns beschirmen
in Christum Amen.

Abb. 412. Bericht von einem wunderlich großen Hagel zu Dordrecht in Holland 1552.

could not be thrown by any ordinary means. One of the rocks weighs 16 ounces. They are not of meteoric origin, as seems to have been hinted, because two of them show signs of cementation, either natural or artificial, and no meteoric factor was ever connected with a cement factory."

In March 1922 the San Francisco *Chronicle* published a series of accounts of the stones. They had been falling in Chico, the paper said, on and off for the past four months, usually on the roofs of two adjoining warehouses. A "downpour of oval-shaped stones" was described, and "a heavy shower of warm rocks." One writer, Miriam Allen de Ford, reported: "I looked up at the cloudless sky, and suddenly saw a rock falling straight down, as if becoming visible when it came near enough. This rock struck the roof with a thud, and bounced off on the track beside the warehouse, and I could not find it." On March 17 one person in a crowd was said to have been injured by a falling stone. (Charles Fort, *The Complete Books of Charles Fort*, pp.533-35) For an account of a heavy fall of small fishes at Chico, see the report of 1878.

During a heavy snowstorm in 1922 "thousands of exotic insects resembling spiders, caterpillars and huge ants" fell on a number of slopes in the Swiss Alps, according to a report. (Charles Fort, *The Complete Books of Charles Fort*, p.535)

A ball of limestone fell from the sky near Bleckenstad, Sweden, on April 11, 1925. On landing, it burst into fragments, among which fossil shells and some evidence of a creature resembling a trilobite were found by Professor Hadding of Lund University. (John Michell and Robert J. M. Rickard, *Phenomena: A Book of Wonders*, p.17)

Tiny frogs fell by the hundreds on Trowbridge, Wiltshire, England, on the afternoon of June 16, 1939, during a shower of rain. (*The Meteorological Magazine*, 74:184-85, July 1939)

Numerous silver coins fell in the Meshchera region in central Russia during a storm in August 1940. (John Michell and Robert J. M. Rickard, *Phenomena: A Book of Wonders*, p.19)

Between 7 and 8 A.M. on October 23, 1947, freshwater fish fell in great numbers on the town of Marksville, Louisiana. The weather at the time was calm and somewhat foggy; the fish—largemouth black bass, sunfish, hickory shad, and minnows—were "abolutely fresh and fit for human consumption." Some were frozen and some were merely cold. The fish fell in an area approximately 1,000 feet long and 75 or 80 feet wide, some of them striking pedestrians. There was no rain at the time, and the New Orleans weather bureau had no report of tornadoes in the vicinity, though numerous miniature tornadoes, or "devildusters," had been observed the day before. (*Science*, 109:402, April 22, 1949)

Among the numerous reports of "angel hair"—a general name for a variable substance described as resembling spiderwebs, cotton, and silk—is an interesting subgroup that associates falls of this fibrous material with the appearance of unidentified flying objects. The following report by P. L. Lewis was published in *Weather*, April 1949:

Sunday, September 26, 1948. Port Hope, Ontario.
This day was warm and the sky cloudless. We had had dinner in the garden and I was lying on my back on the lawn, my head just in the shade of the house, when I was startled to see an object resembling a star moving rapidly across the sky. The time was 2 o'clock Eastern Standard Time.

At first it was easy to imagine that recent reports of "Flying Saucers" had not been exaggerated.

More of these objects came sailing into view over the ridge of the house, only to disappear when nearly overhead. With field glasses I was able to see that each was approximately spherical, the centre being rather brighter than the edges. The glasses also showed quite a number at such heights that they were invisible to the naked eye.

With only a gull flying in the sky for comparison, I should estimate the elevation of the lower objects to be about 300 ft and the higher ones 2000 ft; the size was about one foot in diameter and the speed about 50 mph, in a direction SW to NE.

Also visible every now and then were long threads, apparently from spiders. Some of these were seen to reflect the light over a length of three or four yards, but any one piece may of course have been longer. Each was more or less horizontal, moving at right angles to its length. In one case an elongated tangled mass of these gave the appearance of a frayed silken cord. These threads appeared only in the lower levels.

It is reasonably certain that these objects were balls of spiders' threads, possibly with thistledown entangled in them, but the way in which they caught the rays of the sun and shone so brightly was very striking. [*Weather*, 4:121-22, April 1949]

SINCE 1950

Police officers John Collins and Joe Keenan were cruising the streets of Philadelphia in their patrol car on the night of September 26, 1950. As they made their way down a quiet side street near Vare Avenue and 26th

The Rot of the Stars

A microscopic view of plasmodium

"Star jelly" is one of several names for a gelatinous substance supposedly found at the place where a falling star has landed. Other old names for the same thing are star slough, star shot, and, in Welsh, *pwdre ser,* "the rot of the stars." Since star jelly is usually said to evaporate before a thorough analysis can be made of it, attempts to identify the substance are conjectural, and conclusions vary. What they all have in common is the assumption that the material, whatever it may be, has no connection with the stars.

The two main contenders for the leading role in the star jelly mystery are Nostoc and plasmodium. Nostoc is one of the blue-green algae and grows in beadlike strings within a gelatinous mass on soil or floating in water; colonies can be microscopic or as large as walnuts. Plasmodium is a general name for gelatinous congregations of slime molds or certain kinds of fungi.

Other kinds of gelatinous substances that are generally agreed to have fallen from the sky have been described as the egg masses of insects or amphibians but, having no apparent connection with the fall of luminous bodies, are not classed as star jelly. It has, however, been suggested that egg masses are what people see when they think they have found star jelly. Another idea is that the material may be the gelatinous slime of partly digested fish disgorged by seagulls.

Some, or even all, of these materials might account for the star jelly phenomenon. What none of them explain, except by invoking coincidence and faulty observation, is why, for hundreds of years, so many people making their way to where they suppose a star has fallen should stumble on a mound of jelly.

Street, their headlights picked up a strange, shimmering object that seemed to be coming to earth in an open field about half a block ahead of them.

When they went to investigate, their flashlights revealed a domed disk of quivering purple jelly, six feet in diameter, one foot thick near the center and an inch or two at the edge. They had a curious feeling that the thing was alive. They turned off their flashlights and saw it glow with a faint, purple light. And then they radioed for help.

They were soon joined by Sgt. Joe Cook and Patrolman James Cooper. Sergeant Cook suggested that they try to pick the thing up, but when Officer Collins attempted to do this it fell apart in his hands, like gelatin. The fragments that stuck to his hands soon evaporated, leaving behind only a sticky, odorless scum. Within half an hour after Cook and Cooper arrived on the scene, the whole thing had evaporated. (Frank Edwards, *Strange World,* p.344)

A carpenter, working on the roof of his house near Düsseldorf, Germany, on January 10, 1951, died after being impaled by a shaft of ice. It was six feet long, six inches in diameter, and fell from the sky. (Frank Edwards, *Strangest of All*)

On October 17, 1952, the people of Oloron-Ste.-Marie, in the French Pyrenees, saw a cigar-shaped object flying at an angle of 45° above their town. Accompanying it were 30 smaller, saucer-shaped craft. Ten days later about 100 people saw the same spectacle in the sky above Gaillac. On both occasions a substance like gossamer fell from the unidentified objects, but when people tried to collect samples it turned gelatinous and sublimated. (Aimé Michel, *The Truth About Flying Saucers,* p.64)

Several cars were damaged by a heavy fall of ice along American Avenue in Long Beach, California, on June 4, 1953. The statement of H. A. Boyd, who was working in a used-car lot at the time, was given in the following account by the *Los Angeles Examiner:*

> "I had just finished polishing that car [one whose hood and fender were knocked off by a piece of ice] and was about fifty feet away when I heard a zizzing sound, looked up and saw the air full of white stuff coming down. A big piece of ice that looked to me almost as big as a man, hit the car, shattered, and fragments of ice flew all over."
>
> Across the street from the car lot was the office of Charles Roscoe, a former P-38 pilot. He heard the crash of ice and ran outside to see what was happening. Just as he reached the door of his office at 1461 American Avenue, he told authorities, "something hit the roof of the office with a wham like a big rock landing on it. I looked up and I could see the sun shining on big pieces coming from 2000 feet up. They rolled and twisted and shimmered like some waterfall. I looked for a plane and couldn't see any."

Although meteorologists did theorize that the ice had fallen from a plane, no plane was seen, and if there had been one, it would have been difficult for it to fly with so much ice on the wings. Also, the icefall, which lasted for about two minutes, was concentrated on a relatively small area. If it had come from a moving plane, it seems reasonable to assume that it would have been spread more widely. (The *Los Angeles Examiner*, June 5, 1953)

A downpour of frogs (or toads) "of all descriptions" fell on Leicester, Massachusetts, on September 7, 1953. Paxton Avenue was alive with them, and children gathered them up by the bucketful with their bare hands. A great many were found on roofs and in gutters, thereby tending to discredit the explanation that they had hopped into the streets from an over-flowing pond. (The Worcester *Telegram and Gazette*, January 6, 1959)

Ed Mootz was working in the garden of his house on Boal Street, Cincinnati, Ohio, at 5:30 P.M. on July 22, 1955. Suddenly a few drops of warm, red liquid fell on his arms and hands. In a few moments the red rain was falling all around him. Out of the cloud came a dark protuberance, and it was from this that the red "rain" was falling—right onto a peach tree in his garden.

Edward Mootz of Cincinnati examines the shriveled fruit and brown, defoliated branches of his peach tree, which died overnight after a fall of red rain on July 22, 1955.

"I looked up," said Mr. Mootz "and hanging directly over me about 1000 feet in the air was the strangest cloud I had ever seen. It wasn't a big cloud, but it certainly did have odd colors. It was dark green, red and pink. The red in it matched the color of the substance which hit me and the tree. I could see that whatever it was that was raining down on me was coming from that cloud.

I watched the cloud for a minute trying to figure it out and then my bare arms and hands where the drops had hit me began to burn. They really hurt, too. It felt like I had put turpentine on an open cut. I ran for the house and washed it off real good with strong soap and hot water."

In fact, the "rain" looked like blood. It was somewhat oily and sticky to touch.

The following morning Ed Mootz discovered that his peach tree had died along with the grass beneath it, and all the young fruit had shriveled on the stem.

There were no planes in the area at the time of the rain, and it seems unlikely that a chemical plant or factory could have produced a cloud capable of hovering over a single spot for several minutes. Representatives of the U.S. Air Force came to interview Mr. Mootz and removed samples of the tree, fruit, and grass. If they discovered anything, they kept it to themselves, and the nature of the deadly rain remained a mystery. (The Cincinnati *Enquirer*, August 28, 1955; *The Cincinnati Post*, February 3, 1975)

Pennies and halfpennies fell around children leaving school in Hanham, a suburb of Bristol, England, one day in 1956. (John Michell and Robert J. M. Rickard, *Phenomena: A Book of Wonders*, p.19)

"Thousands" of 1,000-franc notes rained down on Bourges, France, in 1957. No one claimed the notes or reported any loss. (John Michell and Robert J. M. Rickard, *Phenomena: A Book of Wonders*, p.19)

A light crossed the night skies over the Irish county of Westmeath in February 1958 and was seen to land in a field. A number of people rushed to the landing site, where they found only a mass of gelatinous material. (John Michell and Robert J. M. Rickard, *Phenomena: A Book of Wonders*, p.15)

On a November afternoon in 1958 rain fell for 2½ hours onto a 10-foot-square area of the home of Mrs. R. Babington in Alexandria, Louisiana. The sky was quite clear at the time, and neither the local weather bureau nor the nearby England Air Force Base could offer any explanation of the phenomenon. (The *Alexandria Daily Town Talk*, November 11, 1958)

Numbers of sooty shearwaters fell on the town of Capitola, California, on August 18, 1961. Here a policeman examines some of the birds that were injured and unable to fly.

Carpenters working on the roof of a house in Shreveport, Louisiana, on July 12, 1961, had to take shelter from a brief deluge of green peaches; they were about the size of golf balls and were seen to fall from a thick cloud. According to the local weather bureau, the conditions around Shreveport that day were not sufficient to produce whirlwinds, tornadoes, waterspouts, or any other kind of updraft strong enough to carry even young peaches up into the sky. (Jim Brandon, *Weird America*, p.98)

Sooty shearwaters are large oceanic birds that migrate by the millions from their breeding grounds in Australia, New Zealand, and South America to spend the summer and early fall in the coastal waters of the North Atlantic and Pacific, from California to Alaska, Greenland to Labrador. Though they spend most of their time at sea, the birds are sometimes driven toward the coast by harsh weather.

On August 18, 1961, tons of dead and injured sooty shearwaters fell on the coast of California, from Pleasure Point to Rio Del Mar, along Monterey Bay. Thousands of corpses, the bodies 16 inches long, the wings spanning more than three feet, littered the roads, highways, and beaches, festooning power lines and fences and impaled on TV antennas. Several thousand birds were still alive but unable to fly; the local people took them down to the ocean, where most of them recovered.

A number of explanations for the fall were offered: Perhaps the birds had become confused in the fog and headed for the city lights—but why over this area rather than one of the more brightly lit coastal cities? And why wasn't the fall of dazzled seabirds a regular occurrence? Perhaps food poisoning or some sudden disease had killed the birds—but autopsies revealed no sickness: the birds had simply been killed by the fall, and the reason for it remained a mystery. (The *Santa Cruz Sentinel*, August 18, 1961)

On August 28, 1962, while Grady Honeycutt of Harrisburg, North Carolina, was fishing in his state in a lake near Concord, he saw a shining globe fall slowly into the water. He rowed toward it and soon saw the object resting on the lake bed below him.

Through the clear water he could distinguish its features easily: it was about the size of a bowling ball, it glittered, and was covered with short spikes. He rowed for the shore and called the sheriff's office. By the time Deputy Sheriffs Ted May and Bob Eury were on the scene, the thing seemed to have disintegrated into a tangle of shiny wire. They called for more help.

Three divers were dispatched to them from the Armed Services Explosive Disposal Unit No. 2; but by the time they arrived, at seven the next morning after the splashdown, the thing had completely dissolved, and though they searched the lake bed the divers could find only some strips of aluminum foil of the kind dropped by the air force to distort radar. (*The Concord Tribune*, August 29, 1962)

The *Roxburgh Castle* was moored to her berth in Montreal on October 10, 1962. The captain, Mr. R. H. Pape, was taking the air on deck when he noticed "fine white filaments of unknown kind" draped around the railings and stanchions.

> Calling the attention of the Chief Officer, I pulled one of these strands from a stanchion and found it to be quite tough and resilient. I stretched it but it

would not break easily (as, for instance, a cobweb would have done) and after keeping it in my hand for three or four minutes it disappeared completely; in other words it just vanished into nothing.

Looking up [the captain continued] we could see small cocoons of the material floating down from the sky but as far as we could ascertain there was nothing either above or at street level to account for this extraordinary occurrence. [*The Marine Observer*, 33:187, October 1963]

A loud noise at 2 P.M. on February 5, 1968, at the home of Mr. and Mrs. Charles Morris, 89 Elmira Avenue SW in Washington, D.C., brought the neighbors rushing out to see what had happened. The Morrises were not at home at the time. What people saw was a piece of aluminum torn loose from an awning on the house, and ice scattered on the lawn. There was a hole in the metal about 7 or 8 inches in diameter, obviously made by the impact of a falling object. It was guessed that a chunk of ice "the size of a grapefruit" had torn through the awning, hit an iron railing, and shattered.

An understandable assumption would be that the ice had fallen from an aircraft. But the Morris house is about half a mile away from the nearest landing pattern. And even if a plane had strayed, it would have been too low for icing. The temperature at the time was in the upper 40's, and there was a light haze.

Except for a visit to the site by the local police, there was no official investigation of this phenomenon. A spectroscopic analysis was made of some meltwater, however, and it was found to be unusually pure and free of organic material. This might indicate that the ice was created by some meteorological means.

A curious aspect of this case was the mark on the aluminum at the apparent point of impact—a raised, glassy spot that seemed to be partly burned. How ice could have left a heat mark is mystery enough, not to mention where the ice might have come from. (*Info Journal*, 1:17–19, Spring 1968)

On August 27, 1968, blood and flesh fell on an area of about one-third of a square mile between the Brazilian towns of Cacapava and São José dos Campos. The fall was reported to have lasted about five to seven minutes. (John Michell and Robert J. M. Rickard, *Phenomena: A Book of Wonders*, p.15)

During the year 1968 a deluge of mud, wood, glass, and broken pottery fell four times on the town of Pinar del Río, Cuba. (John Michell and Robert J. M. Rickard, *Phenomena: A Book of Wonders*, p.19)

Hundreds of badly injured ducks—canvasbacks, red-heads, and scaup—fell on St. Mary's City, Maryland, in

This is the awning that was damaged by a fall of ice at the home of Mr. and Mrs. Charles Morris of Washington, D.C. The origin of the ice is unknown.

January 1969. They were judged to have received their injuries—broken bones and hemorrhages—while flying, but what might have caused the damage was unknown. (*The Enterprise,* January 30, 1969)

She doesn't know how or why, but about a half pint of rocks fell from the sky on Mrs. Thomas Potter in San Diego, California, on August 31, 1969. Mrs. Potter said, "I went outside about 7:30 P.M. and we were peppered with these red rocks. They came with a gust of wind from the north—in two bunches."

Mrs. Potter poured the "sky rocks" from an empty instant-coffee jar where she had placed them. They were lightweight, like pumice, rough to the touch, pitted with small pockmarks and holes, and dark red in color. The largest pebble was about the size of a quarter.

"They fell and bounced off parked cars," Mrs. Potter said. "It was like hail for a few seconds." She and her husband, Thomas Potter, gathered up as many as they could find.

"I don't know what they are," said Potter. "But no airplane was flying over at the time, and no cars or trucks went by when it happened." (The *San Diego Union,* September 2, 1969)

Banknotes to the value of 2,000 marks fluttered down from a clear sky at Limburg, West Germany, in January 1976 and were picked up by two clergymen. (The *Bath and West Evening Chronicle,* January 6, 1976)

UNIDENTIFIED FLYING OBJECTS

Millions of people have seen objects in the sky that they could not identify, and many thousands have taken the time and trouble to submit written reports about them. The vast majority of these sightings could well be of such things as meteors, planets, stars, weather balloons, swamp gas, and atmospheric disturbances. There remains, however, a significant body of experiences that are truly inexplicable.

There is no doubt that disk-shaped objects (cigar-shaped in profile) have been seen by a great many honest, sober, and mystified men and women. The objects have been tracked by ground-based and airborne radar and have been photographed by still and movie cameras in black and white and color. The craft have been observed to hover, move straight up or down, and accelerate and maneuver at speeds far beyond the capability of any known airplane.

To the best of our knowledge the UFO's have inflicted no damage except to the psyche and reputation of some of the observers and to certain preconceptions we hold about the universe and the laws of physics. The experiences reported on the following pages are in chronological order to 1948. After this date they are subdivided into the categories devised by the astronomer and UFO investigator Dr. J. Allen Hynek.

BEFORE 1800

The sighting of strange objects in the sky may actually predate the emergence of modern man. Perhaps the earliest depictions of cylindrical objects resembling spacecraft, with what might be their extraterrestrial occupants, are those carved on a granite mountain and on rocks on an island in Hunan province, China. They have been assigned a tentative age of 47,000 years, which puts them within the time-span of Neanderthal man, predating modern *Homo sapiens.* (Jacques Vallee, *UFO's in Space: Anatomy of a Phenomenon,* p.1)

One of the first written accounts of a UFO sighting—a fleet of flying saucers, perhaps—is the following excerpt from an Egyptian papyrus—part of the annals of Thutmose III, who reigned around 1504–1450 B.C.:

In the year 22, of the 3rd month of winter, sixth hour of the day . . . the scribes of the House of Life found it was a circle of fire that was coming in the sky. . . . It had no head, the breath of its mouth had a foul odor. Its body one rod long and one rod wide. It had no voice. Their hearts became confused through it; then they laid themselves on their bellies. . . . They went to the Pharaoh . . . to report it. His Majesty ordered . . . [an examination of] all which is written in the papyrus rolls of the House of Life. His Majesty was meditating upon what happened. Now after some days had passed, these things became more numerous in the skies than ever. They shone more in the sky than the brightness of the sun, and extended to the limits of the four

supports of the heavens. . . . Powerful was the position of the fire circles. The army of the Pharaoh looked on with him in their midst. It was after supper. Thereupon, these fire circles ascended higher in the sky towards the south. . . . The Pharaoh caused incense to be brought to make peace on the hearth. . . . And what happened was ordered by the Pharaoh to be written in the annals of the House of Life . . . so that it be remembered for ever. [Brinsley Le Poer Trench, *The Flying Saucer Story,* pp.81–82]

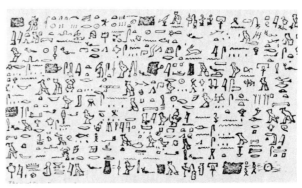

This Egyptian papyrus, more than 3,400 years old, records the sighting of numerous brilliant round objects in the sky by Pharaoh Thutmose III, his army, and his scribes.

The prophet Ezekiel's "vision," recorded in the Bible, is thought by some to be a UFO sighting. His description is of a strange "vehicle" coming from the sky and

Ezekiel's vision of the landing of a wheeled vehicle with four occupants, each of whom had four faces and four wings, is depicted in this 19th-century engraving.

landing near the Chebar River (or Canal) in Chaldea (now Iraq) in the fifth year of the Judean captivity (592 B.C.) under Nebuchadnezzar II of Babylon:

> As I looked, behold, a stormy wind came out of the north, and a great cloud, with brightness round about it, and fire flashing forth continually, and in the midst of the fire, as it were gleaming bronze.

What kind of "machine" was this? Ezekiel continues:

> And from the midst of it came the likeness of four living creatures. And this was their appearance: they had the form of men, but each had four faces, and each of them had four wings. Their legs were straight, and the soles of their feet were like the sole of a calf's foot; and they sparkled like burnished bronze. Under their wings on their four sides they had human hands . . . each had the face of a man in front; the four had the face of a lion on the right side . . . the face of an ox on the left side, and . . . the face of an eagle at the back. . . . And their wings were spread out above; each creature had two wings, each of which touched the wing of another, while two covered their bodies. And each [creature] went straight forward . . . without turning as they went. . . . And the living creatures darted to and fro, like a flash of lightning.

Who were these humanoid "occupants"? Space-helmeted, space-suited astronauts with a strapped-on flying device? Or, perhaps, extraterrestrial flying robots? The account goes on:

> Now as I looked at the living creatures, I saw a wheel upon the earth beside the living creatures, one for each of the four of them. As for the

appearance of the wheels and their construction: their appearance was like the gleaming of a chrysolite . . . being as it were a wheel within a wheel. . . . The four wheels had rims and they had spokes; and their rims were full of eyes round about. And when the living creatures went, the wheels went beside them; and when the living creatures rose from the earth, the wheels rose.

Were these humanoids going back and forth into a green-glowing spacecraft surrounded by a ring of portholes? But there is more:

> . . . there was the likeness of a throne, in appearance like sapphire; and seated above the likeness of a throne was a likeness as it were of a human form. And upward from . . . his loins I saw as it were gleaming bronze, . . . and there was brightness. . . . Like the appearance of the bow that is in the cloud on the day of rain, so was the appearance of the brightness round about. . . . And when I saw it . . . I heard the voice of one speaking.

Ezekiel is told that the Israelites have transgressed and are to be punished unless they obey the Lord's commandments. Ezekiel is selected as the messenger to his people and is taken on board ("the Spirit lifted me up"). The spacecraft takes off ("I heard . . . the sound of the wheels . . . that sounded like a great earthquake"), and Ezekiel is carried to Tel-abib where his fellow exiles are and where he sits "overwhelmed among them seven days," traumatized by his experience. (Ezekiel 1–3) (As we shall see from contemporary UFO encounters, this could be interpreted as an almost classic report of the abduction and return of humans.)

The Roman author Julius Obsequens, believed to have lived in the fourth century A.D., drew on Livy as well as other sources of his time to compile his book *Prodigiorum liber*, which describes many peculiar phenomena, some of which could be interpreted as UFO sightings. Here are just a few examples:

> [216 B.C.] Things like ships were seen in the sky over Italy. . . . At Arpi (180 Roman miles, east of Rome, in Apulia) a *round shield* was seen in the sky. . . . At Capua, the sky was all on fire, and one saw figures like ships. . . .
> [99 B.C.] When C. Murius and L. Valerius were consuls, in Tarquinia, there fell in different places . . . a thing like a flaming torch, and it came suddenly from the sky. Towards sunset, a round object like a globe, or round or circular shield took its path in the sky, from west to east.
> [90 B.C.] In the territory of Spoletium (65 Roman miles north of Rome, in Umbria) a globe of fire, of golden colour, fell to the earth, gyrating. It then seemed to increase in size, rose from the earth, and ascended into the sky, where it obscured the disc of

the sun, with its brilliance. It revolved towards the eastern quadrant of the sky. [Harold T. Wilkins, *Flying Saucers on the Attack*, pp.164–69]

A later chronicler of inexplicable phenomena, one Conrad Wolffhart (a professor of grammar and dialectics who under the pen name of Lycosthenes wrote the compendium *Prodigiorum ac Ostentorum Chronicon*, published in 1567), mentions the following events:

[A.D. 393] Strange lights were seen in the sky in the days of the Emperor Theodosius. On a sudden, a bright globe appeared at midnight. It shone brilliantly near the day star (planet, Venus), about the circle of the zodiac. This globe shone little less brilliantly than the planet, and, little by little, a great number of other glowing orbs drew near the first globe. The spectacle was like a swarm of bees flying round the bee-keeper, and the light of these orbs was as if they were dashing violently against each other. Soon, they blended together into one awful flame, and bodied forth to the eye as a horrible two-edged sword. The strange globe which was first seen now appeared like the pommel to a handle, and all the little orbs, fused with the first, shone as brilliantly as the first globe. [This report is similar to modern accounts of UFO formations.] [Harold T. Wilkins, *Flying Saucers on the Attack*, pp.174, 177]

A rare typeset book from 1493, now preserved in a museum at Verdun, France, contains what may be the earliest pictorial representation of a UFO in Europe. Hartmann Schedel, author of the book *Liber Chronicarum*, describes a strange fiery sphere—seen in 1034—soaring through the sky in a straight course from south to east and then veering toward the setting sun. The illustration accompanying the account shows a cigar-shaped form haloed by flames, sailing through a blue sky over a green, rolling countryside. (Jacques Vallee, *UFO's in Space: Anatomy of a Phenomenon*, p.9)

A term equivalent to our "flying saucer" was actually used by the Japanese approximately 700 years before it came into use in the West. Ancient documents describe an unusual shining object seen the night of October 27, 1180, as a flying "earthenware vessel." After a while the object, which had been heading northeast from a mountain in Kii province, changed its direction and vanished below the horizon, leaving a luminous trail. (Jacques Vallee, *Passport to Magonia*, pp.4–5)

Here is a classical description from *William of Newburgh's Chronicle* of a flying saucer seen in England toward the end of the 12th century:

At Byland, or Begeland Abbey (the largest Cistercian abbey in England), in the North Yorkshire Riding, while the abbot and monks were in the refectory, a flat, round, shining, silvery object ["discus" is the word used in the Latin account] flew over the abbey and caused the utmost terror. [Harold T. Wilkins, *Flying Saucers on the Attack*, p.185]

What might be called the first official investigation of a UFO sighting occurred in Japan in 1235. During the night of September 24, while General Yoritsume and his army were encamped, they observed mysterious lights in the heavens. The lights were seen in the southwest for many hours, swinging, circling, and moving in loops. The general ordered a "full-scale scientific investigation" of these strange events. The report finally submitted to him has the "soothing" ring of many contemporary explanations offered for UFO phenomena. In essence it read: "the whole thing is completely natural, General. It is ... only the wind making the stars sway." (Jacques Vallee, *Passport to Magonia*, p.5)

Many unusual celestial events were recorded in Japanese chronicles during the Middle Ages. As in Western society, such occurrences were usually considered "portents," often resulting in panics and other social disturbances. Here are some examples:

... on September 12, 1271, the famous priest Nichiren was about to be beheaded at Tatsunokuchi, Kamakura, when there appeared in the sky an object like a full moon, shiny and bright. Needless to say, the officials panicked and the execution was not carried out.

In 1361, a flying object described as being "shaped like a drum, about twenty feet in diameter" emerged from the inland sea off western Japan....

... on March 8, 1468, a dark object, which made a "sound like a wheel," flew from Mt. Kasuga toward the west at midnight. [Jacques Vallee, *Passport to Magonia*, pp.5–6]

The European record of possible UFO sightings continued throughout the 14th and 15th centuries:

[A.D. 1322] In the first hour of the night of Novr. 4 ... there was seen in the sky over Uxbridge, England, a pile (pillar) of fire the size of a small boat, pallid and livid in colour. It rose from the south, crossed the sky with a *slow and grave motion*, and went north. Out of the front of the pile, a fervent red flame burst forth with great beams of light. Its speed increased, and it flew thro' the air....
[A.D. 1387] In Novr. and Decr. of this year, a fire in the sky, like a burning and revolving wheel, or round barrel of flame, emitting fire from above, and others in the shape of a long fiery beam, were seen through a great deal of the winter, in the county of Leicester, Eng., and in Northamptonshire.
[A.D. 1461] On November 1, a fiery thing like an

The clouds in this part of Pierro della Francesca's 15th-century fresco "The Legend of the True Cross" may simply be lenticular formations but have been interpreted as UFO's.

iron rod of good length and as large as one half of the moon was seen in the sky, over . . . Arras, France for less than a quarter of an hour. This object was also described as being "shaped like a ship, from which fire was seen flowing." [Jacques Vallee, *UFO's in Space: Anatomy of a Phenomenon,* p.9; Harold T. Wilkins, *Flying Saucers on the Attack,* pp.187, 188]

The following description from 1733 is another almost classical account of one of those gleaming, silvery bodies today referred to as flying saucers:

> Something in the sky which appeared in the north, but vanished from my sight, as it was intercepted by trees, from my vision. I was standing in a valley. The weather was warm, the sun shone brightly. On a sudden it re-appeared, darting in and out of my sight with an amazing coruscation. The colour of this phenomenon was like burnished, or new washed silver. It shot with speed like a star falling in the night. But it had a body much larger and a train longer than any shooting star I have seen. . . . Next day, Mr. Edgecombe informed me that he and another gentleman had seen this strange phenomenon at the same time as I had. It was about 15 miles from where I saw it, and steering a course from E. to N.

The witness of this event was a Mr. Cracker of Fleet, a small township in Dorset, England. Mr. Cracker said that he saw his "flying saucer" in broad daylight on December 8, 1733. (*Fate,* April 1951, p.24)

A fellow of the Royal Society in London was about to cross St. James's Park on his way home from a meeting on December 16, 1742, when he was startled by the appearance of a remarkable celestial object:

> . . . a light arose from behind the trees and houses, to the south and west, which at first I thought was a rocket, of large size. But when it rose 20 degrees, it moved parallel to the horizon, and waved like this —he draws an undulating line—and went on in the direction of north by east. It seemed very near. *Its motion was very slow.* I had it for about half a mile in view. A light flame was turned backward by the resistance the air made to it. From one end, it emitted a bright glare and fire like that of burning charcoal. That end was a frame like bars of iron, and quite opaque to my sight. At one point, on the longitudinal frame, or cylinder, issued a train in the shape of a tail of light more bright at one point on the rod or cylinder, and growing gradually fainter at the end of the rod or cylinder; so that it was transparent for more than half of its length. The head of this strange object seemed about half a degree in diameter, and the tail near three degrees in length.

The observer signed himself "C. M.," probably preferring to remain anonymous to avoid the expected skepticism and scoffing of his fellow members. (Harold T. Wilkins, *Flying Saucers on the Attack,* p.206)

This account of a most unusual sighting was reported by Monsieur de Rostan, an amateur astronomer and member of the medicophysical society of Basel, Switzerland. On August 9, 1762, at Lausanne, Switzerland, he observed through a telescope a spindle-shaped object crossing and eclipsing the sun. Monsieur de Rostan was able to observe this object almost daily for close to a month. He also managed to trace its outline with a camera obscura and sent the picture to the Royal Academy of Sciences in Paris. Unfortunately, this image—probably the first one ever obtained of a UFO—no longer exists.

A friend of Monsieur de Rostan, living at Sole near Basel, also observed the spindle-shaped object against the sun, but it seemed to present more of an edge and was not quite as broad. Oddly enough, the UFO was not visible to a third astronomer, a Monsieur Messier who studied the sun, during the same time, from Paris—an indication that the object was not a sunspot, since it was visible only from certain angles. (Harold T. Wilkins, *Flying Saucers on the Attack,* pp.211–12)

The last year of the 18th century had its share of celestial phenomena. An issue of *Gentleman's Magazine* contained the following story:

> On Sep. 19 [1799], all England saw, at 8:30 P.M., a beautiful ball blazing with white light, and which passed from N.W. to S.E. It moved rapidly with a gentle tremulous motion, and noiselessly. The light cast by it was very vivid, and a few red sparks detached themselves from it.... On Nov. 12, something like a large red pillar of fire passed north to south over Hereford, and alarmed people in the Forest of Dean, some miles away. Flashes of extremely vivid electrical sort preceded its appearance, and at intervals of half an hour, several hours before. This was at 5:45 A.M. ... On this night, the moon shone with uncommon vividness, when between 5 and 6 A.M., bright lights in the sky became stationary. They then burst with no perceptible report, and passed north leaving behind them beautiful trains of floating fire. Some were pointed, some radiated. Some sparkled and some had large columns.... Nov. 19, at 6 A.M., folk of Huncoates, Lincolnshire, were alarmed by vivid flashes lasting 30 seconds, from a ball of fire passing in the sky. [Harold T. Wilkins, *Flying Saucers on the Attack*, p.211]

FROM 1800 TO 1948

With the beginning of the 19th century, reports of UFO's proliferated in the scientific publications of several Western countries. Here is an account from one journal of the sciences and the arts, written by John Staveley of Hatton Garden, London, after observing what he quite naturally assumed were meteors during a thunderstorm on August 10, 1809:

> I saw many meteors moving around the edge of a black cloud from which lightning flashed. They were like dazzling specks of lights, dancing and traipsing thro' the clouds. One increased in size till it became of the brilliancy and magnitude of Venus, on a clear evening; but I could see no body in the light. It moved with great rapidity, and coasted the edge of the cloud. Then it became stationary, dimmed its splendour, and vanished. *I saw these strange lights for minutes, not seconds.* For at least an hour, these lights, so strange, and in innumerable points, played in and out of this black cloud. No lightning came from the clouds where these lights played. As the meteors increased in size, they seemed to descend. [Harold T. Wilkins, *Flying Saucers on the Attack*, p.215]

At Embrun, France, on September 7, 1820, a most puzzling celestial event, a formation of moving objects, was observed by numerous witnesses, as follows:

> ... during an eclipse of the moon, strange objects [were seen] moving in straight lines. They were equally spaced and remained in line when they made turns. Their movements showed a military precision. [Jacques Vallee, *UFO's in Space: Anatomy of a Phenomenon*, p.11]

On March 22, 1870, the British vessel *Lady of the Lake* was off the coast of Río de Oro, northwest Africa, when Capt. F. W. Banner beheld a most remarkable object in the sky. Called by his crew to take a look at it, he observed "a 'cloud' of circular form, with an included semi-circle divided into four parts, and a central shaft running from the centre of the circle and extending far outward and curving backward...."

What convinced everyone that the phenomenon was not a "cloud" was the fact that it was *travelling against the wind.* It approached from the south and "settled right into the wind's eye." Captain Banner watched this UFO for about half an hour, while it remained visible below the clouds. When it grew dark, the object could no longer be seen. The captain made a drawing of it that "looked like a half-moon with a long shaft radiating from the centre." (Harold T. Wilkins, *Flying Saucers on the Attack*, p.217)

A shape resembling an enormous trumpet, about 425 feet long, was seen swaying in the sky at Oaxaca, Mexico, on July 6, 1874. According to one report, it was visible for several minutes.

The first appearance in print of the term "saucer" was in 1878—nearly 70 years before the famous Arnold sighting (see page 215) made the term almost synonymous with an unidentified flying object. On January 24 of that year John Martin, a Texas farmer who lived just south of Denison, saw a dark, disk-shaped object sailing high in the heavens "at a wonderful speed." When relating what he saw, he described the thing as a "saucer." The story was published the next day in the *Denison Daily Herald.* (Jacques Vallee, *UFO's in Space: Anatomy of a Phenomenon*, p.1)

Two "giant luminous wheels" estimated as about 130 feet in diameter were observed spinning above the surface and then slowly descending into the waters of the Persian Gulf by the crew of the ship *Vulture* on May

15, 1879. In May of the following year a British East India Company steamer, the *Patna*, sighted "wheels" of a similar sort and in the same part of the ocean. In the latter case a phosphorescent glint was seen in the waters surrounding these whirling objects.

A number of years later several other such reports added to this mystery. A huge rotating wheel was observed in the Persian Gulf by the S.S. *Kilwa* at 8:30 P.M. on April 10, 1901. In 1906 a giant wheel was reported by a British steamer in the Gulf of Oman, and in 1909 a similar sighting was made by a Danish captain in the China Sea. According to the captain, the wheel, which rotated on and just below the surface of the water, was illuminated and had a hub. Finally, still another wheel—appearing as a horizontal disk of light over the water—was observed in August 1910 in the South China Sea by the Dutch steamer *Valentijn*.

These semiaquatic spinning wheels have been thought by some to originate in the oceans or possibly to be submersible spacecraft. (Jacques Vallee, *UFO's in Space: Anatomy of a Phenomenon*, p.13; Harold T. Wilkins, *Flying Saucers on the Attack*, p.221)

The spot at the top left of this photograph of the sun, taken by José Bonilla, director of Mexico's Zacatecas Observatory, is but one of hundreds of such images recorded on his film.

In 1906 the crew of a British steamer saw a huge illuminated wheel, seemingly larger than their ship, spinning just above the waters of the Persian Gulf near Oman.

On the morning of August 12, 1883, Senor José A. Y. Bonilla, director of the Zacatecas Observatory in Mexico, was making a study of sunspots when, to his amazement, he noticed a small luminous body crossing the solar disk. No sooner had he taken a photograph of this object than he was startled to see a whole succession of these singular bodies, in ones and twos or in groups of 15 to 20 and separated by short intervals, crossing the sun in the same direction. In the course of two hours he

counted 283 bodies, most of which he photographed. The majority of them appeared dark or black when seen against the brightness of the sun, but according to Senor Bonilla they threw out "brilliant trains of light" as they crossed the solar disk. The next day, from 8 A.M. to 9:45 A.M., he saw another 116 of these UFO's crossing his field of vision as he faced the sun. Senor Bonilla contacted other observatories in Mexico, but none of them saw the mysterious bodies.

Some members of the scientific community of the time interpreted these moving objects as insects, birds, or dust in the upper atmosphere, but this is not a very likely explanation. Bonilla remained convinced that these mysterious bodies were "*travelling in space near the earth* but not so far as the moon." (Harold T. Wilkins, *Flying Saucers on the Attack*, pp.218-19)

In 1896 and 1897 dozens of reports of strange flying lights and cigar- or barrel-shaped "airships" appeared in U.S. and Canadian newspapers. The dates of these remarkably consistent UFO reports precede by several years any documented flights of airplanes.

Beginning in November 1896, UFO's were being sighted chiefly in California but also in Washington state and Canada. One night at Tulare, California, hundreds of witnesses saw something descend and then rise and abruptly veer to the west. Whatever it was emitted red, white, and blue lights.

By January 1897 the California sightings ended, but by mid-February of that year reports of unknown craft and mysterious lights in the night skies issued from many parts of Nebraska. By March, sightings were made in neighboring Kansas and in Michigan. And in April, 10,000 residents of Kansas City, Missouri, watched a great black airship hovering in the sky. "Object appeared very swiftly, then appeared to stop and hover over the city for ten minutes at a time, then after flashing green-blue and white lights, shot upwards into space," reported the *Chicago Record* of April 2, 1897. People in Everest, Kansas, described the object as resembling a 25- to 30-foot-long Indian canoe with "a searchlight of varying colors."

Descriptions of the "airships" were within the general framework of "cigar-shaped" and "metallic" but varied as to the kinds of appendages seemingly attached to the body: wings, propellers, and fins were all described by different witnesses. Both daytime and nighttime sightings were reported, and in the case of the latter, brilliant lights were seen.

Reports of sightings continued through May 1897 and came from almost every state of the Union east of the Rockies, with a concentration in the Midwest. (*The Encyclopedia of UFOs*, Ronald D. Story, ed., pp.8-11)

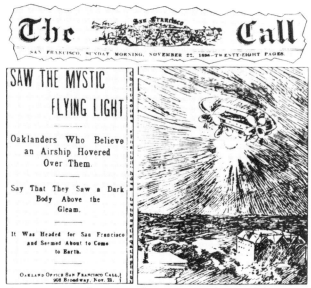

A great wave of UFO sightings occurred in California in the late 1800's. This story and illustration appeared in a San Francisco newspaper on November 22, 1896.

Another wave of "airships" was reported from New Zealand during 1909. For six weeks, from late July to early September, hundreds of people observed cigar-shaped airships over North Island and South Island. Sightings occurred in daytime and nighttime.

The early 20th century was a time of experimental aircraft. The dirigible balloons being built by Graf Ferdinand von Zeppelin in Germany were still in an early stage of development, and so were the balloons being tested in France. These craft could not possibly have found their way to New Zealand. Thus the 1909 reports of "airships" from that part of the world remain as much in the realm of the unexplained as the 1896 and

1897 U.S. sightings. (Brinsley Le Poer Trench, *The Flying Saucer Story*, pp.73-74)

In his travel diary of 1926 Nicholas Roerich, a well-known artist and explorer, told of a strange sighting in northern China:

On August 5th—something remarkable! We were in our camp in the Kukunor district not far from the Humboldt Chain. In the morning about half-past nine some of our caravaneers noticed a remarkably big black eagle flying above us. Seven of us began to watch this unusual bird. At this same moment another of our caravaneers remarked, "There is something far above the bird." And he shouted in his astonishment. We all saw, in a direction from north to south, something big and shiny reflecting the sun, like a huge oval moving at great speed. Crossing our camp this thing changed in its direction from south to southwest. And we saw how it disappeared in the intense blue sky. We even had time to take our field glasses and saw quite distinctly an oval form with shiny surface, one side of which was brilliant from the sun. [Nicholas Roerich, *Altai-Himalaya: A Travel Diary*, pp.361-62]

Nicholas Roerich was a Russian landscape painter and archeologist who traveled widely in India and Asia from 1923 until 1928. New York City's Roerich Museum houses several hundred of his paintings.

Sir Francis Chichester, a yachtsman and a pilot who became world famous for his courageous solo crossings of sea and sky in the late 1920's and the 1930's, described his encounter with a UFO while trying to get his bearings after a storm on June 10, 1931. He was alone in his Gypsy Moth airplane somewhere over the Tasman Sea, having taken off from Lord Howe Island several hours previously on a long flight between New Zealand and Australia:

Suddenly, ahead and thirty degrees to the left, there were bright flashes in several places, like the dazzle of a heliograph. I saw a dull grey-white airship coming towards me. It seemed impossible, but I could have sworn that it *was* an airship, nosing toward me like an oblong pearl. Except for a cloud or two, there was nothing else in the sky. I looked around, sometimes

catching a flash or a glint, and turning again to look at the airship I found that it had disappeared. I screwed up my eyes, unable to believe them, and twisted the seaplane this way and that, thinking that the airship must be hidden by a blind spot. Dazzling flashes continued in four or five different places, but I still could not pick out any planes. Then, out of some clouds to my right front, I saw another, or the same, airship advancing. I watched it intently, determined not to look away for a fraction of a second: I'd see what happened to this one, if I had to chase it. It drew steadily closer, until perhaps a mile away, when suddenly it vanished. Then it reappeared, close to where it had vanished: I watched with angry intentness. It drew closer, and I could see the dull gleam of light on its nose and back. It came on, but instead of increasing in size, it diminished as it approached. When quite near, it suddenly became its own ghost—one second I could see through it, and the next it had vanished. I decided it could only be a diminutive cloud, perfectly shaped like an airship and then dissolving, but it was uncanny that it should exactly resume the same shape after it had once vanished. I turned towards the flashes, but these too, had vanished. All this was many years before anyone spoke of flying saucers. Whatever it was I saw, it seems to have been very much like what people have since claimed to be flying saucers. [Francis Chichester, *The Lonely Sea and the Sky*, p.165]

"Ghost Rockets" were seen over the northern regions of Europe in 1946. The occurrences were first recognized officially on February 26, when the Helsinki radio announced "inordinate meteor activity" in northern Finland near the Arctic Circle. More and more reports streamed in, describing an object "spewing a trail of smoke" and leaving a luminous afterglow as it raced through the night sky over Helsinki at an altitude of 1,000 feet; "an unidentified luminous body giving off glowing vapor [that] had approached the Finnish coast from . . . the Baltic, only to turn sharply and retrace its course"; and flying objects presumed to be bolides (a kind of meteorite) that "appear and disappear, vanishing into the deepness of space with an infernal roaring."

Others were seen flying horizontally, diving, climbing, barrel-rolling, and backtracking, sometimes cross-

The Mysterious Foo-Fighters

On November 23, 1944, crew members of a B-29 bomber on a nighttime mission over Germany saw some distant starlike points that became more clearly visible as 10 or so balls of light, changing from orange to red as they approached the plane. This was the first of many reports of the mysterious fireballs that appeared over Germany toward the end of World War II. The following report (given in Harold T. Wilkins's book, *Flying Saucers on the Attack*) describes how the lights appeared one night to pilot Lt. David McFalls:

> At 0600 hours [6 A.M.] near Hagenau, at 10,000 feet altitude, two very bright lights climbed towards us from the ground. They levelled off and stayed on the tail of our 'plane. They were huge, bright orange lights. They stayed there for two minutes. . . . They *were under perfect control.* Then they turned away from us, and the fire seemed to go out.

Similar reports began to come from Germany and then from the Pacific theater of war as well. The objects were always a glowing ball of orange, red, or white light, seemingly under intelligent control, that followed an aircraft for a while, then turned away and disappeared from view.

After the war it was found that the Japanese pilots also encountered the phenomenon and assumed that it was some secret American or Russian device used, perhaps, to baffle radar. By the same token, U.S. intelligence supposed that they were of German make. Their true nature has never been determined.

"Where there's foo, there's fire," a favorite expression of comic strip character Smokey Stover, not only provided the name for these objects but gave as good an explanation as any concerning their source.

ing the sky at great speeds and sometimes moving in a "leisurely" fashion. Both round and elongated objects were reported—those referred to as a "luminous body," "shining ball," "huge soap bubble," or "rotating object emitting sparks"; and those described as being "football shaped," "cigar shaped," "missilelike," "elliptical," and "like a squash racket."

By July 1946 Sweden was experiencing a wave of mysterious missilelike lights that the newspapers soon began to call ghost rockets. Hundreds of these strange objects were reported over the skies of southern Sweden.

The aerial phenomenon shifted southward, as the year progressed, eventually reaching Tangier, Italy, Greece, and even India by September. But of all the nations affected, Sweden, with as many as 1,000 sightings, was the most concerned. The Swedish government suspected Soviet interference of some kind, and the country's armed forces were put on alert. There was never any solid evidence of damage or bombardment, however, and searches conducted after reported explosions of "ghost rockets" revealed only hard-to-identify fragments of dark-colored, slaglike material or in some cases nothing at all.

The sightings tapered off in autumn. In a final military communiqué released October 10, 1946, the Swedish government stated that, although most accounts of sightings were vague, many reports were "clear unambiguous observations," and something definite had registered on different instruments. It was concluded that 20 percent of the ghost-rocket reports could not be explained either as known aircraft or as natural phenomena. That is to say, they were unidentified flying objects.

In 1948 the London *Times* published a report that ghost rockets were again traversing the skies of several Scandinavian countries. Norwegian airline pilots reported missilelike objects that emitted bluish-green flames and flew as fast as 6,700 mph at altitudes ranging from 25,000 feet down to the level of treetops.

Ghost-rocket UFO's are still being reported sporadically around the world and remain as mysterious as they were in 1946. (*The Encyclopedia of UFOs*, Ronald D. Story, ed., pp.147–49; Jacques Vallee, *UFO's in Space: Anatomy of a Phenomenon*, p.47)

A classic case in the history of UFO's is the Kenneth Arnold sighting of June 24, 1947, which finally caused the U.S. Air Force to take official notice of the phenomena. Arnold, a civilian pilot and the owner of a fire-control equipment company in Boise, Idaho, took off from the Chehalis (Washington) airport at 2 P.M. in his own single-engine plane to search for a Marine C-46 transport that had crashed somewhere in the Cascade mountain range.

It was a beautiful, sunny afternoon with excellent visibility. Arnold had been aloft for about an hour in the vicinity of Mount Rainier and had started to make a wide turn when a brilliant light suddenly flashed on the side of his plane. He looked around but saw nothing except for a DC-4 much too far away to his left and rear to have been the source. The flash suddenly occurred again, and this time Arnold was able to trace it. To his amazement, he saw nine gleaming objects coming south from the direction of Mount Baker, swerving around the highest peaks and flying in echelon formation with two parallel rows of four and five "craft" respectively. As they flew by, Arnold happened to be in a good position to triangulate their speed between Mount Rainier and Mount Adams, 45 miles to the south. His calculations indicated an astonishing

To Kenneth Arnold the objects he reported looked much like these shown on the cover of his book, The Coming of the Saucers. *He saw them, however, from a great distance.*

velocity of about 1,600 mph, nearly three times as fast as the capability of any aircraft of those days.

Arnold described the objects as being "flat like a pie pan and so shiny they reflected the sun like a mirror." Their motion was also strange, comparable to that of "speedboats on rough water" and flying "like a saucer would if you skipped it across the water," he said. They were within view for about three minutes.

An interesting postscript was provided on July 4, only 10 days after the Arnold sighting: Capt. E. J. Smith of United Airlines and his copilot, Ralph Stevens, had just taken off from the Boise, Idaho, airport when they saw a formation of five similar objects. After a minute or so, the five "saucers" took off at an astounding speed and four more appeared. Was this perhaps *the same group of UFO's* Kenneth Arnold had observed in Washington a few days earlier? (*The Encyclopedia of UFOs*, Ronald D. Story, ed., p.25; Brinsley Le Poer Trench, *The Flying Saucer Story*, pp.23–24; Jacques Vallee, *UFO's in Space: Anatomy of a Phenomenon*, p.55)

Investigating UFO's

The history of the official documentation of UFO's began in 1948 when the U.S. Air Force created Project Sign. The following year this was reorganized into Project Grudge, and then into Project Blue Book.

The purpose of Project Blue Book was to investigate and evaluate UFO reports within the United States and at its stations and properties in other countries with regard to any potential threat to national security, whether from foreign powers or from outer space. Critics claimed that the project lacked a scientifically qualified staff and that it was simply a "cover-up" operation meant to reassure an alarmed public.

Project Blue Book proved to be quite effective, however. During its 18 years of activity it accumulated more than 12,600 reported cases in its files, almost all of which were eventually explained as mistaken natural phenomena or as known aircraft. But 701 sightings remained classified as "unidentified."

In 1966 the U.S. Air Force sponsored an independent, stepped-up investigation of UFO's by a team of scientists from the University of Colorado under the direction of Dr. Edward U. Condon, a prominent physicist and former head of the American Association for the Advancement of Science. Of the 59 cases they selected for serious investigation during the next two years, 23 eluded explanation. In his final report, in 1969, Condon nevertheless concluded that a total of 21 years of UFO study had added nothing to scientific knowledge and that "further extensive study" probably was not warranted. He also stated that "it is safe to assume that no ILE [intelligent life elsewhere] outside of our solar system has any possibility of visiting Earth in the next 10,000 years." To date, no one has determined the basis for Condon's estimate.

Following publication of the Condon report, the U.S. Air Force agreed that UFO's posed no threat to national security and that there was no evidence the sighted objects were of extraterrestrial origin. Project Blue Book was then terminated, and all of its files were declassified. But the fact that some other documents on UFO's remained classified prompted a few private UFO investigative groups to press for their release on the ground that the public is entitled to know all.

Even today many UFO buffs believe that the real investigation of UFO's was—and is—being secretly conducted by high-level government personnel. But at this time only private organizations are involved in serious UFO research. Among the membership groups the best known are the Mutual UFO Network (MUFON), founded in 1969; the National Investigations Committee on Aerial Phenomena (NICAP), founded in 1956 in Washington, D.C.; and the Aerial Phenomena Research Organization (APRO), founded in 1952 by Jim and Coral Lorenzen. A highly regarded nonmembership organization is the Center for UFO Studies (CUFOS), founded in 1973 by astronomer Dr. J. Allen Hynek, who for years was the scientific consultant to Project Blue Book. By 1982 CUFOS had amassed a computerized list of 70,000 reported sightings from all over the world. It was found that about 80 percent of these were easily explained and dismissed; the other 20 percent remain subject to further investigation.

Other countries, notably France, Britain, and Australia, also have civilian organizations that collect and seriously investigate UFO reports. Although awareness of the phenomenon is kept alive solely by private enterprise, reports of unidentified flying objects from all over the world continue to accumulate and further compound the most elusive mystery of our time.

SINCE 1948

The modern age of flying saucers began with the Arnold sighting. Although it was by no means an isolated incident in 1947, it was the most extraordinary. Arnold's story, soon transmitted worldwide by the radio and the press, prompted the U.S. Air Force to begin its investigation of UFO reports.

To facilitate the study, Dr. J. Allen Hynek, the astronomer who for 20 years was to serve as consultant for the U.S. Air Force on Projects Sign and Blue Book, divided the many reports of UFO's into categories.

The first major category included sightings of UFO's at a distance of more than 500 feet. These were subdivided into three kinds: *Nocturnal Lights*—well-defined lights that cannot be explained in terms of conventional light sources; *Daylight Disks*—oval or saucerlike metallic-appearing objects; and *Radar Visuals*—unidentified blips on radar screens that confirm simultaneous visual sightings.

The second major category, for sightings from a distance of less than 500 feet, was broken down as follows: *Close Encounters of the First Kind*—those in which there is no interaction between the UFO and the environment; *Close Encounters of the Second Kind*—those manifesting some interaction, such as interference with car ignition systems, burns on the ground, and physical effects upon animals or humans; and *Close Encounters of*

Dr. J. Allen Hynek, formerly an astronomer at Northwestern University, became involved with UFO's as a consultant to the air force's Project Blue Book. He began as a skeptic but found that about 20 percent of the sightings were unidentified.

the Third Kind—those in which UFO occupants from outer space are reportedly seen.

In recent years UFO witnesses have described personal contact with the occupants, and even temporary detainment. These cases are often referred to as *Close Encounters of the Fourth Kind.*

The following accounts, chosen for interest and credibility, are arranged by category and are but a fraction of literally thousands of UFO reports stemming from every part of the globe over the last 35 years.

NOCTURNAL LIGHTS

The Gorman "dogfight" as it is called, which for 27 minutes involved Lt. George F. Gorman of the North Dakota Air National Guard and a UFO over Fargo, North Dakota, on the night of October 1, 1948, is one of the early classics of the genre.

Gorman, who had been on a cross-country flight with his squadron, had decided to stay up after the other planes had landed and log some more night-flying time. At about 9 P.M. he was preparing to land when the control tower informed him of another craft—a Piper Cub—in the vicinity. Gorman could see this plane clearly below him, but then what appeared to be the taillight of another plane flashed by him on the right. When the tower informed him that they knew of no other plane in the vicinity, Gorman decided to investigate. He pulled his F-51 up and toward the moving light. When he was within about 1,000 yards of it, he could see the object clearly:

> It was about six to eight inches in diameter, clear white, and completely round without fuzz at the edges. It was blinking on and off. As I approached, however, the light suddenly became steady and pulled into a sharp left bank. I thought it was making a pass at the tower.
>
> I dived after it and brought my manifold pressure up to sixty inches but I couldn't catch up with the thing. It started gaining altitude and again made a left bank. I put my F-51 into a sharp turn and tried to cut the light off in its turn. By then we were at about 7000 feet. Suddenly it made a sharp right turn

and we headed straight at each other. Just when we were about to collide, I guess I got scared. I went into a dive and the light passed over my canopy at about 500 feet. Then, it made a left circle about 1000 feet above, and I gave chase again.

Gorman cut sharply toward the light, which again was coming straight at him. Just when collision seemed unavoidable, the UFO streaked straight up in a steep climb and disappeared. When Gorman tried to pursue the object, his plane went into a power stall at about 14,000 feet, and he did not see the object again. The total chase had lasted from 9 P.M. to 9:27 P.M.

Gorman was so distraught by his encounter that he had trouble landing his plane. He said he had noticed no sound, odor, or exhaust trail from the UFO and no deviation on his instruments.

Corroboration of the incident was provided by the two traffic controllers on duty, Lloyd D. Jensen and H. E. Johnson, who saw the strange light at the same time they saw the Piper Cub. They described it in very much the same terms as Gorman—"a round light, perfectly formed, with no fuzzy edges or rays leaving its body"—and they noted its apparent high rate of speed. Two further witnesses, the pilot of the Piper Cub and his passenger, not only saw the swiftly moving light while in radio communication with the tower, but after landing they also observed the object and Gorman's plane in pursuit.

Gorman stated that he was convinced that the UFO demonstrated "thought" in its maneuvers and that he was chasing an extraordinary "guided" craft of some kind. No satisfactory conventional explantion for the Gorman "dogfight" has ever been offered. (*The Encyclopedia of UFOs*, Ronald D. Story, ed., pp.151–52)

A whole series of nocturnal lights, some of them having the general outlines of wing-shaped "craft," was reported in and around Lubbock, Texas, in 1951, during the months of August and September. Hundreds of people saw the lights and one man photographed them; they were also tracked on radar.

The first sighting was made over Albuquerque, New Mexico, on the evening of August 25, 1951. An employee of the Atomic Energy Commission and his wife reported watching a huge "wing-shaped" UFO, with bluish lights on the rear edge, pass overhead. The UFO was only 800 to 1,000 feet up, they said. They could see that the "wing" was sharply swept back and was about 1½ times the size of a B-36. Dark bands ran from the front to the back, and the "wing lights" were a softly glowing blue-green.

On the evening of the New Mexico sighting, but somewhat later, several college professors sitting on a porch in Lubbock, Texas, saw a roughly semicircular

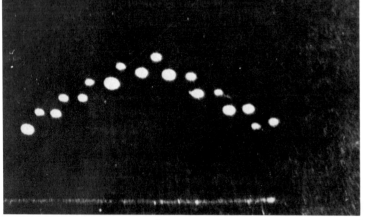

This photograph of the Lubbock "lights" was taken by Carl Hart, Jr., in August 1951. Air force investigators studied the sightings but could never provide a satisfactory explanation.

formation of lights sweep rapidly overhead. After several hours, the lights reappeared and were observed to be softly glowing bluish objects moving in a more open formation than the first time. That same night a woman in Lubbock also saw what she called a giant "winglike" craft with bluish lights on the back moving silently over her house. This report was only minutes after the sighting in Albuquerque, about which the woman could not possibly have known.

During the next two weeks in Lubbock the fast-moving night lights were seen on several occasions. Observers agreed that the "flights" always appeared about 45 degrees above the northern horizon, traveled through 90 degrees of sky often in just over three seconds, and disappeared about 45 degrees above the southern horizon. Among the viewers was a Dr. George, a physics professor who had made extensive studies of the atmosphere and, along with the other professors, could not arrive at a scientific explanation of what they had all seen.

What were probably the same lights were photographed by an amateur photographer named Carl Hart, Jr., on the evening of August 31. One of his photographs, showing a series of bright disklike objects in a roughly V-shaped formation against the night sky, appeared in a local newspaper.

The air force made a thorough investigation of the Lubbock "lights" but could never arrive at a satisfactory explanation. The Hart negatives proved to be genuine, and dozens of witnesses confirmed sightings of soft, bluish lights zipping from one horizon to the other. Sometimes the objects—reportedly from three to several dozen in number—were in precise V-formation, but other times they appeared in more random arrangements. Such "natural" causes as reflections from newly installed mercury-vapor street lamps or reflections from the glistening white chests of flying birds (plovers) were suggested to explain the lights, but these hardly seemed likely to those who observed them. (*The Encyclopedia of UFOs,* Ronald D. Story, ed., pp.215–18)

The *Centaurus* incident of 1954 is one of the best examples of a fairly typical kind of UFO sighting. It occurred over Labrador on the night of June 29. The observations were made by Capt. James Howard and his crew on board a BOAC *Centaurus* (a Boeing Stratocruiser) on its way to London from Idlewild (Kennedy) Airport, New York.

At 9:05 P.M. Labrador time the captain and his copilot, First Officer Lee Boyd, sighted UFO's. They observed that there was one big lighted object with six smaller ones in attendance. The objects, about five miles away, were flying parallel to the *Centaurus*. These UFO's stayed with the *Centaurus* for 18 minutes and a distance of 80 miles. The big object would change its shape—or perhaps only appeared to do so because of an altered angle of flight—and at that time the smaller UFO's rearranged themselves around it.

After a few minutes of these startling observations, Captain Howard contacted flight personnel at Goose Bay. They replied that a fighter pilot was being sent up to investigate. By now the big UFO had changed its original inverted-pear shape to that of a flying arrow and then to what looked like "a giant telephone receiver the size of an ocean liner."

By this time all 8 members of the crew and 14 of the passengers who were awake were observing the phenomenon, when the smaller UFO's started to disappear. George Allen, the navigating officer who had been watching closely the entire time, later reported that "it looked to me as though they went inside the big one." Finally the big object departed "at tremendous speed."

Captain Howard told the arriving jet interceptor about the gradual disappearance of the UFO fleet and its accompanying "base ship." The captain later wrote in the December 11, 1954, issue of *Everybody's Weekly:* "There is no rational explanation—except on the basis

A large elongated craft accompanied by six smaller disk-shaped objects, visible in the lower-right corner, kept pace with a Boeing Stratocruiser over Labrador.

of space ships and flying saucers. On that basis it must have been some weird form of space ship from another world." He remained convinced that what he saw were solid objects, "maneuverable and controlled intelligently—a sort of base ship linked somehow with those smaller attendant satellites." (Brinsley Le Poer Trench, *The Flying Saucer Story,* pp.34–36)

A fleet of four Portuguese jet fighter-bombers under the command of Capt. Jose Louis Ferreira also had an encounter with a UFO "mother ship" and its attendant "satellites." The planes were flying at 25,000 feet between Granada, Spain, and Portalegre, Portugal, on the night of September 4, 1957, when the captain noticed an object resembling a very bright star, "unusually big and scintillating with a colored nucleus which changed color constantly, going from deep green to blue and then passing through yellowish and reddish colors of the spectrum." The other pilots also saw the object. Suddenly the UFO appeared to enlarge, growing to five or six times its original size. Then the object seemed to shrink to a barely visible yellow point. These expansions and contractions were repeated several times. Captain Ferreira thought that these changes in size might have been due to shifts in position.

The bombers now changed their line of flight, but the object maintained its position at 90 degrees to their left. The UFO was now bright red. Suddenly the pilots noticed a small circle of yellow light emerging from it. They then saw three other similar yellow objects to the right of the main UFO. After further maneuvers, the small objects began to disappear.

All the pilots agreed that what they had witnessed had no rational explanation. Speaking for everyone, Captain Ferreira stated: "After this please do not give us the old routine of Venus, balloons, aircraft and the like which has been given as a general panacea for almost every case of UFOs." (Brinsley Le Poer Trench, *The Flying Saucer Story,* pp.39–41)

The Jimmy Carter UFO sighting occurred on January 6, 1969, in Leary, Georgia, at about 7:15 P.M. The former U.S. president, who was at the time governor of Georgia, was standing outdoors waiting to address the local Lions Club, and a group of about a dozen people were with him. Here is the president's report as quoted in the *National Enquirer,* June 8, 1976:

> I am convinced that UFOs exist because I've seen one.... It was a very peculiar aberration, but about 20 people saw it.... It was the darndest thing I've ever seen. It was big; it was very bright; it changed colors; and it was about the size of the moon. We watched it for 10 minutes, but none of us could figure out what it was....

Filing a report of a UFO that he had sighted while governor of Georgia, Jimmy Carter described a round, self-luminous object that first appeared bluish, then turned reddish. The first page of the report is reproduced above.

In October 1973 Governor Carter filled out a detailed report form for the National Investigations Committee on Aerial Phenomena (NICAP). In it he estimated the object to have been about 30 degrees above the horizon, about as bright as but somewhat smaller than the moon and perhaps 300 to 1,000 yards distant. He said that it moved closer and then farther away several times before disappearing. (*The Encyclopedia of UFOs,* Ronald D. Story, ed., pp.63–65)

Tasmania experienced a wave of "nocturnal lights" from February through October 1974. The earlier sightings were from the north and northwestern part of the island, while the later sightings, from May through October, were mainly from the northeastern portion. Here are some of the more interesting reports:

In the Derwent Valley area, on February 25, Mr. M. noticed a round light in the northeastern sky about 4:20 in the morning. The glow increased in brilliance and soon the witness saw directly above his car a dazzling white light with a flat surface and an ill-defined orange ring near the outer edge. Mr. M. estimated the UFO to be 15 feet in width. The UFO "paced" his car for many miles before it disappeared.

Near Latrobe on February 27, at 9:45 P.M., Greg Thornton and his girl friend Sally Lamprey saw an orange dot in the sky move toward their car. It increased in size to about the diameter of a tennis ball and looked like "a triangle with rounded corners" at first, but then it turned on its side and "appeared as a straight orange line, like a pencil at a 45 degree angle." Another witness saw the same object a few minutes later. Judging from its apparent size and distance, he estimated it to have an actual diameter of 20 feet.

On May 25 three witnesses from Boobyalla Estate (a group of houses and stockyards) saw from their car what they first thought to be the moon but soon realized was a strange, stationary light "shaped roughly like a large banana, but fatter in the middle. It was a bright orange below, and more of a fire-red in the middle, blending to bright yellow on top. The object was only 20 feet above the ground." It began to move toward the witnesses to about 200 yards in front of them. They estimated the UFO to be approximately 100 feet long. Frightened, they left the area.

Two nights later (May 27) about a dozen residents of Boobyalla saw the same or a remarkably similar object, described this time as a banana or a half-moon on its side. All the witnesses agreed that it was low to the ground and emitted a strong glow that lit up the cattle pens. (*Flying Saucer Review*, 21:47–50, November 1975)

People in Teheran, Iran, started calling the Iranian Air Force command post at around midnight on September 19, 1976, with reports of a strange object in the sky. Descriptions ranged from "birdlike" and "bright light" to "helicopter with a shining light." B. G. Yousefit, assistant deputy commander of operations, decided to send up an F-4 jet from Shahrokhi Air Force Base to investigate and possibly intercept the UFO. This plane, however, lost all communications instrumentation about 40 miles along its intercept path. The pilot headed back and another F-4 was sent up.

As this second plane approached the UFO, radar contact was made, and the radar return was reported to be about what would be expected from a Boeing 707 aircraft. When the second F-4 reached the point at which the first jet had lost its communications, the UFO suddenly increased its speed, making it impossible for the pilot to close the distance although the F-4 was flying at a speed greater than that of sound. The pilot and other crew members noted the great brilliance of the UFO, which, they said, appeared as a rectangular pattern of flashing colored lights.

Suddenly, as the F-4 continued in its pursuit of the UFO, a smaller brilliant object, emerging from the UFO at high speed, headed directly for the pursuing F-4. The pilot was about to fire a missile at the approaching object, but his weapons-control panel went off and he also lost all communications. The pilot turned and started to dive to avoid what he assumed was a projectile from the UFO. But the small object changed course too, trailed the jet briefly, and then climbed back to rejoin the large UFO. The F-4 now renewed the chase. Suddenly a second object left the side of the UFO; it dived at great speed toward the earth and appeared to land gently in the hills far below. The large UFO now increased its speed to many times the speed of sound and disappeared. As they made a long landing approach to the base, the F-4 crew noticed a cylindrical object about the size of a jet fighter approaching from a higher altitude. There were bright lights at each end of the object and a flashing light at its center. Control tower personnel knew of no other aircraft in the area but confirmed the sighting visually. Brought to the attention of the U.S. Defense Intelligence Agency, the incident was considered exceptionally important in the study of UFO's. (*The Encyclopedia of UFOs*, Ronald D. Story, ed., pp.358–60)

DAYLIGHT DISKS

At Farmington, New Mexico, on March 18, 1950, the entire populace of some 5,000 inhabitants—including the mayor, newspapermen, and highway patrolmen—watched "hundreds of strange objects" performing aerial acrobatics in the sky for more than an hour in the late morning. Some of the objects, described as spaceships, streaked by at speeds calculated at more than 1,000 mph and participated in group "formation" flying. The UFO's disappeared before noon but were back again in the afternoon. Newspapers reported "incredible maneuverability and acute control in split-second timing by their ability to avoid collisions." (Brinsley Le Poer Trench, *The Flying Saucer Story*, p.27; Harold T. Wilkins, *Flying Saucers on the Attack*, p.128)

A strange disk-shaped object was photographed by Paul Trent on May 11, 1950, in Oregon. The two photographs are of great importance in UFOlogy because of their clarity and because of the amount of research undertaken to establish their credibility. The present consensus is that an extraordinary object of the kind described below did indeed fly within the view of Mr. and Mrs. Paul Trent.

What the Trents observed on their farm in the township of McMinnville, Oregon, was "a strange thing like a very large lid of a dustbin, with a sort of spur on the top of the curved rim over it." Mr. Trent

In 1950 Paul Trent took two of the clearest photographs of a UFO ever made (top and center). The negatives were analyzed and appeared to show no evidence of fraud. An enlargement of the UFO alone is shown at bottom left.

said the flying object was "shining like burnished silver, was noiseless, and gave off no smoke or vapour. After a few minutes, it went off to the northwest and vanished over the skyline." He saw it in the evening and estimated it to have been about 30 feet in diameter. When it first came into view, it was flying slowly but did not seem to be rotating. (*The Encyclopedia of UFOs*, Ronald D. Story, ed., pp.223–26; Harold T. Wilkins, *Flying Saucers on the Attack*, pp.131–32)

During October 1952 two remarkable and almost identical daylight sightings took place at the towns of Oloron-Ste.-Marie and Gaillac in southwestern France.

The sightings occurred within 10 days of each other, and hundreds of people witnessed both events.

On October 17, at about 12:50 P.M., Monsieur Yves Prigent, the general superintendent of the Oloron high school, was preparing to sit down to lunch with his wife and children when one child, lingering at the window, suddenly yelled out: "Oh papa, come look, it's fantastic!" The rest of the family rushed to the window, and this is Monsieur Prigent's account of what they saw:

> In the north, a cottony cloud of strange shape was floating against the blue sky. Above it, a long narrow cylinder, apparently inclined at a 45° angle, was slowly moving in a straight line toward the southwest. I estimated its altitude as 2 or 3 kilometers [about 1¼ to 1¾ miles]. The object was whitish, non-luminous, and very distinctly defined. A sort of plume of white smoke was escaping from its upper end. At some distance in front of the cylinder, about thirty other objects were following the same trajectory. To the naked eye, they appeared as featureless balls resembling puffs of smoke. But with the help of opera glasses it was possible to make out a central red sphere, surrounded by a sort of yellowish ring inclined at an angle. The angle was such as to conceal almost entirely the lower part of the central sphere, while revealing its upper surface. These "saucers" moved in pairs, following a broken path characterized in general by rapid and short zigzags. When two saucers drew away from one another, a whitish streak, like an electric arc, was produced between them.
>
> All these strange objects left an abundant trail behind them, which slowly fell to the ground as it dispersed. For several hours, clumps of it hung in the trees, on the telephone wires, and on the roofs of the houses.

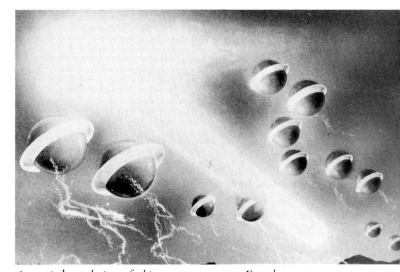

An artist's rendering of objects seen over two French towns by hundreds of witnesses in 1952 shows a large tubelike shape, ringed spheres moving in pairs, and trailing filaments.

These gossamerlike fibers, sometimes found in conjunction with UFO sightings, are referred to as angel hair. They resemble wool or nylon thread but tend to disintegrate rapidly. (See page 188 for more about this.)

On October 27, at 5 P.M., a similar spectacle was seen in the sky at Gaillac, a town 150 miles distant from Oloron-Ste.-Marie. About a hundred witnesses gave the same description of the 20-minute-long event:

> [A] long plumed cylinder inclined at 45°, progressing slowly to the southeast in the midst of a score of "saucers" which shone in the sun and flew two by two in a rapid zigzag. The only difference [in the Gaillac sighting was] that here some pairs of saucers occasionally descended quite low, to an altitude estimated by the observers as 300–400 meters [approximately 1,000 to 1,300 feet].

Again the witnesses saw angel hair fall and again this substance disappeared soon after it was collected. (Aimé Michel, *The Truth About Flying Saucers,* pp.145–50]

An off-duty policeman, Ernst W. Akerberg, and his wife, Karin, were leaving their summer cottage on the island of Gotland, Sweden, on the evening of August 5, 1957, when they both saw a disk-shaped object heading in their direction from the sea. When the UFO reached the shore several hundred yards away it made a sharp turn, tilted on its edge, and swayed for a few moments. The disk then continued on for about half a mile, made another sharp turn, and flew out of view. Almost immediately, another object approached from the same direction and executed the same maneuvers. Both objects made the water ripple and the treetops sway as they passed at a height of some 200 yards. The Akerbergs estimated the width of the objects to be about 25 or 26 yards. They had the shape of a streamlined "bicycle bell" and were a metallic silver-gray. Riveted joints could be seen on the bottom. The upper section seemed to rotate slowly over the lower part. Both of the disks had a glowing "cherry-red tube," and their edges had a "fuzzy, glimmering shine." The objects made a repeated "clicking" noise much like the sound made by winding an alarm clock.

After investigating this sighting, the Swedish Air Force classified the objects as "Unidentified." (*The Encyclopedia of UFOs,* Ronald D. Story, ed., pp.152–53)

The closing months of 1978 marked some very unusual UFO-associated events for the Australian sector of the globe. The tragic case of Frederick Valentich is the starting point of a whole series of visual, radar, and filmed recordings of bizarre flying objects.

"[I]t's approaching from due east of me," radioed the young Australian pilot 50 minutes after he had taken off from Moorabbin Airport, Victoria, on a solo flight in a

Guido Valentich holds a portrait of his son, Frederick, who disappeared without a trace while flying a small plane over Bass Strait south of Australia. Because Frederick reported a strange craft hovering over him just before radio contact was broken, his father believes he was abducted by beings from another planet.

Cessna 182 aircraft across Bass Strait to King Island. His terse message continued:

> It seems to be playing some sort of game. Flying at speed I cannot estimate. . . . It is flying past. It has a long shape . . . coming for me right now. . . . It has a green light and sort of metallic light on the outside.

Valentich was reporting back to Melbourne air flight service controller Steve Robey, after he had radioed a request for confirmation of a large craft with "four bright lights" and been told that there were no reported aircraft in the area.

> [T]he thing is orbiting on top of me.

The Cessna's engine now began to rough-idle and cough, and Valentich called in to announce:

> Proceeding King Island. Unknown aircraft now hovering on top of me.

With these words, the young pilot signed off. A loud metallic sound was heard at ground reception for 17 seconds, and then communications went dead. No sign of either Valentich or his plane was ever found, and the mystery remains unsolved to this day. (*The Encyclopedia of UFOs,* Ronald D. Story, ed., p.379; *Flying Saucer Review,* 24:3–5, March 1979)

RADAR VISUALS

Two radar operators from the White Sands Missile Range, New Mexico, picked up a fast-moving unidentified object on the morning of July 14, 1951. A tracker on the ground who happened to be watching a B-29 with binoculars saw a large UFO near the plane. A second ground observer with a 35mm camera shot 200 feet of film of the object. Reports have it that the film showed a round, bright spot, but the film somehow disappeared and has never been seen since. (Brinsley Le Poer Trench, *The Flying Saucer Story,* p.28)

Seven strange spots suddenly appeared on a radarscope at the Washington National Airport late Saturday evening, July 19, 1952. Unable to identify the blips, air traffic controller Edward Nugent asked his supervisor, Henry G. Barnes, to take a look. The following is an excerpt from the report later made by Barnes:

> The "things" which caused Ed to call me over to the scope were seven pips [blips] clustered together irregularly in one corner . . . the pips showed up as pale violet spots. . . . The seven pips indicated that the objects—or whatever they were—were in the air over an area about nine miles in diameter, fifteen miles south-southwest of Washington. We knew immediately that a very strange situation existed. . . . We tracked the seven pips for about 5 minutes and quickly determined that they were moving between 100 and 130 miles per hour while we could observe them. But their movements were completely radical compared to those of ordinary aircraft. They followed no set course, were not in any *formation,* and we only seemed to be able to track them for about three miles at a time. . . .

Barnes instructed the air force to dispatch jet fighters and then continued to watch the radar screen. By now some of the incoming pilots were radioing in that they could see unidentified lights in the sky. Andrews Air Force Base also began to pick up strange returns on its radarscopes, which correlated with those at Washington National. Ground personnel saw a "bright orange light." A commercial airline pilot reported receiving visual images, one of which included six lights. Each light corresponded to a radar blip. Several hours after Barnes's call, jet fighters finally arrived, but they could find nothing—and by then the strange blips were no longer seen on the radar screen.

But as soon as the fighters left, the radar targets again

Three air traffic controllers watch a radarscope at National Airport, Washington, D.C., in July 1952. Twice between July 19 and July 26 there appeared a series of strange radar blips, coinciding with visual reports of unidentified lights.

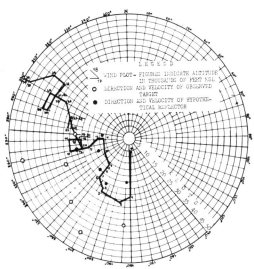

The erratic pattern of blips on the National Airport radar screen in Washington, D.C., on July 26, 1952, was plotted by the U.S. Air Force. Radar experts claim that these blips could not have been caused by temperature inversion.

appeared on the airport screens. Both visual and coincident radar reports continued through the night.

Exactly a week later, on Saturday, July 26, a similar series of mysterious blips was seen on the airport's radar screen and was confirmed visually by numerous aircraft. This time jet interceptors arrived quickly, but only one pilot saw anything. He attempted to close with four lights in the distance but failed.

The incident was played up in newspaper headlines across the country. One of them ran: "The Day the Saucers Visited Washington, D.C." The air force investigators, however, concluded that both incidents "were due to mirage effects created by a double-temperature inversion"—a conclusion denied by Dr. James E. McDonald, a University of Arizona meteorologist who had conducted his own investigation. (*The Encyclopedia of UFOs,* Ronald D. Story, ed., pp.388–89)

In the control room at Orly Airport, Paris, on the evening of February 19, 1956, the radar screen suddenly showed a blip with an echo twice as large as that of the largest known aircraft. The radar image behaved in a very erratic manner, slowing down, hovering, and then accelerating dramatically, quite unlike anything the operator had ever seen before.

At that point a more familiar blip showed up on the screen and was soon identified as an Air France Douglas Dakota airliner on its regular Paris-London run. The control tower radioed the craft that a UFO was in its path. The radio officer who received the message looked through a porthole and was amazed to see an enormous indistinct outline with a red glow. He and the captain watched the UFO for a full half-minute before it disappeared. In his report, the captain stated that the object they saw carried none of the required

223

navigation lights. At Orly, radarmen followed the UFO's strange flight for four hours on their screen. Then it disappeared. An odd twist to this story is that neither Le Bourget Airport nor the Paris Observatory picked up this UFO on their radar screens. (Brinsley Le Poer Trench, *The Flying Saucer Story*, pp.38–39)

A classic in UFO literature is the story of the RB-47 radar sighting of July 17, 1957. This is how it is summarized in the introduction of a long and detailed account of the incident in *Astronautics & Aeronautics* magazine published by the UFO Subcommittee of the American Institute of Aeronautics and Astronautics:

> An Air Force RB-47, equipped with electronic countermeasures (ECM) gear and manned by six officers, was followed by an unidentified object for a distance of well over 700 miles and for a time period of 1.5 hours, as it flew from Mississippi, through Louisiana and Texas and into Oklahoma. The object was, at various times, seen visually by the cockpit crew as an intensely luminous light, followed by ground-radar and detected on ECM monitoring gear aboard the RB-47. Of special interest in this case are several instances of simultaneous appearances and disappearances on all three of those physically distinct "channels," and rapidity of maneuvers beyond the prior experience of the aircrew.

The full report runs for five pages in the magazine, listing all the details of the radar and visual observations. The repeated sightings, coinciding with unidentified radar blips, consisted of an "intense white light" that seemed to be "following" the aircraft at times. Attempts to intercept the UFO failed.

Project Blue Book finally dismissed the case by identifying the UFO as American Airlines Flight 655—a completely unfounded conclusion according to many experts, including the officers of the RB-47. (*Astronautics & Aeronautics*, 9:66–70, July 1971; *The Encyclopedia of UFOs*, Ronald D. Story, ed., pp.297–98)

A most dramatic encounter was confirmed by radar on May 3, 1975, over Mexico City. Carlos Antonio de los Santos Montiel was approaching the city in his Piper PA-24 when the plane began to vibrate for no apparent reason. Just beyond his right wing tip he was amazed to see a dark gray disk-shaped object about 10 to 12 feet in diameter. But that was not all. To his left was another disk, and most frightening of all was a third UFO coming at him head on. This disk actually scraped the underpart of De los Santos Montiel's fuselage, jolting the plane as it did so.

At this point De los Santos Montiel discovered that the controls were not working, yet somehow the plane continued to fly relatively smoothly at 120 mph. The

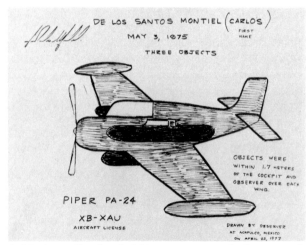

A Mexican pilot sketched his encounter with three UFO's. In the proximity of the dark objects the controls and instruments of his small plane were inoperative.

flier was in tears when he finally radioed to the tower at Mexico City airport. The UFO's had by now disappeared, and the plane's instrumentation was working again so that he could land safely.

The controllers took De los Santos Montiel's report seriously because they had tracked the three objects on radar at the same time the pilot was describing his encounter. One controller told a reporter:

> The objects made a 270-degree turn at 518 m.p.h. in an arc of only three miles. Normally a plane moving at that speed needs eight to 10 miles to make a turn like that. In my 17 years as an air traffic controller I've never seen anything like that.

(*Flying Saucer Review*, 24:8, January 1979)

The early hours of December 31, 1978, have gone down in the annals of UFO research as the first time that on-the-spot tape recordings were made while UFO's were being observed, filmed, and simultaneously tracked on radar both on the ground and in the air.

This event occurred just east of New Zealand's South Island. An Argosy cargo plane, carrying a three-member Melbourne television crew headed by Channel O reporter Quentin Fogarty, was retracing the flight path between Wellington and Christchurch, a route along which bright, unidentified lights had been observed by aircraft crews for several weeks.

On the flight down, the evening of December 30, the team saw some mysterious lights that moved too erratically to catch on film. But the flight back from Christchurch to Blenheim was more rewarding. At 2:15 A.M. something approached within 10 miles of the cargo plane. It was described by one of the TV crew as having a "brightly lit base and a sort of transparent dome." The object was picked up by the craft's radar, and—what was most exciting—it was successfully photographed on 16mm color film. The UFO maintained a certain distance from the plane for a time, then it moved to the front, to the left, and finally sped away. Ground radar confirmed unidentified blips near the plane at the time.

Some 23,000 frames of film were turned over for analysis to Dr. Bruce Maccabee, an optical physicist employed by the U.S. Navy. The film showed several brief sequences of strange, unidentifiable images, one of which had the bell-shaped form mentioned by the cameraman. Another frame showed the track of the UFO as it described a figure-eight loop, and still another sequence showed an object changing from a large, bright, yellowish round shape to a dim, more reddish, triangular shape. Dr. Maccabee estimated that one of the objects was 60 to 100 feet in diameter and emitted a light equivalent to the candlepower of a 100,000-watt bulb. The UFO executing the loop was estimated to be traveling at roughly 3,000 mph.

The film and other documentation were later submitted to a score of U.S. scientists, experts in optics, biophysics, radar, optical physiology, and astronomy. Despite several previous official statements rejecting the observations as natural phenomena, this team unanimously agreed that the recorded lights were not explicable in terms of Venus or other planets, stars, meteors, high-altitude balloons, off-course aircraft, satellites, atmospheric illusions, reflected lights, or even a hoax. The things seen, filmed, and trailed by radar between Christchurch and Blenheim were without question unidentifiable flying objects. (*The Encyclopedia of UFOs*, Ronald D. Story, ed., pp.393-95)

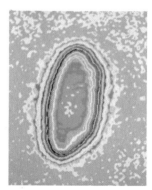
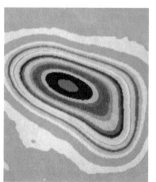
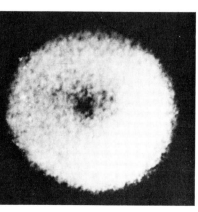

Above are two computer-enhanced frames from a film taken of a UFO over New Zealand in the predawn of December 31, 1978. At left is a photograph of another unidentified flying object, seen on January 3, 1979.

CLOSE ENCOUNTERS OF THE FIRST KIND

One of the earliest reports of a close look at a passing UFO was that of two Eastern Airlines pilots, Clarence S. Chiles and John B. Whitted, on July 24, 1948.

At 2:45 A.M., 20 miles west of Montgomery, Alabama, they saw an aircraft streaking toward them and thought that it was a jet fighter:

> It was heading southwest, exactly opposite our course. Whatever it was flashed down towards us with terrific speed. We veered to the left. It veered sharply, too, and passed us about 700 feet to the right. I saw then it had no wings.

Such was Chiles's report. The mysterious craft passed on Whitted's side, so it was he who had the better view of it. According to him:

> It was about 100 feet long, cigar-shaped and wingless, about twice the diameter of a B-29 with no protruding fins.

Officer Chiles added to the description:

> An intense dark blue glow came from the side of the ship and ran the entire length of the fuselage—like a blue fluorescent light. The exhaust was a red-orange flame....

When the air force investigated the UFO seen by two airline pilots in 1948, they agreed that "it is not of domestic origin," an opinion supported by this illustration. In the 1960's the sighting was reclassified as a meteor. In light of the reports, that explanation seems unlikely.

Both noticed rows of windows and a brilliant light inside the object. Chiles also observed a "snout" protruding like a radar pole from the front of the craft. As the UFO passed, it pulled into some broken clouds and was lost from view.

Chiles then visited the cabin to check the passengers. Clarence McKelvie was the only one awake. He too had seen a brilliant flash of light pass by the window. "[I]t looked like a cigar with a cherry flame going out the back. There was a row of windows.... It disappeared very quickly," McKelvie said. Air force investigators, unable to identify the craft, eventually called it a meteor and closed the case. (Robert Emenegger, *UFO's Past, Present and Future*, pp.36–41; Brinsley Le Poer Trench, *The Flying Saucer Story*, pp.24–25)

Near Amiens, France, some 70 miles north of Paris, around 7:15 A.M., two masons came upon an unusual sight on September 7, 1954. Emile Renard and Yves Degillerboz were bicycling to work when they had to stop to fix a flat tire. Their attention was attracted by an odd-looking haystack some 200 yards away in a field. It looked as though it was "unfinished," with an "upside-down plate on top."

Then, to their amazement, the "haystack" began to swing back and forth and oscillate slowly. As the masons dropped their bicycles and ran toward it, the object took off at a slant, moving diagonally upward for about 50 feet and then flying straight up. They watched the UFO for about three minutes before it disappeared in the clouds. Renard recalled:

> The object flew without making any noise, letting out a little smoke underneath, at the right. It was a bluish-gray color, and might have been about thirty feet in diameter and about 10 feet high—as I said before it looked like a dish turned upside down. On the left side of the bottom we could see a sort of plate, like a door, wider than it was high. It was about a hundred and fifty yards away from us when it took to the air. . . .

The masons told their story to a local constable, who much against their will made them repeat their experience to the police in the neighboring town.

On the same day, in villages scattered over an area of 18 miles in the vicinity of this encounter, many people sent in reports of seeing an object corresponding in all details of time, dimensions, and color with the masons' report. (Aimé Michel, *Flying Saucers and the Straight-Line Mystery,* pp.35–38)

Duty Officer Reg Toland of the Exeter, New Hampshire, police station, was surprised when a badly frightened young man stumbled into the station at 2:24 A.M. on September 3, 1965. His name was Norman Muscarello and he was almost hysterical. He had been hitchhiking to his home in Exeter when, after crossing the state line into New Hampshire, he suddenly saw a round object 80 or 90 feet in diameter with flickering red lights around the rim come "floating down from the sky" toward him. It "wobbled, yawed, and hovered" overhead, making no sound whatever, and Muscarello, afraid it was going to crush him, dove into a ditch beside the road. But the UFO moved slowly away, pausing to hover for a while over one of the two nearby houses. Then it abruptly "flew off."

Muscarello, in a state of panic, hitched a ride to the Exeter police station. Officer Toland wrote down the account, not knowing what to believe. But being a thorough police officer, he called in a patrol car to

Exeter, New Hampshire, policemen David Hunt (left) and Eugene Bertrand saw a UFO with pulsating lights at close range. Both were certain it was not an ordinary aircraft.

investigate. The officer who responded to the call, Eugene Bertrand, told Toland that he had just spoken to a woman in a parked car who was terrified because she too had seen a "low-flying, large, round object with flashing red lights."

Bertrand drove Muscarello back to the place where the latter had seen the UFO. As they walked across the field, Bertrand, who thought the object reported was just a helicopter, saw it for himself. It had returned and was silently hovering about 100 feet above the ground. After a few minutes another patrol car, summoned by radio and driven by David Hunt, arrived. The UFO was still there, and the two officers and Muscarello watched as the brilliant red lights flickered on and off in sequence, casting a scarlet glow over the ground. It finally began to move away, stopping at intervals before it rose and disappeared to the east.

This UFO was seen not only by Muscarello and the two police officers but by several other people in the Exeter area, who also reported having observed what was seemingly the same object.

The case was investigated by the air force but was never explained in terms of natural phenomena or known aircraft. (*Look,* 30:36–42, February 22, 1966; Len Ortzen, *Strange Stories of UFOs,* pp.129–31)

In the early morning of April 17, 1966, near Ravenna, Ohio, four policemen took part in an hour-long chase after a brightly lit object "as big as a house." The first policemen involved were Deputy Sheriff Dale Spaur and his assistant, Wilbur Neff, who just before daybreak saw the object coming toward them low over the woods. The UFO was so bright that they were forced to look down. As it hovered overhead, making a humming sound, the two policemen dove into their car for protection. Finally the UFO moved off and Spaur called headquarters to report the incident. He was told

UFO's—Illusion or Reality?

Scientists find ready explanations for most UFO incidents in terms of known physical phenomena, such as celestial bodies, electrical occurrences in the atmosphere, the warping of light rays, and weather balloons. But in the meantime the complexity of the UFO phenomena has provoked a relatively new approach to the whole question of their reality.

Could it be that accounts of UFO's are related to the many psychic and paranormal experiences recounted by human beings throughout history? Certainly the reports of these strange objects, and their odd occupants who sometimes convey social messages to humans, have a mythical and often visionary quality.

In his book *Passport to Magonia*, Jacques Vallee, a computer scientist and student of UFOlogy, traces the many parallels between the ancient myths of all cultures and today's stories of UFO's. He goes on to propose that UFO experiences are paranormal in nature and are the space-age equivalent of a phenomenon that assumes different guises in different historical contexts. Vallee suggests that human life is controlled by imagination and myth and that paranormal experiences are the means by which man's ideas about himself and his universe are constantly shaped. Such experiences, he adds, become especially important in times of social stress. In his view the UFO phenomenon is the present-day "tool" in this control system. The great mystery is whether this control is part of man's genetic makeup or whether it is imposed upon him from without—through alien intervention.

Psychiatrist Carl G. Jung, who is widely known for his theories concerning the human psyche, also proposed a "supranormal" explanation for UFO's. In a book published in 1958, *Flying Saucers: A Modern Myth of Things Seen in the Skies,* Jung suggested that the UFO phenomenon is a manifestation of man's "collective unconscious," a repository of archetypal images and impressions that surface in symbols, dreams, and myths and predispose man to produce very similar ideas, regardless of time or place. He pointed out the parallels between the ancient religious symbol he called the mandala—a circular pattern representing "the idea of the universal"—and the round shape of most UFO's. Jung regarded UFO's as a psychological projection of man's hopes and fears in an uncertain world. Thus he deprived them of physical reality.

Vallee's ideas are similar to Jung's in many respects; but he differs by accepting the reality of UFO's, in the sense that UFO witnesses have been exposed to a real event. In the February 1978 issue of *Fate,* he suggests that what they experienced is some sort of change in electromagnetic energy in their immediate vicinity. This change in energy may be produced by the witness himself, internally and spontaneously, or by some external agency. In any case, says Vallee:

> What they [the witnesses] tell us is that they've seen a flying saucer [or had an encounter with aliens]. Now they may have seen that or . . . the image of a flying saucer or they may have hallucinated it under the influence of microwave radiation, or any of a number of things may have happened. The fact is that the witnesses were exposed to an event and as a result they experienced a highly complex alteration of perception which caused them to describe the object or objects that figure in their testimony.

Jung's and Vallee's theories seem supported by an analysis of the stories told by UFO "abductees." (Under hypnosis, those who experienced "time loss" are able to "remember" all the details of their sojourn aboard an alien vessel.) Although their accounts vary greatly in detail, they describe a similar chain of events: the person sees a shining light, is guided to the vessel, often in a semiconscious, almost "out-of-body" state, is physically examined, enters into telepathic communication with the "aliens," and finally returns home.

What is truly fascinating is that the same sequence of events is described by hypnotized subjects who have never had the experience of a UFO encounter but have simply been told to *imagine* one. This in no way denies the validity of the testimony of the "real" witnesses—rather it suggests that the human mind is "programmed" to think in a certain way in response to certain stimuli. Apparently any number of stimuli can produce the particular state of consciousness susceptible to UFO-like experiences. Such stimuli might be mind-altering drugs, a brush with death, perhaps the physical charge of ball lightning, or—an actual physical encounter with a flying saucer.

The events described by people who have returned to a normal state of consciousness—whether from death's door or from a hallucinatory or hypnotic state or a religious trance—are amazingly similar, incorporating the light, the "guide" or "abductor," the examination, the messages, and so forth.

All this suggests the likelihood of some common matrix in the mind that can be triggered to allow paranormal experiences of the kind involving UFO's. To what degree such experiences can be called real becomes a question of semantics. However, the "paranormal" theory offers a new look at what remains an inexplicable phenomenon.

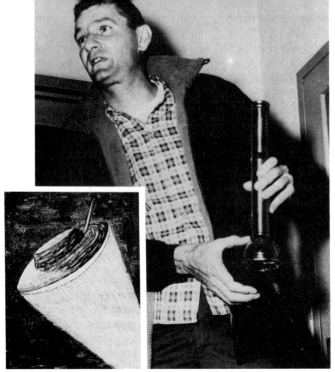

Deputy Sheriff Dale Spaur described the UFO he chased as shaped like the head of the flashlight he is holding. The drawing (inset) was made from Spaur's sketches.

to pursue the object. It was flying slowly, heading into Pennsylvania. Spaur and Neff chased it for some 40 miles when they met Officer Wayne Huston, who also had the object in view. He watched the UFO pass overhead and joined in pursuit. The following is an excerpt from Officer Huston's report:

> I watched it go right overhead. As near as I can describe it, it was shaped something like an ice-cream cone. The point of the cone was underneath; the top was like a dome. Spaur and Neff came down the road right after it. I fell in behind them. We were going eighty to eighty-five miles an hour. . . . It was right straight ahead. . . .

The two cars raced on for another 40 miles when they saw another police car parked by the road. Officer Frank Panzanella, standing by his car, was watching the UFO in utter amazement. He later said he had been observing the object for about 10 minutes:

> [It] was very bright and about twenty-five to thirty feet in diameter. The object then moved out . . . and went straight up real fast to about 3,500 feet . . . [it] continued to go upward until it got as small as a ballpoint pen. . . . We all four watched the object shoot straight up and disappear. . . .

The four officers' sworn statements matched in all details. Just before the UFO disappeared, each saw a plane from the Pittsburgh airport pass below it.

After a lengthy investigation the U.S. Air Force dismissed the sighting as "misinterpretations of con-

ventional objects and natural phenomena"—an unlikely explanation in view of the sequence of events. (*The Encyclopedia of UFOs,* Ronald D. Story, ed., pp.271–72; Len Ortzen, *Strange Stories of UFOs,* pp.59–63)

A road near Gdansk (formerly Danzig), Poland, was the scene of a startling encounter with a UFO on September 5, 1980. At about 3:30 A.M. an ambulance, with Dr. Barbara Piazza, a driver, and a stretcher bearer on board, was rushing Mrs. Elzbieta Pluta, who was in labor, to the local hospital. Suddenly Dr. Piazza noticed a big red ball in the sky. She asked what it might be, and they all joked about its being a UFO. The ball grew larger until it was about the size of the moon, which was then visible. Soon the UFO was at the level of the treetops and some 650 feet away. The driver accelerated, but the object, as the doctor said, "was under intelligent control. We just could not lose it. It was racing after us!" The red ball suddenly appeared about 200 yards ahead of the ambulance and blocked the way, its edges overlapping the 19-foot-wide roadway by a half-yard on each side.

Everyone saw the curved bands on the surface, the irregular black lines going up and down in each direction, and the yellow-orange patches on the crimson exterior. Two guards at the nearby railroad crossing were also looking at the UFO. Mrs. Pluta's contractions were now coming in short intervals. The doctor radioed the police, reporting a UFO "blocking the way." In desperation, she told the driver to flash his headlights. He flashed them twice. Then, at one moment they saw the UFO right in front of them and the next moment it vanished "like a TV set when switched off." The ambulance reached the hospital 10 minutes later, and Mrs. Pluta gave birth to a healthy six-pound girl. (*Flying Saucer Review,* 26:2–4, March 1981)

CLOSE ENCOUNTERS OF THE SECOND KIND

The "Florida scoutmaster" story is one of the earliest American reports of a UFO leaving tangible evidence on the ground. On the night of August 19, 1952, Mr. C. S. Desverges was driving three scouts home when he noticed a light just above a palmetto thicket. The scoutmaster stopped the car, told the boys to go for assistance if he did not return in 15 minutes, and went ahead on foot with a flashlight to investigate what he thought might be a small aircraft making an emergency landing. According to the statement Desverges later made to a sheriff and air force officials, he became aware of a pungent odor and felt a sudden rise in temperature after hacking his way into the thicket with a machete to the spot where he thought he had seen the light. He continued on for about 30 yards into a clearing. Here

C. S. Desverges is shown reading a story about his encounter. Air force investigators decided it was a hoax but could not explain how it might have been perpetrated.

the heat became almost unbearable. When he looked up at the sky to get his bearings, a dark shape overhead totally obscured his view. He backed away and shone his flashlight at the object, which was hovering 30 to 40 feet above the ground. It was disk shaped, with a smooth, gray surface. The underpart was concave, and the upper portion had a dome in the center. Along the edges of the object were vanes with small openings in between. Then he heard a sound "like the opening of a well-oiled safe door," and a small red ball that expanded into a red, misty cloud drifted toward him. As the mist closed in, he fainted.

The three boys had been watching their scoutmaster's progress through the thicket by the light of his flashlight. After 10 minutes, they said in their later statements, they could see him shine his flashlight upward; then a red ball of fire enveloped him and they saw him fall. They got out of the car and ran to a neighboring farmhouse for help.

By the time the deputy sheriff and a constable arrived, Desverges had recovered consciousness and was stumbling back onto the road. He told his story in a coherent manner and everyone went back to the clearing, but other than finding Desverges's flashlight and machete on the ground, and some flattened grass, nothing out of the ordinary was visible. It was only later, driving back in the car, that Desverges noticed that the hair on his arms was singed and that there were slight burns on his arms and hands; his cap was also slightly charred.

Desverges's injuries remained unexplained, however, as did the tiny holes and scorch marks, which appeared to have been made by electrical sparks, on his cap. (*The Encyclopedia of UFO's*, Ronald D. Story, ed., pp.128–31; Len Ortzen, *Strange Stories of UFOs*, pp.28–33)

The following statement was made by Pedro Saucedo and confirmed by a fellow driver who was with him on a Texas highway the night of November 2, 1957:

I was driving my truck on route 116, going north. Four miles out of Levelland (Texas) I saw a big flame ahead. . . . I thought it was lightning, but when this object had reached my position it was different, because it put my truck motor out and the lights. . . . It looked like a torpedo, about 200 feet long, moving at about 600 to 800 miles an hour.

When the blazing lights of the UFO vanished into the distance, the truck's headlights came on again and the engine started up easily.

Patrolman A. J. Fowler, who received the initial, somewhat hysterical phone call from Saucedo reporting the incident, recorded 15 more calls that night from persons who had seen some kind of a large UFO at the same time their car engines had died out. According to the signed statement made later by one of the callers:

I . . . noticed an oval-shaped object—flat on the bottom—sitting on the road ahead . . . about a hundred twenty-five feet long . . . glowing with a bluish-green light. The object seemed to be made of an aluminum-like material, but no markings. The object finally rose into the air—almost straight up.

(Robert Emenegger, *UFO's Past, Present and Future*, p.54; Len Ortzen, *Strange Stories of UFOs*, pp.40–41)

A banana grower, George Pedley of Tully, North Queensland, Australia, was driving his tractor through Albert Pennisi's neighboring cane farm at 9 A.M. on January 19, 1966, when he saw a "spaceship" rise out of Horseshoe Lagoon, a swamp about 26 yards in front of him. He described the ship as bluish-gray, about 25 feet wide, and 9 feet high. Pedley also reported:

It spun at a terrific rate as it rose vertically to about 60 feet, then made a shallow dive and rose sharply. Traveling at a fantastic speed, it headed off in a southwesterly direction. It was out of sight in seconds.

When Pedley investigated the spot where the UFO was seen, he found a depressed circular area about 30 feet in diameter. Within the circle the reeds

were without exception bent below water level, dead and swirled around in a clockwise manner, as if they had been subjected to some terrific rotary force.

Pedley later said that he had noticed a sulfurous odor in the area around the "nest" after the UFO departed.

Investigation of the circular area revealed a nine-inch layer of reeds within it, torn out by the roots and floating on five feet of water. Three large holes were discovered under the "nest." These were thought to be "landing indentations." Two other "nests" were later discovered only 25 yards from the first one.

This "saucer nest" in Australia shows a well-defined perimeter and a pattern of broken reeds, suggesting that a spinning object might have ascended from here.

The official verdict was that the "nests" were "the results of severe turbulence, which normally accompany line squalls and thunderstorms prevalent in North Queensland at that time of year." The weather, however, was fine that day. (*The Encyclopedia of UFOs*, Ronald D. Story, ed., pp.370–71)

Near Delphos, Kansas, 16-year-old Ronald Johnson was tending sheep on his father's farm with his dog on the evening of November 2, 1971. Suddenly he saw a mushroom-shaped object, with multicolored lights covering its surface. The UFO was only 25 yards away, hovering within 2 feet of the ground. Ronald estimated its diameter to be about nine feet. The object sounded much like "an old washing machine which vibrates." Before it took off, an intense light issued from its base, temporarily blinding Ronald. When he regained his sight after a few minutes, he rushed into the house to call his parents. The whole family went outside and they all said they saw the object, "now high in the sky," before it vanished.

At the site where the UFO had hovered, the three witnesses saw "a glowing ring on the ground" and luminescence on parts of the surrounding trees. One investigator said that the texture of the soil "felt strange, like a slick crust, as if the soil was crystallized." Ronald's mother, a nurse, reported that her fingers felt numb, "as if a local anesthetic had been applied," after touching the UFO trace. This condition lasted for two weeks. A month later snow fell and melted on the ground except on the ring, which remained white. On examination, it was found that the ground beneath the ring was impermeable to water and "dry to a depth of at least one foot." Also, a soil sample from the ring area

A glowing white ring with a crusty surface was found by the Johnson family on their farmland in Kansas. The ring, believed to have been caused by a hovering UFO, remained visible for more than a month during the winter.

contained a high concentration of a primitive organism of the genus *Nocardia*, which is often found growing with a fungus that is at times fluorescent. If energy emanating from a UFO had triggered their coincidental growth, this could explain the glowing ring.

Every evening for about two weeks after the event, the sheep would jump out of their pen and run wildly. The dog, too, would desperately try to get into the house at sunset. Ronald was also affected, suffering eye irritation, headaches, and a recurring nightmare, from which he would awaken screaming. (Jacques Vallee, *The Invisible College*, pp.35–38)

Some interesting traces were found of a UFO landing in the Transylvanian Alps, Romania, on the night of September 27, 1972. An elderly night watchman from the parish of Posesti had seen a mysterious object moving through the sky and then settling down on a hillside. The next morning villagers went to the place where the watchman thought the UFO had landed, and found a cornfield with a clump of cornstalks bent over about 3¼ feet from the ground. The patch of bent corn formed a circle about 20 feet in diameter, and in the center of this circle was a narrow, 8-foot-deep cylindrical hole apparently bored into the earth. Radiating from it were three evenly spaced long rectangular imprints in the soil. The local people received the impression that a rounded object with three ground supports had dropped down into the cornfield.

An investigating team from Bucharest University arrived a few weeks later. They measured the imprints, photographed the site, studied the topography, and took away some 20 samples of soil and vegetation for analysis. The investigators concluded that some very heavy object had indeed landed, resting on a three-footed pad. Since the corn had not been flattened, it was assumed that the body had been about a yard off the ground. The UFO must have made a vertical landing and takeoff between three apple trees that remained undamaged. The soil analysis revealed unusual radioactivity, and the sample of grass taken from the circle proved to be scorched. It was also found that the biological rhythm of the moles living close by had been disturbed. Although it was only autumn, they were beginning to come out of hibernation, unlike other members of their species farther away from the site. (Len Ortzen, *Strange Stories of UFOs*, pp.38–39)

CLOSE ENCOUNTERS OF THE THIRD KIND

The first sighting of UFO occupants to be reported after the Arnold case happened on July 23, 1947, near Bauru, Brazil. José C. Higgins, working on a survey crew, heard a piercing high-pitched whistle just before he saw a large disk-shaped object land. He estimated it to be 150 feet in diameter. It seemed to be made of grayish-white metal with a distinct three-foot-wide rim around it and was resting on curved legs. The other members of the crew all fled, and Higgins found himself alone with three entities, each seven feet tall. They wore "transparent suits covering head and body, and inflated like rubber bags" and had "metal boxes" on their backs. Their clothing, which could be seen through the outer suits, resembled colored paper.

The occupants all looked alike. They had huge round eyes and large round, bald heads without eyebrows or beards. Their bodies were similar to ours except that the legs were longer in proportion. They seemed very beautiful in a sexless kind of way to Higgins. One of them used a stick to make eight holes in the ground that suggested a solar system with seven planets. He pointed to the outermost one as being their home and called it Orque. (Some UFO buffs interpret this to mean that they came from Uranus.) They tried to lure Higgins into their craft, but he managed to get away. Hiding for about 30 minutes in a thicket, he watched them leaping and gamboling, playfully throwing huge stones about. Then they boarded the disk, whick took off and disappeared toward the north. (*The Humanoids*, Charles Bowen, ed., pp.88–89)

One of the more frightening of the early landing reports came from Flatwoods, West Virginia, in 1952. A group of youngsters saw what looked like a "meteor" land on top of a hill on the night of September 12 and went to the site with a neighbor, her two sons, and a National Guardsman. All the witnesses claimed that they observed a globe as large as a house making a throbbing, hissing sound. When one of the group shone a flashlight at what he thought were animal eyes in the branches of a tree, the whole crowd saw a huge figure, about 10 or 15 feet tall, with a "blood red 'face' " and odd, "glowing, greenish-orange 'eyes.' " The monster "floated" slowly toward the witnesses, who fled hysterically down the hillside. Later on, two parallel skid marks and a large circle of flattened grass were found on the site, and a strange lingering odor was detected. (*The Encyclopedia of UFOs*, Ronald D. Story, ed., pp.127–28; *The Humanoids*, Charles Bowen, ed., pp.144–45)

Mrs. Kathleen May holds an artist's drawing of the Flatwoods Monster that she and six others vowed they saw on a West Virginia hilltop. Note the size of the creature in relation to the human figure.

At Ranton, near Shrewsbury, England, on October 11, 1954, at 4:45 P.M., Mrs. Jennie Roestenberg and her two children watched a disk-shaped aluminum-colored UFO hovering above their house. She claimed that she could see two "men" through two transparent panels on the side of the object. The occupants were very pale, had long, shoulder-length hair, and foreheads so disproportionately high that all the features seemed concentrated in the lower half of their faces. They wore turquoise-blue outfits resembling ski suits and transparent helmets. While the UFO was hovering at an angle, the two humanoids surveyed the scene "sternly, not in an unkindly fashion, but almost sadly, compassionately." (*The Humanoids*, Charles Bowen, ed., p.16)

On November 28, 1954, at 2 o'clock in the morning, two truckdrivers, Gustavo González and José Ponce, found their vehicle blocked by a shining sphere, about nine feet in diameter, hovering some six feet above the roadway outside Caracas, Venezuela. On investigating, González was attacked by a bristly, hairy dwarf with claws and glowing eyes. When he tackled the creature, González found it to be very light in weight but remarkably strong, for it threw him a distance of some 15 feet. When González stabbed at the dwarf with his knife, the blade glanced off the body as though it was made of steel. A similar creature, emerging from the sphere, blinded González with a "dazzling light from a small tube." During the scuffle Ponce watched two other dwarfs emerge from the side of the road, carrying what appeared to be rocks and dirt in their arms. They leaped lightly up into the sphere through an opening in the side. Alarmed, Ponce ran to the local police station close by. He was in the middle of his story when González, "overcome with exhaustion and fright," arrived. González had a "long deep red scratch" on his side. The two men were sedated and kept under observation for several days. One of the doctors treating them later claimed that he had seen the entire scuffle, exactly as the two men had described it, as he drove by on his way home from a night call. (*The Humanoids*, Charles Bowen, ed., p.93)

Joe Simonton, a master plumber of Eagle River, Wisconsin, received four "pancakes" from the hands of one of the occupants of a UFO that hovered over his yard. Simonton tells of hearing a sound, on April 18, 1961, like "knobby tires on a wet pavement" before seeing a silvery object like "two wash bowls turned face to face" just a few inches off the ground. When he approached, a six-foot-high hatch opened and he saw three "men" inside. They appeared young and about five feet tall with dark hair and hairless dark faces. One of them handed Simonton a silver-colored jug with

The illustration above was drawn from Joe Simonton's description of the craft carrying small, dark beings that he said landed by his farmhouse. When Simonton saw them "cooking," he requested and received what looked like four flat cookies, one of which he is holding at right.

two handles and indicated with a motion that he wanted water. Simonton filled the jug and handed it back. He then saw a man "cooking" on some kind of flameless stove. Seeing a stack of small, perforated cookielike objects next to the "griddle," Simonton motioned that he wanted one. An occupant picked up four of the "pancakes" and gave them to Simonton. Then the UFO took off at a 45-degree angle, creating a great rush of wind that bowed over the pine trees nearby. Simonton ate one of the cookies. He said later that it "tasted like cardboard." He kept a second one and gave the remaining two to various UFO investigation committees. The group from Northwestern University apparently said that the cookie they had checked contained "flour, sugar and grease." (*The Encyclopedia of UFOs*, Ronald D. Story, ed., pp.107–08; *The Humanoids*, Charles Bowen, ed., pp.161–63)

A shiny, egg-shaped object about 20 feet long and 15 feet wide was seen by dairy farmer Gary T. Wilcox of Newark Valley, Tioga County, New York, in his field at 10 A.M., April 24, 1964. Two dwarfs, about four feet tall, suddenly appeared, wearing seamless clothing and a hood that covered their faces completely. Each was carrying a tray containing samples of soil with alfalfa and grass. One of them spoke to Wilcox in faultless English, telling him that they were from Mars. The conversation continued for two hours. It seemed that since their people obtained their food from the atmosphere, they knew very little about regular agriculture. They wanted a bag of fertilizer to take with them. After the Martians took off, Wilcox got some fertilizer from the barn and left it in the field. The next day it was gone. When asked if he thought the Martians had returned for it, he replied: "Well, anybody who would walk all the way to that field to get an eighty-cent bag of fertilizer would be crazy." (*The Encyclopedia of UFOs*, Ronald D. Story, ed., pp.246–48; *The Humanoids*, Charles Bowen, ed., pp.163–64)

The Socorro affair, as it was called, caused a great stir in 1964. On the same evening (April 24) the Wilcox encounter took place in New York state, New Mexico patrolman Lonnie Zamora was chasing a speeder when he saw a blue flame in the sky in the direction of an isolated dynamite shack south of the town of Socorro. When he approached the mesa near the spot where the flame seemed to have settled, he got a glimpse of an object in an arroyo some 450 feet away. The UFO was elliptical in shape and had supporting legs. Next to it were two forms "like a young boy or small adult" in white or beige clothing. One of the figures seemed to look toward him in surprise. When Zamora got out of his car for a better look, the UFOnauts reentered their vehicle and took off with an ear-splitting roar.

He ran back to his car and called the dispatcher for someone to come to the site. The officer who arrived found Zamora pale and white and covered with sweat. Both men then saw some burning brush and several marks on the ground. On close examination it was seen that these "tracks" consisted of "four squarish imprints arranged in a trapezoid pattern." Presumably they were made by the legs of the craft. There were four burned areas, three of them within the imprints. (*The Encyclopedia of UFOs*, Ronald D. Story, ed., pp.341–44; *The Humanoids*, Charles Bowen, ed., p.164)

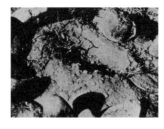

The photograph above shows one of the four imprints found near Socorro where a UFO and its occupants (illustrated) were reportedly seen in 1964.

CLOSE ENCOUNTERS OF THE FOURTH KIND

Definitions of this category vary, but the common denominator is extremely close contact with alien creatures from a UFO. Here are some personal accounts of incidents involving abduction into an alien vessel. Most witnesses can recall the actual details of abduction only under time-regression hypnosis.

If the story of Antonio Villas Boas, a 23-year-old Brazilian farmer, is to be believed, he could very well be

The Extraterrestrial Connection

The idea that earth is being visited or has been visited by intelligent beings from outer space is regarded with skepticism by the scientific community. Such visitations are highly improbable, according to some astronomers, although they also say it is likely that advanced civilizations exist among the billions of galaxies in the universe.

In our own galaxy, the Milky Way, there are perhaps 200 billion stars, a small fraction of which probably have planets on which life is feasible. On some of these it is not unlikely that intelligent beings have evolved and developed civilizations with technologies far superior to ours. In his book *The Cosmic Connection: An Extraterrestrial Perspective*, astronomer Carl Sagan makes an "optimistic estimate" that within the Milky Way there might be a million such instances.

Why, then, apart from the lack of concrete evidence, do scientists find it hard to believe that interstellar spaceships have visited earth?

For one thing, we have only just announced our existence—by radio, in the last 30 or so years—to the rest of the universe. We live on the edge of our galaxy, and our closest neighbors may be hundreds or thousands of light-years away. It is going to be some time before the good news reaches them. Probably they would respond by radio, but they may have the technology for travel close to the speed of light (186,000 miles per second) and decide to drop by for a look at us. Even so it would take another several hundred or thousand years in planetary time for their spaceships to reach us and return home.

Furthermore, the notion that intelligent beings from outer space are making daily, or even yearly, rounds to see us is presumptuous to say the least. Given

a million possible destinations with advanced civilizations, our planet with its comparatively primitive beings could hardly be of more than anthropological interest. Still, we might merit an occasional field trip. If so, on that basis outer space must be heavily trafficked with UFO's dispatched hither and yon.

But one of the main reasons why science is so skeptical about extraterrestrial visitations is that, in Sagan's words, the accounts of spaceships and their occupants are "stodgy in their unimaginativeness." Our reports of close encounters ascribe to these visitors our own technology, whereas, Sagan points out, theirs would be "so far beyond our present capabilities as to be indistinguishable from magic."

Also, the UfOnauts themselves are too much like earthlings. Even though life forms elsewhere in the universe are probably composed of atoms and molecules as we are, given the random factors operating in the evolutionary process, Sagan says, it could be assumed that extraterrestrial beings would be totally different from us. Even the least imaginative of the science-fiction writers would not suggest a humanoid so uninteresting as the reported saucerians.

For these and other reasons it is hard for science to imagine all these starfolk popping in and out of our atmosphere in the erratic manner ascribed to UFO's. It is even more difficult to suppose that any technically advanced beings who have so convincingly conquered time and space would not establish contact with us in a more efficient way.

To all of this, convinced UFO enthusiasts simply reply that the ways of the aliens are not necessarily ours and that so far as believers are concerned, their visits are indeed indistinguishable from magic.

---

the father of an extraterrestrial child. According to the deposition made before Dr. Olavo Fontes, who examined and treated Villas Boas for what he thought looked like radiation poisoning, the key elements of this strange and very intimate encounter, are the following:

At 1 A.M. on October 15, 1957, Villas Boas was tilling a field with his tractor when a "luminous egg-shaped object" about 35 feet long and 23 feet wide hovered over him and landed nearby. As three metal "legs" came out from under the machine, Villas Boas's tractor lights failed and the engine went dead. Four helmeted figures then dragged him up a ladder into the craft. There were five humanoids inside, who "talked" in "a series of barks, slightly resembling the sounds made by a dog." Villas Boas noted their "light-coloured eyes, which appeared to me to be blue" through lenses set into the

helmets. They were a little over five feet tall and were "dressed in very tight-fitting overalls." Villas Boas was stripped naked and his captors took blood from his chin, but he felt "no pain or prickling." (During Villas Boas's physical examination by Dr. Fontes, two dark scars were clearly visible on his chin.)

A little later, said Boas, a beautiful naked woman entered the room. After going into considerable detail about his seduction by the woman, he went on:

Shortly after we had separated, the door opened. One of the men appeared on the threshold and called the woman. Then she went out. But, before going out, she turned to me, pointed at her belly and then pointed towards me and with a smile (or something like it), she finally pointed towards the sky—I think it was in the direction of the south.

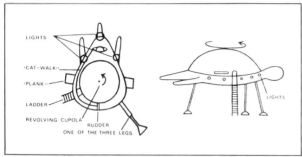

Antonio Villas Boas drew these diagrams of the spaceship into which he said he was taken. He was given a tour of the ship and then introduced to a beautiful woman.

One of the men now returned and handed Villas Boas his clothes. The only thing missing was his Homero lighter. Villas Boas was now given a tour of the craft, which he described in great detail, especially the great "dish-shaped cupola" overhead that whistled like the "sound of air being drawn in by a vacuum cleaner" as it revolved. His guide then pointed to the metal ladder on which Villas Boas had entered the craft, and he disembarked. He watched the UFO rise slowly as the "legs" retreated. The cupola spun more and more rapidly, lights flashing and changing color. "Then, listing slightly to one side, that strange machine shot off like a bullet towards the south. . . ."

The entire adventure lasted from 1:15 A.M. to 5:30 A.M., according to Villas Boas.

Dr. Fontes's physical examination given four months later revealed the two scars on Villas Boas's chin and several healed purplish lesions on various parts of his body. He concluded that Villas Boas might have had a case of "radiation poisoning." (*The Encyclopedia of UFOs,* Ronald D. Story, ed., pp.382–83; *The Humanoids,* Charles Bowen, ed., pp.200–38)

The Barney and Betty Hill encounter with a UFO in 1961, and their subsequent abduction revelations—brought out under hypnosis by a Boston psychiatrist in 1964—were sensational front-page news and the subject of books for several years. Here is what happened around midnight, September 19, 1961:

Betty and Barney Hill were returning to their home in Portsmouth, New Hampshire, after a vacation in Canada. They were driving south on U.S. Route 3 and had just passed the village of Lancaster, when they saw a moving light in the sky. Stopping the car and getting out, they noticed that the object was moving on a very erratic course. They then drove on, stopping every now and then to check the moving, soundless light. As they reached the White Mountains, the object, now appearing much larger, seemed to be moving in a course parallel to their car. Near Indian Head it suddenly appeared directly in front of them. Leaving the engine running, Barney got out of the car to observe the object with a pair of binoculars. He saw 5 to 11 figures moving behind a double row of windows. Betty, watching her husband from her side of the car, heard him repeating, "I don't believe it! I don't believe it!" adding, "This is ridiculous!" She herself did not see the descent of the UFO nor the humanoid figures observed by Barney. They were dressed in shiny black uniforms that looked like leather and wore black caps with visors. They moved with odd military precision.

By now the UFO was only about 70 feet overhead and some 100 feet distant. Barney dashed back to the car, yelling, "They are going to capture us," pushed down the gas pedal, and drove off as though possessed. As they streaked away, Betty still could not see the object, but Barney thought it was directly above them. Suddenly they heard a "beeping" noise, like the sound of a tuning fork. And then they felt very drowsy.

They found themselves driving, about two hours later, in the vicinity of Ashland, 35 miles south of Indian Head. They drove home, feeling puzzled and uneasy about the missing two hours.

The next day they reported their experience to Pease Air Force Base, and the incident was carefully recorded. A few days later Betty got in touch with the National Investigations Committee on Aerial Phenomena (NICAP) in Washington, D.C. A special investigator was sent out to document both their stories. Ten days after the incident, Betty began to experience recurring nightmares. In them a group of 8 to 11 men, dressed in matching uniforms and "military" caps, would stand in the middle of the road to stop the Hills's car. The "leader" would assure the couple that they would not be harmed. Then the Hills would be led aboard a disk-shaped craft and examined. Samples of hair, fingernails, and scrapings of skin would be taken from Betty. Afterward the couple would be returned to their car and allowed to drive home.

The UFO experience resulted in unbearable feelings of persistent anxiety for both Hills. Eventually they consulted Dr. Benjamin Simon, a prominent Boston psychiatrist who specialized in treating personality disorders and amnesia through hypnotherapy.

While they were driving through the White Mountains of New Hampshire late one night in 1961, Betty and Barney Hill had a frightening encounter with a UFO, depicted here, and its occupants.

Dr. Simon treated the Hills for six months, starting in January 1964. During this period, under time-regression hypnosis, some amazing details were revealed. The Hills's stories about their abductors' appearance and actions seemed to match closely. The gist of what they remembered under hypnosis was very much like the content of Betty's nightmares: their abduction so that they might be physically examined.

One of the most fascinating aspects of the case concerns the "star map" the leader showed Betty when she asked him where he was from. This map was drawn by Betty under posthypnotic suggestion. Several years later an astronomical investigation, based on newly published data (data that was not known in 1961), revealed a cluster of stars near two stars called Zeta Reticuli that is amazingly close in configuration to the "map" drawn by Betty. This "match" has become a very controversial subject among UFO investigators and several members of the scientific community.

Dr. Simon has expressed the professional opinion that the Hills's account of their abduction by UFOnauts was a fantasy. The reason Barney's account matched Betty's so closely was that he absorbed and believed all the details Betty experienced in her dreams and then recounted to him. People do not necessarily tell the factual truth while they are under hypnosis—all they tell is what they *believe* to be the truth. (*The Encyclopedia of UFOs*, Ronald D. Story, ed., pp.172–77; *The Humanoids*, Charles Bowen, ed., pp.239–41)

On the evening of October 11, 1973, Calvin Parker and Charles Hickson were fishing near Pascagoula, Mississippi, when they both saw a bright, 20-foot-long oval object land nearby. Three occupants emerged and advanced toward them. The five-foot-tall creatures were pale gray in color with horribly wrinkled skin. They had no neck, their arms ended in clawlike hands with only two fingers, and their legs seemed to be fused together. The sight made Parker faint. Hickson was carried off by one of the creatures, while another took the unconscious Parker. They "floated" toward the UFO and entered the craft. Hickson found himself in a very brightly lit room where a large "eyelike" device "examined" him minutely. Afterward Hickson and Parker were both "floated" out of the UFO and deposited back on the riverbank. The two men, after some hesitation and a few drinks, told their story to a sheriff, and the incident became headline news. A lie detector test that supposedly corroborated their account was later questioned. Hickson then refused to take another test. Since both men were afraid of hypnosis and would not submit themselves to it, no additional insights could be gained by that technique. (*The Encyclopedia of UFOs*, Ronald D. Story, ed., pp.260–62)

Carlos Alberto Diaz, a 28-year-old waiter in the town of Ingeniero White, Argentina, was found lying by the side of the road about 7 A.M., January 5, 1975. His scalp was exposed in spots where tufts of hair were missing. He was driven some 30 miles to a hospital in Buenos Aires (about 350 miles from his hometown), and there Diaz claimed that his hair had been forcibly removed by three humanoids with rubbery "moss green" skin and stumpy arms with suckers. Forty-six doctors and specialists and several police investigators questioned and examined Diaz, who quietly and believably adhered to his story of abduction.

He stated that he had left work in the predawn that morning. On his walk home he was crossing a deserted railroad yard when he saw a very bright but "broken" beam of light, which he took for lightning and which temporarily blinded him. When his sight returned he found himself paralyzed, and he heard a persistent "hum" in the air. Suddenly he felt himself being *"drawn and absorbed upwards"* by what he described as the "windy humming of the beam." Then he fainted.

He awoke inside a smooth, shining unfurnished "sphere" about 8 feet wide and 10 feet high. Three entities "slid" into the room and started pressing their peculiar arms against his long hair, somehow "sucking up" whole tufts of it at a time but without causing any pain. The heads of these beings were half the size of ours and totally hairless; their moss-green faces were featureless, lacking eyes, nose, mouth, and ears. They were about five feet seven inches tall and had slim bodies covered with soft, pale, cream-colored "rubber." While they "extracted" clumps of Diaz's hair, they jumped up and down gleefully. After working on his head, the entities started to remove tufts of hair from his chest. Diaz fainted again.

Some hours later Diaz found himself stretched out on the grass in the bright morning sunlight. The bag he had been carrying was lying next to him. Glancing at his watch, he saw that it had stopped at 3:50 A.M., whereas it was now obviously much later. He felt nauseous and began to vomit. At that point a motorist noticed him and came to his aid.

The medical examination established that some of Diaz's head and chest hair had indeed been removed. Some of it seemed to have been "sheared off," but quite a bit had been extracted by the roots, leaving the surrounding capillary tissues completely clean. How this could have been done is uncertain. One theory is that the "beings" created enough suction to "dilate" the capillary bulbs around the roots so that the individual hairs came out smoothly. Other than the missing hair and the nausea, which persisted for several days, the medical team found nothing else wrong with D (*Flying Saucer Review*, 21:39–42, November 1

HEAVENS ABOVE: ATMOSPHERIC AND ASTRONOMICAL ODDITIES

The heavens have always been a screen on which people projected their deepest beliefs and hopes in the order of the cosmos. Weather might be unpredictable, but the regular cycle of the seasons stood behind every thunderbolt and hurricane. Meteors and comets flared above, but the "fixed stars" wheeled beyond them every night.

The heavens were, until recent times, seen as a unified system; the atmospheric events we call "weather" were not clearly separated from celestial events, and events that regularly occurred together were seen to have cause-and-effect relationships. The "dog days" of summer can be traced back to the Egyptian observation that the rising of Sirius, the Dog Star, meant a period of hot, still weather. In all parts of the world the orientation of the crescent moon has been interpreted as signifying rain or drought. Not all such beliefs should be dismissed as superstition: the links between sunspots and climate and between the moon's position and storms are being intensively studied today; both are thought to work through interactions in the thin upper atmosphere and through subtle "air tides" similar to the tides of the sea.

Large-scale weather could not be understood until good maps and communications were available to trace the movements of the air. Today the international network of weather stations and satellites gives reliable long-range forecasts of large weather patterns, but, in a seeming paradox, forecasters cannot tell us whether a given cloud will rain on us, on the next county, or not at all. The general laws and statistics that apply to large-scale weather are of little help on a small scale. The continent-sized loops of moving air that shape whole seasons are generally stable from year to year. The smaller loops that can tighten into hurricanes tend to follow repetitive tracks but can swerve with little warning. Tornadoes are dangerously capricious; and whirlwinds and dust devils are totally unpredictable.

So it is the local, unpredictable, sometimes bizarre and incomprehensible atmospheric events that are recorded here: waterspouts, abnormal fogs, inexplicable mirages, thunder and other noises that seem to come from nowhere, ball lightning, strange auroral effects, and more. Some of these events are now well documented and classified. Others are so rare that they must be considered inexplicable until chance brings together the right observers, instruments, and circumstances.

BEFORE 1700

On June 18, 1178, a group of men saw the upper cusp of the new moon "split in two." According to the chronicler Gervase of Canterbury:

> From the midpoint of this division a flaming torch sprang up, spewing out, over a considerable distance, fire, hot coals, and sparks. Meanwhile the body of the moon which was below writhed, as it were, in anxiety.... This phenomenon was repeated a dozen times or more, the flame assuming various twisting shapes at random and then returning to normal.

> Then after these transformations the moon from horn to horn ... took on a blackish appearance. The present writer was given this report by men who saw it with their own eyes....

Almost 800 years later, space scientist Jack Hartung put the medieval account together with modern calculations and realized that Gervase may well have recorded the lunar meteor impact that created the 12-mile-wide crater Giordano Bruno. (*Meteoritics*, 11:187–94, September 30, 1976)

"A luminous cloud was seen, driven with some violence from E. to W., where it disappeared below the horizon" on the same day an earthquake occurred at Florence, Italy, on December 9, 1731. Like many accounts of earthquake lights, this one is tantalizing because it lacks detail that would identify it either as escaping gas or as some auroral display stimulated by magnetic effects of the earthquake. (*Report of the Twenty-second Meeting of the British Association for the Advancement of Science,* 22:129, 1852)

Before dawn on October 23, 1740, James Short, an expert optician and a Fellow of the Royal Society, was watching the sky:

> Directing a reflecting telescope of 16.5 inches
> focus . . . towards Venus, I perceived a small star
> pretty nigh her; upon which I took another telescope
> of the same focal distance, which magnified about
> fifty or sixty times. . . . Finding Venus very distinct,
> and consequently the air very clear, I put on a
> magnifying power of 240 times, and to my great
> surprise found this star put on the same phasis with
> Venus [that is, it showed the same phase or pattern
> of sunlight and shadow, indicating that it was near
> Venus rather than a distant star]. . . . Its diameter
> seemed about a third, or somewhat less, of the
> diameter of Venus; its light was not so bright or
> vivid, but exceeding sharp and well defined. . . . I
> saw it for the space of an hour several times that
> morning; but the light of the sun increasing, I lost it
> altogether about a quarter of an hour after eight. I
> have looked for it every clear morning since, but
> never had the good fortune to see it again.

Short was a premier telescope maker and would hardly have been deceived by a "ghost Venus"—an internal reflection within the eyepiece—as some have suggested. Others who saw an apparent satellite of Venus included Gian Domenico Cassini, the discoverer of four of Saturn's moons, in 1672 and 1686; Andreas Meier in 1759; T. W. Webb in 1823; and M. Stuyvanert in 1884. Today there is no trace of any satellite of Venus. (*Nature,* 14:193-94, June 29, 1876)

Phantom soldiers appeared on and above a mountain in Scotland on June 23, 1744. Twenty-seven witnesses, some of whom gave sworn testimony to a local magistrate, watched the aerial maneuvers for up to two hours before darkness ended the display. Sir David Brewster, in his *Letters on Natural Magic,* suggested that it must have been a mirage of troops on the far side of the mountain and linked the hypothetical troops to the Scottish rebellion of the following year. (*Notes and Queries,* 1:7:304, March 26, 1853)

There were earthquakes at many points in England and throughout Europe in 1750. Several days before the March 2 tremor in London, "there were reddish bows in the air, which took the same direction as the shock." At the moment of the April 2 quake in Warrington, England, the Reverend Sedden saw "an infinite number of rays of light, proceeding from all parts of the sky, to one point near the zenith." An aurora accompanied the August 23 quake at Spalding, England, and Northampton felt the earth shudder on September 30. Dr. Doddridge reported a fireball that morning, a red sky the following night, and the night after that "the finest aurora he ever saw." (*Magazine of Natural History,* 7:300-01, July 1834)

An extraordinary fog astonished the colonists in Connecticut one morning in 1758. One of them wrote:

> . . . about sun-rise, at this place was a fog of so
> strange and extraordinary appearance, that it filled
> us all with amazement. It came in great bodies, like
> thick clouds, down to the earth, and in its way,
> striking against the houses, would break and fall
> down the sides in great bodies, rolling over and over.

Our First Century, a book published in 1874, included this 1780 engraving entitled "Wonderful Dark Day," which shows daytime farm workers carrying lanterns.

Mariner 10 *photographed Venus from 450,000 miles away on February 6, 1974. No recent observations of Venus have detected any satellites of the planet.*

It resembled the thick steam rising from boiling wort [a plant used in making soap], and was attended with such heat that we could hardly breathe. When first I saw it I really thought my house had been on fire, and ran out to see if it was so; but many people thought the world was on fire, and the last day come. One of our neighbors was then at Sutton, 100 miles to the eastward, and reports it was much the same there. [*Annual Register,* 1:90–91, 1758]

A large number of luminous globes filled the air on the day of an earthquake at Boulogne, France, in 1779. (Felix Sestier, *De La Foudre,* Vol. 1, p.169)

Subterranean "thunder" was heard at Guanajuato, Mexico, in 1784, although there was no earth tremor. (*Philosophical Magazine,* 5:49:58, January 1900)

A "bright ball of fire and light" accompanied a hurricane that struck England on September 2, 1786. If it was ball lightning, it was unusually persistent, lasting a full 40 minutes. (Charles Fort, *The Complete Books of Charles Fort,* p.100)

After Sir William Herschel's observations of "volcanoes" on the moon in 1783 and 1787, a German astronomer named Johann Hieronymus Schröter saw something even stranger. In 1788 he noted, to the east of the lunar Alps and in their shadow, "a bright point, as brilliant as a fifth-magnitude star, which disappeared after he had watched it for fifteen minutes." After the moon had turned enough to bring the site into full sunlight, Schröter saw a round shadow, varying from gray to black, where it had been.

Johannes Hevelius's Selenographia *(1647) contained this early detailed map of the lunar surface. Some of his names for lunar features, including the Alps, are still in use.*

It has been proposed that Schröter saw first a mountain peak projecting above the shadow cast by the adjacent lunar Alps and then a shadow cast by the mountain itself, but as a selenographer esteemed enough to have another crater named for him in later years, would Schröter have failed to make that identification himself? And how could a steep mountain cast a round shadow under light from any direction? (*The Popular Science Monthly,* 34:158–61, December 1888)

A mirage of a walled town was seen at Youghal, Ireland, in October 1796, again the following March, and in June 1801 there appeared a mirage of an unknown city—mansions surrounded by shrubbery with a forest behind them. (Charles Fort, *The Complete Books of Charles Fort,* p.391)

FROM 1800 TO 1830

A weird marine noise was heard by naturalist Alexander von Humboldt and other members of his expedition to South America:

On the 20th of February, 1803, toward seven in the evening, the whole crew were astounded by an extraordinary noise, which resembled that of drums beating in the air. It was at first attributed to the breakers. Speedily it was heard in the vessel, and especially toward the poop. It was like a boiling, the noise of the air which escapes from fluid in a state of ebullition. They then began to fear that there was some leak in the vessel. It was heard unceasingly in all parts of the vessel, and finally, about nine o'clock, it ceased altogether.

Humboldt's French contemporary Baron Cuvier confidently ascribed the sound to fish of the group called the sciaenoids, but this was later studied and found to be unlikely (see the second entry for 1870 on page 243). (*Nature,* 2:46, May 19, 1870)

Lewis and Clark, on their 1804–06 expedition to the far west of the United States, heard booming noises like cannon at a site near what is now Great Falls, Montana. A party outfitted by John Jacob Astor heard similar noises in the Black Hills of South Dakota and Wyoming a few years later. (*Nature,* 53:487, March 26, 1896)

The light that filled the London sky for a few seconds one December night in 1814 was attributed to a meteor by the editors of *Annals of Philosophy.* Their informant, John Wallis, described it:

. . . at about 20 minutes before 11, I was walking in an open part of the village of Peckham. . . . The night was cloudy and dark, the lower part of the atmosphere clear and calm. . . . Suddenly I was surrounded by a great light. I remember that at the

Lights on the Moon

William Herschel, the German-born English astronomer who has been called the greatest observer in the history of the science, was observing the dark portion of the new moon on April 19 and 20, 1787, when he saw three spots of light that he called volcanoes, "two of them . . . either already nearly extinct, or otherwise in a state of approaching eruption . . . the third [showing] an actual eruption of fire, or luminous matter." He compared the light of the third source to "a small piece of burning charcoal, when it is covered by a very thin coat of white ashes." Three years later, during an eclipse, he noticed more than 150 "red, luminous points . . . small and round."

In 1822 *The American Journal of Science and Arts* printed reports from two observers of spots of light in the crater Aristarchus, concluding that "the hypothesis of volcanoes in the moon is not modern, and at present it is almost rejected." Instead, it was proposed that light from earth was being reflected from an unusually flat, smooth area of the lunar surface.

Other reports have accumulated over the years, so that in 1965 astronomer Zdenek Kopal could sum up 16 observations of lights near Aristarchus and a handful more in other lunar regions. But by then volcanoes seemed less likely than ever. Much smaller than the earth, the moon must have lost its internal heat more rapidly. If there is molten rock at all, it is almost certainly too deep to reach the moon's surface in eruptions.

Kopal and his colleagues obtained color pictures of the moon through red, green, and infrared filters. These images showed distinct brightening of large areas, especially the region of the crater Kepler. The luminescence faded within half an hour, only to reappear later that night. Noting that powerful solar flares had occurred shortly before, Kopal attributed at least some instances of light from dark regions of the moon to the effect of high-speed solar particles on the moon's dusty soil. His calculations did not, however, explain the reports of excess light from sunlit regions, where much more energy would be needed to create a

Sir William Herschel and his sister Caroline, both noted astronomers, worked together in their observatory.

noticeable glow: "This gives rise to a suspicion that the effects of solar activity may depend on processes that are not yet understood."

Another possibility was set forth a few years later by A. A. Mills, who had studied experimental "fluidized beds" of fine dust churned up by gas from below. (Such an arrangement is used, more mundanely, as an efficient way of burning coal.) He wrote in *Nature*:

> The generation of considerable electrostatic potentials in fluidized beds has been reported. On a larger scale, many industrial accidents have been traced to the movement of dust-laden air generating potential differences sufficient to promote an incendiary spark. Natural dust storms cause violent disturbances of the terrestrial electric field.

If there are gases trapped within the moon's crust, then, and if they are occasionally released by tidal strains or by shock waves from a meteor impact, they could create a momentary fluidized bed in the lunar dust. That, in turn, could generate a hazy "glow discharge" of static electricity. Well and good—but could such a transient phenomenon account for Herschel's observations on successive nights? Could Kopal's explanation account for the wide variety of colors, from bluish-purple through orange, ascribed to the mysterious lunar lights over the years? Perhaps several mechanisms will have to be combined to account for what Herschel thought were volcanoes . . . or perhaps Herschel saw just what he thought he saw, and the moon is not geologically "dead" after all.

---

instant I shrunk downward and stooped forward; as I was apprehensive of some danger behind me, I instantly ran a few paces. I turned about in a few seconds. . . . But I saw nothing to cause this light. It did not give me the idea of the force and intensity of lightning; its brilliancy was not so instantaneous and fierce; but it was a softer and paler kind of light, and lasted perhaps three seconds. I could discover no noise, though immediately I expected an explosion.

The strength of the light was nearly equal to that of common day-light; all near objects were distinctly visible. . . . None of the persons I met that night thought it to be lightning, though none of them saw anything but the light. [*Annals of Philosophy,* 5:235–36, March 1815]

At Comrie, Scotland, mysterious booming noises have been reported since 1597. In 1816 a resident observed "a large luminous body, bent like a crescent, which stretched itself over the heavens." (*The Edinburgh New Philosophical Journal,* 31:117, April–October 1841)

"Strange, howling noises" in the air and large spots obscuring the sun were reported along with an earthquake at Palermo, Italy, in April 1817. (*Report of the Twenty-fourth Meeting of the British Association for the Advancement of Science,* 24:111, 1854)

What seemed to be an unknown planet was seen crossing the sun's disk by the German astronomer Stark in Augsburg on October 9, 1819. He observed the same thing again on February 12, 1820. The second appearance was described as "a singular and well-defined circular spot with indications of an atmosphere, which was not visible in the evening of the same day"—as any planet with an orbit inside the earth's should have been. (*Monthly Notices of the Royal Astronomical Society,* 20:98–101, January 13, 1860)

One of the most widespread "dark days" of history came to eastern Canada and New England on November 10, 1819. There had been a heavy, soaplike rain on November 8, which left behind a sooty residue. Then, in Montreal:

> On the morning of Tuesday, the 10th, heavy clouds again covered the sky, and changed rapidly from a deep green to a pitchy black, and the sun, when occasionally seen through them, was sometimes of a dark brown or an unearthly yellow color, and again bright orange, and even blood red ... the day became almost as dark as night, the gloom increasing and diminishing most fitfully. At noon lights had to be burned in the courthouse, the banks, and public offices of the city. Everybody was more or less alarmed. ...
>
> About the middle of the afternoon a great body of clouds seemed to rush suddenly over the city, and the darkness became that of night. A pause and hush for a moment or two succeeded, and then one of the most glaring flashes of lightning ever beheld flamed over the country, accompanied by a clap of thunder which seemed to shake the city to its foundations ... [and] then came a light shower of rain of the same soapy and sooty nature as that of two days before. ... Another rush of clouds came, and another vivid flash of lightning, which was seen to strike the spire of the old French parish church and to play curiously about the large iron cross at its summit before descending to the ground. A moment later came the climax of the day. Every bell in the city suddenly rang out the alarm of fire, and the affrighted citizens rushed out from their houses into the streets. ... Directly the great iron cross, together with the ball at its foot, fell to the ground with a crash, and was shivered to pieces ... the real night came on, and when next morning dawned everything was bright and clear, and the world was as natural as before.

The rain's strange texture suggests a distant volcanic eruption or forest fire—the usual explanation for dark days. But the accompanying electrical storm hints at something more than just smoke. Meteorologists do not yet know much about the effects of such rarely occurring clouds of smoke and ash upon the weather. (*Scientific American,* 44:329, May 21, 1881)

At the village of Babino Polje in the center of a valley in Mljet Island in the Adriatic Sea remarkable sounds were heard. They started on March 20, 1822:

> They resembled the reports of cannon, and were loud enough to produce a shaking in the doors and windows of the village. They were at first attributed to the guns of some ships of war, at a distance, in the open sea, and then to the exercise of Turkish artillery, on the Ottoman frontiers. These discharges were repeated four, ten, and even a hundred times in a day, at all hours and in all weathers, and continued to prevail until the month of February, 1824, from which time there was an intermission of seven months. In September of the same year, the detonations recommenced, and continued, but more feeble and rare, to the middle of March, 1825, when they again ceased. [*The American Journal of Science and Arts,* 1:10:377, February 1826]

In 1829, on an expedition into what became New South Wales, Australia, Captain Sturt's expedition heard cannonlike noises on a clear, calm day in flat, wooded country along the Darling River. "To this day the singularity of such a sound, in such a situation, is a matter of mystery to me," Sturt wrote. (*Nature,* 81:127, July 29, 1909)

Capt. Charles Sturt and his party were pictured in a small sailboat and a difficult situation in Romance of Australia. *Sturt led three expeditions into the Australian interior.*

The mysterious cannonlike sounds at Comrie, Scotland, began a two-year "barrage" in October 1839. Almost 250 blasts, many accompanied by earth tremors, were heard between then and October 1841. (*The Edinburgh New Philosophical Journal*, 32:106–09, October 1841–April 1842)

At Forest Hill, Arkansas, the sky was clear on December 8, 1847. Then, in midafternoon, turbulent clouds formed suddenly, appearing "like a solid black fleece lighted from above by a red glare as of many torches." A loud explosion shook houses and rang the bell of the church, and a barrel-sized flaming body crashed into the earth just outside the town, making a hole eight feet deep and more than two feet in diameter. The rock that was found at the bottom of the hole smelled of sulfur and was hot enough to boil away water thrown on it. Inside of 20 minutes the sky cleared and the sun shone again.

Fulgurites are formed when lightning strikes sand or rock and vitrifies it. Sand fulgurites characteristically have branched, tubular forms, as shown above.

Was the phenomenon at Forest Hill a meteorite impact? If so, there is no plausible explanation for the clouds beforehand; a meteorite passes through the entire atmosphere within a few seconds and cannot affect the air over its impact zone while still scores or hundreds of miles away. Is it possible that lightning fused the soil into a solid mass at the bottom of the hole? Such a stone, known as fulgurite, is not uncommon, but barrel-sized chunks are unheard of. (*The American Journal of Science and Arts*, 2:5:293–94, May 1848)

A phantom battle was reported at the village of Büderich in Westphalia, on January 22, 1854:

> Shortly before sunset, an army, of boundless extent, and consisting of infantry, cavalry, and an enormous number of waggons, was observed to proceed across the country in marching order. So distinctly seen were all these appearances, that even the flashing of the firelocks, and the colour of the cavalry uniform, which was white, could be distinguished. This whole array advanced in the direction of the wood of Schafhauser, and as the infantry entered the thicket, and the cavalry drew near, they were hid all at once, with the trees, in a thick smoke. Two houses, also, in flames, were seen with the same distinctness. At sunset the whole phenomenon vanished. As respects the fact, government has taken the evidence of fifty eye-witnesses, who have deposed to a universal agreement respecting this most remarkable appearance.

Local citizens considered it a supernatural "replay" of a battle that had taken place nearby some years earlier. There were no battles anywhere in Germany in January 1854, so the suggestion that it was a mirage of a faraway scene is scarcely more credible. (*Notes and Queries*, 1:9:267, March 1854)

A planet closer to the sun than Mercury was observed on March 26, 1859, by a French country doctor and amateur astronomer named Lescarbault. He watched it begin its transit across the sun's disk and, after an interruption to attend a patient, finished timing the transit and chalked his observations on a pineboard. Lescarbault's evidence was good enough to convince Urbain Jean Joseph Le Verrier, the most illustrious astronomer in France, of its existence. Le Verrier proposed that the gravitational pull of Vulcan would explain the advance of Mercury's perihelion (its closest point to the sun), observed to be 43 inches every hundred years. Unfortunately, Lescarbault's planet—also called Vulcan—has never been proved to exist, and today most astronomers think that the country doctor and hundreds of others over the years were somehow mistaken. (*The American Journal of Science and Arts*, 2:29:415–17, May 1860)

A commemorative medallion struck in honor of Urbain Jean Le Verrier had his portrait on one side and, on the other, 10 planets, including Vulcan, revolving around the sun.

Vulcan: The Once (and Future?) Planet

Prehistoric skywatchers noticed that five bright points of light did not move with the wheeling of the fixed stars. These planets—Mercury, Venus, Mars, Jupiter, and Saturn—were woven into astrology and legend. Around A.D. 1600 the earth itself came to be recognized as another member of the sun's family. Sir William Herschel (see page 239) discovered Uranus in 1781. In the 1840's Urbain Jean Joseph Le Verrier and John Couch Adams independently analyzed small irregularities in Uranus' orbit, which led to the discovery of Neptune in 1846; then 84 years later a similar study of Uranus and Neptune pointed the way to frigid Pluto, the outermost known planet.

Along the way, however, a 10th planet had made a brief appearance. The existence of Vulcan, a small planet supposedly orbiting even closer to the sun than Mercury, was affirmed in 1859 by no less an authority than Urbain Le Verrier. His suspicion had been aroused by Mercury's tiny deviation from its predicted path. Combing the records, he found many reports of a small black disk seen fleetingly against the sun. From these reports Le Verrier selected the most consistent and computed that Vulcan must orbit about 13 million miles from the sun, with a year of only 20 earth days.

It was clear that further observations of Vulcan would require both luck and skill. Most of the time it would be lost in the sun's glare. Only during solar eclipses or during its periodic "transits" of the sun—when it could easily be mistaken for a sunspot—would it stand out. Le Verrier predicted that the best viewing date would be on March 22, 1877.

In the years that followed, further scattered reports were published, and some textbooks added Vulcan to the list of planets. Thus it was discouraging when not one of the many astronomers poised to observe it in 1877 was able to find Vulcan. But hopes rose again the following year, when two American astronomers observing an eclipse from separate sites in Wyoming and Colorado spotted something that was not a known star very near the sun. A writer in *Popular Science* said:

> The interesting observations of Prof. Watson and Mr. Swift will not only stimulate astronomers to renewed search for the planet so fortunately detected, but must lead also to a more thorough examination of the space within Mercury's orbit. It is not improbable that the detection of Vulcan may be merely the first in a series of similar discoveries.

Alas for optimism. The Watson and Swift observations were not repeated, and other astronomers—having been burned often enough to be very shy indeed of any alleged Vulcan—questioned the accuracy of the Americans' sightings.

When Le Verrier's calculations proved to be faulty, the French began to satirize his efforts, as illustrated by these two caricatures of the astronomer.

FROM 1860 TO 1880

A superheated whirlwind passed through Cheatham County, Tennessee, one summer day in 1869:

> On the farm of Ed. Sharp, five miles from Ashland, a sort of whirlwind came along over the neighbouring woods, taking up small branches and leaves of trees and burning them in a sort of flaming cylinder that travelled at the rate of about five miles an hour, developing size as it travelled. It passed directly over the spot where a team of horses were feeding and singed their manes and tails up to the roots; it then swept towards the house, taking a stack of hay in its course. It seemed to increase in heat as it went, and by the time it reached the house it immediately fired the shingles from end to end of the building, so that in ten minutes the whole dwelling was wrapped in flames. The tall column of travelling caloric [the chemical "substance" of fire, according to a theory already outmoded in 1869] then continued its course over a wheat field that had been recently cradled, setting fire to all the stacks that happened to be in its course. Passing from the field, its path lay over a stretch of woods which reached the river. The green leaves on the trees were crisped to a cinder for a breadth of 20 yards, in a straight line to the Cumberland. When the "pillar of fire" reached the water, it suddenly changed its route down the river, raising a column of steam which went up to the clouds for about half-a-mile, when it finally died out. Not less than 200 people witnessed this strangest of strange phenomena, and all of them tell substantially the same story about it. The farmer, Sharp, was left houseless by the devouring element,

and his two horses were so affected that no good is expected to be got out of them in future. Several withered trees in the woods through which it passed were set on fire, and continue burning still. [*Symons's Monthly Meteorological Magazine,* 4:123, September 1869]

This phenomenon combines the most peculiar aspects of whirlwinds—their self-contained nature, apparently unconnected to clouds and large-scale weather—and of tornadoes, which are often accompanied by a variety of odd electrical discharges. It is worth noting that to set fire to straw and shingles, heated air alone (assuming no electrical sparks) would have to be at 400°F or more.

Changing patterns of lights appeared in the lunar crater Plato from the late 1860's through 1871. Reputable selenologists saw them often enough to assign them numbers and chart their dimming and brightening. More than 1,600 such observations were collected by selenographer W. R. Birt and deposited in the library of the Royal Astronomical Association. (*Report of the Forty-first Meeting of the British Association for the Advancement of Science,* 41:60–97, 1871)

On March 22, 1870, the crew of the bark *Lady of the Lake,* located in the mid-Atlantic, watched a strange, umbrella-shaped cloud climb from the southeastern sky near to the zenith, then sink to the northeast, retaining its shape for more than 20 minutes. "Its general appearance was similar to that of a halo round the sun or moon," according to the ship's log, "of a light grey colour, and though distinctly defined in shape, the patches of cirro-cumulus at the back could be clearly seen through." (*Quarterly Journal of the Royal Meteorological Society,* 1:157, 1873)

In 1870 several correspondents to *Nature* took up the question of the "Grey Town Noises," heard on the Atlantic coast of Costa Rica and Nicaragua and near Trinidad. Charles Dennehy reported that the "peculiar metallic vibratory sound . . . musical . . . with a certain cadence, and a one-two-three time tendency of beat," was heard only in iron rather than wooden ships and seemed to come through the iron from the water:

> By English sailors it was considered to be caused by the trumpet fish, or what they called such (certainly not the *Centriscus scolopax,* which does not even exist here). . . . But if caused by any kind of fish, why only at one place, and why only at certain hours of the night? . . . What is, then, this nocturnal music? Is it the result of a molecular change or vibration in the iron . . . ?

C. Kingsley replied that he had heard the sound, "like a locomotive in the distance rattling as it blows off

steam," from the shore of Trinidad and that it could be heard on wooden ships as well:

> The natives told me that the noise was made by a fish, and a specimen of the fish was given me, which is not *Centriscus scolopax,* the snipe-fish, but the trumpet-fish, or *Fistularia.* I no more believe that it can make the noise than Mr. Dennehy believes (and he is quite right) that the *Centriscus* can make it.

(*Nature,* 2:25–26, May 12, 1870; 2:46, May 19, 1870)

The longspine snipefish has been named as a possible noisemaker. Its long, tubular snout and thick body suggest another common name for it, the bellows fish.

What may have been ball lightning appeared to a woman in Remenham, England, on a cold day in 1871. "The wall paper and furniture of the room . . . were suddenly flushed with rose colour, which gradually deepened into crimson, passing through bright gold into orange, lilac and deep violet." She looked out the window and saw "air bubbles" a few inches in diameter rising from the level snow outside. They took on the same hues seen inside and bobbed up and down before a breeze blew them away, only to be replaced by another group. There were no apparent sparks or electrical odors. (*Quarterly Journal of the Royal Meteorological Society,* 13:306, October 1887)

Ball lightning can pass through windows, then exit through the door without doing damage. A storm in Salagnac, France, in September 1845 produced this phenomenon.

Similar bubbles were observed in very different weather at Ringstead Bay, England, in August 1876. A mother and daughter were walking near a seaside cliff on a hot, sultry afternoon marked by sheet lightning but no thunder:

> Over the crest of the ground, surrounding them on all sides, and extending from a few inches above the surface to 2 or 3 feet overhead, numerous globes of light, the size of billiard balls, were moving independently and vertically up and down, sometimes within a few inches of the observers, but always eluding the grasp; now gliding slowly upwards 2 or 3 feet, and as slowly falling again, resembling in their movements soap bubbles floating in the air. The balls were all aglow.... Their numbers were continually fluctuating; at one time thousands of them apparently enveloped the observers, and a few minutes afterwards the numbers would dwindle to perhaps as few as twenty, but soon they would be swarming again as numerous as ever. Not the slightest noise accompanied this display.
>
> The ladies sauntered up to the quarry and down again several times along the edge of the cliff, viewing the phenomenon for upwards of an hour.... About 10 P.M. a severe thunderstorm, attended with torrents of rain, came up from the sea.... [*Quarterly Journal of the Royal Meteorological Society*, 13:305, October 1887]

FROM 1880 TO 1900

At Clarens, Switzerland, an 1880 thunderstorm was more than typically terrifying. According to the London *Times* correspondent,

> ...a tremendous peal of thunder shook the houses of Clarens and Tavel to their foundations. At the same instant a magnificent cherry-tree near the cemetery, measuring a metre in circumference, was struck by lightning. Some people who were working in a vineyard hard by saw the electric "fluid" play about a little girl who had been gathering cherries and was already 30 paces from the tree. She was literally folded in a sheet of fire. The vine-dressers fled in terror from the spot. In the cemetery six persons, separated into three groups, none of them within 250 paces of the cherry-tree, were enveloped in a luminous cloud. They felt as if they were being struck in the face with hailstones or fine gravel, and when they touched each other sparks of electricity passed from their finger-ends. At the same time a column of fire was seen to descend in the direction of Le Châtelard, and it is averred that the electric fluid could be distinctly heard as it ran from point to point of the iron railing of a vault in the cemetery ... neither the little girl, the people in the cemetery, nor the vine-dressers appear to have been hurt;

> the only inconvenience complained of being an unpleasant sensation in the joints, as if they had been violently twisted, a sensation which was felt with more or less acuteness for a few hours after ... the trunk of the cherry-tree is as completely shivered as if it had been exploded by a charge of dynamite. [*Nature*, 22:204, July 1, 1880]

The "Yellow Day" that came to New England and New York State on September 6, 1881, has been ascribed—like many other such phenomena—to a prairie fire or forest fire in the Far West, its smoke at high altitude being concentrated by local atmospheric eddies. Be that as it may, no specific fire has been associated with the Yellow Day.

According to the Springfield (Massachusetts) *Daily Republican*, the day began with a heavy ground fog before sunrise; "as the sun rose invisibly behind, the vapours became a thick, brassy canopy, through which a strange yellow light pervaded the air." Natural colors were distorted, yellow flowers appearing gray and the grass bluish. Gas and electric lights were turned on throughout the city, although both seemed to emit an unnatural light themselves. "There was a singular luminousness on every fence and roof-ridge, and the trees seemed to be ready to fly into fire." The strange light deepened and brightened until it finally began to pass in midafternoon. Even then the sun looked like a rouge-colored ball surrounded by yellow clouds. "The temperature throughout the day was very close and oppressive, and the physical effect was one of heaviness and depression." (*Nature*, 24:540, October 6, 1881)

On the night of July 3, 1882, the moon was almost full. About 45 minutes after moonrise several residents of Lebanon, Connecticut, noticed a strange spectacle:

> Two pyramidal luminous protuberances appeared on the moon's upper limb. They were not large, but gave the moon a look strikingly like that of a horned owl or the head of an English bull terrier. These points were a little darker than the rest of the moon's face. They slowly faded away a few moments after their appearance, the one on the right and southeasterly quarter disappearing first. About three minutes after their disappearance two black triangular notches were seen on the edge of the lower half of the moon. These points gradually moved toward each other along the moon's edge, and seemed to be cutting off or obliterating nearly a quarter of its surface, until they finally met, when the moon's face instantly assumed its normal appearance. When the notches were nearing each other the part of the moon seen between them was in the form of a dove's tail. [William R. Corliss, *Strange Universe*, p.A1-132]

Four people on an avenue in Davidson's Mains, a suburb of Edinburgh, Scotland, had an unclassifiable experience on the evening of July 23, 1885. As one of them described it:

> . . . we saw a feebly-luminous flash appear on the ground at a distance of some thirty yards down the avenue. It rushed towards us with a wave-like motion, at a rate which I estimate at thirty miles an hour, and seemed to envelop us for an instant. My left hand, which was hanging by my side, experienced precisely the same sensation as I have felt in receiving a shock from a weak galvanic battery. About three minutes afterwards we heard a peal of thunder. . . .
>
> Another of the party says that he observed what seemed to be a luminous cloud running up the avenue with a wavy motion. When it reached the party it rose off the ground and passed over the bodies of two of them, casting a sort of flash on their shoulders . . . the gardener . . . saw a flash of lightning in the direction of [the luminous cloud], but sideways; also that the top of the cloud seemed to be three or four feet from the ground, and it gradually rose higher as it came along. When the cloud reached the party he saw one of them distinctly by its light. . . . [*Nature*, 32:316–17, August 6, 1885]

No forest fire can be blamed for whatever happened in Oshkosh, Wisconsin, on March 19, 1886. At 3 P.M. on a cloudy day, midnight darkness settled down over a five-minute period. It was startling enough to disturb horses and send people rushing through the streets. After 10 minutes it was gone. According to the local newspaper, "cities to the west say the same phenomenon was observed there in advance of its appearance here, showing that the wave of darkness passed from west to east. Nothing could be seen to indicate any air currents overhead." There was no solar eclipse on that day. (*Monthly Weather Review*, 14:79, March 1886)

Soft, inexplicable airborne sounds were heard by Edwin Linton, a scientist for the U.S. Fish Commission, when he worked at Yellowstone Lake, Wyoming, in 1890. He and a guide heard sounds like echoes, slightly metallic reverberations, from the air over the Shoshone Lake. The sounds seemed to begin overhead and move southwest, lasting for 30 seconds at a time. Sometimes they sounded like wind, but there was no evidence of a wind on the lake or in the surrounding trees.

Others who heard the sound were F. H. Bradley in 1872 and Hugh M. Smith in 1919. It was considered "real" enough to merit an entry in the *Ranger Naturalists' Manual* but has never been explained. (*Science*, 22:244–46, November 3, 1893; 63:586–87, June 11, 1926; 71:97–99, January 24, 1930)

Strange sounds were heard near this eerie landscape of Yellowstone National Park. West Thumb Geyser Basin is in the foreground and Yellowstone Lake in the background.

A luminous arch in the night sky startled passengers on a Houston & Texas Central train in 1890:

> The luminous mist was first observed by the engineer, when it was still several hundred yards ahead of the train, and thinking it a prairie fire, he slowed up, thus arousing the passengers, who, with the crew, crowded to the windows and on to the platforms to look at the vast, hueless rainbow spanning the heavens. As the arch was more closely approached its dim, white radiance was seen to be clearly defined against the sky as though painted there by the sweep of a brush dipped in white fire. The stars could be seen shining close against the rim of it, and all around and under the arch. It was in form the half of a perfect circle, one leg resting on the earth, while the other appeared to have been broken off near the base. It seemed to gradually increase in size.
>
> The arch rose directly over the track, and as the train approached it seemed to gather a greater luster . . . under the bridge of light, the surrounding country spanned by it became plainly visible, appearing to be bathed in pale moonlight.
>
> A curious feature of the luminosity was that while it gave all objects a weird, unreal aspect, the shadows which it caused them to throw were black and as clearly defined as silhouettes. In a few minutes after the train passed under the arch it seemed to fade away, melting gradually into the starlit sky. The night was fair and fogless. There was no moon, so the arch must have been self-luminous. [*The American Meteorological Journal*, 8:35, May 1891]

This description seems to rule out a lunar halo or other rainbowlike phenomenon. Auroral displays have been reported this close to earth only in the far north.

Barisal Guns, Mistpoeffers, and Airquakes

Mysterious detonations—booming noises apparently unrelated to thunder or earthquakes—are among the most widespread and puzzling phenomena of nature. Long before the days of dynamite or sonic booms, fishermen in the North Sea were familiar with *mistpoeffers*, their name for the distant rumblings they heard on calm, foggy days. In India's Ganges Delta, the Barisal guns have long been familiar. G. B. Scott's 1896 account in *Nature* expresses well his puzzlement when he tried to trace them:

> The villages are few and far between and very small, firearms were scarce, and certainly there were no cannon in the neighbourhood, and fireworks were not known to the people. I think I am right in saying I heard the reports every night while south of Dhubri, and often during the day ... more distinctly on clear days and nights.
>
> I specially remember spending a quiet Sunday, in the month of May, with a friend at Chilmari, near the river-bank. We had both remarked the reports the night before and when near the hills previously. About 10 A.M. in the day, weather clear and calm, we were walking quietly up and down near the river-bank, discussing the sounds, when we heard the booming distinctly, about as loud as heavy cannon would sound on a quiet day about ten miles off, down the river. Shortly after we heard a heavy boom very much nearer, still south. Suddenly we heard two quick successive reports, more like horse pistol or musket (not rifle) shots close by. I thought they sounded in the air about 150 yards due west of us over the water. My friend thought they sounded north of us. We ran to the bank, and asked our boatmen, moored below, if they heard them, and if so in what direction. They pointed south!

Albert G. Ingalls, who discussed these mysterious sounds in *Science* magazine in 1934, grew up with the sound of the "guns of Seneca Lake" in upstate New York but had no better luck as an investigator: "Their direction is vague, and like the foot of a rainbow, they are always 'somewhere else' when the observer moves to the locality from which they first seemed to come."

Similar noises are called either *marina* or *brontidi* in Italy; to Haitians they are the *gouffre*. Early settlers in the Connecticut River valley (where the towns of Moodus and East Haddam now stand) were told by the Indians that the sounds represented the Indian god's anger at the English god. Unlike many other such noises, those heard in Connecticut often involved earth tremors as well:

> The effects they produce, are various as the intermediate degrees between the roar of a cannon and the noise of a pistol. The concussions of the earth, made at the same time, are as much diversified as the sounds in the air. The shock they give to a dwelling house is the same as the falling of logs on the floor. The smaller shocks produced no emotions of terror or fear in the minds of the inhabitants. They are spoken of as usual occurrences, and are called Moodus noises. But when they are so violent as to be heard in the adjacent towns, they are called earthquakes.

None of the usual signs of earthquakes accompanied the Moodus noises, however, so it may be questioned whether "the concussions of the earth" were a cause or an effect of the atmospheric phenomena.

Scientific attempts to explain such sounds began in earnest in the 1890's, when a Belgian, Ernest Van den Broeck, collected hundreds of pages of testimony about *mistpoeffers* from Iceland to the Bay of Biscay. He also drew the attention of Sir George Darwin, Charles Darwin's son and an expert on the tides, to the problem. That led to publication of many more reports in physical and meteorological journals throughout the English-speaking world.

Soon there were almost as many explanations as there were names for the mysterious noises. Van den Broeck himself believed that the most likely causes were "some peculiar kind of discharge of atmospheric electricity" (in other words, thunder—but from clear skies?), while one of his colleagues, M. Rutot, thought the origin to be internal to the earth, comparing the noise to "the shock which the internal fluid mass might give to the earth's crust." The latter theory was barely plausible even at the time. Although the molten interior zones of the earth certainly transmit earthquake waves, the liquid rock, or magma, cannot possibly slosh around as Van den Broeck's colleague seems to have imagined.

Others suggested that because many of the noises were associated with coastal regions and river deltas, perhaps they came from occasional settling of the earth beneath the steadily accumulating weight of sediment washed to sea. Such settling, though, should have produced large and noticeable waves and probably tidal waves, or *tsunamis*, as well.

246

Rock bursts—the fracturing of boulders or subterranean strata as ancient stresses are relieved—were advanced as a possible cause, but rock bursts produce a higher-pitched noise than that of most of the reported cases—a crack rather than a boom. In any event, most of the areas where rock bursts are common are mountainous regions, where sharp temperature changes can add their effects, rather than lowlands such as the Ganges Delta.

Another theory was offered by Father Saderra Maso, who had studied earthquakes in the Philippines for years before turning his attention to the distant noises that his native parishioners attributed to waves:

> It is a common opinion among the Filipinos that the noises are the effect of waves breaking on the beach or into caverns, and that they are intimately connected with changes in the weather, generally with impending typhoons. Father Saderra Maso is inclined to agree with this view in certain cases. The typhoons in the Philippines sometimes cause very heavy swells, which are propagated more than a thousand kilometres [away], and hence arrive days before the wind acquires any appreciable force. He suggests that special atmospheric conditions may be responsible for the great distances to which the sounds are heard, and that their apparent inland origin may be due to reflection, possibly from the cumulus clouds which crown the neighboring mountains, while the direct sound-waves are shut off by walls of vegetation or inequalities in the ground.

Father Saderra Maso may have been correct, but a theory that depends on distant typhoons, breaking ocean swells, special (unspecified) atmospheric conditions, reflection of sounds by clouds, and strategically placed hills could explain virtually anything.

Similarly, when residents of the northeastern coast of the United States heard booming noises from the Atlantic in the winter of 1977, they were told that a few cases could be traced to sonic booms from Concorde airliners and that the rest were probably more distant sonic booms carried hundreds of miles by special atmospheric conditions. Air layers of a certain temperature and density can unquestionably conduct sounds much farther than usual, just as they can produce mirages of scenes beyond the horizon. However, they are unlikely to last until a scientific investigation can be made, which makes them conveniently untestable as explanations.

In the summer of 1897 the duke of Abruzzi led an expedition to Mount St. Elias, in a glacial region near the Alaskan coast. There they searched out the "Silent City of Alaska," a mirage that many prospectors and Indians had reported seeing over a glacier. C. W. Thornton, a member of the expedition, later wrote: "It required no effort of the imagination to liken it to a city, but was so distinct that it required, instead, faith to believe that it was not in reality a city." Earlier another spectator had written in *The New York Times:* "We could plainly see houses, well-defined streets, and trees. Here and there rose tall spires over huge buildings which appeared to be ancient mosques or cathedrals." Some people believed the apparition to be an image of Bristol, England, which is 2,500 miles across the pole from the site of the extraordinary mirage. Its appearance was reported each year between June 21 and July 10. (*Quarterly Journal of the Royal Meteorological Society,* 27:158–59, April 1901)

The "Silent City of Alaska," a remarkably clear and unusual mirage, is commemorated by this illustration in Alaska, *written by Miner Bruce and published in 1899.*

FROM 1900 TO 1920

Mountains that hurled fire at each other were described to Ellsworth Huntington, a geologist on a field trip in Turkey's Taurus Mountains at the turn of the century. Villagers told him that Keklujek Mountain and Ziaret Mountain "fought" with fireballs across the Euphrates River, sometimes several times a year. Huntington was at first skeptical, but "after hearing substantially the same story from ten or twelve men whom I saw in five different places separated by an extreme distance of 40 or more miles," he said, "I became thoroughly convinced of its truth. . . . One observer said that a glow remained after the flash, but all the rest contradicted this. Another said that the ball of fire was first small, but grew larger as it passed over, and then grew smaller again...." (*Monthly Weather Review*, 28:286–87, July 1900)

The summer of 1902 brought drought and dust storms to Australia, with trade winds blowing the dust so thickly over the Malay Archipelago that navigation was hindered.

On November 12, fireballs began to strike all over the continent. The dust in the air thickened until residents of Sydney were forced to carry lanterns through the streets. Exploding fireballs—meteoric, electrical, or something else—were reported from Parramatta and Carcoar. On November 20 Sir Charles Todd traced a fireball for four minutes over the Adelaide Observatory; any meteor moving that slowly should scarcely have been heated enough to glow. The last explosion came over Ipswich, Queensland, on November 23. (Vincent Gaddis, *Mysterious Fires and Lights*, pp.81–82)

An apparent dust storm or cloud on Mars was observed in late May 1903 both by W. F. Denning in England and Percival Lowell in Arizona. Interestingly, although Lowell's many straight Martian "canals" eventually proved to be an illusion, his observations of transient changes in the planet's colors are among the best of their time. (*Nature*, 68:353, August 13, 1903; 69:160, December 17, 1903)

The astronomer Percival Lowell was best known for his study of Mars and for his belief in intelligent life on the planet, based on what he thought were irrigation canals and vegetation. He was among the first of the astronomers to realize that the best sky views would be from sites at high altitude with clear air, well away from city lights and smoke, and built an observatory on a 7,200-foot mesa near Flagstaff, Arizona.

A white spot appeared on Jupiter on December 17, 1903, growing from a point to a "bright oblique rift" within five minutes. The observer in Ceylon, a Major Molesworth, wrote the Royal Astronomical Society that "with a lengthy experience in observing Jupiter, [he had] never before noticed any such change in this region of the planet, but [was] perfectly assured that the phenomenon was real." If it was real, an extraordinarily large area had changed color in an unbelievably short time. (*Nature*, 72:207, June 29, 1905)

A brief and inexplicable darkness fell on Wimbledon, England, one April day in 1904. It continued for 10 minutes; there was no sign of rain clouds or of any abnormal amount of smoke. (*Symons's Meteorological Magazine*, 39:69, May 1904)

A beach burst into flames at Kittery Point, Maine, on September 1, 1905:

> ... the guests at the Hotel Parkfield were startled by the appearance of flames rising from the beach and from the surface of the water, an event of so remarkable and unusual a character as to excite great curiosity and some alarm. The conflagration occurred between seven and eight o'clock in the evening, and lasted for upwards of forty-five minutes. The flames were about one foot in height. They were accompanied by a loud and continuous crackling noise which could be distinctly heard one hundred yards away, while at the same time there was a very strong liberation of sulphurous acid fumes which penetrated the hotel, drove the proprietor and his staff from the office and filled the other rooms to such an extent as to cause great inconvenience to the guests. One guest of an investigating turn of mind secured some of the sand in his hand, but was obliged to drop it on account of the heat. When some of the sand was taken into the hotel and stirred in water, bubbles of gas were liberated and produced flame as they broke at the surface in contact with the air.

D. P. Penhallow examined the beach and concluded that a layer of buried seaweed had fermented, creating pockets of "carburetted and phosphuretted hydrogen" and other gases. His explanation is so plausible that one can only wonder why blazing beaches are not a common seaside attraction. (*Science*, New Series 22:794–96, December 15, 1905)

G. H. Martyn wrote to *Nature* magazine in 1906 concerning a thunderstorm he had witnessed in South Tottenham, England:

> ... two of the peals began with a musical note of distinct and definite pitch ... for about two seconds in each case, and the frequency of the note was both times about 400 per second.... I listened carefully to determine that the note had its origin outside and was not due to resonance within the room, and in the second peal it was certainly outside.... [*Nature*, 74:200, June 28, 1906]

A **startling aerial display** unfolded before four witnesses in Burlington, Vermont (one of them a former governor of the state), one day in 1907. They heard a thunderous explosion and looked down the street to see "a torpedo-shaped body . . . about six feet long by eight inches in diameter" floating 50 feet in the air. Its surface was dark, "with here and there tongues of fire issuing from spots on the surface resembling red-hot unburnished copper." The apparition was surrounded by a dim 20-foot halo. There was no sound after the initial blast. Twenty minutes later a heavy downpour without thunder or lightning began. One witness wrote:

> Four weeks have past . . . but the picture of that scene and the terrific concussion caused by it are vividly before me, while the crashing sound still rings in my ears. I hope I may never hear or see a similar phenomenon, at least at such close range.

(*Monthly Weather Review*, 36:310–11, July 1907)

Colored, glowing night skies so bright that newsprint could be read at midnight were remarked all over the United Kingdom and in many parts of Europe on June 30, 1908, and succeeding nights. They appeared steadier than any aurora. L. A. Kulik, the Soviet scientist in charge of the first expedition to the site of the June 30 blast in the Tunguska Basin (variously attributed to the midair explosion of a comet head, a giant meteorite, a black hole, antimatter, and a nuclear blast), believed that meteoritic dust scattered by a gigantic blast was responsible for these "night dawns." (*Nature*, 206:861–65, May 29, 1965; *Popular Astronomy*, 45:559–62, December 1937; *Quarterly Journal of the Royal Meteorological Society*, 34:202, July 1908)

Virtually every tree within 20 miles of the Tunguska blast was knocked down, people were badly burned 40 miles away, and some 400 miles away horses were thrown off their feet.

A gust of wind proved fatal for a schoolgirl in Bradford, England. The *Yorkshire Observer* reported that on February 23, 1911, one witness saw the girl headed for the playground by the school. Another then saw her in the air, parallel with the 20-foot balcony, "her arms extended, and her skirts blown out like a balloon." Later she was carried in, dead of a fall. (*Symons's Meteorological Magazine*, 46:54, April 1911)

In October and November 1911 L. J. Wilson of Nashville, Tennessee, observed a number of brilliant white spots on Mars, near the region labeled Hesperia. (*Nature*, 89:17, March 7, 1912)

A transient "shadow" on the moon was observed by Dr. F. B. Harris on January 27, 1912:

> About 10:30 Eastern time I was surprised to see the left cusp showing the presence of an intensely black body about 250 miles long and fifty wide, allowing 2000 miles from tip of cusp to cusp. The appearance was fully as black comparatively as marks on this paper, and in shape like a crow poised.
>
> Of course dark places are here and there on the lunar surface, but not like this. Not to be tedious I will say that every effort was made to eliminate any error of vision or other mistake. . . . The moon is very tricky and it is very unlikely that anything of this character will be seen in many years or hundreds of years even. I cannot but think that a very interesting and curious phenomenon happened.
> [*Popular Astronomy*, 20:398–99, June–July 1912]

Halos around the moon can be round or occasionally elliptical, single, or multiple, and ideal atmospheric circumstances can create multiple images and even moonbows. But no existing optical theories can account for the *square* halo, three moon diameters on a side with one corner down toward the horizon, that was ob-

Paraselenae (left), rings of light around the moon, are the result of light rays filtering through or striking ice crystals. Lunar coronas (right) are close to the moon and diffuse.

served from the R.M.S. *Balmoral Castle* on the night of January 21, 1913, off the coast of equatorial Africa. In a masterpiece of understatement, Lewis Evans wrote: "I pointed out the halo to some of the ship's officers, none of whom seems to have seen one like it before, so it may be very uncommon." (*Quarterly Journal of the Royal Meteorological Society*, 39:154, April 1913)

Forty to 60 fireballs, apparently meteoric but moving so slowly that some were visible for 40 seconds, passed over Canada and the Atlantic Ocean on February 9, 1913. From more than 140 reports, W. F. Denning established that the total path observed was 5,500 miles, or almost a quarter of the way around the earth. He judged they were moving in near-orbital paths.

The point of origin of a meteor shower (known as the radiant) should in theory move across the sky as the earth follows its curving path around the sun. However, W. F. Denning, who observed meteors and plotted their radiants throughout the late 19th and early 20th centuries, drew attention to showers that seemed to come from the same region of the sky, night after night, for months. In 1913 he wrote in *The Observatory*:

> A few astronomers, in fact, recognizing the insuperable difficulties in explaining stationary radiants, reject them as unproven and suspect them as brought about by many succeeding but distinct showers from directions forming the same apparent radiant during long intervals. But such sceptics wilfully neglect the very real and tangible evidence which supports the fixed radiation of meteors. It is a thing that lives indelibly in the sky, and though previous attempts to account for it are not generally accepted, no observations have succeeded or will succeed in obliterating it from the firmament.

We know much more about meteors today, but Denning's puzzle remains unsolved. Most meteor showers behave as they should, with radiants moving across the sky during the night and the dominant trajectory shifting from night to night as the earth passes through an orbiting stream of cosmic debris—but there is still no good explanation why some do not. (*Nature*, 92:87–88, September 18, 1913; 97:181, April 27, 1916; *The Observatory*, 36:334–39, August 1913; *Popular Astronomy*, 30:632–37, December 1922)

A white spot on Jupiter, which appeared to project above the edge of the planet as the clouds' swift rotation carried it around, was seen on two successive nights in January 1919 by Frank Sargent of Bristol, England. (*Nature*, 102:432, January 30, 1919)

A sky-spanning auroral arch that resembled "the rays of a powerful searchlight" caught the attention of

Auroras—Or Are They?

The aurora borealis, or northern lights, is a breathtaking, eerie spectacle. Its flickering streams and curtains of light, usually from 60 to 250 miles above the ground, have been the inspiration for legends and folklore since prehistoric times. It is almost impossible not to see some image or portent from a supernatural world in the display.

The lights can take a variety of vivid forms, the most common of which have been recognized at least since the time of the Roman writer Seneca:

> the abysses, when beneath a luminous crown the heavenly fire is wanting, forming as it were the circular entrance to a cavern; the turns, when a great rounded flame in the form of a barrel is seen to move from place to place, or to burn immovable; the gulfs, when the heaven seems to open and to vomit flames . . . sometimes these fires are high enough to shine among the stars; at others, so low that they might be taken for the reflection of a distant burning homestead or city. [Seneca, the Younger (Lucius Anneaus), quoted in Richard A. Craig, *The Edge of Space*, pp.117–18]

And a Norseman of the Viking era, speculating boldly as befitted one whose people sailed waters where the ghostly phenomenon can be seen on every clear night, gave some very plausible explanations:

> Some people maintain that this light is a reflection of the fire which surrounds the seas of the north and of the south [clearly he knew of the aurora australis, the southern lights, as well]; others say that it is the reflection of the sun when it is below the horizon; for my part I think that it is produced by the ice which radiates at night the light which it has absorbed by day.

Today, having probed the auroras with satellites, balloons, and various instruments, scientists know they are the result of charged particles streaming out from the sun, which are caught by the earth's magnetic field and funneled toward the poles. There they collide with the scattered gas molecules of the upper atmosphere, "exciting" them to higher energy states so that they give off characteristic colors: the deep red, blue, and violet of nitrogen, the green and pink of oxygen. Solar activity that sends shock waves outward through the "wind" of charged particles and disturbances in the earth's magnetic field can expand the auroral zone southward by many hundreds of miles, even as far as Rome, where (as Seneca reports) the troops of the

The arch (above) is a rare form of the aurora borealis; this was the view from Guilford, England, on October 24, 1870. Below is a photograph of an aurora as seen in Denali National Park in Alaska.

What, then, would account for the experience of the man at a government radio station in northern Canada who watched the light extend itself down until it played about his hands and he had to stoop to walk under a "coloured fog"? And what of the people who have heard a hissing, crackling noise or smelled the ozone of an electrical discharge while the lights shimmered above?

A writer in *Nature* said of these phenomena in 1931: "Inability to understand their physical nature is not a sufficient ground, in the present state of knowledge, for rejecting the possibility of such occurrences." Fifty years later some atmospheric physicists still deny that sounds or smells could be associated with the aurora, preferring to believe that those who report them are deluded because they *expect* electrical sounds or smells, not knowing they are "impossible." But there are surely more things in heaven and earth than current theories allow for—especially in the aurora, where heaven and earth combine to create a glow that has lost little of its mystery over the centuries.

An illustration for a planetarium show places a Norse ship in front of the curtain aurora to indicate that this is generally a northern phenomenon.

emperor Tiberius once rushed from their barracks toward the port of Ostia because they thought it to be on fire. Undoubtedly, these spectacular displays can account for many of the strange lights seen in the heavens over the centuries, but not all occurrences fit the theory of auroras.

There are many reliable reports of auroral activity *near the ground* (for one such account, see page 245, for example). Those reports are difficult or impossible to explain, because the aurora requires a near vacuum: that is, the dense air at ground level should be as "dead" as a leaky neon tube or television picture tube.

William H. Wagner in West Reading, Pennsylvania, on May 2, 1919:

> The light was very steady, with no evidence of flickering or rapid movement.... The beam slowly changed its form, one side fading out.... It was perfectly transparent but grew very bright at times, having at one time almost blotted out the second magnitude star Gamma Leonis. [*Popular Astronomy*, 27:405, June–July 1919]

FROM 1920 TO 1940

About 1920 C. S. Bailey was living at Stockton Heath, England, near the Manchester Ship Canal, where he had noticed a persistent breeze going inland. One July evening he became aware that the air had grown strangely still:

> Gazing down the road, I saw a small black thundercloud gathering along the length of the Canal, and about 30 or 40 ft. above it. It was approximately 100 yards long and perhaps 6 ft. thick. As I gazed at this strange formation, a dazzling lightning flash raced through the entire cloud, i.e. parallel to the water, and a bang like the discharge of field artillery followed immediately. About 40 seconds later, another flash and report occurred: then the cloud thinned and dispersed in about four minutes. [*Weather*, 4:267, August 1949]

Two eminent astronomers, W. W. Campbell, director of the Lick Observatory, and H. N. Russell, director of the Princeton Observatory, were at Campbell's residence on Mount Hamilton, California, in early August 1921. They spotted an object brighter than Venus in the sunset sky. Through binoculars it showed none of the hazy cloud or tail to be expected of a comet. Observers in Detroit and in England saw it too, and telegrams alerted observers all over the world, but the object was not seen again. (*English Mechanic and World of Science*, 1:114:47, August 19, 1921; *The Journal of the Royal Astronomical Society of Canada*, 15:364–67, December 1921)

On June 30, 1922, a waterspout on Lake Victoria, Uganda, came within 100 yards of G. D. Hale Carpenter and his wife on the shore. Both noticed that outside the central core was a "sheath," or second concentric layer, of whirling water vapor, separated from the core by a layer of clear air. A commentator wrote:

> [This] would appear to require a discontinuity of water content of the air, symmetrical about the axis of the whirl. It does not appear possible to explain it even as the effect of discontinuities of velocity within the whirl. No physical explanation of this clear space can be suggested. [*Nature*, 110:414–15, September 23, 1922]

Lightning during a thunderstorm on July 9, 1923, left a bleached silhouette image of a wastebasket on the wooden floorboards of an office in London. The wicker basket's ribs were clearly visible in the image. The office was in a glassed-over space between two buildings used by a firm of rice merchants. As the image was discovered the morning after the storm, there was no way to tell whether it had been caused by a bolt of lightning or by intense light. (*The Meteorological Magazine*, 58:166–67, August 1923)

This image of a wastebasket on the "bare, unpolished, ordinary flooring boards" was of such interest that it was cut out and placed in a science museum in London.

An audible display of northern lights took place on the Arctic coast, north of Cape Prince of Wales, during the winter of 1925–26. Clark M. Garber, who had until then believed the Eskimos' reports of auroral noises to be superstitions, watched for more than an hour with his driver:

> As we sat upon the sled and the great beams passed directly over our heads they emitted a distinctly audible sound which resembled the crackling of steam escaping from a small jet ... [or] the cracking sound produced by spraying fine jets of water on a very hot surface of metal ... the continuous beam would often emit the sound for a minute or more. [*Science*, 78:213–14, September 8, 1933]

An exceptionally fast—or close—comet was seen by an astronomer in Cracow, Poland, on September 1, 1926. It moved at 15° per hour, fast enough to pass from horizon to horizon in 12 hours. "I do not think there is any record of a celestial object, other than a meteor, showing such a rapid apparent motion across the sky," wrote one astronomer who attempted without success to spot it on the following nights. (*Popular Astronomy*, 34:538–39, 1926)

A mysterious round black dot crossed the disk of the sun to the surprise of a Hamburg astronomer on March 15, 1927. "The slowness of the motion [passing over the sun's face in six seconds] makes it probable that the distance, and therefore the size, of the object were considerable." (*Nature*, 120:201, August 6, 1927)

"Parasitic" rain clouds were noted in two widely separated places in mid-1928. On May 10, watchers on board H.M.S. *Herald*, in the South China Sea, saw a peculiar cumulus formation:

> It appeared as if a heavy rainfall was taking place from one cloud to another. It was quite apparent that no rain was falling into the sea. . . . This rain was "funnel"-shaped, and it is considered that a small waterspout had formed in the sky and was sucking rain from a heavy cumulus cloud to another cloud (small, fluffy and whitish) above it.

A month later the S.S. *Dryden*, en route from Liverpool to Montevideo, Uruguay, sailed near a nimbus cloud "connected to a bank of cumulus cloud by two waterspouts, which did not reach sea, but merely stretched between the two cloud-banks." (*The Marine Observer*, 6:102, May 1929; 6:127, June 1929)

Early in August 1928 Jupiter's south-tropical cloud belt seemed to emit a number of small dark spots that traveled faster than the general rotation of the clouds in that zone. Most passed north of the Great Red Spot, but a few entered it and disappeared. Like the observations of 1903 and 1919 (see pages 248 and 250), this hints at disturbances more sudden than anything seen during the Voyager probes' flyby visits to Jupiter. (*Nature*, 122:743, November 10, 1928)

Lights seen during the Izu Peninsula earthquake in Japan on November 26, 1930, resulted in more than 1,500 reports:

> At one place on the east side of Tokyo Bay, the light resembled auroral streamers diverging from a point on the horizon. . . . Others describe the lights as like that of fireballs . . . when the earthquake was at its height, a straight row of round masses of light appeared in the southwest.

Earthquake lights have been linked with escaping gas, large-scale frictional effects, lightning, and auroras. General agreement on their reality has come only recently, but no mechanism proposed so far can account for all forms of the lights. (*Bulletin of the Seismological Society of America*, 63:2177–78, December 1973)

The S.S. *Nova Scotia* was crossing the North Atlantic on May 24, 1931. At 1:35 A.M. Greenwich time, it was observed that "sea and sky were suddenly quite brilliantly lit for about three seconds with a flickering purplish light, which did not appear to emanate from any particular point." The only clouds were scattered altostratus—not lightning clouds, and not dense enough to diffuse the glare of a bright meteor. (*The Marine Observer*, 9:93, May 1932)

Bright flashes against the new moon were seen on June 17, 1931, by a Riverside, California, couple, who described them as appearing like lightning. The Mount Wilson Observatory "courteously discounted" the observation. A later commentator suggested that the flashes were faint meteors that would have been invisible against the summer evening sky but visible against the unlit portion of the moon's surface. The brightness of the two backgrounds does not in fact differ enough to make this credible. (*Science*, 104:146, August 9, 1946; 104:448–49, November 8, 1946)

A rumbling mini-thunderstorm appeared over Cache Lake, Ontario, in July 1932. Witness John Zeleny saw "a very long, low, narrow, tenuous cloud, resembling a squall cloud." He heard a rumbling noise coming from it, although the cloud's diameter was only 200 feet and he could detect no lightning flashes. "The noise could not have come from the rattle of hail because the cross-section of the cloud was too small to give time for hail formation; and in any case no hail fell." (*Science*, New Series 75:80–81, 1932)

Jupiter's Great Red Spot, photographed by Voyagers 1 *and 2 in 1979, is about three times the size of Earth and is the coldest spot on the planet.*

An orange ray projected upward from the moon for 15 minutes on the night of May 2, 1933, according to observers aboard S.S. *Transylvania* in the North Atlantic. They had seen auroras several hours before. (*The Marine Observer*, 11:49, April 1934)

A white spot on Saturn was seen by astronomers in Germany, England, and the United States in August 1933. The spot, observed in several places along the equatorial belt, covered an area from one-tenth to one-fourth the diameter of the planet. Similar to one detected in 1876, it was presumed to be an atmospheric storm. (*Nature*, 132:285, August 19, 1933)

One of the strangest lightning displays on record was seen in 1936 by M. D. Laurenson of New Zealand:

> Travelling alone by car from Hamilton to Tauranga, I reached the top of the Kaimai Road, and was greatly struck with the vivid lightning display over the Bay of Plenty.... At about 10:10 P.M. I noted, due east, a faintly glowing light.... I mentally registered the impression that it was a bit high up for a house or a car. (I am well acquainted with the district, so that I am fairly sure as regards localities and directions.)
>
> Some minutes later, a bright flash from the north lit up the sky, and I was more than amazed to realise that the glowing light actually proceeded from the upper surface of a black bank of cloud.... Before I had time to conjecture what that could mean, I witnessed one of the most weird and uncanny sights I have ever seen. It suddenly seemed to pulsate, it took definite shape as a molten ball of soft light ... [with] an indescribably bright, greenish white light, or rather radiance. This radiance lit up the whole of the upper surface of the cloud bank and showed the ball of light balanced on a finger of cloud.... Then it pulsated again (seeming to slightly contract and expand once or twice) and almost immediately became much enlarged.... For the 15 minutes that I saw it, it did not move in the sky....
>
> After the glowing light had finally disappeared, one particular display of lightning emanating from the northern cloud flashed across the sky. One jagged fork was travelling horizontally above the spot where the ball had been. Suddenly this jagged fork resolved itself into an absolutely straight line, and drove itself directly into the spot where the ball had been. [*The Meteorological Magazine*, 71:134–36, July 1936]

Bright spots on the south polar cap of Mars, "some of the spots coalescing to swell into a brilliant white spot which quickly became yellow, then red-yellow," were observed in Nashville, Tennessee, on May 30, 1937. (*Popular Astronomy*, 45:430–32, October 1937)

The south polar cap of Mars appears at the top of this photograph because refracting telescopes invert images. The sizes of the caps vary with the Martian seasons.

A mirage projected over more than 300 miles was seen from the schooner *Effie M. Morrissey* on July 17, 1939. The ship was between Cape Farewell, the southern tip of Greenland, and Iceland. Capt. Robert Bartlett, who had sailed polar waters for 40 years, had never seen so clear a mirage:

> At 4 P.M. with sun in the southwest ... the Snaefells Jökull (4,715 feet) and other landmarks [of Iceland] ... were seen as though at a distance of twenty-five or thirty nautical miles [instead of the actual 335 to 350 statute miles]. "If I hadn't been sure of my position and had been bound for Rejkjavik [Captain Bartlett said], I would have expected to arrive within a few hours. The contours of the land and the snow-covered summit of the Snaefells Jökull showed up almost unbelievably near." [*Science*, 90:513–14, December 1939]

FROM 1940 TO 1960

World War II had begun and England had survived the worst of the blitz by November 1940. E. Matts of Coventry was working in his garden shortly after noon in clear weather when suddenly:

> I seemed to be in the centre of intense blackness and looking down observed at my feet a ball about 2 feet across. It was of a pale blue-green colour and seemed made of a mass of writhing strings of light, about ¼ inch in diameter.

After a few seconds the ball rose from the ground, cleared a row of houses, and landed a quarter mile away, damaging a pub as it exploded. "As a matter of interest," Matts concluded, "I felt no alarm whatever, but this may be explained by the fact that we had experienced considerable bombing in Coventry at that period." (*Weather*, 19:228, July 1964)

On the night of August 13–14, 1942, detectors in London registered an unprecedented burst of cosmic rays, the very-high-energy particles that pervade intergalactic space. There was no evidence of a solar or terrestrial "magnetic storm" to account for it. Because cosmic rays travel so far and their direction changes so many times, they usually have a very smooth, even distribution. A sudden burst would require a very strange and violent phenomenon to explain it. (*Nature*, 151:308–09, March 13, 1943)

Upward **lightning bolts,** beginning at the top of a thundercloud and branching like a tree's roots into the clear sky above, were observed by a weather officer of the Royal Australian Air Force at Broome in February 1945. He described them as purple and lasting unusually long, from half a second to one second. (*Weather*, 6:64, February 1951)

The types of lightning include forked (shown here), sheet, ribbon, bead, and ball lightning; and even, as mentioned above, flashes that go upward from a cloud.

A tornado—or an accompanying fireball—dug a trench in a hard-packed clay tennis court at Curepipe, Mauritius, in the Indian Ocean, on May 24, 1948:

A trench running in a north-south direction, 60 feet long and 1 to 2½ feet wide, was cut in the bare surface of the court to a depth varying from 1 to 4 inches. The material lifted from the trench was all thrown to the west to a distance of 50 feet; pieces weighing about one pound were thrown as far as 30 feet. The surface material was slightly blackened as if by heating, and a crackling like that of a sugar-cane fire was heard for two or three minutes. . . . One [witness] claims to have seen a ball of fire about two feet in diameter which crossed from a football pitch to the tennis court through a wire-netting fence without leaving any evidence of its passage. . . . [*Weather*, 4:156–57, May 1949]

From a physicist's point of view, this is one of the strangest fireball reports on record. It is hard to imagine *any* theory that could explain electrically charged gases that would pass through metal netting without effect, then interact with clay.

A freakish blast of heat swept over the towns of Figueira da Foz and Coimbra, Portugal, on July 6, 1949. It lasted only two minutes, but a naval officer at Figueira da Foz reported that the temperature shot up from about 100°F to 158°F within that time. Many barnyard fowl were killed, and the Mondego River was reported to have dried up in several places. (Vincent Gaddis, *Mysterious Fires and Lights*, p.74)

An electrical "pool" swept over a witness in Yellowstone National Park in early September 1949. William B. Sanborn watched a "hazy patch of blue light," about 50 yards wide and five times that long, sweep across a marsh and toward him, moving several feet per second under a low cloud:

When the patch was but a few yards away, I noted a sudden calm in the air and a marked change in temperature, as well as what I believe was the odor of ozone. . . . It kept low to the ground, actually "flowing around" everything that it came in contact with, coating it with a strange pulsating light. Each twig on the sagebrush was surrounded by a halo of light about two inches in diameter. It covered the automobile and my person but did not cover my skin. There was a marked tingling sensation in my scalp, and brushing my hair with the hand caused a snapping of tiny sparks. . . . I obtained no shock from touching any object on the ground or the outside of the car. [*Natural History*, 59:258–59, June 1950]

A strange combination of the aurora australis and lightning was observed by officers of the M.V. *Mel-*

bourne Star in June 1952 south of Madagascar in the Indian Ocean. An aurora so brilliant that the sky resembled sunrise was followed a few hours later by overcast and lightning flashes that left colored streaks in the sky, some of them lasting for three to five minutes—almost certainly too long for afterimages from the lightning. (*The Marine Observer*, 23:81–82, April 1953)

Marine phosphorescence that showed up on radar was noted aboard the M.V. *Malaita*, sailing off the eastern tip of New Guinea in September 1954. At two in the morning, what seemed to be a "loom" of light from beyond the horizon appeared ahead. The radar screen showed the trace of a rain squall, but as the ship moved on, the captain and second officer could see only a patch of light in horizontal streaks, such as is often caused by glowing plankton. They sailed through the radar "squall" without noticing any increase in wind or in the light rain that was falling. (*The Marine Observer*, 25:149–50, July 1955)

Straight, slow lightning from an almost clear sky was reported by two observers on the S.S. *Oronsay*, sailing off the west coast of Africa on October 17, 1956. A full moon was shining, revealing high patches of cirrus clouds and a few low "fair weather" cumulus clouds:

> Lightning started to flash from a point slightly behind the Ci [cirrus] and travelled in a path about 30° from the vertical in an absolutely straight line, at what seemed to be a comparatively slow speed, towards the small Cu [cumulus]. It appeared to enter the Cu and then reappear, moving downwards in a different direction at normal speed. The lightning track from the Cu, which had a greenish glow when "hit," did not seem to be so wide as the original one. Similar flashes occurred at regular intervals of between 2–3 min and each followed the same path to the Cu.

Dr. B.F.J. Schonland, an expert on lightning, noted that while lightning flashes between clouds are not unheard of, they are not usually so regular and repetitive. And while strokes which do not reach the ground are often slower than usual (because they consist of "leader" currents rather than the much more powerful upward return stroke), such leaders are usually very irregular rather than straight. (*The Marine Observer*, 27:208–09, October 1957)

A possible natural earth satellite was first sighted on November 17, 1956, a year before Sputnik. Seven more reports up to 1965 led J. P. Bagby to propose that a meteor may have approached the earth at just the right angle and speed to be pulled into orbit for nine years before burning up. (*Nature*, 211:285, July 16, 1966)

An uncanny stretch of clear water in the midst of a storm eased the passage of the motor yacht *Yvancha* on September 16, 1958. The captain had rounded Portugal's Cape St. Vincent and was heading north for Lisbon against rough seas and northwest winds of force 5–6 (20–30 mph):

> However, by reducing speed from 10 knots to about 6, the going was made more comfortable.... We were still having a pretty horrible time when there appeared ahead quite a calm patch with no broken water and a little more than half an hour's steaming brought us up to it.
> I was quite dumbfounded.... This calm patch was at least a cable [608 feet] wide and stretched away in a north-easterly direction for about 30 miles. I was able to steam along it for three hours in almost a complete calm at full speed, while on either side of me was a steep sea. The lane was absolutely dead straight and the demarcation line of where the broken water flattened itself out into this marine *autobahn* had to be seen to be believed. Needless to say, I kept in it and steamed right into Setubal without even any spray on deck.
> ... I have spent over 30 years at sea and have made the passage to the Mediterranean on many occasions, but I have never experienced such a phenomenon as this before. It was most definitely not an oil slick; there was no sign of any oil and the lane was dead straight for 30 miles with clearly defined sides on both port and starboard sides. Had it come from an oil leakage I am sure it would have been curved from the source as it was blown away by the wind.... I shall look forward with interest to any explanation, if such is possible. [*Weather*, 16:86–87, March 1961]

A brief sky brightening on December 1, 1959, puzzled Capt. J. Williams of the M.V. *Trevean*. His ship was sailing through stiff winds, under low cloud, in the mid-Atlantic, when "a bright blue diffused light suddenly grew." He thought at first it was an electrical short-circuit in the wheelhouse. Finding nothing amiss there, he went back out on deck to witness the gradual fading of the blue light. (*The Marine Observer*, 30:194, October 1960)

SINCE 1960

An eight-inch globe of ball lightning—about as bright as a 10-watt bulb, and giving off no perceptible heat—emerged from the pilot's cabin and floated down the aisle of an airliner on a New York-to-Washington flight on March 19, 1963, just after lightning had struck the plane. Passenger R. C. Jennison was especially struck by its perfect symmetry and "almost solid appearance." (*Nature*, 224:895, November 29, 1969)

Strange atmospheric spirals marked the path of a Centaur rocket launched from Cape Kennedy on November 27, 1963. Three ships in the Atlantic sighted them. The curves may have been formed by strong wind vortices in the rocket's wake or by the same upper-atmosphere magnetic effects that cause particles from solar storms to spiral in the earth's magnetic field. (*The Marine Observer*, 34:181–83, October 1964)

On March 3, 1964, meteorologists J. B. Matthews and D. O. Staley watched an odd electrical display during a snowstorm in Tucson, Arizona (an odd event in itself). From the 80-foot observation tower of the Institute of Atmospheric Physics they could see single, short flashes of light originating at or near the ground all across the city. The flashes were less flickering and intense than normal bolts. There was neither thunder nor radio static. Matthews speculated that discrete amounts of electric charge were carried down with the unusually large, wet flakes. "Clearly," Matthews added, "this leaves many unanswered questions." (*Weather*, 19:291–92, September 1964)

Survivors of a 1965 tornado in Toledo, Ohio, reported:

> We were shaken up and our trailer along with others was dented badly from hail the size of baseballs. The beautiful electric blue light that was around the tornado was something to see, and balls of orange and lightning came from the cone point of the tornado. The cone or tail of the tornado reminded me of an elephant trunk. It would dip down as if to get food then rise up again as if the trunk of an elephant would put the food in his mouth. While the trunk was up the tornado was not dangerous, just when the point came down is when the damage started. My son and I watched the orange balls of fire roll down the Race Way Park then it lifted and the roof came off one of the horse barns. . . . [*Science*, 153:1213–20, September 9, 1966]

Another report of electrical light, in a 1968 tornado, came from Gene Elkins of Tuckerman, Arkansas, who was about 75 feet from the point where the funnel first touched down. He reported a "kind of a green glowish light," bright enough to illuminate objects in the store where he was sheltered. "I don't know if that was kind of a solid bolt of lightning or where that light was coming from. It lasted 2 or 3 seconds." (*Weatherwise*, 23:129, June 1970)

A "semicircle of milky-white light" swelling above the western horizon on March 20, 1969, was reported by observers on two ships southeast of Bermuda. Viewed from the *Otaio*, the light appeared to swell and become fainter until it reached more than halfway to the zenith

and spanned almost one-fifth of the horizon. Watched from the *Port Victor*, it seemed to begin as "a sharply-defined globular area of light" that became irregular as it expanded, eventually enveloping the crescent moon. (*The Marine Observer*, 40:17–18, January 1970)

Sparks stood straight up from the tops of gypsum sand dunes in White Sands National Monument, New Mexico, as a thunderstorm passed overhead. Their properties were measured by instruments set up in 1971 by A. K. Kamra, who found that friction of the wind and blowing sand generated astonishingly high static voltages. (*Nature*, 240:143–44, November 17, 1972)

The dunes at White Sands National Monument in New Mexico are between 10 and 60 feet high. They are formed and re-formed by wind. Friction of the windblown gypsum sand creates static electricity.

The first X-ray bursts from outer space were detected by the *Cosmos 428* satellite in 1971. Scientists have since found many more fluctuating X-ray sources—some a million times more powerful than the sun at all wavelengths. Many of them are believed to be binary (paired) stars in which one partner strips gas from the surface of the other, but no one knows why they seem to be concentrated in the dense star-clouds known as globular clusters or why their bursts follow irregular schedules rather than showing the clocklike precision of pulsars. (*Nature*, 261:542, June 17, 1976)

A purple-blue, four-inch ball surrounded by a flame-colored halo appeared above the stove in a Smethwick, England, home during a thunderstorm in 1975. The witness brushed it away from her, feeling heat around her gold wedding band. It "burned" a two-by-four-inch hole in her dress and tights as it disappeared with a bang. The fabric around the hole was shriveled but not charred, and the print was faded. (*Nature*, 260:596–97, April 15, 1976)

IN THE REALM
OF
MIRACLES

When things occur that cannot be explained by the laws
of nature or science, the popular recourse is to
assign them to the world of the supernatural.
The miracles most readily believed are those having to do
with dramatic recoveries by the ill and disabled.
The documented examples are literally countless.
Another more challenging category of the miraculous is
that in which the well-established laws of
gravitation are somehow violated and levitation
occurs. And what are we to make of pictures that weep
and statues that move? To say that the witnesses of
these events are victims of mass hallucination is to propose
a miracle as puzzling as the ones they experienced.

The hand of God reaches toward Adam in the ultimate miracle, the creation of man.

CURES AND IMMUNITIES

Sooner or later everyone prays—or perhaps just hopes—for a miracle. And since time and disease subdue, and finally destroy, all living things, the miracles most in demand are those that reverse the course of a fatal or crippling illness or confer immunity from some perilous conspiracy of the elements.

Prayers sometimes seem to be answered, and hopes fulfilled, in hopeless circumstances. Or, putting it in a way less offensive to hardened skeptics, a desperate need and the circumstances that relieve it sometimes come together in a context of prayer, ritual, or hope. The victims of a shipwreck, for example, dying of thirst, drift into an area of fresh water in the middle of the ocean. The rope around a condemned man's neck breaks unaccountably before he hangs. A fire walker prays, waves a wand of leaves, and walks safely on a bed of red-hot stones. A tumor bathed in water from Lourdes gradually disappears.

From the skeptic's point of view, such events are simply matters of coincidence. But this is little more than a semantic shuffle, for one man's coincidence is another's miracle. As Dr. William Temple, the late archbishop of Canterbury, is said to have noted: When I pray, coincidences tend to happen; when I don't, they don't.

The skeptic, of course, has a more frontal attack at his disposal. Where miraculous cures are concerned, he can say that the initial diagnosis was wrong (the condition was something other than terminal); or that the illness was functional rather than organic (it was produced by hysteria and was therefore subject to cure by suggestion); or that the disease was naturally subject to spontaneous remission (as is sometimes the case with cancer and tuberculosis, for example).

To these undoubtedly valid observations the believer can only reply that there are cases where these things seem not to apply and that, in a religious context, the revelation of a diagnosis as inaccurate, the alleviation of hysterical symptoms, or the remission of a deadly complaint constitutes a miraculous coincidence. To which the skeptic may reply that this would be more convincing if the percentage of recoveries attributable to such causes in a large hospital were not much the same as at Lourdes. And the skeptic's motivation may well be of the most humane kind.

Advocates of miraculous healing rarely keep records of their failures, but both skeptic and believer will probably agree that for every paralytic who leaps from his wheelchair at a revival meeting, there are numerous unrecorded others who must be wheeled away without cure. For these, and their loved ones—for the parents of the incurably ill child as well as for the paralytic who must return to his wheelchair a few days after the healing service—the fallacious hope of recovery fostered by healers may be a grave disservice, especially if it prevents the patient from seeking orthodox medical help. But where there is desperate need there will always be charlatans and hypocrites willing to offer promise for a price or self-deluded saviors asking no more in return than a token offering and respect for their skill.

All this is true. And yet there is a residuum of cases where none of these things seem to apply, and they occur in a field—medicine—where honest practitioners freely admit the narrow scope of their knowledge. Above all is the incontrovertible truth that the capacities of the body and mind are still deeply and confoundingly mysterious.

The Death of Saint Polycarp

One of the earliest Christian martyrdoms for which an eyewitness account survives is that of Saint Polycarp, the bishop of Smyrna (today known as Izmir, in Turkey). Condemned to die at the stake because he would not recognize the divinity of the Roman emperor, he was put to death in the stadium at Smyrna in A.D. 155, when he was 86 years old. The manner of his death is described in a letter of unquestioned authenticity written by members of the church in Smyrna:

> When he had offered up the Amen and finished his prayer, the firemen lighted the fire. And a mighty flame flashing forth, we to whom it was given to see, saw a marvel, yea and we were preserved that we might relate to the rest what happened. The fire, making the appearance of a vault, like the sail of a vessel filled by the wind, made a wall round about the body of the martyr; and it was there in the midst, not like flesh burning but like gold and silver refined in a furnace. For we perceived such a fragrant smell, as if it were the wafted odour of frankincense or some other precious spice.
>
> So at length the lawless men, seeing that his body could not be consumed by fire, ordered the executioner to go up to him and stab him with a dagger. And when he had done this there came forth a quantity of blood so that it extinguished the fire, and all the multitude marvelled that there should be so great a difference between the unbelievers and the elect.

After Saint Polycarp died the fire was lit again, and his body was cremated. (Herbert Thurston, *The Physical Phenomena of Mysticism*, pp.171, 222–23)

A 19th-century French engraving shows Saint Polycarp at the stake, impervious to the flames beneath. The martyr had been appointed bishop of Smyrna by Saint John.

The Saintly Ordeal of Peter Igneus

In 1068 the citizens of Florence, Italy, took to the streets to protest the appointment of their new bishop, a man well known to have purchased the office at the cost of an enormous bribe. Only the judgment of Heaven, it was decided, could settle the matter and bring the rioting to an end, and with that in mind Saint John Gualbert, abbot of Vallombrosa, ordered one of his monks, Peter Aldobrandini, to submit to God's judgment in an ordeal of fire.

Two mounds of wood, 10 feet long with a narrow passage between them, were duly made ready for the test. When the wood was burning fiercely, Peter, who had prepared himself by saying Mass, removed his outer vestment and walked slowly between the two infernos along a pathway now strewn with red-hot embers. He emerged from the fire unharmed, his hair unsinged, his priestly robe unscorched. He then volunteered to go back through the fire again, but the crowd was convinced: God had made His will plain.

The bishop was deposed (and later came to repent his actions), and Peter Aldobrandini eventually became a cardinal. He was canonized as Saint Peter Igneus—Saint Peter Fire. (Herbert Thurston, *The Physical Phenomena of Mysticism*, p.172)

The Lankadas Fire Dance

Around the year 1250 the church of St. Constantine in the Thracian village of Kosti caught fire. It was said that some of the villagers heard the icons groaning, dashed into the blazing church to rescue them, and, miraculously, emerged unharmed. Since then the icons of Saint Constantine and Saint Helen have been passed down from one generation to the next, and every year on the feast day of the saints (May 21) the descendants of the early parishioners have honored them with a fire dance.

In the early 1900's some of the fire walkers moved to Lankadas, Greece, taking the icons with them. There they continued their ritual celebration.

The fire, which covers an area some 12 feet square, is lit early in the morning, while those who are to dance prepare themselves. For several hours they contemplate the icons in rapt concentration, and as they meditate, the ancient music of drum and lyre is played. At length, when the fire is glowing cherry-red, a dancer rises to his feet, enters the flames, and begins to dance. Another follows him, and then another, each carrying reproductions of sacred pictures. For half an hour they dance, treading on the logs and embers until the flames are finally extinguished.

The temperature of the coals, recently measured by Dr. Christo Xenakis of Athens General Hospital, ranged from 500° to 850°F. "I would have expected third-degree burns in all cases," Dr. Xenakis said. But he found that only a few of the fire dancers were harmed, suffering blistered feet. (A young American who joined in the fire dance, George Mills was, however, hospitalized with third-degree burns on both feet after his attempt.)

"It is almost exclusively a question of faith," said the village's chief fire walker, 50-year-old Constantine Kitsinos, adding that one must first "overcome the feeling that it is impossible."

> Once guided by faith and concentration, the actual dancing on the burning coals is painless. You feel something but it is no more than like walking in a prickly field. Despite the heat the strange thing is that your feet sometimes even feel cool.

(Vincent H. Gaddis, *Mysterious Fires and Lights*, pp.126–27; *National Enquirer*, July 14, 1981)

Saint Francis the Fire Handler

For some saints immunity to fire seems to be a special mark of grace, while for a few less exalted men and women the same immunity seems a natural and habitual thing. One saint who handled fire as easily as other men handle a shovel or a walking stick was Francis of Paola, who died in 1507.

Francis was born of Italian peasant stock, and many of the stories about him are set in ordinary, workaday situations. Once, for example, he came into a blacksmith's forge just as the smith was finishing a shoeing job, to inquire about some work he needed done. Would there be enough iron left over, Francis asked. The smith indicated a large scrap of red-hot iron that remained, and Francis, without more ado, bent over and picked it up. "By your leave," he said to those screaming at him in horror to stop, "I am just holding it to warm myself."

On another occasion Francis seems to have conferred his immunity to fire on someone else. A lime kiln used in the construction of new monastic buildings near Paterno Calabro had been fired and seemed in danger of collapse. The entrance was perhaps too small for Francis himself to enter, for he instructed a small monk to go into the furnace and prop up the ceiling with a stick. The monk did as he was bidden, suffered no injury, and the kiln was saved. (In this case, Saint Francis must have extended his immunity not only to the monk but to the stick used as a prop.)

Another example of the way that Francis applied his unworldly immunity to worldly tasks occurred when he helped some men in the process of making charcoal. They had covered their stack of wood with earth so ineptly that flames were breaking through in several places. While the men fetched more earth to plug the holes, Francis used his bare feet to control the flames.

An illustration from an old book depicts the humble Saint Francis of Paola, who often used his miraculous immunity to fire in mundane ways. He was canonized in 1519.

It was not, however, such stories as these that first brought Francis to the attention of church officials but his reputation for leading a life of extreme austerity and deprivation. In due course two church dignitaries were sent to examine and test him.

"It is quite easy for you to do these things," they told him, "because you are a peasant and used to hardship. But if you were of gentle blood you would not be able to live in this way."

Francis replied: "It is quite true that I am a peasant, and if I were not, I should not be able to do things like this." A large fire was blazing nearby. He reached into it with both hands and scooped up some burning sticks and red coals. Holding them, he said to the canon: "You see, I could not do this if I were not a peasant."

The canon then prostrated himself on the ground and sought to kiss Francis's hands and feet, but the saintly peasant would not allow it. (Herbert Thurston, *The Physical Phenomena of Mysticism*, pp.174–75)

Imperishable Eloquence

Saint Anthony of Padua (1195–1231), a Franciscan preacher and theologian who was canonized a year after his death, was renowned not only for his sanctity but for his eloquence. Some 400 years after his death, his coffin was disinterred and opened. In the pile of gray dust inside it—the remains of the saint's body—lay his tongue, as soft, pink, and fresh as though it were still living. (*Pursuit*, 10:3:69, Summer 1977; Herbert Thurston, *The Physical Phenomena of Mysticism*, p.243)

Saint Anthony of Padua, portrayed here by a 16th-century artist, was renowned for his brilliant, persuasive sermons and for his humanitarianism. He is considered to be one of the greatest preachers of all times.

A Sinister Entertainment

From the diary of Englishman John Evelyn comes the following account of a performance by a famous 17th-century fire handler named Richardson. It suggests that the audience may have witnessed something other than a display of stage magic:

> Oct. 8, 1672. I tooke leave of my Lady Sunderland, who was going to Paris to my Lord, now ambassador there. She made me stay dinner at Leicester House, and afterwards sent for Richardson the famous fire-eater. He devoured brimston [sulfur] on glowing coales before us, chewing and swallowing them; he mealted a beare-glasse [beer glass] and eate it quite up; then taking a live coale on his tongue, he put it on a raw oyster, the coal was blown on with bellows till it flames and sparkled in his mouth, and so remained until the oyster gaped and was quite boiled; then he melted pitch and wax with sulphur, which he drank downe as it flamed; I saw it flaming in his mouth a good while . . . then he stood on a small pot, and bending his body, took a glowing yron with his mouth from between his feete, without touching the pot or ground with his hands; with divers other prodigious feates. [Herbert Thurston, *The Physical Phenomena of Mysticism*, p.178]

The Bad and Good Luck of Johannes Osiander

When British author George Orwell was recovering from a bullet wound in the neck during the Spanish Civil War, he was surprised to find that people were congratulating him on his good luck—the bullet had narrowly missed his carotid artery. What puzzled Orwell was the thought that there was *anything* lucky about being shot in the neck.

The Reverend Johannes Osiander (1657–1724), of Tübingen, Germany, might have sympathized with Orwell. Among his misfortunes were the following: he was charged and knocked down by a wild boar but sustained no injury; during a severe flood his horse fell, trapping him beneath it, but he emerged without a bruise or broken bone; he escaped a fusillade of gunfire

by bandits and was buried by an avalanche but climbed out unharmed; a wild blizzard blew him off his feet and into the icy water of the Rhine, but the adventure is said to have left him without even a sniffle. On another occasion a tree fell on him with an impact that would have crushed someone less resilient; the Reverend Johannes merely picked himself up and walked away unscathed. At sea he was as unlucky, or lucky, as on land: he survived a shipwreck only to be plowed under the waves by the ship intent on his rescue; needless to say, he survived this indignity as a matter of course and popped to the surface again unharmed. (Josef Fordrer, *Sie Pregten*, p.147; George Woodcock, *The Crystal Spirit: A Study of George Orwell*, p.168)

An Eloquent Ordeal

In 1685 King Louis XIV of France revoked the civil liberties and religious freedom of all Protestants in France. After some years of dissatisfaction a state of guerrilla warfare broke out in 1702. It was called the Camisard rebellion, probably so named for the long shirts worn by the Protestants in their night raids against the king's troops.

Among the Camisard leaders was a man by the name of Claris, who chose to demonstrate the righteousness of his cause by enduring an ordeal of fire.

A pyre was built, and Claris, in a state of religious ecstasy climbed upon it, all the while declaiming to a crowd of about 600 people. The fire was lit, and as the flames licked around him and his wife screamed in terror, Claris continued to speak. The flames engulfed him, leaping high above his head, and still his voice was heard; even as the flames declined, his voice did not falter. Not until the wood was all consumed was Claris silent. He stepped from the ashes unscathed, with not a burn or scorch mark on his clothes.

But sadly for the Protestants, Louis was as immune to Claris's fiery eloquence as Claris had been to the flames, and in 1704 the rebellion was broken by vague concessions and the offer to the principal general of the Camisards of a command in the royal army. (Vincent H. Gaddis, *Mysterious Fires and Lights*, p.117)

The Incorruption of Andrew Bobola

Saint Andrew Bobola, a Polish Jesuit who became renowned for his successful missionary work among the Russian Orthodox, was brutally murdered by marauding Cossacks in 1657, when he was 67 years of age. After the Cossacks had withdrawn, Father Bobola's tortured and mutilated body was recovered from the dung heap where they had thrown it and quickly buried in the vault of the Jesuit church in Pinsk.

Forty-four years after the murder, the rector of the Jesuit College in Pinsk was directed in a dream, or vision, to disinter the body, and when he did so it was found to be not only unmarred by any decay but still as soft and flexible as the body of a living person.

Then in 1730 the body was officially examined by a panel of six ecclesiastics and five medical experts, who unanimously confirmed its unnatural state of preservation, still showing, 73 years after death, no trace of rigor or decomposition.

Several members of the examining panel were careful to note that none of the other bodies buried in the same vault as Father Bobola had been similarly preserved. (Herbert Thurston, *The Physical Phenomena of Mysticism*, pp.262-63)

Holy Fragrance
The body of the Blessed Maria Anna (Ladroni) of Jesus was exhumed 107 years after her death during the process of investigation in 1731 that ultimately led to her beatification. Eleven doctors and surgeons were present to examine the remains, which were discovered to be not only free from decomposition but still soft and supple, though no signs of embalming were found—and exuding a remarkable and pleasing fragrance of balsam. This seemed to be produced by a strange oily substance that moistened both the skin and internal organs and with which the nun's clothing was saturated.

The astonishment of the medical experts was so great at these findings that they made "an absolute dissection" of the body in their efforts to discover some secret means by which it had been preserved. They discovered nothing of the kind, however, only—the more they cut and probed—a richer fragrance, so pleasing that one surgeon afterward refused to wash his hands for several days for fear of losing the trace of it. (Herbert Thurston, *The Physical Phenomena of Mysticism*, pp.260-61)

The Man Who Wouldn't Hang
In 1803 a policeman in Sydney, Australia, died from wounds inflicted on him by a thief, or thieves, he had discovered stealing a small desk containing a bag of gold and silver coins. Before long Joseph Samuels, "a man of ill-repute," was arrested and, when some of the missing coins were discovered in his pocket, was charged with the murder. Samuels claimed that he had won the coins gambling and produced witnesses who swore that he had not only been helplessly drunk when the robbery occurred but miles away from the scene of the crime. At last, though, under police pressure, Samuels confessed to the robbery but stoutly maintained that he was innocent of murder. Nevertheless, he was promptly found guilty of the murder and sentenced to death.

Samuels's accomplice in the robbery, a man named Isaac Simmonds, was also being held in custody at this time but had refused to confess to anything. In the hope of shocking a confession out of him, the provost marshal ordered Simmonds to be brought to Samuels's execution, to take place in public.

On the appointed day Samuels was brought to the gallows in a horse-drawn cart, and the noose was placed around his neck. When the signal was given, the horses would be driven forward, leaving the condemned man to swing until dead.

A large crowd had gathered for the occasion, and Samuels was allowed to address them briefly before the sentence was carried out. Yes, he said, he had helped to steal the desk, but he had had no part in the murder. The real murderer, he went on quite calmly, was standing there in the crowd under police guard: Isaac Simmonds was the murderer.

As soon as he heard his name, Simmonds began to shout, trying to drown out the words of his accuser. But the crowd had heard enough and began to clamor for Samuels's release and Simmonds's trial. As they rushed forward, a guard jabbed the horses and the beasts lumbered off, leaving Samuels dangling from the rope. But only for an instant. Then the rope broke.

The guards surrounded the condemned man while the hangman prepared a second rope. The crowd was in a dangerous mood, but the provost marshal, a man who knew where his duty lay, had the half-conscious Samuels hoisted back into the cart and the noose again placed around his neck. The order was quickly given, the cart was pulled away, and again Samuels, who had been sitting on a barrel since he was too weak to stand, dangled from the rope. But this time the rope began slowly to unravel, until Samuels's feet brushed the floor—just enough to save him from being strangled.

By now the crowd was convinced that they had witnessed divine intervention, and a cry went up to cut the condemned man down. And cut down he was— only to have yet a third rope placed around his neck.

This time the rope broke just above Samuels's head, and the provost marshal's nerve at last failed him. He mounted his horse and rode at a gallop to the governor's office to report what had happened. The governor immediately reprieved the condemned man.

Still skeptical, the provost marshal carefully examined and tested the three ropes. They showed no sign of tampering, and the last of them, which had been brand-new, was tested in drop after drop with a weight of nearly 400 pounds. Even when two of the three strands of rope were deliberately cut, the remaining strand still held the full weight; yet all three strands had snapped like sewing thread when the much lighter Samuels had dangled from them.

Isaac Simmonds was eventually brought to trial and hanged for the policeman's murder. Once at liberty, Samuels returned to his old ways and before long was imprisoned again, this time in Newcastle. There he and a group of fellow convicts stole a boat and made their escape by sea. Nothing more was heard of him, and he and his companions were presumed to have drowned. (Frank Edwards, *Strange People*, pp.236–39)

Medium Cool: Home on the Range

The most famous medium of the late 19th century—the golden age of mediums and spiritualistic phenomena— was a Scottish-American named Daniel Dunglas Home (1833–86), whose distinctions included never having been discovered in any kind of fraud. (For an account of Home's frequently performed levitations, see pages 293–95.) The following report of a séance given at Norwood, England, in 1868 was written by Lord Adare, later the earl of Dunraven. He describes how Home entered a trance and seemed to become fascinated by the fire, which he frequently approached and stirred with a poker. He returned to the fire again,

> and with his hand stirred the embers into a flame; then kneeling down, he placed his face right among the burning coals, moving it about as though bathing it in water. Then, getting up, he held his finger for some time in the flame of the candle. Presently, he took the same lump of coal he had previously handled and came over to us, blowing upon it to make it brighter. He then walked slowly round the table, and said, "I want to see which of you will be the best subject. Ah! Adare will be the easiest, because he has been most with Dan." [Home is here referring to himself as Dan.] Mr. Jencken held out his hand, saying, "Put it in mine," Home said, "No no, touch it and see," he touched it with the tip of his finger and burnt himself. Home then held it within four or five inches of Mr. Saal's and Mr. Hurt's hands, and they could not endure the heat. He came to me and said, "Now, if you are not afraid, hold out your hand"; I did so, and having made two rapid passes over my hand, he placed the coal in it. I must have held it for half a minute, long enough to have burned my hand fearfully; the coal felt scarcely warm. Home then took it away, laughed, and seemed much pleased. As he was going back to the fire-place, he suddenly turned round and said, "Why, just fancy, some of them think that only one side of the ember was hot." He told me to make a hollow of both my hands; I did so, and he placed the coal in them, and then put both his on the top of the coal, so that it was completely covered by our four hands, and we held it there for some time. Upon this occasion scarcely any heat at all could be perceived.

In fact, demonstrations of this kind were not extraordinary for Home, as Lord Lindsay, later the earl of Crawford and Balcarres, testified to the Committee of

the Dialectical Society in 1869, during their investigation of spiritualistic phenomena:

> I have frequently seen Home [he said], when in a trance, go to the fire and take out large red-hot coals, and carry them about in his hands, put them inside his shirt, etc. Eight times I have myself held a red-hot coal in my hands without injury, when it scorched my face on raising my hand. Once, I wished to see if they really would burn, and I said so, and touched a coal with the middle finger of my right hand, and I got a blister as large as a sixpence [i.e., the size of a dime]; I instantly asked him to give me the coal, and I held the part that burnt me, in the middle of my hand, for three or four minutes, without the least inconvenience. A few weeks ago, I was at a séance with eight others. Of these, seven held a red-hot coal without pain, and the two others could not bear the approach of it; of the seven, four were ladies.

As these (and many other) accounts make clear, Home was able to extend his own immunity to fire to others on numerous occasions. The most dramatic involved his old friend Samuel Carter Hall, who for years had been editor of *The Art Journal*. Hall, as his wife relates, was an old man when Home enlisted him in an outrageous and, from one point of view, preposterous demonstration. There were several people present at the séance, in addition to the Halls, when Home, in a trance, seized a lump of burning coal from the fireplace—it was so large that he needed both hands to hold it—and placed it on Samuel Hall's head. "Is it not hot?" someone asked. "Warm, but not hot!" Hall replied. Home, meanwhile, was gathering up his friend's white hair and bunching it around and above the coal, which was still glowing red. Hall still did not find it too hot. Home then placed the coal in Mrs. Hall's left hand, and she too reported that it felt warm but not painfully hot—though several others who tried touching it burned their fingers.

Home's power to confer his own immunity to fire on others was variable, depending on his own state of mind and the mental attitude of the other person. To prepare himself for these exploits he apparently conferred with spirits, by whom he believed his immunity was granted. A description of one of these spirit conferences has been preserved in notes made by W. Stainton Moses, himself a notable medium:

> [Mr. Home] then went to the fireplace, removed the guard, and sat down on the hearthrug. There he seemed to hold a conversation by signs with a spirit. He repeatedly bowed, and finally set to work to mesmerise his head again. He ruffled his bushy hair until it stood out like a mop, and then deliberately lay down and put his head in the bright wood fire.

The hair was *in* the blaze, and must, under ordinary circumstances, have been singed off. His head was in the grate, and his neck on a level with the top bar. This was repeated several times. He also put his hand into the fire, smoothed away the wood and coal, and picked out a live coal, which he held in his hand for a few seconds, but replaced soon, saying the power was not sufficient. He tried to give a hot coal to Mr. Crookes, but was unable to do it.

The Mr. Crookes mentioned here, later Sir William Crookes, was one of the leading chemists and physicists of his time. His own account of the incident, which occurred in London on April 28, 1873, is as follows:

> ... Mr. Home told me to leave my seat and come with him to the fire. He asked me if I should be afraid to take a live coal (ember) from his hand. I said, No, I would take it if he would give it to me. He then put his hand among the hot coals (embers), and deliberately picked out the brightest bit and held it in his hand for a few seconds. He appeared to deliberate for a time, and then returned it to the grate, saying the power was too weak, and he was afraid I might be hurt. During this time I was kneeling on the hearthrug, and am unable to explain how it was he was not severely burnt. ... After Home had recovered from the trance I examined his hand with care to see if there were any signs of burning or of previous preparation. I could detect no trace of injury to the skin, which was soft and delicate like a woman's.

(*Proceedings of the Society for Psychical Research*, 9:306–08, 1894; 35:132–36, 281–82, 1926; Herbert Thurston, *The Physical Phenomena of Mysticism*, pp.181–86)

Nathan Coker: The Cool Blacksmith

Nathan Coker was born into slavery in the town of Hillsborough, Maryland, in about 1814. His owner, Henry L. Sellers, sold him to a Bishop Emary. When Coker was in his early teens, Emary leased his services to a lawyer named Purnell. Purnell treated the boy badly in various ways and deprived him of enough food. Nathan, therefore, was always hungry, and it was hunger that prompted the discovery of his unusual gift.

> I shied around the kitchen one day [Nathan said later] and when the cook left I shot in, dipped my hand into the dinner pot, and pulled out a red hot dumpling. The boiling water did not burn and I could eat the hot dumpling without winking; so after [that] I often got my dinner [that] way. I has often got the hot fat off the boiling water and drank it. I drink my coffee when it is boiling, and it does not give me half so much pain as it does to drink a glass of cold water. I always likes it just as hot as I can get it.

At length Coker left the service of Purnell and became a blacksmith in the town of Denton, Maryland. And in his pursuit of this trade his early indifference to heat assumed prodigious proportions. The following account appeared in the *New York Herald* in 1871. It describes a demonstration that Coker gave before a number of prominent citizens of Easton, Maryland (including two local newspaper editors and four physicians), in the office of a Dr. Stack:

> A brisk fire of anthracite coal was burning in a common coal stove, and an iron shovel was placed in the stove and heated to a white heat. When all was ready the negro pulled off his boots and placed the hot shovel upon the soles of his feet, and kept it there until the shovel became black. His feet were then examined by the physician, but no burns could be found, and all declared that no evidence of a heated substance having come in contact with them was visible.
>
> The shovel was again heated red hot, taken from the stove and handed to him. He ran out his tongue as far as he could, and laid the heated shovel upon it, licking the iron until it became cooled. The physician examined the tongue, but found nothing to indicate that he had suffered in the least from the heated iron.
>
> A large handful of common squirrel shot ... was next placed in an iron receptacle and heated until melted. The negro then took the dish, poured the heated lead into the palm of his hand, and then put it into his mouth, allowing it to run all around his teeth and gums. He repeated the operation several times, each time keeping the melted lead in his mouth until solidified. After each operation the physicians examined him carefully, but could find nothing upon his flesh to indicate that he had been in the least affected. ... [Then] he deliberately put his hand into the stove, in which was a very hot fire, took therefrom a handful of hot coals and passed them about the room to the gentlemen present, keeping them in his hand some time. Not the slightest evidence of a burn was visible upon his hand after he threw the coals back into the stove.

The account also describes Coker's other astounding feats, including working with red-hot iron without the use of tongs. But for Nathan Coker—who was a working blacksmith, not an entertainer, visionary, or medium—such things were an everyday part of his life. "... I often take my iron out the forge with my hand when red hot," he said, "but it don't burn. Since I was a little boy I have never been afraid to handle fire." (The *New York Herald*, September 7, 1871)

Faith Rewarded

In 1867 Pierre de Rudder, a Belgian, had his leg broken by a falling tree. His leg became infected, and doctors urged him to let them amputate it. Pierre refused, even though the injury was agonizing and rendered him almost immobile. He endured the pain year after year, but never lost hope that somehow he might be cured. Then, in 1875, his employer arranged for him to make a pilgrimage to the Shrine of Our Lady of Lourdes in Oostakker, Belgium; the date set was April 7.

In January Pierre visited a specialist, Dr. Van Hoestenberghe, for a final diagnosis. His condition was described in these words:

> Rudder had an open wound at the top of the leg. In this wound one could see the two bones separated by a distance of three centimeters [about 1.2 inches]. There was no sign of healing. . . . The lower part of the leg could be moved in all directions. The heel could be lifted in such a way as to fold the leg in the middle. It could be twisted, with the heel in front and the toes in back, all these movements being only restricted by the soft tissues.

This description was confirmed by another doctor and by several other witnesses who saw Rudder's bandages being changed a few days before the pilgrimage.

At Oostakker Pierre found the shrine crowded with pilgrims. He was in great pain after his journey and unable, though he tried twice, to walk around the shrine. He therefore sat and prayed, in a state of exhaustion. Suddenly a strange, overwhelming emotion arose in him: without thinking, he walked to the statue of Our Lady of Lourdes and knelt down before it. Then, realizing what he had done, and overcome with joy, he began to walk around the shrine. When his wife saw what he was doing, she fainted.

At a house nearby, the leg was examined. The wound had healed, the bone was mended, and his legs were again the same length. When he arrived home his younger son, who had never seen him without crutches, refused to believe this was his father. Two physicians, Dr. Affenaer and Dr. Van Hoestenberghe, confirmed the obvious: the leg was restored.

Pierre continued to walk normally until his death in 1898. To document the miracle fully, Dr. Van Hoestenberghe exhumed the body and examined the leg on May 24, 1899. The photographs taken clearly showed a remarkable growth of bone at the fracture point. A report of the autopsy was published in the *Revue des Questions Scientifiques* in October 1899. (Jacques Vallee, *The Invisible College*, pp.158–62)

An Ocean Oasis

Sometime in 1881 Capt. Neil Curry set sail from Liverpool for San Francisco in the sailing ship *Lara*. His wife and two children were traveling with him. All

Dreaming of fresh water while adrift on the ocean 1,500 miles from shore is not mysterious, but Capt. Neil Curry's dream of a green freshwater oasis in the endless expanse of blue came true in every detail.

went well on the voyage until the *Lara* was about 1,500 miles off the west coast of Mexico, when a fire broke out and forced the captain, his family, and 32 crew members to abandon the ship in three lifeboats.

Before long the agonies of thirst began. Those strong enough struggled to row, hoping to sight another ship and in the meantime vainly setting their course for Mexico. But no ship appeared; no sign of human life broke the vast blue solitude of the Pacific Ocean. Exhaustion set in, and soon 7 of the 36 were unconscious. Captain Curry later reported:

> We dreamed . . . and in the midst of one of our dreams, we imagined the water beneath us had turned from the blue of the sea to green. . . . I managed to muster up strength to let out a container. I tasted the water and it was fresh.

Then Captain Curry noticed a change: their boats had wandered into an area of green water, marked like a meadow in the surrounding blueness. He reached down and tasted: the water was fresh! They had found a mysterious upwelling of pure water—an unaccountable, lifesaving oasis in the endless sea.

Twenty-three days after they had abandoned ship, Captain Curry, his wife, children, and all the crew members made a safe landfall. (Charles Fort, *The Complete Books of Charles Fort,* pp.972–73; *The Sun* [New York], October 9, 1931)

The Trap That Wouldn't Spring
On the morning of February 23, 1885, John Lee was taken from his cell at Exeter prison, England, and led to the gallows in the prison yard. He had been condemned to death for murdering his employer, a wealthy old woman named Emma Ann Keyse, who had been found with her throat cut and her head battered by a hatchet. It had been a brutal murder, and Lee's guilt had seemed evident. He had a criminal record, and it was obvious that he hated Miss Keyse.

Now he climbs the steps onto the scaffold. His arms are pinioned behind him, and the hangman, a Mr. Berry, puts a white bag over his head and guides him onto the trapdoor. The noose is placed around his neck. Has he any last words? "No," he says. "Drop away." The sheriff of Exeter gives the signal. Mr. Berry pulls back the bolt on the trapdoor.

At this point the trap should open, Lee should fall, should be jerked by the tightening noose, and die of suffocation or a broken neck.

The bolt is pulled. Nothing holds the trapdoor in place. It does not open. Lee stands there, the bag over his head, the noose around his neck.

They shuffle him to one side and try the trap. It opens smoothly as soon as the bolt is pulled. Again they

maneuver Lee onto the door. The sheriff signals and Mr. Berry again withdraws the bolt. Again John Lee stands there, poised above eternity on a trapdoor that refuses to open. They take him back to his cell.

Now the sheriff investigates. The trap works perfectly. To make absolutely sure, the hangman stands on it, hanging onto the rope with his hands. When the bolt is pulled, the door opens and he falls through.

They send for Lee again. Again the bag, the noose, the signal. Again nothing; the door will not budge.

Someone suggests that the door has been swollen by the recent rains. Its edges are planed to increase the clearance. The morning is cold, and the witnesses—there are newspapermen among them—shiver.

John Lee is shivering too. They stand him on the trapdoor and pull the bolt. He remains there, as though an immovable mountain were beneath his feet. The bolt has slid away as it should. Nothing supports the trap, but it supports John Lee as though a mountain of rock wedged it in place. They take Lee back to his cell.

The sheriff, baffled, writes to the home secretary, who orders a stay of execution. From one end of England to the other the newspapers are full of the story: John Lee, the man they can't hang! The situation is without precedent and is debated at length in the House of Commons.

Eventually John Lee's sentence was changed to one of life imprisonment, and after 22 years, in December 1907, he was released on parole. He married (unsuccessfully) and ended his days as a junk dealer in London. He is thought to have died in 1943.

The official explanation for Lee's escape, as detailed in the *Annual Register* for 1885, was that rain had caused the trapdoor of the gallows to swell and had made it inoperative. A more colorful (and less patently fictitious) explanation, given by former convict Frank Ross, was that the gallows had been built by a highly skilled joiner, himself previously condemned to death and then reprieved, who had engineered the trap to be jammed by the weight of the chaplain standing next to the condemned man. If this was the case, it was never discovered during the minute official investigation of the scaffold, and it seems unlikely that during all the successful tests of the door no one should have happened to activate the jamming mechanism—or that the prison chaplain should have stood in exactly the right spot to activate it throughout each of the four attempts to execute John Lee. (Charles Fort, *The Complete Books of Charles Fort,* pp.1052–55; David Wallechinsky and Irving Wallace, *The People's Almanac #2,* p.1182)

The Lava Walk of Dr. William Brigham
One of the few westerners to perform a traditional fire walk, and perhaps the only westerner to perform the

walk on red-hot lava, was Dr. William Tufts Brigham of the Bishop Museum of Ethnology in Honolulu. His account of the walk, which he performed in the 1880's under the guidance of three kahuna friends—native Hawaiian priests—was told to Max Freedom Long:

Until noon we climbed upward under a smoky sky and with the smell of sulphur fumes growing stronger and stronger. . . . At about three o'clock we arrived at the source of the flow.

It was a grand sight. The side of the mountain had broken open just above the timber line and the lava was spouting out of several vents—shooting with a roar as high as 200 feet, and falling to make a great bubbling pool.

The pool drained off at the lower end into the flow. An hour before sunset we started following it down in search of a place where we could try our experiment. . . .

Coming down to the rain forest without finding a place where the flow blocked up and overflowed periodically, we bedded down again for the night. In the morning we went on, and in a few hours found what we wanted. The flow crossed a more level strip perhaps a half-mile wide. Here the enclosing walls ran in flat terraces, with sharp drops from one level to the next. Now and again a floating boulder or mass of clinker would plug the flow just where a drop commenced, and then the lava would back up and spread out into a large pool. Soon the plug would be forced out and the lava would drain away, leaving behind a fine flat surface to walk on when sufficiently hardened.

Stopping beside the largest of three overflows, we watched it fill and empty. The heat was intense. . . .

As we wanted to get back down to the coast that day, the kahunas wasted no time. They had brought *ti* leaves with them and were all ready for action as soon as the lava would bear our weight. (The leaves

Dr. William T. Brigham, who was the director of the Bishop Museum of Ethnology at Honolulu from 1888 to 1918, undertook the lava walk in a moment of madness when he was a young man. His boots were burned to a crisp, but his feet were unharmed.

A traditional fire walk over red-hot stones was photographed at the University of Hawaii in 1949. Both native Hawaiians and haoles (Caucasians) performed the walk.

of the *ti* plant are universally used by fire walkers where available in Polynesia. They are a foot or two long and fairly narrow, with cutting edges like saw-grass. They grow in a tuft on the top of a stalk resembling in size and shape a broomstick.)

When the rocks we threw on the lava surface showed that it had hardened enough to bear our weight, the kahunas arose and clambered down the side of the wall. It was far worse than a bake oven when we got to the bottom. The lava was blackening on the surface, but all across it ran heat discolorations that came and went as they do on a cooling iron before a blacksmith plunges it into his tub for tempering. I heartily wished that I had not been so curious. The very thought of running over that flat inferno to the other side made me tremble. . . .

The kahunas took off their sandals and tied *ti* leaves around their feet, about three leaves to the foot. I sat down and began tying my *ti* leaves on outside my big hob-nailed boots. I wasn't taking any chances. But that wouldn't do at all—I must take off my boots and my two pairs of socks. The goddess Pele hadn't agreed to keep boots from burning and it might be an insult to her if I wore them.

I argued hotly—and I say "hotly" because we were all but roasted. I knew that Pele wasn't the one who made fire-magic possible, and I did my best to find out what or who was. As usual they grinned and said that of course the "white" kahuna knew the trick of getting *mana* (power of some kind known to kahunas) out of air and water to use in kahuna work, and that we were wasting time talking about the thing no kahuna ever put into words—the secret handed down only from father to son.

The upshot of the matter was that I sat tight and refused to take off my boots. In the back of my mind I figured that if the Hawaiians could walk over hot lava with bare calloused feet, I could do it with my heavy leather soles to protect me. . . .

The kahunas got to considering my boots a great joke. If I wanted to offer them as a sacrifice to the gods, it might be a good idea. They grinned at each other and left me to tie on my leaves while they began their chants.

The chants were in an archaic Hawaiian. . . . It was the usual "god-talk" handed down word for word for countless generations. All I could make of it was that it consisted of simple little mentions of legendary history and was peppered with praise of some god or gods.

I almost roasted alive before the kahunas had finished their chanting, although it could not have taken more than a few minutes. . . . One of the kahunas beat at the shimmering surface of the lava with a bunch of *ti* leaves and then offered me the honor of crossing first. Instantly I remembered my manners; I was all for age before beauty.

The matter was settled at once by deciding that the oldest kahuna should go first, I second and the others side by side. Without a moment of hesitation the oldest man trotted out on that terrifically hot surface. I was watching him with my mouth open and he was nearly across—a distance of about a hundred and fifty feet—when someone gave me a shove that resulted in my having a choice of falling on my face on the lava or catching a running stride.

I still do not know what madness seized me, but I ran. The heat was unbelievable. I held my breath and my mind seemed to stop functioning. I was young then and could do my hundred-yard dash with the best. Did I run! I flew! I would have broken all records, but with my first few steps the soles of my boots began to burn. They curled and shrank, clamping down on my feet like a vise. The seams gave way and I found myself with one sole gone and the other flapping behind me from the leather strap at the heel.

That flapping sole was almost the death of me. It tripped me repeatedly and slowed me down. Finally, after what seemed minutes, but could not have been more than a few seconds, I leaped off to safety.

I looked down at my feet and found my socks burning at the edges of the curled leather uppers of my boots. I beat out the smouldering fire in the cotton fabric and looked up to find my three kahunas rocking with laughter as they pointed to the heel and sole of my left boot which lay smoking and burned to a crisp on the lava.

I laughed too. I was never so relieved in my life as I was to find that I was safe and that there was not a blister on my feet—not even where I had beaten out the fire in the socks.

There is little more that I can tell of this experience. I had a sensation of intense heat on my face and body, but almost no sensation in my feet. When I touched them with my hands they were hot on the bottoms, but they did not feel so except to my hands. None of the kahunas had a blister, although the *ti* leaves which they had tied on their feet had burned away long since.

My return trip to the coast was a nightmare. Trying to make it in improvised sandals whittled from green wood has left me with an impression almost more vivid than my fire-walking.
[Max Freedom Long, *The Secret Science Behind Miracles*, pp.31–39]

The Unknotted Noose

On February 7, 1894, young Will Purvis was taken to be hanged for the murder of a farmer in Columbia, Mississippi. The trapdoor opened, and Will Purvis plunged to his doom—or would have, if the noose had not become unknotted and slipped over Purvis's head. As it was, Purvis emerged from beneath the scaffold relatively unharmed.

But he had been sentenced to hang, and hang he would. The deputies led him back up the steps of the gallows, and the noose, reknotted, was again placed around his neck. By this time, though, the crowd of 3,000 had other ideas: they had seen a miracle, and as far as they were concerned Will had been reprieved by the highest judge of all. Singing, shouting, and praising the

Sentenced to hang for a murder committed by another man, Will Purvis was miraculously saved when the noose slipped. Some said it was because the rope was made of grass too wiry to keep a knot; another claimed it had been greased. Upon his vindication years later, Mississippi rewarded Purvis with the sum of $5,000.

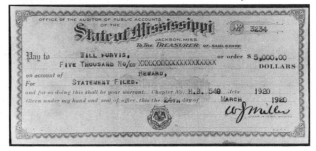

Lord, they treated Purvis as a hero. Utterly bewildered, Sheriff Irvin Magee led him back to his cell.

Purvis's attorneys filed several appeals with the state supreme court, but to no avail. A new date of execution was set for December 12, 1895. A few nights before the hanging was to take place, the lad's friends spirited him out of jail and he went into hiding. A month later Mississippi inaugurated a new governor who was sympathetic to Will. He then surrendered himself and on March 12, 1896, the governor commuted his sentence to life imprisonment. By now Purvis was famous and thousands of letters poured into the state house demanding a full pardon. Toward the end of 1898 this was granted and Purvis was freed.

Many years passed. Then, in 1917, a dying man named Joseph Beard confessed to the murder and Purvis was at last exonerated.

During the trial Purvis had sworn that he was innocent, and when the 12 jurors returned their verdict of "guilty" he was stunned with disbelief. It was said that he cried out, "I'll live to see the last one of you die!" Purvis died October 13, 1938, three days after the death of the last juror. People still speculate about his miraculous reprieve. (*The Clarion Ledger*, June 26, 1955; The Jackson, Mississippi, *Daily Clarion-Ledger*, March 11, 1917; *The New York Times*, February 9, 1894; *Times-Picayune New Orlean State Magazine*, April 13, 1947)

Charbel Makhlouf

Soon after Charbel Makhlouf, a Maronite monk at the St. Maroun monastery at Annaya, Lebanon, was buried in 1898, strange lights were seen around his grave. He had been buried, like others of his order, without a coffin, and after the lights had been seen for several weeks his body was disinterred. Heavy rains had flooded the grave, but despite this the body was found to show no trace of decomposition. It was washed, dressed in new clothes, and placed in a wooden coffin in the monastery chapel. Before long a strange oily liquid was noticed suffusing the body. It smelled of blood and seemed to be a mixture of blood and sweat, but whatever it was, it seeped through the skin in such quantities that the body's clothing had to be changed twice a week. Strips of the saturated cloth were said to have remarkable healing properties.

Twenty-nine years after Charbel's death, his body was examined by doctors and pronounced free from corruption. Their report, together with the testimony of other eyewitnesses, was sealed in a zinc tube and placed with the body in a wood-lined zinc coffin, which was then placed in the monastery wall and bricked over. That was in 1927.

In 1950 pilgrims noticed that a curious liquid was seeping through the wall in front of the coffin. The tomb was broken open, the coffin removed, and, again in the presence of ecclesiastical and medical authorities, opened for examination of the body.

By every appearance Charbel might have been merely asleep. His clothing was partly rotted and was soaked in the oily fluid, much of which had congealed inside the coffin. The zinc tube containing the evidence of the previous examination was badly corroded.

Since 1950 the body has been examined and the oily exudation, which had accumulated to a depth of about three inches, has been removed from the coffin for curative dispensation. Charbel Makhlouf was canonized in 1977. (*The Unexplained: Mysteries of Mind Space & Time*, Vol. 4, Issue 39)

Colonel Gudgeon in Rarotonga

"I knew quite well that I was walking on red-hot stones and could sense the heat," wrote Colonel Gudgeon,

> yet I was not burned. I felt something resembling slight electric shocks, both at the time and afterward. I did not walk quickly across the oven, but with deliberation, because I feared to tread on a sharp stone as my feet were very tender. My impression, as I crossed the hot stones, was that the skin would all peel off my feet. Yet all I felt afterward was a tingling sensation lasting for some seven hours. I do not know that I would recommend anyone to try it. A man must have *mana* to do it.

Colonel Gudgeon's mana—magical power—came to him, in a sense, at third hand. In 1899 he and three other Englishmen had been watching a fire walk on the tiny island of Rarotonga (the largest of the Cook Islands in the South Pacific), where he had the status of British resident. After the natives had completed the walk, their leader turned to one of the Englishmen, a man named Goodwin, and handed him his wand of ti leaves, saying, "I hand my *mana* to you; lead your friends through the oven."

To a man, the Englishmen removed their shoes and socks and set out after Goodwin across the stones. Goodwin, Gudgeon, and a Dr. George Craig were unharmed by the walk, but Craig's brother William disobeyed the clear instructions he had been given and looked back before he had completed the traverse. His feet were severely burned, and he was unable to walk for several weeks.

Thirty minutes after the walk, Colonel Gudgeon and his friends, perhaps scarcely believing what they had accomplished, began to speculate as to what the temperature of the stones might actually be. In response, the native leader tossed his wand of green ti leaves onto the stones, and the Englishmen had the satisfaction of seeing it flame almost at once. (Vincent H. Gaddis, *Mysterious Fires and Lights*, pp.144–45)

Almost Immune to Death

"If I am killed by common assassins, and especially by my brothers the Russian peasants, you . . . have nothing to fear," wrote the "mad monk" Grigori Yefimovich Rasputin in December 1916 to his protector, Czar Nicholas II of Russia.

> But if I am murdered by Boyars (nobles), and if they shed my blood, their hands will remain soiled with my blood. . . . Brothers will kill brothers and they will kill each other and . . . there will be no nobles in the country.

Rasputin, a filthy, rude-mannered, lecherous, hard-drinking peasant renowned for his hypnotic powers and healing skills, was the most feared and detested person in Russia because of his sway over the royal family. The czar and especially the czar's wife, the empress Alexandra, who believed he had miraculously saved the life of their hemophiliac son, were devoted to him.

In 1914 Rasputin had survived being knifed in the stomach by a peasant woman. Now, even as he wrote of his anticipated murder, several palace noblemen led by Prince Felix Yusupov were busy plotting it.

Inviting Rasputin to Yusupov's palace the night of December 29, 1916, they arranged that he should be the first to arrive and laid out wine and cake for him. While he awaited the others, he helped himself generously to both, not suspecting that the refreshments

Rasputin's mesmerizing eyes, a key to his power, were once described by Prince Yusupov, who later claimed to be the "monk's" murderer: "[His] eyes shone before me like a kind of phosphorescent light. From them came two rays that flowed into each other and merged into a glowing circle. . . . I was gradually falling into the power of this mysterious man."

were loaded with potassium cyanide. When Yusupov arrived and found his guest unaffected by the cyanide, he shot him in the back. Rasputin crumpled to the floor and was pronounced dead. A while later the conspirators returned to pick up the corpse and take it to the Neva River. But Rasputin sprang to life and, crawling

on his hands and knees, pursued the terrified Yusupov up a flight of stairs. Shot twice more, the "monk" fell.

Certain that he was finally dead, the nobles kicked and battered him, took his body to the river, smashed a hole in the ice, and shoved him into the frigid water. To their disbelief, Rasputin was still breathing as they did so. When his body was retrieved two days later, his right hand was found upon his chest with three fingers in a sign of benediction.

His predictions of what would follow his death and his curse on his murderers were soon realized with the Russian Revolution of 1917. (For the prophecy of the manner of Rasputin's death, see page 27.) (*Out of This World,* Perrott Phillips, ed., pp.98–102)

Padre Pio

Giovannino—Little John—could only crawl on his hands and knees through the streets of his hometown, Foggia, in southern Italy. He was nine years old and had been born a hunchback. An object of contempt to children of his own age, and an object of pity to his elders, he was unable even to dress himself, for the curve of his spine brought his chin almost to the ground. To his parents, Giovannino's loneliness and deformity were a source of daily and enduring heartbreak.

One day as Giovannino was crawling along a street in Foggia, he felt someone touch his back. Unused to human contact in the street, he was startled. Suddenly he found himself standing upright, and he caught a brief glimpse of the bleeding hand of the monk who had just touched him. "Padre Pio!" Giovannino called, "Padre Pio!"—but the monk had gone.

Giovannino ran and leaped like a lamb.

At the door of his home, his mother asked him, in a formal manner, what he wanted. Then she recognized him and fell to her knees in prayer. "Padre Pio touched me with his hands!" her son said again and again.

Padre Pio was born in 1887 in the village of Pietrelcina, near Benevento in southern Italy. When he was 17 he joined the Capuchins, an order of Franciscan monks, and for 11 years lived the quiet life of a novice. Then, on September 20, 1915, he began to experience pains in his hands, feet, and side. Doctors could find no reason for these pains and had no reason to suspect that they were the prelude to something extraordinary.

On September 20, 1918, Padre Pio collapsed in agony during his prayers at the altar of the church in Foggia. His brother monks found him there, unconscious and bleeding from his hands, feet, and side. The wounds of the crucified Christ had been duplicated in his flesh. They were to defy every medical effort to heal them, and he would bear them for the rest of his life.

Among the many who viewed Padre Pio as a fraud, an attention-seeking trickster, was a Dr. Ricciardi who lived in the town of San Giovanni Rotondo, not far from Padre Pio's monastery. One day Dr. Ricciardi was unable to rise from his bed. He sent for two colleagues, Dr. Merla and Dr. Juva. They concurred in their diagnosis. He had an incurable brain tumor.

Dr. Ricciardi was a rationalist, a scientist, and a skeptic. If his relatives brought a priest to see him, he said, he would throw him out of the house—especially Padre Pio. All he wanted was to die in peace.

But dying came hard to Ricciardi, for he found much pain and fear in it, and little peace.

One day, when death was not far off, the doctor looked up to see Padre Pio standing in the doorway of his bedroom. Who had sent for him, Ricciardi moaned, who had sent for him?

Padre Pio stepped to his bedside and began to pray in Latin: "Peace to this house and to those who inhabit it. Enter, Oh Lord, together with us, and with our humble entrance let come in everlasting happiness, Divine prosperity, joy, and fruitful charity. Let the demons run out. Let the angels come." Then Padre Pio asked Ricciardi if he would accept from him the holy oil used to anoint the dying.

Ricciardi reached out and clutched the monk's hands, oblivious of the wounds in them.

"I accept," he said.

"Your soul is right," Padre Pio told him, "and in a few days your body too will be right again."

That Christmas Dr. Ricciardi, his health fully recovered, attended Mass at the church of St. Mary of the Graces. The year was 1929.

As the century wore on, Padre Pio's fame spread across the world, though he rarely left the seclusion of his monastery. Many claimed to have been visited by him when he was actually many miles away, and a prodigious number of cures were attributed to him. His personal manner was said to be down-to-earth and often humorous. He died on September 28, 1968, and his devotees impatiently await his canonization. (Oscar De Liso, *Padre Pio, The Priest Who Bears the Wounds of Christ*, pp.114–18; *National Review*, 20:138–39, February 13, 1968; Reader's Digest, eds., *Strange Stories, Amazing Facts*, pp.382–83)

A Burning Invitation

In the early spring of 1921 the Roman Catholic bishop of Mysore, in southern India, was invited by the local maharajah to attend an exhibition of fire walking at his summer palace. The performance was set for 6 P.M., but the bishop, Monsignor Despatures, who was eager to witness both the event and all the preparations for it, arrived at the palace early.

The master of ceremonies was a Muslim from northern India, and on his instructions a trench some 13 feet long, 6 feet wide, and nearly a foot deep had been dug. On the instructions of the maharajah, however, who seems to have been as suspicious of the whole affair as the bishop, the Muslim himself had not been allowed to have any hand in the actual preparation of the pit. As far as Monsignor Despatures could tell, the fire walk had no religious overtones but was regarded, at least by the educated Indians present, as no more than a spectacle or curiosity.

In due course a fire was lit in the trench, and the heat produced was so great that the maharajah, his family, and guests could sit no closer than 25 yards from the trench. The account continues in the bishop's words:

> The Mohammedan, according to Indian usage, came and prostrated himself before the sovereign and then went straight to the furnace. I thought that the man was going to enter the fire himself, but I was mistaken. He remained about a yard from the brink, and called upon one of the palace servants to step into the brazier. Having beckoned to him to come forward, he made an appeal into which he seemed to put all his powers of persuasion, but the man never stirred. In the meanwhile, however, the Mohammedan had drawn closer to him, and then unexpectedly taking him by the shoulders he pushed him into the little lake of glowing ashes. For the first moment or two the Indian struggled to get out of the fire; then suddenly the look of terror on his face gave place to an astonished smile, and he proceeded to cross the trench lengthwise, without haste and as if he were taking a constitutional, beaming contentedly upon those who were standing round on either side of him. His feet and legs were perfectly bare. When he got out, his fellow servants crowded round him to ask what it felt like. His explanations must have been satisfactory, for one, two, five, and then ten of the palace household plunged into the trench. After this it was the turn of the bandsmen of the Maharajah's band, several of whom were Christians. They marched into the fire three by three. At this juncture several cartloads of dried palm-leaves were brought down and thrown upon the embers. They blazed up at once, breaking into tongues of flame higher than a man's head. The Mohammedan induced others of the palace servants to pass through the flames and they did it without taking harm. The bandsmen went through a second time, carrying their instruments in their hands and with their sheets of music on top. I noticed that the flames which rose to lick their faces bellied out round the different parts of the instruments and only flickered round the sheets of music without setting them on fire. There must, I think, have been two hundred people who passed over the embers, and a hundred who went right through the middle of the flames. Beside me were standing two Englishmen, the head of the Maharajah's police force (a

Catholic), and a civil engineer. They went to ask the royal permission to try the experiment themselves. The Maharajah told them that they might do it on their own responsibility. Then they turned to the Mohammedan and he motioned to them to go forward. They crossed without any sign of burning. When they came back into my neighbourhood, I asked them what they thought of it. "Well," they said, "we felt we were in a furnace, but the fire did not burn us." When the Maharajah stood up to mark the close of the proceedings, the Mohammedan, who was still standing close to the trench, fell writhing upon the ground, as if in an agony of pain. He asked for water; they brought it and he drank greedily. A Brahmin who stood near me remarked: "He has taken upon himself the burning of the fire."

Two weeks later the Muslim gave another exhibition in the city of Mysore, at which many people walked through the fire with impunity. But at the end of the event, after the maestro had warned that no one else should make the walk, three people forced their way into the trench. They were badly burned and had to be hospitalized. In conclusion, the bishop wrote:

> I was in full possession of my faculties. I went round the trench before the proceedings began; I went back to it again after all was over; I spoke with those who passed through the fire, and I even said a Hail Mary or two with the view of arresting any exhibition of diabolic power.... It was beyond doubt a real burning fire which consumed the charcoal and sent up in flames the cartloads of palm leaves that were thrown upon it, but it was a fire which had lost its power of injuring those who crossed it and all that they took with them.... How can we account for it all? I do not think any material cause can explain it. No expedient, at any rate, had been employed to produce such an effect. I am forced to believe in the influence of some spiritual agency which is not God.

Monsignor Despatures's description of this event was made in a letter to Olivier Leroy, the French author of a study of such cases entitled *Les Hommes Salamandres* ("Human Salamanders"). With the bishop's permission and help Leroy checked the story with others who had been present. All agreed with the main points of the bishop's story but differed in some details. An Englishman named Macintosh, for example, estimated the length of the trench at 30 yards (though perhaps he meant feet) and the number of fire walkers at 500. Mr. Lingaraj Urs, on the other hand, recalled the trench as being 4 feet wide, 15 feet long, and 5 feet deep. Leroy also discovered that Mr. Urs and a Mr. J. C. Rollo, the principal of Mysore College, kept their boots on to negotiate the fire. Neither pair of boots was damaged, and neither man experienced any burning sensation. (Herbert Thurston, *The Physical Phenomena of Mysticism*, pp.187–89)

The Sudden Health of Jack Traynor

In World War I Jack Traynor, of Liverpool, England, suffered two bullet wounds. One left a hole in his skull that refused to heal, and the other, which severed nerves that not even a most skillful surgeon could join, had left him with a paralyzed and atrophied right arm. He was awarded a total-disability pension.

By 1923 Traynor had begun to suffer from epilepsy, probably triggered by the head wound. He was now unable to walk. That same year he was taken on a pilgrimage to Lourdes, France, where he was lowered bodily into the communal bath.

Four days later he jumped out of bed, washed and shaved himself, and walked out of the hospice unaided. After he returned to England he went into business as a coal merchant, married, fathered two children, and lived a normal life for the next 20 years, until his death of pneumonia in 1943. During this time the Ministry of Pensions, refusing to believe that someone who had been pronounced totally disabled could become mysteriously totally cured, continued to pay Traynor the full disability pension. Although it was never declared miraculous by the Catholic Church, the cure is inexplicable. (*CMA Journal*, 111:1255, December 7, 1974; *The Journal of Religion and Psychical Research*, 4:1:31–32, January 1981; *Parapsychology Review*, 8:5:25, September–October 1977)

Tibetan Yogis and Body Heat

"To spend the winter in a cave amidst the snows, at an altitude that varies between 11,000 and 18,000 feet, clad in a thin garment or even naked, and escape freezing, is a somewhat difficult achievement," observed Alexandra David-Neel in the late 1920's. And yet, she wrote, "numbers of Tibetan hermits go safely each year through this ordeal." In her book about the 14 years she spent in Tibet, she gives an account on "The Art of Warming Oneself Without Fire up in the Snows." The endurance of these monks, she said, "is ascribed to the power which they have acquired to generate *tumo*." She went on to explain:

> The word *tumo* signifies heat, warmth, but is not used in Tibetan language to express ordinary heat or warmth. It is a technical term of mystic terminology....
> It is kept secret by the lamas who teach it, and they do not fail to declare that information gathered by hearsay or reading is without any practical result if one has not been personally taught and trained

by a master who is himself an adept. . . .

Sometimes, a kind of examination concludes the training of the *tumo* students.

Upon a frosty winter night, those who think themselves capable of victoriously enduring the test are led to the shore of a river or lake. If all the streams are frozen . . . a hole is made in the ice. A moonlight night, with a hard wind blowing, is chosen. . . .

The neophytes sit on the ground, cross-legged and naked. Sheets are dipped in the icy water, each man wraps himself in one of them and must dry it on his body. As soon as the sheet has become dry, it is again dipped in the water and placed on the novice's body to be dried as before. The operation goes on in that way until daybreak. . . .

It is said that some dry as many as forty sheets in one night. One should perhaps make large allowances for exaggeration, or perhaps for the *size* of the sheets which in some cases may become so small as to be almost symbolical. Yet I have seen some *respas* dry a number of pieces of cloth the size of a large shawl. . . . [Respas wear but a single cotton garment in all seasons at any altitude.]

It is difficult for us to get a perfectly correct idea about the extent of the results obtained through *tumo* training, but some of these feats are genuine. Hermits really do live naked, or wearing one single thin garment during the whole winter in the high regions I have mentioned. I am not the only one who has seen some of them. It has been said that some members of the Mount Everest expedition had an occasional glimpse of one of these naked anchorites. [Alexandra David-Neel, *Magic and Mystery in Tibet,* pp.216–29]

The Internal Control of Body Heat

Descriptions have long existed of yogis in Tibet and India who habitually survive extreme cold by practicing certain yogas that allow them to control the body's ability to produce heat.

In 1981 Westerners were allowed to investigate this phenomenon. By invitation of the dalai lama, a group of scientists from Harvard Medical School, led by Dr. Herbert Benson, went to India to perform experiments in collaboration with three Tibetan Buddhist monks. Temperature sensors were attached to various parts of the monks' bodies. By means of meditation, all were able to raise the temperature of their fingers and toes substantially—sometimes by as much as 15°F. Other skin areas registered lesser increases, and internal temperatures remained normal.

Dr. Benson believes that the monks, through their yoga, are able to dilate the small blood vessels in the skin, thus increasing blood flow and raising the surface temperature. Such feats are all the more amazing, he says, because the normal body response to cold (such as in Tibet) is to constrict those blood vessels and lower the temperature at the extremities.

Prof. Herbert Benson monitors the surface body temperature of a Tibetan Buddhist monk while he practices tumo, *the yoga that enables him to produce heat.*

The Human Cork

On August 13, 1931, the *New York Herald Tribune* published the obituary of Angelo Faticoni, who had died a few days before at Jacksonville, Florida. According to the obituary—which was headlined "'Human Cork' Is Dead, His Secret Unrevealed"— Faticoni had been phenomenally and unnaturally buoyant. He could stay afloat, for example, for 15 hours with 20 pounds of lead tied to his ankles:

Faticoni could sleep in water, roll up into a ball, lie on his side or assume any position asked of him. Once he was sewed into a bag and then thrown head foremost into the water, with a twenty-pound cannonball lashed to his legs. His head reappeared on the surface soon afterward, and he remained motionless in that position for eight hours. Another time he swam across the Hudson tied to a chair weighted with lead.

Some years ago he went to Harvard to perform for the students and faculty. He had been examined by medical authorities who failed to find support for their theories that he was able to float at such great length by the nature of his internal organs, which they believed were different from those of other men.

Faticoni had often promised to reveal the secret of how he became "the Human Cork," but he never did. [The *New York Herald Tribune*, August 13, 1931]

Angelo Faticoni, "the human cork," was photographed floating easily while tied to a weighted chair. Doctors could find nothing to account for his extraordinary buoyancy.

The Virgin and the Anarchist

Twelve-year-old Mariette Beco was looking out of the window of her home in Banneux, Belgium, on the evening of January 12, 1933. It was about 7 P.M. and her young brother was due home from his friends. Suddenly Mariette saw a light outside in the garden: shining in the night was the luminous bright figure of a woman, her posture erect, her head inclined slightly to one side. Mariette called for her mother.

Mrs. Beco also saw the strange figure. "It must be the Blessed Virgin," she said half-jokingly to her daughter's repeated questions. Soon the vision faded, at least as far as Mrs. Beco was concerned. But her daughter could still clearly see the shining woman and she began to say her rosary. At last the figure disappeared, and when Mariette's father came home, he laughed at his daughter's experience.

The Becos were one of the poorest families in the area and, although nominally Catholics, had little time for churchgoing. Despite this Mariette began to attend catechism at the local church. The priest, Abbé Jamin, listened to her story of the shining lady and at first put it down to a vivid imagination encouraged by the recent apparitions of the Virgin that were reportedly seen at Beauraing, not many miles away.

On Thursday, January 19, Mr. Beco found his daughter praying on the garden path. He was worried and went to solicit Abbé Jamin's help. The priest was out, so Beco got a neighbor instead. They came upon Mariette as she was leaving the garden and tried to

induce her to come indoors. "She's calling me," she answered, and set off down the road. Together they followed along behind the child.

Soon she came to a small roadside spring and knelt down beside it. Seemingly listening to something the two men could neither hear nor see, she plunged her hands into the water. "This spring is set apart for me," the child murmured, as though repeating something she had been told by an invisible presence.

Later, in the garden, she again saw a vision and asked: "Who are you, Madame?" The girl then replied, as though answering her own question, "... the Blessed Virgin of the poor."

Nearly 14 months before these events in Banneux, Benito Pelegri Garcia's right arm had been seriously injured in a boiler explosion in Barcelona. Medical efforts in Spain, Italy, and Germany had failed to heal the arm, and Garcia was unable to work. His wife, a Belgian woman, urged him to make a pilgrimage to Banneux, where the healing spring of the Virgin of the Poor had become well known. But Benito was an anarchist and would have nothing to do with such superstitions. At last Garcia's daughter, who had turned 13, threatened to find work in domestic service to help the family unless her father consented to try the healing powers of the spring.

Garcia could only succumb to such pressure and reluctantly agreed to make the pilgrimage. As a token of willingness, if not good faith, he also vowed to abstain from alcohol and tobacco during the journey.

On July 4, 1933, the Garcias set out on foot for the Belgian shrine. They had no money for lodgings and very little for food, except for the small amounts Mrs. Garcia managed to earn by obtaining occasional knitting jobs when they stopped to rest for the night.

As they neared Banneux, Garcia's nerves were thoroughly frayed. If nothing happened at the shrine, he promised, he would leave his wife there and go back to Spain alone. Finally, when they were no more than half a mile from their goal, his resolution failed: he slipped away from his wife, found a kindred anarchist who was willing to lend him 100 francs, and was gone for several hours. Mrs. Garcia became frantic.

With the help of the police she found him and persuaded him that it was foolish to have come so far only to turn back. Together they made their way to the spring, Garcia in a mood as far removed from faithful confidence as possible. As he approached the spring, Garcia was given a bucket of its water. He placed his right hand into the bucket and was surprised to find that the water was almost boiling. Then he dipped his uninjured left hand in it. To his amazement the water now felt cool. A doctor at the scene suggested that he not touch the water from the common pool because it might make his wound more septic. Still unbelieving, Garcia therefore placed his arm into a fresh bucket of spring water and appealed: "If you are 'the Virgin of the Poor,' prove it. Here is a poor man who has come all the way from Spain."

To his stupefaction, and to the amazement of those around him, the wounded arm healed visibly in the water. Benito Garcia, a poor man without faith, had been cured. (Herbert Thurston, *Beauraing and Other Miracles,* pp.25–44)

The Fire Virgins of Surinam
Not an ordeal but an orgy: that was how Rosita Forbes described the traditional fire dance of Surinam (Dutch Guiana) that she witnessed in the mid-1930's. Only men take part in the ceremony, but their immunity to the waist-high flames in which they cavort, to the blazing boughs they embrace, and to the glowing embers they chew is bestowed by a virgin priestess.

As long as she remains in a trance, the dancers are safe. But when the trance ends, so does the immunity, and when she gives the signal terminating the

spell, the men quickly leap from the fire to safety.

The role of the virgin priestess is not hereditary, and the young women selected for it receive no special training. Instead, they are chosen by their parents when they demonstrate, as children, an ability to walk on or stick their feet in the fire burning in the hearth or pick up and play with the live coals.

Those who participate in the fire dance are said to gain the power of healing the sick. (Vincent H. Gaddis, *Mysterious Fires and Lights,* pp.129–30)

Fire Walkers and Water Babies
The people of Mbengga, one of the smaller of Fiji's tropical islands, harvest coconuts, lemons, and bananas and, once a year, observe one of the world's most astonishing religious ceremonies.

The night before the ceremony takes place, those who are to participate offer prayers to Tui Namoliwai, the water god. Meanwhile others line the bottom of a pit 25 feet long, 10 feet wide, and 6 feet deep with stones, most of them about 10 inches in diameter. On these a layer of logs is laid, then a layer of brush, then

For the fire-walking ceremony on Mbengga, an island in Fiji, stones are heated in a pile of burning brush and logs until they glow, after which they are leveled with rakes fashioned from long poles and twisted vines.

more stones, and on top a second layer of logs. The fire is lit and left to burn all night. By morning the heat is so intense that those who tend the fire—pulling partially burned logs out of the way and smoothing the bed of stones—must do so with long poles. By now the stones are aglow with heat, and the participants in the ceremony are gathered in a hut to offer final prayers.

Leaving the hut, their leader unhesitatingly enters the pit. His companions follow, and together they circle the pit. They are barefoot and keep their balance with some difficulty on the irregular stones. Their faces show no flicker of emotion. They leave the pit at the point where they entered it and make their way back to the hut. As they do, the onlookers applaud and toss the roots of dracaena plants into the pit, then cover the roots with leaves and dirt. The ceremony is over for another year, and if the men have properly prepared themselves—mentally or spiritually—they will have suffered no harm. If they have not, the consequences can be disastrous. In the 1940's one fire walker was so badly injured that both his legs had to be amputated.

And yet the preparations in no way involve any kind of physical protection for the feet. In 1950 Dr. Harry B. Wright of Philadelphia published an account of his observation of one fire walk. He found that the feet of two of the walkers, examined shortly before they ventured onto the glowing stones, were sensitive to the approach of a burning cigarette or to a pinprick and showed no sign of having been coated with any kind of protective substance. After the walk the feet were covered with ash but were not at all burned or blistered and were still sensitive to the cigarette and pin test.

When Dr. Wright asked for an explanation of what he had witnessed, the leader of the walk said that "the water god sent hundreds of water babies to spread their bodies over the stones, and the men walked on the cool backs of the water babies." (Vincent H. Gaddis, *Mysterious Fires and Lights,* pp.133–35)

No License to Heal

The story of the Brazilian healer Arigo, one of the most mystifying figures in the history of occult medicine, began with dreams, headaches, and a political campaign. It ended with a crowd of some 20,000 mourners and a controversy as unresolved today as it was when Arigo was alive.

Arigo's given name was José Pedro de Freitas. He was a farmer's son, born in the Belo Horizonte district of Brazil in 1918. His nickname, Arigo, by which he was known, was given him while he was still a child; it can be roughly translated as "country bumpkin."

When he was at school, Arigo was occasionally troubled by strange hallucinations. He would see a blinding light and sometimes he would hear a voice speaking in a strange language. As a young man, Arigo went to work in one of the nearby iron mines and by the time he was 25 he had been elected president of the union local. After leading a strike in protest against the brutal working conditions, he was fired. Arigo next began to earn his living as the manager of a bar in the mining town of Congonhas do Campo.

The dreams that now began to plague him nightly, often leaving him with a severe headache, were more difficult to deal with than those of his adolescence. In them he saw the operating room of a hospital, where a stout, baldheaded man addressed a group of doctors and nurses in the same guttural voice that he had first heard as a child. Deeply disturbed by the insistence of the dreams and headaches, Arigo often went to pray for help at the church of Bom Jesus do Matosinho.

Then the dream doctor revealed his identity. He was Dr. Adolpho Fritz, he told Arigo, and he had died during World War I. His own work had been cut short by his death, and he had chosen Arigo, who was, he knew, a compassionate man, to continue it for him. Henceforward, he said, Arigo would only find peace by helping the sick and distressed people around him.

For several years the vivid nightmares and fierce headaches continued. Then, in 1950, events passed out of Arigo's control.

Elections were being held that year, and one of the campaigners to visit Congonhas was Lúcio Bittencourt, a supporter of the iron miners in their struggle for better conditions. In Congonhas he met Arigo and was so impressed by his passionate advocacy of the miners' cause that he invited him to attend a political rally in Belo Horizonte, the nearest city. When the rally was postponed, Bittencourt invited Arigo to spend the night at the hotel where he was staying, the Hotel Financial.

Unknown to Arigo, Bittencourt was suffering from lung cancer and his doctor had advised an immediate operation in the United States.

As Bittencourt was about to fall asleep that night, the door of his room opened and someone put on the light. It was Arigo; his eyes were "glazed," and he was holding a razor. Strangely enough, Bittencourt was unafraid. Arigo began to speak in a thick German accent and in a tone quite unlike his ordinary voice. There was an emergency, he said; there would have to be an operation. Then Bittencourt lost consciousness.

When he came to, he found that his pajama jacket was slashed and bloodstained and that a neat incision had been made toward the back of his ribcage. He dressed and went into Arigo's room.

At first Arigo thought Bittencourt was drunk. But in Bittencourt's room he saw the incision and bloodstained pajamas and realized that an operation of some kind must have taken place. He had no memory, however, of

Arigo (behind desk, right) concentrates on one of his patients during a consultation. He was unable to explain his healing powers, but thousands attested to his success.

going to Bittencourt's room and denied having had any part in the bizarre affair. Shaken, Bittencourt caught the first available plane to Rio de Janeiro to see his doctor.

Now Arigo was afraid. Perhaps he had performed the operation while in some kind of trance; perhaps this was what the dreams and voices had been leading to. He could only pray that Bittencourt had come to no harm.

He did not have to wait long for news. The doctor had taken X-rays and was highly satisfied with the result of what he presumed was American surgery. The tumor had been removed, he explained to an astonished Bittencourt, "by a technique unknown in Brazil," and the patient's chances of recovery were now excellent. Then Bittencourt told his doctor what had happened, and not only his doctor but anyone else who would listen. Newspapers all over Brazil carried the story.

In Congonhas, Arigo's priest, Father Pernido, took the story seriously enough to warn him to perform no more operations. But how could he stop doing something he had no memory of having done, Arigo asked. Local spiritists hailed him as a genuine medium, but though he rejected their acclaim, the persistent visions of Dr. Fritz continued.

During the next six years Arigo saw as many as 300 patients a day and, to contain the crowds, had to move his "clinic" from his house to an empty church across the street. Then in 1956, under pressure from the medical establishment and the Catholic Church, he was charged with practicing "illegal medicine."

"How do you go about your practice?" Judge Eleito Soares asked him.

"I start to say the Lord's Prayer," Arigo answered. "From that moment, I don't see or know about anything else. The others tell me I write out prescriptions,

but I have no memory of this." He spoke earnestly.

"What about the operations?" the judge asked.

"It is the same with them. I am in a state I do not understand. I just want to help the poor people."

"But you are doing what you are charged with, are you not?"

"I am not the one who is doing this," Arigo replied. "I am just an intermediary between the people and the spirit of Dr. Fritz."

The judge was unimpressed. Could Arigo make this Dr. Fritz appear in the courtroom for questioning? All over Brazil newspapers carried reports of the trial and numerous testimonies on Arigo's behalf. According to J. Herculano Pires, a professor of the history and philosophy of education, it was "simply ridiculous to deny that the phenomenon of Arigo exists. Medical specialists, famous journalists, intellectuals, prominent statesmen have all witnessed the phenomena at Congonhas. We cannot possibly deny the reality of his feats."

Despite the favorable publicity, Arigo was sentenced to 15 months in jail and fined 5,000 cruzeiros (approximately $270). The court of appeals later reduced the sentence to eight months and allowed Arigo a year of probation before beginning his imprisonment. During this period he would be allowed to leave Congonhas only with the judge's permission and would have to stop his practice completely.

For a time he did stop his practice, and the headaches began again. After a while, since the local police seemed to look the other way, he began to see his patients covertly but, at least at first, refrained from operating. In May 1958 President Juscelino Kubitschek granted Arigo a presidential pardon.

In 1961 Kubitschek was no longer in office, and the religious and medical authorities again pressed for legal action against Arigo. But witnesses willing to testify on the prosecution's behalf were hard to find, and for months the new investigation made little headway. Then, in August 1963, Arigo performed surgery on an American investigator, Dr. Andrija Puharich. The operation brought him back into the national headlines.

Puharich, an investigator of psychic phenomena who had a medical degree from Northwestern University in Illinois, had heard stories of Arigo's remarkable cures and had come to Congonhas to see for himself. Arigo told him that he and his three companions were welcome to observe him for as long as they wished and to interview any of his patients.

On the first day of their investigation Puharich and his friends found a crowd of nearly 200 people waiting for Arigo to open his clinic at 7 A.M. After they had all filed into the abandoned church, Arigo told them that although it was Jesus who effected the cures he was credited with, he had no interest in the religious beliefs of those present. "All religions are good. Is this not true?" he said, then asked everyone to join him in repeating the Lord's Prayer. After this, he withdrew into a private cubicle for a few moments.

When Arigo reappeared, Puharich was struck by the change in his manner. His bearing was now formal and commanding and his speech sharp. The interpreter noticed a heavy German accent in his Portuguese and a "sprinkling" of simple German words and phrases. Arigo summoned the investigators into his treatment room. "Come," he said. "There is nothing to hide here. I am happy to have you watch."

What Puharich saw that day staggered him. The first patient was an elderly man whom Arigo brusquely pushed against the wall. He then took a four-inch-long stainless steel paring knife and inserted it between the man's left eyeball and eyelid, scraping and pressing upward into the socket with a forcefulness that Puharich found shocking. But the patient seemed quite unperturbed. At length Arigo withdrew the knife, noted a smear of pus on the blade, and told the old man he would get well. Then he wiped the blade on his shirt and summoned the next patient. Puharich examined the eye. He found no bleeding and no wounds. The operation had taken less than a minute.

Throughout the morning Arigo worked in this manner, never using an anesthetic or taking any precautions against infection. As far as the investigators could see, he employed no form of hypnotic suggestion. Bleeding was invariably minimal, and the patients appeared to feel no pain. More often than not, the treatment consisted only of the writing of a prescription, which Arigo did at high speed and without hesitation. At 11 A.M. he announced that the session was over and that he would be back that afternoon after he finished working at his regular job in the government welfare office (so far as is known, Arigo never accepted payment of any kind for his medical work). As soon as he left the clinic, the German accent and imperious manner left him and his usual down-to-earth amiable character emerged again.

That evening Puharich and a journalist from São Paulo, Jorge Rizzini, set up a movie camera in the treatment room. If Arigo was a sleight-of-hand expert, they would try to catch his deception on film. That night Arigo worked until 1 A.M. In a single day he had treated some 200 people.

Puharich was completely baffled. He knew that a convincingly thorough study of this amazing man's work would require far more time, money, and equipment than was presently available. What other tests could he make before he returned to the United States? On the inside of his right elbow was a small tumor, benign but annoying, known as a lipoma. Tomorrow,

he decided, he would ask Arigo to remove it. He would be his own guinea pig.

Arigo unhesitatingly agreed to perform the operation. "Of course," he said. "Has anyone here got a good Brazilian pocketknife to use on this Americano?" Several were offered, and Arigo quickly chose one. Puharich felt a sudden chill of alarm, but there was no way now for him to withdraw. He looked to see if Rizzini had the movie camera ready.

"Just roll up your sleeve, Doctor."

Puharich did as he was told and braced himself to watch Arigo make the incision. Arigo, however, told him to look the other way.

Less than 10 seconds later Puharich felt Arigo slap something wet and slippery into his hand. It was the excised lipoma. Glancing down at his forearm, he saw a neat half-inch slit oozing the barest trickle of blood. There had been no pain at all.

That afternoon the Americans left Congonhas. Puharich kept a careful watch on the wound in his arm; Arigo had used no antiseptics, and he was on the alert for the first signs of blood poisoning. They never appeared. Despite the unhygienic conditions and the fact that no stitches had been used to close the incision, it healed quickly and cleanly.

In São Paulo, Puharich and his friends watched the movies Rizzini had taken. They could find no evidence

Arigo, who was jailed in 1964, had antagonized the Catholic Church and the medical establishment for performing magic and practicing medicine without a license.

of trickery in them. Soon the newspapers were again buzzing with Arigo's name and details of his operation on the American doctor.

Now the courts were spurred into action, and on November 20, 1964, Arigo was sentenced to 16 months in jail. He was allowed to leave the courtroom only to say good-bye to his wife and children, for the sentence was to begin immediately. He went home, made his farewells, and waited for the police to come.

But not a single man in the Congonhas police force was willing to take Arigo to jail, and the state police were reluctant to drive through the crowd that had gathered outside his house. As the evening wore on, Arigo became impatient and finally walked over to the prison by himself.

Even in jail Arigo managed to carry on his work. After he quelled a riot, the warden gave him the freedom to leave whenever he wished. Arigo took advantage of this dispensation only rarely and always to visit the sick. While the guards looked the other way he began treating sick prisoners and then the crowds of people who waited in the alley outside.

Arigo was released from jail in November 1965. Soon afterward Puharich returned to Congonhas with a research assistant. His plan was to test Arigo's ability to diagnose his patients' complaints, an activity not likely to rouse the anger of the Brazilian Medical Society. In the test Arigo gave an immediate verbal diagnosis of each patient who stepped in front of him. Of 1,000 such patients, chosen at random, 545 had brought their official medical records with them. In 518 of these cases Arigo's spontaneous diagnosis matched that of the patient's own doctor.

How could he possibly make such diagnoses and state them in modern medical terminology, Puharich asked. "That's easy," Arigo said. "I just listen to what the voice of Dr. Fritz tells me and repeat it. I always hear it in my left ear."

More tests of Arigo's ability followed, this time employing a battery of instruments—an electroencephalograph, an electrocardiogram, X-ray and blood-typing equipment, a microscope, tape recorders and cameras. Tests were made on the patients before, during, and after their treatment, and Arigo's surgical technique was demonstrated for the cameras on a variety of tumors, cysts, cataracts, and other complaints.

The press discovered what was going on, and a horde of reporters and cameramen descended on Congonhas. It was impossible to continue the research. Puharich returned to São Paulo with his evidence and showed it to a number of interested professionals, including an ophthalmologist, a nuclear physicist, a medium, a psychiatrist, and a cardiologist. They could only agree that Arigo's cures were a fact.

When he returned to New York, Puharich showed color films of Arigo's surgery to Dr. Robert Laidlaw, former director of psychiatry at Roosevelt Hospital. Laidlaw observed that Arigo's face assumed a quite uncharacteristic expression when he operated, that his hands and fingers moved with astonishing speed and dexterity when he worked, even when he was looking elsewhere, and that the incisions he made seemed to "glue" themselves together without stitches. Laidlaw could not explain how Arigo had acquired surgical skills that were beyond the abilities of many trained surgeons. He too was baffled.

Against the possibility that Arigo was a skilled magician are the following facts: that he indisputably cured numerous people (or, to be quite precise, that numerous people experienced cures immediately or soon after his treatment); that he made real incisions, which bled little and healed despite the unhygienic conditions attending them; that his patients experienced little or no pain during or after his surgical procedures, despite the lack of anesthetics; that he was able to diagnose illnesses at a glance and write accurate prescriptions, despite having had little formal and no medical education; and that, so far as is known, he never accepted money for his medical work but supported his family by working at an ordinary job.

José Pedro de Freitas, known to the world as Arigo, died in a car accident on January 11, 1971. (*Reader's Digest*, 106:635:214–39, March 1975)

Holy Water

Joe Riker of New Haven, Connecticut, refused to have an operation in 1974. The cancer had made a hole in his skull and laid bare the brain itself.

"You're going to get meningitis," said the surgeon who dressed the wound for him every week. "Any day now. And die. That thing is going to get your brain."

"No operation," Joe said.

One week Joe did not come to have his wound dressed, nor did he come the week after. A month went by, and the surgeon who had been treating him went over to the diner where Joe was a short-order cook.

Joe was behind the counter, wearing his fedora as usual. Yes, he said, he would come to the surgeon's office later that afternoon.

When he arrived he took off his hat and inclined his head. Instead of the hole in his skull there was now a fragile bridge of new skin.

"What happened?" the surgeon asked.

"You mean that?" Joe pointed to the top of his head. "Oh well," he said, "the wife's sister, she went to France, and brought me a bottle of water from Lourdes. I've been washing it out with that for a month." (*Harper's*, 252:75–76, January 1976)

SIGNS AND WONDERS

There is a community of men and women who set themselves resolutely against the established order. Some of them focus their rejection on the multiways of sin, both their own and the world's; others are resolved to rid all beings of the suffering inherent in conventional existence; still others refuse to be persuaded by the rhetoric of appearance; and some seek a transcendence in their lives of all three conditions: sin, suffering, and illusion.

This community, whose history is probably as old as the records of human behavior, is the community of penitents and saints, of yogis, shamans, and enlightened ones: the community of those in search of, and in touch with, the miraculous.

Around this strange company another community is informally gathered. Its members are all those who from time to time find the inexplicable intruding into their lives and who have sometimes been required by common sense to accept the uncommon. They have also discovered that the cold hard facts of life are sometimes far from that: are, indeed, often warmly shimmering (or icily adamantine) creatures that cannot be safely assigned to either the subjective or the objective world. This second group of people includes priests and farmers, firemen and truck drivers, nurses and criminals, presidents, blacksmiths, and tree surgeons, of whatever age and circumstance.

For this second community of ordinary people the miraculous comes unbidden, leavens the stodgy repetitions of daily life, and in many cases alleviates the gloomy uncertainties of death.

For the community of saints the world may seem to be a body of light, and the trucker and the tree surgeon may be indistinct from angels.

The miraculous comes in many forms. A mass-produced Madonna, all plaster and bright paint, wets with her copious tears the uniform of the policeman who takes her into safekeeping; a stone arm bends in benediction; a giant, silvery cross, appearing from nowhere, floats above a crowd of startled French parishioners.

If such wonders as these are signs of the miraculous, what is the miraculous itself? When something unquestionably lifeless stirs with the appearance of life, or when the laws of gravity are held at bay, we perceive a transcendence of physical laws, and all our expectations become open to question. But since even modest technology can produce seemingly miraculous results for an unsophisticated audience, is it sufficient to define the miraculous merely as whatever seems to cause suspension of the laws of physics? It might be, if we had precise knowledge of these laws—but we do not.

The fact is, whatever name we give to the miraculous only adds a new term to our battery of preconceptions.

But the miraculous is a destroyer of preconceptions and fixed ideas. A miracle, by definition, must fly in the face of common sense and reason. Thus it becomes the touchstone by which our fondest concepts can be proved wrong. Somewhere beyond this desperate apprehension lie all the possibilities of the unknown forces that we fear—or hope for.

To keep them in historical perspective, the following case histories of extraordinary events are presented in chronological order.

The Sign of Conquest

An aerial vision of the cross is said to have been instrumental in establishing Christianity as the religion of choice in Europe.

In A.D. 312 there were two principal contenders for the title of Emperor of Rome: Maxentius, who had held the office, though uneasily, since 306, and Constantinus, a man with imperial family connections and whose army had declared him the true emperor.

On the eve of their confrontation Constantinus and his troops saw a great cross in the sky, bearing the legend *In Hoc Signo Vinces* ("In This Sign Thou Shalt Conquer"). That night Christ appeared to Constantinus in a dream and instructed him to take the cross as his emblem. In the morning Constantinus ordered his troops to inscribe the Christian monogram (the Greek letters Chi and Rho) on their shields.

In the battle that followed, at the Milvian bridge spanning the Tiber not far from Rome, Maxentius was defeated. Constantinus eventually became emperor and became known to history as Constantine the Great.

In 313, soon after his victory at the Milvian bridge, Constantine issued the Edict of Milan, revoking the laws under which Christians had previously been persecuted, granting Christians full religious freedom and civil rights, and restoring to them previously confiscated property. (Lord Kinross and Newsweek Book Division, eds., *Hagia Sophia*, pp.16–17)

A 19th-century engraving by Alonzo Chappel depicts the cross in the sky seen by Constantinus and his troops on the eve of battle with the Romans at the Milvian bridge.

A Cross Above Golgotha

In the year 351 Bishop Cyril (later, Saint Cyril) wrote to the emperor Constantine II:

> For in these holy days of the Pentecostal season on the nones of May [May 7], about the third hour, a great luminous cross appeared in the sky over the holy hill of Golgotha, extending as far as the Mount of Olives, and it was seen most plainly, not by one or two people alone, but by the whole population of the city [Jerusalem]. Nor was it, as one might be tempted to think, a cross conjured up by the fancy, which was quick to disappear, but for many hours together it hung above the earth visible to all, outshining with its brilliant refulgence the rays of the sun.... And so the whole people, penetrated alike with awe and with joy at this heavenly portent, crowded at once into the church, old and young, men and women, even maidens from their bed-chambers, natives and foreigners, Christians and idolaters, and all of them as with a single voice proclaimed the glory of our Lord Jesus Christ, the only Son of God, the worker of all marvels. [Herbert Thurston, *Beauraing and Other Apparitions*, pp.100–01]

The Exaltation of Saint Francis

After Saint Francis of Assisi had received the stigmata on Mount Alverna in 1224, he sometimes allowed Brother Leo to visit him there. What the visiting monk saw is described in the following account from *The Little Flowers of St. Francis*:

> And from that hour forth, the said Brother Leo with great purity and with good intention began to keep watch upon and to observe the life of S. Francis: and for his purity's sake, he merited to see S. Francis full many and many a time rapt in God and uplifted from the earth, at one time to the height of three cubits, at another to that of four, at another to the height of the beech tree: and at another time he beheld him lifted up in the air so high, and surrounded with such splendour, that he scarce could see him. And what did this simple brother do, when S. Francis was uplifted from the earth but a little way, so that he could reach him? He went softly to him and embraced his feet and kissed them, and spake with tears: "My God, have mercy on me a sinner, and through the merits of this holy man grant me to find Thy grace." [*The Little Flowers of St. Francis*, T. W. Arnold, trans., p.172]

The Madonna of the Prisons

On July 6, 1484, the Blessed Lady appeared to an eight-year-old boy in Prato, a city near Florence, Italy. Soon after that she appeared to a youth named Nicholas Giudetto. Their stories about the Madonna aroused great interest, and her portrayal as the "Madonna delle Carceri" ("Madonna of the Prisons") in the church at Prato soon became an object of devotion.

Then, one day when the vicar general and many others were present, it was noticed that the expression on the Virgin's face began to change: her eyes opened and closed and even shed tears.

Even larger crowds came to venerate the picture, and many miracles were said to stem from it. Ridolfo, the infant son of the painter Domenico Ghirlandaio, for example, was believed to have been suddenly cured of a serious illness in this way.

The manifestations at Prato were witnessed without variation by all those present in the church when they occurred: if the Virgin was smiling and joyous, thus was she universally observed; if pale and sad, so she appeared to one and all. In 2½ years, according to Father Gumppenberg, "forty-seven days were counted on which the Blessed Mother looked upon her clients with a countenance transformed." (Herbert Thurston, *Beauraing and Other Apparitions*, p.67)

The Fire of Love

During her last illness, which began in January 1510 and ended with her death in September of the same year, Saint Catherine of Genoa was subject to sensations of fierce internal heat. One day, for example, "she was stabbed with a still sharper arrow of divine love. . . . The wound was so poignant that she lost speech and sight, and abode in this manner some three hours." In her helplessness she gestured to indicate that she felt as if red-hot pincers were attacking her heart and other internal parts. Eventually the day came

> when she suffered such an intensity of burning that it was impossible to keep her in bed. She seemed like a creature placed in a great flame of fire, so much so that human eyes could not endure the spectacle of such a martyrdom.

As her death approached, these attacks of burning, which were interpreted as evidence of the great love the saint bore for her Savior, increased in severity and began to manifest themselves in the external world. For example, a large silver cup full of cold water was brought to her

> for refreshing her hands, in the palms of which, because of the great fire that burned within her, she felt intolerable pain. And on putting her hands into it, the water became so boiling that the cup and the very saucer were greatly heated.

Between September 13 and her death two days later on the 15th, Saint Catherine's condition deteriorated rapidly and she lost a great deal of blood, which was so hot that it scalded her body wherever it flowed, and which so heated the vessels in which it was caught that one silver cup left a permanent mark on the surface where it was set down.

Catherine of Genoa was canonized in 1737. (Baron Friedrich von Hügel, *The Mystical Element of Religion*, pp.196–97, 452; Herbert Thurston, *The Physical Phenomena of Mysticism*, pp.213–17)

Saint Teresa of Ávila

Among the best-documented levitations by a Christian are those of Saint Teresa, a Carmelite nun. Her own brief statements on the subject occur in Chapter 20 of her autobiography (entitled *Life* and completed in 1565), in which she discussed the distinction between the mystical states of Union and Rapture. Rapture, she said, "comes, in general, as a shock, quick and sharp, before you can collect your thoughts, or help yourself in any way, and you see and feel it as a cloud, or a strong eagle rising upwards and carrying you away on its wings." Nor, as it proves, was she speaking here only of the spirit. She continued:

> I repeat it; you feel and see yourself carried away you know not whither. For though we feel how delicious it is, yet the weakness of our nature makes us afraid at first . . . so trying is it that I would very often resist and exert all my strength, particularly at those times when the rapture was coming on me in public.

"The Ecstasy of Saint Teresa," painted by Giovanni Cignaroli, captures the spiritual beauty of the nun, whose intelligence, candor, and humor endeared her to others.

I did so, too, very often when I was alone, because I was afraid of delusions. Occasionally I was able, by great efforts, to make a slight resistance; but afterwards I was worn out, like a person who had been contending with a strong giant; at other times it was impossible to resist at all; my soul was carried away, and almost always my head with it—I had no power over it—*and now and then the whole body as well, so that I was lifted up from the ground.*

Although the words here are unambiguous, it might be supposed that in her spiritual exaltation she had merely fancied herself to be lifted into the air. That this was not the case is attested by those who saw her levitations. One of these, according to her friend and biographer, Bishop Diego de Yepes, was the bishop of Ávila, Don Álvaro de Mendoza. On this occasion Bishop Mendoza was serving Communion to Teresa and her nuns through an aperture made for that purpose in the wall of the choir. Teresa, however, was gripped by rapture before the Communion could be given her and she rose into the air some distance above the opening. Her own description, possibly of the same occasion, is as follows:

This (the being lifted into the air) has not happened to me often: once, however, it took place when we were all together in choir, and I, on my knees, on the point of communicating. It was a very sore distress to me; for I thought it a most extraordinary thing and was afraid it would occasion much talk; so I commanded the nuns—for it happened after I was made Prioress—never to speak of it.

Despite her unwillingness to be distinguished from her sisters in this way, however, the levitations continued. Once during a sermon on a feast day, when some noble ladies were present at the convent, she felt the rapture coming on and flung herself to the ground to resist it. The nuns gathered round to help hold her down, "but still," she said, "the rapture was observed." Saint Teresa humbly described her sensations and emotions on being lifted into the air:

It seemed to me, when I tried to make some resistance, as if a great force beneath my feet lifted me up. . . . I confess that it threw me into a great fear, very great indeed at first; for when I saw my body thus lifted up from the earth, how could I help it? Though the spirit draws it upwards after itself, and that with great sweetness, if unresisted, the senses are not lost; at least, I was so much myself as to be able to see that I was being lifted up. . . . I have to say that, when the rapture was over, my body seemed frequently to be buoyant, as if all the weight had departed from it; so much so that now and then I scarcely knew that my feet touched the ground.

The experience was thus frightening, but "with great sweetness, if unresisted." Nonetheless, Teresa prayed that these visible signs of grace be withheld from her, "for it was a grievous affliction to me that people should make so much of me, and because His Majesty [God] could honour me with his favours without their becoming known." Her prayer was answered, she wrote, "for I have never been enraptured since." But she then admitted that no great length of time had elapsed.

Thirteen years after her death (which occurred in 1582), eyewitnesses to her levitations were still living and able to provide sworn testimony to them. One of these witnesses was Sister Anne of the Incarnation. Her deposition stated:

On another occasion between one and two o'clock in the daytime I was in the choir waiting for the bell to ring when our holy Mother entered and knelt down for perhaps the half of a quarter of an hour. As I was looking on, she was raised about half a yard from the ground without her feet touching it. At this I was terrified and she, for her part, was trembling all over. So I moved to where she was and put my hands under her feet, over which I remained weeping for something like half an hour while the ecstasy lasted. Then suddenly she sank down and rested on her feet and turning her head round to me she asked me who I was and whether I had been there all the while. I said yes, and then she ordered me under obedience to say nothing of what I had seen, and I have in fact said nothing until the present moment.

But perhaps the most touching evidence in the story of Saint Teresa's levitations bears as much on her humility as on her supernatural flights. The witness on this occasion was Bishop Yepes. The saint had just received Communion. Struggling against an onset of rapture, she grasped the bars of the grille (through which Communion had been served) as she rose into the air, calling out to God: "Lord, for a thing of so little consequence as is my being bereft of this favour of Thine, do not permit a creature so vile as I am to be taken for a holy woman." (Saint Teresa, *Life*, David Lewis, trans., pp.161–63, 169; Herbert Thurston, *The Physical Phenomena of Mysticism*, pp.9–12)

A Theologian's Rapture

Francisco Suárez, a Spanish member of the Society of Jesus, was one of the great theologians of the Roman Catholic Church and, though neither beatified nor canonized, was known as a man of pure and holy life. He lived from 1548 to 1617. The following incident in his life was described by a brother Jesuit:

I, Brother Jerome da Silva, S.J., hereby certify that I have written this document by order of my confessor, Fr. Anthony de Morales, and that the same Father has commanded me to give it to no one, nor let it be read, but to keep it closed in an envelope with an endorsement absolutely forbidding anyone to open it until after the death of Father Francis Suárez. . . .

Brother Jerome went on to explain that he himself would probably not live long and then described finding Father Suárez in ecstasy on two occasions. His account of the second one follows:

Another day at the same hour—it was about two in the afternoon—Don Pedro de Aragon (the Rector of the University of Salamanca) [where Suárez taught] asked me to request Fr. Suárez to be good enough to go with him to the monastery of Santa Cruz. As the Father had bidden me summon him whenever this gentleman called, I went up at once. Across the door of his room I found the stick which the Father usually placed there when he did not wish to be interrupted. Owing, however, to the order I had received I removed the stick and entered. The outer room was in darkness [the shutters were closed]. I called the Father but he made no answer. As the curtain which shut off his working room was drawn, I saw through the space left between the curtain and the jambs of the door a very great brightness. I pushed aside the curtain and entered the inner apartment. Then I noticed that a blinding light was coming from the crucifix, so intense that it was like the reflexion of the sun from glass windows, and I felt that I could not have remained looking at it without being completely dazzled. This light streamed from the crucifix upon the face and breast of Father Suárez and in this brightness I saw him in a kneeling position in front of the crucifix, his head uncovered, his hands joined, and his body in the air lifted three feet above the floor on a level with the table on which the crucifix stood. On seeing this I withdrew, but before quitting the room I stopped bewildered, and as it were beside myself, leaning against the door-post for the space of three Credos [about 1½ minutes]. Then I went out, my hair standing on end like the bristles on a brush, and I waited, hardly knowing what I did, beside the doorway of the outer room. A good quarter of an hour later I heard a movement within, and the Father, coming to take the stick away, saw me standing there. I then told him the gentleman was waiting. He asked me why I had not let him know. I answered that I had come to the inner room and called him but that he had not replied. When the Father heard that I had entered the inner room, he seized me by the arm, made me come right inside again, and then, clasping his hands and with his eyes full of tears, he implored me to say nothing of what I had seen, at any rate as long as he lived. On my

part I asked permission to consult my confessor. To this he readily consented, for my confessor was also his. My confessor advised me to write this account in the form above explained, and I have signed it with my name, because all that it contains is the simple truth. And if it should please God that I die before Father Francis Suárez, those who read this may believe it as if they had seen everything with their own eyes. Otherwise if our Lord should will that Father Suárez die first, I shall be able to confirm the whole on oath so far as may be necessary.
JEROME DA SILVA

(Herbert Thurston, *The Physical Phenomena of Mysticism*, pp.27–28)

María of Agreda

She would have preferred to sit in the pillory, María Coronel of Agreda said when she discovered that her nuns had displayed her to strangers while she was in a state of trance. They had even gone so far as to remove her veil for them. Like many other mystics, María had a horror of exhibitionism and of being considered "holy," and she resisted her ecstatic levitations so fiercely that she sometimes vomited blood. Her good friend Bishop Ximenes Samaniego gave the following account of her:

The raptures of the servant of God were of this nature. The body was entirely bereft of the use of the senses, as if it were dead, and it was without feeling if violence were done to it; it was raised a little above the ground and as light as if it had no weight of its own, so much so that like a feather it could be moved by a puff of breath even from a distance. The face was more beautiful than it normally appeared; a certain pallor replaced the naturally swarthy hue. The whole attitude was so modest and so devout that she seemed a Seraph in human form. She frequently remained in this state for two or even for three hours.

María Coronel (1602–65) was even more famous for her alleged feats of bilocation, which allowed her to preach to the North American Indians while remaining in her cell at Agreda, than she was for her occasional levitations. (Herbert Thurston, *The Physical Phenomena of Mysticism*, pp.28–29)

Saint Joseph of Cupertino

One of the most unusual Christian saints, and the most susceptible to levitation, was Joseph Desa. Canonized as Saint Joseph of Cupertino, he was born to poor parents in southern Italy in 1603. His childhood years were marked by unusual piety and a kind of spiritual absentmindedness that caused his schoolmates to nickname him Open Mouth. As he grew older, Joseph practiced increasingly harsh austerities. By the time he was 17, he was wearing a hair shirt and had taken to

When 10 workmen had difficulty erecting a heavy cross near his hometown, Saint Joseph of Cupertino "rose like a bird into the air," easily lifted the cross, and set it in place.

sprinkling his food—a few vegetables, which he ate sparingly at infrequent intervals—with a bitter powder to make it less palatable and enjoyable.

In 1620 the Capuchin order admitted him as a lay brother. At first he was set to work in a dining room, but his absentmindedness, fits of ecstasy, and careless ways with the crockery soon had him demoted to odd jobs in the kitchen. Even as a carrier of firewood, though, Joseph was found wanting, and after eight months he was dismissed from the order.

At Grottaglie, near his hometown, Joseph found his way into the order of Conventual Franciscans as a mulekeeper. This time he was better at his work, and in 1625 he was received into the clerical state. Two years later he became a novice in the monastery at Grottaglie, and on March 28, 1628, he was ordained a priest—largely because his classmates did so well in their oral examination that the bishop, believing all the candidates in the group must be equally well prepared, did not bother to ask Joseph any questions.

In the monastery Joseph was able to devote himself to his austerities. He scourged himself so forcefully that the walls of his cell were blood-spattered, and he became so proficient at making his food unpalatable that a fellow monk who gingerly tasted it was nauseated for three days. Joseph's ecstasies, moreover, had rapidly become so disruptive that he was forbidden to join the other monks in the choir or the dining room.

These peculiarities, and the increasing rumors of miracles associated with him, brought Joseph to the attention of the ecclesiastical authorities, and he was ordered to Naples to face an examination by the Holy Office. The inquisitors found nothing to censure him for and allowed him to worship in their own Church of Saint Gregory of Armenia, and there something remarkable happened.

Joseph had said Mass in a private chapel and had then withdrawn to a corner of the church to pray. Suddenly, and without warning, he rose into the air and, uttering a sharp cry, flew to the altar, his body upright and his arms outstretched. Seeing him alight on the altar amid the burning candles, several nuns began to scream: "He will catch fire! He will catch fire!" But Joseph's companion, Brother Lodovico, who seemed to have had some familiarity with such sights, urged the nuns to greater faith and assured them that Joseph would not be burned. And sure enough, after a short time Joseph gave another cry and flew back from the altar, this time in a kneeling position, in which he landed safely on the church floor. Then, to the further astonishment of the nuns, he leaped to his feet in a whirling dance, crying out, "Oh! Most Blessed Virgin, Most Blessed Virgin!"

One other levitation was witnessed by the pope himself. Joseph had gone to Rome, where it had been arranged for him to see Pope Urban VIII. Joseph was quickly moved to ecstasy by the presence of the Holy Father and rose into the air where he remained until the father general of his order brought him to his senses. Witnessing this, the pope remarked that if Joseph should die before him, he himself would testify to the truth of what he had seen.

But now Joseph's strange fortunes changed. From Rome he was summoned in April 1639 to Assisi, where the custos of his order—the second in command—had become suspicious of his raptures and eccentricities. In Assisi he was subjected to scathing criticism, was repeatedly called a hypocrite in public and private, and was bullied, threatened, and humiliated. For two years this treatment continued. Joseph bore it with patience and humility, but at the cost of severe self-doubt. During this period he suffered a siege of hallucinations.

At last news of his condition reached the father general of his order, who called him to Rome. A short time later Joseph returned to Assisi, where the local people greeted him with great enthusiasm. There now began a period when Joseph's ecstasies and levitations were so frequent as to become his normal behavior. Music, in particular, was apt to provoke an ecstatic flight. One Christmas Eve some shepherds, who at Joseph's suggestion were playing their pipes in the church at Grottaglie, saw the saint so moved to joy by their music that he began to dance. Then, sighing and uttering a cry, he rose into the air and flew some 20 yards to the high altar, where he embraced the tabernacle and knelt for 15 minutes or so amid the burning candles. Then he flew back to the floor.

Sometimes Joseph's flights took place outdoors. One day, for instance, he was walking in the kitchen garden with a priest, who remarked on the beauty of the heaven God had created. In response Joseph gave his high-pitched cry and promptly flew to the top of an olive tree, where he remained for about half an hour, kneeling on a slender branch. On this occasion the rapture deserted him before he regained the ground, and the priest had to get a ladder to help him down.

At other times Joseph was able to lift others with him into the air and was once said to have thus cured a violent madman, Baldassare Rossi, of his lunacy. Joseph's treatment was to place a hand on Rossi's head, saying, "Sir Baldassare, do not be in doubt but commend yourself to God and to His most holy Mother," and then, seizing Baldassare by the hair with that same hand, to rise into the air with him and remain there for about a quarter of an hour.

Reports like these, especially when they occur in great numbers, inevitably have the quality of a fable or folktale. In fact, though, Joseph's fame was such that many illustrious people in Europe sought him out and testified to the miracles they saw him perform.

In 1645, for instance, the Spanish ambassador to the papal court visited Joseph in his cell at Assisi and afterward told his wife that he had "seen and spoken to another St. Francis." His wife was eager to enjoy the same privilege, and so Joseph was ordered to go down to the church to speak with her. "I will obey," Joseph said, "but I do not know whether I shall be able to speak with her." What followed was testified to, under oath, by numerous eyewitnesses during the process that led to Joseph's canonization:

> In point of fact no sooner had he entered the church than his eyes rested on a statue of Mary Immaculate which stood over the altar, and he at once flew about a dozen paces over the heads of those present to the foot of the statue. Then after paying homage there for some short space and uttering his customary shrill cry he flew back again and straightway returned to his cell, leaving the Admiral, his wife, and the large retinue which attended them speechless with astonishment.

Another eminent witness of Joseph's flights was Johann Friedrich, duke of Brunswick, who visited Assisi in 1651 and greatly wished to see the famous friar. He and two companions were taken to a room from which they could secretly observe Joseph saying Mass. As they watched, the monk gave his customary cry and rose in a kneeling position into the air, moved backward five paces or so and then forward toward the altar, where he remained suspended in ecstasy for some time.

The duke, a Lutheran, was most anxious to see this phenomenon again, and since there seemed some possibility that he might thereby be converted to Catholicism, he was allowed to watch Joseph at Mass on the following day as well. This time he saw Joseph floating about 10 inches above the altar step. His doubts resolved, the duke embraced the Catholic faith.

As Joseph's fame grew, so did the numbers of those hoping to see him perform a miracle. In 1653 he was ordered to leave Assisi and go to a Capuchin monastery at Pietra Rossa in the Duchy of Urbino. He spent three months there and was then transferred to a series of monasteries. Wherever he went, the news of his presence soon spread, and crowds of miracle seekers gathered. And the miracles continued. Finally he was sent to the monastery of Osimo, not far from Ancona, and there, in the summer of 1663, he succumbed to his final illness. During his last months he was attended by the surgeon Francesco Pierpaoli, who described how, when he was cauterizing Joseph's leg one day, the saint passed into a rapture and was raised a hand's breadth above the chair throughout the operation.

Joseph died on September 18, 1663. His last words, before passing into the ecstasy in which he remained until his death, were "Oh! what chants, what sounds of Paradise! What perfumes, fragrance, sweets and tastes of Paradise!" He was canonized on July 16, 1767. (A. Butler, *The Lives of the Saints*, pp.587–91; Eric John Dingwall, *Some Human Oddities*, pp.9–29; Herbert Thurston, *The Physical Phenomena of Mysticism*, p.16)

The Odor of Sanctity

Christian nuns are considered, and consider themselves, to be the brides of Christ and in token of this put on a wedding ring at the time of their final vows. After the mystical wedding of Sister Giovanna Maria della Croce, of Rovereto, Italy, which took place about 1625, her ring finger "exhaled a delicious fragrance, which she was unable to hide, and which all the community soon became aware of." Her biographer continues:

> The perfume which it gave out was so powerful that it communicated itself to the touch and persisted for a considerable time. Thus it happened that Sister Mary Ursula, having touched that finger in the holy nun's first illness, her hand for several days afterwards retained an exquisite fragrance. This scent was particularly perceptible when Giovanna Maria was ill, because she could not then take any precautions to disguise it. From her finger the perfume extended

gradually to the whole hand and then to her body, and communicated itself to all the objects which she touched. It could not be compared to any earthly scent because it was essentially different, and transfused soul and body with an indescribable sweetness. It was more powerful when she came back from Communion. It exuded not only from her body but also from her clothes long after she had ceased to wear them, from her straw mattress and from the objects in her room. It spread through the whole house and betrayed her comings and goings and her every movement. The religious who were in the choir were aware of her approach from the perfume which was wafted before her before she came into view. This phenomenon, which lasted for many years, was the more remarkable because naturally she could not endure any form of scent. It was necessary to keep all such things as musk and amber out of the house altogether, because they acted upon her from a considerable distance even though they were hidden in the cellar, and produced a most distressing effect, so much so that she would even faint away on the spot. The only scent which did her no harm was that which breathed from her own person. [Herbert Thurston, *The Physical Phenomena of Mysticism*, pp.229-30]

A Furnace of Love

Sister Maria Villani, a Dominican nun of Naples who believed that she had been pierced in the side and heart "by a fiery spear of love," was 86 years old when she died in the latter 1600's. At the moment of death her flesh was dark and shriveled, but afterward it changed miraculously, becoming "fresh-coloured and supple like that of a living person."

Nine hours after her death an autopsy was performed, the first incision being made in the chest. But when this was done, smoke arose from the heart, to the great astonishment of those watching, and with it so much heat that the surgeon had to stand back. At length he moved his hand toward the incision again to withdraw the heart from the body, but the heat was still intense, and he was burned several times before being able to extract it.

Those present were then able to see and explore an open wound in the heart of exactly the same shape and size that Maria had herself once sketched of the puncture. "This wound (in the heart)," her biographer says, "I have seen and touched and examined. The lips of the wound are hard and seared, just as happens when the cautery is used, to remind us, no doubt, that it was made with a spear of fire."

Sister Maria's biography, which was published only four years after her death, not only contains formal affidavits to the above facts by the surgeons responsible for the autopsy, Domenico Trifone and Francesco Pinto, but also sworn depositions by three of her confessors, to the effect that they had been allowed to see and probe the supernatural wound in her side. Of these confessors, one, Leonardo di Lettere, was a man whose moral and spiritual quality was so much above suspicion that after his own death he became a candidate for beatification. (Herbert Thurston, *The Physical Phenomena of Mysticism*, pp.219-20)

A Warm Heart

The Venerable Serafina di Dio, a Carmelite nun who lived in the 17th century in Capri, was renowned in her time for the ardor of her devotion to Christ, which, according to the testimony of other nuns, brought an incandescent glow to her face when she was at prayer. Her flesh, they noted, was so hot that if they touched it, even on a cold winter's day, they were scorched. By her own report, they said, she felt "consumed with a living fire and that her blood was boiling."

As her death approached, Serafina, like Saint Catherine of Genoa (see page 284), "lost great quantities of blood through the nostrils or by the mouth"—so much, indeed, that all were astonished she could survive the loss, being then quite old and emaciated. But the greatest wonder occurred after the nun's death:

> For the space of twenty hours the body retained so great a heat, particularly in the region of the heart, that one could comfortably warm one's hand by holding it there, as many of the nuns discovered on making the experiment. Indeed, the warmth was perceptible for thirty-three hours after death, though somewhat less in degree, in spite of the fact that the month was March and the weather chilly. The corpse did not completely lose its heat until it had been opened and the heart extracted.

(Herbert Thurston, *The Physical Phenomena of Mysticism*, pp.218-19)

The Fragrant Ways of Mary of the Angels

During the hearings that led to the beatification of the Blessed Maria degli Angeli, who died in Turin, Italy, in 1717, the following evidence was given under oath by a a princess of the royal house of Piedmont:

> As a proof of the holiness of this servant of God I would appeal to the incomparable fragrance which made itself manifest in the places where she lived or through which she passed. The sweetness of this perfume resembled nothing earthly. The more one breathed it the more delicious it became. It was specially perceptible on the feasts of our Lady, of St. Joseph, of St. Teresa, during solemn novenas and at the holy seasons of Christmas, Easter and Pentecost. The ladies of my suite were conscious of it as well as myself, and what astonished me more than all else

was the fact that after the death of the servant of God I noticed and still continue to notice this perfume in the cell she occupied, although every object which it formerly contained has been taken out of it.

Other witnesses at the hearing gave similar testimony. One of the nuns at Maria's convent said: "When we wanted Reverend Mother, and could not find her in her cell, we tried to track her by the fragrance she had left behind." Like many people of saintly achievements, however, Sister Maria was at pains to conceal the evidence of the grace granted her and would often keep malodorous objects in her cell to disguise her fragrance. The ruse was useless, though, for the unworldly perfume would not be hidden. (Herbert Thurston, *The Physical Phenomena of Mysticism,* pp.231–32)

A Fiery Blessing

Every Whitsunday for seven years the Venerable Rosa Maria Serio, prioress of the Carmelite convent of Fasano, Italy, was visited by an extraordinary manifestation of fire. On the first occasion, her nuns saw a ball of fire descend on her. Removing her robes, they found that the undergarments covering the breast had been burned in the shape of a heart. The same sort of burning occurred six more times before the saintly woman's death in 1725, though the ball of fire was observed only once. (Herbert Thurston, *The Physical Phenomena of Mysticism,* p.221)

The Madonnas of Rome

In March 1796 Napoleon's army swept across northern Italy with a speed and efficiency that left the defending opposition helpless. He occupied Milan on May 14 and by July was laying siege to Mantua.

As the French Army approached Rome, its inhabitants experienced waves of fear, patriotism, and an increased readiness to place themselves under Heaven's protection. On July 9, a Saturday, a painting of the Virgin Mary known as the "Madonna dell'Archetto" was seen to assume a sorrowful expression and to open and shut its eyes. Within a short time some 20 other paintings of the Madonna in different neighborhoods had shown similar signs of animation. Statues of saints shifted position, and the closed eyes of Christ on several crucifixes opened. A great upsurge of piety turned Rome into a city of penitents.

A typical description of just how the Madonnas moved their eyes is provided by a Father Goani, who had been summoned to observe the Madonna dell'- Archetto on the first occasion of the phenomenon. At first Father Goani saw nothing unusual, but he kept vigil for about three-quarters of an hour. Then:

On a sudden, when I least expected it, I perceived a visible and manifest motion in both the eyes. I observed that the ball of the eye moved, that the pupils ascended by degrees, and so far concealed themselves under the upper eyelids, that nothing but the white of the eyes could be seen. I saw, moreover, after a very short interval, the same pupils with a slow and uniform motion descend to their prior position. . . . This perpendicular movement I observed two other times successively. . . . I must not omit some other circumstances that accompanied the prodigy. The first is, that at the instant the ball of the eye began to move, I perceived a very thin shade that rather darkened the white. But this shade was instantly dissipated, for at the moment of the elevation of the pupils, I observed again the same white just as before. The second circumstance is that the movement was attended with much grace and majesty. . . . The third that at the precise moment I observed the supernatural movement it was attested by the extraordinary cries, prayers and acclamations of all there present.

Pretending to take care of a guttering candle, Father Goani then climbed some steps to examine the picture more closely. He "perceived the varnish to be perfectly smooth without the least vestige of any fraud." Two days later he pursued his examination with the aid of a set of compasses:

While the pupil was almost concealed under the superior eye-lid I applied one point of the compass to its lower extremity, then barely visible, and I fixed the other point to the rim of the lower eye-lid. By this operation I was qualified to take the exact dimensions of the white part or cornea of the eye which appeared, and I found it to be about five lines or half an inch. The pupil of the eye soon re-occupying its former position, no portion of the white was any longer visible, as the pupil touched the inferior eye-lid.

Several paintings were subjected to the same close scrutiny that Father Goani had applied to the Madonna dell'Archetto. In one church a painting of the Madonna Addolorata was removed from its frame for examination, and the people beseeched the priest to bless them with it. He did so, and as he was about to replace the picture on the altar, the eyes moved again, inducing such a surge of emotion that he fainted. Late in the summer of 1796 Napoleon obtained a favorable treaty from the pope and by the following spring had withdrawn his troops beyond the Alps. (Herbert Thurston, *Beauraing and Other Apparitions,* pp.68–76)

The Miraculous Sky-Cross of Migné

Between two and three thousand people had gathered outside the parish church of Migné, near Poitiers,

Hallucination and Hysteria

By far the most common explanation—or dismissal—of miraculous phenomena runs as follows: the laws of nature cannot be suspended; those who claim otherwise (who claim, for instance, to have seen stone hands move or painted eyes shed tears) must therefore be lying or the victims of hallucination. Moreover, this theory continues, religious practice in which the themes of guilt, fear, and the repression of normal human impulses are powerful elements is likely to produce such hallucinations.

The first part of this argument, however, is neither self-evident nor axiomatic. A law of nature exists only as a scientific formulation and stands in a given form only until further observations or competing theories render it either obsolete or incomplete, at which time it is modified or abandoned. A well-known example is the Newtonian description of gravity, which seemed unassailable for more than 200 years before Einstein and others revealed its deficiencies.

In more general terms, the question of whether the laws of nature have been historically consistent (on a time scale of billions of years) is not only unanswered but is a question that science at present hardly knows how to approach. Similar uncertainties exist about the operation of natural laws in extreme physical circumstances, in the "black holes" in outer space, for example.

It may, however, be argued that by "the laws of nature" something more pragmatic is meant, such as "what people normally experience." But such a formulation defeats the argument that depends on it, for being essentially statistical and empirical, it admits of exceptions—such as those who claim that stone statues move. On the other hand, if the phrase means "what everyone always experiences," it begs the question, since this is the point in dispute.

On the grounds of science and common sense, then, the statement in the hallucination argument regarding the fixity of the laws of nature is not unassailable.

The next assertion, that those who report miraculous events must be lying or hallucinating, is probably true in some instances, if only because lies and hallucinations are an established part of human nature. But the case histories of many miraculous events—those at Rimini in 1850 and at Limpias in 1919, for example—

are replete with the testimony of those who feared they were suffering a delusion and made strenuous efforts to discover whether this was so or not. Whether a hallucination can coexist with rational and determined efforts by several people to discern it as such is uncertain, but seems unlikely, unless such experiences as those at Rimini and Limpias are taken as proof; but this again begs the question.

As for those instances in which different people have observed different manifestations of the same image at the same time, while others close to them have discerned nothing unusual, no one asserts that a simple objective manifestation is occurring. But to admit this is not to admit that a collective hallucination is at work; sincere eyewitnesses often provide very varied accounts of the same event without being accused of hallucinating. What such cases do suggest is that each witness reports accurately what he or she sees from one viewpoint of a complex and unorthodox phenomenon and that what some witnesses see is nothing. To admit that this viewpoint is psychological yields nothing to the delusion argument, since all perception (except the perception of mental events) is the result of a mental component and a physical occasion.

The final stage of the hallucination argument is that religious practice fosters fear and repression, which in turn give rise to delusion. Without questioning the Freudian dogma that lurks in this supposition, the following observations may be made here.

First, there are good grounds for supposing that religious practice develops fearlessness just as often as it does fear. Second, the notion that religiously inspired abstinence is a cruel and repressive imposition is one that comes naturally to those who view such abstinence with a sense of horror and personal aversion. The fact is that for many people the keeping of vows and the practice of austerity are a joy in themselves and are seen as a source of clarity and tranquillity. This is not to say that fear, repression, and delusion never occur in a religious context. Obviously they do, just as they occur in armies, schools, corporations, football teams, and wherever humans gather with common goals: even, perhaps, in congregations of atheists, scientists, and psychoanalysts.

France, to listen to Abbé Marsault preach the final sermon of a week-long mission. It was December 17, 1826, a year proclaimed an "extraordinary" jubilee by the Roman Catholic Church, and at the close of the celebrations in Migné, Abbé Marsault was to bless and consecrate a large wayside cross that had been set up outside the church's west door. The abbé had reached the part of his address in which he referred to the cross that had miraculously appeared in the air before Constantine's defeat of Maxentius at the Milvian bridge (see page 283). Suddenly the people of Migné saw a luminous cross more than 100 feet long floating horizontally about a hundred feet above them. No sound or burst of light had signaled its appearance, and Abbé Marsault was unaware of what was happening until his fellow missioners pointed to the sky:

> It would be impossible [Abbé Marsault wrote later] to describe the intense impression produced by this astounding vision upon the minds and hearts of those who were present. I can only assure you that at that moment I could perceive one portion of the crowd crouching down upon the muddy ground . . manifestly terror-stricken, and the rest gaping open-mouthed with their arms raised towards the sky. I took the opportunity to entone the hymn "Vive Jésus! Vive sa croix!" ["May Jesus live! Long may His cross reign!"] and this was sung amid a trouble and agitation of mind which was shared by us all.

A multitude was gathered at Migné, France, to hear the Abbé Marsault's sermon. The luminous cross that appeared in the sky seemed miraculous to all those who witnessed it.

Before long the cross began to disappear from the base upwards; by the time Abbé Marsault had given the blessing, there was little of it left to be seen. Within five days a statement about the occurrence signed by 50 witnesses was dispatched to the bishop of Poitiers, leading him to a commission of inquiry. Among its members were the mayor of Migné, the vicar general of the area, and a Protestant professor of physical science at the Collège Royale de Poitiers, M. Boisguiraud.

The commission was painstaking in its inquiry, interviewing numerous witnesses and comparing the eyewitness accounts. The following details emerge from their report, which was issued on February 9, 1827:

- The sun had set when the cross appeared and the sky was cloudless.
- The color of the cross was silver (or, according to many witnesses, silvery white tinged with pink) and contrasted well with the still blue color of the sky. It was not dazzling.
- The arms of the cross appeared to be perfectly

equal in length, the edges of the figure as crisp as if cut with a saw.
- The length of the stem was estimated at about 140 feet and its breadth between 3 and 4 feet.
- The cross was estimated to be 100 to 200 feet above the ground.

The commission's report created a considerable stir throughout France and was roundly attacked as evidence of the gullibility of the clergy and the parishioners. The attempts of the skeptics to provide an explanation were a good deal less forceful, however, than their invective. Some suggested that a huge kite was responsible for the phenomenon—but the witnesses were in agreement that the air was absolutely still when the cross appeared. The notion of solar or lunar rainbows was introduced—but as the astronomer Jean-Dominique Cassini pointed out, rainbows do not appear in a cloudless sky or when the sun and moon are below the horizon.

Professor Boisguiraud, the member of the commission most knowledgeable in science, said he had no hesitation, after thoroughly examining the evidence, "to challenge anyone to offer any natural explanation of the phenomenon; and even if such an explanation were forthcoming, I should nevertheless still believe that the appearance of the cross was miraculous, on account of the circumstances which attended it."

The bishop of Poitiers declared himself to be of the same opinion as Professor Boisguiraud, and on April 18, 1827, Pope Leo XII pronounced that the vision could not be attributed to natural causes. (Herbert Thurston, *Beauraing and Other Apparitions,* pp.94–100)

The Moving Eyes of the Madonna

At the Church of Santa Chiara, in Rimini, Italy, in 1850, the eyes in a painting of the Madonna appeared to move as the Countess Baldini, her adopted daughter, and another young woman gazed upon her. The two girls returned to the church the next day and along with several other women and the priest again saw the Madonna raise her eyes until only the whites showed.

Pilgrims flocked to Santa Chiara, and the bishop of Rimini ordered that the painting be removed to St. Augustine's, one of the largest churches in the city. The triumphal procession in which the Madonna was carried to her new home halted in Rimini's main square while the bishop of Faenza blessed the people with her image. Again the eyes were seen to move.

Many eminent members of the nobility and clergy testified to the fact of the moving eyes. Cardinal Ciacchi swore that he had seen the left eye of the Madonna look upward seven or eight times: "I believe that on one occasion I noticed a similar movement of the right eye, but I do not feel so sure of it as to be able to swear to the fact," he added. The governor of Urbino saw the eyes move gently from left to right and vice versa. The bishop of Pesaro, who was nearsighted, climbed on a table in broad daylight to see the wonder, having seen nothing the previous evening. He was not disappointed:

> While I was in this position, five minutes or more passed without my being deemed worthy to perceive any change in the sacred eyes, although the faithful, crowded below, testified by the ardent piety of their exclamations that they saw more than I did. Accordingly I addressed an earnest prayer to our Lady, begging her . . . that I might witness, if only once, this evidence of her sovereign power. At that moment—and the tears fill my eyes as I recall it—I saw the sacred pupils gleam as they passed from left to right and back again, and then I perceived that the left pupil turned upwards towards the eyelid so far that it was almost entirely hidden, and left only the opaque white of the cornea in its place. My emotion was something I cannot describe. A flood of tears burst from my eyes and I trembled so violently in all my limbs that I was compelled to descend with the aid of two priests standing by.

The bishop of Pesaro then added that he had returned to Rimini with a large number of pilgrims from his own diocese and had spent long hours in devotion before the picture of the Madonna, but he "never saw anything more, save with the eye of faith."

The bishop of Cesena reported that the Virgin raised and lowered her eyes and then gazed upon him "for a moment with so tender a look that I could not keep back my tears." Canon Canzi of Bologna, after failing to perceive any movement in the picture through opera glasses, borrowed a pair of powerful binoculars that enabled him to see the familiar moving glance.

Although Joseph Pini, the parish priest of San Gregorio in Bologna, beheld some movement of the eyes when he first entered the church, he was sufficiently skeptical to go up to the altar to examine the painting for signs of trickery and fraud. He remained there, obstructing the view of the faithful congregation for so long that they began to mutter impatiently. He drew to one side, and the crowd soon exclaimed that they again saw the movements. Father Pini related:

> I was convinced that nothing of the sort had happened. . . I could not help saying aloud: "No, no; we must not delude ourselves. That would do no pleasure to our Lady. Certainly at this moment there is no movement." On this the cries ceased. Oh! how my doubts redoubled! Who knows, I said to myself, if I have not so far been quite mistaken in what I thought I saw? Who knows if it is not all pure imagination?—then, suddenly, after a moment's interval, I saw with the utmost possible clearness the two pupils directed towards Heaven, and almost

entirely disappearing under the eyelids, until only a tiny rim of black could be discerned, while the white expanded and filled a large space.

The most determined experiment with the Madonna's painting was made after the manifestations of movement—which had occurred frequently for about six months—had almost ceased and the picture had been returned to the Church of Santa Chiara. The test was made by seven devout persons, three of whom were priests. Two needles were stuck into the frame of the picture, and a white thread was stretched between them in such a way as to mark the lower edge of the pupils. With the thread in place, the seven, who had determined to watch the painting all night, began their prayers. When the words "Turn then, most gracious advocate, your eyes of mercy towards us" were reached in the Salve Regina (Hail Holy Queen), the Madonna's eyes began to move from side to side. Each of the seven in turn climbed on a table and verified that when the eyes were raised, a noticeable gap appeared between the thread and the bottom of the pupil, only to disappear as the eye was lowered.

A few witnesses at Rimini claimed that the face of the Madonna changed color, alternating between pale and rose. Some were positive that they saw the lips move, while Fathers Constantino and Da Forli, both Capuchins, swore that they saw a tear well up and trickle from the Virgin's right eye.

The bishop of the Rimini diocese—who had appointed a commission to check the facts—examined the bulky report on the happenings at Santa Chiara and St. Augustine, together with a huge number of sworn depositions, including those of a cardinal, three bishops, various other clergy, members of the nobility, artists, lawyers, and doctors. And on January 11, 1851, he issued a decree stating that "the truth of the prodigious movement of the eyes in the picture of the Mother of Mercy has been proved" and might be regarded as a well-established historical fact. (Herbert Thurston, *Beauraing and Other Apparitions*, pp.76–85)

Home in the Air

The medium Daniel Dunglas Home was observed to levitate numerous times over a period of 40 years and was never discovered in any fraud. The first account of his unusual ability was given by F. L. Burr, editor of the *Hartford Times*:

> Suddenly, without any expectation on the part of the company [or on Home's part—he was 19 years old, and this was his first, involuntary experience of levitation] Home was taken up in the air. I had hold of his hand at the time and I felt his feet—they were lifted a foot from the floor! He palpitated from head to foot with the contending emotions of joy and fear

which choked his utterances. Again and again he was taken from the floor, and the third time he was carried to the ceiling of the apartment [the Connecticut home of Ward Cheney, a silk manufacturer], with which his hands and feet came into gentle contact.

That was in 1852. Later Home learned to control his flights and demonstrated them before audiences including such notables as the emperor Napoleon III and Mark Twain. His popularity was enormous, and he habitually moved in the aristocratic circles of society, especially in England, where he gave one of his most celebrated performances. Those present were Lord Adare, his cousin Capt. Charles Wynne, and the master of Lindsay, later earl of Crawford and Balcarres. Lindsay told the story:

> I was sitting on December 16, 1868, in Lord Adare's rooms in Ashley Place, London, S.W., with Mr. Home and Lord Adare and a cousin of his. During the sitting, Mr. Home went into a trance, and in that state was carried out of the window in the room next to where we were, and was brought in at our window. The distance between the windows was about seven feet six inches, and there was not the slightest foothold between them, nor was there more than a 12 inch projection to each window, which served as a ledge to put flowers on. We heard the window in the next room lifted up, and almost immediately after we saw Home floating in the air outside our window. The moon was shining full into the room; my back was to the light, and I saw the shadow on the wall of the windowsill, and Home's feet about six inches above it. He remained in this position for a few seconds, then raised the window and glided into the room feet foremost and sat down.
>
> Lord Adare then went into the next room to look at the window from which he had been carried. It was raised about 18 inches; and he expressed his wonder how Mr. Home had been taken through so narrow an aperture. Home said (still in trance) "I will show you," and then with his back to the window he leaned back and was shot out of the aperture head first, with the body rigid, and then returned quite quietly. The window is about 70 feet from the ground.

The hypothesis of a mechanical arrangement of ropes or supports outside has been suggested, but does not cover the facts as described.

Some researchers have considered this event suspect for a number of reasons. In the first place, there are several discrepancies between the accounts given by Adare and Lindsay. Some of these concern the dimensions and configuration of the windows and their height above the ground and whether the night was dark or moonlit. Lord Adare, moreover, gave inconsistent accounts of the event at different times. Captain Wynne's statement was simple and straightforward: "The fact of Mr. Home having gone out of one window and in at another I can swear to: anyone who knows me would not for a moment say I was a victim of hallucination or any other humbug of the kind."

But the omission of any reference to flight or levitation is regarded by some as significant—perhaps Captain Wynne was not convinced that Home had levitated and confined his statement to the simplest fact of the exit and entry. Finally, an examination of what seems likely, though not certain, to have been the house in question has shown that a tightrope could have been stretched between the two balconies.

Researchers have therefore questioned whether or not Lindsay and Adare were too bemused on the evening of December 16 to know what Home was really up to or whether he had resorted to trickery.

But although their versions of the event differed, Adare and Lindsay clearly agreed on its most important feature—that Home *flew*, and was seen to fly in through the window and, later, to fly both out and in. They may have been bemused and imagined the whole thing, but at least they agreed on what they imagined.

As for Captain Wynne's terse statement and its omission of any direct reference to flight, it seems clear that he understood himself to be describing something quite out of the ordinary—for he denied being the victim of a hallucination or of humbug.

Daniel Dunglas Home, among the most sought-after mediums of his day, was well known for his levitations before groups of witnesses. An eminent scientist who tested Home's extraordinary performance found no fraud.

The suspicion that a mechanical device such as a tightrope might have been used was dismissed by Lindsay at the time: it "does not cover the facts as described." In particular, such an explanation does not answer the assertion that Home floated through the window feet first or that he later leaned backward and shot out of the window head first.

This leaves us with the more usual objections to reports of levitation: that the witnesses were lying or were bewitched, hysterical, too imaginative, or not really observant.

And since it can never be proved that a hallucination has not taken place, this objection can never be fully answered. But when numerous people of good faith and good reputation testify to having seen a certain thing, and when no certain proof is found that what they saw was achieved by trickery, we must suppose—according to the hallucination theory—that all these people were weak-minded or that the subject of the reports possessed a supernatural gift for inducing mass hallucinations or a talent for persuading large numbers of people to lie on his behalf with no gain to them.

In 1871, the year in which Lindsay wrote his account of the Ashley Place levitation, Home was observed to levitate by Sir William Crookes, an eminent scientist who later became president of the prestigious British Association for the Advancement of Science. His statement, printed in the *Quarterly Journal of Science,* concisely describes the dilemma into which honest people were put by Daniel Dunglas Home:

The phenomena I am prepared to attest are so extraordinary, and [so] directly oppose the most firmly-rooted articles of scientific belief—amongst others, the ubiquity and invariable action of the force of gravitation—that, even now, on recalling the details of what I witnessed, there is an antagonism in my mind between *reason,* which pronounces it to be scientifically impossible, and the consciousness that my senses, both of touch and sight, are not lying witnesses.

(Jean Burton, *Heyday of a Wizard,* pp.36–38, 213–30; *The Unexplained: Mysteries of Mind Space & Time,* Vol. 2, Issue 20)

The Statue That Lost Its Head

Upon unlocking the door of a vaulted chamber at Turner's Waxwork Theater one morning, the janitor was startled to find that one of the wax figures had changed its position during the night and its head lay on the floor behind it.

The theater, which opened in Sacramento in 1857, was the inspiration of Richard Turner, an entrepreneur who had just visited Madame Tussaud's exhibition in London and thought such a show would be popular with the newcomers pouring into town in the wake of the California gold rush. The nucleus of his new show was a dimly lit guillotine scene with the figures of several French men and women executed during the French Revolution: an aristocratic couple (clothed in the now-faded finery they had worn to their beheading), a curé, a young lady-in-waiting, and a colorless-looking man in a black suit. The label on the podium of this black-suited effigy identified him as Nicodème Léopold-Lépide, and it was later learned that he had been a tax collector who had unscrupulously lined his pockets with the money of the poor. It was the figure of M. Léopold-Lépide that had moved during the night.

The show, which was an instant success, had been open only one week when the janitor, Ezra Potter, came to Turner with his strange story. Turner took extra precautions to keep the door locked at night and had the building patrolled, but the occurrence continued. Finally, after several weeks, Turner and Potter spent a night in the room with the guillotined figures. They fell asleep, only to find on awakening that once again the effigy of the tax collector had moved. The next night they managed to stay awake, and this is what Turner reported seeing:

It was remarkable; a little before 2:30 in the morning the figure of Monsieur Nicodème Léopold-Lépide began to move. First the arms and then the legs stirred. After a moment we saw the wax face take on a more flesh-and-blood image, and the brows frowned as if in anger and then we heard a voice.

The figure spoke in French, which Turner could not understand, but he repeated the words as best he could to a French Canadian, who translated them as follows:

Is it not possible to get some peace at night? The people came to see us die, now they come to see our spirits encased in wax. Come here no more during the hours of darkness or you will regret it.

Word of this reached a Sacramento journalist who asked to spend a night in the chamber with the waxworks. Turner consented, and the young man was locked in the room for the night with Potter posted at the door. At 2:31 the janitor scrambled to his feet, aroused by hysterical screams and pounding on the door. He quickly unlocked it, and the journalist fell into his arms in a dead faint.

The newspaperman wrote a detailed account of his experience, describing the room and each of the five figures on their podiums. He continued:

As I sat in the gloom of the lamps, the dim wavering light fell on the rows of figures which were so uncannily like human beings that the silence and stillness of their forms made them seem even more unnatural and ghastly. I greatly missed the sound of breathing, the rustle of clothes and the perpetual sequence of noises one hears even when a deep silence has fallen over a vast crowd.

For an hour or two I sat facing the sinister figures boldly enough. They were, after all, only waxworks. . . .

Waxworks don't move. But every time I looked away from the taxman, when I looked back again he seemed to have struck a slightly different pose. I kept on looking and this time I saw something. The waxwork's arm did move. Slowly at first, then more rapidly to suddenly flick off its head! I stared . . . petrified, gripping the chair. . . . To my added horror where the waxwork head had been a ghostly visage now formed, with a cruel, rapacious leer.

It turned towards me and moved off its podium. I jumped up to face it, and the waxwork-ghost made towards me. What frightened me the most was the way I could see through its head!

Backing to the door I tapped on it to get the janitor to see the phenomena. There was no answer. I banged hard this time, as the waxwork-ghost moved closer. I turned and started to bang my fists on the door. I screamed too as I felt the horrid wax hands close round my neck. I screamed again and can't remember any more, only the welcoming face of Ezra Potter.

I would swear by all that is holy that this that I have written is true.

In the morning the wax head of M. Léopold-Lépide was found on the floor beside the other figures, but the body was in a heap by the door. The fingers were said to be flat and out of shape.

The journalist's story was apparently suppressed (it did not come to light until the 1930's, sometime after his death). But the figure of the tax collector was melted down and replaced by another, after which the disturbance ended. Turner's Waxwork Theater continued its successful operation until 1885. (Raymond Lamont Brown, *Phantoms of the Theater*, pp.26–30)

"Entirely Supernatural and Miraculous"

A most critical phase in the unification of Italy by King Victor Emmanuel II was his seizure of Rome and the Papal States in 1870. The act created difficulties between the church and state that were only resolved by the Lateran Treaty (which established the Vatican as an independent state) in 1929.

During this crisis an extraordinary event took place in the Church of St. Dominic at Soriano Calabro, in southern Italy. The story is told by Father H. M. Cormier, general of the Dominican order:

It was the 15th of September, the day when the feast of St. Dominic is kept at Soriano. After the High

Mass, about midday, the statue of the Saint, which was exposed for veneration on the right of the altar, began to move as if it had been a living person. The worshippers who remained in the church were stricken with astonishment; to astonishment succeeded terror, and to terror admiration. Their feelings could not be suppressed; all cried out with a common impulse, "Saint Dominic! Saint Dominic! Miracle! Miracle!" The other inhabitants ran to the spot. In their presence the statue continued to move, at one time advancing, then retiring, at one time moving to the right and then returning to the left as if to trace out the figure of a cross, indeed there were moments when it detached itself completely from its pedestal. Often it lifted and lowered the right hand and arm like a man preaching, and the left arm, which grasped a lily, vibrated in harmony. If any effort was made to check these movements, those who attempted it, far from succeeding, were compelled to follow them, overpowered by some mysterious force. The face itself, like that of a living person, assumed an expression full of meaning, alternately flushing and then turning pale; the forehead was puckered and the eyes at one moment looked down reproachfully upon the people, at another, turned sideways with an appealing glance directed towards the statue of our Lady of the Rosary; even the lips were seen to move like those of a man who is speaking with intense feeling.

A commission of inquiry into these events was ordered by the diocesan bishop of Mileto, whose judgment on the matter was delivered February 11, 1871. He concluded his statement with these words:

Considering, moreover, that it is within our knowledge, and proved by the Commission of enquiry, that remarkable favours, even in the temporal order, have been granted, and that the moral effects produced have been excellent, not only amongst the people of Soriano itself, but throughout the diocese, after invoking the holy name of God, we pronounce that the movements of the statue of St. Dominic, as we have described them, which took place on September 15, 1870, were entirely supernatural and miraculous.

(Herbert Thurston, *Beauraing and Other Apparitions*, pp.102–05)

Rose, Sandalwood, and Verbena

Those who undertake a spiritual or spiritualistic practice always do so, if conditions permit, under conditions appropriate to their venture. A quiet place is chosen, for example, suitable images are displayed, candles are lit, incense burned, and so on: whatever will enhance the setting is employed. For W. Stainton Moses, a former clergyman and one of Victorian England's

W. Stainton Moses, an Oxford-educated curate in the Church of England, left the clergy in 1872 when he developed the overriding interest in spiritualism that would last the rest of his life.

foremost mediums, the appropriate atmosphere for a séance was always achieved by the use of perfumes of one kind or another, most often those fragrances provided by flowers.

This habit led to some curious consequences, according to Moses (and to the testimony of several reputable people who witnessed the same thing in his presence), for the invisible beings in attendance took the use of flowers as a cue and scattered fragrances of all kinds on those present. "No séance passes," Moses wrote, "without perfumes being showered upon us, or perfumed waves of air being wafted round the circle."

Moses continued his story in a letter to *The Spiritualist* newspaper for January 1, 1875:

> These perfumes are of various kinds, rose, sandalwood, and verbena, being favourites. Any sweet-scented flowers in the room are utilised and their perfume extracted. This is notably the case in the country. We have noticed in such cases that the presence of a particular flower in the room would determine the prominent spirit odour; and that particular blossoms would have all the perfume extracted from them for the time, though the odour would return on the following day. Sometimes, however, a perfectly distinct odour would be extracted from—or, more precisely, be put upon—a particular flower. In this case the flower invariably withered and died in a short time.

For W. Stainton Moses, however, more was in store than mysteriously scented drafts in closed rooms. His own body, too, began to exhale an unaccountable fragrance, he noted:

> It is now some months since I first noticed the presence of a perfumed atmosphere round myself, especially during times when I was suffering pain. I have been liable to neuralgia, and at such times those around me have noticed the presence of perfume of various kinds, such as those we observe during our séances. One evening I was standing at an open window through which the air was blowing, and the perfume of rose was so marked that friends who were present endeavoured to trace it. . . . It was found to be localised in a spot no bigger than a shilling [roughly the size of a quarter] at the top of my head. The spot was perceptibly wet with perfume, which oozed out more freely on pressure.

Moses went on to observe that his own experience is probably not different from what has traditionally been called the "odour of sanctity." Since, however, he disclaimed any sanctity in his own person, he regarded such perfumes as evidence not of saintliness but of mediumistic ability, which, he believed, the saints had in full measure. But in making this point, Moses ignored a feature of those cases where a saintly person has been accompanied by a mysterious fragrance, for such perfumes have almost invariably been characterized as unearthly and indescribable. The perfumes associated with W. Stainton Moses, on the other hand, were all highly specific and immediately identifiable by those around him. Nor is there any suggestion that the perfume he exuded was capable of impregnating his surroundings and the objects he touched for long periods after his departure from them, whereas this was commonly the case with fragrant saints. (See pages 288–90.) (*Proceedings of the Society for Psychical Research*, 9:269–73, 1894; 10:224–26, 1895)

An Omen in the Sky

Gen. George A. Custer and his 7th Cavalry Regiment, about 600 strong, were assigned in mid-May 1876 to join an expedition against the Sioux Indians in what is now southeastern Montana. As the residents saw the command marching out of Fort Abraham Lincoln in a cloud of dust, they observed a strange omen of the fate that would befall the regiment. While they watched in wonder, almost half the regiment appeared to ride off into the sky and vanish.

A little more than a month later, at the Battle of the Little Bighorn on June 25, Custer and 264 of his men

Although he was graduated at the bottom of his class at West Point, Gen. George A. Custer earned a reputation for daring and aggressiveness during the Civil War. The disaster at Little Bighorn is now referred to as Custer's "Last Stand."

were outflanked and killed by the forces of the Sioux chiefs Sitting Bull and Crazy Horse. As the vision, or mirage, had indicated, about half the regiment was lost. (Fairfax Downey, *Indian Fighting Army*, pp.195–96)

A Prodigy at Campocavallo

In 1892 the chapel at Campocavallo, about six miles from Loreto in Italy, occupied a converted outbuilding on a farm of the same name. It was used by people from the surrounding countryside and was visited by a priest who regularly came to say Mass. The only decorations in this humble chapel were two colored reproductions, one of which was Bartolomé Esteban Murillo's portrayal of the Virgin Mary as the Sorrowing Mother.

On June 16, the feast day of Corpus Christi, a few devout women were praying before this picture when they noticed beads of moisture on the face, some of which had begun to trickle down. They informed the person in charge of the chapel, who, after satisfying himself that this was so, went to tell the priest.

The priest was skeptical, but the next morning he broke his usual schedule and visited the church to say Mass. There he saw the moisture for himself. By afternoon a small crowd had gathered at the chapel, all anxious to kneel as close to the picture as possible. As the people prayed, the eyes of the Madonna began to move. News of this soon reached the bishop of Osimo, Egidio Mauri, in whose diocese the chapel was. The bishop promptly cautioned his clergy to avoid encouraging the people in their taste for these marvels and appointed a commission of inquiry into the matter.

But the pilgrims were not to be restrained. By December 10 they had donated enough money for the bishop to lay the foundation stone of a new church to be built at Campocavallo.

A year later the bishop was named archbishop of Ferrara (later he became a cardinal). In his farewell address to the people of Osimo the new archbishop paid tribute to our Lady of Campocavallo, making clear his conviction that the prodigies associated with her picture were supernatural:

> Twenty months ago, O dear Madonna of Campocavallo, you were unknown to the world; but one day the eyes in a poor picture of you moved in a marvelous way, and from that moment millions and millions of lips have called you blessed.

(Herbert Thurston, *Beauraing and Other Apparitions*, pp.87–89)

The Miraculous Statue of Mellieha

In the 1890's the English Jesuits ran a boys' boarding school not far from the town of Valletta on the island of Malta. On March 20, 1893, the young boarders were taken on a picnic to Mellieha, a village in the northwest corner of the island. The excursion was in the charge of Father John McHale and Father John Gordon, with the assistance of lay brothers Noonan and Ellingworth.

According to Father McHale, Mellieha was chosen as the picnic site purely as a matter of convenience. But on the way there, in one of the carriages hired for the outing, some of the older boys told him of a statue at Mellieha that moved miraculously of its own accord.

The party arrived at the village a little early for lunch, so it was decided to visit the church. Across the road from the church two flights of stone steps led into a cave known as the Grotta della Madonna. Following these steps, several boys and Father McHale found themselves confronting a larger-than-life statue of the Virgin Mary. Father McHale described what happened:

> I went forward in the direction of the statue, leaving the other Father with a number of the boys near the entrance. . . . My eyes by this time had grown accustomed to the dim light of the cave, and on reaching the railing I saw the statue before me. I was deeply impressed by its majestic and dignified appearance. It is an old statue carved out of the common stone of the country—a soft whitish limestone. In her left hand our Lady is holding the Divine Infant, while her right hand is free and extended some distance from her side in a very conspicuous position. The fingers were resting on each other and bent forward in the shape of a hook. The sacristan lit two large candles and placed them in front of the statue. . . . Whilst closely examining the statue I asked some of the boys who stood near me, which hand was supposed to have moved. They told me it was the right hand, and I turned my eyes to look at it. It was perfectly still. But almost immediately I was startled by seeing the little finger move gently backwards. This was followed by the next two fingers, then by the forefinger, and last of all by the thumb. When the fingers had assumed a very graceful position, the whole hand moved gently upwards some ten or twelve inches, came slowly down again and ended by forming a beautiful cross. The fingers then resumed their original hook-like position, and after a pause of a few minutes the gesture was again repeated.

When the boys with Father McHale saw the Madonna's hand move, they called out, "A miracle! A miracle!" and the others came running to see. Father Gordon (who had traveled in a different carriage and knew nothing of the statue) was studying the inscription near the cave entrance. McHale called up to him to come see the statue:

> He came up immediately and saw the hand moving. He tried several positions, but in each beheld the

hand in motion. Fearing lest it might be his own head that was moving, he stood near to the wall, leaning up against it for support, and fixed his eyes on one of the cross-bars of the railing. He then distinctly saw the hand rise above the bar and slowly descend below it. To prevent my own head from moving I tightly squeezed it between two of the bars of the railing, and I can vouch for the movement being precisely the same.

McHale then asked a Protestant boy named Frederic Clothier, about 14 years old, to look at the right hand and tell him what he saw. The boy confirmed everything the father saw and then drew his attention to the hand of the Holy Child. Father McHale recalled:

I looked up and saw the tiny hand of the Child blessing us. The little head too was moving gently from side to side, and the appearance of the face seemed to change. When the head and hand were moving the expression very much resembled that of a little child crying for joy. This may have been due to my own imagination. . . . When the hand was at rest there was certainly nothing extraordinary about the appearance of the face. We stayed in the cave about half an hour and the hand continued to move the whole time we were there. . . .

The movement of the hand was anything but uniform. Sometimes the fingers would open out one after the other, and close in the same manner, or again would open out together and close one after the other. The hand, too, would at one time rise ten or twelve inches, at another only half that distance, while the motion was constantly changing. . . . No matter how the gestures varied there was something so gentle and attractive about the movement that the feeling almost amounting to fear, which came over me when I first saw the fingers moving, speedily disappeared, and I felt irresistibly drawn to pray to our Lady.

At the end of May Father McHale returned to the cave at Mellieha with some of the other fathers from the college. The sacristan told them that from the time of their visit in March until the end of April the statue had been still but that during May it had motioned almost daily. On inspecting the statue, the fathers were convinced that the figure was carved from a single block of stone, with no joints whatever. They waited and watched in the cave for a long time but saw no movement. A further visit, on June 1, the day of the feast of Corpus Christi, was more rewarding:

Looking up at the statue, I saw the hand gently moving. This time it did not rise more than five or six inches. The movement, too, was very slow. After completing the cross the hand was still. What next followed seemed to me to have been done by our Lady to convince us that she had really given us her

blessing. The thumb and the forefinger were about an inch apart from each other. Though the hand did not move, the thumb joined the forefinger, opened out again, then rose about an inch above it, after which it descended the same distance below it and ended by rising to its original position. This continued for some minutes. The other fingers also kept moving from time to time.

A colleague present with McHale proposed placing his own finger between the statue's moving finger and thumb to feel the motion. "For fear lest there should be any irreverence or undue curiosity in the action," McHale said, "I strongly advised him not to do so. He yielded to my suggestion." Soon after this the movements ceased, and after offering prayers of thanksgiving McHale and his colleagues departed.

John McHale, who died in 1911, is described by Herbert Thurston, a leading scholar and writer in the field of psychic and mystical phenomena, as "a man of acute perceptions and shrewd in all the practical affairs of life" who was "scrupulously honest and direct in all his methods." Father John Gordon, who died in 1913, is described as "a matter-of-fact Scotsman, without a trace of romance in his composition." His obituary referred to "his hatred of deceit and shams, his simple and honest nature."

After McHale's death, his story was confirmed by one of the pupils present, Frederic Clothier, but it was qualified by another pupil, Testaferrata Bonici, later marquis. In 1920 Bonici wrote the following note in response to a request for information:

Together with other college boys I was once taken by the late Father McHale . . . to Melleha [sic] Parish Church to pay a visit to our Lady. While we were praying before the famous statue, Father McHale, and many of the boys with him, cried out that our Lady was shaking her hand and blessing us. I regret I did not have the privilege of seeing myself the statue move. But I can guarantee the incident in so far as Father McHale and many of the boys exclaimed that our Lady was blessing us.

Brother Ellingworth confirmed that he and Brother Noonan had entered the grotto after lunch and had seen the statue move, though not so much or for so long as McHale and Gordon had.

Does anything other than these testimonies lend weight to this improbable story?

On August 13, 1887, Father Angelo Portelli and a number of Dominican novices saw the Virgin of Mellieha move. So did another priest named Portelli, no relative of the first. Their affidavits precisely describing the movements of the right arm "upward and downward . . . and also toward the breast" were filed at Sliema in Malta. (*The Month*, 79:360–69, September–

December 1893; Herbert Thurston, *Beauraing and Other Apparitions*, pp.106–16)

A Magician Meets His Match

Howard Thurston (1869–1936) was one of the most famous magicians of his day and, like the great majority of magicians, knew full well how easily the public can be duped to believe any of the stories of psychic phenomena that the numerous mediums of the period were generating.

Of these mediums, few were more controversial than Eusapia Palladino, an Italian whose debut in North America had been arranged by Dr. Hereward Carrington, a notable psychical researcher. Eusapia had been exposed as a fraud by professors at Columbia University. It was said that she would resort to trickery when her gift faltered, but Carrington was convinced that she could indeed perform supernatural acts.

Carrington offered to prove this to the skeptical Thurston at a private séance to be held in Eusapia's hotel room. Thurston recorded what he observed:

> With no expectation whatever, except the old story of fraud and its exposure, Mrs. Thurston and I repaired to the hotel. . . . Eusapia kept us waiting, and in the interval before her appearance Mrs. Thurston and I took the opportunity to make a complete examination of the room. . . . But all our searching was unrewarded; we found nothing even remotely suspicious.
>
> Particularly I examined the table which she was to use. I scrutenized [*sic*] every inch of that piece of furniture; I do not recall ever having seen a more innocent object.

When Eusapia Palladino arrived, she seemed utterly exhausted. Her eyes were glassy, her complexion was unnaturally pale, and her hands were sweating. More lights were turned on, and the séance began:

> I do not believe that ever before in the history of the world had a magician and a sceptic been privileged to behold what I then looked upon. I saw Eusapia replace her hands on that table I had examined so carefully. I saw it lift up and float, unsupported in the air; and while it remained there I got down on my knees and crawled around it, seeking in vain for some natural explanation.
>
> There was none. No wires, no body supports, no iron shoes, nothing—but some occult power I could not fathom. My pride was wounded. . . . I was not ready to surrender my faith in rationalism. I demanded more proof, and with bewildering willingness the strange old lady agreed. Mrs. Thurston held her feet. I held her arms. And even then, thus guarded and a prisoner, the table rose again!
>
> When it finally crashed back to the floor again

A photograph taken during a séance in Munich on March 15, 1903, shows Eusapia Palladino (facing camera) levitating the small table and accordion in the background.

> before my very eyes I was a defeated sceptic. Palladino had convinced me! There was no fake in what she had showed me. . . . If after reading what I have said of this adventure into the realm where my magic cannot penetrate, the reader doubts, not my word, but my observation, let me say this: "My career has been devoted consistently to magic and illusions. I believe I understand the principles governing every known trick. I would be willing to sail around the world just to behold one feat I could not explain."
>
> In all my seance examinations I train all my faculties against the Medium, watching for the slightest evidence of trickery. I am willing to stake my reputation as a magician that what this Medium showed me was genuine. I *do* insist that woman showed genuine levitation, not by trickery but by some baffling, intangible, invisible, force, that radiated through her body and over which she exercised a temporary and thoroughly exhausting control. [Eric John Dingwall, *Very Peculiar People*, p.211; Sylvan Muldoon, *Psychic Experiences of Famous People*, pp.54–56]

The Miracle at Fátima

On May 13, 1917, a vision appeared to three shepherd children near the village of Fátima in Portugal. On a cloud that hovered above an oak tree they saw the shining figure of a woman, "a beautiful Lady from Heaven." The lady told the children—Lucia, 10, Francisco, 9, and Jacinta, 7—to meet her in the same place on the 13th of each month until October.

A month later, about 50 people gathered to see the apparition. Some of them claimed to see a cloud above the tree, but only the children saw the lady herself. A larger crowd assembled the following month, but again the lady was invisible to all but the children. By now there was considerable opposition to the story and the unwelcome publicity it was bringing to the district, and on August 13 the children were arrested by the local prefect. Two days of interrogation failed to make them change their testimony. On the 19th of the month the lady again appeared to them, this time, at Valinhos, not far from Fátima, and told them that they would see her again for the last time on October 13.

A crowd of 50,000 gathered, on a wet and dismal day, to see the last apparition. This time the shining lady, again invisible to all but the children, announced her identity: she was Our Lady of the Rosary, and she told them three "secrets" about the future.

Then something shocking happened.

The rain suddenly stopped and the sun came out. At first it seemed to start spinning and then it began to plunge crazily toward the earth. The crowd was terrified. After a moment the sun returned to its normal position and then, twice more, repeated the same maneuver. Later, people found that their clothing, which had been soaked in the downpour, was quite dry.

The two younger children, Francisco and Jacinta, died during the influenza epidemic of 1918-19. Lucia learned to read and write and recorded the "secrets" the lady had told her. The first was a vision of hell. The second may be a reference to World War II:

> The war [World War I] is coming to an end. But if people do not cease to offend the Lord, another and more terrible one will break out during the next pontificate. When you see the night lit up by a great, unknown light, know that it is a sign that God gives you of that punishment of the world by another war, famine and persecution of the Church and of the Holy Father.

Soon after their miraculous vision at Fátima, Jacinta Marto (left), her brother Francisco, and Lucia dos Santos, their cousin, solemnly faced the camera for this photograph.

During the next pontificate, that of Pius XI, Hitler annexed Austria. In January 1938, two months before this prelude to World War II, the people of western Europe beheld an extraordinary display of lights in the night sky. They lasted for two hours and were so bright that in the Alps night workers were able to see without artificial light. The lights were described as a rare form of the aurora borealis.

In accordance with Lucia's instructions, her record of the lady's third secret was, reportedly, opened by Pope John XXIII in 1960. What the message said has never been made public, but according to one account, the pope told some of those closest to him in the Vatican that what he read there almost made him faint with horror. (Cyril Charlie Mardindale, *The Message of Fátima*, pp.30–35, 77–78, 159)

The Eyes of Christ

Dominating the altar in the parish church of Limpias, a small town near Santander in northern Spain, is a finely carved wooden crucifix. The eyes of this wooden figure, which is somewhat larger than life size, are made of porcelain. On March 30, 1919, a girl about 12 years old saw them move.

She was so startled that she ran up to one of the two missionary Capuchins then visiting the church to tell him what she had seen. The Capuchin father, who could see nothing untoward in the figure, assumed the child was imagining things, until several other children also said they saw the eyes move.

Then several adults joined the chorus: not only were the eyes moving, but Christ's face and neck were wet, as though He were sweating.

On April 2 the parish priest, Don Eduardo Miqueli, wrote to his bishop, describing what his parishioners claimed to have seen and the religious fervor that had subsequently gripped his church. To his letter he appended the names of two children, two workmen, two ladies, and two gentlemen of independent means who had been permitted, as representatives of a much larger group of witnesses, to make sworn depositions. As for himself, the priest said, he had made no comment one way or the other on the possibly miraculous nature of what had been reported.

Despite a high level of excitement in Limpias, nothing else was seen for two weeks. On May 4, however, 1,500 pilgrims came from Santander on special trains to visit the church. Triumphal arches were built, bells were rung, and firecrackers lit. The excitement was intense, and the manifestations now became more various and startling. According to the Reverend Baron von Kleist, who chronicled the events at Limpias:

> Many said that the Savior looked at them—at some in a kindly manner, at others gravely, and at yet

others with a penetrating and stern glance. Many of them saw tears in His eyes; others noticed that drops of blood ran down from the temples pierced by the crown of thorns; some saw froth on His lips and sweat on His body; others again saw how He turned His head from side to side and let His gaze pass over the whole assembly of people; or how at the Benediction He made a movement of the eyes as if giving the blessing; how at the same time He moved the thorn-crowned head from one side to the other. Others had the impression that a deep, submissive sigh was wrested from His breast; some believed they saw Him whisper—in short the most varied manifestations were discerned in this crucifix.

Hundreds of people of all kinds—rich and poor, educated and uneducated, devout and agnostic—gave sworn testimony to having witnessed manifestations of the kind described by the Reverend Baron von Kleist. Some of these people were so affected by what they saw that they fainted. Others, seeing Christ look sternly at them, ran from the church in a panic and could not be persuaded to return. Many devout men and women saw nothing, though they spent hours watching. (In fact, the majority of those who visited the church—3,000 or 4,000 a day for more than two years—saw nothing at all.) Thus, while one person would see the most vivid and dramatic signs of life in the figure, his neighbor might see nothing whatsoever or might see something quite different.

There is therefore no question that what was seen at Limpias was subjective and somewhat conditioned by the observer's experience. Those with a medical background, for instance, seem to have been disposed to witness in detail the progressive agony of Christ's death. Such an experience was described by Dr. Gutierrez de Cossio of Santander, who saw clearly every stage of death's approach in his Savior's face. "In the whole of my medical practice," he said, "nothing has ever made such a deep impression on me, not even the sight of the first corpse which I saw as a young student. . . ."

To say that what was seen in the crucifix was not objectively present does not, of course, detract from the

The Crystal Vision

When the eyes of a painting, print, or statue move we may discern the will of God, a hyperactive imagination, or an instance of the phenomenon known as scrying, or crystal gazing.

Scrying (the term comes from the word *descry*, meaning to perceive things at a distance) has been practiced all over the world in every period of history, and scryers have employed not only crystal balls but mirrors, pools of water, thumbnails, inkblots, and virtually anything that shines. Not everyone has the gift, but those who have can see all manner of wonderful things by staring into the chosen shiny surface. The experience was well described by Andrew Lang, a turn-of-the-century Oxford scholar known for his research in this area:

It is almost universally found, in cases of successful experiment, that the glass ball takes a milky or misty aspect, that it then grows black, reflections disappearing, and that then the pictures emerge. Some people arrive at seeing the glass ball grow milky or misty, and can go no further. Others see pictures of persons or landscapes, only in black or white, or motionless. Others see in the glass coloured figures of men, women and animals in motion; while in rarer cases the ball disappears from view and the scryer finds himself apparently looking at an actual scene. In a few attested cases two persons have shared the same vision. In experiments with magnifying glasses and through spars [lustrous minerals], the ordinary effects of magnifying and of alteration of view are sometimes produced; sometimes . . . not.

How, or why, the scryer sees things is unknown, but a partial explanation, in Lang's view, is that the effort involved in crystal gazing objectifies images consciously or unconsciously held in the mind of the gazer. Similarly, the great Arab historian Ibn Khaldun, who studied the phenomenon 500 years earlier, wrote that scryers concentrate all their perceptions in a single sense, that of sight: "fixing their gaze on an object . . . they regard it with attention until they perceive the thing that they wish to announce."

The number of people who have the gift in some latent form may be greater than one might think. If so, this may explain how on many occasions large numbers of people have claimed to see movement in the often shiny eyes of religious images (the figure of Christ at Limpias, for example, had porcelain eyes). Although this explanation removes such events from the realm of the miraculous, it invokes an almost equally mysterious phenomenon. And it does not explain why outbreaks of spontaneous scrying by numerous people occur only rarely. Nor does it negate the possibility that this curious human capacity may sometimes be the vehicle chosen for divine revelation.

extraordinary, or even miraculous, nature of what happened at Limpias; for why it happened remains deeply mysterious. And those who recognized that their experiences were subjective, even as they were occurring, could neither control them nor avoid responding to them as though they were physically real. For example, Dr. Maximilian Orts, who was a medical officer, examined the face of the statue through binoculars from a distance of seven or eight yards. He saw a drop of bright red blood trickle from the right eye down into the carved lock of hair below the ear:

> The blood gradually disappeared until the tract of skin it had crossed was left quite clear. . . . To the surprise occasioned by the sight of this phenomenon, there succeeded a spirit of revolt. It was humiliating for a man of my age, with my large professional experience, to be made the victim of an hallucination. I am a Catholic, but I am not a fanatic. Worried by the abnormality of what I had witnessed, I rested a while, I collected my thoughts and then turned to look again, confident that the phenomenon would have disappeared. It was not so. The blood continued to gleam and to trickle on. I compared this blood with that which came from the wound of the left hand and that which showed on the right breast of the figure, and the comparison proved to me that the latter was black blood, painted blood, while the other was crimson, blood which had movement and life in it. . . .

Dr. Orts told himself that it was all an optical illusion. But he saw the hair glisten with sweat, the bright blood trickle into the hair. He moved from the nave to a side chapel, but there too he saw the process repeated. Finally, convinced despite himself, he cried out, loudly enough for those around him to hear: "There can't be a doubt; it *is* blood." (Herbert Thurston, *Beauraing and Other Apparitions*, pp.46–65)

The Bleeding Statues of Templemore

The year 1920 was one of violence in Ireland. The British government had outlawed the Sinn Fein (the Irish nationalist movement) and the Dail (the Irish assembly), and the nationalists were now waging a fierce guerrilla war with the authorities, especially against the infamous Black and Tan troops sent to restore order. Bombings, burnings, murder, terrorism, hanging, and bloodshed were the order of the day.

On August 15 the Town Hall at Templemore, County Tipperary, was burned down, and several other buildings were destroyed as the violence continued. Six days later all the religious statues and pictures in the homes of Thomas Dwan and his sister-in-law, Mrs. Maher, began to bleed simultaneously.

News of the miracle spread through the surrounding

The pilgrims who thronged to Templemore ascribed curative powers to the bleeding images. Here Mrs. Thomas Dwan touches the eyes of a blind man with one of the statues.

countryside, and the initial trickle of pilgrims increased to a torrent. Special excursion trains from Dublin to Templemore were organized, and the Thomas Cook Travel Agency inquired if the local inns could accommodate 2,000 pilgrims. Similar inquiries came from the United States, South Africa, and Japan, and one group of pilgrims came from India. A sea of tents, dubbed Pilgrimsville, surrounded Templemore on all sides.

In Mrs. Maher's house lived James Walsh, a devout teenager. In the earth floor of his room a hollow the size of a teacup miraculously filled with water from an unknown source. Pilgrims took gallons of it away with them, but always the water was replenished. At first people were admitted to the two houses in groups of 50, for five minutes at a time. Later, the statues were displayed in the windows; processions of pilgrims trooped past the houses, and by night they carried torches. It was estimated that by the time the statues had stopped bleeding, roughly a month after they had begun, close to 1 million people had visited Templemore. (Charles Fort, *The Complete Books of Charles Fort*, pp.585–88)

An Uncommissioned Portrait

In the summer of 1923 the portrait of a well-known Oxford cleric, Dean Henry Liddell, became visible on the plaster wall of Christ Church Cathedral, Oxford, close by a tablet that had been erected to his memory. The cleric had died in 1898.

Three years later—on September 11, 1926—*T.P.'s and Cassell's Weekly* of London described the portrait as "a faithful and unmistakable likeness" and noted:

> One does not need to call in play any imaginative faculty to reconstruct the head. It is set perfectly

This conventional portrait of Oxford cleric Dean Henry Liddell hangs in the Hall of Christ Church, Oxford. New construction has since covered the likeness of Dean Liddell that appeared spontaneously on the wall of Christ Church Cathedral in 1923.

straight upon the wall, as it might have been drawn by the hand of a master artist. Yet it is not etched; neither is it sketched, not sculptured, but it is there plain for all eyes to see.

In 1931 the dean's face was still "beautifully clear," according to Mrs. Hewat McKenzie, president of the British College of Psychic Science. But the following year a new altar built across the wall completely concealed it. Whether the portrait still remains is unknown. (Nandor Fodor, *Between Two Worlds,* pp.243–44; Charles Fort, *The Complete Books of Charles Fort,* pp.961–62)

The Power of Thought?
In February 1932 the "clearly discernible" figure of Christ appeared in the marble of the sanctuary wall at St. Bartholomew's Church in New York City. It was discovered by the rector, the Reverend Dr. Robert Norwood, just as he concluded a Lenten talk on "The Mystery of Incarnation":

> . . . I happened to glance at the sanctuary wall and was amazed to see this lovely figure of Christ in the marble. I had never noticed it before. As it seemed to me to be an actual expression on the face of the marble of what I was preaching, "His Glorious Body," I consider it a curious and beautiful happening.

The figure, about 1½ feet tall, was well delineated in the veining and variegations of the rich sepia-toned marble directly above the sanctuary door. On close inspection Dr. Norwood saw that the figure of Jesus, which was clad in white robes, was emerging from a tomb hewn in a rock. A primitive cross was visible in the background of the scene.

News of the Christ-like figure appeared in some of the New York newspapers on February 23, and crowds of people pressed into the church to see it. *The New York Times,* whose story appeared the following day, inter-

viewed the rector in his study at the church. Discussing the appearance of the figure, Dr. Norwood commented:

> I have a weird theory that the force of thought, a dominant thought, may be strong and powerful enough to be somehow transferred to stone in its receptive state. How this Christ-like figure came to be there, of course, I don't know. It is an illusion that grows before the vision. Has thought the power of life? People can scoff, but the figure is there.

(*The New York Times,* February 24, 1932)

"And a Wild Look in His Eye"
In 1936 P. T. Plunkett, a tea planter, published an account and photographs in the *Illustrated London News* of a levitation he had observed in southern India:

> The time was about 12:30 P.M. and the sun directly above us so that shadows played no part in the performance. . . . Standing quietly by was Subbayah Pullavar, the performer, with long hair, a drooping moustache and a wild look in his eye. He salaamed to us and stood chatting for a while. He had been practising this particular branch of yoga for nearly 20 years (as had past generations of his family). We asked permission to take photographs of the performance and he gave it willingly, thus dispelling any doubt as to whether the whole thing was merely a hypnotic illusion.

The demonstration began with Pullavar sprinkling a ring of water around a small tent, which he then entered. After a few minutes the tent was removed and the yogi was observed lying horizontally in the air, his hand resting lightly on top of a cloth-wrapped stick. Plunkett and his friends walked around him and passed their hands beneath him. Apart from the stick "the man had no support whatsoever."

About four minutes later the tent was put up around the yogi again, but the fabric was thin and Plunkett saw Pullavar's descent:

> After about a minute he appeared to sway and then very slowly began to descend, still in a horizontal position. He took about five minutes to move from the top of the stick to the ground, a distance of about three feet. . . . When Subbayah was back on the ground his assistants carried him over to . . . [us] and asked if we would try to bend his limbs. Even with assistance we were unable to do so.

A few minutes of massage and dousing with cold water brought the yogi back to his normal consciousness and the demonstration was over. Plunkett and his companions were positive that what they had seen had not involved trickery. (Francis Hitching, *The Mysterious World: An Atlas of the Unexplained,* pp.104–06)

The most legendary *of the feats of levitation attributed to Indian magicians is the rope trick: a rope is thrown into the air and supposedly remains there, rigid enough for a man to climb. But it seems to be a clever hoax—the rope is said to be hooked onto a concealed cord and suspended. This photograph purportedly showing the trick was taken by an Englishman in India in about 1930.*

Tears for Hiroshima

Among the art objects collected by Allen Demetrius, a Pittsburgh businessman, was the bronze bust of a Japanese girl, which rested on a stone pedestal in his living room. On the evening of August 6, 1945, the day the atom bomb was dropped on Hiroshima, Demetrius

This bronze bust, which is more than 100 years old, is said to have shed tears on the day that the atomic bomb was dropped on Hiroshima. Allen Demetrius, the owner, had never noticed anything unusual about the statue previously. In 1969 streaks were noticed where the tears had flowed down the cheeks.

happened to glance at the statue and saw tears in its eyes. "The teardrops ran down the cheeks. I was astonished. I can't explain how it happened," he later told Jim Lewis of the *Pittsburgh Press.*

In 1969 Demetrius presented the bust to his daughter, Annabelle Sollon, who lived in Canonsburg, Pennsylvania. While she was cleaning house one day, Mrs. Sollon noticed green streaks tracing the course of tears down the cheeks of the bronze maiden. She told her father about it. Examining the figure on his next visit, Demetrius concluded that the streaks were caused by a chemical reaction to the tears.

Mrs. Sollon later returned the weeping statue to her father, who proposed that it be displayed in the United Nations as "a warning against war." (The *Pittsburgh Press,* March 18, 1979; February 26, 1980)

The $3 Madonna

When Antonietta and Angelo Iannuso, of Syracuse, Italy, were married in the spring of 1953, one of their wedding presents was a small figure of the Madonna. The fact that this was not a work of art—but was mass-produced in plaster by a Sicilian factory and sold for only $3—was neither here nor there as far as the 20-year-old bride was concerned. In whatever guise, the Madonna was worthy of veneration.

Not long after her marriage, Antonietta became pregnant and began to suffer from agonizing headaches and temporary loss of sight. On August 29, during such an attack, Antonietta looked toward the Madonna. The Virgin's face was streaming with tears.

"It was incredible. For a moment I thought I was mad. She was crying like a child. Then I began to shout, '*La Madonnina piange* [The little Madonna is weeping]!'" Thinking that Antonietta had become hysterical with pain, her mother and her sister-in-law tried to soothe her. Then they too saw the tears. Soon after the weeping began, Antonietta's attacks ceased.

For four days huge crowds passed through the Iannusos's apartment. One visitor took the figure down from the wall to examine it closely. The wall behind it was dry. "I unscrewed the statue from its base," he said, "and thoroughly dried it. Then two tears, like pearls, began to appear in the eyes of the Madonna."

Even when the Madonna was taken to police headquarters, the weeping continued—in sufficient quantities to wet the uniform of the policeman who carried it. A chemical analysis showed the tears to be similar to human tears. But if someone suffering from a seemingly incurable complaint was merely brushed with a piece of cloth that had been soaked in the tears, he or she might be cured: a 49-year-old man with a crippled left arm regained the use of it, and an 18-year-old girl who had been mute began to speak.

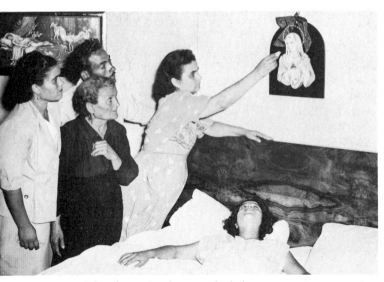

The plaster Madonna, which hung over Antonietta Iannuso's bed while she was ill, wept when she suffered pain. Here her mother wipes away the Madonna's tears.

A month after the weeping began, the little Virgin was carried at the head of a procession of 30,000 people to a railway shed and there enshrined in a glass case. Within five years many thousands of pilgrims had visited the shrine, among them 72 bishops and archbishops and 3 cardinals. A litter of abandoned crutches testified to the number of cripples cured. (*Information*, 74:7-8, October 1960; *Time*, January 6, 1958, p.50)

The Tearful Icon

Pagona Catsounis, a devout woman, was 22 years old, and she lived with her husband, Pagionitis, in an attic apartment in Island Park, New York. She said her evening prayers every night before a six- by eight-inch colored reproduction of an icon of the Blessed Virgin.

On the evening of March 16, 1960, Pagona Catsounis was frightened. While she was saying her prayers the Virgin had started to weep, and the picture was wet with her tears.

Pagona called out for her husband. Pagionitis Catsounis saw the tears too.

When George Papadeas, the Catsounis's pastor at St. Paul's Greek Orthodox Church in Hempstead, New York, answered the telephone that night and heard the plea for help and advice from two members of his congregation, he was simultaneously concerned for the couple, and mindful of the possibility of a hoax.

"When I arrived," he said, "a tear was drying beneath the left eye. Then just before the devotions ended, I saw another tear well in her eye. It started as a small, round globule of moisture in the corner of her left eye, and it slowly trickled down her face."

As far as George Papadeas was concerned, he had witnessed a miracle.

During the following week 4,000 people, and reporters from every newspaper in metropolitan New York, poured through the Catsounis's home. All week long the Virgin continued to shed copious tears. For the young couple, whose small apartment was now constantly invaded, life became a misery.

On March 23 the icon was taken to St. Paul's for safekeeping and to give the Catsounises some much needed relief from the publicity. Although the weeping had ceased by then, each day brought 3,500 people to St. Paul's to pray before the miraculous Virgin, whose picture had been enshrined on the altar (with the permission of Archbishop Iakovos, head of the Greek Orthodox Church in North and South America). (*Information*, 74:2-7, October, 1960)

A Bleeding Crucifix

In 1968, in a church at Pôrto Alegre, Brazil, a large wooden crucifix some 300 years old suddenly began to exude a red substance, as if it were bleeding. The substance was tested and did, indeed, prove to be blood.

The appearance of blood or tears on religious symbols is a phenomenon with a long recorded history. And notwithstanding all the modern equipment that is now available for testing and investigation, many of these miraculous occurrences cannot be disproved, nor can they be explained. They persistently remain in the realm of mystery. (*The Unexplained: Mysteries of Mind Space & Time*, Vol. 4, Issue 42)

In the Brazilian church where this wooden crucifix shed blood, many cures were reported. Cures are often associated with objects that manifest miraculous properties.

BIBLIOGRAPHY

ALBERS, MICHAEL D. *The Terror.* New York: Manor Books, Inc., 1979.

ALEXANDER, MARC. *Phantom Britain.* London: Frederick Muller Limited, 1975.

AMERICAN COUNCIL OF LEARNED SOCIETIES. *Dictionary of American Biography.* New York: Charles Scribner's Sons, 1927.

BACH, RICHARD. *Nothing by Chance.* New York: William Morrow & Company, 1969.

BARRETT, SIR WILLIAM F. *On the Threshold of the Unseen.* New York: E. P. Dutton & Company, 1917.

BASEDOW, HERBERT. *The Australian Aboriginal.* Adelaide: F. W. Preece and Sons, 1925.

BECK, THEODORIC R. and JOHN B. *Elements of Medical Jurisprudence.* Albany, N.Y.: Little & Company, 1851.

BEGG, PAUL. *Into Thin Air.* London: David & Charles, Limited, 1979.

BEIERLE, FREDERICK P. *Man, Dinosaur and History.* Prosser, Wash.: Frederick Beierle, 1980.

BOLTÉ, MARY. *Haunted New England: A Devilish View of the Yankee Past.* New York: Weathervane Books, 1972.

BORD, JANET and COLIN. *Alien Animals.* London: Granada Publishing Limited, 1980.

BOWEN, CHARLES, ed. *The Humanoids.* Chicago: Henry Regnery Company, 1969.

BRADFORD, GERSHOM. *The Secret of Mary Celeste, and Other Sea Fare.* Barre, Mass.: The Barre Publishing Co., 1966.

BRANDON, JIM. *Weird America.* New York: E. P. Dutton, 1978.

BREWSTER, SIR DAVID. *Letters on Natural Magic.* London: W. Tegg, 1856.

BROAD BROOK GRANGE NO. 151, ed. *Official History of Guilford, Vermont, 1678–1961.* Guilford, Vt.: Town of Guilford and Broad Brook Grange No. 151, 1961.

BROUGHTON, GEOFFREY, ed. *Climbing Everest.* London: Oxford University Press, 1960.

BROWN, RAYMOND LAMONT. *Phantoms of the Theater.* Nashville, Tenn.: Thomas Nelson Inc., 1977.

BROWN, RAYMOND LAMONT. *Phantom Soldiers.* New York: Drake Publishers, Inc., 1975.

BRYAN, JOSEPH III. *The Sword Over the Mantel.* New York: McGraw Hill, 1960.

BUITENEN, J.A.B. VAN, ed. and trans. *The Mahābhārata.* Chicago: The University of Chicago Press, 1975.

BURTON, JEAN. *Heyday of a Wizard: Daniel Home, the Medium.* New York: Alfred A. Knopf, 1944.

BUTLER, ALBAN. *Butler's Lives of the Saints,* rev. and supp. Herbert J. Thurston and Donald Attwater. Westminster, Md.: Christian Classics, 1981.

BYRNE, PETER. *The Search for Bigfoot: Monster, Myth or Man?* New York: Pocket Books, 1976.

CARRINGTON, HEREWARD. *Essays in the Occult.* New York: T. Yoseloff, 1958.

CARRINGTON, RICHARD. *Mermaids and Mastodons.* New York: Rinehart & Company, Inc., 1957.

CAVENDISH, RICHARD, ed. *Man, Myth & Magic.* New York: Marshall Cavendish Corporation, 1970.

CAZEAU, C. J., and STUART D. SCOTT, JR. *Exploring the Unknown.* New York: Plenum Press, 1979.

CHEETHAM, ERIKA. *The Prophecies of Nostradamus.* New York: Capricorn Books, G. P. Putnam's Sons, 1975.

CHICHESTER, FRANCIS. *The Lonely Sea and the Sky.* New York: Coward-McCann, 1964.

CHURCHILL, ALLEN. *They Never Came Back.* Garden City, N.Y.: Doubleday & Company, Inc., 1960.

COCHRAN, JACQUELINE, and FLOYD ODLUM. *The Stars at Noon.* Boston: Little, Brown & Co., 1954.

CORLISS, WILLIAM. *Ancient Man: A Handbook of Puzzling Artifacts.* Glen Arm, Md.: The Sourcebook Project, 1978.

CORLISS, WILLIAM. *Strange Universe.* Glen Arm, Md.: The Sourcebook Project, 1975.

COSTELLO, PETER. *In Search of Lake Monsters.* New York: Coward, McCann & Geoghegan, Inc., 1974.

CRAIG, RICHARD A. *The Edge of Space.* Garden City, N.Y.: Doubleday & Company, Inc., 1968.

CYRANO DE BERGERAC, SAVINIEN. *Voyages to the Moon and the Sun.* London: Routledge, 1927.

DAVID-NEEL, ALEXANDRA. *Magic and Mystery in Tibet.* Baltimore, Md.: Penguin Books, 1971.

DE LISO, OSCAR. *Padre Pio, the Priest Who Bears the Wounds of Christ.* New York: McGraw Hill, 1960.

DELOUISE, JOSEPH, and TOM VALENTINE. *Psychic Mission.* Chicago: Henry Regnery Company, 1971.

DINGWALL, ERIC JOHN. *Some Human Oddities.* London: Home and Van Thal Ltd., 1947.

DINGWALL, ERIC JOHN. *Very Peculiar People: Portrait Studies in the Queer, the Abnormal, and the Uncanny.* London, New York: Rider, 1950.

DINSDALE, TIM. *Loch Ness Monster.* London: Routledge and K. Paul, 1972.

DINSDALE, TIM. *Monster Hunt.* Washington, D.C.: Acropolis Books, 1972.

DOWNEY, FAIRFAX. *Indian-Fighting Army.* New York: Charles Scribner's Sons, 1941.

DREJOVIĆ, DRAGOSLAV. *Europe's First Monumental Sculpture: New Discoveries at Lepinski Vir.* New York: Stein and Day, 1972.

DUDLEY, EDWARD, and MAXIMILLIAN E. NOVAK, eds. *The Wild Man Within: An Image in Western Thought From the*

Renaissance to Romanticism. Pittsburgh: University of Pittsburgh Press, 1972.

EBON, MARTIN. *Prophecy in Our Time.* New York: The New American Library, Inc., 1968.

EBON, MARTIN, ed. *Demon Children.* New York: The New American Library, Inc., 1978.

EBON, MARTIN, ed. *Exorcism: Fact Not Fiction.* New York: The New American Library, Inc., 1974.

EDDINGTON, SIR ARTHUR. *The Nature of the Physical World.* New York: The Macmillan Company, 1928.

EDSALL, F. S. *The World of Psychic Phenomena.* New York: David McKay Company, Inc., 1958.

EDWARDS, FRANK. *Strange People.* New York: Lyle Stuart, 1961.

EDWARDS, FRANK. *Strangest of All.* New York: Citadel Press, 1956.

EDWARDS, FRANK. *Strange World.* New York: Lyle Stuart, 1964.

ELLENBERG, AL, ed. *Abduction: Fiction Before Fact.* Containing the text of Harrison James, *Black Abductor.* New York: Grove Press, 1947.

ELLIS, KEITH. *Prediction and Prophecy.* London: Wayland (Publishers) Ltd., 1973.

EMENEGGER, ROBERT. *UFO's Past, Present and Future.* New York: Ballantine Books, 1974.

FISHER, JOE. *Predictions.* New York: Van Nostrand Reinhold Company, 1980.

FLAMMARION, CAMILLE. *The Atmosphere.* New York: Harper and Brothers, 1873.

FLAMMARION, CAMILLE. *The Unknown.* New York: Harper and Brothers, 1900.

FLEMING, PETER. *Brazilian Adventure.* New York: Charles Scribner's Sons, 1934.

FODOR, NANDOR. *Between Two Worlds.* West Nyack, N.Y.: Parker Publishing Company, Inc., 1964.

FORT, CHARLES. *The Complete Books of Charles Fort.* New York: Dover Publications, Inc., 1974.

FRANCIS OF ASSISI, SAINT. *The Little Flowers of St. Francis,* trans. T. W. Arnold. London: J. M. Dent and Company, 1903.

GADDIS, VINCENT H. *Mysterious Fires and Lights.* New York: David McKay Company, Inc., 1967.

GARDNER, MARTIN. *The Incredible Dr. Matrix.* New York: Charles Scribner's Sons, 1967.

GARRISON, OMAR V. *The Encyclopaedia of Prophecy.* Secaucus, N.J.: Citadel Press, 1978.

GEDDA, LUIGI, and GIANNI BRENCI. *Chronogenetics: The Inheritance of Biological Time,* trans. Louis Keith. Springfield, Ill.: C. C. Thomas, 1978.

GODWIN, JOHN. *Unsolved: The World of the Unknown.* Garden City, N.Y.: Doubleday & Company, Inc., 1976.

GOERNER, FRED. *The Search for Amelia Earhart.* Garden City, N.Y.: Doubleday & Company, Inc., 1966.

GREEN, JOHN. *On the Track of the Sasquatch.* Aggassiz, B.C., Canada: Cheam Publishing Ltd., 1968.

GREEN, JOHN. *The Sasquatch File.* Agassiz, B.C., Canada: Cheam Publishing Ltd., 1973.

GREEN, JOHN. *Year of the Sasquatch.* Agassiz, B.C., Canada: Cheam Publishing Ltd., 1970.

GREENHOUSE, HERBERT R. *Premonitions: A Leap Into the Future.* New York: Bernard Geis Associates, Inc., 1971.

GREY, IAN. *The Romanovs.* Garden City, N.Y.: Doubleday & Company, Inc., 1970.

GURNEY, EDMUND, and others. *Phantasms of the Living.* London: Rooms of the Society for Psychical Research; Trübner and Company, 1886.

HALL, ANGUS. *Signs of Things to Come.* London: Aldus Books Ltd., 1975.

HARE, AUGUSTUS J. C. *The Story of My Life.* London: George Allen, 1896.

HARPER, CHARLES G. *Haunted Houses.* Philadelphia: J. B. Lippincott Company, 1924.

HARRISON, MICHAEL. *Fire From Heaven: A Study of Spontaneous Combustion in Human Beings.* New York: Methuen, Inc., 1976.

HAYMAN, LEROY. *Thirteen Who Vanished.* New York: Julian Messner, 1979.

HEUVELMANS, BERNARD. *In the Wake of the Sea-Serpents,* trans. Richard Garnett. New York: Hill & Wang, Inc., 1968.

HEUVELMANS, BERNARD. *On the Track of Unknown Animals,* trans. Richard Garnett. New York: Hill & Wang, Inc., 1959.

HITCHING, FRANCIS. *The Mysterious World: An Atlas of the Unexplained.* New York: Holt, Rinehart and Winston, 1978.

HOLROYD, STUART. *Dream Worlds.* Garden City, N.Y.: Doubleday & Company, Inc., 1976.

HOPKINS, TIGHE. *The Man in the Iron Mask.* Leipzig, Germany: B. Tauchnitz, 1901.

HÜGEL, BARON FRIEDRICH VON. *The Mystical Element of Religion.* London: J. M. Dent & Co.; New York: E. P. Dutton & Co., 1909.

HUME, DAVID. *A Treatise of Human Nature.* London: Longmans, Green, 1874.

HUTTON, J. BERNARD. *On the Other Side of Reality.* London: Baker (Howard) Press, 1969.

JUNG, CARL G. *Flying Saucers: A Modern Myth of Things Seen in the Skies.* Zurich, Switzerland: Rascher & Cie. AG., 1958.

JUNG, CARL G. *Synchronicity: An Acausal Connecting Principle.* New York: Bollingen Foundation, 1960.

JUNG, CARL G., and W. PAULI. *The Interpretation of Nature and the Psyche.* New York: Pantheon Books, 1955.

KEEL, JOHN A. *The Mothman Prophecies.* New York: Saturday Review Press, E. P. Dutton & Co., Inc., 1930.

KINROSS, LORD, and EDITORS OF THE NEWSWEEK BOOK DIVISION. *Hagia Sophia.* New York: Newsweek, 1972.

KOESTLER, ARTHUR. *The Roots of Coincidence.* New York: Random

House, 1972.

KUSCHE, LAWRENCE DAVID. *The Bermuda Triangle Mystery—Solved.* New York: Warner Books, 1975.

LAIR, PIERRE-AIMÉ. *Essai sur les Combustions Humaines.* Paris: Crapelet, 1800.

LE POER TRENCH, BRINSLEY. *The Flying Saucer Story.* New York: Ace Books, 1966.

LEROY, OLIVIER. *Les Hommes Salamandres: recherches et réflexions sur l'incombustibilité du corps humain.* Paris: Desclée, de Brouwer et Cie, 1931.

LEWIS, DAVID. *Saint Teresa.* Brooklyn, N.Y.: International Catholic Truth Soc., 19—.

LIVY, TITUS. *From the Founding of the City,* trans. B. O. Foster. London: William Heinemann; New York: G. P. Putnam's Sons, 1919.

LOCKHART, J. G. *Curses, Lucks and Talismans.* London: Geoffrey Bles, 1938.

LONG, MAX FREEDOM. *The Secret Science Behind Miracles.* Los Angeles: Kosmon Press, 1948.

MACKAL, ROY P. *Searching for Hidden Animals.* Garden City, N.Y.: Doubleday & Company, Inc., 1980.

MACKAY, CHARLES. *Extraordinary Popular Delusions and the Madness of Crowds.* New York: Harmony Books, 1980.

MACKENZIE, ANDREW. *A Gallery of Ghosts.* New York: Taplinger Publishing Company, 1973.

MAGRE, MAURICE. *Magicians, Seers, and Mystics,* trans. Reginald Merton. New York: E. P. Dutton & Co., Inc., 1932.

MALONE, DUMAS. *The Sage of Monticello.* Boston: Little, Brown & Company, 1981.

MANNING, MATTHEW. *The Link.* Gerrards Cross, England: Colin Smythe Ltd., 1974.

MARDINDALE, CYRIL C. *The Message of Fátima.* New York: Kenedy, 1950; London: Burns, Oates & Washburne, 1950.

MAY, HERBERT G., and BRUCE M. METZGER, eds. *The New Oxford Annotated Bible.* Revised Standard Version. New York:

Oxford University Press, Inc., 1962.

MELLAND, FRANK H. *In Witchbound Africa.* London: Seeley, Service & Co., Ltd., 1923.

MEREDITH, DENNIS L. *Search at Loch Ness.* New York: Quadrangle/The New York Times Book Co., 1977.

MÉTRAUX, ALFRED. *Voodoo in Haiti,* trans. Hugo Charteris. London: Sphere Books, Ltd., 1974.

MICHEL, AIMÉ. *Flying Saucers and the Straight-Line Mystery.* New York: Criterion Books, 1958.

MICHEL, AIMÉ. *The Truth About Flying Saucers.* New York: Criterion Books, 1956.

MICHELL, JOHN, and ROBERT J. M. RICKARD. *Phenomena: A Book of Wonders.* London: Thames & Hudson Ltd., 1977.

MORGENSTERN, JULIAN. *Some Significant Antecedents of Christianity.* Leiden, The Netherlands: E. J. Brill, 1966.

MOSKOWITZ, SAM. *Explorers of the Infinite.* Cleveland and New York: The World Publishing Co., 1957.

MULDOON, SYLVAN. *Psychic Experiences of Famous People.* Chicago: The Aries Press, 1947.

NAPIER, JOHN. *Bigfoot, the Yeti and the Sasquatch in Myth and Reality.* London: Jonathon Cape Ltd., 1972.

NASH, JAY ROBERT. *Among the Missing.* New York: Simon and Schuster, 1978.

NICOLA, REV. JOHN H. *Diabolical Possession and Exorcism.* Rockford, Ill.: TAN Books and Publishers, Inc., 1974.

NICOLSON, HAROLD. *Small Talk.* New York: Harcourt, Brace and Co., 1937.

NOORBERGEN, RENE. *Secrets of Lost Races.* Indianapolis: Bobbs Merrill, 1977.

NOUËT, NOËL. *Tokyo.* Tokyo: La Maison Franco-Japonaise, 1937.

ORTZEN, LEN. *Strange Stories of UFOs.* New York: Taplinger Publishing Company, Inc., 1977.

OWEN, HAROLD. *Journey From Obscurity, Wilfred Owen, 1893-1918,* Vol. 3. London:

Oxford University Press, 1965.

OWEN, ROBERT DALE. *Footfalls on the Boundary of Another World.* Philadelphia: J. B. Lippincott & Co., 1875.

PALMER, LYMAN L. *History of Napa and Lake Counties, California.* San Francisco: Slocum, Bowen & Co., 1881.

PHILLIPS, PERROTT, ed. *Out of This World: The Illustrated Library of the Bizarre and Extraordinary.* London: Phoebus Publishing Company, 1976.

PHOTIUS, SAINT. *Myriobiblon.* Geneva, Switzerland: P. Stephanus, 1612.

PONTOPPIDAN, ERIK L. *The Natural History of Norway,* trans. from the Danish. London: A. Linde, 1755.

PRIEST, JOSIAH. *American Antiquities and Discoveries in the West.* Albany, N.Y.: Hoffman & White, 1833.

PURCHAS, SAMUEL. *Purchas his pilgrimes.* London: W. Stansby, for H. Fetherstone, 1625.

READER'S DIGEST EDITORS. *American Folklore and Legend.* Pleasantville, N.Y.: The Reader's Digest Association, Inc., 1978.

READER'S DIGEST EDITORS. *Folklore, Myths and Legends of Britain.* London: The Reader's Digest Association Limited, 1973.

READER'S DIGEST EDITORS. *Strange Stories, Amazing Facts.* Pleasantville, N.Y.: The Reader's Digest Association, Inc., 1976.

RIDGWAY, JOHN, and CHAY BLYTH. *A Fighting Chance.* Philadelphia: J. B. Lippincott Company, 1967.

Ripley's Believe It or Not! New York: Warner Books, 1976.

Ripley's Believe It or Not Ghost Stories and Plays. New York: Scholastic Book Services, 1968.

Ripley's Giant Book of Believe It or Not! New York: Warner Books, 1976.

ROBERTSON, MORGAN. *Futility.* New York: M. F. Mansfield, 1898.

RODEWYK, ADOLF. *Possessed by Satan.* Aschaffenburg, Germany:

Paul Pattloch Verlag, 1963.

ROERICH, NICHOLAS. *Altai-Himalaya: A Travel Diary*. New York: Frederick A. Stokes, 1929.

ROGO, D. SCOTT. *An Experience of Phantoms*. New York: Taplinger Publishing Company, 1974.

ROGO, D. SCOTT. *The Haunted Universe*. New York: The New American Library, Inc., 1977.

ROGO, D. SCOTT. *The Poltergeist Experience*. New York: Penguin Books, Inc., 1979

ROLL, WILLIAM G. *The Poltergeist*. New York: The New American Library, Inc., 1974.

ROLL, WILLIAM G., and others, eds. *Research in Parapsychology*. Metuchen, N.J.: The Scarecrow Press, Inc., 1973.

ROMMEL, KENNETH M., JR. *Operation Animal Mutilation*. Report of the District Attorney, First Judicial District State of New Mexico, June 1980.

ROOSEVELT, THEODORE. *The Wilderness Hunter*. New York: G. P. Putnam's Sons, 1893.

ROSE, RONALD. *Living Magic*. New York, Chicago, San Francisco: Rand McNally & Company, 1956.

SAGAN, CARL. *The Cosmic Connection: An Extraterrestrial Perspective*. Garden City, N.Y.: Anchor Press, 1973.

SAGAN, CARL, AND I. S. SHKLOVSKI. *Intelligent Life in the Universe,* trans. Paula Fenn. San Francisco: Holden-Day, 1966.

SANDERSON, IVAN, *Abominable Snowmen*. Radnor, Pa: Chilton Book Company, 1961.

SEABROOK, WILLIAM B. *The Magic Island*. New York: Harcourt, Brace and Company, Inc., 1929.

SHATTUCK, ROGER. *The Forbidden Experiment*. New York: Farrar, Straus & Giroux, Inc., 1980.

SHERMAN, C. E. *Land of Kingdom Come*. Columbus, Ohio: Privately published, 1936.

SINGH, JOSEPH, and ROBERT M. ZINGG. *Wolf Children and Feral Man*. New York: Harper & Brothers, 1942.

SITCHIN, ZECHARIA. *The Twelfth Planet*. New York: Stein and Day, 1976.

SMITH, FREDERICK W. *Cattle Mutilation: The Unthinkable Truth*. Cedaredge, Colo.: Freedland Publishers, 1976.

SMYTH, FRANK. *Ghosts and Poltergeists*. London: Aldus Books Ltd., 1976.

SOTHERN, EDWARD H. *My Remembrances: The Melancholy Tale of "Me."* New York: Charles Scribner's Sons, 1916.

STEAD, WILLIAM T. *More Ghost Stories*. (London) New York (Publishing Office of the Review of Reviews), 1892.

STEIGER, BRAD. *Mysteries of Time and Space*. Englewood Cliffs, N.J.: Prentice-Hall, Inc., 1974.

STEPHEN, SIR LESLIE, and SIR SIDNEY LEE. *Dictionary of National Biography*. London: Oxford University Press, 1917.

STERN, PHILIP VAN DOREN, comp. *The Breathless Moment*. New York: Alfred A. Knopf Inc., 1935.

STORY, RONALD D., ed. *The Encyclopedia of UFO's*. Garden City, N.Y.: Dolphin Books, Doubleday & Company, Inc., 1980.

SYMONS, JULIAN. *A Pictorial History of Crime*. New York: Crown Publishers, 1966.

TCHERNINE, ODETTE. *The Yeti*. London: Neville Spearman, 1970.

TEMPLE, ROBERT. *The Sirius Mystery*. New York: St. Martin's Press, 1976.

THURSTON, HERBERT. *Beauraing and Other Apparitions*. London: Burns Oates & Washbourne Ltd., 1934.

THURSTON, HERBERT. *The Physical Phenomena of Mysticism*. Chicago: Henry Regnery Company, 1952.

TREVOR-ROPER, HUGH R. *The Last Days of Hitler*. New York: The Macmillan Company, 1947.

UNDERWOOD, PETER. *Haunted London*. London: George G. Harrap & Co. Ltd., 1973.

VALLEE, JACQUES. *The Invisible College*. New York: E. P. Dutton, 1976.

VALLEE, JACQUES. *Passport to Magonia*. Chicago: Henry Regnery Company, 1969.

VALLEE, JACQUES. *UFO's in Space: Anatomy of a Phenomenon*. Chicago: Henry Regnery Company, 1965.

VAUGHAN, ALAN. *Incredible Coincidence*. New York: J. B. Lippincott Company, 1979.

VELIE, LESTER. *Desperate Bargain*. New York: Reader's Digest Press, 1977.

WADDELL, LAURENCE A. *Among the Himalayas*. Philadelphia: J. B. Lippincott Company, 1900.

WALLECHINSKY, DAVID, and IRVING WALLACE. *The People's Almanac*. Garden City, N.Y.: Doubleday & Company, Inc., 1975.

WALLECHINSKY, DAVID, and IRVING WALLACE. *The People's Almanac #2*. New York: Bantam Books, 1978.

WEAVER, WARREN. *Lady Luck: The Theory of Probability*. New York: Anchor Books, 1963.

WHITE, GILBERT. *The Natural History of Selborne*. Edinburgh: Constable and Company, 1829.

WILKINS, HAROLD T. *Flying Saucers on the Attack*. New York: Citadel Press, 1954.

WILLIAMS, ROGER L. *Gaslight and Shadow: The World of Napoleon III, 1851–1870*. New York: The Macmillan Company, 1957.

WILLIAMSON, HUGH ROSS. *Enigmas of History*. New York: The Macmillan Company, 1957.

WILSON, COLIN. *Enigmas and Mysteries*. London: Aldus Books Limited, 1976.

WINER, RICHARD, and NANCY OSBORN. *Haunted Houses*. New York: Bantam Books, Inc., 1979.

WOODCOCK, GEORGE. *The Crystal Spirit: A Study of George Orwell*. Boston: Little, Brown & Co., 1966.

WOOLLCOTT, ALEXANDER. *While Rome Burns*. New York: The Viking Pres, 1934.

YOUNG, THOMAS. *An Account of Some Recent Discoveries in Hieroglyphical Literature and Egyptian Antiquities*. London: John Murray, 1823.

INDEX

Page numbers in **bold** type refer to illustrations.

Page numbers in **bold** type refer to illustrations.

Page numbers in **bold** type refer to illustrations.

Page numbers in **bold** type refer to illustrations.

Page numbers in **bold** type refer to illustrations.

Acknowledgments

Acropolis Books Ltd. Excerpts from THE SEARCH FOR BIGFOOT: MONSTER, MYTH OR MAN? by Peter Byrne. Reprinted by permission of Acropolis Books Ltd. *E. Wing Anderson.* Excerpts from THE SECRET SCIENCE BEHIND MIRACLES by Max Freedom Long. Reprinted by permission of E. Wing Anderson. *Bantam Books, Inc.* Excerpts from HAUNTED HOUSES by Richard Winer and Nancy Osborn. Copyright © 1979 by Bantam Books, Inc. Reprinted by permission of the publisher. *Bobbs-Merrill Co., Inc.* Excerpts from SECRETS OF LOST RACES by Rene Noorbergen. Copyright © by Rene Noorbergen. Used with the permission of the publisher, The Bobbs-Merrill Company, Inc. *Chatto & Windus Ltd.* Excerpts from MERMAIDS AND MASTODONS by Richard Carrington. Copyright © 1957 by Richard Carrington. Reprinted by permission of Chatto & Windus Ltd. and the author's Literary Estate. *Cheam Publishing Ltd.* Excerpts from ON THE TRACK OF THE SASQUATCH by John Green; from THE SASQUATCH FILE by John Green; and from YEAR OF THE SASQUATCH by John Green. Reprinted by permission of Cheam Publishing Ltd. *Chilton Book Co.* Excerpts from ABOMINABLE SNOWMEN by Ivan T. Sanderson. Copyright © 1961, 1968 by Ivan Sanderson. Reprinted by permission of Chilton Book Co. *Coward, McCann & Geoghegan, Inc.* Excerpts from IN SEARCH OF LAKE MONSTERS by Peter Costello. Copyright © 1974 by Peter Costello; excerpts from THE LONELY SEA AND THE SKY by Francis Chichester. Copyright © 1964 by Francis Chichester. Reprinted by permission of Coward, McCann & Geoghegan, Inc. *Doubleday & Co., Inc.* Excerpts from ENCYCLOPEDIA OF UFO's, ed. Ronald D. Story. Copyright © 1980 by Ronald D. Story. Reprinted by permission of Doubleday & Co., Inc.; excerpts from SEARCHING FOR HIDDEN ANIMALS by Roy P. Mackal. Copyright © 1980 by Roy P. Mackal. Reprinted by permission of Doubleday & Co., Inc., and Gentry Books Ltd. *E. P. Dutton & Co., Inc.* Excerpts from PHANTOMS OF THE THEATER by Raymond Lamont Brown. Copyright © 1977 by Raymond Lamont Brown; excerpts from WEIRD AMERICA by Jim Brandon. Copyright © 1978 by Jim Brandon Associates. Reprinted by permission of E. P. Dutton & Co., Inc. *John Farquharson Ltd.* Excerpts from IN SEARCH OF LAKE MONSTERS by Peter Costello. Copyright © 1974 by Peter Costello; excerpts from THE LONELY SEA AND THE SKY by Francis Chichester. Copyright ©1964 by Francis Chichester. Reprinted by permission of John Farquharson Ltd. *Fate.* Excerpts from April 1951 and September 1981 *Fate.* Reprinted by special permission from *Fate* magazine. *Flying Saucer Review.* Excerpts from *Flying Saucer Review.* Reprinted by permission of *Flying Saucer Review.* *Granada Publishing Ltd.* Excerpts from ALIEN ANIMALS by Janet and Colin Bord. Copyright © 1980 by Janet and Colin Bord. Reprinted by permission of Granada Publishing Ltd. *Harper & Row, Publishers, Inc.* Excerpts from ARIGO: SURGEON OF THE RUSTY KNIFE by John G. Fuller (Thomas Y. Crowell Publishers). Copyright © 1974 by John G. Fuller; excerpts from INCREDIBLE COINCIDENCE by Alan Vaughan (J. B. Lippincott Co., Inc.). Copyright © by Alan Vaughan. Reprinted by permission of Harper & Row, Publishers, Inc. *George G. Harrap & Co. Ltd.* Excerpts from HAUNTED LONDON by Peter Underwood. Reprinted by permission of George G. Harrap & Co. Ltd. *Hill & Wang.* Excerpts from IN THE WAKE OF SEA-SERPENTS by Bernard Heuvelmans. Translation copyright © 1968 by Rupert Hart-Davis; excerpts from ON THE TRACK OF UNKNOWN ANIMALS by Bernard Heuvelmans. Copyright © 1959. Translated by Richard Garnett. Reprinted by permission of Hill & Wang. *Hippocrene Books, Inc.* Excerpts from PHANTOM SOLDIERS by Raymond Lamont Brown. Copyright © 1971. Reprinted by permission of Hippocrene Books, Inc. *Holt, Rinehart & Winston.* Excerpts from THE MYSTERIOUS WORLD: AN ATLAS OF THE UNEXPLAINED by Francis Hitching. Copyright © 1978 by Francis Hitching. Reprinted by permission of Holt, Rinehart & Winston, Publishers. *Macmillan Publishing Co., Inc.* Excerpts from A TREATISE OF HUMAN NATURE by David Hume. Introduction by Antony Flew. Copyright © by Macmillan Publishing Company, Inc., 1962. Reprinted by permission of Macmillan Publishing Co., Inc. *Manor Books, Inc.* Excerpts from THE TERROR by Michael D. Albers. Reprinted by permission of Manor Books, Inc. *Harold Matson Co., Inc.* Excerpts from UNSOLVED: THE WORLD OF THE UNKNOWN by John Godwin. Copyright © 1976 by John Godwin. Reprinted by permission of Harold Matson Co., Inc. *David McKay Co., Inc.* Excerpts from THE WORLD OF PSYCHIC PHENOMENA by F. S. Edsall. Copyright © 1958. Reprinted by permission of David McKay Co., Inc. *Scott Meredith Literary Agency.* Excerpts from MYSTERIOUS FIRES AND LIGHTS by Vincent H. Gaddis. Copyright © 1967 by Vincent H. Gaddis. Reprinted by permission of Scott Meredith Literary Agency. *New American Library.* Excerpts from DEMON CHILDREN, ed. Martin Ebon. Copyright © 1978; excerpts from EXORCISM: FACT NOT FICTION, ed. Martin Ebon. Copyright © 1974; excerpts from THE POLTERGEIST by William G. Roll. Copyright © 1972 by William G. Roll. Reprinted by arrangement with New American Library. *The New York Times.* Excerpts from 6/30/76, 1/5/80, and 10/4/81 *The New York Times.* Copyright © 1976/80/81 by The New York Times Company. Reprinted by permission. *Oxford University Press.* Excerpts from JOURNEY FROM OBSCURITY, WILFRED OWEN, 1893-1918 by Harold Owen. Reprinted by permission of Oxford University Press. *Prentice-Hall, Inc.* Excerpts from MYSTERIES OF TIME AND SPACE by Brad Steiger. Copyright © by Brad Steiger. Reprinted by permission of Prentice-Hall, Inc. *D. Scott Rogo.* Excerpts from THE POLTERGEIST EXPERIENCE by D. Scott Rogo (New York, Penguin, 1979) are reprinted by permission of the author. *St. Martin's Press, Inc.* Excerpts from THE SIRIUS MYSTERY by Robert Temple. Copyright © 1976 by Robert Kyle Grenville Temple. Reprinted by permission of St. Martin's Press, Inc. *Search Press Ltd./Burns & Oates Ltd.* Excerpts from BEAURAING AND OTHER APPARITIONS by Herbert Thurston. Reprinted by permission of Search Press Ltd./Burns & Oates Ltd. *Simon & Schuster.* Excerpts from AMONG THE MISSING by Jay Robert Nash. Copyright © 1978. Reprinted by permission of Simon & Schuster, a Division of Gulf & Western Corporation. *SITU/Pursuit.* Excerpts from *Pursuit*, 2nd quarter, 1981. Reprinted by permission of SITU/Pursuit. *Neville Spearman Limited.* Excerpts from THE FLYING SAUCER STORY by Brinsley Le Poer Trench. Reprinted by permission of Neville Spearman Limited. *Sphere Books, Ltd.* Excerpts from VOODOO IN HAITI by Alfred Métraux, trans. Hugo Charteris. Reprinted by permission of Sphere Books, Ltd. *Lyle Stuart, Inc.* Excerpts from ENCYCLOPAEDIA OF PROPHECY by Omar V. Garrison. Copyright © 1978 by Citadel Press; excerpts from FLYING SAUCERS ON THE ATTACK by Harold T. Wilkins. Copyright © 1954 by Citadel Press; excerpts from STRANGE WORLD by Frank Edwards. Published by arrangement with Lyle Stuart, Inc. *Taplinger Publishing Co., Inc.* Excerpts from STRANGE STORIES OF UFOs by Len Ortzen. Copyright © 1977 by Len Ortzen. Reprinted by permission of Taplinger Publishing Co., Inc. *Thames & Hudson Ltd.* Excerpts from PHENOMENA: A BOOK OF WONDERS by John Michell and Robert J. M. Rickard. Reprinted by permission of Thames & Hudson Ltd. *Warner Books.* Excerpts from RIPLEY'S BELIEVE IT OR NOT! Reprinted by permission of Warner Books.

Picture Credits

The editors are grateful for the contributions of these individuals and organizations in picture research: Colin and Janet Bord; Hilary Evans; Wide World Photos; UPI; MacDonald and Company, Ltd.; Jean-Loup Charmet; Culver Pictures; Bishop Museum; Jack L. Walper; Simone D. Gossner; NASA; Yugoslav Press and Cultural Center; The American Museum of Natural History.

THE ENDLESS SEARCH FOR ANSWERS 2–3 Wide World Photos. **BEYOND THE WALLS OF TIME 11** Alinari/Editorial Photocolor Archives. **13** The Mansell Collection. **14** Jean-Loup Charmet. **16** BBC Hulton Picture Library. **18** *top left* The Mansell Collection; *lower left to right:* Mary Evans Picture Library; Culver Pictures; Jean-Loup Charmet. **20** Mary Evans Picture Library. **22** Culver Pictures. **23** Mary Evans Picture Library. **24** The Bettmann Archive. **26** Collection of E. L. Dieckmann. **27** Wide World Photos. **28** *top* BPCC/Aldus Archive; *bottom* The Bettmann Archive. **30** Chicago Tribune Photos, used with permission. **32** *top* Michael Laughlin/Sygma; *below* Wide World Photos. **33** UPI. **35** New York Public Library, Science and Technology Research Center. **36** *left* Jack L. Walper; *right* Cecil Dougherty. **37** *upper* U.S. Army Photo; *bottom*

Marc Cohen based on material courtesy of the U.S. Army White Sands Missile Range. **38** From *Mysteries of Time and Space* by Brad Steiger, Dell Books. **39** *left* New York Public Library, Science and Technology Research Center; *top* Nature. **40** Ivan P. Goodman photo courtesy of Dr. George W. Gill, associate professor of anthropology, University of Wyoming. **41** Ruth Tipton/Humboldt Museum. **44** BBC Hulton Picture Library. **46** *left* From *World Before Our Own* by Brad Steiger, Berkley-Putnam Publishing Corporation; *right* Flash's Studio, Red Lodge, Montana. **47** From *Mysteries of Time and Space* by Brad Steiger, Dell Books. **49** *top* Reproduced courtesy of Srpska Knjizevna Zadruga, Belgrade; *bottom* Jack Fields/Photo Researchers. **50** *top to bottom:* Jason Laure/Woodfin Camp & Associates; Reproduced from *The World Atlas of Mysteries* by Francis Hitching, published by Pan Books Ltd., London; Irving W. Lindenblad/U.S. Naval Observatory. **53** Michael Holford Photographs. **54** Staatliche Museen zu Berlin. **55** *both* Robert V. Gentry, Columbia Union College, Takoma Park, Maryland. **57** *left* Jean-Loup Charmet; *top right* The Granger Collection, New York; *bottom right* Independence National Historical Park Collection. **58** *left* Culver Pictures; *right* The Bettmann Archive. **59** Jean-Loup Charmet. **60** Culver Pictures. **61** Mary Evans Picture Library. **63** The Allen G. Falby Collection of the Special Collections Department, the University of Texas at El Paso Library. **64** UPI. **65** *left* The Meserve Collection; *right* Photri/ Courtesy of the Bureau of Engraving and Printing. **66** David Page. **67** *left* Richard Harrington/Photo Trends; *right* The Washington Post. **68** *top* Ira Berger; *bottom* Jean-Loup Charmet. **69** *left* The Bettmann Archive; *right* The Granger Collection, New York. **70** *left* Reproduced by courtesy of the Trustees of the British Museum; *bottom* The Bettmann Archive. **71** *left* Culver Pictures; *right* The Bettmann Archive. **72** New York Public Library, Picture Collection. **73** *both* Reprinted with the permission of *The New Yorker* as it appeared in the magazine. **74** *left* John Frost Historical Newspaper Service; *top right* UPI; *lower right* Syndication International/Photo Trends. **75** Pictorial Parade. **77** *left* The Granger Collection, New York; *right* Mark Gerson/Photo Trends. **UNEARTHLY FATES 79** Alinari/Editorial Photocolor Archives. **81** Jean-Loup Charmet. **83** Mary Evans Picture Library. **86** Reproduced by permission of Great Grimsby Borough Council (W.E.R. Hallgarth Collection, Welholme Galleries). **88** Mary Evans Picture Library. **89** *all* Culver Pictures. **93** Ray Skibinski. **95** René Magritte "La Reconnaissance Infinie" © by ADAGP, Paris 1983. **96** Wide World Photos. **98** Adams State College. **100** *left* Howard Burgess; *right* Dan McCoy/Rainbow. **101** Frank Fisher/Liaison. **103** Archiv für Kunst und Geschichte, Berlin. **105** UPI. **108** Axel Poignant. **111** *top* UPI; *remainder* Charles Moore/Black Star. **113** Vincent Eckersley/Skyline Features. **115** *left* BPCC/Aldus Archive; *bottom* BBC Hulton Picture Library. **117** *top* BBC Hulton Picture Library; *bottom* BPCC/Aldus Archive, courtesy of Viscount Bledisloe. **118** The Bettmann Archive. **119** Jean-Loup Charmet. **121** Mary Evans Picture Li-

brary. **122** BPCC/Aldus Archive. **123** W. G. Lucas/Hebridean Press Service, Stornoway. **124** *both* Culver Pictures. **125** *left* Culver Pictures; *bottom* Wide World Photos. **127** *both* UPI. **129** *top* The Bettmann Archive; *remainder* Wide World Photos. **130** *left* The Granger Collection, New York; *right* Wide World Photos. **131** George Buctel. **132** *both* Wide World Photos. **133** Wide World Photos. **134** *lower right* Reprinted from *The Investigator* June 1981, published by the Federal Bureau of Investigation; *remainder* Wide World Photos. **135** *top right* Photo Trends; *remainder* UPI. **MONSTERS AND MORE 137** Alinari/Editorial Photocolor Archives. **139** The Mansell Collection. **140** *top* Mary Evans Picture Library; *bottom* Jean-Loup Charmet. **142** René Dahinden/Fortean Picture Library. **143** *left* Tim Dinsdale/ UPITN Film Library, London; *top* Wide World Photos. **144** Illustration by Melanie Arwin; photo inset courtesy of Central Press/Pictorial Parade. **146** *left* Newport Daily Independent; *right* Photographers International/Pictorial Parade. **147** *both* Academy of Applied Science/Photo Trends. **148** *top left* Wide World Photos; *bottom left* Academy of Applied Science/ Photo Trends; *upper and lower middle* London Daily Express/Pictorial Parade; *top right* P. A. MacNab/Photo Trends; *bottom right* Anthony Shiels/Fortean Picture Library. **149** Wide World Photos. **150** Sandra Mansi/Liaison. **151** Artwork by Wilcock Riley Graphic Art for Weidenfeld & Nicolson, London. **152** Fortean Picture Library. **153** Miriam Schottland. **155** René Dahinden/Fortean Picture LIbrary. **156** *both* René Dahinden/Fortean Picture Library. **158** *upper* BBC Hulton Picture Library; *bottom* UPI. **160** *upper* Wide World Photos; *remainder* Photo Patterson/Gimlin © 1968 René Dahinden/Fortean Picture Library. **162** © by The New York Times Company, reprinted by permission. **163** J. S. Whyte. **165** Fortean Picture Library. **167** Frances Pellegrini **168** BBC Hulton Picture Library. **170** *left to right:* Illustration by Charles G. Harper from *Haunted Houses* by Charles G. Harper, published by J. B. Lippincott Company, republished by Tower Books, 1971; BBC Hulton Picture Library; John H. Cutten Associates. **171** Mary Evans Picture Library. **172** Mary Evans Picture Library. **173** *left* Culver Pictures; *top* Published with permission from *Fate* Magazine. **174** Courtesy of Jessica Strong. **175** Mary Evans Picture Library/ Society for Psychical Research. **178** Richard Winer, author, *Haunted Houses*, Bantam Books, 1979. **THE UNQUIET SKY 183** Scala/Editorial Photocolor Archives. **185** Mary Evans Picture Library. **186** *top* Mary Evans Picture Library; *bottom* Alinari/The Mansell Collection. **187** Culver Pictures. **188** Wide World Photos. **190** Mary Evans Picture Library **194** BPCC/Aldus Archive. **195** E. R. Degginger/Bruce Coleman Inc. **199** Marc Cohen. **201** The Mansell Collection. **203** William H. Amos/Bruce Coleman Inc. **204** The Cincinnati Enquirer. **205** Vester Dick Photography, Santa Cruz, California. **206** By permission of INFO (the International Fortean Organization), College Park, Maryland. **207** ICUFON. **208** Jean-Loup Charmet. **210** Mary Evans Picture Library. **211** © 1982 Peter Angelo Simon. **212** *left* Chris Foss/© BPCC/Aldus Ar-

chive; *top* ICUFON. **213** *left* Courtesy of the San Francisco Public Library; *right* Wide World Photos. **214** Wide World Photos. **215** Mary Evans Picture Library. **217** Wide World Photos. **218** *top* Popperfoto; *bottom* Chris Foss/© BPCC/Aldus Archive. **219** *top* ICUFON; *lower* Wide World Photos. **221** *top to bottom right:* UPI; Popperfoto; Fortean Picture Library; Editions du G.E.O.S./Mary Evans Picture Library. **222** UPI. **223** *top* U.S. Air Force Photo; *bottom* Wide World Photos. **224** Mutual UFO Network, Inc. **225** *bottom left* Wide World Photos; *right* Editions du G.E.O.S./Mary Evans Picture Library; *remainder* Global Communications. **226** © 1966 James H. Karales. **228** *both* Wide World Photos. **229** UPI. **230** *top* Fortean Picture Library; *bottom* Mutual UFO Network, Inc. **231** Fortean Picture Library. **232** *lower left* Fortean Picture Library; *lower right* Mary Evans Picture Library; *remainder* Philip Daly. **234** *top* Flying Saucer Review of West Malling, Maidstone, Kent, England; *bottom* Mary Evans Picture Library. **237** *left* NASA; *right* Mary Evans Picture Library. **238** Culver Pictures. **239** Culver Pictures. **240** Mary Evans Picture Library. **241** *left* Courtesy of the American Museum of Natural History; *remainder* Courtesy of Simone D. Gossner/Photos by R. Taylor States. **242** *both* Jean-Loup Charmet. **243** *upper* Zig Leszczynski/Animals Animals; *bottom* Fortean Picture Library. **245** M.P.L. Fogden/Bruce Coleman Inc. **246–247** *headlines* © 1977–78 by The New York Times Company, reprinted by permission. **247** *lower* Courtesy of the New York Public Library. **248** Lowell Observatory Photograph. **249** *left* UPI; *remainder* Mary Evans Picture Library. **251** *top left* Ann Ronan Picture Library; *lower left* Peter G. Sanchez; *bottom right* Courtesy of the American Museum of Natural History. **252** Science Museum, London. **253** *both* NASA. **254** Courtesy of the American Museum of Natural History. **255** David Baumhefner/National Center for Atmospheric Research/National Science Foundation. **257** National Park Service Photo. **IN THE REALM OF MIRACLES 259** Alinari/Editorial Photocolor Archives. **261** Jean-Loup Charmet. **262** Roger-Viollet. **263** The Bettmann Archive. **265** Miriam Schottland. **269** *both* Bishop Museum. **270** *upper* The Clarion-Ledger, Jackson, Mississippi; *bottom* The Mississippi Department of Archives and History. **272** Culver Pictures. **275** John W. Lehmann. **276** UPI. **277** Pictorial Parade. **279** Manchete/Pictorial Parade. **280** Manchete/Pictorial Parade. **283** Culver Pictures. **284** The Mansell Collection. **287** Mary Evans Picture Library. **292** Jean-Loup Charmet. **294** Mary Evans Picture Library. **297** *top* Mary Evans Picture Library; *bottom* National Archives. **300** Jean-Loup Charmet **301** National Catholic News Service. **303** UPI. **304** BBC Hulton Picture Library. **305** *left* Mary Evans Picture Library; *right* Marlene Karas/Pittsburgh Press Photo. **306** *top* Wide World Photos; *bottom* Manchete/Pictorial Parade.

Efforts have been made to contact the holder of the copyright for each picture. In several cases these sources have been untraceable, for which we offer our apologies.